International Commercial Agreements and Electronic Commerce

International Commercial Agreements and Electronic Commerce

Sixth Edition

William F. Fox

Wolters Kluwer

Published by:
Kluwer Law International B.V.
PO Box 316
2400 AH Alphen aan den Rijn
The Netherlands
E-mail: international-sales@wolterskluwer.com
Website: lrus.wolterskluwer.com

Sold and distributed in North, Central and South America by:
Wolters Kluwer Legal & Regulatory U.S.
7201 McKinney Circle
Frederick, MD 21704
United States of America
Email: customer.service@wolterskluwer.com

Sold and distributed in all other countries by:
Air Business Subscriptions
Rockwood House
Haywards Heath
West Sussex
RH16 3DH
United Kingdom
Email: international-customerservice@wolterskluwer.com

Printed on acid-free paper.

ISBN 978-90-411-7005-7

e-Book: ISBN 978-90-411-7008-8
web-PDF: ISBN 978-90-411-7009-5

Printed in the United Kingdom.

Table of Contents

Preface

The first edition of this book was published in 1986. As I complete the manuscript for the sixth edition, I remain fascinated by all the issues that go into the drafting, negotiating, and disputing of international commercial agreements. One of the things that I struggled with in 1986 was the relative dearth of good literature on any of the important subtopics in this field. As I mentioned in the preface to the first edition, I found only two types of sources: a handful of law journal articles and poorly-indexed, badly-collated multivolume treatises. Almost all of the literature consisted of writings by experts talking to other experts. There seemed, at the time, to be nothing in print that tried to explain the important concepts of international business transactions in terms that a lawyer or business executive new to the field could understand and use.

Such is no longer the case. Most recently, I have been struck by the enormous growth in the available literature. There has been an explosion of books, law journal articles, websites, and government sources. For this, I hope all of us are grateful. Perhaps the most striking development is the sheer volume of information available in electronic form and retrievable by computer. Unlike my travels—and travails—in the early 1980s, I no longer have to explore musty shelves in back corners of bricks and mortar libraries to find rules of arbitration or requirements for international letters of credit. These days, I sit at my desk, stare at my computer monitor, and explore the riches of the Web.

But even with all the new information, I think there is still a need for a book such as this. With this edition and the earlier versions I have tried to create a text that can be read and understood by *both* lawyers and business executives. More importantly, it is intended as a book that can be applied to actual business deals, rather than a book whose abstractions are of interest only to academics. This book should be helpful to someone with an immediate specific problem or someone who just wants to become better acquainted with the field before he or she steps into an actual transaction.

The sixth edition applies the same technique that I developed for the original manuscript. The text contains a great deal of solid basic information on a wide variety of issues and concepts that people will encounter in putting together international commercial agreements. For those readers who wish to delve more deeply into any of the topics discussed, the extensive and up-to-date references in the footnotes will provide additional depth and clarification.

Acknowledgment

As always, I owe a strong debt of gratitude to a number of research assistants, all of whom are now highly successful practicing lawyers: Scott Squillace and Andrew Palmieri for the first edition; Erin Sullivan for the second edition; Stephen Harris for the third edition, for the fourth edition: Brian Tannenbaum, Drew Tannenbaum, and, especially, Roman Majtan, and for the fifth edition, Mustafa Yagci and Qasim Murad. Because I am now semi-retired, I served as my own research assistant for the sixth edition.

CHAPTER 1

Introduction

§1.1 INTERNATIONAL TRADE AND THIS BOOK

International trade is a fundamental requirement for survival in an economically interdependent world. While trade among different countries and regions has often waxed and waned depending on economic and political conditions, overall figures show that trade between nations is now worth trillions of dollars a year and will continue to increase in both volume and monetary value as the world's population continues to grow. This does not mean that international trade is completely unfettered. The idea of completely free world trade is a notion whose time has not yet come. Barriers set up through tariffs and through the so-called nontariff trade barriers continue to inhibit world trade. Countries with grievances against other countries sometimes invoke sanctions or embargoes.

No country has ever been completely consistent on matters of trade. Most countries have shifted back and forth over the years from the extreme of protectionism to the uninhibited exchange of goods and services. These shifts in position often depend on how the internal political climate of that country meshes with the worldwide economic climate. At the same time, every country has at least *some* exports and imports. Accordingly, no country in the world is completely cut off from international trade. As the Sixth Edition of this book goes to press we are seeing more turmoil and dissonance on trade than anytime since World War Two.

Governments frequently intervene in matters of international trade even though the vast majority of individual transactions take place between two private entities or between a private entity and a national government (or component of government). Because these transactions involve firms in two or more different countries and often directly affect the economy of both the exporting and importing nation, it is generally impossible for national governments *not* to get involved. Every national government imposes some controls on the export and import of goods and services—controls that are usually implemented by requiring firms to secure government permission in the form of a license to export or import the good or service in question.

Some government controls are imposed to protect domestic businesses. There are controls that purport to establish a level playing field by policing the importation of goods carrying prices below market costs and, by way of antidumping and countervailing duty sanctions, imposing penalties on the exporters. Some countries attempt to extend certain of their domestic commercial principles, such as antitrust regulations, to international transactions. A few countries have even attempted to impose standards of fair and ethical dealing, normally restricted to purely domestic business transactions, to their companies' business practices abroad. For example, under a 1977 statute called the Foreign Corrupt Practices Act, the United States has been particularly aggressive in policing acts of bribery of foreign public officials on the part of U.S. companies that seek to do business in foreign countries. The United States, until just a few years ago, was unique in its treatment of foreign corrupt practices. Now there are a number of important international agreements on bribery and corruption, as well as significant legislation prohibiting international commercial bribery enacted by individual countries.

Many countries have other forms of government regulation of international trade that often must be addressed in forming a valid international commercial agreement. This book takes up a number of issues of government regulation of trade but when it comes to forming a specific agreement, the only effective way to deal with and understand government regulation is on a case-by-case, country-by-country basis.

Regional and international trade agreements are increasingly important in international trade. To this end, governments have cooperated on both a regional (e.g., the European Union and the North American Free Trade Agreement) and a worldwide basis (the World Trade Organization incorporating virtually all of the earlier General Agreement on Tariffs and Trade) to promote free trade. Many countries have negotiated and ratified *bilateral investment treaties* (BITs). Modern BITs are often based on concepts that were historically included in an older treaty form, the treaty of friendship, commerce and navigation (FCN). Both BITs and FCNs have, as their primary purpose, a statement of the rights of the nationals of each country to trade, invest, or establish and operate businesses in the other country. Virtually all of the major trading nations have entered into BITs or FCNs with each other. The United States, for example, has ratified at least 130 such treaties.

Virtually all the major trading nations recognize the concept of *most-favored nation*, a term of art in international trade that attempts to promote nondiscrimination in trade by giving the same trade benefits to any country that the host country extends to any other country. The status of most-favored nation sometimes becomes a bone of contention between countries. A number of years ago there was a singular dispute between the United States and the Peoples Republic of China on the issue of most-favored nation—a dispute eventually resolved by the United States granting China most-favored nation status.

But even given a layer of government regulation and oversight, day-to-day international trade remains primarily a private matter—that is, an undertaking between two or more private businesses based on a contract drafted and negotiated between the contracting parties to be performed by the parties with the occasional assistance of other private entities such as financial institutions, insurance companies, and freight carriers. This book concentrates on the private dimensions of international trade, and more precisely, on the contractual aspects of that trade. On occasion, we will touch on other matters, such as the need to secure government permission to export or import goods or services or antitrust concerns or corruption, but we will do so only insofar as those peripheral matters are important to drafting and performing a valid contract.

Most private international transactions involve contracts for the sale of tangible objects or *goods*. For that reason, a significant part of the text concentrates on issues relating to the sale of goods. But this book does not ignore the wide variety of other international commercial transactions such as contracts for *sale of services* (e.g., engineering, architectural, or telecommunications services), *licenses* for the transfer of patents and other types of intellectual property, *joint ventures*, *franchise* agreements, and foreign direct investment. There are many instances when it is preferable for the contracting parties to create a wholly separate entity such as a franchise or a joint venture, rather than merely selling the goods themselves. Subsequent chapters discuss drafting contracts to cover a wide variety of business relationships, not merely purchase and sale transactions. Because intellectual property has become such an important component of international trade this edition contains a separate chapter on the nature of intellectual property and licensing agreements. With the explosion of commerce conducted electronically through the Internet, lawyers and business executives must now deal with issues that arise in electronic commerce. Accordingly, the reader will find a substantial amount of information and discussion on international electronic commerce both in separate chapters and within chapters on more general topics.

§1.2 AN OVERVIEW OF INTERNATIONAL COMMERCIAL TRANSACTIONS

A business executive entering into an international commercial transaction is mainly interested in drafting an agreement that satisfies all of the parties and that will be performed as promised. The expectation of *performance* is the first principle of contract negotiation and drafting. People in business rarely enter into a business transaction assuming that the contract will never be performed or that one or more of the parties will violate some aspect of the agreement. Indeed, many if not most business transactions, both domestic and international, are fully and quietly performed by the parties.

This first principle also reflects a basic consideration in contract negotiation: parties sign contracts because they *want* to do business, not because they want to fight with each other in court or in an arbitration hearing after the other party violates the contract. There may be a few occasions when it is important to dig deeply into the motives of the contracting parties; but in most circumstances, motive is usually very easy to discern. Almost always, the parties want to make a *profit*, in some fashion, from the transaction. It may be a small or a large profit. The profit may be short-term or long-term. It may be tied to a series of transactions rather than a single business event. But however structured, profit lies at the heart of every agreement. Put a bit more crassly: people do business with each other to make money.

While many transactions are fully performed as agreed, the possibility of *breach* or nonperformance must always be taken into account at the beginning of the process—i.e., when parties negotiate and draft the original agreement. As distasteful as it may seem to happy, enthusiastic parties who are just concluding what appears to be a brilliant agreement, *dispute resolution* must be addressed at the outset, not when the dispute occurs. Indeed, just as it is usually more effective to draft a person's last will and testament when that person is still healthy and mentally alert, it is usually more effective to consider dispute resolution when the parties are enjoying the warm glow of friendship and cooperation that developed during the contract drafting and signing stage.

To draft successful agreements, the parties and their counsel must understand how contracts are formed. This understanding must include at least a basic appreciation of both the "law" of contracts and a grasp of the technical aspects of the specific transaction entered into. For example, if a contract is for the sale of telecommunications equipment, the contract itself, or documents appended to the contract ("exhibits" or "annexes"), will invariably contain technical specifications for the equipment. Persons negotiating and drafting the contract should have a good understanding of the equipment's technical capabilities or be able to call on experts who have the technical answers because these details often figure importantly in the negotiation, drafting, and performance of the agreement.

Contract drafters need to be sensitive to the differences between international contracts and contracts that are to be performed domestically. It is a mistake to assume that the two are exactly alike. Numerous considerations enter into the drafting and execution of an international agreement that are not pertinent to contracts between domestic companies. For example, in the United States purely oral contracts (what we often refer to as "handshake" agreements) for more than modest sums of money are extremely rare. This is due to a U.S. principle of contract law (also recognized in a number of other countries, particularly those in the common law tradition), known as the *statute of frauds*. This is a legal obligation that requires all but the smallest contracts to be evidenced by some kind of writing.

By contrast, many countries make oral contracts just as enforceable as written contracts; and cultural assumptions in those countries frequently favor oral dealings. The element of trust—the idea that a person's word or handshake is her bond—is often carried into the country's law of contract. Even so, almost all international commercial agreements are evidenced by some kind of writing, ranging from the exchange of simple e-mails and facsimile transmissions to multipage documents in which each clause is separately negotiated.

In contrast to purely domestic transactions, the language differences between the parties to international contracts often demand that the parties agree to a single, official language for the contract, even if the document is translated into other languages for the convenience of the parties. Cultural differences frequently require different negotiating styles and techniques.

Many international contracts involve substantial amounts of money. These sums usually justify a separately negotiated agreement tailored to the specific deal, rather than the use of standard forms. Nonetheless, standard form contracts or agreements concluded by the exchange of purchase and sale orders (frequently leading to what law professors call *the battle of forms*) are not prohibited internationally and, indeed, are quite common for small-scale transactions.

International contracts tend to be longer and more comprehensive in an attempt to ensure that each party's rights are protected and that the writing sets out virtually all important details of the agreement. But length can sometimes be counterproductive and proposed contracts that are too lengthy can kill the deal in its inception. Lawyers in the United States seem particularly prone to writing contracts that are considered excessively long and suspicious by lawyers and business executives in other countries. In more than a few instances, the author has seen deals poisoned by the submission of a 100-page draft agreement when the non-U.S. party was expecting fifteen or twenty pages.

Even so, there are considerations in international transactions that promote length over brevity. Business practices differ from country to country, so many of the assumptions and understandings (what we frequently refer to as a *course of dealing*) that might not necessarily be written into a domestic agreement may need to be fully spelled out in an international contract. The parties often have never done business together, so they have not developed the degree of trust present in many domestic settings. When there is a great deal of trust between the parties, they can often do a much shorter written agreement.

The parties' geographical separation can cause problems, although the advent of e-mail, videoconferencing, and the Internet that have accompanied the vast improvement in worldwide telecommunications make mere distance much less of a factor now than it might have been in the past. Particularly when the elements of prior acquaintance or personal trust are missing, the dispute resolution clause of the contract becomes a matter of major importance. All of these matters must be addressed in some fashion if the contract is to have a solid foundation.

Negotiation is intimately related to the drafting process even though the timing of the negotiation can differ from transaction to transaction. Parties occasionally sit down with a blank piece of paper and hammer out the entire agreement on a face-to-face basis. Some agreements are launched over the telephone or by facsimile or e-mail exchanges followed by the exchange of rudimentary confirming memoranda.

Some transactions begin with one side submitting a *letter of intent* or a draft contract for the other side's consideration. The parties then negotiate only those provisions in the draft over which there is genuine disagreement. This is normally the most efficient process, but it also can have the effect of giving the negotiating momentum to the party who writes the draft, in the same way that the outcome of a meeting can often be dictated by the person who writes the agenda for that meeting. Parties sometimes spar with each other to see who gets to go first.

Careful lawyers and business executives must spend some time considering the *process* of negotiation to achieve the best possible result. There are certain techniques of negotiation and certain guidelines for preparing for negotiation that should be taken into account prior to doing the actual negotiation. Thinking about negotiation generally and planning the negotiation at hand, sometimes even to the point of actually rehearsing a forthcoming negotiation, often pays off in better results. One of the premises of this book is that many negotiation techniques may be reviewed and analyzed even though some traditionalists view good negotiation as purely a matter of extensive personal experience. Although most experienced negotiators will agree that prescribing elaborate and rigid doctrinal rules for negotiation—and especially for cross-cultural negotiation—is a formula for disaster, as much thought as possible should be given to the negotiation process before the negotiation itself begins.

The end result of the negotiation is normally the drafting and execution (the signing) of the final agreement. That agreement is often performed without incident. However, some transactions unravel; and when they unravel, the issue of dispute resolution becomes of paramount importance. In business agreements, there is no limit to the possible reasons for a party's failure to perform. Typically, these include shifts in the financial circumstances of a party, changes in underlying economic conditions, loss of sources of supply or of customers, the repeal of necessary government permissions, and wholly unanticipated events that we sometimes refer to as *acts of God*. Long-term contracts are especially vulnerable to changes in the conditions necessary for performance and often call for the insertion of clauses that will permit the contract to adapt to these changes without the need for either renegotiation or some other type of dispute resolution. Properly drafted *adaptation* clauses, such as flexible price and supply terms and force majeure clauses, permit the contract to flex with those underlying changes without destroying the contractual relationship itself. But if the adaptation clauses prove unequal to the task, and if the parties still wish to continue the relationship, one of the best devices to preserve the contract is simple *renegotiation*—that is, a process by which the parties get back together and craft additions and modifications to the contract that allow the transaction to go forward.

Sometimes the breach is so immense and injurious to one of the parties that neither adaptation nor renegotiation will suffice to avoid a breach. When this occurs, the dispute resolution mechanisms built into the agreement (or agreed to later or imposed by law) come into play. Most written international commercial agreements specify the precise dispute resolution device to be used and many of the details that accompany that device. For a number of reasons, including ease of enforcement, *arbitration* is the device of choice for many parties to international contracts. If the contracting parties choose to include an arbitration clause, attention must be devoted to the procedures to be followed in the arbitration. Such considerations usually include a selection of one or another of the major arbitral rules systems, a determination of the physical location of the arbitration hearing, and a statement of the law to be applied to the dispute. Some commercial arbitrations are managed entirely by the parties themselves under procedural rules and other requirements set out in the contract itself (so-called ad hoc arbitration). Many others are conducted under the supervision of and under rules promulgated by domestic entities such as the Stockholm Chamber of

Commerce, the American Arbitration Association, or an international body such as the International Chamber of Commerce. This form of supervision and assistance is known as *institutional* arbitration.

If the arbitration goes forward and an arbitration hearing is held, the parties present their cases and the arbitrator (or arbitration panel) renders a decision in the form of an arbitral *award*. Most arbitrations are final in the sense that the losing party simply pays up and goes away. But there are instances in which choosing arbitration does not guarantee that the dispute will not reach the courts. For example, when a dispute arises under a contract one of the parties may refuse to abide by the arbitration clause and thereby force the other side to seek the assistance of a court to compel arbitration. If the losing party does not comply voluntarily with the terms of the award, the award must be enforced by some court, normally a court having jurisdiction over the losing party.

If the contract is silent on dispute resolution or if the contract's dispute resolution clause does not specify arbitration, the injured party may seek to litigate the dispute in an appropriate court. There are no international courts that deal with private commercial matters so any court selected is, by definition, a domestic court within a particular country. International commercial litigation is difficult and complicated because the jurisdiction of domestic courts normally does not extend to parties physically outside that country who do not own property in that country. Nonetheless, if the difficulties can be worked out, litigation has certain advantages of process, certainty, and finality not enjoyed by other forms of dispute resolution.

Many dispute resolution experts who are committed to the idea of international commercial arbitration view litigation as evidence that the parties' dispute resolution planning process has failed. However, it need not be regarded as such. Disputes can occur under the most competently drafted contracts. When disputes occur, litigation in domestic courts has a significant number of advantages over arbitration along with a substantial number of pitfalls, defects, and disadvantages. Unplanned litigation may indeed be attributable to a failure to plan; but a conscious decision to resolve a dispute by litigation can frequently be cost-effective in the long run. As one might expect, litigation is also a favorite dispute resolution mechanism of lawyers.

Litigation and arbitration are not the only choices. Parties who wish to preserve a continuing business relationship may profit from the effective use of the less adversarial devices such as mediation/conciliation or minitrial. Indeed, members of some cultures react so negatively to the rigid, adversarial, never-give-an-inch posture of U.S.-style litigation that even the threat of litigation can destroy an ongoing relationship. These milder dispute resolution devices are often ignored because they have only recently become part of the international dispute resolution vocabulary. In many cases, these techniques are far less expensive, stressful and time-consuming, and frequently promote a more satisfactory solution.

Sadly, the use of the less confrontational settings of mediation and conciliation are not used as often as they should be. There is some hope for the future, however. Many entities that deal with international commercial dispute resolution such as the International Chamber of Commerce, the United Nations Commission on International Trade Law (UNCITRAL), and the American Arbitration Association have promulgated rules for various processes, such as mediation and minitrial that can have advantages over both litigation and arbitration. While each of these techniques has its own advantages and disadvantages, the less-drastic alternatives are sometimes not considered because lawyers advising on international business transactions often take a very traditional view of dispute resolution. They advocate commercial arbitration, or litigation in domestic courts, because those are the only two devices they have experience with. A far better approach is to be aware of and take into consideration all of the dispute resolution possibilities.

§1.3 HOW TO USE THIS BOOK

This book is to be read and used as a practical guide for negotiating, drafting, and resolving disputes in international commercial agreements. The author has not assumed that the every reader will read the book from preface to final chapter. Instead, he assumes that most readers are interested in obtaining guidance and information relating to a specific transaction or problem. This book can help a lawyer or business executive plan and carry out individual transactions even when that person is not interested in a full-blown understanding of the entire landscape of international contracts.

Within each chapter and each section of the book, readers requiring more depth on a topic will be directed by the footnotes to appropriate additional sources. These sources include treaties, rules, statutes, and other primary sources of the law, the multivolume treatises that deal with these topics, and numerous journal articles that provide additional depth and clarification. Most of these materials are English language materials, although materials from and citations to appropriate literature in languages other than English have also been included. Business executives who are not lawyers will find that this book gives them the understanding and perspective necessary to work effectively with the legal experts. The Internet and the World Wide Web have had a massive impact on dissemination of information and on the conduct of business and legal research. This edition contains a large number of websites that the reader may find helpful as he or she pursues and concludes a transaction.

This book organizes commercial agreements according to the three stages of an agreement: entering into, performing, and disputing a contract. For example, it begins with the premise that almost all international commercial transactions start not with a dispute but rather with the negotiating and drafting of a contract by two parties who wish to do business with each other. That business may involve the sale of goods, the establishment of an agency relationship, the transfer of intellectual property such as patents and copyrights through a license, or the providing of engineering or construction services. Contracts may run from one-time purchase and sale agreements involving small amounts of money to long-term arrangements worth millions of dollars.

Because international contracts are legal instruments, anyone seeking to understand the basis for an agreement must know a little about the various legal systems in the world and something of the general law of commercial transactions. Persons lacking this knowledge should turn first to Chapters 2 and 3. Immediate guidance on drafting commercial agreements and suggestions for specific contractual language can be found in Chapter 4. With this background, readers unfamiliar with some of the new thinking on negotiation would do well to read Chapter 5 before walking into a negotiation session. That chapter discusses many negotiation techniques and practice tips that can help a session go much more smoothly. Chapter 5 should be especially helpful for readers who are inexperienced negotiators. The chapters premise assumes that good negotiation can be studied and mastered and is more than simply a matter of personal experience. Chapter 6 provides for in-depth discussion of the important basic concepts for Internet-based agreements and electronic commerce, which has made giant leaps in international business and now warrants separate treatment. Chapter 7 acknowledges the exponential growth of trade in the various forms of intellectual property and the special considerations inherent in drafting licensing agreements—the contractual vehicle by which intellectual property rights are conveyed.

Some contracts do not stand the test of time and must be taken through a dispute resolution process. Chapters 8 through 13 discuss a large number of issues and concepts relating to dispute resolution. At this point, the author will make his standard plea to readers of this book to at least consider some of the less-drastic forms of dispute resolution such as mediation and conciliation. Many of those mechanisms are discussed in Chapter 8. Contracts that have been breached and are about to become the subject of arbitration are covered in Chapters 9, 10, and 11.

Readers with specific interest in dispute resolution in a particular area of the world will obtain additional guidance on some of those distinctions in Chapter 11. Arbitration in Latin America is often different from arbitration in London. Commercial dispute resolution in China, a country now at the top of the list of major trading nations, is often a unique and sometimes trouble-filled experience for many companies. Business executives and lawyers who fail to appreciate and allow for these regional differences may face unanticipated trouble.

Litigation is described and analyzed in Chapter 12, but considerations of time and space do not permit a full-blown excursus into all the different forms of litigation that exist in various countries. Readers should take note of the fact that the immense differences in the judicial systems of various countries make large-scale generalizations very deceptive. Litigation is such a specialized undertaking that only lawyers trained and qualified in the procedures of a particular country are equipped to deal with it.

Chapter 14 is perhaps the bravest of the chapters. In this chapter, the author attempts to predict a number of future trends in international commercial arrangements—a tricky, risky, fraught-with-uncertainty undertaking at best. It is also one of the shortest chapters for the same reasons.

As mentioned earlier, this edition has a substantial amount of material on the Internet, the World Wide Web, and electronic commerce. Indeed, some international transactions, such as letters of credit, are now mainly executed in electronic form. As we move toward the third decade of the twenty-first century, it is not too much to say that persons without access to the Internet will be at a near-total disadvantage in pursuing and performing international commercial agreements.

CHAPTER 2
Sources of the Law of International Commercial Agreements

§2.1 INTRODUCTION

Where does one find the rules of the game? The sources of the applicable law for a contract are numerous but not infinite. Some of the law is to be found in the contracts themselves in the form of principles negotiated between the parties and stated expressly as provisions in the contract. This process of party-to-party formation of legal principles, often referred to as *private ordering,* is developed mainly through the process of negotiation and drafting and is discussed below.[1] But everyone should understand that under the traditional contract doctrines of party autonomy and *pacta sunt servanda* (contracts are to be respected and enforced) such provisions are just as compelling as any other command in the law so long as these provisions do not contradict legal principles imposed by the domestic law of a country or by treaty provisions. Because contracts do not exist in a legal vacuum, they almost always must reflect certain considerations imposed by external forces. These limiting provisions have several sources: the domestic law of a country that bears some relationship to the contract, or in certain instances principles of international commercial conduct and behavior.

It is difficult to generalize accurately about the domestic law (occasionally referred to as *municipal law*) of various countries even though it is the domestic law that prescribes most of the legal principles governing commercial arrangements. To establish some predictability, most parties to international commercial agreements provide that their contracts are to be governed by the law of a particular country to

1. For a lengthy and fascinating inquiry into the impact of a single, albeit very large, American corporation on global trading practices and principles by way of the corporation's contracting and business activities, *see*, Larry Cata Backer, *Economic Globalization and the Rise of Efficient Systems of Global Private Law Making: Wal-Mart as Global Legislator*, 39 Conn. L. Rev. 1739 (2007).

insure that the applicable legal principles will be readily understood and applied. Most of the major trading nations have extensive and detailed systems of commercial law that are remarkably similar despite having domestic legal systems that sharply differ in origin.

It is sometimes possible to frame a few general observations about the applicable law from an analysis of the placement of a country's legal system in one or another of the broad categories or *families* of law in the world. When faced with a choice as to whether to incorporate a particular country's law into a contract—or perhaps even the more basic decision whether to do business in a particular country—lawyers can sometimes gain insights from an inquiry into where that legal system fits when compared with other legal systems often referred to, by comparative legal scholars, as *families* of law.

§2.2 PROMULGATION AND ENFORCEMENT OF PRINCIPLES OF COMMERCIAL LAW

There are four basic instruments for developing and promulgating principles of commercial law external to the contract itself: (1) treaties; (2) statutes; (3) court decisions (and occasionally decisions by arbitral bodies); and (4) government regulations. Most international scholars also believe that legal principles can emerge from pronouncements of international organizations such as the UN and through the growth of international custom; but in most instances, these latter sources have less to do with actual day-to-day commercial arrangements then the four basic sources first enumerated.

Treaties. Treaties are documents that control relationships between nations. They may be negotiated and executed between two countries (*bilateral* treaties) or among a number of countries (*multilateral* treaties). Conceptually, they are devices by which each country voluntarily surrenders some sovereignty in order to enter into the agreement. There appears to be no power currently in existence (other than perhaps victory in war) that can compel a country to enter into a treaty; but once a country enters into the treaty, it generally becomes bound to the terms of that treaty. There are, of course, occasional problems of enforcement of treaty obligations. The International Court of Justice at The Hague (sometimes referred to as the *World Court*) is viewed as an appropriate body to adjudicate disagreements under a treaty, but many countries, including on occasion the United States, consider themselves free, in certain circumstances, to ignore the court's jurisdiction.

There are three steps in implementing a treaty. First, the terms of the treaty are negotiated and the participating countries prepare a final draft. Second, the final version is signed by the participating countries as a signal that they approve the final version of the negotiated document. This does not mean, however, that the treaty becomes immediately enforceable. Third, the treaty is ratified by each country's government. The process of ratification differs from country to country. Some countries permit ratification decisions to be made by the executive authority. In other countries, such as the United States, a legislative body (e.g., the U.S. Senate) must give its approval before the ratification process is complete. Fourth, treaties enter into force when a sufficient number of countries (a number generally spelled out in the treaty itself) ratify the agreement. A country may accede to a treaty, thus considering itself bound by the treaty's terms, without formal ratification.

There are many different types of treaties that affect commercial relationships. One of the most common is the Bilateral Investment Treaty (BIT), a newer form of agreement that has eclipsed the older treaty form known as a Treaty of Friendship, Cooperation and Navigation (frequently referred to as an FCN).[2] Such treaties spell out many of the details of one country's commercial relationship with another. Multilateral treaties can have an impact on commercial relations among countries. For example, one of the most important treaties governing the enforceability of international commercial arbitral awards is the New York Convention on the Recognition and Enforcement of Arbitral Awards of 1958, discussed at length in Chapter 8. Another multilateral treaty, discussed at the end of this chapter, is the Vienna Convention on the International Sale of Goods (CISG). The World Trade Organization, a group created by this treaty to implement the General Agreement on Tariffs and Trade is having an increased impact on barriers, both tariff and nontariff, to trade in goods and services around the world. One of the most important regional treaties is the North American Free Trade Agreement, discussed in Chapter 4.

Statutes. As used in this section, the term *statute* refers to the promulgation of principles of law by the governments of individual countries that govern commercial transactions as a whole. In some countries, these principles are stated as part of the civil code. In the United States, private commercial dealings are governed mainly by statutes enacted by the legislatures of the individual states, rather than by the national government. All states except Louisiana have enacted a comprehensive set of commercial statutes called the Uniform Commercial Code (UCC), which controls, among other things, the sale of goods, commerce in negotiable instruments, and the creation of secured transactions.

Court decisions. In virtually all countries a great deal of commercial law is developed by courts' deciding individual cases brought by parties who claim to have suffered some legal injury in the context of a specific commercial undertaking. Many disputes arising out of international commercial agreements are first decided in the

2. For further reading on BITs and FCNs, *see*, Ahmad Ghouri, *The Evolution of Bilateral Investment Treaties, Investment Treaty Arbitration and International Investment Law*, 14 Int'l Arb. L. Rev. 189 (2011); Kenneth J. Vandevelde, *Bilateral Investment Treaties: History, Policy, and Interpretation* (2010); Rudolf Dolzer & Margrete Stevens, *Bilateral Investment Treaties* (1994); United Nations Centre on Transnational Corporations, *Bilateral Investment Treaties* (1988). *See*, e.g., Mark Kantor, *Little Has Changed in the New US Model Bilateral Investment Treaty*, 27 ICSID Rev.—For. Inv. L.J. 335 (2013); Megan Wells Sheffer, *Bilateral Investment Ttreaties: A Friend or Foe to Human Rights?* 39 Denver J. Int'l L & Policy 483 (2011); Efraim Chalamish, *The Future of Bilateral Investment Treaties: A De Facto Multilateral Agreement?*, 34 Brooklyn J. Int'l L. 335 (2009); Symposium, *Romancing the Foreign Investor: BIT by BIT*, 12 U.C. Davis J. Int'l L. & Pol'y 1 (2005); Jeswald W. Salacuse & Nicholas P. Sullivan, *Do BITs Really Work?: An Evaluation of Bilateral Investment Treaties and Their Grand Bargain*, 46 Harv. Int'l L.J. 67 (2005); J. Steven Jarreau, *Anatomy of a BIT: The United States-Honduras Bilateral Investment Treaty*, 35 U. Miami Inter. Am. L. Rev. 429 (2004); Kenneth J. Vandevelde, *U.S. Bilateral Investment Treaties: The Second Wave*, 14 Mich. J. Int'l L. 621 (1993).

context of an arbitration proceeding, after which the winning party takes the arbitral award to some court for enforcement. In a common law system, the cumulation of individual court decisions leads to the development of legal principles (so-called judge-made law) that are just as valid as anything enacted by the country's legislature. Even in countries outside the common law system, the resolution of individual cases in court often helps fill in the gaps in that country's civil and commercial code.

Government regulations. In many countries with a centralized system of government, there is really no difference between government regulations and statutes since virtually all authority flows directly from the central government. By contrast, in countries such as the United States, there is often a sharp distinction drawn between statutes (which in the United States are enacted by the legislative branch of government, i.e., the state legislatures or the Congress) and regulations promulgated by government agencies within the executive branch of government such as the Department of the Treasury or the Bureau of Customs. In many countries, such as the United States, the basic principles of commercial law are usually developed through statutes and court decisions, while the peripheral aspects of commercial undertakings such as the imposition of taxes and export and import controls are implemented by government agencies.

For the most part, this book deals with private arrangements between individuals as set out in their negotiated written agreements. These agreements are generally tailored to the specific problems and issues faced by the parties; and in most countries, the parties are relatively free to work out their own deals. However, there is virtually no private deal that is totally exempt from external controls. Lawyers and business executives who seek to draft enforceable contracts must have an understanding both of what they and the other side hope to accomplish privately and what will be permitted by the various governments involved.

§2.3 THE WORLD'S MAJOR LEGAL SYSTEMS

Virtually all international commercial agreements choose some body of law to govern the contract. Knowing something about the different national legal systems makes it a little easier to understand why so many contracting parties affirmatively choose law rather than leave the decision on governing legal principles to a court or arbitrator. An understanding of the legal system of another country may also help negotiators better appreciate the context within which the other side is negotiating. At the same time, this is one of the areas of law in which too much generalization can be dangerous. This section is not intended to be an exhaustive inquiry into the fascinating area of comparative law, but rather is a relatively brief overview to demonstrate how each system accommodates commercial undertakings.[3]

3. Readers wishing additional depth in these topics may wish to review: *The Oxford Handbook of Comparative Law* (Mathias Reimann & Reinhard Zimmermann eds., 2007); Geoffrey Samuel, *An Introduction to Comparative Law Theory and Method* (2014); Mary Ann Glendon, Paolo G. Carozza & Colin B. Picker, *Comparative Legal Traditions: Text, Materials and Cases on Western Law* (4th ed., 2014); International Encyclopedia of Comparative Law; P.D.V. Marsh, *Comparative*

Most comparative law scholars agree that there are at least four broad classifications (occasionally referred to as *families*) of law: the civil law, the common law, socialist law, and Islamic law. Viewed even more deeply, one can discern subcategories such as: Latin American law, generally derived from a mixture of the various versions of European civil law; hybrids such as Japanese law—a mixture of indigenous rules and customs, the German civil code, and United States law; and aboriginal systems such as African tribal law.

The common law systems have their roots in the British law and include virtually all present and former members of the British Empire plus the largest trading nation, the United States. The United States has developed separately from Britain for the last 200 years and now has an internal system of commercial law known as the UCC. The UCC, as it is generally referred to in the United States, has become a national system of commercial law by virtue of its enactment by all the states except the state of Louisiana.

The civil code countries are primarily the countries of the European continent and those countries, such as most of Latin America whose legal systems derive either from the French or German systems. Socialist legal systems (a set of legal principles derived from the tenets of Marxism) are a dying breed as we move toward the third decade of the twenty-first century. Formerly, the major socialist legal systems comprised the Soviet Union, the Peoples Republic of China and those countries of Eastern Europe and Asia that found themselves under Soviet domination. However, as China modernizes its economy and its system of external legal principles, with the demise of the Soviet Union, and as the countries of eastern Europe join the European Union (EU), the concept of a socialist legal system is nearly an anachronism. The Islamic systems, principally but not exclusively located in the Middle East, obtain their commercial doctrines from the teachings of the Koran and other Islamic religious teachings.

In recent years, there has been some movement toward development of commercial law principles on a regional basis. For example, the EU, formerly referred to as the EC or "Common Market" promulgates certain commercial and antitrust principles applicable to all the countries of the EU. The countries in Latin America's MERCOSUR trading group and the Association of Southeast Asian Nations (ASEAN) of the Far East have also started discussing regional economic and commercial practices. The last half of the twentieth century saw the formation of a number of regional trade groupings such as the North American Free Trade Agreement. These regional trade groups have developed commercial principles applicable to all participating countries.

While there may be a great deal of controversy with regard to the economic wisdom of regional trade groupings, these trends appear to have promoted a great deal of trade law uniformity thus eliminating much of the uncertainty one traditionally encountered in putting together an international business transaction. Still, when one

---

Contract Law: England, France, Germany (1994); Michael Bogdan, *Comparative Law* (1994); *Introduction to Foreign Legal Systems* (Richard A. Danner ed., 1994); Rene David & John E.C. Brierley, *Major Legal Systems in the World Today* (3d ed., 1985). Any reader searching for materials on international law, comparative law, and the law of individual countries may profitably consult the United States Library of Congress and its fabulous law library, including all of its web-based information sources. The Library of Congress' website is: www.loc.gov. The Library of Congress' law library sources may be accessed at www.loc.gov/law/find.

searches for the "law" governing the deal, he or she will of necessity look to the domestic law of individual countries. Often the law of an individual country may be better understood if a lawyer or business executive can place that country within a particular family of comparative law.

In a book such as this it is impossible to illustrate every conceivable nuance of commercial law within each of the four families of law. Some examples, however, are instructive to demonstrate how each system deals with certain fundamental issues of commercial practice. The discussion of each of the families of law set out below will address, among other things, how legal systems within that family deal with three important commercial concepts: (1) impossibility or frustration of performance; (2) the requirement of good faith in commercial dealing; and (3) the application of trade usage or course of dealing to the interpretation of contracts.

Impossibility of performance or *frustration* are encountered when events occur that impede performance of the contract or make performance totally impossible. International lawyers frequently refer to this as a force majeure event.[4] For example, fire or shipwreck may destroy the goods that are subject to the contract. An earthquake or volcanic eruption may destroy the factory where the goods are manufactured. War or insurrection may inhibit the shipment of goods or the delivery of services. Many force majeure events are what people frequently refer to as acts of God. But mere mortals may also play a role. For example, a government may take some action that limits or prohibits the transaction in question as when a country forbids the sale or consumption of alcohol. Governmental action of this sort is sometimes referred to as a *supervening illegality*, but is also normally recognized as a force majeure event.

Good faith may be difficult to define in the abstract but comprises one of the fundamental assumptions of modern commerce. If merchants cannot presume good faith on the part of the other contracting party, they probably will not agree to the transaction in the first instance. But even if the concept of good faith is elusive and theoretical, it can become important in allocating blame and risk when a dispute arises under the contract.

Trade usage is difficult to define in the abstract but is often of vital importance in resolving dispute. Even the best-drafted contracts contain ambiguities. Contracts that are to be performed over a long period of time may develop ambiguities even when the original language seems clear at the point of contract formation. When ambiguities have to be addressed, it is often helpful to see how other members of the same industry or business conduct their activities. However, not all systems of law permit reference to an industry's usage of trade or course of dealing as a tool for determining normal practices within an industry. To the extent that a legal system does not comprehend reference to terms outside the contract it may not have the necessary flexibility to be a good system for dealing with commercial matters.

4. *See* generally, Symposium, *In the Wake of the Storm: Nonperformance of Contract Obligations Resulting from a Natural Disaster*, 31 Nova L. Rev. 551 (2007).

§2.4 THE CIVIL LAW SYSTEM

The civil law system traces its origins to Roman law and, more specifically, to probably the most distinguished contemporaneous compilation of Roman law, the sixth century Corpus Juris Civilis of Justinian (the Justinian Code). This compilation of law was revived for both study and application as the Western European countries began to develop mature, modern legal systems. The Justinian Code set the stage for many of the concepts of the present civil law system, and has many of the attributes of a modern legal system.[5] For example, it was intended to be a complete and exhaustive statement of the law, a concept that led directly to the modern idea of a civil code as an exhaustive and fully integrated body of law.

Certain concepts of canon law also affected the development of Roman law; but these principles, while generally accepted in most of Europe for a number of centuries, proved not especially suitable for commercial transactions. Because some of the early legal principles did not lend themselves easily to commercial practices, merchants began creating informal modes of dealing with each other that eventually hardened into legal principles accepted by the domestic courts of the various countries.

As the European nation-states proliferated in the eighteenth and nineteenth centuries, national legal systems emerged through the process known as codification, a movement that began in the Scandinavian countries and later found its way into the remainder of Europe. The codification movement culminated in the two most prominent codes in existence today, both of which provide the basis for today's civil law tradition. The Code civil des francais (often referred to as the Code Napoleon) was promulgated in 1804 and was followed nearly a century later by the German Civil Code of 1896.

The French Code has been adopted by or has significantly influenced a large number of domestic legal systems, including the legal systems of Belgium and Luxembourg, the Netherlands Civil Code of 1838, the Portuguese Civil Code of 1867 (now replaced with a new code promulgated in 1967), the Spanish Civil Code of 1888, some of the Eastern European countries including Poland and virtually all of France's colonial possessions. The German code, drafted almost 100 years later, was created in a different political atmosphere and under a far different tradition of legal scholarship. While the French code was viewed as a kind of everyman's law—written in general terms so that it could be read and understood by the average citizen—the German Code (*Burgerliches Gesetzbuch*) grew out of so-called scientific legal scholarship and resulted in a highly detailed set of provisions drafted with specific reference solely to Germany. The German Code is a distinguished work of legal scholarship by any standard but is one that, as one set of commentators stated, "was not built to travel."[6] Nevertheless,

5. *See*, e.g., John Henry Merryman, David S. Clark & John Owen Haley, *Comparative Law: Historical Development of the Civil Law Tradition in Europe, Latin America, and East Asia* (2010); John Henry Merryman & Rogelio Perez-Perdomo, *The Civil Law Tradition* (3d ed., 2007); Andrew Harding, *Comparative Law in the 21st Century* (2002); Franz Wieacker, *The Importance of Roman Law for Western Civilization and Western Legal Thought*, 4 B.C. Int'l & Comp. L. Rev. 257 (1981).
6. Glendon, *supra* n. 3.

the German code has had a substantial influence on a number of countries including Greece, Switzerland, Brazil and, perhaps most importantly, Japan.

Codification in these countries was only the first step, however. As the nations developed more sophisticated forms of government, and as the work of government became more complicated, the judiciary began to affect the law contained in the codes by deciding individual cases. This led inexorably to a body of judge-made law that exerts a strong influence on the legal system, even though, in theory, in civil law systems courts are not permitted to modify the code by judicial decision-making. One comparative law scholar, Professor Ferdinand Stone has identified four basic goals of a code system: (1) that the law be written essentially in the form of statutes, rather than in the form of court opinions; (2) that the provisions of the code be drafted and arranged systematically (e.g., organizing contract principles beginning with the formation of the contract and perhaps concluding with remedies for breach of contract); (3) that the code be dealt with by courts and subsequent legislatures in a unified fashion (a "seamless web" as it were); and (4) that the code be constructed by experts rather than lay persons.[7]

Have all these goals been achieved? Not exactly. Is a code system the perfect system of law? Probably not. Most codes have as many disadvantages as advantages.

Generally, the civil code systems try to separate the law into public law and private law, but with little success in preventing a great deal of overlap. In addition, although a civil code governs a large number of issues of private law it is not necessarily an exhaustive treatment of all possible questions. For example, France adopted a separate commercial code, the Code de Commerce, in 1807 shortly after adopting the Code Napoleon because the Code Napoleon simply did not address all the issues that a modern commercial system requires. German courts have historically recognized certain principles of Handelsrecht (commercial law) standing separate and apart from the main codification. Today, the most important aspects of civil and commercial law are merged in most civil code countries. Professor Rene David notes "[t]he Civil law has been commercialized to such a degree in all economically developed nations that there are hardly any rules left in which commercial obligations are treated differently from civil obligations."[8]

Because the civil codes grew up in nations with strong traditions of business and contract, the codes are generally sympathetic to the formation and performance of contracts. For example, both the French and German codes recognize both bilateral (promises made by both contracting parties) and unilateral (a promise made by one party yet enforceable by the other party) contracts. Article 1101 of the French Code defines contract as "an agreement through which one or more persons obligate themselves to one or more other persons to give, or to do or not to do, something." Article 1102 provides: "A contract is synallagmatic or bilateral when the contracting parties mutually obligate themselves each toward the other." Article 320 of the German Civil Code elaborates on the duties of persons who are parties to bilateral contracts: "A

7. Ferdinand F. Stone, *A Primer on Codification*, 29 Tul. L. Rev. 303 (1955).
8. David & Brierley, *supra* n. 3, at 90.

person who is bound by a mutual contract may refuse to perform his part until the other party has performed his part, unless the former is bound to perform his part first."

Both systems explicitly recognize impossibility of performance (the excuse of performance when it becomes impossible for one or the other party to live up to his obligations), require good faith and recognize common business practices (course of dealing or usage) in commercial arrangements. Note, for example, the following extracts from both the French and German Codes:

(1) *Impossibility and frustration of performance*: Under the French Code, Article 1134 states that contracts "cannot be revoked except by mutual consent or on grounds allowed by law."[9] Most courts and commentators have viewed the general article on contracts as a firm, virtually inflexible command of performance irrespective of unanticipated changes in circumstances. There are, of course, additional provisions in the Code such as Article 1147: "An obligor shall be ordered to pay damages [for nonperformance] ... whenever he does not establish that the nonperformance is due to a foreign cause that cannot be imputed to him. ... " But these provisions have never been used as a basis to override Article 1134's fundamental duty of performance.

The German Code was substantially revised in 2002, but most of its basic provisions, while somewhat differently phrased, remain largely intact in purpose and intent. The current German code contains a number of provisions suggesting that performance under a contract might be forgiven or adjusted due to unforeseen circumstances.[10] For example, Article 275 states: (1) "A claim for performance cannot be made in so far as it is impossible for the obligor or anyone else to perform." Article 275 goes on to provide that "the obligor may refuse to perform in so far as performance requires expenditure which, having regard to the subject-matter of the obligation and the principle of good faith, is manifestly disproportionate to the obligee's interest in performance. When determining what may reasonably be required of the obligor, regard must be had as to whether he is responsible for the impediment."

While the language of each of these articles is reasonably clear, even in civil code jurisdictions courts will adjudicate the application of code provisions to specific facts. In both the French and German systems forgiveness of performance has generally been allowed only if the event that impedes performance was not reasonably foreseeable and when the performance is humanly

9. *See* generally, John Bell & Sophie Boyron, *Principles of French Law* (2008); Barry Nicholas, *The French Law of Contract* (2d ed., 1992).

10. *See* generally, Ernest Joseph Schuster, *The Principles of German Civil Law* (2015); Sir Basil Markesinis, Hannes Unberath & Angus Johnston, *The German Law of Contract: A Comparative Treatise* (2006); Reinhard Zimmerman, *The New German Law of Obligations: Historical and Comparative Perspectives (2006). Key Aspects of German Business Law: A Practice Manual* (Michael Wendler, Bernd Tremmi & Bernard John Buecker eds., 3d ed., 2006).

impossible. Moreover, the event that makes the contract nonperformable must not be attributable to any action by one of the contracting parties.[11]

(2) *Good Faith and Custom and Usage*: The French Code states: "[Contracts] must be performed in good faith" (Article 1134) and "ambiguous provisions are to be interpreted in accordance with the usage of the region in which the contract is concluded" (Article 1159). The German Code provides: "The obligor must perform in a manner consistent with good faith taking into account accepted practice" (Article 242).

These extracts make clear that a great deal of the two codes was written to promote commercial dealings by providing both stability and predictability for contracting parties. Stability and predictability largely flow from the establishment of clear and easily understood rules that allow people in business to draft and negotiate their own agreements without heavy-handed interference by either legislature or courts. As such, the French and German civil codes enhance rather than impede the formation of contracts and the honoring of business obligations.

Impossibility of performance, good faith, and custom and usage are not the only legal concepts encountered when dealing with companies in civil code countries. While the influence of the codes is great, of equal importance for modern commercial practice, is the overlay of regulatory provisions that affect such issues as licensing, antitrust, intellectual property and consumer protection measures.

§2.5 THE BRITISH COMMON LAW SYSTEM

Although the common law and civil law systems share roots in Roman law, the evolution of the common law system has taken a different path. Most scholars begin an analysis of the common law systems with the Norman conquest of England in 1066 and the subsequent work of the royal courts of justice. The general principles of the common law grow not out of codification, but rather out of the deciding of specific cases by individual judges over a long period of time.

Through the doctrine of *stare decisis* these decisions, properly read and categorized, eventually result in discernible, generally applicable principles on which future court decisions must be based. *Stare decisis* itself requires at least three assumptions: (1) that a court will render a principled and properly articulated decision—that is, that a court will give sound reasons for its decision; (2) that decisions will be published in some fashion so that other courts dealing with similar cases will know-how earlier cases came out; and (3) that the judicial system will be set up as a hierarchy, with the lower courts required to abide by the decisions of the higher courts.

---

11. *See*, e.g., *Durlach v. Grandgerard, Cour de cassation, Chambre des requetes*, July 3, 1918 (a lease would not be vacated simply because the city of Nancy was under enemy bombardment since the plaintiff did not show that the premises themselves were uninhabitable). German courts may on occasion revise the contract if the parties were agreeable to a revision. *W. v. K., Deutsches Reich, Reichsgericht*, Fifth Civil Senate, January 6, 1923, 106 ERG (Z). *See also*, John P. Dawson, *Judicial Revision of Frustrated Contracts: Germany*, 63 B.U. L. Rev. 1039 (1983).

By definition, the common law system concentrates enormous power in the courts and gives primary influence within the system to lawyers (the system's legal specialists) because lawyers are the only professionals properly schooled in the methods of the common law. At the same time, decisions were not rendered blindly or without regard for history and tradition. The early common law judges searching for a reasoned basis for substantive legal rules often consulted Roman sources. For example, the sanctity of contract doctrine (*pacta sunt servanda*) that was developed to its highest degree in England is historically a principle of Roman law. English commercial law has other roots in the conventional practices of business people, just as in the civil law systems. In 1666, an English court noted: "the law of merchants is the law of the land, and the costume is good enough generally for any man, without naming him merchant."[12] This had the effect of recognizing judicially what had probably been the case for centuries—that the basis for the development of a comprehensive, judge-made body of commercial law lies largely in those common trade practices and usages known as *lex mercatoria* or the law merchant.[13]

For those not familiar with the common law tradition, it is sometimes difficult to understand the immense influence of the courts on commercial practices in the common law countries. A short example may be helpful. In England prior to the mid-1800s it was not entirely certain whether lost profits could be awarded to a company that was injured by another company's breach of a contract. Unquestionably, the British Parliament could have passed a statute establishing some rule on point. However, because Parliament did not do so at that time—and at that point in history rarely legislated on commercial topics in any event—the development of an applicable principle of law was left to the British courts.

In the classic case in point, *Hadley v. Baxendale*,[14] a crankshaft in a mill broke and the mill owners had to send off to the manufacturer for a new shaft. The owners contracted with a transportation company to carry the new shaft from the manufacturer to the mill. The shipment was delayed and as a result the mill did not operate for several days. The mill owners sued the transportation company not only for the price of the shipment (a sum of two pounds, four shillings) but also for the lost profits over those days when the mill did not operate, a far greater sum of money.

The case eventually made its way to the Exchequer Court. The court determined the issue, and announced its decision in the form of a written judicial opinion, only after litigation between the parties. The court concluded:

> Where two parties have made a contract which one of them has broken [here the contract for the transportation of the mill shaft], the damages which the other party ought to receive...should be such as may fairly and reasonably be considered either arising naturally, i.e., according to the usual course of things, from such

12. *Woodward v. Rowe*, 2 K.B. 132, 84 Eng.Rep.84 (1666).
13. *See* generally, Leon E. Trakman, *The Twenty-First Century Law Merchant*, 48 Am. Bus. L. J. 775 (2011); Leon E. Trakman, *The Law Merchant: The Evolution of Commercial Law* (1983); Richard A. Epstein, *The Empirical and Theoretical Underpinnings of the Law Merchant: Reflections on the Historical Origins and Economic Structure of the Law Merchant*, 5 Chi. J. Int'l L. 1 (2004); Celia Wasserstein Fassberg, *Lex Mercatoria—Hoist with Its Own Petard?* 5 Chi. J. Int'l L. 67 (2004).
14. 9 Exch. 341 (1854).

> breach of contract itself, or such as may reasonably be supposed to have been made in the contemplation of both parties, at the time they made the contract.

The court went on to determine that the lost profits had not been contemplated by the parties, because there had been no discussion of profits—or of the consequences of a delay in the shaft's shipment—when the transportation contract was entered into. Consequently, profits were not "reasonable" damages and thus could not be recovered by the mill owners.

Once this decision was announced, the principle of *stare decisis* required that other courts follow the rule of *Hadley v. Baxendale* in all similar cases. The vast majority of British commercial law principles, even those applicable today, were constructed in this fashion. Eventually, over a long period of time, an entire body of commercial law was developed that is probably as good as any other in the world. The doctrines of impossibility of performance, good faith and the use of commercial custom and usage so easily spotted in the French and German civil codes are firmly established in British law by way of case decisions rather than statutes. So, for example, impossibility in British law is a nearly absolute concept, forgiving a party's performance of a contract only when matters become either physically impossible (e.g., when the entire supply of goods is destroyed in a fire) or legally impossible (a legislature makes it a crime to sell alcoholic beverages), not when matters become merely impracticable (such as a mere rise in price).[15]

Even so, the common law method for creating commercial rules is viewed by many continental legal scholars as inefficient and somewhat haphazard since it depends on the decision of only those cases that parties chose to litigate. It is also exceptionally time-consuming. The length of the court's opinion in the *Hadley* case is as long as dozens of French or German code provisions put together. Moreover, readers of court opinion sometimes find it difficult to separate grain from chaff and even more difficult to determine whether a court might apply an earlier case in a new situation in which the facts are just slightly different. This means that most of the system is in the hands of lawyers. Laypersons cannot normally perform these feats of analysis on their own. In theory, but often not in practice, civil codes were promulgated to eliminate many of these difficulties.

At the end of the nineteenth century, the British parliament entered the arena of commercial law by enacting two detailed statutes, the Bills of Exchange Act (1882) and the Sales of Goods Act (1893). These two statutes began as reform movements but ended as attempts to merely reproduce in statutory form, the existing judge-made principles of commercial law.[16] Since then, Parliament has occasionally legislated in specific areas of commercial transactions such as import and export matters, but has left most of British commercial law in the hands of the courts. Fortunately, the case law is well parsed and most fundamental principles of contract are so well established that

15. *See*, e.g., *Ford & Sons, Ltd. v. Henry Leetham & Sons, Ltd.*, 21 Comm. Cas. 55 (1915).
16. The 1979 English Sale of Goods Act has been replaced by the 2015 Consumer Rights Act. *See*, e.g., David Campbell, *Contract Law and Contract Practice: Bridging the Gap Between Legal Reasoning and Commercial Expectation*, L.Q.Rev. 526 (2014). Mackenzie D.E.S. Chalmers, *Sale of Goods Act* (14th ed., 1963).

British merchants have virtually the same sense of stability and predictability as enjoyed by their counterparts in the code countries. Today, British contract and commercial law is highly developed and exceptionally sophisticated, as one might expect of one of the world's major trading nations.

§2.6 COMMERCIAL LAW IN THE UNITED STATES OF AMERICA

U.S. commercial law is derived from the British common law but has lately moved in the direction of codification and national uniformity. This movement toward significant national uniformity has developed in a context that is often not familiar to persons from outside the U.S. To analyze U.S. commercial principles, one must begin with the understanding that, to a large extent, the individual states that make up the United States of America have sovereignty to develop their own commercial law principles. Accordingly, when one looks for commercial "law" in the U.S., one normally does not look to the laws enacted by the national government. This means that there is no absolute uniformity within U.S. commercial law. However, the differences among the various states tend to be relatively small and insubstantial. Over the past sixty years, a great deal of uniformity has been created by state-by-state adoption of the UCC.

The UCC is now the law in 49 states and the District of Columbia. The one state that has not adopted the UCC is Louisiana, a state that entered the Union as a former French colony and that derives some of its commercial principles from the Code Napoleon. But even with Louisiana taking a somewhat different course in developing commercial principles, the differences create very few problems in commercial dealings involving businesses in Louisiana.

It is uncertain whether the UCC was intended to develop as a true code in the French and German sense. Many U.S. legal scholars disagree on this issue. Karl Llewellyn, sometimes regarded as the father of the UCC, saw the UCC as a kind of hybrid "case-law Code" that would set a firm—and uniform—basis for commercial rules, but that would permit the courts to fill in any gaps in the UCC by case law. Other scholars disagree with Llewellyn's view but are still of the opinion that the promulgation of the UCC has been a one of the most important developments in U.S. commercial law.[17]

The UCC is separated into nine articles, dealing variously with sales of goods (Article 2),[18] leases (Article 2A), commercial paper and bank deposits and collections

17. *See* generally, Allen R. Kamp, *Uptown Act: A History of the Uniform Commercial Code: 1940-49*, 51 SMU L. Rev. 275 (1998); George A. Hisert, *Uniform Commercial Code: Does One Size Fit All?* 28 Loy. L.A. L. Rev. 219 (1994); Student Note, *Commercial Law and the American Volk: A Note on Llewellyn's German Sources for the Uniform Commercial Code*, 97 Yale L.J. 156 (1987). For an intense discussion of the Llewellyn position and opposition thereto *see*, Grant Gilmore, *In Memoriam: Karl Llewellyn*, 71 Yale L.J. 813 (1962); William D. Hawkland, *Uniform Commercial "Code" Methodology*, 1962 U.Ill.L.F. 291 (UCC is a true code) and Homer Kripke, *The Principles Underlying the Drafting of the Uniform Commercial Code*, 1962 U.Ill.L.F. 321 (UCC is merely a proper restatement of common law principles). One of the best basic treatises on the UCC is James White & Robert Summers, *Uniform Commercial Code (Hornbook)* (6th ed., 2010).
18. The full text of Art. 2 is available at numerous state law websites. For example, the District of Columbia UCC may be found at www.dc.gov (dclaws).

(Articles 3 and 4), letters of credit (Article 5), bulk transfers (Article 6), documents of title (Article 7), investment securities (Article 8), and secured transactions (Article 9). A number of provisions in Article 2 on sales of goods address the same matters examined under French, German and British law.

Under the UCC, impossibility of performance has been transmuted into a concept of *impracticability of performance* (§2-615) by providing:

> Delay in delivery...by a seller...is not a breach of his duty under a contract for sale if performance as agreed has been made impracticable by the occurrence of a contingency the nonoccurrence of which was a basic assumption on which the contract was made or by compliance in good faith with any applicable foreign or domestic governmental regulation.

The official comments to the UCC make clear that the use of the term *impracticable* is intended to include circumstances that are less onerous than absolute impossibility of performance, although there is a serious question whether section 2-615 excuses performance of a contract merely because of increases in prices.[19]

Similarly, section 1-203 establishes a fundamental obligation of good faith for all transactions governed by the Code by providing: "Every contract or duty within this Act imposes an obligation of good faith in its performance or enforcement." Section 2-208 permits a contract to be construed in terms of the merchants' course of performance and the general usages of trade unless the contract provides otherwise.

The UCC is not the sum total of U.S. commercial law, however. Even though the UCC is one of the primary sources of commercial law in the United States, and even though it has had an impact far beyond the boundaries of the United States because it is so often incorporated as the law applicable to international commercial agreements, there is a great deal of American commercial practice that is not covered by the Code. For example, the UCC does not cover contracts for the purchase and sale of services. It has virtually nothing to do with the purchase and sale of real estate. Until an Article 2A was added about twenty years ago, the UCC did not apply to leases of goods. For the law governing these matters, American lawyers look to the common law of each state and statutes in the various states apart from the UCC that may affect the subject matter of the transaction. Looking to the common law, as in the British system, requires the analysis of numerous court decisions.

§2.7 SOCIALIST LEGAL SYSTEMS

As we move through the first decade of the twenty-first century, this section is something of an anachronism. Nonetheless, because a few socialist states remain, a

19. *See* generally, Paula Walter, *Commercial Impracticability in Contracts*, 61 St. John's L. Rev. 225 (2012); Stephen G. York, *The Impracticability Doctrine of the U.C.C.*, 29 Duq. L. Rev. 221 (1991); Jonathan A. Eddy & Peter Winship, *Commercial Transactions: Text, Cases & Problems* (1985), 543–552 and Richard E. Speidel, *Excusable Non-Performance in Sales Contracts: Some Thoughts About Risk Management*, 32 S.Car. L. Rev. 241 (1980). *See also*, Carla Spivak, *Of Shrinking Sweatsuits and Poison Vine Wax: A Comparison of Basis for Excuse under U.C.C. §2-615 and CISG Article 79*, 27 U.Pa.J. Econ. L. 757 (2006).

reader may encounter a socialist legal system in practice. Cuba, North Korea and perhaps one or two other countries are avowedly socialist.

This system of law had its origins in the 1917 political revolution in Russia which set the stage for a parallel revolution in its legal system that, in turn, has affected a number of other countries when those countries adopted socialism as their form of government. Under Marxist theory, the government—and by implication, the law—was eventually to wither away. However, in the interim all socialist countries have developed highly sophisticated systems of legal controls that affect not only the conduct of individuals within those societies, but also the nature and course of commercial practices in those countries.

In theory, the concept of a private contract is antithetical to a socialist system. Under socialism, the state has three tasks: (1) to provide for national security; (2) to enhance economic development so that each person receives goods and services according to his need; and (3) to eliminate the acquisitive tendencies of human beings that are characteristic of capitalist societies and that are so detrimental to the building of a truly fair and just society. None of these goals comprehends commercial contractual relationships between private persons. To the extent that the state must engage in international trade either with other collective systems or with private companies outside the socialist country, those contracts are executed and performed by the government, not by individuals.

Of course, theory gives way to reality in most systems of government. In all socialist systems, the law springs primarily from the central government in the form of legislation and proclamations. The following is an illustration, based on practices in the former Soviet Union that typifies a socialist legal systems development of commercial legal principles.

As a byproduct of the central government's economic activities, many countries, including the former Soviet Union, established a concept of internal contracting that was based on various economic plans written by the government. Within the strictures of the economic plan, each affected economic enterprise is required to enter into a plan contract with another related enterprise for the supply of the raw materials needed for it to meet its production plan. Thus, for example, an enterprise that produces automobiles will be required to contract with an enterprise that produces tires.[20]

Disputes that arise under these plan contracts are typically handled through a system of economic courts that function in much the same way as a Western arbitration system. They review disputes in terms of state economic goals rather than in terms of narrow principles of contract law and are frequently dissociated from the regular courts of the country.[21]

These arbitral bodies are generally limited to internal disputes between governmental entities. Contracts between the national government and foreign private companies are negotiated and performed between the private companies and a governmental body referred to as a foreign trading organization or foreign trading

20. Glendon, *supra* n. 3, at 766–767. For an excellent general work on Soviet law *see*, John Hazard, William Butler & Peter B. Maggs, *The Soviet Legal System* (3d ed., 1977).
21. *Id.*

commission. The foreign trading commission functions much like a private party in that it negotiates and signs contracts and participates in various types of dispute resolution.[22] In the former Soviet Union, such contracts were often standard form contracts of adhesion. If the western participant chose to enter the deal, it either accepted the standard clauses proffered by the foreign trading commission or did not do the deal.

§2.7.1 Life after the Soviet Union

The more difficult, yet fascinating question is what happens when a country throws off its socialist legal system. In Eastern Europe and in many of the republics of the former Soviet Union (sometimes referred to as the Commonwealth of Independent States), the governments, with Western assistance, rushed to develop modern systems of commercial practice and regulation.

In Russia there is a body of law that now forms the basis for a new system of contract law.[23] There are many useful provisions to be found in the basic civil code for the Russian Republic, a code with heavy Germanic influences that appears to have outlived socialism. For example, the Article 130 of the Russian civil code prescribes that a contract must contain the following elements to be valid: "the subject matter of the contract, the price, the time, as well as all other particulars with respect to which, according to the preliminary declaration of either party, agreement was to be reached." The civil code contains a flavor of impossibility and frustration in Article 144 that provides, in part: "If performance of a bilateral contract by one of the parties becomes impossible owing to circumstances for which neither party is liable, then, unless the law or contract provides otherwise, such party shall have no right to claim any benefits under the contract from the other party." Article 235 provides: "An obligation is terminated by impossibility of performance, if the impossibility is caused by a circumstance for which the obligor is not responsible. ..."

It is impossible to predict the final dimensions of the political and economic systems of Russia or the former Soviet Republics. A large part of the Soviet Bloc countries, such as Poland, the Czech Republic and Hungary, have taken their seats within various western European institutions including the EU. To the extent that these trends continue, western European models are surely the best predictions of future

22. *See* e.g., Olga Schwartz & William Burnham, *Law & Legal System of The Russian Federation* (6th ed., 2015). A book on the Russian economy and political system is: Erik Berghof, Andrei Kunov, Julia Shvets & Ksenia Yadaeva, *The New Political Economy of Russia* (2003). Years ago the best work on trade with the former USSR, now dated but with some fascinating excursions on the Russian personality and character, is Thomas W. Hoya, *East-West Trade: Comecon Law, American-Soviet Trade* (1984). Mr. Hoya is also the author of several law review articles on the same subject that are now incorporated in his book. *See*, e.g., Thomas W. Hoya & Daniel D. Stern, *Drafting Contracts in U.S.-Soviet Trade*, 7 Law & Pol'y Int'l Bus. 1057 (1975). *See also*, Harold J. Berman & George L. Bustin, *The Soviet System of Foreign Trade*, 7 Law & Pol'y Int'l Bus. 987 (1975).
23. *See* Schwartz & Burnham, *supra* n. 22. *See also A Legal Guide to Doing Business in Russian and the Former Republics of the U.S.S.R.* (Aviva Yakren ed., 2000).

business and legal trends. To the extent that countries such as Cuba and North Korea persist in maintaining a socialist legal system, they may be even further isolated from the community of trading nations.

§2.7.2 China

As we move toward the second decade of the twenty-first century, China has become one of the world's major trading nations.[24] The current Chinese government is quite enthusiastic about expanding its trade opportunities and has developed modern legal regimes to govern contracts with private companies outside China. Indeed, many regions of China, particularly the province of Guandzhou, are now functioning almost independently of the central government and have instituted market mechanism economic principles—and related legal reforms—that have greatly enhanced economic growth in those regions. China has accepted the Vienna CISG, the Berne Copyright treaty and a number of other important international agreements that are intended to promote and harmonize world trade. In 2002 China became joined the World Trade Organization. In 2008 China hosted the Summer Olympics—a significant mark of international status and achievement.

But just a few years ago, some of the shadows of socialism and central control could still be found in the Chinese system. In years past, China followed the basic Soviet approach of insisting that contracts be with a governmental contracting entity. In addition, the terms and conditions of the contract were imposed, in part, through a series of Chinese government pronouncement that resemble administrative agency regulations in the United States. So, for example, the 1979 joint venture law promulgated by the government of the Peoples Republic contained only 15 articles covering such matters as registration of the joint venture, taxation of the venture, marketing and distribution arrangements, and a kind of "buy-Chinese" provision that obligated the joint venture to seek raw materials in the first instance from Chinese sources.

This very rudimentary enactment, primitive by Western legal standards, was hailed as a breakthrough in Chinese attitudes toward the West and toward entrepreneurial activities in 1979. It was followed by a number of increasingly sophisticated legal instruments—for example, the Foreign Economic Contract Law and the Joint Venture Law of 1985—initiatives that that confirmed China's desire to become a major trading nation.

Even more dramatic innovations followed as China sought membership in the World Trade Organization, most-favored nation status with the United States and a role as a powerful trading nation. In 1999 China promulgated the Uniform Contract Law (UCL) as one component of a series of initiatives to qualify for World Trade Association

24. *See* generally, Chao Xi & Tim Ambler, *Doing Business in China* (4th ed., 2016). Freshfields China Business Group, *Doing Business in China* (2004); Stanley Lubman, *Looking for Law in China*, 20 Colum. J. Asian L. 1 (2006); John H. Matheson, *Convergence, Culture and Contract Law in China*, 15 Minn. J. Int'l L. 329 (2006); Patricia Pattison & Daniel Herron, *The Mountains Are High and the Emperor Is Far Away: Sanctity of Contract in China*, 40 Am. Bus. L.J. 459 (2003).

membership.[25] The enactment of the UCL expressly repealed the earlier Economic Contract Law, the Foreign Economic Contract Law and the 1987 Technology Contract Law.[26] The UCL draws heavily on Western legal instruments such as the International Institute for the Unification of Private Law (UNIDROIT) principles and the CISG (*see* Chapter 4). The avowed purposes of the UCL are unexceptional while still paying lip service to China's socialist groundings—that is, "protecting the legitimate rights and interests of the parties to contracts, maintaining the socioeconomic order and promoting the socialist modernization."

While too voluminous to discuss fully in this book, the UCL contains 129 separate articles dealing with general contracting requirements (the "General Principles") and an additional 299 articles that deal with specific types of contracts (the "Specific Provisions"). It attempts to place domestic and international contracts on an equal footing. It recognizes certain electronic commerce devices. Echoing the CISG, it permits oral as well as written contracts in certain instances. It contains an express statement of good faith: "The parties shall observe the principle of good faith in exercising their rights and fulfilling their obligations."[27] The UCL is premised on full performance of contractual obligations: "The parties shall fulfill fully their respective obligations as contracted."[28] But it also recognizes and addresses the possibility and the consequences of breach: Article 107 provides: "[I]f a party fails to perform its obligations under a contract, or rendered nonconforming performance, it shall bear the liabilities for breach of contract by specific performance, cure of the nonconforming performance, or payment of damages." The Specific Provisions get into the details of, for example, sale of goods, gifts, and construction contracts.

Most observers believe that the UCL is a good start and a healthy development for the future. However, there are so many other components of doing business in China that must be addressed, it is only a piece of the puzzle. Some of these other pieces of the puzzle, such as intellectual property in China (Chapter 6) and dispute resolution (Chapter 11) are discussed elsewhere in this book.

§2.8 ISLAMIC LEGAL SYSTEMS

Most Islamic legal systems are a mixture of civil codes (the Code Napoleon has had particular influence in the Middle East) and the principles of law that grow out of the fundamental tenets of the Islamic religion. To the extent that a predominantly Islamic country conducts its commercial business by civil code devices, it will not differ all that much from the basic concepts discussed in §2.3 above. However, to the extent that a

25. The text of the UCL (promulgated by the National People's Congress on March 15, 1999 with an effective date of October 1, 1999) can be found in English language translation in Chinese Civil Law Forum, www.cclaw.net.
26. *See* generally, Preston Torbert, *Globalizing Legal Drafting: What the Chinese Can Teach Us About Ejusdem Generis and All That*, 41 Scribes J. Leg. Writing (2007). Feng Chen, *The New Era of Chinese Contract Law: History, Development, and a Comparative Analysis*, 27 Brook. J. Int'l L. 153 (2001).
27. UCL, Art. 6.
28. *Id.*, Art. 60.

particular country has returned to a theocratic base for its legal system, an understanding of some basic principles of Islam is necessary even if one's only interest is in the commercial area.

The Islamic legal system is normally referred to as the Shari'a (a literal translation of which is "way to follow"). The Shari'a prescribes detailed codes of conduct for Muslims in all areas of their life, both personal and commercial. As a consequence there are few of the sharp distinctions between private matters, such as, say, domestic relations, and commercial law that are common in Western societies.

The Shari'a flows from four sources. The Qur'an is the cornerstone of Islam—a recitation of the words spoken by God to Mohammed. The Sunna is what might be regarded as the pronouncements of Mohammed himself and includes descriptions of his activities while he was alive and his statements on various human activities. The Ijma is the work of Islamic scholars who attempted to fill gaps in the principles set out in the Qur'an and the Sunna; and the Qiyas is another work of scholarship by which various principles are derived by analogy from the pronouncements in the Qur'an and the Sunna.

It is not inappropriate to refer to these writings as a sort of codification of legal principles. However, the application of the principles themselves is almost always on a case-by-case basis with few individual decisions committed to writing. To analogize, perhaps too broadly, to American law, the Shari'a is something like a system based on the UCC without reported court decisions construing the UCC's individual provisions.

Westerners frequently blanch at the use of a theologically based system of law in a commercial setting, while conveniently forgetting that more than a little Western law (e.g., certain prohibitions on usury and the enforcement of certain unilateral promises in some civil code countries) has definite religious underpinnings. In many countries, the Shari'a has evolved to the point where it has some utility in controlling mercantile behavior.[29]

However, it does take some getting used to under the best of circumstances. For example, a number of precepts in the Shari'a prohibiting certain forms of interest as usurious, have inhibited the negotiation and execution of a number of commercial

29. *See* generally, David Powers, *Islamic Legal Thought* (2013); Gil Feiler, *The Middle East in the New Millennium: Economic Development and Business Law* (2000); George N. Sfeir, *Modernization of the Law in Arab States: An Investigation into Current Civil, Criminal and Constitutional Law in the Arab World* (1998); *Islamic Law and Legal Theory* (Ian Edge ed., 1996); Nayla Comair-Obeid, *The Law of Business Contracts in the Arab Middle East: A Theoretical and Practical Comparative Analysis* (1996); International Bar Association, *Arab Comparative and Commercial Law: The International Approach* (1987); Noel J. Coulson, *Commercial Law in the Gulf States: The Islamic Legal Tradition* (1984). For some articles addressing these and other issues, *see*: Emilia Justyna Powell & Stephanie J. Rickard, *International Trade and Domestic Legal Systems: Examining the Impact of Islamic Law*, 36 Int'l. Interactions 335 (2010); Faisal Kutty, *The Shari'a Factor in International Commercial Arbitration*, 28 Loy. L.A. Int'l & Comp. L. Rev. 565 (2006); John H. Donboli & Farnaz Kashefi, *Doing Business in the Middle East: A Primer for U.S. Companies*, 38 Cornell Int'l L.J. 413 (2005); Irshad Abdal-Haqq, *Islamic Law: An Overview of Its Origins and Elements*, 7 J. Islamic L. & Culture 27 (2002); Ali Ahmad, *The Role of Islamic Law in the Contemporary World Order*, 6 J. Islamic L. & Culture 157 (2001); H.S. Shaaban, *Commercial Transactions in the Middle East: What Law Governs* ? 31 Law & Pol'y Int'l Bus. 157 (1999).

transactions. By contrast, a number of principles to be found in the Qur'an and the Sunna admonish Muslims to abide by their promises and obligations and extend the protections of the Shari'a to both Muslims and non-Muslims. This suggests that an elaborate document freely consented to by the parties will go a long way toward preserving an agreement.

The tenets of the Shari'a tend to preserve an obligation of good faith, but also insist upon a literalist approach to the contract, which often forbids cancellation or revision based on impossibility or frustration. To this extent, it is a more inflexible system than, say, the American UCC. However, the incorporation of the Shari'a is often insisted upon by government entities in Islamic countries and as a consequence cannot always be avoided.

Impossibility and frustration are generally recognized through the doctrine of *Riba* which seeks to protect against risk and uncertainty, but which is normally fleshed out in the context of individual cases in the Islamic courts. It appears to be a much more relaxed doctrine than the doctrine of impossibility in Western courts (which, as noted above, usually forgives performance only in instances of absolute inability to perform, rather than mere inconvenience or impracticability). In the view of some commentators *Riba* may have impeded commercial development by making it too easy for a contracting party to avoid his obligations under the contract.[30] One recent development of concern to Western business executives is the use of some of the pronouncements in the Shari'a on the collection of interest on a loan (generally forbidden by the Shari'a) as grounds for avoiding loan contracts whose interest rates are deemed excessive by courts in Islamic countries. Some Saudi Arabian courts have suggested that interest-bearing loan agreements would not be enforceable in Saudi courts.[31]

This observation is not, of course, intended to cast aspersions on the legitimacy of the Islamic system of law. As noted earlier, most Western systems also have a historical basis in religion and religious practices. It is rather to illustrate some of the often unanticipated difficulties which arise when a contract is grounded in a system of law with which one of the parties may be unfamiliar.

§2.9 THE IMPACT OF INTERNATIONAL PRINCIPLES OF COMMERCIAL LAW

§2.9.1 International Law Generally

International law is also beginning to contribute significant principles for the execution and performance of international commercial agreements. These principles have been developed on the international level through two separate sources. The first is the body

30. *See*, M. Cherif Bassiouni & Gamal M. Badr, *The Shari'ah: Sources, Interpretation, and Rule-Making*, 1 UCLA J. Islamic & Near E.L. 135 (2002); Chibli Mallat, *Commercial Law in the Middle East: Between Classical Transactions and Modern Business*, 48 Am. J. Comp. L. 81 (2000); Nayla Comair-Obeid, *The Law of Business Contracts in the Arab Middle East: A Theoretical and Practical Comparative Analysis* (1996); *Book Review of Commercial Law in the Gulf States*, 20 Int'l Law. 442, 447 (1986).
31. *See*, e.g., 8 *International Lawyers' Newsletter* 1 (May/June 1986).

of law known as public international law. As Wolfgang Friedmann recognized more than fifty years ago: "private corporations are now active participants in the evolution of public international law. This is mainly the result of the manifold international economic activities of private corporations coupled with the emergence of a large number of economically underdeveloped countries claiming [sovereignty] over their natural resources but needing foreign financial, technical and managerial assistance" in the development of those resources.[32]

Within public international law there are a number of sources of doctrine. These sources are now recognized in codified form in Article 38(1) of the Statute of the International Court of Justice and include:

(1) international conventions (treaties), whether general or particular, establishing rules expressly recognized by the contesting states;
(2) international custom, as evidence of a general practice accepted by law;
(3) the general principles of law recognized by civilized nations; and, in certain circumstances;
(4) judicial decisions and the teachings of the most highly qualified publicists of the various nations.

Most commentators regard Article 38(1) as an exclusive statement of the sources of international law. Even though the sources are not expressly stated to be a hierarchy, most scholars regard sources 1 and 2 as the most important.[33] Within the last three categories lies the genesis of a special system of international commercial law which some scholars refer to as *lex mercatoria* (the law merchant)—a synthesis of generally held and generally accepted commercial principles that may be expected to be applied to contracts among the major trading nations.

The substantive general principles that have emerged are essentially threefold: (1) a merchant must deal in good faith; (2) an agreement between merchants is binding on them—a principle derived from the old Roman doctrine known as *pacta sunt servanda*; and (3) if a dispute arises, a merchant is obligated to abide by the decision of a merchants' court (an early form of arbitration) or face commercial ostracism.[34] Whether the *lex mercatoria* really exists, however, is not fully certain. At least one commentator suggests that it is simply a reflection "of the increasing uniformity of commercial laws in the major jurisdictions and of a judicial tendency to uphold

32. Wolfgang G. Friedmann, *The Changing Structure of International Law* 375 (1964).
33. Ian A. Brownlie, *Principles of Public International Law* 3 (3d ed., 1979). Following Professor Brownlie's death, the book was revised by Professor James Crawford. It is now: *Brownlie's Principles of Public International Law* (8th ed., 2012).
34. *See*, e.g., Gilles Cuniberti, *Three Theories of Lex Mercatoria*, 52 Colum. J. Transnatl L. 369 (2012); Alex Stone Sweet, *The New Lex Mercatoria and Transnational Governance*, 13 J. Eur. Pub. Policy 627 (2006); Leon E. Trakman, *The Evolution of the Law Merchant: Our Commercial Heritage*, 12 J. Mar. L. & Com. 1, 153 (1980); Harold J. Berman & Colin Kaufman, *The Law of International Commercial Transactions (Lex Mercatoria)*, 19 Harv. Int'l L.J. 221 (1978); Ernst von Caemmerer, *The Influence of the Law of International Trade on the Development and Character of the Commercial Law in the Civil Law Countries*, in *The Sources of the Law of International Trade* (Clive Schmitthoff ed., 1964).

international contracts."[35] Some commentators see a new *lex mercatoria* arising from the decisions of arbitrators in international commercial arbitrations.[36]

In recent years the UN has taken the lead in developing more uniformity in international commercial law through various conventions and agreements primarily encouraged through the actions of the United Nations Commission on International Trade Law (UNCITRAL). The UN's work in developing the Vienna CISG, its work in developing the UNCITRAL Model Law of International Commercial Arbitration and other ventures have begun to unify much of the law and practice of international trade.[37]

It is clear that one might compose a fairly lengthy list of commercial principles on which most nations would agree. But such a list does not necessarily constitute an articulable or enforceable body of law. In all likelihood most lawyers and business people would agree with the comment that transnational law is something of a misnomer, or at least a "phrase without meaning" and a recognition that the existing bodies of law are not quite up to coping with international commercial dealings in the last few years of the twentieth century.[38] There is, however, one relatively recent development that cannot be ignored and which may ultimately provide a true, enforceable set of commercial law principles to govern international contracts—the Vienna CISG.

§2.9.2 The UNIDROIT Convention and the UNIDROIT Contract Principles

Between World War One and World War Two the League of Nations established the *UNIDROIT*, one of whose primary missions was to develop a uniform set of legal principles governing international sales of goods. The demise of the League of Nations and World War Two interrupted the work of UNIDROIT and deprived the Institute of its between-the-wars momentum.[39] Although considerably eclipsed by the work of the UN, UNIDROIT still exists as a separate entity with headquarters in Rome. The UNIDROIT contract principles, ratified by a much smaller number of countries than

35. Philip Wood, *The Law and Practice of International Finance* (2008).
36. Bernardo Cremades & Steven L. Plehn, *The New Lex Mercatoria and the Harmonization of the Laws of International Commercial Transactions*, 2 B.U. Int'l L.J. 317 (1984).
37. *See*, e.g., Sergie Cigoj, *International Sales: Formation of Contracts*, 23 Netherlands Int'l L. Rev. 257 (1976); Leonard Lazar, *Transnational Economic and Monetary Law* (1981).
38. Lazar, *supra* n. 37, at 103.
39. *See*, e.g., Ralf Michaels, *The UNIDROIT Principles as Global Background Law*, 19 Unif. L. Rev. 643 (2014); Bruno Zeller, *The UNIDROIT Principles of Contract Law: Is There Room for Their Inclusion into Domestic Contracts?*, 26 J. Law & Commerce 115 (2008); Michael J. Bonnell, *From UNIDROIT Principles 1994 to UNIDROIT Principles 2004: A Further Step Towards a Global Contract Law*, 37 U.C.C. L.J. 49 (2004). M del Pilar Perales Viscasillas, *UNIDROIT Principles of International Commercial Contracts: Sphere of Application and General Principles*, 13 Ariz. J. Int'l & Comp. L. 381 (1996); Michael Joachim Bonell, *The UNIDROIT Principles of International Commercial Contracts: Why? What? How?* 69 Tul. L. Rev. 1121 (1995). Joseph M. Perillo, *UNIDROIT Principles of International Commercial Contracts: The Black Letter Text and a Review*, 63 Fordham L. Rev. 281 (1994).

have ratified the UN conventions, have support in many European countries. The UNIDROIT principles were most recently amended and clarified in 2004.[40]

The UNIDROIT principles are promulgated with an understanding that they can be incorporated merely by reference in a contract and thereby "they not only save time, but are also able to take advantage of provisions which are drafted by specialists in the respective trade sector or area of law and successfully tested in practice."[41] They have the additional advantage of having been drafted by international legal scholars and thus are essentially "neutral" in scope and effect.[42]

The Principles comprise ten separate chapters which are broken down into articles within each chapter. The ten chapters include: Chapter 1 (General Provisions); Chapter 2 (Formation and Authority of Agents); Chapter 3 (Validity); Chapter 4 (Interpretation); Chapter 5 (Content and Third Party Rights); Chapter 6 (Performance); Chapter 7 (Non-Performance); Chapter 8 (Set-Off); Chapter 9 (Assignment of Rights, Transfer of Obligations, Assignment of Contracts); and Chapter 10 (Limitation Period). While too voluminous to set out here, some representative provisions include:

> Article 1.3: "A contract validly entered into is binding upon the parties. It can only be modified or terminated in accordance with its terms or by agreement or as otherwise provided in these Principles."
> Article 1.7: "(1) Each party must act in accordance with good faith and fair dealing in international trade. (2) The parties may not exclude or limit this duty."
> Article 2.1.1: "A contract may be concluded either by the acceptance or an offer or by conduct of the parties that is sufficient to show agreement."
> Article 3.1: "These Principles do not deal with invalidity arising from (a) lack of capacity; [or] immorality or illegality."
> Article 4.4: "Terms and expressions shall be interpreted in the light of the whole contract or statement in which they appear."
> Article 5.1.6: "Where the quality of performance is neither fixed by, nor determinable from, the contract a party is bound to render a performance of a quality that is reasonable and not less than average in the circumstances."
> Article 6.1.10: "Where a monetary obligation is not expressed in a particular currency, payment must be made in the currency of the place where payment is to be made."
> Article 7.1.1: "Non-performance is failure by a party to perform any of its obligations under the contract, including defective performance or late performance."

No international contract lawyer will find any of these provisions terribly disturbing. They clearly reflect common international understandings and practices.[43] As noted, the UNIDROIT Principles could easily be made an express part of any contract or may be incorporated by reference in the agreement. Once so incorporated the provisions become just as binding and enforceable as anything expressly set out in the contract.

---

40. The full text of the UNIDROIT principles may be found at www.unidroit.org.
41. Michael J. Bonnell, *Soft Law and Party Autonomy: The Case of the UNIDROIT Principles*, 51 Loy. L. Rev. 229, 231 (2005).
42. *Id.*
43. The UNIDROIT website also contains an extensive annotation to the UNIDROIT Principles that readers may find helpful in understanding each of the individual provisions.

§2.9.3 The European Contract Principles

Beginning in the 1980s the EU gathered a body of legal experts from the Member States to write a set of contract principles that reflect much of the common understanding of contract within the EU.[44] The contract principles are viewed as the first step in developing a European Civil Code. At the moment, the principles are regarded only as "soft law"—i.e., provisions which contracting parties may adopt and refer to but which are not mandatory since they are not yet components of the actual law of any EU country.

The European Principles are divided into three parts. Parts I and II cover formation, authority of agents, validity, interpretation, content, performance, nonperformance or breach, and remedies. Part III covers plurality of parties, assignment of claims, substitution of new debt, transfer of contracts, set-off, prescription, illegality, conditions and capitalization of interest. A few representative provisions are:

> Article 1:102(1): "Parties are free to enter into a contract and to determine its contents, subject to the requirements of good faith and fair dealing and the mandatory rules established by these Principles."
> Article 2:101: "(1) A contract is concluded if: (a) the parties intend to be legally bound; and (b) they reach a sufficient agreement without any further requirement. (2) A contract need not be concluded or evidenced in writing nor is it subject to any other requirement as to form. The contract may be proved by any means, including witnesses."
> Article 4:101: "This chapter does not deal with invalidity arising from illegality, immorality or lack of capacity."
> Article 5:104: "Terms which have been individually negotiated take preference over those which are not."
> Article 6:104: "Where the contract does not fix the price or the method of determining it, the parties are to be treated as having agreed on a reasonable price."
> Article 8:107: "A party who entrusts performance of the contract to another person remains responsible for performance."

Much like the UNIDROIT principles—and for that matter the UCC and the discussion of the CISG that follows—these principles clearly reflect some common understandings among international business executives and lawyers and are not terribly controversial. All of these efforts taken together have been seen by some commentators as the first steps in a truly global contract law.[45]

---

44. The voluminous work product can be found in Commission on European Contract Law, Principles of European Contract Law, Parts I and II (1999 and 2001). The basic materials may be accessed electronically at https://www.trans-lex.org/400200/_/pecl/. *See also*, Zeeshan Mansoor, *Principles of European Contract Law: An Autonomous Lex Mercatoria or Part of a Universal Lex Mercatoria?*, 6 Int'l J. Private L. 24 (2013).
45. *See*, e.g., Ole Lando, *CISG and Its Followers: A Proposal to Adopt Some International Principles of Contract Law*, 53 Am. J. Comp. L. 379 (2005). Professor Lando also comments on a new venture to develop a law of contract for a number of African countries through the work of The Organization for the Harmonization of Business Law in Africa.

§2.9.4 The 1980 Vienna Convention on Contracts for the International Sale of Goods

The 1980 Convention on Contracts for the International Sale of Goods (occasionally referred to as the *Vienna Convention*, but more often abbreviated as CISG) is best understood both with reference to its historical context and by way of its specific provisions. In 1951, at the instigation of the Dutch government, a group of countries convened at The Hague to draft a Uniform Law on the International Sale of Goods and a Uniform Law on the Formation of Contracts for the Sale of Goods. These early efforts were the subject of some interest but lacked a broad base of international support.

It was only in 1966, when the UN formed the UNCITRAL with a far larger membership than was the case with the earlier efforts, that the world had a decent chance for a truly international and enforceable body of contract law. Shortly after the formation of UNCITRAL, work began anew on a unified international sales law. In 1980, the final convention was prepared and by September 1981, twenty-one countries had signed the agreement (signing a convention is a step leading toward ratification but which does not constitute ratification itself). The United States ratified the CISG on January 1, 1987. CISG formally entered into force on January 1, 1988. As of early 2008 over seventy countries, including most of the major trading nations, had ratified CISG.[46] Perhaps the most notable absence from the list is the United Kingdom.

As a consequence of the treaty's entering into force and ratification by most of the major trading nations, CISG shows all the signs of becoming the unifying thread that so many international legal scholars and practitioners have been waiting for. As such it bears close attention by persons who may draft or negotiate international sales contracts for the foreseeable future.[47] The CISG is probably best understood by working through some of its major provisions.

---

46. As of late 2017, the countries are: Albania Argentina, Armenia, Australia, Austria, Azerbaijan, Bahrain, Belarus, Belgium, Benin, Bosnia and Herzegovina, Brazil, Bulgaria, Burundi, Cameroon, Canada, Chile, China, Colombia, Congo, Costa Rica, Croatia, Cuba, Cyprus, Czech Republic, Denmark, Dominican Republic, Ecuador, Egypt, El Salvador, Estonia, Fiji, Finland, France, Gabon, Georgia, Germany, Ghana, Greece, Guinea, Guyana, Honduras, Hungary, Iceland, Iraq, Israel, Italy, Japan, Kyrgyzstan, Latvia, Lebanon, Lesotho, Liberia, Lithuania, Luxembourg, Madagascar, Mauritania, Mexico, Mongolia, Montenegro, Netherlands, New Zealand, Norway, Paraguay, Peru, Poland, Republic of Korea, Republic of Moldova, Romania, Russian Federation, Saint Vincent & the Grenadines, San Marino, Serbia, Singapore, Slovakia, Slovenia, Spain, Sweden, Switzerland, Syrian Arab Republic, The former Yugoslav Republic of Macedonia, Turkey, Uganda, Ukraine, United States, Uruguay, Uzbekistan, Venezuela, Vietnam, and Zambia. An up-to-date list may be obtained from the UNCITRAL website: www.uncitral.org/. This same website contains a significant amount of material on CISG including the full text of the Convention and a compendium of interpretations and court decisions construing CISG. Probably the best private sector website on CISG is administered by Pace Law School, located in Westchester, New York: www.cisg.law.pace.edu. The Pace website contains the full text of the treaties, virtually the whole of CISG scholarship, CISG case law from all over the world and a number of other very helpful items for persons interested in the CISG.
47. An enormous amount of literature has been generated on the 1980 Convention. The definitive book-length work is: John Honnold & Harry M. Fletcher, *Uniform Law for International Sales Under the 1980 United Nations Convention* (4th ed., 2009). *See also* Schlechtriem & Schwenzer, *Commentary on the UN Convention on the International Sale of Goods* (4th ed., 2016); Clayton P. Gillette & Steven D. Walt, *The UN Convention on Contracts for the International Sale of Goods:*

[1] Scope

The Convention is not intended to be a comprehensive statement of commercial principles. It applies on its terms only to the sale of certain goods. In this respect the CISG is analogous, but not identical to Article 2 of the UCC. Among other things, the CISG does not apply to sales of ships or aircraft, sales of stock or negotiable instruments, or sales of goods purchased for personal or household use (Article 2). This suggests that it is to be a device applicable only between merchants and is not to be regarded as some kind of international consumer protection statute.

The Convention becomes the applicable law automatically only when the buyer and the seller both reside in countries which have adopted the Convention (Article 1). So, for example, since the United States and Germany have ratified the Convention, it will govern a transaction for the sale of widgets between XYZ, Inc. (an American corporation) and MMM AG of Germany. However, if only one of the countries has ratified, the Convention would not apply, and the parties would have to resort to other legal principles to identify the law applicable to the contract if the contract does not specify a choice of law.

An interesting question not yet fully resolved by international legal scholars is whether contracting parties could "choose" the 1980 Convention as the applicable law even if it would not be applicable on its own terms. (A longer analysis of choice of law is set out in §4.4.2 in Chapter 4.) The converse—whether contracting parties may exclude provisions of the 1980 Convention by specific language—is covered in Article 6: "The parties may exclude the application of this Convention or, subject to Article 12 (the requirement of a writing), derogate from or vary the effect of any of its provisions." As a consequence of this last provision, the United States Department of State recommends the following language to be inserted into any contract that the parties do not wish governed by CISG: "The rights and obligations of the parties under this agreement shall not be governed by the provisions of the 1980 UN Convention on Contracts for the International Sale of Goods; rather these rights and obligations shall be governed by the law of ___________."

Theory and Practice (2d ed., 2016); Bruno Zeller, *Damages Under the Convention on Contracts for the International Sale of Goods* (3d ed., 2009); Larry A. DiMatteo & Lucien Dhooge, *International Sales Law: A Critical Analysis of CISG Jurisprudence* (2005); Alina Kaczorowska, *International Trade Conventions and Their Effectiveness Present and Future* (1995) (approximately one-half of this book is devoted to the CISG). For some representative articles *see*: Jianming Shen, *The Remedy of Requiring Performance under the CISG and the Relevance of Domestic Rules*, 13 Ariz. J. Int'l & Comp. L. 253 (1996); Franco Ferrari, *Interpretive Decision Applying CISG: Issues of Applicability and Private International Law*, 15 J. L. & Com. 159 (1995); Richard E. Speidel, *The Impact of Internationalization of Transnational Commercial Law: The Revision of UCC Article 2 in Light of the United Nations Convention for the International Sale of Goods*, 16 J. Int'l L. Bus. 165 (1995); Ronald A. Brand & Harry M. Flechtner, *CISG: Arbitration and Contract Formation in International Trade*, 12 J. L. & Com. (1993) (NOTE: The University of Pittsburgh's Journal of Law and Commerce has become perhaps the best compendium of regular commentary on the CISG); Symposium, *International Sales of Goods Convention*, 18 Int'l L. 3 (1984). This symposium contains an extensive bibliography on the Convention collected by Professor Peter Winship. An updated bibliography appears regularly in the American Bar Association, Section of International Law publication: International Law.

There are other possibilities. If the parties wish to use the CISG as the primary law governing the document but to resort to, say, the UCC as a gap-filling device, the State Department recommends, as an example: "This agreement shall be governed by the CISG. However, any ambiguities or items not covered by the CISG shall be governed by the UCC of the State of New York." Most persons who have compared the CISG and the UCC find the UCC more detailed on matters such as fraud, mistake, warranties, and damages.

[2] Individual Provisions

The Convention contains 101 individual articles which might best be analyzed in terms of five general categories: (1) application of the Convention; (2) interpretation of the Convention; (3) contract formation; (4) provisions relating the obligations of seller and buyer, breach, and risk of loss; and (5) provisions relating to adoption, reservations and ratification. Viewed generally, the Convention makes it relatively easy to form contracts, is relatively well-balanced between the rights of the seller and the rights of the buyer, and contains those crucial seeds of flexibility and predictability so necessary to the doing of business on an international basis.

In analyzing CISG, a good starting point is to recognize that CISG does not prohibit oral contracts. To use the U.S. term it does not contain a statute of frauds and thus purely oral undertakings may be enforced under CISG (although individual signatory nations may take a reservation against oral contracts). Article 11 provides expressly: "A contract of sale need not be concluded in or evidenced by writing and is not subject to any other requirement as to form. It may be proved by any means including witnesses." Beyond that, course of dealing or usage may be relevant to a contract. Article 9 provides: "The parties are bound by any usage to which they have agreed and by any practices which they have established between themselves." Article 9(2) amplifies this: "[The parties are bound by] a usage of which the parties knew or ought to have known and which in international trade is widely known to, and regularly observed by, parties to contracts."

Contract formation is somewhat different from conventional practice. Article 14 defines offer as any proposal that is "sufficiently definite and indicates the intention of the offer to be bound in case of acceptance." The same article defines sufficiently definite as a proposal that "indicates the goods and expressly or implicitly fixes or makes provision for determining the quantity and the price." An offer become effective when it reaches the offeree (Article 15); but silence may not be construed as an acceptance. An acceptance, like an offer, is effective only when it reaches the offeror (Article 18). The acceptance of the offer must be the *mirror image* of the offer (Article 19): "A reply to an offer which purports to be an acceptance but contains additions, limitations or other modifications is a rejection of the offer and constitutes a counter-offer."

Warranties under the CISG may prove troublesome. The CISG warranty provisions are not as nearly detailed as the UCC. The basic seller's warranty is merely (Article 35):

> The seller must deliver goods which are of the quantity, quality and description required by the contract.... The goods do not conform with the contract unless they (a) are fit for the purposes for which goods of the same description would ordinarily be used [or] are fit for any particular purpose expressly or impliedly made known to the seller at the time...of the contract.

By contrast, the buyer has an obligation to inspect the goods (Article 37) and (Article 39) "loses the right to rely on a lack of conformity of the goods if he does not give notice...within a reasonable time after he has discovered [the nonconformity] or ought to have discovered it." Both the seller and buyer have various remedies available to them including the remedy of strict performance (Article 46: "the buyer may require performance by the seller...unless the buyer has resorted to a remedy which is inconsistent with this requirement.") Article 62 is the parallel remedy for the seller.

Compensatory damages permit the recovery of profit in certain circumstances (Article 74): "Damages for breach of contract...consist of a sum equal to the loss, including loss of profit...[but] such damages may not exceed the loss which the party in breach foresaw or ought to have foreseen...as a possible consequence of the breach." The nonbreaching party, as in virtually all legal systems, has the obligation to mitigate damages (Article 77): "A party who relies on a breach of contract must take such measures as are reasonable in the circumstances to mitigate the loss, including loss of profit, resulting from the breach."

There is now a burgeoning body of CISG scholarship and case law. One important development since the promulgation of the treaty is the work of the CISG Advisory Council (AC), a group of highly regarded academic lawyers, identified and supported by the Institute of International Commercial Law at Pace University School of Law, who have promulgated (at the time of this writing) six AC Opinions on important aspects of the CISG. While technically not part of the treaty language and therefore not binding, the AC Opinions are both clarifying and persuasive.[48] AC Opinion Number 1 resolves any lingering doubts about electronic contracts under the CISG. AC Opinion Number 1 is more fully discussed in Chapter 6, but in essence provides: "A contract may be concluded or evidenced by electronic communications" and "The term 'writing' in CISG also includes any electronic communication retrievable in perceivable form."

AC Opinion Number 2 deals with examination of goods and notice of nonconformity and concludes, among other things: "Although a buyer must examine the goods, or cause them to be examined, within as short a period as is practicable under the circumstances, there is no independent sanction for failure to do so." Opinion Number 3 clarifies that the parole evidence rule has not been included in the CISG and that virtually all of the parties' understandings and behavior, including negotiations, may be used to interpret a CISG contract unless the parties expressly provide otherwise

48. The full text of each advisory opinion—and a truly overwhelming amount of additional information on the CISG—may be found at the Pace University Law School's website: www.cisg.law.pace.edu/cisg.

in the contract. Opinion Number 4 addresses the question of whether the CISG applies to contracts that are partially for sale of goods and partially for some other economic undertaking. The Opinion states:

> In interpreting the words "substantial part" under Article 3(1) CISG, primarily an "economic value" criterion should be used....Article 3(2) CISG governs mixed contracts. Whether the different obligations as to goods and services are agreed upon in one mixed contract or in several contracts is a matter of contract interpretation....In interpreting the words "preponderant part" under Article 3(2) CISG, primarily an "economic value" criterion should be used....

Opinion Number 5 establishes that a buyer may avoid the contract if any failure of the seller to perform amounts to a fundamental breach of the contract. Opinion Number 6 deals with calculation of damages under CISG Article 74 and provides that Article 74, generally, reflects the principle of full compensation.

Opinion Number 7 deals with exemption of liability for damages under CISG Article 79. This opinion points out that Article 79 exempts a party from liability for damages when the party has failed to perform any of its obligations. It notes that Article 79(1) continues to be the controlling provision on exemption of liability even when a contracting party has engaged a third party to perform some or all of the underlying contract. However, a contracting party may be exempted if the contracting party was not able to choose or control the third party. Moreover, there may be occasions when certain changes in circumstances may be deemed the "impediment" under Article 79(1) if those changed circumstances make performance "excessively onerous." In such cases, a nonperforming party may argue "hardship" even if performance is not "absolutely impossible."

The text of the CISG is not completely clear on the issue of calculation of damages under Articles 75 and 76. Advisory Opinion Number 8, sheds some additional light on this issue. First, Articles 75 and 76 do not replace Article 74. Instead, they provide parties with alternative methods for calculating damages. The Opinion makes clear that nothing in either Article 75 or 76 may be used to place the aggrieved party in a "better" position than he or she would have been in had the contract not been breached. Nonetheless, under Article 75, the aggrieved party is permitted to recover the difference between the contract price and the price of a substituted transaction. Under Article 76, an aggrieved party is entitled to recover the difference between the price fixed by the original contract and the current price.

Advisory Opinion Number 9 deals with the consequences of avoidance of the contract. The opinion makes clear that any right to damages for nonperformance survive avoidance of the contract, irrespective of whether the damages were accrued prior to avoidance or from any future nonperformance. Moreover, the contract's provisions survive avoidance if they assist in the winding-up of the contract.

Advisory Opinion Number 10 addresses what are generally referred to as "liquidated damages" in American contract literature and case law. In general, the contracting parties may agree to clauses in the contract that provide "for the payment of agreed sums for failure to perform." But the opinion goes on to exhibit a great deal of sensitivity as to any underlying national principles regarding the "reasonableness, excessiveness, or proportionality" of the specified amounts of money. As the opinion states: "Legal systems may establish formal requirements for agreed sums; legal systems may fix the maximum amount of agreed sums; legal systems may deny enforceability to agreed sums classified as penalties; legal systems may provide for the reduction of excessive sums." In such instances, the CISG is expected to be interpreted and applied consistently with these underlying "domestic protection" requirements.

The CISG is not a perfect code. No such perfect sales code has ever existed. Nonetheless, it serves some very important purposes and deserves all the attention international lawyers and business executives choose to give it. First, it is sufficiently comprehensive and balanced that parties electing its provisions should feel comfortable with its terms. Second, it is a creation of the UN, so even contracting parties in developing countries should feel free to use its provisions without the worry that this is an unbalanced, made-in-the-west body of law imposed on them by patronizing major trading nations. Third, it is consistent with traditional principles of sales, and in that sense, may be regarded as a codification of the *lex mercatoria*. The drafters of this convention may justifiably take pride in their work. Conversations between the author and numerous international lawyers suggest that more and more contracts are either affirmatively choosing CISG or at least not opting out of it. If the reported case law and commentary can be believed, the CISG is now beginning to prove its value to the international business community.

§2.9.5 The 1974 UN Convention on the Limitation Period in the International Sale of Goods

Readers should also be aware of another UN convention, the UN Convention on the Limitation Period in the International Sale of Goods. entered into force in August 1988 and was ratified by the United States in 1994. This treaty is considered to be a companion to the CISG and provides time limits (in general terms of four years) in which to bring claims for any breach of an international contract for the sale of goods.[49] As of late 2017, the Limitation Convention has been ratified or acceded to by only thirty nations and, accordingly, has limited effect and applicability.[50] Nonetheless, it is regarded as an important international statement on the crucial issue of limitations of actions for breach of international contracts.

49. The 1980 Protocol amending the convention on the limitation period may be found at 19 I.L.M. 671. This protocol seeks to align the limitations convention and the CISG. For some commentary on the limitations convention *see*, Anita F. Hill, *A Comparative Study of the United Nations Convention on the Limitation Period in the International Sale of Goods and Section 2-725 of the Uniform Commercial Code*, 25 Tex. Int'l L.J. 3 (1990).
50. The countries are: Argentina, Belarus, Belgium, Benin, Bosnia & Herzegovina, Brazil, Bulgaria, Burundi, Costa Rica, Cote d'Ivoire, Cuba, Czech Republic, Dominican Republic, Egypt, Ghana, Guinea, Hungary, Liberia, Mexico, Mongolia, Montenegro, Nicaragua, Norway, Paraguay, Poland, Republic of Moldova, Romania, Russian Federation, Serbia, Slovakia, Slovenia, Uganda, Ukraine, United States of America, Uruguay, and Zambia. The full list may be found at the UNCITRAL website: www.uncitral.org/uncitral/en/uncitral_texts/sale_goods/1974Convention_status.html.

The Limitations Convention defines an "international" contract for the sale of goods as one, "if at the time of the conclusion of the contract, the buyer and the seller have their places of business in different States" (Article 2). Echoing the CISG, the Limitations Convention does not apply to mixed contracts in which the "preponderant part of the obligations of the seller consists in the supply of labor or other services" (Article 6). The basic limitation period is four years (Article 8). The limitations period begins running from the date on which a claim arises (Article 9) and, for example, a claim for breach of contract begins running from the date on which the breach occurs (Article 10(1)). By contrast, a claim of fraud begins running "on the date on which the fraud was or reasonably could have been discovered" (Article 10(3)). If the time period has expired, "no claim shall be recognized or enforced in any legal proceedings commenced after the expiration of the limitation period" (Article 25).

CHAPTER 3

Planning International Commercial Agreements

§3.1 INTRODUCTION

By definition, international commercial agreements transcend national boundaries. This feature creates a number of problems for the lawyers and business executives who plan, negotiate, and draft the agreement because it introduces complications and uncertainties that typically do not exist in domestic commercial arrangements. For example, it is often uncertain which country's commercial law governs the transaction. In many cases, methods of payment for goods and services that are taken for granted in a domestic context are often too insecure and too slow for deals that involve businesses in more than one country. If a dispute arises under an international agreement, access to a legitimate, principled court system is never a sure thing.

This section lays the foundation for some of the more sophisticated issues discussed in later sections in this chapter and subsequent chapters. Readers not fully acquainted with basic principles of contract law should look closely at §3.2 before moving to subsequent discussion and analysis. Readers who contemplate entering into one of the more complex undertakings such as a franchise agreement or a joint venture should spend some time considering the issues discussed in §3.3 and later chapters before venturing further. This edition also covers foreign direct investment in-depth in §3.3.6.

For the purposes of this book, an international commercial agreement or transaction is defined as some kind of business arrangement reflected in a contract, either written or oral:

(1) between a company or individual in one country and a company or individual in another country; or

(2) in certain circumstances, between a private company or individual and a foreign government or some component of a government such as a state-owned trading company.

This definition is deliberately broad, but it excludes, with a few exceptions, those intergovernmental transactions between sovereign entities that legal scholars often refer to as international relations and whose rules are set by the body of law normally referred to as *public international law*. The transactions analyzed in this chapter are essentially private commercial transactions. For the most part, transactions analyzed for this book are transactions between people in business (or, as some of the commercial codes put it "between merchants"). Accordingly, there is very little inquiry into consumer protection laws in the discussion that follows.

The final general assumption made throughout the remainder of this book is that the commercial agreement, whatever its nature, will be evidenced by some kind of writing. Oral agreements in international commercial transactions are seen occasionally (indeed within certain cultures they are commonplace) but they are so unusual as to be relatively insignificant in terms of total dollar value. Many systems of national law such as the United States' Uniform Commercial Code (UCC) normally require a writing for a contract to be enforceable—a doctrine known in Anglo-American law as the *Statute of Frauds*. By contrast, Article 11 of the Convention on the International Sale of Goods (CISG) does not require a writing for a contract to be valid and enforceable—thus permitting the existence of an agreement to "be proved by any means, including witnesses." As the CISG takes hold, it is possible that the world will see more oral contracts. But in all likelihood, the vast majority of international commercial agreements will continue to be evidenced by some kind of writing.

A writing is important for a number of reasons. As noted, a written document promotes enforceability of the agreement as a whole, but also accomplishes other goals. For example, a writing removes a great deal of uncertainty. When agreements are oral, memories fade and minds change over time. A writing is something that can be referred to a long time after the agreement is concluded for proof of what the parties said and what they intended. Eliminating uncertainty greatly reduces the risk in a transaction. As Professor Andreas Lowenfeld points out, there are risks inherent in all commercial dealings, but there are special risks in international trade, including war, the dangers of carriage on the high seas, expropriation, currency fluctuations, boycotts, and changes in governmental controls such as tariffs and export and import regulations.[1] Parties who have never dealt with each other may feel insecure about payment or about delivery of the goods or services. A written agreement with appropriately drafted provisions can deal expressly with many of these issues and, accordingly, remove many of the hazards in the transaction.

Any number of different types of commercial arrangements may be negotiated between businesses, including the sale or lease of goods, the sale of services, the licensing of patents, copyrights or trademarks, the selling of franchises, or the creation

1. Andreas F. Lowenfeld, *International Private Trade* 2–3 (3d. ed., 1996).

of joint ventures. Because we presume that each of these arrangements is sparked by a profit motive, each agreement also involves money (or something else of value) changing hands—which, in turn, requires some analysis of the proper method of payment for the transaction. The payment component of an agreement may add another party to the transaction (typically a bank), a whole new set of legal principles (generally those principles governing negotiable instruments or other payment devices), and the creation of financing documents (such as bank checks, money orders, negotiable bills of lading, and one of the mainstays for payment of international transactions—the irrevocable letter of credit).

Contracts that involve the sale of goods, and occasionally contracts that provide for the delivery of certain types of services, also involve a transportation component, which introduces yet another player—the transportation company or carrier—and another piece of paper, such as a bill of lading or warehouse receipt that is in effect a separate contract between the seller or buyer and the carrier. If the parties desire more protection against loss than the carrier is willing to provide as part of the costs of transportation, they may elect to purchase insurance to cover the goods or services, generating yet another separate contract with an insurance company.

In certain circumstances, government agencies will underwrite all or part of the transaction. In the United States, the Export-Import Bank was created to help fund certain types of transactions. The Overseas Private Investment Corporation (OPIC) provides insurance for United States' businesses against certain types of overseas losses for selected transactions. A new component of the World Bank, the Multilateral Investment Guarantee Agency (MIGA) has been established to perform functions parallel to OPIC under the World Bank's umbrella.

Finally, because international commercial agreements are often of considerable interest to the governments of both the seller and the buyer's countries, both seller and buyer will frequently have to obtain import and export permissions from government agencies and will often have to cope with other facets of government regulation such as taxes, the imposition of antitrust laws, dumping and countervailing duty principles and, on occasion, the enforcement of various public health and safety measures such as consumer safety and employee protection standards. These issues are discussed below.

§3.2 SOME FUNDAMENTAL PRINCIPLES OF CONTRACT LAW

It is virtually impossible to begin a discussion of planning and drafting an international contract without some idea of what the contract must contain in order to be valid and enforceable.[2] However, the validity and enforceability of a commercial agreement

2. There are a large number of books on contract law. Indeed, there are so many that no purpose would be served by trying to cite them in a single footnote. Nonetheless, readers who wish some additional basic grounding in general concepts of contract law may profitably consult the following: Gareth Spark, *Vitiation of Contracts: International Contractual Principles and English Law* (2013); Larry A. Dimatteo, *The Law of International Contracts* (2d ed., 2009); Henry Deeb Gabriel, *Contracts for the Sale of Goods: a Comparison of U.S. and International Law* (2008); Tadas

normally turns on the commercial principles developed within the country whose law is to be applied to the agreement. This issue sometimes causes a chicken and egg dilemma: the parties cannot draft a contract whose validity they have faith in without understanding the principles of law applicable to that particular agreement. And yet, in some instances, the applicable law is determined long after the contract is drafted when some dispute arises that forces a court or an arbitrator to investigate and resolve the issue of applicable law.

This issue, normally referred to as *choice of law*, is discussed extensively in Chapter 4. This section will concentrate on some fundamental concepts of contract law that are common to or at least not incompatible with most legal systems. However, once again the reader should understand that the resolution of some of these issues may differ significantly depending on the law applicable to the specific contract under examination.

The classic definition of contract in Anglo-American jurisprudence is "a promise, or set of promises, for breach of which the law gives a remedy, or the performance of which the law in some way recognizes as a duty."[3] In most systems of law, this basic definition gives rise to two other fundamental propositions. First, unless other laws make a contract or any portion of a contract illegal (such as the selling of alcoholic beverages in countries that forbid such sales), the parties are free to make whatever agreement they wish. This concept, normally referred to as *party autonomy* or freedom of contract, suggests that a contract can say nearly anything; and, if it is otherwise valid, the parties will be held to the terms of their agreement. Second, once a contract is formed, the parties must perform the bargain as agreed. This proposition, *sanctity of contract* (sometimes referred to in civil law systems by its Latin name, *pacta sunt servanda*) means that, absent extraordinary circumstances, the parties must perform as agreed even if performance becomes uncomfortable or inconvenient.

Flowing from these basic propositions, an international contract normally includes provisions (either in the language of the contract itself or provided by way of external legal principles that fill in gaps not covered by the contract), covering the following five issues: (a) formation and subject matter; (b) performance; (c) breach; (d) remedy; (e) dispute resolution. Each of these components is discussed separately below. A number of more specific contract principles and some sample clauses are set out in Chapter 4.

Klimas, *Comparative Contract Law: A Transystemic Approach with an Emphasis on the Continental Law* (2006); Michael H. Whincup, *Contract Law and Practice: The English System with Scottish, Commonwealth and Continental Comparisons* (5th ed., 2006); B.S. Markensinis, Hannes Unberath & Angus Johnston, *The German Law of Contract: A Comparative Treatise* (2d. rev. ed., 2006); *Calamari & Perillo on Contracts* (5th ed., 2003); *Id., Principles of Existing EC Contract Law* (2003); Edward Allan Farnsworth, *United States Contract Law* (1999). For a book on contract law that also connects with other themes in this book *see*, Thomas R. Haggard, *Contract Law from a Drafting Perspective* (2002).

3. *1 Williston on Contracts* §1 (3d ed., 1957).

§3.2.1 Formation and Subject Matter

Although not all legal systems use the same terminology, a contract is normally formed through the acts of offer and acceptance. Illustrated simply, a seller writes to a potential buyer: "I will sell you fifteen telescopes for $150.00 per telescope." The buyer writes back saying: "I accept. I will buy your fifteen telescopes for $150.00 each." In the Anglo-American legal system and in most civil code systems, once this exchange of writings has taken place, a contract has been formed and becomes a legally enforceable obligation for both parties because there has been an offer and an acceptance and the subject matter of the contract is not unlawful. The mutual promises (*"I promise to sell"* and *"I promise to buy"*) also satisfy the requirement of *consideration*—the third vital ingredient of a contract in the Anglo-American system.

Problems arise in a number of ways. Occasionally, persons who purport to enter into a contract do not have the proper capacity to agree. In all systems, contracts with children or mentally ill persons are generally not enforceable. On the international level, the problem of capacity is a little different. When business executives are dealing across international boundaries with entities that they do not know personally, it is sometimes difficult to ascertain precisely which person in a company has the necessary authority to sign a contract that binds the company. It is difficult to create any generalizations about this dimension of capacity because businesses around the world have varying organizational structures. However, as a general rule, the higher the rank of the officer signing the contract the more likely it is that the officer has the necessary power to sign enforceable contracts.

There are other areas of potential trouble. Consider, for example, what might happen if the offer is made by the seller's sending a preprinted form to the buyer. The form contains a price for the goods that is effective only if the buyer pays the transportation charges from seller's factory to buyer's place of business. The buyer then tries to accept, not by signing or endorsing the seller's form, but by sending the buyer's own preprinted form. The buyer's form says: "I accept at seller's price if the seller pays for the transportation of the goods to my place of business."

In traditional contract law, for example, under Article 19 of the CISG—and in many legal systems outside the United States—to be effective an acceptance must be the *mirror image* of the offer. That is, the buyer cannot append any conditions to the acceptance that were not part of the original offer. If the buyer attempts to do so, the buyer's form is construed not as an acceptance but rather as a counteroffer, which the seller must then affirmatively accept before a valid contract is formed.[4]

In the United States, the UCC handles this problem in a slightly different fashion. In section 2-207 (the famous *battle of the forms* section), the UCC provides that an

4. *See*, e.g., Louis F. Del Duca, *Implementation of Contract Formation, Statute of Frauds, Parol Evidence, and Battle of Forms: CISG Provisions in Civil and Common Law Countries*, 25 J. L. & Com. 133 (2005); Kevin C. Stemp, *A Comparative Analysis of the "Battle of the Forms,"* 15 Transnat'l L. & Contemp. Probs. 243 (2005); Peter Winship, *Formation of International Sales Contracts Under the 1980 Vienna Convention*, 17 Int'l Law. 1 (1983); Note, *The United Nations Convention on Contracts for the International Sale of Goods: Contract Formation and the Battle of the Forms*, 21 Colum. J. Transnat'l L. 529 (1983).

acceptance that varies from the precise terms of the offer may still operate as an acceptance unless the offer expressly states that the acceptance must exactly conform to the offer or unless the terms of the acceptance *materially alter* the offer. If the offer does not expressly require conformity, or if the new conditions in the acceptance do not materially alter the deal, the new conditions become proposals by the buyer for additions to the contract. In our hypothetical, the shift in the obligation to pay for transportation charges has a substantial impact on the total price of the contract and thereby would, in all likelihood, be considered a material alteration. If the acceptance is considered a material alteration, the acceptance (as under traditional contract law) operates as a counteroffer that is not effective unless the seller accepts the new terms.

By contrast, assume that the buyer's form simply adds: "All disagreements under this sale shall be resolved by arbitration." The UCC itself is not clear as to what types of alteration constitute a material alteration, and United States courts disagree on whether merely adding an arbitration clause constitutes a material alteration.[5] Many U.S. legal scholars believe that the mere addition of a dispute resolution clause does not materially alter the basic agreement—the purpose of which is to buy and sell goods. Interestingly, under the CISG, the result would be about the same, but the analytical process is somewhat different. Under CISG Article 19(2), nonmaterial changes contained in the acceptance become part of the contract unless the offeror objects to these changes either orally or in writing in a timely fashion. However, the CISG deems an arbitration clause to be a material addition to the contract. Since the CISG requires an acceptance that is the mirror image of the offer, an acceptance that contains an arbitration clause when the offer is silent on arbitration would be construed only as a counteroffer.

Consider another common problem in contract formation. The seller's letter says: "I offer to sell you fifteen telescopes for $150.00 per telescope. This offer is open until July 29, 1993." The buyer writes back: "I accept your offer" and mails her letter on July 29. However, the buyer's letter (the "acceptance") is not received by the seller until July 31, 1993. On July 30, the seller sells the telescopes to another company. In most domestic systems of contract law and under the CISG, an acceptance is not effective until it is received by the seller.[6] There would, accordingly, be no enforceable contract between the original seller and buyer.

However, under British contract law as delineated in the case of *Adams v. Lindsell*[7] and under the contract law of a few states in the United States, an acceptance may be effective when the letter of acceptance is mailed (i.e., put into the hands of the postal authorities).[8] This is the so-called *mail box* rule. The rule was initially based on the supposition that once a letter is placed in the post the sender of the letter loses control over the letter. In our case, courts applying the mail box rule would likely

5. *See*, e.g., Edward Allan Farnsworth, *Contracts* 157–166 (1982). For a discussion of the battle of the forms under the CISG *see*, Del Duca & Stemp, *supra* n. 4, and Francois Vergne, *The "Battle of the Forms" under the 1980 United Nations Convention on Contracts for the International Sale of Goods*, 33 Am. J. Comp. L. 233 (1985).
6. *See*, Winship, *supra* n. 4.
7. 1 B. & Ald. 681, 106 Eng. Rep. 250 (K.B. 1818).
8. Farnsworth, *supra* n. 5, at 166–170.

determine that the seller bound herself to the agreement when she put the letter into the mail box. While the basic supposition is not necessarily true today (many postal systems permit a sender to retrieve correspondence), it has nonetheless remained a provision in the contract law of a few jurisdictions.

The UCC is somewhat more ambiguous on this point. Under the UCC, an offer may demand a particular type of acceptance (i.e., a statement in the offer to the effect that "acceptance of this offer is effective only when the acceptance is received by offeror"). Conversely, if the offer does not make such a statement, an offer will be construed "as inviting acceptance in any manner and by any medium reasonable in the circumstances."[9]

Many other problems can arise when contracts are being formed. The illustrations of offer and counteroffer and the problem of acceptance set out above are merely two examples of problems that can occur when sellers and buyers are operating at some distance from each other. Note that all of the possible solutions have both advantages and disadvantages. None of them is necessarily commanded by reference to some higher principle of ethics or morality. They are simply a practical, realistic way to deal with common business problems. In most business transactions, we have learned that the most important thing is simply to tell the business executives what the rules are—or, in certain cases, to inform them that there are no external rules and that they are free to agree between themselves. Once people in business understand the rules, they usually can accommodate their behavior or their contracts to the terms of the rules.

There is a message here for persons about to begin a contract drafting exercise. The contract itself may be drafted to overcome many of these problems. So, for example, a Seller's offer may state: "Buyer may not alter the terms of this offer in any way." This language requires a mirror-image response for a valid contract to be formed. Similarly, an offer can state: "Your acceptance is effective only when it is actually received by us." This inserts an *actual receipt* provision in the contract that supplants the mailbox rule in British and certain U.S. jurisdictions. The provision also makes clear in the contract what would otherwise be an ambiguity under the UCC.

These two exercises further illustrate another major point that will be constantly reiterated through the remainder of this book. Contracting parties may either negotiate and draft provisions of their choosing (remember the doctrine of freedom of contract) or may let the contract law of a particular jurisdiction fill in those matters not specifically addressed in the contract. If a seller is in a business situation in which she absolutely must receive notice of acceptance, it would be silly and possibly dangerous not to insist on an "acceptance effective only when received" clause in the contract. By contrast, if the seller has a large and rapid manufacturing capability for his products and can sell those products to many buyers at any given time, he may be happy with mailbox rule. A manufacturer in this position would operate on the assumption that he can always make more products if he has already sold, to another buyer, the quantity promised to a buyer whose acceptance was received later than he expects.

9. UCC §2-206(1)(a).

The subject matter of a contract sometimes poses problems in drafting international commercial agreements. Among the major trading nations, contracts for the sale of most goods are almost always valid, unless the sale of the product in question (e.g., alcohol, firearms, explosives and other dangerous commodities) is prohibited under other laws of either the seller or the buyer's country. For example, a contract between a Nepalese company and an American furrier to purchase the pelts of the Himalayan snow leopard for import to the United States is unenforceable in the United States because the U.S. government has placed the snow leopard on its list of endangered species and thus made the importation of snow leopard pelts illegal.

Problems with the subject matter of a contract occasionally arise when contracting parties wish to enter into some of the other forms of business arrangement such as a franchise, licensing or joint venture agreement. Many countries do not permit certain types of services contracts. For example, for-profit employment services occasionally run into prohibitions within a particular country that make it a crime to accept a fee for finding employment for workers.

A number of developing countries are less-than-enthusiastic about externally owned manufacturing operations and prefer licensing agreements, technology transfer arrangements, or carefully structured joint ventures that keep the business itself—and most of the proceeds generated by the business—in the hands of the country's own citizens. In many cases, business arrangements may not be concluded unless a national of the host country is involved as a major actor in the business operation. Other countries, such as India, do not forbid foreign entities from entering the country per se, but provide special benefits and concessions for those businesses in which Indian nationals participate.

The Anglo-American doctrine of *consideration* is a special inquiry into a contract's subject matter.[10] Unilateral promises under British and American law are almost never valid. That is, merely saying to another "I will make you a telescope" is not normally construed as an enforceable agreement. The Anglo-American system instead contemplates some sort of mutuality of obligation such as "I will make and sell you a telescope if you pay me USD150" to which the offeree replies, "Okay." Consideration in this instance is evidenced by the mutual promises of offeror and offeree: Seller promises to make the telescope and buyer promises to pay USD 150. In the British and U.S. legal systems, the notion of consideration is normally indispensable to a valid contract.

At the same time, Anglo-American courts rarely inquire into the amount (sometimes referred to as the *adequacy* of consideration). So, for example, even if an automobile's fair market value is USD 20,000, a court will still enforce a contract for the sale of that automobile for USD 200, if that is what the parties fairly agreed to. This explains why, on occasion, people will enter into a contract based on an express payment of USD 1. Such a contract is valid, all other things being equal, because the *adequacy* of the consideration for the contract is normally not something that a court will examine. Keep in mind the underlying principle of party autonomy. People may

10. *See*, e.g., Robert A. Prentice, *"Law" and Gratuitous Promises*, Ill. L. Rev. 881 (2007); Seana V. Shiffrin, *The Divergence of Contract and Promise*, 120 Harv. L. Rev. 708 (2007).

make whatever bargains they please so long as those bargains do not involve an unlawful subject matter and so long as one is not committing fraud on the other.

Another problem that can arise regarding subject matter is the issue of mistake.[11] Mistakes occur every now and then in domestic contracts and perhaps even more often in international contracts where differences in language and culture sometimes interfere with a proper understanding of the matter under negotiation.

Mistakes involving language differences are easy to imagine. But serious mistakes can occur just as easily when the only difference between the parties is a matter of culture and normal business practices. Consider a contract between a U.S. paper manufacturer and an English stationer that calls for the sale of "1,000 reams of bond business stationery" without mentioning the precise size of the paper. Conventional business stationery in the United States is eight and one-half inches wide and eleven inches long. Conventional business stationery in Great Britain is the so-called A4 paper, which is approximately eight and one-quarter inches by eleven and three-quarter inches. The actual difference is relatively small, but the consequences of a mistake are enormous. Photocopiers and computer printers must be readjusted. Business envelopes do not fit. Filing cabinets must often be reorganized. In short, even small differences in paper size can create considerable inconvenience and discomfort for the average business. For these reasons, stationery cut to American dimensions is not a very attractive commodity in Britain.

Most legal systems recognize two different types of mistake in contracts. The first is a mistake on the part of only one of the contracting parties, referred to as *unilateral* mistake; and the second is a mistake shared by the parties known as *bilateral* mistake. An 1864 British court addressed the question of bilateral mistake in a case called *Raffles v. Wichelhaus*,[12] in which a contract called for shipment of goods to the United States on the ship Peerless. It turned out that there were two ships named Peerless. Unfortunately, the U.S. buyer expected the goods to be shipped on the Peerless scheduled to arrive in October, while the seller shipped the goods on the Peerless that arrived in New York in December. A law suit for breach of contract ensued in England. The British court held that the contract was ambiguous and that the mistake was essentially bilateral because it was a jointly held misunderstanding. It therefore concluded that no contract had been formed.

In the case of the improperly sized office paper, if both the American paper manufacturer and the English stationer were simply unaware that each country had a different size of paper for business stationery, the result might well be the same as in the *Raffles* case. No contract would have been formed and the parties would simply go their own way.

---

11. *See*, e.g., James Gordley, *Mistake in Contract Formation*, 52 Am. J. Comp. L. 433 (2004); Melvin A. Eisenberg, *Mistake in Contract Law*, 91 Calif. L. Rev. 1573 (2003); Eric Rasmusen & Ian Ayres, *Mutual and Unilateral Mistake in Contract Law*, 22 J. Legal Studies 309 (1993). For a comparative analysis *see* Nils Jansen & Reinhard Zimmerman, *Contract Formation and Mistake in European Contract Law: A Genetic Comparison of Transnational Model Rules*, 31 Oxford J. Leg. Stud. 625 (2011).
12. 2 H. & C. 906, 159 Eng. Rep. 375 (1864).

The result is often different, however, when only one party makes the mistake or if only one party is aware of the ambiguity and could have taken steps to resolve the ambiguity. In these instances, courts deal with the issue in a number of different ways. Traditionally, courts have imposed the doctrine of *caveat emptor* against buyers of goods or services. In other words, a buyer has the obligation to investigate the deal before he agrees to buy and any misunderstanding on his part will be assessed against him. On occasion, the same doctrine is levied against a seller who is not aware of the true worth of the thing she is selling—as for example, the person who inadvertently sells an original Rembrandt painting for USD 10 after finding the painting in the attic of her grandmother's house and after mistakenly concluding that the painting has no value when it is actually worth millions of dollars. Under traditional legal concepts, the seller would have had to live up to her bargain, however much money she lost in the transaction.

Recently, courts have been taking a harder and more sophisticated look at unilateral mistake. On occasion courts will reason as follows: (1) contracts imply a duty of good faith on the part of both parties; (2) there are instances in which one party was aware of the ambiguity and failed to disclose it to the other party or failed to take steps to reduce the harm that ensues because of the mistake; (3) accordingly, the burden should be levied against the party with the superior knowledge who could have corrected the mistake but did not. In the case of the mistake as to the size of the office paper, a traditionally minded court might simply invoke the doctrine of caveat emptor against the British buyer and enforce the contract as written. Thus, the buyer would have to pay for the paper and take on the additional burden of getting rid of the unwanted paper. The court's reasoning would be something to this effect: The buyer could have inquired or investigated further as to the size of the paper but did not. Therefore, he must live with his failure to inquire.

By contrast, under some of the newer theories of unilateral mistake, if the British stationer had never before done business with a U.S. manufacturer and the U.S. manufacturer had frequently sold to British businesses and, in the past, had frequently encountered mistakes as to paper size, a court might impose some kind of burden on the U.S. manufacturer to bring up the question of paper size knowing that he was dealing with an unsuspecting British customer. In this case, not having made the disclosure, the ambiguity might well be assessed against the manufacturer and the contract would be held not enforceable.

The doctrine of mistake illustrates the vital necessity of getting all the important facts straight before signing an agreement. It is particularly important when parties are dealing with each other over long distances and when differences in language or culture are likely to impede a full understanding on both sides. Perhaps more than any other concept under discussion, it shows the vital need for proper precontract planning.

§3.2.2 Performance

Performance is the centerpiece of any contract. By definition, it is the reason why the parties entered into the agreement in the first instance. In most international contracts of any size, performance is spelled out in considerable detail in the contract itself or in related documents. For example, a contract for the sale of cellular telephones between an American manufacturer of communications devices and a Brazilian purchaser will normally state the quantity, the price, the shipment dates, the quality of the goods (usually by way of spelling out the precise engineering and performance specifications for the telephones), any warranties that the seller is providing the buyer, the duration of the contract, and any special conditions that might attach to the bargain—as, for example, "this sale is contingent on buyer's obtaining permission to import the goods from the Brazilian government" or "this agreement will continue in effect so long as the Brazilian government permits the importation of U.S.-manufactured cellular telephones."

A large body of law, both judge-made and statutory, has helped develop the doctrine of performance and the related concept of conditions in virtually all major trading nations. It is difficult to generalize further on these points because performance in the context of a contract for the sale of goods is vastly different from performance under a franchise contract, which in turn is different from the type of performance that one might expect in the context of a manufacturing joint venture.

Nonetheless, it may be helpful at this point to distinguish between promises and conditions and to introduce the concept of standard contract clauses, sometimes referred to as *conditions*, that are imposed or recommended in a number of international transactions, such as international construction contracts. In the past, contracts negotiated in the countries that made up the former Soviet bloc were almost always drafted on the basis of standard conditions, the language of which was not negotiable.

In this context, it is helpful to attempt some preliminary definitions. A promise in a contract is the obligation to which one or the other parties commits himself. For example, in a transaction involving the sale of a computer, the buyer will likely say: "I promise to pay you $100,000 for your Model 2007-A computer." The seller will state: "I promise to sell you my Model 2007-A computer for $100,000." These two promises are regarded by legal scholars as unconditional—that is, they are dependent on nothing other than themselves.

But rarely are sophisticated commercial dealings this simple. Most business dealings are made contingent on a number of occurrences that must take place before the deal is finally consummated. For example, our computer buyer, being a typically cautious business executive, might say: "I promise to pay you $100,000 for your Model 2007-A computer if the computer passes a government-imposed quality test." The additional requirement—that the device pass the test—is regarded as a *condition* to the agreement.[13] Stated a bit differently, the buyer's promise is now conditional rather than unconditional.

13. The discussion of basic concepts of conditions in Farnsworth, *supra* n. 5, at 538–574 is especially lucid.

The possibilities for conditions may well be infinite. The condition imposed in our computer contract presumably requires an affirmative act on the part of the seller: the Model 2007-A computer must be submitted to the appropriate government authority for testing, and the computer must pass that test. Of course, the buyer could probably protect his interest just as easily by stating the condition in negative: "I will pay you $100,000 for the Model 2007-A computer unless the computer fails the appropriate government inspection." The consequence of either type of condition is just about the same. If the computer does not pass muster with the government, the buyer has no obligation to purchase. In the parlance of contracts, her performance is thereby excused.

There is another way to look at conditions that fascinate professors of contract law. A condition may be stated so that it must occur before a party's obligation under the contract is triggered—a happening referred to as a *condition precedent*. The condition of the government inspection in our computer contract is a condition precedent. The buyer has no obligation to purchase until and unless the computer passes. By contrast, performance on a contract can be required until some event occurs. This is the concept of a *condition subsequent*. If the computer contract contained a provision that buyer would buy one computer each month for five years "unless the government withdraws its approval of the Model 2007-A computer" the contract would be viewed as containing a condition subsequent. The buyer's performance obligation continues until the government fails to approve the computer.

Reams of commentary have been written on these issues. It is usually only the smallest and briefest international contracts that do not contain both conditions precedent and conditions subsequent. For example, a contract's government approval clause is normally stated either as a condition precedent ("I will buy your widgets if you get your government's permission to export the widgets.") or a condition subsequent ("I will continue to buy your widgets so long as your government grants export permission."). A government permission clause can be written as *both* a condition precedent and a condition subsequent: "This contract goes into effect when the Kenyan government gives permission to import the goods and will continue in effect so long as the Kenyan government approves the import of the goods."

Readers must also be aware that there is a somewhat different use of the term *conditions* in international business. Because of the singular dangers involved in bicultural, bilingual international commercial transactions, a number of international bodies have developed standard clauses for contracts that are often referred to as *conditions* even though not every one of these standardized provisions would be regarded as a true condition by legal scholars. Many of these standardized terms and conditions are discussed further in Chapter 4; but for the purposes of this discussion a few illustrations will suffice.

For example, the International Chamber of Commerce (ICC) has developed a set of standardized provisions, known as *Incoterms*, that set out many rules for the transportation of goods across international boundaries. These terms provide standardized definitions for such things as free alongside ship (FAS) and free on board (FOB) and may be inserted into international contracts at the election of the parties.[14] The International Federation of Consulting Engineers (FIDIC), an international body of construction engineers, has developed so-called conditions for international construction contracts that contain standard definitions of such crucial terms as *employer* and *contractor*. The FIDIC has standard clauses on virtually all other matters of interest to contracting parties such as site inspection, insurance, payment, and settlement of claims.[15]

Some governments and groups of governments have also developed sets of standard clauses and standard form contracts. The Economic Commission for Europe has published standard form contracts to try to more equitably balance the relative bargaining power of contracting parties.[16] In the former Soviet bloc, the now-defunct Council for Mutual Economic Assistance (referred to as CMEA or CEMA in most of Europe and more often as COMECON in the United States) promulgated mandatory standard conditions for incorporation into commercial contracts with the foreign trade organizations of any of these countries. Because a few socialist states remain in the world, international contract negotiators may continue to encounter the COMECON standard forms even if the organization itself no longer exists.[17]

Whether parties use standard clauses or draft tailor-made provisions for their contract, the terms of performance will be set out in the various documents underlying the agreement, and the vast majority of transactions are fully performed without incident. Many contracts are written with sufficient clarity and foresight that no problems of performance ever arise. The difficult cases are those in which one party seeks to be excused from performance for various reasons or in which one party simply refuses to perform. These problems are best discussed under the next heading, breach of contract and excuse.

§3.2.3 Breach of Contract and Excused Performance

Breach of contract, and its first cousin, excused performance, are exceptions to the normal expectation of full performance that underlies every contract. These two concepts are evaluated in terms of the express language of the contract and the law that governs the contract. Obviously, if full performance has occurred there is usually no

14. INCOTERMS 2010, International Chamber of Commerce. Information on INCOTERMS and many other ICC products may be found at the organization's website: www.iccwbo.org.
15. FIDIC, *Conditions of Contract for Construction* (1st ed., 1999). More information on the FIDIC and their many publications may be found at: www1.fidic.org. *See also*, Ellis Baker, Ben Mellors, Scott Chalmers & Anthony Lavers, *Fidic Contracts: Law and Practice* (2009); Axel-Volkmar Jaeger & Gotz Sebastian Hok, *Fidic: A Guide for Practitioners* (2009).
16. *See*, e.g., Georges R. Delaume, *Transnational Contracts*, part 5 (Booklet 2) at 4–5 (1983).
17. *See* generally, Thomas W. Hoya, *East-West Trade: Comecon Law and American-Soviet Trade* (1984). As the fifth edition of this book goes to press, North Korea and Cuba claim to have retained their socialist systems, so COMECON-style conditions may possibly be encountered when trading with those countries, although Cuba, unlike North Korea, has recently signaled its interest in becoming less isolated and more mainstream as a trading nation. Cuba's troubled relationship with the United States may be easing somewhat as we find ourselves in the second decade of the twenty-first century.

further issue that can arise under the contract. So, for example, if a contract calls for the purchase of 100 facsimile machines at USD 300 per unit, the contract is concluded when the machines are delivered, determined to be satisfactory under the terms of the contract, and final payment is made. Any further dealings between the parties will normally spring from a new contract.

Similarly, if a contract calls for the sale of "100 compact disc (CD) players per month so long as the buyer's government permits the sale of CD players, or for five years, whichever period is longer" the contact is concluded if the buyer's government prohibits the sale of CD players or at the end of the fifth year of the contract. If either of these acts occurs (denial of government permission or the expiration of the five-year period) the contract is concluded without any breach. Put another way, the manner in which performance is described in the contract frequently is used as the primary factor determining whether breach has occurred.

However, when a party does not perform all the terms of the contract that party will often be deemed to be in breach of the contract. If the parties cannot work out their differences on their own through renegotiation or some form of mediation, they will probably take the dispute before a court or arbitrator. When a dispute arises, the party arguably in breach may respond by disclaiming any breach or by arguing that his performance is excused for some reason. Much less frequently, one party to a contract who seeks to be excused from performance will go before a court or arbitrator for what amounts to a declaration that further performance is not required. In either case, some decisional authority must determine whether the contract should be performed as written, whether the contract should in some fashion be modified (the civil code term for certain types of modification is *revision*), or whether performance should be excused entirely.

Difficult issues arise when one of the parties performs almost all of the agreement but for some reason refuses to or cannot perform the remainder of the agreement; or when performance is prevented or diminished because of some external event such as a strike or a war. On these points, it is important not to forget the doctrine of party autonomy. Most of the time, the parties can spell out the consequences of these occurrences in the contract itself, and that language will normally be honored by a court or arbitrator. If the contract is not clear on these occurrences, quite often the applicable law will provide some answers.

Assume, for example, that a contract calls for the sale of 1,200 telescopes over a one-year period. The contract provides expressly that 100 telescopes shall be shipped to the buyer each month. The seller ships 1,100 telescopes in each of the first eleven months of the contract, ships fifty telescopes in the twelfth month and then refuses or is somehow unable to ship the final fifty telescopes. Assume further that the contract calls for payment in full at the end of the twelfth month, rather than for installment payments. Would it be possible for the buyer to keep the 1,150 telescopes and refuse to pay for any of the telescopes because of the seller's breach—that is, because the seller refused to deliver the last fifty telescopes?

In most legal systems, the answer is "no." As a matter of common sense, the law recognizes what the Anglo-American system calls *substantial performance* and would most likely require payment for the goods actually received *unless* it was absolutely clear from the circumstances that the goods were totally useless unless all 1,200 were shipped and received and that both parties understood this at the inception of the contract. Even then the court might order the telescopes returned to the seller, even if the buyer's obligation to pay is forgiven and even if the buyer might be compensated for the consequences of the seller's breach. The reason for this is that virtually all systems of contract law forbid *unjust enrichment* on the part of one or the other parties. The buyer's keeping the 1,150 telescopes and paying nothing is clearly an instance of unjust enrichment.

Under U.S. contract law, the doctrine of substantial performance is not simply a matter of mechanics. Courts almost never establish a specific fixed level of performance, say, 60%, that is always deemed to be substantial performance. Each case is examined on its facts and a determination of substantial performance is measured in terms of many factors—such as the hardship on the parties, the willfulness or negligence involved in the failure to perform, and the benefit that accrues to the injured party from the performance actually accomplished.[18] But once again, this is a situation in which the parties can take care of any problem by contract language. If the buyer absolutely insists on all 1,200 telescopes, the contract can be written to include language such as: "payment under this contract is due if and only if the seller delivers all 1,200 telescopes in good condition within the twelve month period." Of course, even with this kind of provision, if a court or arbitrator were to determine that the 1,150 telescopes in the hands of the buyer had some intrinsic worth, it is doubtful that the buyer would be permitted to keep them while still paying nothing. At the very least, the buyer would probably be instructed to ship the telescopes back to the seller at the seller's expense. Most courts and arbitrators try to do justice to both parties in this kind of situation.

Parties frequently seek to be excused from all or part of their performance when performance becomes impossible or even when performance becomes somewhat more difficult than the party anticipated. More often than not, the idea of *impossibility of performance* or *frustration* of the contract's purposes is addressed in the contract through specific clauses (such as "Seller will ship the computers so long as the Nigerian government approves the shipments") or through a general force majeure clause that excuses performance on the part of either of the parties because of, for example, acts of God, war, insurrection and other unforeseen events. While some courts and legal scholars have sought to distinguish sharply between impossibility and frustration, for the purposes of this discussion, they will be regarded as synonyms. Moreover, while many legal systems have different names for excused performance, the concepts themselves are viewed similarly, if not identically, by virtually all systems. For purposes of convenience and efficiency, the following discussion will consider excuse in terms of U.S. contract law.[19]

18. Restatement Contracts §275.
19. For a good up-to-date review of almost all of these concepts, *see* Melvin A. Eisenberg, *Impossibility, Impracticability and Frustration*, 1 J. Leg. Analysis 207 (2009); For some interesting discussion involving terrorism and excuse *see*, Mark B. Baker, *"A Hard Rain's A Gonna Fall"—Terrorism and Excused Contractual Performance in a Post September 11th World*, 17 Transnat'l. L. 1 (2004). For a discussion of excuse in other systems *see*, e.g., Gerhard Wagner,

The United States legal system recognizes a number of instances in which contract performance will be forgiven. For example, the UCC permits a buyer to reject goods that on inspection after delivery do not conform to the specifications in the contract.[20] When a contract calls for the sale of specific, nonfungible goods and those goods are destroyed through no fault of the buyer or seller before the risk of loss passes to the buyer, the buyer's performance will be forgiven.[21] Contract law in the United States also excuses all or part of the performance when the contract is impossible to perform or when the purposes of the contract become frustrated even when a force majeure clause is not in the contract.

To evaluate an argument that the contract has become impossible to perform, American courts generally apply what is referred to as the *objective* standard of review. In other words, the court must determine not merely that the specific party to the contract could not perform, but that no person, faced with the same problems, could have performed the agreement.

There are two types of impossibility, impossibility because of supervening illegality and impossibility because the subject matter of the contract has been destroyed. A supervening illegality is a change in the law that makes performance unlawful. For example, assume that a U.S. furrier and an African seller enter into a ten-year contract for the sale of the hides of the white rhinoceros at a time when it is perfectly legal to ship those hides into the United States. Eight years after the contract is signed, the U.S. government puts the white rhinoceros on its list of endangered species (thus making it illegal to import the hides into the U.S.). The hide contract will be deemed impossible to perform because of a supervening illegality. Any further obligation to perform on the part of the African shipper will be forgiven, and the parties will simply go their own way.

If a British construction firm promises to build a hotel on an island in the Pacific Ocean and the entire island is destroyed or rendered totally and permanently

In Defense of the Impossibility Defense, 27 Loy. U. Chi. L.J. 55 (1995); Michael G. Rapsomanikis, *Frustration of Contract in International Trade Law and Comparative Law*, 18 Duq. L. Rev. 551 (1980) and Hans Smit, *Frustration of Contract: A Comparative Attempt at Consolidation*, 58 Colum. L. Rev. 287 (1958); Samir A. Saleh, *Note, Some Aspects of Frustrated Performance of Contracts Under Middle Eastern Law*, 33 Int'l & Comp. L. Q. 1046 (1984). For comments on the CISG *see*, e.g., Donald L. Grace, *Force Majeure, China and the CISG: Is China's New Contract Law a Step in the Right Direction?* 2 San Diego Int'l L.J. 173 (2001); Dionysios P. Flambouras, *The Doctrines of Impossibility of Performance and Clausula Rebus Sic Stantibus in the 1980 Convention on Contracts for the International Sale of Goods and the Principles of European Contract Law—A Comparative Analysis*, 13 Pace Int'l L. Rev. 261 (2001); Barry Nicholas, *Force Majeure and Frustration*, 27 Am. J. Comp. L. 231 (1979). For a comparative note, *see*, J. Barrigan Marcantonio, *Unifying the Law of Impossibility*, 8 Hastings Int'l & Comp. L. Rev. 41 (1984). For an excellent article containing a very sophisticated discussion of many of these issues *see*, A.H. Puelinckx, *Frustration, Hardship, Force Majeure, Imprevision, Wegfall der Geschaftsgrundlage, Unmoglichkeit, Changed Circumstances: A Comparative Study in English, French, German and Japanese Law*, 1 J. Int'l Arb. 47 (1986). For an article on the related issue of price reduction in a contract under the CISG, *see* Sanne Jansen, *Price Reduction under the CISG: A 21st Century Perspective*, 32 J. L. & Commerce 325 (2014).

20. UCC §2-601.
21. UCC §2-613.

uninhabitable by a typhoon, the subject matter of the contract has been destroyed and performance made impossible. In this instance, both U.S. and British courts would excuse performance.

Except in the context of the sale of goods under the UCC (which forgives performance in certain instances of mere *impracticability*, rather than impossibility), U.S. and British courts generally require two things to be present before performance will be excused: (1) the event must be unforeseeable; and (2) performance must be physically or legally impossible in an absolute sense. Moreover, if performance is only temporarily inhibited (e.g., the island could be restored to human habitation or hides that are in transit will be permitted to enter the U.S.) the parties must generally perform to the extent that they are capable of performing.

By comparison, commercial impracticability under §2-615 of the UCC, while not contemplating mere inconvenience, may forgive performance even for certain substantial increases in the costs of performance when "the rise in cost is due to some unforeseen contingency which alters the essential nature of the performance."[22] But readers should not interpret this provision too expansively. The official comments to §2-615 make clear that the section is to be applied only to cases in which the inhibiting event could not reasonably be foreseen at the time of contracting; and most importantly, the UCC provides that the contracting parties can bind themselves to a different standard of behavior by express language in the contract.[23]

There are other interpretative questions associated with the doctrine of excuse of performance. The specific language of the force majeure clause may cause problems. For example, some courts have had trouble excusing performance because of, say, labor strife if the contract's force majeure clause contains only those events that are naturally occurring—flood, typhoon, earthquake, and so forth. By contrast, as is discussed in Chapter 2, German courts between World War One and World War Two occasionally forgave performance because of the rampant inflation that occurred under the Weimar Republic. The courts determined that inflation of such drastic proportions was unforeseeable by the parties. For these reasons, parties who may have some worries about their ability to perform may try to negotiate very lengthy force majeure clauses containing all sorts of excuses for performance. Of course, the other side will likely insist on the narrowest possible force majeure for the same reasons. Contract drafters should always keep in mind the basic rule: a contract requires performance; excuses are rarely accepted.

§3.2.4 Remedy

What happens when a party is in breach of contract and the breach is not forgiven? All legal systems have developed rules for compensating the person who suffers because

22. Official Comment Number 4 to UCC §2-615. For further reading on commercial impracticability under the UCC *see*, Melvin Eisenberg, *Impossibility, Impracticability and Frustration*, 1 J. Leg. Analysis 207 (2009); Richard E. Speidel, *Excusable Non-Performance in Sales Contracts: Some Thoughts about Risk Management*, 32 S.C.L. Rev. 241 (1980).
23. Official Comment Number 8 to §2-615.

of the breach. In the Anglo-American system, the basic rule of compensation, frequently referred to as the principle of compensatory damages, is that the injured party should be placed in the same position he would have been in had the contract been fully performed.[24] Normally, this means that the injured party will be given monetary compensation.

In most instances, money damages will include the additional expenses the injured party incurred to restore his position, known as incidental and consequential damages, to the extent that those expenses are reasonable and foreseeable.[25] To illustrate, the buyer who received 1,150 of 1,200 telescopes would be permitted to pay for only 1,150 telescopes. In certain circumstances, the seller would have to compensate the buyer for his expenses in seeking out and purchasing the remaining fifty telescopes from some other manufacturer.

But at the same time, the law seeks to give both parties the benefit of their bargain. In the 1,150 telescope case, a court or arbitrator would likely not find the fifty telescope shortage a substantial breach of the contract, absent unusual circumstances, and thus would require the buyer to compensate the seller for the value to him of the 1,150 telescopes received. When evaluating damage claims courts are always concerned about avoiding situations that result in unjust enrichment for one party or the other.

Moreover, courts normally require a party who is injured to take reasonable steps to reduce his injury. This doctrine, normally referred to as the requirement of mitigation, prohibits a court from awarding damages to a party if he simply sat back and did nothing while the injury continued to accrue. In this regard, consider a slight change in the facts of the 1,150 telescope case. Assume that the 1,200 telescopes obtained from the seller will be used by the buyer to complete a separate contract that the buyer formed with the American Arbitration Association (AAA) School for Astronomers. The second contract is to be completed by July 1, 1992 or buyer is liable for a penalty of USD 1,000 per day for each day after July 1 that the contract is unfulfilled. Further assume that buyer could readily obtain the additional fifty telescopes from another company with only two days lost time on the second contract. Instead, buyer

24. *See*, e.g., Farnsworth, *supra* n. 5, at 811–816. For a fine piece of writing on contract damages generally, *see* Charlie Webb, *Performance and Compensation: An Analysis of Contract Damages and Contractual Obligation*, 26 Oxford J. Leg. Stud. 41 (2006). For a discussion of remedies under the CISG *see*, Rolf Herber, *The Rules of the Convention Relating to the Buyer's Remedies in Cases of Breach of Contract*, 7 Dig. Com. L. 104 (1980). *See also*, Bruno Zeller, *Damages under the Convention on Contracts for the International Sale of Goods* (2009); Ralph Cunnington & Saidov Djakhongir, *Contract Damages: Domestic and International Perspectives* (2008).

25. Readers of this book who reside outside the United States may find some of the U.S. thinking on the economic consequences of contract damage awards fascinating. *See*, e.g., Adam Kramer, *The Law of Contract Damages* (2014); One of the principal works is the fourth chapter of Professor (and for many years Judge) Richard Posner's, Economic Analysis of the Law (9th ed., 2014). *See also*, Damien Nyer, *Withholding Performance for Breach in International Transactions: An Exercise in Equations, Proportions or Coercion?* 18 Pace Int'l L. Rev. 29 (2006); Steven Shavell, *Specific Performance Versus Damages for Breach of Contract: An Economic Analysis*, 84 Tex. L. Rev. 831 (2006); John H. Barton, *The Economic Basis of Damages for Breach of Contract*, 1 J. Leg. Stud. 277 (1972); Robert L. Birmingham, *Breach of Contract, Damage Measures, and Economic Efficiency*, 24 Rutgers L. Rev. 273 (1970).

sits around for ten additional days doing nothing to purchase the last fifty telescopes, thus performing the second contract twelve days late. Under the contract between buyer and AAA School of Astronomy, buyer will be assessed a USD 12,000 penalty. Assume finally that seller was notified and fully aware of the existence of the second contract and the importance of the 1,200 telescopes to the second contract. This knowledge on the part of the original seller arguably makes the penalty suffered by buyer a matter of incidental or consequential damages.

However, the doctrine of mitigation applies here. If buyer were to seek to recover the full USD 12,000 from seller because of seller's failure to ship all 1,200 telescopes, his claim would almost surely be denied. Under the principle of mitigation a court or arbitrator is very unlikely to give B any more than two days lost time compensation (USD 2,000) since she delayed ordering the replacement widgets for ten days for no good reason. By contrast, the two-day delay was directly attributable to the fault of the seller and the seller knew about the related School of Astronomy contract and the penalties, in that contract, that would be incurred for late performance. The two-day penalty would probably be held to be foreseeable by the seller and to the extent that the USD 1,000 per day penalty clause was seen as reasonable, the court or arbitrator would likely award USD 2,000 to the buyer as part of her incidental and consequential damages.

Occasionally, parties will be seriously injured through some type of willful and malicious conduct on the part of the other party and will ask a court for punitive or exemplary damages. While not totally unheard of in cases of breach of contract, this type of damage award is rare, particularly in the context of an international commercial agreement. Indeed, the CISG does not mention exemplary damages, although it is arguable that the Convention's silence does not exclude them. Moreover, there are instances in the United States in which punitive damages have been awarded even by arbitrators for particularly egregious breaches of contract.[26]

Many contracts are silent on the issue of damages. But some contracts try to anticipate the consequences of a breach by providing a specific formula for computing damages or by establishing a specific figure (known as a liquidated damages clause) that both parties agree at the outset is proper compensation for breach. Most courts and arbitrators in both common law and civil systems will honor a formula for a liquidated damages clause so long as the amount is not excessive or seen to be a penalty and so long as it bears some reasonable relation to the injuries actually suffered.[27]

There are occasions when the subject matter of a contract is so unique that mere monetary damages are not sufficient to compensate the injured party. For example, in

---

26. *See*, e.g., Cedric Vanjleenhove, *Punitive Damages in Private International Law: Lessons for the European Union* (2016); Charles Calleros, *Punitive Damages, Liquidated Damages, and Clauses Penales in Contract Actions: A Comparative Analysis of the American Common Law and the French Civil Code*, 32 Brook. J. Int'l L. 67 (2006); International Chamber of Commerce, *Guide to Penalty and Liquidated Damages Clauses (International Contracts)* (1990); Glower W. Jones, *Punitive Damages in Arbitration in the USA*, 14 Int'l Bus. Law. 188 (1986); Timothy J. Sullivan, *Punitive Damages in the Law of Contract: The Reality and the Illusion of Legal Change*, 61 Minn. L. Rev. 207 (1977).

27. *See*, e.g., Farnsworth, *supra* n. 5, at 895–904; UCC §2-718(1).

the case of real estate transactions, a contract to purchase a particular plot of land on which the buyer expects to erect a hotel cannot normally satisfied by giving the buyer money. A buyer who needs and contracts for unique goods that can be manufactured only by one company cannot be properly compensated except by receiving these unique goods. Injured parties involved in agreements involving this kind of product often seek the remedy known as specific performance by which a court orders the other party to perform the contract as written, no matter what the inconvenience or expense might be to the party in breach.[28]

§3.2.5 Dispute Resolution

Virtually all international commercial agreements contain some type of dispute resolution clause. The clause can call for arbitration, for litigation in a particular country's judicial system, or for some less-drastic resolution procedure such as mandatory renegotiation or mediation. The pros and cons of each of these procedures are discussed at length in §3.4. For the purposes of this section, it is sufficient to understand that the parties will generally be expected to adhere to the dispute resolution device or devices specifically set out in the contract. In many instances, the parties may be compelled to engage in the selected procedure even if one party has changed its mind since the contract was drafted.

§3.3 THE DIFFERENT FORMS OF INTERNATIONAL COMMERCIAL AGREEMENT

The contract principles and concepts discussed in §3.2 are generally applicable to virtually any type of commercial agreement even though most of the examples used were drawn from agreements involving the sale of goods—still the most prevalent form of international commercial transaction. But the sale of goods is not the only form of agreement that exists at the international level. Particularly over the past few years, many private parties and government agencies have executed contracts for franchises, for joint ventures, for the transfer of technology in the form of licensing agreements, for the sale of services and for foreign direct investment.

Each of these types of agreement is designed to accomplish a specific goal and each has its own complications and intricacies. In understanding the general nature of each type of agreement the reader will go a long way towards understanding the entire gamut of international commercial agreements. The different types will be addressed in the following order: contract for the sale of goods or services, agency and distributorship, franchise, licensing, joint venture and foreign direct investment.

---

28. *See*, e.g., Theodore Eisenberg & Geoffrey P. Miller, *Damages Versus Specific Performance: Lessons from Commercial Contracts*, 12 J. Empirical Leg. Stud. 29 (2015); Steven Shavell, *Specific Performance Versus Damages for Breach of Contract*, Harvard Law & Economics Discussion Paper No. 532 (2005).

§3.3.1 Sales of Goods or Services

[1] The Sale of Goods Generally

The sale of goods is one of the most common international commercial transactions and has been extensively discussed in previous portions of this chapter. By definition, it is the sale of some tangible object for a specified price. Most principles of law that address the definition of a good tend to define it as a residual concept. For example, the CISG defines the sale of goods as being sales of something other than, among other things: ships, aircraft and hovercraft, goods bought for family or personal use, or goods bought at auction.[29] The UCC defines goods as "all things...which are movable at the time of identification to the contract ..."[30] Problems related to payment for the sale of goods and peripheral issues such as dumping and countervailing duty problems and antitrust issues are discussed below.

[2] Barter and Countertrade

There are other commercial transactions, generally referred to as barter and countertrade that are becoming more frequent and that resemble the sale of goods in that the primary goal of each transaction is to obtain a particular good. The exchange of another good is simply used as a payment substitute—that is, another good is provided by the buyer in lieu of a monetary payment. While the international trading community has not completely resolved these terms as words of art some attempt at defining each term is helpful. As used by many lawyers and business executives countertrade is a set of at least two separate buy and sell agreements negotiated between the same two parties, both of which agreements must be performed to satisfy the entire obligation.[31] Put a little more colloquially, it is a situation in which A says to B (both companies in the hospital supply business, "I will buy your test tubes if you agree simultaneously to buy

29. CISG, Art. 2. For some special perspectives on "distance" sale of goods (also discussed extensively in Chapter 6, *infra*) *see* Rafal Manko, *Contracts for Online and Other Distance Sales of Goods*, European Parliamentary Research Service (2016).
30. UCC §2-105(1).
31. *See*, e.g., Dalia Marin & Monika Schnitzer, *Contracts in Trade and Transition: The Resurgence of Barter* (2002). *See also*, Andrew J. Horowitz, *NOTE: Revisiting Barter under the CISG*, 29 J. L. & Com. 99 (2010); Robert Howze, *Beyond the Countertrade Taboo: Why the WTO Should Take Another Look at Barter and Countertrade*, 60 U. Toronto L.J. 289 (2010); Scott J. Lochner, *Countertrade and International Barter*, 19 Int'l Law. 725 (1985); Clive M. Schmitthoff, *Countertrade*, J. Bus. L. 115 (1985) and Thomas B. McVey, *Countertrade: Commercial Practices, Legal Issues and Policy Dilemmas*, 16 L. & Policy Int'l Bus. 1 (1984). Two good book-length works on countertrade are Pompilis Verzariu, *Countertrade, Barter & Offsets* (1985) and Leo G.B. Welt, *Trade Without Money: Barter & Countertrade* (1984). UNCITRAL has issued a one-volume set of standard clauses for countertrade agreements. For a good discussion of the World Trade Organization and barter and countertrade *see* Robert Howze, *Beyond the Countertrade Taboo: Why the WTO Should Take Another Look at Barter and Countertrade*, 60 U. Toronto L.J. 289 (2010).

my surgical gloves." While each contract theoretically can stand on its own two feet, both parties enter into the agreement only on the expectation that both agreements will be fully performed.

Barter is a concept related to countertrade and is often defined in its traditional sense as an exchange of one thing for another, with each thing serving as payment for the other. In other words, "I will give you 10,000 test tubes if you give me 20,000 surgical gloves." Or, as Boeing agreed several years ago in what may have been the largest (by dollar amount) barter in history: "We will give you X number of airplanes if you, Saudi Arabia, will give us X barrels of oil." Barter serves virtually the same purposes as countertrade by preserving scarce hard currency and enhancing export volumes and market penetration. Much like countertrade, it is really just a substitute for the payment of money. The bartered goods, by definition, constitute payment for each other.

The United Nations Commission on International Trade Law (UNCITRAL) has proffered a somewhat more cumbersome definition: "A countertrade transaction...is an economic transaction in which one party supplies, or procures the supply of, goods or other economic value to the second party and in return, the first party agrees to purchase or procures to be purchased from the second party, or from a party designated by the second party, goods or other economic value, so as to achieve an agreed ratio between the reciprocal performances."[32] Under the UNCITRAL definition, barter (described below) is a subset of countertrade. Under the UNCITRAL definition, parties can engage in either a bilateral arrangement (A ships computers to B; B ships telescopes to A) or the transaction can be multi-legged: A ships computers to B, B ships telescopes to C, C ships running shoes to A. It is at least theoretically possible for the transaction to have even more than three components; but as the following discussion shows, each new actor in the transaction simply compounds the difficulty of putting together a fully satisfactory agreement. Recall that the economic rational of barter and countertrade is that each of the goods constitutes payment for the other.

Barter and countertrade transactions are popular in countries that have limited hard currency resources because an exchange of goods dispenses with the need to expend hard currency to obtain those products. These transactions are also viewed as devices to assist fledgling businesses in one country to penetrate the markets of more developed countries without huge expenditures of funds for such things as agents and advertising. While barter and countertrade are innovative—and frequently beneficial devices to do business—they do not really affect or require the alteration of basic principles of contract law. The exchange transaction is in reality merely a substitute for the payment of money for goods.

There are a number of pitfalls that business executives may encounter in setting up barter or countertrade transactions. First, a proper comparative valuation of both products is vitally important to the deal. In other words, the parties must each have a solid understanding of how many pairs of surgical gloves equal how many test tubes in

32. UNCITRAL, *Preliminary Study of Legal Issues in International Countertrade* (1988).

the example set out above. If either party makes an erroneous valuation of either her product or the product offered by the other side, the economic value (the profit, as it were) of the deal is placed in jeopardy.

Second, most barter and countertrade transactions need to be performed almost simultaneously. Otherwise the party who receives the goods late winds up giving what amounts to an interest-free loan to the other side. Consider the following example: X agrees to ship Y 100 computers in exchange for 300 telescopes. The standard assumption in a barter transaction is that X need not be paid in cash because he can sell the telescopes in his own market for an amount of money that results in a profit after taking into consideration all of his costs involved (including purchase price) from his shipping the computers to Y. If X ships the computers on day 1 and Y receives them on day 10, Y can put the computers immediately to use or resell them. If Y delays the shipment of the telescopes, X will not have the use of the telescopes or be able to resell them, but having shipped the computers is obliged to pay for the computers. Over the time that X has shipped the computers but has not received the telescopes, he is in essence subsidizing the transaction in favor of Y. A barter contract can incorporate language that alleviates this problem. It could, for example, contain a clause that assesses some kind of penalty against Y (or against X if he is the delaying party) for every day that one shipment of goods is delayed after the other side receives its goods. However, because of the inherent nature of barter, many barter agreements are oral undertakings conducted over the telephone with perhaps a few documents transmitted by telex or facsimile machine. Getting both sets of goods shipped at about the same time is usually a primary consideration in barter and countertrade.

A third factor to consider is the issue of quality control. Recall that the essence of a barter arrangement is the notion that a certain number of computers is equal to a certain number of telescopes. That valuation presumes that both the computers and the telescopes are manufactured and perform up to certain standards. If, upon receipt, one of the sets of products proves to be defective, the receiving party is stuck with either suing his counterpart for breach of contract or having to take steps—frequently costly steps—to bring those products up to an appropriate quality standard for resale. For all of these reasons, the reader should be aware that barter and countertrade have their own special problems and pitfalls. Many lawyers and business executives avoid such transactions completely. They are not normally preferred transactions for persons new to international commercial agreements.[33]

[3] The Sale of Services

The sale of services across national borders is becoming increasingly common. The traditional service contract was a contract for engineering and construction services, or

33. For a much longer discussion of all these issues, see the three articles in the symposium: Montague, *An Introduction to Countertrade*; van Dort, *Some Conceptual Problems of Countertrade*; and del Campo Wilson, *Advantage and Disadvantage of Countertrade: The Argentine View, as an Importing Country*, 17 Int'l Bus. Law. 360–372 (1989). *See also*, Cedric Guyot, *Countertrade Contracts in International Business*, 20 Int'l L. 921 (1986).

in many instances, a mixed service and goods construction contract that constitutes a "turnkey" arrangement (by which an entire facility such as an electric power plant is built and placed in operation by a foreign company and the key to the project turned over to the host government or the purchasing company).[34] These days contracts for the sale of services can run the gamut from financial and data processing services to employment services to expert consulting services. Countries that participate in the General Agreement on Tariffs and Trade (GATT) are now beginning to negotiate free trade provisions governing the sale of services.[35] The North American Free Trade Agreement (NAFTA), following on the model of the United States-Canada Free Trade Agreement (USCFTA), contains some innovative provisions on the sale of services among the United States, Canada, and Mexico.[36]

Construction and engineering services contracts are so common around the world that they frequently incorporate standard provisions and clauses (discussed more extensively in Chapter 4) developed by the FIDIC and by the European Development Fund. More recently, the UN has promulgated a comprehensive set of construction contract provisions, entitled Legal Guide on Drawing Up International Contracts for the Construction of Industrial Works.[37] While focusing on the construction of factories and other similar construction projects, many lawyers who have read through the Legal Guide believe it is helpful for virtually any kind of construction project. The Legal Guide identifies a number of elements that are normally contained in a construction contract: description of the work, guarantees, technology transfer, pricing, payment, scheduling, role of the consulting engineer,[38] subcontracting, inspection, completion, acceptance, risk of loss, security (including guarantees of performance by the contractor and guarantees of payment by the purchaser), delays, damages (including liquidated damages), excusability, changes, suspensions, terminations, post-construction obligations (such as the provision on training programs and spare parts), choice of law and dispute resolution. Large-scale construction contracts are usually massive documents with exceptionally detailed contract provisions. They are not matters that are usually put into the hands of beginners.

---

34. For a good commentary on some of the issues involved in turnkey projects *see*, Mark Frilet, *Price and Terms of Payment in Large International Turnkey Contracts*, 18 Int'l. Bus. L. 362 (1990).
35. *See*, e.g., Lazar, *Services and the GATT: US Motives and a Blueprint for Negotiations*, 22 J. World Trade L. 135 (1989); Kakbadse, *Trade in Services and the Uruguay Round*, 19 Ga. J. Int'l & Comp. L. 384 (1989). For a European perspective on services contracts (and other forms of agreement) *see* Rafael Illescas Ortiz & Pilar Perales Viscasillas, *The Scope of the Common European Sales Law: B2B, Goods, Digital Content and Services*, 11 J. Int'l Trade L. & Pol'y, 241 (2012).
36. *See*, e.g., Joel P. Trachtman, *Trade in Financial Services under GATS, NAFTA and the EC: A Regulatory Jurisdiction Analysis*, 34 Colum. J. Transnat'l L. 37 (1995); A. Keith Tuomi, *The Canada-U.S. Free Trade Agreement: Implications for the Bilateral Trade Balance*, 13 Maryland J. Int'l L. & Trade 105 (1988).
37. UNCITRAL, *Legal Guide on Drawing Up International Contracts for the Construction of Industrial Works* (1988).
38. For excellent analysis of both the underlying contract and performance of a construction contract *see*, William Godwin, *International Construction Contracts* (2013); Wendy Venoit Kennedy, *Construction Law: a Guide for Cross-Border Transactions and Legal Disputes* (2009); Bryan Morgan, *International Construction Contract Management: a Compendium of Knowledge* (2005). For additional commentary on the crucial functions performed by the engineer *see*, U. Hochuli, *Role of the Engineer under FIDIC Standard Contracts*, 19 Int'l Bus. L. 542 (1991).

One type of service contract increasingly popular in developing countries is the management contract—an agreement by which a host country can take advantage of foreign expertise without giving over valuable natural resources, as it might have to in the context of a conventional concession agreement.[39] A company involved in the purchase of a management contract is in essence buying expertise which is to be applied to some activity in the purchaser's operation. A management contract can be, for example, an agreement to operate a country's data processing services or to operate a system of cellular telephones.

It is not uncommon for a management contract to be coupled with a long-term licensing agreement. The management contract insures that the process subject to the license will be performed properly from the beginning by persons who know what they are doing while permitting nationals in the host country to be trained to eventually perform the operation themselves. Since a portion of the funds flowing from a management contract will be expended in the host country for the support and well-being of the management personnel in the form of salaries and living expenses, the host country gets to keep more of its money in-country than might otherwise be the case.

§3.3.2 Agency and Distributorship Agreements

These arrangements are common on the international level and are usually associated with contracts for the sale of goods or services. Companies that wish to sell goods abroad have a number of ways to get the goods into the hands of the ultimate purchasers. The company may establish a branch office or a foreign subsidiary under the rules and regulations pertaining to the organization and registration of subsidiaries in the target country. The company's goods may then be marketed through the subsidiary. This is often a risky operation since the capital investment and the expenses associated with starting up and maintaining the business can be considerable without any guarantee that the product will catch on among the target country's consumers. Moreover, many countries establish significant regulatory barriers to this type of undertaking.

A company that wishes to explore the possibilities of marketing a good or service in a foreign country without the need to commit huge amounts of money to the undertaking may decide to appoint an agent in that country or to contract with a company in the host nation to serve as a distributorship for the company's products. A distributorship is distinguished from an agency agreement mainly by the method of compensation for the distributor or agent.[40]

39. *See*, e.g., *Petroleum Investment Policies in Developing Countries* (Nicky Beredjick & Thomas Walde eds., 1988); James Westring, *Construction and Management Contracts*, in *The Transnational Law of International Commercial Transactions* 184–190 (Norbert Horn & Clive M. Schmitthoff eds., 1982).

40. For a good discussion of numerous issues involving agency and distributorship agreements *see*, Marianne Dickstein & Christelle Albaric, *International Commercial Agency and Distribution Agreements: Case Law and Contract Clauses* (2d ed., 2017); Geert Bogaert & Ulrich Lohmann, *Commercial Agency and Distribution Agreements* (3d ed., 2000), Thomas F. Clasen,

An agent brings the product of the seller to the attention of potential purchasers by contacting potential customers, showing and demonstrating samples of the products and soliciting orders. However, the actual sales contract is executed directly between the seller and the purchaser. An agent is normally compensated for his efforts on a percentage commission for products actually sold. Often, the agent does not even see the product change hands and works on the basis of samples, models, and printed specifications. The actual goods are shipped by the seller directly to the purchaser.

A distributorship, by contrast, is a commercial arrangement by which the distributor undertakes to sell the foreign company's product in the target country and takes as remuneration a profit on the goods sold, bearing virtually all the risks for obtaining products, selling those products and receiving payment from the ultimate purchasers. In this instance, the sales contract is between the distributor and the purchaser.

In virtually every country there are principles of law specially developed for the agent-principal relationship. For example, in the Anglo-American system, agents are regarded as fiduciaries of their principals, owing them duties such as the duty of loyalty (an agent may not work for a competitor under most circumstances) and the duty of full disclosure (an agent is not supposed to keep secrets from his principal). Because there is a perception in many countries that in-country agents have not been treated properly by their foreign principles, many countries have enacted laws that give certain protections to in-country agents from arbitrary or unreasonable termination by foreign principles.[41] Distributorships, by contrast, are more of an arm's-length transaction that is normally dealt with by the application of conventional rules of contract law.

Agency and distributorship agreements are generally entered into as risk-avoidance devices because the distributor buys the product from the manufacturer and bears the risk of selling the product in the host country. In many countries, such as the United States, foreign distributorships are an attractive way of doing business because of favorable tax treatment of the relationship afforded by one or another of the countries involved.

Distributorship arrangements are not totally free of risks and problems. These arrangements sometimes trigger antitrust problems at home and abroad. Some countries have established regulations on the arbitrary termination of distributorship contracts.[42] Virtually every country in which agents and distributorships are permissible also have tight controls on registration of the arrangement and require detailed

---

International Agency and Distribution Agreements: Analysis and Form (1992). Mr. Clasen has also produced a number of writings on specific areas of the world, e.g., Thomas F. Clasen, *International Agency and Distribution Agreements: Europe* (1994). *See also*, Steven C. Nelson, *Negotiating and Drafting Agency, Distribution and Franchise Agreements* (1992); Richard Christou, *International Agency, Distribution and Licensing Agreements* (6th ed., 2011).

41. *See*, e.g., Joke Sperling, *Termination under Dutch Law of Agency Agreements*, 18 Int'l Bus. L. 462 (1990); David M. Dobson & Rita Gaudenzi, *Agency and Distributorship Laws in Italy*, 20 Int'l L. 997 (1986).

42. *See*, e.g., Valentine Korah, *Group Exemptions for Exclusive Distribution and Purchasing in the EEC*, 21 Com. Mkt. L. Rev. 53 (1984); Robert T. Jones, *Practical Aspects of Commercial Agency and Distribution Agreements in the European Community*, 6 Int'l L. 107 (1972).

and continuous reporting of the activities of the undertaking.[43] Still, even with all the pitfalls and strictures on formation and operation, agency, and distributorship agreements remain a popular form of transnational business relationship.

§3.3.3 Franchises

In scope and concept, a franchise agreement falls somewhere between a distributorship and a licensing agreement.[44] It is a comparatively new and quintessentially U.S. form of doing international business. The relationship itself is fairly simple and is best described in terms of a hypothetical. Assume that XYZ Corporation has designed a new fast food hamburger that has entranced the U.S. public. After massive advertising and exceptionally successful market penetration, consumers in the United States now flock to buy XYZ Burgers. Successes such as these make XYZ want to expand its operation as quickly as possible. The corporation has essentially two options in expanding its hamburger market. It can finance, build, and operate retail outlets wherever it chooses to do business; or it can sell franchises.

Within the United States, creating company-owned facilities in different states is not a difficult undertaking. The U.S. Constitution permits businesses to cross state lines to establish new enterprises. There are relatively few legal impediments to starting a business in New York and eventually opening company-owned outlets in California and Florida. However, the business considerations and the financial consequences may not make sense. Huge numbers of company-owned outlets will require a large capital outlay, possibly greater than the corporation's ability to raise capital funds. The current tax climate may militate against large numbers of company-owned outlets; or the corporation's business strategy may warrant trying to displace some of the risk of starting up large numbers of company-owned outlets in untested markets.

---

43. Henry T. King, Jr., *Legal Aspects of Appointment and Termination of Foreign Distributors and Representatives*, 17 Case W. Res. J. Int'l L. 91 (1985). *See also*, Pilar Perales Viscasillas, *The Good, the Bad, and the Ugly in Distribution Contracts: Limitation of Party Autonomy in Arbitration?*, 4 Penn. St. J.L. & Int'l Aff. 213 (2015). For a continental viewpoint *see*, Ioannis Lianos, *Commercial Agency Agreements, Vertical Restraints, and the Limits of Article 81(1) EC: Between Hierarchies and Networks*, 3 J. Competition L. & Econ. 625 (2007); Utz Toepke, *EEC Law of Competition: Distribution Agreements and Their Notification*, 19 Int'l Law. 117 (1985); Peter Burkard, *Termination Compensation to Distributors under German Law*, 7 Int'l L. 185 (1973).
44. For excellent and thorough discussion of many franchising issues *see*, e.g., Harold Brown & Ebin Sandler, *Franchising: Realities and Remedies* (2016); Rupert M. Barkoff, *Fundamentals of Franchising* (3d ed., 2009); Roger D. Blair & Francine Lafontaine, *The Economics of Franchising (2005); Frank Hoy, Franchising: An International Perspective* (2002); Nelson, *supra* n. 40; A. Konigsberg, *International Franchising* (1991). For an excellent analysis with a regional focus *see*, Viktorija Jarkina, *Franchising in Theory and Practice: A Franchise Agreement in the Framework of Civil Law* (2010); Francoise J. Gamet-Pol, *Franchise Agreements within the European Community* (1997). For some good discussion of narrower issues that arise in the context of franchise agreements, *see* Michael R. Gray & Natalma M. McKnew, *Covenants Against Competition in Franchise Agreements* (3d ed., 2012); Robert W. Emerson, *Franchise Goodwill: Take a Sad Song and Make It Better*, 46 U. Mich. J. of L. Reform 349 (2013); Maureen Brookes & Levent Altinay, *Franchise Partner Selection: Perspectives of Franchisors and Franchisees*, 25 J. Services Mkt. 336 (2011).

XYZ (the franchisor) may prefer to sell franchises by which a private individual (the franchisee) obtains permission to use the XYZ trade name and its proprietary processes so long as these individuals hold themselves out as XYZ Burger outlets, follow company-dictated procedures and practices, and pay the company a percentage royalty for the right to use the XYZ logo. The franchisee usually contributes a substantial sum of money as part of his personal investment and is often required to spend time at the XYZ headquarters receiving training in XYZ methods of business. In the United States, one of the premier hamburger franchises, McDonald's, requires that new franchisees attend "Hamburger University" before operating a new franchise.

Benefits to both franchisor and franchisee are considerable. The franchisor expands its operations faster and wider with far less capital investment and with far less risk than would be the case if it set up wholly owned outlets. The franchisee derives enormous marketing benefits from the nationwide or worldwide reputation and advertising efforts of the franchisor. The royalties paid by the franchisee pays for the use of the franchisor's name and good will. Royalties are sometimes stated as a percentage of gross revenues rather than profits. Thus, the franchisor gets paid whether or not the franchisee makes a profit.

Franchises have become an enormously popular method of doing business in the United States, particularly in the services industries. The most popular franchises in the United States, such as McDonald's, are now exceptionally difficult to obtain, but once obtained are usually gold mines for both parties.

As might be expected, there have been abuses associated with the franchise process. Government agencies in the United States have noticed that there is a considerable disparity in the bargaining power between franchisee and franchisor. The franchisor almost always dictates the precise extent and nature of the agreement, normally proffering a standard form contract that the franchisee must sign. These standardized agreements are weighed heavily in favor of the franchisor, especially in the areas of amount of royalties, strictures on operating arrangements and grounds for termination. In a number of countries, including the United States, this imbalance has led to government-imposed constraints on the entire franchising process.[45] Other locations, such as Hong Kong, are relatively free-wheeling and noninhibitory when franchises are concerned so long as royalty outflow is not excessive.[46]

45. The United States Congress investigated the franchise practices of major American oil companies and decided to impose severe restrictions on the ability of an oil company to terminate a retail gasoline franchise through the Petroleum Marketing Practices Act, 15 U.S.C. §§2801-14 (PMPA). The United States Federal Trade Commission has developed regulations which attempt to equalize imbalances in bargaining power in franchises outside the oil industry. *See*, e.g., 16 C.F.R. Part 436. For a discussion of the PMPA *see*, William Fox, *Federal Regulation of Energy* 364–384 (1983). *See also*, Bryan Schwartz & Leandro Zylberman, *International Franchise Regulation*, 8 Asper Rev. Int'l Bus. & Trade L. 317 (2008).

46. *See*, e.g., Bryan W. Blades, *Franchising in China: A Current Perspective*, 14 Currents Int'l Trade L.J. 20 (2005); Philip D. Woods, *Franchising in Hong Kong*, Int'l Bus. L. 440 (1985).

The European Union (EU) now appears to be interested in strong, yet realistic regulation of franchise relationships.[47] In 1986, the European Court of Justice issued an opinion, now generally referred to as the *Pronuptia* case,[48] that held squarely that franchise relationships were subject to the EU's competition laws. Prompted by the *Pronuptia* decision, the European Commission in Brussels issued EC Guidelines on franchises to conform franchise regulation with the EC's competition policies. These guidelines are too lengthy to restate here, but briefly summarized, they permit a franchisor to safeguard know-how and other trade secrets in the franchise relationship, permit termination of the franchise relationship on a number of grounds yet prohibit price-fixing and certain types of market sharing arrangements.[49]

As popular as they are in the United States, franchise agreements are not uniformly admired elsewhere in the world. Some countries faced with what appears to be an increasingly Americanized retail business sector object to franchises on cultural and social grounds as well as on economic grounds.

Franchises create additional concerns for developing countries because the payment of royalties causes a hard currency outflow. As a consequence, franchising on an international level has developed much more slowly than it has in the United States, although it appears to be of growing interest in virtually every part of the world.

There are any number of ways that an international franchise may be established and administered. It can be a joint venture between the foreign franchisor and a host-country business entity. The franchise may be administered at long-distance from the parent company's location in another country; or the franchisor may establish an administrative office in the host country to manage all the franchises within that country. The parent company may establish operations on a regional basis which in turn have the authority to establish franchises in an established territory.

Depending on the host country selected for the franchising operation, there can be many or few constraints on the business operation.[50] Stated briefly, the primary issues of concern in foreign franchising operations are: protection of intellectual property including both patents, trademarks and know-how (*see* §3.3.4 below); specific regulations on termination of franchises established by the host country; any special matters of taxation applicable to franchises; and any special controls on utilization of personnel in the franchise operation.

---

47. Martijan van Empel, *Franchising and Strict Liability in the EEC*, 18 Int'l Bus. L. 169 (1990). Symposium, *Franchising in Europe, 1987*, 16 Int'l Bus. L. 117 (1988); Roger J. Goebel, *The Uneasy Fate of Franchising under EEC Antitrust Laws*, 10 Eur. L. Rev. 87 (1985).
48. *Pronuptia de Paris GmbH v. Pronuptia de Paris Irmgard Schillgallis*, reported in 1 Com. Mkt. L. Rev. 414 (1986).
49. *See*, e.g., E. Hackemi Aliouche & Udo A. Schlentrich, *International Franchise Assessment Model: Entry and Expansion in the European Union*, 3 Entrepren. Bus. L.J. 517 (2009); Dieter A. Schmitz & Alain Van Hamme, *Franchising in Europe—The First Practical EEC Guidelines*, 22 Int'l L. 717 (1988).
50. The EU, for example, has initiated some comprehensive rules on the creation and operation of franchises within the EU. *See*, Regulation No. 4087/88, Application of the Treaty to Categories of Franchise Agreements (November 30, 1988). *See also*, James W. Kirkconnell, *Franchise Agreements and Adjudication in the United States and the European Union*, 18 Fla. J. Int'l L. 413 (2006).

§3.3.4 Licensing and Technology Transfer

Licensing is a process by which the holder of some form of intellectual property (licensor) such as a patent, copyright, or trademark—each of which is a form of intellectual property that requires formal registration with an appropriate government body—or unpatented trade secrets and commercial processes (sometimes referred to as "know-how") gives permission to another person (the licensee) to make use of the property. The license is normally stated for a term of years or, in certain instances, for the life span of the underlying intellectual property. In return, the licensee uses the intellectual property and pays the licensor royalties for that use. Because licensing agreements are of increasing importance in international trade, this book devotes an entire chapter, Chapter 7, to intellectual property and licensing agreements.

§3.3.5 Joint Ventures

As more and more countries require at least some control over business operations within their boundaries, the older forms of doing business such as the take-over of foreign companies, the establishment of foreign subsidiaries and the execution of concession agreements are giving way to joint ventures. Viewed in its simplest form, a joint venture is a contract that creates a partnership for the purpose of performing some kind of business operation—for example, the sale of goods or the construction of a power plant.[51]

One fundamental characteristic of joint ventures is that they are almost always substantial undertakings. In one instance, an American lawyer was asked whether it would be feasible for an American company with less than USD 1 million in assets even to consider a joint venture given the incredible complexity of the regulatory structure, the time and effort necessary to prepare and execute the agreement itself and the direct start-up investment. He replied: "I would have a very difficult time imagining how [such a company] could get involved in a joint venture outside the United

51. For some excellent writings covering many of the issues involved in joint ventures *see*, Zenichi Shishido & Munetake Fukuda, *Joint Venture Strategies: Design, Bargaining and the Law* (2016); Robert F. Klueger & Jacob Stein, *International Joint Ventures: A Concise Guide for Attorneys and Business Owners* (2014); Ronald Charles Wolf, *The Complete Guide to International Joint Ventures: With Sample Clauses and Contracts* (3d ed., 2011); *Handbook of International Joint Ventures* (John Walmsley ed., 2007); Ronald Charles Wolf, *Effective International Joint Venture Management: Practical Legal Insights for Successful Organization and Implementation* (2000); Aimin Yan & Yadong Luo, *International Joint Ventures: Theory and Practice* (2000); Peter D. Ehrenhaft, *International Joint Ventures: Setting Them Up, Taking Them Apart*, and Franklin C. Jesse, Jr., *International Joint Ventures*, in *International Trade for the Non-Specialist* (ALI-ABA, 2d ed., 1997); Michael B. Nelson, *Critical Analysis and Strategies for U.S. Overseas Businesses Participating as a Foreign Joint Venture Partner*, 9 Transnat'l L. 1 (1996); Michael E. Hooton, *Structuring and Negotiating International Joint Ventures*, 27 Creighton L. Rev. 1013 (1997). For an in-depth analysis of a sample joint venture contract *see* Committee on Negotiated Acquisitions, *Model Joint Venture Agreement with Commentary* (American Bar Association 2007).

States...[Such a business] should do so first with a commissioned agent....[B]usinesses go by stages in international transactions and if you try to get ahead of the stage, you'll go wrong every time."[52]

There are any number of ways to begin an analysis of joint ventures. Professor Detlev Vagts, among others, has developed a framework for categorizing these undertakings.[53] In the first instance, he distinguishes between a joint venture that is merely a partnership (including a partnership between two corporations or between an individual and a corporation) and a joint venture in which the joint venturers, whoever they may be, form a separate corporation to conduct the business of the joint venture.

In addition, a joint venture may comprise: (1) two or more firms from the same country engaging in a joint venture in a second country; (2) a party from country A and another from country B engaging in a joint venture in country C; (3) a joint venture between a party from country A and a party in the country in which the venture takes place; (4) a joint venture between a foreign private party and a government in the host country; and (5) a joint venture established as a free standing business created by investors from abroad and investors in the host country.

These categories suggest some of the problems that may occur in setting up a joint venture. They range from possible antitrust violations, to host-country employment regulations, to those special problems a company faces when the other party to the venture is a government rather than a private entity. Moreover, in terms of current popularity, many developing countries no longer view types 1 and 2 as attractive arrangements since the host country obviously derives far fewer benefits from the venture than might be the case with the latter three types.

There are other ways to categorize joint ventures. The Andean nations define a joint venture as "foreign" if less than 51% of the venture is in the hands of host-country nationals or the host-country government, as "mixed" if the venture is controlled between 51% and 80% by host nationals and "national" if at least 80% of the venture is in the hands of nationals.

These categorizations provide both ways to review joint venture plans and a definitional structure for regulation of the venture by the host government. For our purposes, it is sufficient to note that a joint venture is mainly a matter of who controls the operation and how the profits and risks are to be allocated, rather than a concept which affects the subject matter of the business. Thus, a joint venture may be formed to sell goods or services, to launch and administer a franchise operation or to establish a licensing scheme.

To the extent that a joint venture is affected by legal principles outside the context of specific government regulation (either by the country of origin or the host country), the law to be applied will be the law of partnerships and corporations. Persons planning joint ventures are typically concerned with provisions on duration of the venture, financing, termination, control of the venture, the distribution of profits and the allocation of risks (normally allocated on the basis of percentage participation in

52. John D. Hushon, *Joint Ventures between Multinationals: Government Regulatory Aspects*, 6 N.C.J. Int'l L. & Com. Reg. 207 (1984).
53. Detlev Vagts, *Transnational Business Problems* 421 (1986).

the joint venture), day-to-day management of the venture, destruction of the subject matter of the undertaking and addition, deletion and substitution of parties to the venture.[54]

Transnational joint ventures are increasingly popular. One of the more remarkable breakthroughs in doing business in the People's Republic of China occurred in 1979 when the government of the People's Republic authorized joint ventures between business entities in China and foreign companies.[55] Many developing countries appear to be involved in or on the verge of completely rethinking their joint venture policies.[56]

§3.3.6 Foreign Direct Investment

[1] Some Basic FDI Concepts and Vocabulary

Foreign direct investment (sometimes "FDI") is one of the most important and lucrative vehicles for international business. FDI can take place in any country at any time, although a great deal of the focus in the FDI literature has concentrated on FDI by companies from developed countries investing in business entities in developing countries. The United Nations estimates that FDI represents a significant portion of the global economy. According to the United Nations Commission on Trade and Development (UNCTAD) FDI amounted to USD 1.76 trillion in 2015 with a slight drop in 2016 to USD 1.52 trillion.[57] In the past several years, China has assumed very large profile in worldwide FDI. There is, for example, a great deal of FDI by Chinese enterprises in the United States and a large amount of FDI by U.S. companies in China. In 2016 China invested more than USD 45 billion in the United States.[58] U.S. FDI in China since 2000 has been about USD 220 billion. These are, by any measure, enormous sums of money and reflect the importance of FDI in the global economy.

54. *See*, e.g., Hushon, *supra* n. 52, at 233. *See also*, Jackie Taylor, *Drafting Intellectual Property Joint Venture Agreements with an Eye Toward Termination*, 4 Pittsburgh J. Tech. L. & Pol'y 5 (2004); (Sanjiv K. Kapor, *Structuring and Negotiating International Joint Ventures: Anecdotal Evidence from a Large Law Firm Practice*, 53 Case W. Res. L. Rev. 937 (2003)); Jeanne M. Rickert, *Keep Your Eyes Open: Avoiding Unintended Consequences in Joint Venture Relationships*, 53 Case W. Res. L. Rev. 897 (2003); Richard J. Hoskins, *Antitrust Analysis of Joint Ventures and Competitor Collaboration: A Primer for the Corporate Lawyer*, 10 U. Miami Bus. L. Rev. 119 (2002).
55. *See*, e.g., Xiaowen Tian, *Managing International Business in China* (2016); Asia Briefing, *Setting Up Joint Ventures in China* (3d ed., 2011); Michael Amtmann, *International Joint Ventures in China* (2007); Ralph H. Folsom & W. Davis Folsom, *International Business Agreements in the PRC* (1997); Daniel A. Lapres & Zhang Yuejiao, *Business Law in China: Trade, Investment & Finance* (1995); Wei Jia, *Chinese Foreign Investment Laws and Policies: Evolution & Transformation* (1994); Henry J. Graham, *Foreign Investment Laws of China and the United States: A Comparative Study*, 5 J. Transnat'l L. & Pol'y 253 (1996); Walter S. Surrey, Benjamin P. Fishburne & M. Javade Chaudhri, *Joint Ventures in China: The First Water Stop*, 21 Tex. J. Int'l L. 221 (1986); Paul E. Brace, *Joint Ventures in the People's Republic of China (Non-Corporate Form)*, Int'l Bus. Law. 434 (1985); Craig A. Jaslow, *Practical Considerations in Drafting a Joint Venture Agreement with China*, 31 J. Am. Comp. L. 209 (1983). *See* generally, James A. Dobkin, *International Technology Joint Ventures in the Countries of the Pacific Rim* (1988).
56. *See*, e.g., Heather M. Douglas, *The Watchful Eye: The Role of Joint Ventures, Direct Investment and Subsidiaries in Developing Countries*, 8 New England Int. & Comp. L. Ann. 441 (2002).
57. UNCTAD, *Global Investment Trends Monitor*, February 1, 2017.
58. Financial Times, *Surge in Chinese Corporate Investment into the US*, January 2, 2017.

While some of the definitions of FDI differ depending on the organization in question, most observers are content with the detailed and comprehensive definition offered by the Organization of Economic Security and Development (OECD). The OECD defines FDI as: "establishing a lasting interest by a resident enterprise in one economy (*direct investor*) in an enterprise (*direct investment enterprise*) that is resident in an economy other than that of the direct investor."[59]

The OECD definition of FDI is both qualitative and quantitative. FDI assumes "the existence of a long-term relationship between the direct investor and the direct investment enterprise and a significant degree of influence on the management of the enterprise."[60] Quantitatively, the OECD insists that the direct investor hold at least a 10% voting power interest in the enterprise. OECD does this to ensure statistical uniformity. It is possible that other entities and other organizations would accept less than a 10% control factor. But with less than a 10% interest in any given entity, the outside investor probably lacks the requisite control to have a legitimate instance of FDI.

Beyond this, the investment is regarded as the sum of equity capital, long-term capital and short-term capital and involves the direct investor in the management of the enterprise. FDI can involve investing management activities, organizational expertise, and transfer of technology as well as a simple financial contribution to the enterprise. One of the central characteristics that distinguish FDI from mere investment in a foreign entity is that the FDI direct investor participates in the management and day-to-day operation of the enterprise, rather than simply contributing funds and then waiting passively for dividends.

Depending on the direction of the FDI, most of the literature distinguishes between *inward FDI*—investments coming into a particular country; and *outward FDI*—investments by entities in that country that go into ventures in other countries. The difference between inward and outward FDI is referred to as the *FDI inflow*—which can be either negative or positive.[61]

There is additional vocabulary that the reader should master.[62] Many FDI specialists distinguish between *horizontal* and *vertical* FDI. Horizontal FDI involves simply setting up a business entity in another country that performs virtually all its

59. OECD, *Benchmark Definition of Foreign Direct Investment, Chapter Three (Main Concepts and Definitions of Foreign Direct Investment)* (4th ed. 2008), 48. For some good book-length treatments of FDI *see*, e.g., Hwy-Chang Moon, *Foreign Direct Investment: A Global Perspective* (2015); Marianne Ojo, *Foreign Direct Investment: Theories, Rationale, Costs and Benefits* (2014); Theodore Moran, *Foreign Direct Investment and Development: Reevaluating Policies for Developed and Developing* (2011); Nathan M. Jensen, *Nation-States and the Multinational Corporation: A Political Economy of Foreign Direct Investment* (2008); Stephen D. Cohen, *Multinational Corporations and Foreign Direct Investment: Avoiding Simplicity, Embracing Complexity* (2007). For a sampling of journal articles on FDI, *see* Murat Yulek & Nurullah Gur, *Foreign Direct Investment: Smart Policies and Economic Growth*, 17 Progress in Dev. Stud. 245 (2017); Andrew Myburgh & Jordi Paniagua, *Does International Commercial Arbitration Promote Foreign Direct Investment*, 59 J. of L. & Econ. 597 (2016).
60. OECE Benchmark, *supra* n. 59, at 48.
61. *Id.*
62. These concepts and this vocabulary are found in several of the OECD sources as well as other FDI literature.

activities within the target country. A good example of horizontal FDI is creating a retail establishment to sell clothing or automotive supplies. Vertical FDI involves an investor setting up an FDI activity in one country that then sends its product to another country as a contribution to the investor's overall business enterprise. An example would be an oil company that explores and produces crude oil in one country, that then builds an FDI project, a refinery, say, in another country, which refinery then sends gasoline and diesel fuel to yet another country for sale to the ultimate consumer.

Most investors also distinguish between *greenfield* and *brownfield* FDI projects. A greenfield project comprises a project that is built as an entirely new facility, where no previous operations have existed. A brownfield FDI project is one where the direct investor merely purchases or invests in an operation that is already in existence.

Because a number of companies around the world make a lot of FDI-type investments in many countries, FDI has also led to the recognition of such companies as multinational enterprises (MNE). The growth in MNEs has led, in turn, to wide-ranging discussion as to how best to regulate the activities of MNEs when no individual nation has the juridical power to control the offshore activities of such countries. One such device, discussed below, is the creation of codes of conduct for MNEs.

The OECD has identified a number of characteristics that create a favorable climate for FDI in a particular country. They are:

- a predictable and nondiscriminatory regulatory environment and an absence of undue administrative impediments to business more generally;
- a stable macroeconomic environment, including access to engaging in international trade;
- sufficient and accessible resources, including the presence of relevant infrastructure and human capital;
- protocols that safeguard public sector transparency, including an impartial system of courts and law enforcement;
- rules that ensure free transfer of investments along with protections against arbitrary expropriation;
- adequate frameworks for a healthy competitive environment in the domestic business sector;
- ensuring that public spending is adequate and relevant.[63]

When an entrepreneur looks for FDI opportunities, there are several vehicles for the transaction. An investor can: (a) incorporate a wholly owned subsidiary in the host country; (b) buy an ownership interest in an existing, ongoing business in the host country; (c) arrange a merger or acquisition of a business in the destination country; or (d) establish a joint venture with a host-country partner. Typically, the direct investor is hoping to benefit from a number of incentives offered by the host country such as:

- low tax rates (both corporate and individual);
- preferential tariffs;

63. OECD, *Guiding Principles for Policies Toward Attracting Foreign Direct Investment* (2003), 7–8.

- the benefits of special economic zones;
- real estate subsidies;
- infrastructure subsidies.

There are any number of criteria that influence the decision to engage in FDI in a particular country. Some of those factors are:

- *cost*: how do the costs of production in the target country compare with other countries;
- *logistics*: how do transportation expenses affect the ultimate price of the goods or services;
- *internal market*: is there a significant internal market for the goods or services or will the goods and services be shipped elsewhere;
- *natural resources*: if the business entity requires access to natural resources, where are they and how much to they cost;
- *local know-how*: is there special expertise within the country that justifies setting up the FDI enterprise;
- *competitors*: what is the extent of competition among different companies in the country;
- *ease of establishment*: how easy is it to establish the business entity in the target country—are there lots of government impediments;
- *expatriation of funds*: can the investor easily move profits out of the target country;
- *termination*: how easy or difficult is it to shut down and take apart the FDI entity when the time comes to close the operation.

And, as with all of our other business vehicles, it is axiomatic that the investor seeks to make a profit from the FDI activities.

When a country is found to be hospitable to FDI, what should a business executive do to consummate an FDI project in that country? The following discussion is in the nature of a check list for beginning the project. The place to start is with the government regulations in that country that bear on FDI. Some countries have very rudimentary requirements; others are much more elaborate.

[2] Setting Up a Foreign Direct Investment Project

Assume that you are an investor-entrepreneur based in the United States who manufacturers and operates small unmanned aircraft—i.e., those flying objects that most people refer to as "drones."[64] Drones are no longer toys or jokes. The drone industry is now a multi-billion USD industry and we are finding, almost daily, more and more business applications for drones. Some of the most obvious uses are photography

64. The author is a licensed commercial drone pilot in the United States. Drone pilots who fly drones commercially (i.e., for money) in the U.S. must have a license from the Federal Aviation Administration, a component of the national government.

operations. But drones are now used in facility inspection, such as high towers, bridges, and railroad tracks. Drones are beginning to be used for commodity delivery. In the United States, Amazon is leading the charge on package delivery. Businesses and governments are using drones for surveillance activities. Some African countries are using drones to surveil poachers of protected animal species. You have done some global market research and have determined that it would be profitable for you to establish a business entity in some other country to do three things: (1) sell or rent your drones; (2) establish a training facility to train drone pilots; and (3) create a drone maintenance and repair service. You have done some specific country-by-country market research and have determined that you would like to engage in an FDI project in two countries—one a very large country in Asia (which we will call Dalgesh), and the second a smaller country (Varunda) in Sub-Saharan Africa. Dalgesh has some very intricate rules for FDI; Varunda has a far simpler, rudimentary FDI process. We will compare the FDI process for each of these countries on a side-by-side basis. And—as the most basic requirement—we will have first obtained the services of in-country consultants, lawyers and various other advisers to counsel us on the target country requirements, The following is an FDI roadmap.

Step One: Deciding on the form of business for the FDI enterprise

Varunda:

Varunda permits investors to set up a separate company or branch office or representative office. The branch office or representative office do not protect against liability. There are some important restrictions for a representative office. In Varunda, a representative office may conduct market research and promote the parent company's product. It may not engage in any other activities. There are similar restrictions for the branch office.

Accordingly, your Varunda adviser recommends either a Varunda limited liability company (Ltd) or a Varunda public limited liability company (PLC). Further research tells you that the PLC is best for really large investments so it is probably best to establish a limited liability company. Varunda law permits you to create the company with one shareholder and one director. These two entities can be either individuals or corporate persons and do not have to be either nationals of or resident in Varunda. Also, there are no minimum capital contributions that must be made. The LLC takes approximately 10 weeks to set up. You must also:

(a) Create and register the company's tradename.
(b) Open a company bank account in an approved Varunda bank (takes about five weeks).
(c) Get a tax registration certificate.
(d) File an annual tax return (the Varunda corporate tax rate is 30%).
(e) File an annual financial statement.

In turn, the LLC is permitted to issue sales invoices, to import and export goods, to rent office space, to buy real property in Varunda and to own an equity share in other Varunda companies.

Dalgesh:

Dalgesh is a much larger country with an elaborate system of business regulation. In Dalgesh, a foreign investor is permitted to establish an incorporated entity under the Dalgesh Companies Act by way of setting up a joint venture or a wholly owned subsidiary.[65] An investor may also set up a liaison (representative office), a "project office" or a "branch office" as unincorporated entities.

With regard to making the investment, Dalgesh recognizes either an "automatic route" or a government route" for the investment. A foreign investor may make a 100% investment of funds and assets in any commercial activity except (a) activities that require an industrial license (heavy manufacturing) or (b) certain financial services activities. The government route requires prior government approval from the Dalgesh Foreign Investment Promotion Board which is a component of the Ministry of Finance. There is no fee required for such approval but approval itself can take many months. There are other business activities (e.g., gambling and lottery activities) that are not permitted to FDI investors either under the automatic route or the government route.

An investor who follows the automatic route does not have to obtain prior government approval but must file the appropriate documents of creation (of the incorporated entity) within 30 days of issuing shares to foreign investors. But there are some very peculiar restrictions for FDI in the retail trade. The government of Dalgesh claims to be considering removing some of these restrictions but has not done so to date. This suggests that our foreign investor would be better off buying into an existing Dalgesh business rather than creating a brand-new company. Dalgesh permits foreign investors to purchase shares of a Dalgesh company up to a maximum of a 24% interest in the existing company.

Your Dalgesh consultant and your in-house experts believe that the investment in an existing company would be preferable. You can now search for an appropriate Dalgesh company.

Step Two: Protection of Intellectual Property

We will assume that our foreign investor has a U.S. patent on a certain type of drone, has registered a trademark for its drones, and has produced a large amount of copyrighted training manuals for drone operators and drone maintenance personnel. In both Varunda and Dalgesh these pieces of intellectual property will be properly registered under the relevant patent and copyright procedures in each country.

Step Three: The Business License, Banking and Financial Arrangements

In virtually every country a commercial entity must obtain a business license before it is permitted to engage in any business activities. In Varunda, such a license is obtained from the appropriate local government. The situation is virtually the same in Dalgesh, but because our foreign investor is buying into an existing business, that business will already have a business license. However, our proposed drone activities may be so different from the existing businesses current activities, the license will

65. Dalgesh Companies Act 22-456 (2007).

require amendment. The new company will also have to create a banking relationship with an appropriate bank for various financial activities such as payroll, cash flow, purchases, etc.

Step Four: Visas and Permanent Residence for Critical Personnel

The drone business proposal is one that has no existing counterpart in the target countries. That is, there are no people in-country who are already prepared to engage in any of the proposed business activities. In both Varunda and Dalgesh, the investor will have to take steps to bring into the country a group of experts to do these things. In Varunda, they will presumably become employees of the newly created LLC. In Dalgesh, they will be hired by the already-established Dalgesh company. In any event, the foreign investor will have to satisfy the requirements for visas and permanent residence for these critical personnel. While the business model envisions training indigenous people to perform all the business activities, it will be a long time before that is a realistic possibility. Our in-house experts speculate that it will be at least five to seven years before indigenous personnel will be fully capable. Thus, the crucial need for importing employees.

Step Five: Office Space and Host-Country Employees

In Varunda and Dalgesh, an appropriate physical location for the business activities must be obtained. In this case, the real estate decision is vitally important because the drones will not only be sold, but also demonstrated on the company's premises. It is not as simple as finding a small office for the business. This means that local zoning requirements must be researched. Also, even if the foreign investor brings in key personnel for the first several years of operation, there will still be an immediate need for a number of in-country employees who need to be hired and trained. A smart foreign investor will look into these issues before making a final commitment for the investment.

Step Six: Market Research and Advertising

A major part of the business plan is the selling or renting of drones. This will entail an intense period of market research and subsequent advertising after the market research is completed. Dalgesh is a large country with a well-educated population and has all the standard media vehicles such as television, newspapers, radio, Internet, and the like. Presumably, market research and advertising in Dalgesh will be similar to whatever the investor is currently doing in the United States. But Varunda is a small country just emerging from a tragic period of civil war and tribal unrest. Market research and advertising in Varunda may well be in the form of sales agents who go around the country speaking with potential renters and purchasers.

Step Seven: Follow Up and Monitoring

FDI beginners frequently believe that once the investment is made they can just walk away from the transaction and wait for the profits to roll in. Nothing could be more wrong! FDI investments must be constantly monitored and policed, pretty much for the duration of the investment. Many FDI ventures fail simply because the investor failed to engage in proper follow up and monitoring.

The reader should not consider this list as a comprehensive checklist for engaging in FDI. There are many other issues that have to be considered before signing the final contract and handing over the investment funds. What is set out above are some of the major issues to consider. Countries differ so much from place to place that additional generalization is really not possible. Each FDI is to be handled on a case-by-case, country-by-country basis.

§3.3.7 Other Forms of Agreement

There are a number of other forms of agreement that have been used over time. One of the more important is the natural resource concession agreement—a form of international transaction pioneered by major Western oil companies in the Middle East early in the twentieth century to move oil from the sands of the Middle East to western consumers. The use of concession agreements was later expanded to other regions of the world where developing countries had control of large amounts of unexploited natural resources. A concession agreement (now sometimes referred to as a development agreement) is an agreement that permits a foreign entity to enter the country in which the resources are located and, generally for royalty payments and other remuneration to the host government, permits the company to remove the resources and sell them elsewhere.

The earliest concession agreements are now viewed with considerable disfavor because of the nearly unconscionable terms negotiated between the Western developers and the host countries.[66] Typical provisions gave the foreign company exclusive and long-term exploration and development rights, covered huge amounts of the country's territory, called for the payment of royalties that bore virtually no relationship to the injury to the land and the depletion of nonreplaceable natural resources, and gave the host government virtually no say in the concession's operation.[67]

These days, development agreements tend to be far better balanced and tend to relinquish far less control to the foreign entity while still preserving the developing country's access to both investment funds for development and major markets for sale of the resources. But considerations such as these are mainly matters of public policy and negotiation. The legal principles governing development agreements—which these days often take the form of joint ventures—normally do not differ from those principles applicable to the forms of business discussed above.[68]

66. *See*, e.g., Michael A.G. Bunter, *The Promotion and Licensing of Petroleum Prospective Acreage* (2002); George E. Kronman, Don B. Felio, Thomas E. O'connor & Mindy S. Kronman, *International Oil and Gas Ventures: a Business Perspective* (2000); Zhiguo Gao, *International Petroleum Contracts: Current Trends and New Directions* (1994); David N. Smith & Bouis T. Wells, Jr., *Negotiating Third World Minerals Agreements* (1975); R.D. Vock, *The Evolution of the Legal Relationship Between International Petroleum Mining Companies and Host Countries*, Int'l Bus. Law. 244 (1983).
67. *See*, the excellent history of Middle East oil development, Daniel Yergin, *The Prize: The Epic Quest for Oil, Money and Power* (1992). Mr. Yergin's prize-winning book was presaged by John M. Blair, The Control of Oil (1976). Mr. Yergin has followed "The Prize" with Daniel Yergin, *The Quest: Energy, Security, and the Remaking of the Modern World* (2011).
68. *See*, Beredjick & Walde, *supra* n. 39.

§3.4 PLANNING FOR DISPUTE RESOLUTION

Many persons entering into international agreements for the first time find it difficult even to contemplate something going wrong with the deal. People enter commercial transactions with the expectation that the contracts will be fully performed. Frequently, when a negotiation session is going well and after some decent personal relationships have been formed, it is almost impossible to look across the table and conceive of the other person reneging on the deal. But it is in the planning and drafting process that a party *must* anticipate problems and *must* consider how disagreements might be managed if they do arise.

Dispute resolution is the management and resolution of conflict between the parties that can range over a broad spectrum of different possibilities. It is something that cannot be ducked in international commercial transactions because the parties will be at great distances from each other after the agreement is consummated. The people responsible for drafting and negotiating the agreement are rarely those who have the day-to-day responsibility for performance. Even if the parties have the greatest sense of well-being and security at the time of signing the contract, external conditions can still disrupt the agreement no matter how much personal regard and trust the negotiating parties have for each other.

For this reason, virtually all properly drafted international contracts contain some kind of dispute resolution clause. For those contracts fully performed without incident, the clause is superfluous. However, for those deals that fall apart, the clause can be crucial. A few minutes of inattention to dispute resolution at the planning and drafting stage of an agreement can cost millions of dollars later on when a dispute has to be resolved.

Many dispute resolution clauses are drafted haphazardly and put in as an afterthought and without the consideration that they really deserve. Many less-than-acceptable clauses simply incorporate some boilerplate from a book of forms with very little inquiry into how the clause might actually work if a dispute occurs. Worse, garden-variety dispute resolution clauses often incorporate the more rigid techniques of dispute resolution such as arbitration and litigation without obliging the parties to try to work things out between themselves in a milder, less-threatening setting such as renegotiation or mediation.

A lot of these mistakes are made because many of the people who draft and plan contracts know relatively little about dispute resolution. The following discussion is an introduction to the various forms of dispute resolution for contract drafters and planners. Chapter 4 sets out some useful dispute resolution clauses, and Chapters 8 through 13 of this book contains an extensive discussion of each of these different devices as they are employed in practice.

There is no uniform world view of dispute resolution. Lawyers in the United States have a favorite saying: "One person's delay is another person's due process." Developing proper dispute resolution procedures in domestic controversies now occupies a great deal of the time of many U.S. legal scholars. In international transactions many additional factors, such as cultural and language differences, often affect the dispute resolution process. For example, the antagonism and ferocity of U.S.

litigation is taken for granted in the United States, but is regarded as totally unproductive—perhaps even despicable—by societies in the Far East and elsewhere in the world. Understanding the apprehensions that these cultural differences create might persuade the parties negotiating a contract to opt for some less-drastic dispute resolution mechanism—such as mediation—to be attempted before a more adversarial process such as arbitration or litigation is utilized.

Yet those processes which are less adversarial such as mediation and arbitration are often much less final and certain; and finality of result (i.e., the understanding that a dispute has been conclusively resolved and that the final decision is enforceable against the losing party) is very important in most commercial transactions. Agreeing to engage in a process of dispute resolution that cannot lead, in and of itself, to a final decision may have the effect of lengthening the overall dispute resolution phase of an agreement and multiplying the costs of obtaining a permanent resolution of the dispute.

There are a number of devices regularly used to resolve international commercial matters. They include the device of adaptation by which the contract itself is drafted in a sufficiently flexible fashion to accommodate unanticipated occurrences such as supply shortages, strikes or sharp price increases or decreases. Similarly, since international contracts are normally the product of negotiation, by definition they are always subject to renegotiation. Frequently, adaptation and renegotiation go hand in hand. The twin concepts of mediation and conciliation are essentially processes by which negotiation between the parties takes place in the presence and with the assistance of a third party who is sometimes referred to as a facilitator. The more structured forms of commercial dispute resolution, arbitration and litigation, are probably the best known among the public at large and easily the most frequently utilized devices on the international level. But each of these can still be rigid, costly, time-consuming, totally under the control of specialists, and so adversarial that the parties' relationship is permanently damaged.

§3.4.1 Adaptation

Contract provisions such as force majeure clauses and flexible pricing terms that turn, say, on the increase or decrease of a published cost of living index are provisions that allow a contract to change with new circumstances without provoking a breach or forcing the parties into some kind of formal dispute resolution. Long-term contracts almost always contain a number of adaptation provisions. Frequently, even when the contract does not contain such clauses, the law underlying the contract will supply certain adaptation and gap-filling terms. For example, under the UCC a contract for the sale of goods does not even have to specify a price. If the contract is silent as to price, UCC section 2-305 provides that the price is "a reasonable price at the time of delivery [of the goods.]" The legal doctrines of impossibility and frustration may excuse performance in whole or in part or for a certain period of time even if the contract does not contain a force majeure clause or even if the force majeure clause does not expressly cover the incident that has caused the problems.

§3.4.2 Renegotiation

If the contract cannot itself adapt to changing circumstances, the parties may always renegotiate. Some parties place an express obligation of renegotiation in the contract with the expectation that the parties will not resort to a more formal method of dispute resolution without first trying to talk to each other. Some companies that have a large stake in preserving existing contracts, such as the U.S. airplane manufacturer, Boeing Corporation, insert renegotiation clauses in their contracts that specify that the renegotiation must take place between two high-level corporate officials. In multi-billion dollar contracts to be performed over a period of many years, renegotiation can be a matter of life and death for the contracting parties. Like the initial negotiation, renegotiation is simply a dialogue or discussion between the disputing parties that has as its goal the resolution of the dispute by mutual agreement. Normally, it is cheap, quick and has the advantages of a solution that is neither coerced nor imposed by external entities. One of its best features is that it can be undertaken while the contract continues to be performed. To the extent that a negotiated solution is possible, it is almost always the most advantageous and cost-beneficial device.

§3.4.3 Mediation/Conciliation

The twin devices of mediation and conciliation are, as noted above, negotiation in the presence of or with the help of a third party. In some settings, mediation may be nothing more than a friendly conversation. In other settings, particularly when conducted under formal commercial mediation rules it can rival the formality of commercial arbitration. To a certain extent, mediation has many of the advantages of a negotiated settlement in that it is relatively uncoerced, fast, and confidential; but in complex matters it may take a great deal more time. The addition of the third-party mediator is an additional expense and the educating of that person on the facts of the dispute can lengthen the proceeding. However, to the extent that the parties believe they have worked out the final solution themselves (albeit with the assistance of a third-party mediator), they may find the end result highly satisfactory.

§3.4.4 Arbitration

Most international commercial agreements call for arbitration of any disputes that may arise under the contract by incorporating standard form arbitration clauses. These clauses, in turn, usually incorporate the procedural rules of one or another of the major international arbitral bodies such as the ICC or UNCITRAL. Some clauses incorporation the rules of a national arbitral body such as the AAA or the Japan Commercial Arbitration Association. Some local or regional business entities, such as the Stockholm Chamber of Commerce, promulgate rules and supervise arbitration proceedings.

Under modern procedural systems, arbitration is essentially the litigation of a dispute before an arbitrator rather than a judge. The procedure is adversarial and almost always handled by lawyer-specialists. However, there are many arbitrations in which nonlawyers sit as arbitrators and there is usually no requirement that either the representatives of the parties or the arbitrator be a lawyer. It is just that arbitration is such a complicated undertaking and is so close in concept to Anglo-American style litigation that most parties put themselves in the hands of their lawyers if they have to arbitrate. Often, the arbitration clause will require that the arbitrator be expert in the underlying subject matter. For example, an arbitration clause in, say, a construction contract might call for an arbitrator with at least ten years' experience in the construction industry.

Parties who are worried about the ability or integrity of a single arbitrator, irrespective of whom that person may be, often provide for a three-person arbitration panel with each side choosing one of the arbitrators. The two party-appointed arbitrators then pick the third member of the panel, who normally chairs the panel and presides over the arbitration. Contrary to the beliefs of many lay persons, arbitration is often costly, time-consuming, and far from satisfactory. Especially antagonistic opponents frequently go into court both before, during, and after the arbitration to test the ultimate validity of the process. As a result, arbitration is not always a complete substitute for litigation. The administrative fees that must be paid at the outset merely to commence the arbitration under the supervision of organizations such as the ICC or the AAA are substantial.

There is very little so-called *nonbinding* arbitration in international commercial arbitration. To the extent that this concept exists, it is probably only a species of mediation and is used mainly in the labor relations sector. Thus, the decision of a commercial arbitrator is—at least in theory—final and conclusive. However, in certain instances when the losing party balks at the decision of the arbitrator, who issues her decision in the form of an *arbitral award*, it must be taken into some domestic court system for confirmation and enforcement against the losing party. Sometimes a party will refuse to commence arbitration. Then the party seeking to arbitrate must resort to domestic courts for an order compelling the other party to arbitrate.

Even with these inherent disadvantages, arbitration is generally favored by most commentators and appears to be the dispute resolution device of choice in most international commercial agreements. One of the major reasons for this pride-of-place is that an international treaty, the New York Convention on the Recognition and Enforcement of Foreign Arbitral Awards—permits the enforcement of arbitral awards rendered in one country to be enforced in another country. Except within the EU, there is no parallel treaty for the enforcement of court judgments. As a result, if one is worried about where enforcement might take place, arbitration is often superior to litigation.

§3.4.5 Litigation

Litigation is a formal proceeding conducted in an appropriate court in the country of the buyer or the country of the seller, or in some instances in a country perceived to be neutral by the parties. There is really no such thing as international litigation or an international court for parties to private agreements. The International Court of Justice at The Hague is restricted to disputes between countries, although it has served as the site for arbitration of commercial disputes between the United States and Iran under the Algerian Accords of 1981. As litigation's detractors constantly note, the process is expensive, costly, and often protracted. It can be handled only by lawyer-specialists. Indeed, in many countries no one other than a lawyer may litigate a case.

In many circumstances, litigation can cause additional hostility and antagonisms between the parties. Unlike arbitration or mediation, parties usually do not resort to litigation until and unless the entire agreement has fallen completely apart. By contrast, arbitration and mediation can often be utilized to resolve a dispute that arises within the overall commercial undertaking without terminating the agreement itself. Litigation has some advantages. It is generally final when concluded—that is, there is usually no other forum (other an appeal to a higher court) and no other recourse for the losing party except to honor the judgment of the court. A failure to comply with a court's judgment in most countries creates contempt of court problems for the recalcitrant party.

Litigation is sometimes the mechanism of choice even in international commercial contracts, because a number of lawyers—particularly in the United States—are cynical about the other forms of dispute resolution and conclude that they might as well go into court in the first instance because in all likelihood that is where the parties will wind up in any event. However, there are some special difficulties in using litigation in domestic courts to resolve international commercial disputes. Domestic courts frequently lack jurisdiction over parties in other countries. They also have a great deal of difficulty in enforcing their judgments abroad. To a certain extent, domestic courts can evidence prejudice against foreign parties who come into those courts.

Some contracting parties try to eliminate the problem of local prejudice by providing for litigation in the courts of a third country. To the extent that the third country agrees to hear the case, this maneuver is always a possibility. For example, in one important case eventually decided by the United States Supreme Court, *The Bremen v. Zapata Off-Shore Oil Company,*[69] a dispute arising between a German shipping company and an American oil company, the contract provided for dispute resolution in the High Court of Justice in London. Great Britain had nothing to do with the contract or the two parties. The United States Supreme Court honored that choice of forum even when one of the parties tried to litigate the dispute in a federal court in the United States. Within the EU choice of forum clauses, including clauses that call for litigation in a neutral forum, are generally honored so long as one of the parties is deemed to be domiciled within the jurisdiction of a country that is part of the Union.[70]

69. 407 U.S. 1 (1972).
70. Article 17, EEC Convention on Jurisdiction and Enforcement of Judgments in Civil and Commercial Matters, done, September 27, 1968, reprinted in 8 Int'l Leg. Materials 229 (1969). Choices will not be enforced if a particular court has exclusive jurisdiction or if undue influence or a contract of adhesion (a printed form agreement) is involved.

§3.4.6 Other Forms of Dispute Resolution

There are other forms of dispute resolution worthy of attention that may have increasing utility for commercial disputes even though they are not commonly used by the international business community. For example, businesses in the United States have experimented with a commendable device known as the *minitrial*, a procedure in which lawyers for the contending parties present a summary of each party's case to an important corporate official, such as a corporation vice president, for each of the parties. That official must attend the proceeding with express authority to settle the case. The executives listen to a shortened presentation by the parties' attorneys and are frequently assisted by a third-person referee, often a retired judge. After the abbreviated presentations are concluded—and normally they last only a day or so—the executives and the referee consider the presentations and attempt to negotiate a final agreement.

Some jurisdictions in the United States, notably the State of California, now permit parties to seek out and hire their own judge in a program formally referred to as the California Reference Procedure, but colloquially labeled *rent-a-judge*. No party can be forced into this procedure, but if both parties agree to its use, it is helpful in moving quickly to a resolution of the case because it avoids the congestion of the regular system of state courts (many civil cases in the United States take three to four years to reach a final decision). Moreover, the decision rendered by the judge is binding on the parties just as if it had been rendered in a regular court. There is no evidence that the rent-a-judge procedure has caught on elsewhere in the world, however.

Having set out these elaborate descriptions of the various forms of dispute resolution, it may be helpful to see some of the same ideas presented in pictorial form. The following chart, *see* Figure 3.1, depicts the alternatives in terms of various factors. On the left side of the chart are the factors of time, cost, and finality. Those factors increase as one moves down the chart. For example, the mechanisms become more time-consuming (in terms of how long from start to finish it normally takes to complete the procedure) and more expensive. By definition, litigation—because it is procedurally far more complex and because it is heavily dependent on court-imposed timetables and court-created congestion—is more expensive than mediation. The final factor on the left side of the chart, finality, simply reflects whether the parties may move to another form of dispute resolution if they do not like the result in the mechanism in question.

Put another way, if mediation fails or if an arbitral award is not complied with voluntarily by the losing party, the parties must normally go into court to resolve the dispute. By contrast, there is no subsequent dispute resolution forum after litigation. There the parties receive a final judgment rendered by a court that must be complied with, so long as the court has jurisdiction over both parties. All the mechanisms other than litigation require consent by both parties. Litigation is the only process that one party may utilize without the consent of the other side. (Of course, even this requires a small disclaimer. If the parties have already signed an agreement to arbitrate, they will be held to that agreement even if one party now wishes to litigate.)

The factors on the right side of the chart, party autonomy and confidentiality, decrease as one moves down the list. Party autonomy is the matter of party control. Obviously, the parties have less control over an arbitration or a court proceeding (those devices are much more in the hands and under the control of arbitrators or judges) than over renegotiation. As one moves down the list, the dispute is placed in the hands of neutral, third parties over whom the disputing parties have very little control. The factor of confidentiality is frequently an important one in commercial dispute resolution, particularly for those disputes that involve important commercial or trade secrets. To the extent that one moves down the chart, more and more people become aware of and have knowledge of the parties' dispute.

Figure 3.1 A Dispute Resolution Chart

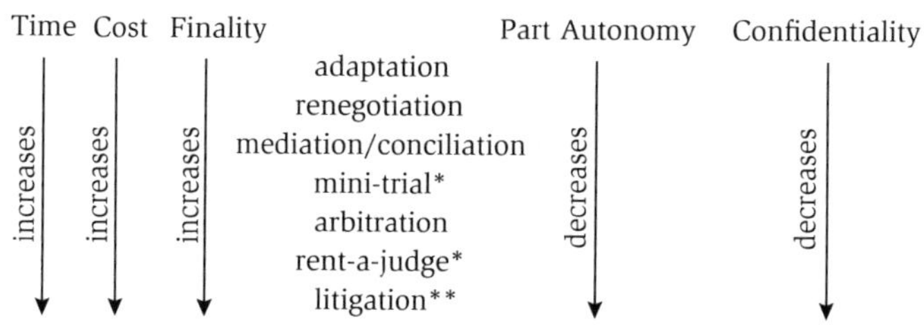

* The procedures of mini-trial and rent-a-judge are too new to make accurate estimates of time and cost.

** Litigation is a non-consensual device; all other devices require the consent of both parties before they may be utilized.

None of these procedures is perfect. No perfect procedure is likely to be discovered. For persons engaged in planning and drafting international commercial agreements, one thing is clear. To the extent that the parties do not choose a method of dispute resolution on their own, one will be imposed on them whenever a dispute arises under the contract.

§3.5 FINANCING AND PAYING FOR INTERNATIONAL COMMERCIAL AGREEMENTS

Securing funds for international commercial agreements is often more difficult than creating the agreements themselves. Since commercial transactions are not charitable undertakings, the efficient securing and transmitting of money is indispensable to the success of the deal. Sales of goods and services require payment for those goods and services. The other forms of agreement normally require investment money flowing from one country to another to get the venture started and, once begun, call for royalty payments that flow back to the country of origin. International businesses and financial institutions have worked out a large number of alternatives for financing and payment. Most of the commonly used payment mechanisms are described in the following subsection.

§3.5.1 Direct Payment

Virtually any method of payment that is used for the payment of obligations under domestic contracts may be used for the payment of obligations in international dealings, including such things as cash, checks, promissory notes, and negotiable bills of lading. But on closer examination, many of these payment devices have serious deficiencies for international transactions. Cash is normally too dangerous a commodity to ship abroad, although it has been used on occasion. A few countries have prohibitions against the export of their national currency. Bank checks are less subject to theft than cash; but just as in domestic transactions, they can be dishonored for insufficient funds and various other reasons. This level of uncertainty can have a stifling effect on transactions that take place over long distances, because buyers typically want their goods quickly while sellers prefer to wait to ship the goods until a bank check clears the buyer's bank—an event that can take an enormously long time between banks in different countries. Promissory notes, generally regarded as negotiable instruments under United States law and often fully acceptable in many other countries, create many of the same problems as checks.

The sporadic nature of many international transactions, the distances involved and the lack of prior business dealings between the parties frequently prompt the seller to look to sources other than the buyer to guarantee payment. There are many ways to protect the seller's interests. The seller can seek government assurances of payment. The United States government on occasion provides payment guarantees for U.S. agricultural interests who sell their produce abroad. Sellers may try to buy private or government-sponsored insurance to protect against certain risks such as expropriation. More commonly, however, the seller may simply insist on one or another of the traditional forms of international payment, such as a letter of credit.

§3.5.2 Payment Devices

Two methods of payment on contracts—*cash in advance* and *payment on account*—are frequently used in domestic transactions but are far less common in international transactions. They are essentially mirror images of each other. Cash in advance (the payment of the contract price in full by the buyer prior to any performance whatsoever by the seller) gives the seller total security and places all the risks of nonperformance on the buyer. A cash in advance term in a contract indicates that the seller's negotiating strength is nearly overwhelming and that the buyer for whatever reason is almost completely at the mercy of the seller but desires the goods or services so desperately that he will agree to this kind of payment term.

Payment on account switches these risks almost completely. Here, the seller ships the goods or provides the services and the buyer pays either periodically or in a lump sum into an account established by the seller. This type of device places the seller almost completely at the mercy of the buyer and again may indicate significantly disparate bargaining power between the parties. Another form of payment that tilts heavily in favor of the buyer is known as a clean draft collection. In this instance, the seller ships the goods, sends the papers relevant to the transaction directly to the buyer and merely presents a draft for payment to the buyer's bank in the same fashion that the buyer's check would ultimately be presented to the buyer's bank for collection. While a little more elaborate in terms of the total number of documents involved, the procedure for a clean draft collection is not much different from that of payment by check.

Given the risks associated with cash in advance and payment on account and the possibility that more equally balanced parties would never agree to them in the first place, international businesses and international banks have worked out two other devices of payment that are much more common. The first is *payment on collection*, sometimes referred to as the process of *documentary collection*. In this case, the seller gathers the relevant documents of the transaction such as bills of lading, invoices, and insurance certificates and sends them to the buyer's bank along with a draft for money payable by the buyer's bank. The bank reviews the documents and approves payment; but unlike a letter of credit, discussed below, the bank does not substitute its credit worthiness for that of the buyer. The bank merely reviews the documents.

The draft can be either a *sight draft* (a negotiable instrument payable as soon as the buyer's bank "sees" it) or a *time draft* (an instrument payable on a particular date). In the case of a sight draft, the buyer's bank will not release the other documents of the transaction (bill of lading, etc.) until the buyer pays the draft. In the case of a time draft, the buyer's payment is due on some fixed date after the other documents are released to the buyer. It is easy to spot the allocation of risks here—sight drafts give solid protection to the seller; time drafts make it easier for the buyer to inspect the goods or services before payment is due.

There are still some problems with this mode of payment. It is more secure than cash in advance or payment on account, but it remains a transaction solely between seller and buyer. If the buyer's financial status is shaky, or if the parties have never done business with each other, a seller might not accept even the relatively secure device of documentary collection as the payment mechanism. Even if this device gives the seller essentially two claims—seller can sue on the underlying contract for breach of contract or separately on the dishonored draft—the seller still has to track the buyer down and move against the buyer directly.

To strengthen the seller's sense of security, international businesses and banks have established a much more secure form of payment that has become one of the most common forms of payment for international commercial agreements, the *irrevocable letter of credit*.

Legal scholars like to distinguish between *revocable* and *irrevocable* letters of credit, and most legal systems recognize both types of instrument. A revocable letter of credit may be changed or canceled by the issuing bank at any time with no notice to the beneficiary. This makes the letter of credit almost worthless as a protective device, and as a consequence revocable letters of credit are virtually unheard of in international commercial agreements. At the same time, the term *irrevocable* does not mean immutable. Irrevocable letters of credit may be changed or canceled but only after all parties to the letter give their consent to the modification or cancellation.

The actual mechanics of a letter of credit are not terribly different from payment on collection. The transaction has several steps and a specialized vocabulary:

- *Step One*: The buyer (normally referred to as the applicant) applies to a bank for a letter of credit. This bank, known as the issuing bank, analyzes the application and if it approves, draws up the letter of credit and sends the letter of credit to a second bank known as the advising bank. The advising bank is normally one used by the seller.
- *Step Two*: The advising bank gets in touch with the seller (usually referred to as the *beneficiary*, i.e., the person who "benefits" from the letter of credit) and notifies the seller of the issuance of the letter of credit and informs the seller of the various documents, such as a bill of lading and a certificate of insurance that must be produced by the seller before payment will be made. This compiling of documents makes this stage of the letter of credit cycle very much like the process known as documentary collection.

  Armed with this information, the seller knows that a letter of credit has been issued and that the issuing bank guarantees payment so long as the goods are shipped and so long as the seller's papers are in order. In other words, the seller may proceed against the bank itself if the letter of credit is dishonored and need not track down the buyer. Since banks are traditionally stable and creditworthy, this pledge of the issuing bank's guarantee provides the seller with vastly more security than he would have if he had only the buyer's assurances that payment would be made.
- *Step Three*: The seller ships the goods and simultaneously gathers all the other documents relevant to the letter of credit, including the sight or time draft, appropriate invoices, export and import permissions (if applicable), documents of insurance and bills of lading, and presents these documents to the advising bank which then forwards the documents to the issuing bank for final collection and payment.

  Under the legal principles applicable to letters of credit, if the documents presented are in order, the issuing bank must pay the draft, irrespective of any change of mind on the buyer's part. The banks will examine the relevant papers in minute detail for their validity and consistency but will not serve as a quality control mechanism with regard to the goods themselves. In other words, even if the buyer discovers that the goods are defective, she cannot renege on the letter of credit.[71]

71. *See*, e.g., James Byrne, *International Letter of Credit Law and Practice* (2015); Thomas J. Ward, *Letters of Credit and Documentary Collections: An Export and Import Guide* (2009); Matti S. Kurkela, *Letters of Credit and Bank Guarantees Under International Trade Law* (2007); Frank Schroder, *Understanding and Handling International Letters of Credit* (2006); R.I.V.F. Bertrams, *Bank Guarantees in International Trade* (1996); Gao Xiang & Ross P. Buckley, *The Unique*

A letter of credit is not cheap. Banks spend a great deal of time and attention on them both as issuing bank and advising bank. The fee for a typical letter of credit is a percentage of the dollar amount of the letter of credit itself. The fee is increased as the individual letter of credit transaction increases in complexity. For example, there are instances in which a seller does not fully trust the issuing bank. In that case, a seller may insist on what is called a *confirmed* letter of credit. The confirmation is normally provided by the advising bank (or some intermediary bank other than the issuing bank) and provides a payment guarantee from both the issuing bank and the confirming bank. In other words, if the issuing bank does not pay, the confirming bank agrees to make the payment. But all of this security can substantially increase costs and fees. For parties seeking to save money on letter of credit transactions, the basic message is: keep it simple.

Letter of credit transactions are subject to both legal constraints and customary banking practices. In the United States, Article 5 of the UCC provides many of the controlling legal principles. For international letters of credit, many of the governing legal principles are provided by a set of rules drafted by the ICC called the Uniform Customs and Practice for Documentary Credits (UCP). When reviewing the UCP, the reader should keep in mind that these are rules that favor banks. Banks are always skittish about substituting their creditworthiness for that of their customers, and they have written the UCP so that their obligations for handling letters of credit are both clearly spelled out and limited in scope. For example, Article 15 provides that the bank's only obligation is to examine the relevant documents on their face. Article 17 specifies that banks do not "assume any liability or responsibility for the description, quantity, weight, quality, condition, packing, delivery, value or existence of the goods represented by any documents." Article 5 of the UCC contains similar but not identical provisions. The UCP and the UCC should be closely consulted by any lawyer working with letters of credit.

The letter of credit transaction described above is a conventional letter of credit. Some international commercial relationships involve transactions in which the parties require some security but for various reasons choose not to use the letter of credit as the payment device itself. In these cases, the parties may negotiate a *standby* letter of credit which follows the same format as the conventional letter of credit but which is

Jurisprudence of Letters of Credit: Its Origin and Sources, 4 Swan Diego Int'l L.J. 91 (2003); Ross P. Buckley, *The 1993 Revision of the Uniform Customs and Practices for Documentary Collections*, 28 Geo. Wash. J. Int'l L. & Econ. 265 (1995); James J. White, *The Influence of International Practice on the Revision of Article 5 of the UCC*, 16 J. Int'l L. & Bus. 189 (1995). For an excellent discussion of letters of credit (again from the American perspective) *see*, James J. White & Robert S. Summers, *Uniform Commercial Code* (6th ed., 2010). For a discussion of a number of issues that arise within letters of credit *see*, e.g., Ebenezer Adodo, *Letters of Credit: The Law and Practice on Compliance* (2014); Deborah Horowitz, *Letters of Credit and Demand Guarantees: Defences to Payment* (2010). For a book-length work on standby letters of credit *see* Jacob E. Sifri, *Standby Letters of Credit: A Comprehensive Guide* (2008).

activated only if one of the parties does not live up to his contractual obligations.[72] A standby letter of credit may be triggered only when one of the parties certifies that the other party did not perform their part the bargain. When triggered, however, the issuing bank guarantees payment as it does under a conventional letter of credit. For these reasons, the standby letter of credit operates more like a performance bond than an irrevocable letter of credit. For transactions to be performed in installments over a long period of time such as an international construction contract, the parties may agree to a *revolving* letter of credit by which the seller draws from the letter of credit account periodically and the purchaser replenishes the account whenever the account falls below a certain level.

The letter of credit device obviously gives the seller tremendous security and the resulting security explains better than anything else why letters of credit are so frequently used. But recall that letters of credit are expensive transactions. Banks charge substantial fees for all the work they do and for the exposure they take on if the deal somehow falls through. Further, because the issuing bank's credit is pledged to the transaction, they put applications under a very high powered microscope even to the point of requiring that the entire amount of the payment term be deposited in an account with the issuing bank before the letter of credit application is approved. Many foreign buyers cannot meet the banks terms. Some foreign buyers in especially strong negotiating positions vis-a-vis the seller will simply not agree to a letter of credit.

Just as importantly, if the parties have not done business with each other and if both parties feel somewhat insecure a buyer might not agree to a letter of credit because the exposure is too great. One of the legal principles underlying letters of credit stipulates that even if the goods or services are completely faulty, the letter of credit must be honored. That leaves the buyer with only a claim against the seller for breach of contract and forces the buyer to track the seller down to bring an action for breach wherever the seller can be found. Over all that time the seller has the enjoyment of the money. Much like virtually every other contract term and condition, the insertion of letter of credit provisions in a contract depend heavily on the respective bargaining power of the parties.

§3.5.3 Insuring Against Risks

There are other devices that parties may use to insure against various risks such as the risk of nonperformance or risks external to the deal itself such as the risk of expropriation. To guarantee performance, parties often negotiate the execution of various types of bonds such as surety bonds. These are issued by private entities such

72. For an excellent description of the differences between surety bonds, bank guarantees and standby letters of credit *see*, Jacob E. Sifri, *Standby Letters of Credit: a Comprehensive Guide* (2008) and David J. Barru, *How to Guarantee Contractor Performance on International Construction Projects: Comparing Surety Bonds with Bank Guarantees and Standby Letters of Credit*, 37 Geo. Wash. Int'l L. Rev. 51 (2005).

as banks and insurance companies and guarantee performance of the contract (or stated a bit more accurately guarantee that the injured party will be compensated in case of failure of performance).[73]

Some government entities may serve as guarantors of certain types of international commercial agreements. For example, the three components making up the World Bank group, the International Bank for Reconstruction and Development (IBRD), the International Development Association (IDA), and the International Finance Corporation (IFC) engage in various activities that can serve as a form of loan guarantee. The IBRD loans money to developing countries for specific development projects, such as construction of large hydroelectric facilities and major transportation projects. The IFC works with private entities to work out underwriting and technical assistance arrangements.

In 1988, the Convention Establishing the MIGA entered into force, creating MIGA as a component of the World Bank. MIGA insures various investments made under World Bank auspices in terms of: (1) currency inconvertibility; (2) expropriation; (3) war, revolution, and civil disturbance; and (4) certain types of breach of contract that cannot be resolved through arbitration proceedings.[74] There are a number of regional development banks such as the African Development Bank, the Asian Development Bank and the Inter-American Development Bank which provide both loans and loan guarantees for projects within their respective regions.[75]

In the United States, the Export-Import Bank (sometimes called the Ex-Im Bank) makes loans to certain foreign importers who could not otherwise qualify for financing to purchase American products and services.[76] A government corporation, the OPIC, provides various types of guarantees against expropriation and other unforeseen circumstances in certain developing countries. Both of these entities produce masses of information on many aspects of U.S. export activity in addition to engaging in the execution of guarantees and contracts of insurance.[77] A consortium of private insurance companies organized as the Foreign Credit Insurance Association writes policies for protection against short-term risks that foreign buyers will not pay for goods or services.[78]

---

73. *See*, e.g., Nicholas Horn, *Securing International Commercial Transactions: Standby Letters of Credit, Bonds, Guarantees and Similar Sureties*, in The Transnational Law of *International Commercial Transactions*, *supra* n. 39, at 275–303.
74. *See*, e.g., Lorin Weisenfeld, *Specialized Sources of Financing and Political Risk Insurance for Trade and Investment Abroad*, in *International Trade for the Non-Specialist* (2d ed., 1997); *Multilateral Investment Guarantee Agency General Conditions of Guarantee for Equity Investments (dated January 25, 1989)*, 4 For. Inv. L.J. 112 (1989). Much more information on MIGA may be found on the agency's website: www.miga.org.
75. *See* generally, Philip Wood, *Law and Practice of International Finance* (University Edition, 2008); Symposium, *Restructuring of Sovereign Debt*, 23 Colum. J. Transnat'l L. 1 (1984); Brian W. Semkow, *Syndicating and Rescheduling International Financial Transactions*, 18 Int'l Law. 869 (1984). *See*, the respective websites for a wealth of additional information: African Development Bank, www.afdb.org; Asian Development Bank, www.adb.org; Inter-American Development Bank, www.iadb.org.
76. *See*, the Export-Import Bank's website: www.exim.gov.
77. *See*, the OPIC website: www.opic.gov.
78. The FCIA's website is: www.fcia.com.

§3.6 OTHER CONSIDERATIONS IN PLANNING COMMERCIAL AGREEMENTS

The planning and drafting of private commercial agreements does not take place in a vacuum. There are a large number of other matters that must be taken into account before a company can be assured that the agreement is sound, lawful, and enforceable. An in-depth analysis of the following topics is beyond the scope of this book but some awareness of each of these issues is necessary to have a well-rounded grasp of all the ingredients of an international commercial agreement.

§3.6.1 Tax Matters

There is no easy way to generalize about matters of taxation. Indeed, generalizations in this area can be dangerous because there is virtually no area of the law that changes with such rapidity and little notice as do the taxation laws of any country. Some brief observations may prove useful, however. Virtually all countries impose taxes of one sort or another on both individuals and businesses. These taxes run the gamut from sales taxes (often referred to as value added taxes outside the United States), property taxes for the use of real estate in a particular country, taxes in the nature of various types of license fees, and perhaps most importantly in the United States, income taxes (imposed on both individuals and corporations).[79]

The United States tax system is incredibly complicated and is frequently subject to revision. Some generalizations will probably hold true for the near future, however. The basic scheme of U.S. income taxation requires the identification of taxpayers (either individuals, corporations or partnerships), requires those entities to report their income (generally all money earned from their activities) and then permits taxpayers to reduce their taxable income by an extraordinarily complicated set of exemptions, exclusions and deductions. For example, the United States tax system permits American corporations to deduct certain taxes paid to foreign governments against the tax they owe to the United States and further permits American citizens living abroad to exclude a certain amount of foreign earnings from U.S. taxation. U.S. law permits

79. Some excellent guides to international taxation written from an American perspective are: Brian Arnold, *International Tax Primer* (3d ed., 2016); Lynne Oats & Angharad Miller, *Principles of International Taxation* (6th ed., 2017); Philip F. Postlewaite, *International Taxation: Corporate and Individual* (10th ed., 2016); Joseph Isenbergh, *International Taxation (Concepts and Insights)* (3d ed., 2009); Roy Rohatgi, *Basic International Taxation (Principles) and Basic International Taxation (Procedure)* (2d ed., 2007); and Joseph Isenbergh, *International Taxation: U.S. Taxation of Foreign Taxpayers and Foreign Income* (1990). For further guidance, *see The International Taxation System* (Andrew Lymer & John Hasseldine eds., 2002); Allison Christians, *Hard Law, Soft Law, and International Taxation*, 25 Wis. Int'l L.J. 325 (2007); Reuven S. Avi-Yonah, *All of a Piece Throughout: The Four Ages of U.S. International Taxation*, 25 Va. Tax Rev. 313 (2005); *See also*, Michael Mulroney, *Foreign Transactions and Persons: United States Income Taxation, A Primer*, in *International Trade for the Non-Specialist* (2d ed., 1997); John E. Bischel, *Fundamentals of International Taxation* (2 vols., 1985).

business entities to establish Domestic International Sales Corporations and Foreign Export Sales corporations that qualify for special tax treatment because of their export activities.[80]

The U.S. also has a number of tax treaties with foreign governments that affect the manner in which U.S. citizens are dealt with under foreign tax schemes.[81] Recently, there has been increasing attention paid to the impact of taxation on business activities in developing countries.[82] When a company plans a transaction with a specific country, a quick and generally accurate summary of that country's taxation laws may be found in World Tax Series.

In the final analysis, advice and information on tax matters both foreign and domestic must be left in the hands of the experts. There is no other area of the law that is trickier and so fraught with hazards for the uninitiated. Nonetheless, tax considerations always have a major impact on an international commercial undertaking.

§3.6.2 Antitrust Issues

Most international transactions create no antitrust problems, but those that do tend to create enormous problems. Like taxation, antitrust is a legal topic on which generalizations are dangerous; but some basic concepts may be helpful.[83] The entire concept of antitrust, both in the United States and abroad, is grounded in a belief that competition among businesses is generally a good thing. As a consequence, most antitrust law seeks to promote competition and prohibits various practices which inhibit or restrain competition. The principal U.S. antitrust law, the Sherman Antitrust Act,[84] prohibits, among many other things, "every contract, combination...or conspiracy, in restraint of trade or commerce among the several States, or with foreign nations ..." The U.S. courts have framed some basic principles that flesh out this statute. For example, two

80. *See*, e.g., Thomas R. Bretz, *Current Developments on DISCs*, 19 N.C.J. Int'l L. & Com'l Reg. 385 (1984).
81. *See*, e.g., IRS, Tax Treaties and Rates (IRS Pub. No. 901, 1985); H. David Rosenbloom, *Tax Treaty Abuse Policies and Issues*, 15 L. & Pol'y in Int'l Bus. 763 (1983).
82. *See*, e.g., Honey Lynn Goldberg, *Considerations for the Elimination of International Double Taxation: Toward a Developing Country Model*, 15 L. & Pol'y in Int'l Bus. 833 (1983).
83. Some excellent sources on the topic of antitrust from a U.S. perspective are: Maher M. Dabbah, *International Antitrust and Competition Law* (2010); Mark R. Joelson, *An International Antitrust Primer: A Guide to the Operation of United States, European Union and Other Key Competition Laws in the Global Economy* (4th ed., 2017); D. Daniel Sokol, *Monopolists Without Borders: The Institutional Challenge of International Antitrust in a Global Gilded Age*, 4 Berkeley Bus. L.J. 37 (2007); Paul B. Stephan, *Global Governance, Antitrust, and the Limits of International Cooperation*, 38 Cornell Int'l L.J. 173 (2005); Anu Piilola, *Assessing Theories of Global Governance: A Case Study of International Antitrust Regulation*, 39 Stan. J. Int'l L. 207 (2003); James F. Rill, *The Status of International Antitrust Enforcement*, 18 Whittier L. Rev. 321 (1997); Spencer W. Waller, *The Internationalization of Antitrust Enforcement*, 77 B.U.L. Rev. 343 (1997); Spencer W. Waller, *Antitrust and American Business Abroad Today*, 44 DePaul L. Rev. 1251 (1995). For a book-length work written from a European perspective *see*, Richard Whish & David Bailey, *Competition Law* (2012); Lennart Ritter & W. David Baum, *European Competition Law: A Practitioner's Guide* (2005); Nicholas Green, Aidan Robertson & Monckton Chambers, *Commercial Agreements and Competition Law: Practice and Procedure in the UK and EC* (2d ed., 1997).
84. 15 U.S.C. §1.

companies that get together to fix prices automatically violate the act. Getting together to divide up sales territories is also what is known as a per se violation of the Sherman Act. For most other situations, the courts apply what is termed a rule of reason to determine whether a company's conduct has violated the antitrust statutes. In 2006, the United States Supreme Court reviewed a fascinating joint venture created by Shell and Texaco. While the two companies had competed fiercely at both the international level and in domestic U.S. oil markets, they decided to set up a joint venture that combined their U.S. refining operations and their gasoline retail marketing networks. A group of gasoline retail dealers sued the companies contending that such a combination—whether or not styled as a joint venture—violated the basic prohibition in the Sherman Act against price-fixing and was, thereby, a per se violation of the Sherman Act. When the case got to the Supreme Court, the Court disagreed, holding that the joint venture was a legitimate business undertaking and that internal deliberations respecting the venture's pricing posture was not a per se violation.[85] Instead, the Court ordered the lower federal courts to consider the controversy under the much more lenient rule of reason principle—which requires courts to take account of the entirety of market conditions and circumstances before ruling that the cited conduct violates the Sherman Act's price-fixing constraints.[86]

The United States government has always taken these principles very serious for purely domestic business enterprises. The problems become far more difficult, however, when they involve companies doing business abroad. First, there is a serious question, not yet resolved, as to whether the United States has the jurisdiction to enforce its antitrust principles abroad in any event. Attempts to do so have greatly offended a number of countries. Second, the U.S. antitrust principles are not identical to those applicable in other countries. If country X is happy to permit American company A to do business on its territory, why should the U.S. government be permitted to interfere through an extraterritorial application of its domestic antitrust laws. Third, the fundamental purpose of the antitrust laws—to promote competition within the United States—may have little consequence when U.S. companies are attempting to increase foreign sales.

The United States Congress recognized this last factor in an early statute, the Webb-Pomerene Act,[87] which provides a partial exception to the Sherman Act for activities abroad. More recently, Congress has enacted the Export Trading Company Act of 1982,[88] a statute that permits American manufacturers, exporters and banking institutions to form export trading companies as a joint activity without having to worry about antitrust violations for these practices.

The U.S. Justice Department has attempted to clarify some of the basic principles as they apply to activities abroad by promulgating guidelines for companies doing business abroad. These principles, entitled the Antitrust Guidelines for International

85. *Texaco v. Dagher*, 547 U.S. 1 (2006).
86. *See*, e.g., Thomas A. Piraino, Jr., *The Antitrust Analysis of Joint Ventures after the Supreme Court's Dagher Decision*, 57 Emory L.J. 735 (2008).
87. 15 U.S.C. §12.
88. 15 U.S.C. §62.

Enforcement and Cooperation[89] caused significant controversy when initially issued in 1977, but are much more realistic in their current configuration. In essence, the Justice Department takes the position that it is not interested in violation of U.S. antitrust principles abroad unless that conduct has a direct impact on U.S. consumers. Justice Department spokesmen strive mightily to confirm that these guidelines are solidly based in an understanding of the U.S. competitive position abroad and in the concept of the rule of reason. However, they are not without their detractors. A former high-ranking Justice Department officer described them as statements that "read more like a preacher's sermon than a counselor's guide."[90] That judgment may be a little harsh. What the Guidelines attempt to do is state a number of hypothetical transactions and to suggest the position that the Justice Department might take in each of those cases. The analysis is somewhat tentative, and perhaps that gives little comfort to business executives and lawyers who are trying to work out a specific compliance posture. There are signals that the Department is becoming more aggressive about extraterritorial application of the U.S. antitrust laws, so anyone setting up a transaction with some connection to the United States should pay attention to the Guidelines.

However, even if companies avoid domestic antitrust problems flowing out of their foreign activities, they may still run into problems under the antitrust laws of the host country. The EU, for example, has some highly developed antitrust principles that it enforces with a great deal of aggressiveness.[91] The Union has become particularly concerned about business merger activity in recent years.[92]

§3.6.3 Antidumping and Countervailing Duty Issues

Most countries impose customs duties on products imported into the country. Many countries also do not wish to see foreign goods enter the country with prices that undercut domestic companies, especially if those prices are set lower than domestic prices for the same product in the country of origin (the idea of dumping) or if those

89. The guidelines were initially issued by the Justice Department in 1977, but substantially revised in 1988, 1995, and 2010. The current guidelines, updated as of January, 2017, may be found on the DOJ's website (antitrust division): www.doj.gov/antitrust.

90. Donald I. Baker & Bennett Rushkoff, *The 1988 Justice Department International Guidelines: Searching for Legal Standards and Reassurance*, 23 Cornell Int'l L.J. 405 (1990). *See also*, Wilber L. Fugate, *The New Justice Department Antitrust Enforcement Guidelines for International Operations—A Reflection of Reagan and, Perhaps, Bush Administration Antitrust Policy*, 29 Va. J. Int'l L. 295 (1989).

91. Articles 85–87 of the Treaty of Rome (establishing the EC) provide the basic foundation. *See*, e.g., Pierre Raoul-Duval, *The EEC Merger Control Regulation*, in *International Trade for the Non-Specialist* (2d ed., 1997); William Brown, *The Impact of European Community Antitrust Law on United States Companies*, 13 Hastings Int'l & Comp. L. Rev. 383 (1990); Ixo Van Bael, *A Practitioner's Guide to Due Process in EEC Antitrust and Antidumping Proceedings*, 18 Int'l Law. 841 (1984).

92. *See*, e.g., Marsha Cope Huie & Stephen D. Hogan, *The New European Community Merger Control Regulation and the Short-Term Horizon of United States Firms*, 6 Am.U.J. Int'l L. & Pol'y 325 (1991).

prices are somehow subsidized by the country of origin in order to give its companies unfair leverage for market penetration in the country of destination (the basis for the imposition of countervailing duties).[93]

The process by which these duties are computed and the administrative procedures by which they are finally adjudicated (in the United States by the International Trade Commission) are too complicated to go into here. Suffice it to say that the pricing of products in a fair and competitive manner is highly important for all contracts for the sale of goods. Artificially low or subsidized prices will likely give rise to protests from competing companies in the country of destination. Those protests could result in the imposition of additional duties which raise the seller's prices. Worse, dumping and subsidization can lead to additional monetary penalties which can make the price of doing business abroad very expensive indeed.

§3.6.4 Export and Import Controls

Virtually every country has strict controls on those things that can be brought into the country and those things that can be taken out. The rationale for these controls may range from an interest in the conservation of natural resources to a desire to protect national security. In the United States, the control of exports is governed mainly by the Export Administration Act of 1979,[94] a statute that requires potential exporters to secure export permission in the form of a validated license (for certain high-technology items and for certain items going to certain countries) or a general license (for other products). The U.S. export controls were greatly eased when the Soviet Union began to collapse and as East-West tensions diminished. In 1989 and with subsequent adjustments, the U.S. sharply reduced the number of items that require a validated license and removed most of the countries of Eastern Europe from the list of countries singled out for special export control treatment.[95] Nonetheless, export and import controls do exist and when applicable must be complied with in the same fashion that other government regulations must be complied with.[96]

Import controls are imposed by the country of destination of the product or service in question. There is no feasible way to generalize about these controls. In private international commercial transactions, both import and export controls are

93. *See* generally, Peter D. Erenhaft, *Remedies Against "Unfair" International Trade Practices*, in *International Trade for the Non-Specialist* (1997).
94. 50 U.S.C. app. §§2401–2420.
95. *See*, e.g., Cecil Hunt, *Export Controls*, in *International Trade for the Non-Specialist* (2d ed., 1997); Joseph P. Griffin, Michael R. Calabrese & John C. Lindsay, *U.S. Department of Commerce Takes Further Steps to Ease Export License Requirements*, 18 Int'l Bus. Law. 42 (1990).
96. *See*, e.g., John R. Liebman & Kevin J. Lombardo, *A Guide to Export Controls for the Non-Specialist*, 28 Loy L.A. Int'l & Comp. L. Rev. 497 (2006); Tara L. Dunn, *Surviving United States Export Controls Post 9/11: A Model Compliance Program*, 33 Denver J. Int'l L. & Pol'y 435 (2005). *See also*, Debra Burke, *At the Intersection of Export Control Regulations and Employment Discrimination Law*, 45 Am. Bus. L.J. 565 (2008) Andrew F. Diamond, *Dueling Over Dual-Use Goods: The U.S. Department of Commerce's Misguided Attempt to Promote U. S. Security and Trade with China Through Restrictive Export Controls*, 3 Brooklyn J. Corp. Fin. & Com. L. 153 (2008).

normally dealt with by requiring the buyer to obtain all necessary government permissions for the importation of the product, by requiring the seller to obtain the parallel export permissions and making a failure to obtain or to continue these permissions grounds for excuse of performance.

§3.6.5 Ethical Considerations

[1] Anti-bribery Measures

In the late 1970s the United States Congress became concerned over a number of documented cases in which U.S. corporations had paid bribes to foreign officials in order to do business in other countries. The outcome of this concern was the Foreign Corrupt Practices Act of 1977 (FCPA),[97] a statute that makes it a crime for any U.S. company to "corruptly" give "anything of value" to any foreign official or foreign political party to induce or assist in "obtaining or retaining business."[98] In 1988, the

97. 15 U.S.C. §78dd-2. The primary website for materials and analysis of corruption is that of Transparency International, a group that has pioneered significant research in this area for a number of years, including the publication of a "corruption index" that ranks individual nations in terms of corruption levels. The TI website is: www.transparency.org. For a really good excursus on international business corruption, *see* generally, the following articles: Jon Jordan, *The Need for a Comprehensive International Foreign Bribery Compliance Program: Covering A to Z in an Expanding Global Anti-Bribery Environment*, 117 Penn St. L. Rev. 89 (2012); Bruce Wiklaw, *A New Strategy for Preventing Bribery and Extortion in International Business Transactions*, 49 Harv. J. Legis. 303 (2012); Carl Pacini, *The FCPA: Taking a Bite Out of Bribery in International Business Transactions*, 17 Fordham J. Comp. & Fin. L. 545 (2012); Symposium, *Rethinking Corruption: An Interdisciplinary Look at a Fundamental Problem*, 20 Pac. McGeorge Global Bus. & Dev. L.J. 237 (2007); Ethan S. Burger & Mary S. Holland, *Why the Private Sector Is Likely to Lead the Next Stage in the Global Fight Against Corruption*, 30 Fordham Int'l L.J. 45 (2006) and Ben W. Heineman, Jr. & Fritz Heimann, *The Long War against Corruption*, 85 For. Aff. 75 (2006). For some excellent comments on the FCPA *see*, Daniel P. Ashe, *The Lengthening Anti-Bribery Lasso of the United States: The Recent Extraterritorial Application of the U.S. Foreign Corrupt Practices Act*, 73 Fordham L. Rev. 2897 (2005); Oren Gleich & Ryan Woodward, *Foreign Corrupt Practices Act*, 42 Am. Crim. L. Rev. 545 (2005); Michael R. Geroe, *Complying with U.S. Antibribery Laws*, 31 Int'l Law. 1037 (1997); Steven R. Salbu, *Bribery in the Global Market: A Critical Analysis of the Foreign Corrupt Practices Act*, 54 Wash. & Lee L. Rev. 229 (1997). Three excellent books on the FCPA and other anti-corruption initiatives are Stuart H. Deming, *The Foreign Corrupt Practices Act and the New International Norms* (2011); J. Ndumbe Anyu, *The Foreign Corrupt Practices Act: A Catalyst for Global Corruption Reform* (2007); Don Zarin, *Doing Business under the Foreign Corrupt Practices Act* (2004). Also worthy of consideration are: Martin Weinstein & Robert T. Meyer, *The Foreign Corrupt Practices Act: Compliance, Investigations and Enforcement* (2016); Mike Koehler, *The Foreign Corrupt Practices Act in a New Era* (2014); Robert W. Tarun, *The Foreign Corrupt Practices Act Handbook: A Practical Guide for Multinational General Counsel* (2013) and Richard L. Cassin, *Bribery Abroad: Lessons from the Foreign Corrupt Practices Act* (2011). The United States Department of Justice has issued *A Resource Guide to the U.S. Foreign Corrupt Practices Act (FCPA): Anti-Bribery Provisions, Definitions, Payments to Third Parties* (2017). For an excellent book-length treatment of business corruption generally *see* Michael S. Auslander & Sarah Hudson, *The Handbook of Business and Corruption: Cross-Sectoral Experiences* (2017).
98. This language, particularly the modifier "corruptly" and the phrase "anything of value" seems to cause a great deal of consternation in first-time readers. In truth, that language is simply taken verbatim from the basic United States bribery statute, 18 U.S.C. §201: "Whoever (1) directly or indirectly, corruptly gives, offers or promises anything of value to any public official...with

FCPA was amended to exclude from its scope a payment for "facilitating or expediting" what the amended Act refers to as the "performance of a routine governmental action." In addition, parties accused of violations of the FCPA may base their defense on either of two other assertions: (1) that the payment is lawful under the written laws and regulations of the foreign country; or (2) that the payment is a reasonable and bona fide expenditure directly related to promotion of products or services or the performance of a contract with a foreign government or agency."[99] These exceptions should not be read too broadly, however. The remainder of the Act and its legislative history state clearly that the FCPA still covers any payments to influence "any decision by a foreign official whether, or on what terms, to award new business to or to continue business with a particular party."[100]

Since the statute contains criminal penalties (businesses may be fined up to USD 2 million and individuals may be fined up USD 100,000 and imprisoned for up to five years), U.S. businesses must pay close attention to compliance matters. Moreover, the FCPA cannot be circumvented by employing a foreign agent or representative to do things which American business people could not themselves get away with.

There have been many assertions that the FCPA (especially before it was amended in 1988) harms the international competitiveness of U.S. businesses since the U.S. is probably the only country in the world with an FCPA. As of 1979 the U.S. Department of Justice estimated that the Act had cost around USD 1 billion in lost business opportunities. That study has not been updated. The Justice Department appears to prosecute only the most egregious examples of bribery of foreign officials. The Department's lukewarm attitude toward the statute was signaled once again in 1990. The 1988 Amendments to the FCPA suggested that the Justice Department might wish to promulgate guidelines for FCPA compliance. In July 1990, the Department announced its conclusion that compliance with the FCPA would not be enhanced by such guidelines. The final story on the FCPA has not yet been written.[101]

Of course, the United States is not the only entity with an interest in ethical business conduct in the context of international transactions. In 2010, the United Kingdom adopted a Bribery Act that reflects a determination (critics say one that was too long coming) that makes bribery of foreign government officials explicitly a U.K. criminal offense. Patterned somewhat on the FCPA, the new statute deals with both bribery itself and with a company's failure to prevent acts of bribery.[102] In late 1997, the

---

intent (A) to influence any official act" is guilty of bribery. This statute has been on the books in the United States for nearly 200 years. Most other countries, and certainly virtually all major trading nations have prohibited bribery of their own public officials for many, many years. *See*, e.g., Ashish S. Joshi, *Britain's Fight Against the "Silver Lance": A Radical Overhaul of the U.K.'s Bribery Laws*, 33 Champion 36 (2009).

99. 15 U.S.C. §78dd-2(c).

100. 15 U.S.C. §78dd-1(f)(3)(B), 78dd-2(h)(4)(B).

101. Indeed, cultural differences greatly affect even discussions of corrupt practices. *See*, e.g., Mohamed A. Arafa, *Corruption and Bribery in Islamic Law: Are Islamic Ideals Being Met in Practice?* 18 Ann. Survey Int'l & Comp. L. 171 (2010); Joongi Kim & Jong Bum Kim, *Cultural Differences in the Crusade against International Bribery: Rice-Cake Expenses in Korea and the Foreign Corrupt Practices Act*, 6 Pac. Rim. L. & Pol'y 549 (1997).

102. The Bribery Act, greatly detailed in actual text, is well described in Peter Alldridge, *The U.K. Bribery Act: "The Caffeinated Younger Sibling of the FCPA,"* 73 Ohio St. L.J. 1181 (2012). For

Organization of Economic Cooperation and Development (OECD) concluded a thirty-four country Convention on Combating Bribery of Foreign Public Officials in International Business Transactions.[103] The convention, joined by all twenty-nine Member States of the OECD plus five nonmembers, commits each signatory country to:

> take such measures as may be necessary to establish that it is a criminal offense under its law for any person intentionally to offer, promise or give any pecuniary or other advantage, whether directly or through intermediaries, to a foreign public official...in order that the official act or refrain from acting in relation to the performance of official duties, in order to obtain or retain business or other improper advantage in the conduct of international business.[104]

This is a magnificent breakthrough in international attempts to police the worst bribery abuses. It may mark the beginning of the end of the frequently stated attitude that "everyone does it." It also means that the United States no longer stands alone in its prohibition of such conduct. But like most treaties it may have perceptible weaknesses and deficiencies. For example, the Convention does not prescribe the exact form that domestic legislation in each signatory country must take in order to comply with the Convention.[105] There may be problems in certain of the definitions. For example, the reach of the term "public enterprise" probably does not reach the operation by public officials of purely commercial enterprises. So, if a foreign government official is also operating a government-run hotel, his hotel-managing activities may not be covered by the Convention.[106] The Convention also does not cover any fee-paying activities that are permitted under the written law of a country or which are characterized as minor "facilitating" payments. These last two provisions are similar to but not identical with the FCPA.

There are now a number other regional and international initiatives to combat bribery and other forms of business corruption that international lawyers and business executives should be aware of. Perhaps the most significant international treaty is the UN Convention Against Corruption which entered into force in 2005 after ratification by thirty countries.[107] As this edition goes to press, more than 165 nations, including the United States and the EU have subscribed to the convention. The significance of the

---

more on U.K. bribery *see* Vivian Robinson & Stuart H. Deming, *The FCPA and the U.K. Bribery Act: A Ready Reference for Business and Lawyers* (2014).

103. The convention is dated December 17, 1997 and the full text of the convention may be found on the OECD website: www.oecd.org.
104. Convention on Bribery, Art. 1(1).
105. Daniel K. Tarullo, *The Limits of Institutional Design: Implementing the OECD Anti-Bribery Convention*, 44 Va. J. Int'l L. 665 (1999). *See also*, Tanya Rolo, *NOTE: Enforcing Enforcement: Is the OECD Antibribery Convention's Peer Review Effective?* 43 Geo. Wash. Int'l L. Rev. 137 (2011).
106. *Id.* The Convention is accompanied by official commentary that provides that activities that "operate on a normal commercial basis in the relevant market, i.e., on a basis which is substantially equivalent to that of a private enterprise, without preferential subsidies or other privileges" are not covered by the Convention. The official commentary may be found on the OECD website: www.oecd.org.
107. S. Treaty Doc. No. 109-6.

U.N. Convention is that it is truly multilateral in approach and design and it is not confined merely to combating bribery. It is a vehicle that may be used to police many other forms of corrupt business practices.

The United Nations Convention establishes a Conference of the States Parties (CSP) to develop cooperation initiatives between the signatories to the Convention and to promote implementation of the Convention. The United Nations Office on Drugs and Crime serves as the CSP's secretariat. The Convention itself begins with a number of provisions on integrity, accountability and international cooperation and technical assistance.[108] The Convention then sets out a number of "preventive measures" that call for the establishment of anti-corruption bodies and transparency in elections and political parties. But most importantly, the preventive measures are directed at both the public sector and the private sector. Among other things, private-sector entities are admonished to develop codes of conduct and practices that promote transparency.

The Convention pushes the anti-corruption envelope by recognizing not only the old forms of corruption such as bribery, embezzlement and money laundering, but also misconduct in the form of trading in influence, obstruction of justice and concealment of illegally obtained assets.[109] The Convention goes on to provide for asset recovery as a "fundamental principle" of the agreement and encourages signatory states to develop measures that enhance the identification, seizure and confiscation, forfeiture and, hopefully, the return of the assets to innocent parties.[110]

The Council of Europe has promulgated the Criminal Law Convention and the Civil Law Convention on Corruption.[111] Both conventions are similar in vocabulary and application. In contrast to the OECD Convention and the FCPA, these conventions are mainly a multilateral framework within which each signatory country commits to combating various forms of bribery and corruption by way of national legislation that implements the very broad provisions of the conventions themselves. Looking at the Civil Law Convention, we find the following:

(1) A definition of "corruption": "Corruption" means requesting, offering, giving or accepting directly or indirectly, a bribe or any other undue advantage or prospect thereof, which distorts the proper performance of any duty or behavior required of the recipient of the bribe, the undue advantage or the prospect thereof.
(2) A commitment to provide injured persons "the right to initiate an action in order to obtain full compensation for such damage."

108. *See* the Convention's General Provisions, Chapter I, Arts. 1–4. The full text of the Convention may be obtained from the Convention's website, www.un.unodc.org.
109. UN Convention, Chapter III, Arts. 15–44.
110. *Id.*, Chapter V, Arts. 51–59.
111. Civil Law Convention on Corruption, November 4, 1999, Europ. T.S. No. 174, and Criminal Law Convention on Corruption, January 27, 1999, Europ. T.S. No. 173, both of which may be found at www.conventions.coe.int/treaty/en/Treaties.

(3) A somewhat unusual provision, entitled "contributory negligence," that permits the government to reduce the compensation to an injured person "if the plaintiff has by his or her own fault contributed to the damage or to its aggravation."
(4) An express provision that any contracts that are procured through corrupt means are to be declared null and void.

A large number of Latin American nations gathered together to formulate the Inter-American Convention against Corruption which entered into force in 1996.[112] The Inter-American Convention addresses several different types of corruption but appears to concentrate mainly on anti-bribery initiatives. It requires signatory nations to develop specific preventive measures to fight corruption including: standards of conduct, systems for policing the income, assets and liabilities of public officers, creation of "oversight" bodies to prevent and detect corrupt practices, and mechanisms to encourage civil society and nongovernmental organizations in efforts to prevent corruption.[113]

The African Union has promulgated the Convention on Preventing and Combating Corruption which entered into force in 2006.[114] The African Union Convention sees bribery and corruption as having exceptionally damaging effects on "political, economic, social and cultural stability of African states," as well as inhibiting "the economic and social development of the African peoples." The Convention divides the fight against corruption into three constituent parts: prevention, criminalization, and international cooperation. Among other things, it requires signatory nations to police the assets of public officials, to create internal bodies to establish and monitor a code of conduct. Much like a number of the other anti-corruption initiatives, it defines bribery as "the solicitation or acceptance, directly or indirectly, by a public official or any other person, of any goods of monetary value, or other benefit, such as a gift, favor, promise or advantage for himself or for another person or entity, in exchange for any act or omission in the performance of his or her public functions."[115]

In recent years, the World Bank and a number of the regional development banks have developed anti-bribery and anti-corruption initiatives in conjunction with their

112. The text of the convention may be accessed at www.oas.org/juridico/english/Treaties. *See*, Patricio Maldonado & Geraldo D. Berthin, *Transparency and Developing Legal Frameworks to Combat Corruption in Latin America*, 10 Sw. J. L & Trade Am. 201 (2004).
113. *See*, e.g., Alexandra R. Harrington, *Natural Integrity: The Relationship Between Anti-Corruption Laws and Natural Resource Protections in Latin America*, 17 Currents Int'l Trade L.J. 13 (2009); Jose Armando Fanjul, *Comment: Corporate Corruption in Latin America: Acceptance, Bribery, Compliance, Denial, Economics, and the Foreign Corrupt Practices Act*, 26 Penn St. Int'l L. Rev. 735 (2008).
114. The text of the convention may be found at 43 I.L.M 5 and www.africa-union.org/root/au/Documents/Treaties/Text/Convention. *See*, Thomas R. Snider & Won Kidane, *Combating Corruption Through International Law in Africa: A Comparative Analysis*, 40 Cornell Int'l L.J. 691 (2007).
115. African Convention, Art. 4(1)(a). For some extensive commentary on the African Convention, *see* John Mukum Mbaku, *The International Dimension of Africa's Struggle Against Corruption*, 10 Asper Rev. Int'l Bus. & Trade L. 35 (2010).

lending activities.[116] A new group, "Sigma," has been formed within the OECD to support governance improvements in approximately 30 countries in the Central and Eastern European area.[117] A very new and very intriguing anti-corruption venture is CleanGovBiz: a new development hosted by the OECD that supports governments, business, and civil society organizations in building integrity and fighting corruption. The CleanGovBiz "toolkit" "offers practical guidance on how corruption can best be tackled in multiple domains. It draws together relevant instruments to support the establishment of healthy systems of governance, prevent corrupt practices, detect corruption, prosecute delinquencies and remedy the consequences of corruption."[118] Parties that avail themselves of the toolkit are given: (1) priority checklists; (2) implementation guidance with examples of good practices, access to existing relevant standards and instruments; and (3) case studies and reviews elaborated by international and civil society organizations.[119]

Those lawyers who despise bribery and who have found it difficult to make clients understand that bribery is not to be tolerated will welcome the all of these initiatives, warts and all. Even if none of the treaties and conventions is perfect they represent a considerable improvement on the total vacuum that existed just a few years ago.[120] At the same time, lawyers in particular must understand that these new legal instruments present some important and difficult counseling problems for them and their clients. Clients now must be informed that corruption, and particularly bribery, is contrary to both domestic and international law and must be avoided. The "see no evil/hear no evil" approach no longer works. Lawyers who do not satisfy their counseling obligations on these issues could, ultimately, be faced with both ethical violations leading to professional discipline and malpractice liability.[121]

Much more work is required before any of us live in a bribery-free world. But these relatively new and somewhat untried initiatives are all significant and very welcome steps toward leveling the playing field.

[2] Codes of Conduct

The UN Conference on Trade and Development (UNCTAD) is developing codes of conduct for transfer of technology and multinational corporations (MNCs) that attempt

116. The World Bank initiatives are described on the Bank's website: www.worldbank.org.
117. The Sigma website is found within the OECD website: www.oecd.org/sigma.
118. The CleanGovBiz website is: www.oecd.org/cleangovbiz.
119. *Id.*
120. Readers should take special note of a very insightful and provocative article that takes a very broad look at international corruption and bribery: Jon Jordan, *The Need for a Comprehensive International Foreign Bribery Compliance Program: Covering A to Z in an Expanding Global Anti-Bribery Environment*, 117 Penn St. L. Rev. 89 (2012).
121. *See*, e.g., Jennifer D. Faucett, *Legal Malpractice and Bribery: The Foreign Corrupt Practices Act and the Pitfalls It Creates for Attorneys*, 29 J. Leg. Prof. 213 (2004).

to place certain limitations on a company's negotiation posture and techniques and to effectuate a proper and equitable dispute resolution mechanism between MNCs and developing countries.[122]

Among many other things, the UNCTAD Codes of Conduct: (1) require that foreign corporations respect the sovereignty of the host government; (2) respect the right of the host government to control its natural wealth and resources; (3) abstain from interference in the internal political affairs of the host country; and (4) remain sensitive to the political, economic and social environment of the host country.[123]

A number of international NGOs, including the International Organization for Standardization have promulgated rules of behavior for international corporations.[124] In the case of the ISO, standard 14000 is an attempt to heighten corporate awareness of environmental harm and to foster business practices to minimize such harm.[125]

In the United States there have been sporadic and as-yet unsuccessful attempts to force the foreign subsidiaries of American companies to comply with health and safety standards abroad that would be imposed on the company if it were operating in the United States.[126] The United States Supreme Court has ruled that the job discrimination statutes of the United States (the U.S. equal employment opportunity laws) do not apply outside the country.[127] But other U.S. laws, including for example, the endangered species act, may have extraterritorial application that has not yet been resolved

122. *See*, e.g., drafts of the codes at 17 Int'l Leg. Materials 453 (1978). A recent journal article that does a good job of surveying the international code of conduct landscape is Mark B. Baker, *Promises and Platitudes: Toward a New 21st Century Paradigm for Corporate Codes of Conduct*, 23 Conn. J. Int'l L. 123 (2007). For book-length works on MNCs and the codes of conduct *see*, *Emerging Standards of International Trade and Investment: Multinational Codes and Corporate Conduct* (Seymour J. Rubin & Gary Clydehufbauer eds., 1984); *Legal Problems of Codes of Conduct for Multinational Enterprises* (Nicholas Horn ed., 1980). *See also*, Patrick M. Erwin, *Corporate Codes of Conduct: The Effects of Code Content and Quality on Ethical Performance*, 4 J. Bus. Ethics 535 (2011); Elodie Bethoux, Claude Didry & Arnaud Mias, *What Codes of Conduct Tell Us: Corporate Social Responsibility and the Nature of the Multinational Corporation*, 15 Corp. Governance: An Int'l Rev. 77 (2007) Pedro Roffe, *Transfer of Technology: UNCTAD's Draft International Code of Conduct*, 19 Int'l Law. 689 (1985).

123. For a lengthy discussion of the Codes of Conduct *see*, Samuel Asante, *The Concept of the Good Corporate Citizen in International Business*, 4 ICSID Rev. For. Inv. L.J. 1 (1989).

124. There is an elaborate discussion of the work of the ISO in Chapter 4, §4.9.2.

125. For additional information on ISO 14000 *see*, the ISO's website: www.iso.org and Thomas Zobel, *The Impact of ISO 14001 on Corporate Environmental Performance: A Study of Swedish Manufacturing Firms*, 59 J. of Envtl Plan. & Mgmt 587 (2015); Henk J. de Vries, Deniz K. Bayramoglu & Ton van der Weile, *Business and Environmental Impact of ISO 14000*, 29 Int'l J. of Quality & Reliability 425 (2012). For information on some of the other nongovernmental attempts to develop codes of conduct *see*, e.g., Sean D. Murphy, *Taking Multinational Corporate Codes of Conduct to the Next Level*, 43 Columb. J. Transnat'l L. 389 (2005); Mark B. Baker, *Promises and Platitudes: Toward a New 21st Century Paradigm for Corporate Codes of Conduct*, 23 Conn. J. Int'l L. 123 (2007).

126. *See*, e.g., Laicold M. Street, *U.S.-Exports Banned for Domestic Use, but Exported to Third World Countries*, 6 Int'l Trade L.J. 95 (1981).

127. *EEOC v. Aramco*, 499 U.S. 244 (1991).

in U.S. courts.[128] One major international topic, global warming, may have a substantial impact on international trade through most of the twenty-first century.[129]

§3.6.6 Criminal Matters

As discussed in the preceding section, the U.S. FCPA and the OECD Bribery Convention impose domestic criminal liability on extraterritorial actions that constitute bribery of a public official. The antitrust concerns discussed in an earlier section can lead to criminal sanctions if engaged in intentionally by a particular company. The United States has imposed a substantial number of trading sanctions prohibiting or restricting trade with certain countries such as Cuba and North Korea.[130] Insider trading activities and environmental offenses may have extraterritorial application. There are many other possibilities too numerous to list here; but potential criminal liability is something every transactional lawyer must confront.[131]

§3.7 SPECIAL REGIONAL CONSIDERATIONS IN PLANNING INTERNATIONAL COMMERCIAL AGREEMENTS

The importance and inevitability of world trade is no longer subject to serious question. Indeed, some journalists and editorial writers have coined a term, *globalization*, to describe the phenomenon. But this does not mean that everything is settled. There is extraordinary ferment in international trade. Countries that had once been part of the Soviet bloc, such as Poland, Hungary and the Czech Republic, have developed democratic political systems and market mechanism economies and are now full-fledged members of the EU.[132] The smaller Baltic states have acted similarly. China and India, while not affiliated with any regional trading group, are proving to be enormous competitors in the world of international trade. Japan remains one of the largest economies in the world. While experiencing a few recent economic hiccups, the United States' economic engine will likely be the strongest in the world for some time to come.

128. *See*, e.g., *Dominic A. Gentile, Note: International Trade and the Environment: What Is the Role of the WTO?* 20 Fordham Envt'l L. Rev. 197 (2009); and the extensive discussion of environmental controls in Michael J. Quinn, *International Environmental Law*, in *International Trade for the Non-Specialist* (2d ed., 1997); Richard A. Phelps, *Environmental Law for Overseas Installations*, 40 A.F.L. Rev. 49 (1996).
129. *See*, e.g., Paul G. Harris, *The European Union and Environmental Change: Sharing the Burdens of Global Warming*, 17 Colo. J. Int'l Envt'l L. & Pol'y 309 (2006); Jeffrey A. Smith, *The Implications of the Kyoto Protocol and the Global Warming Debate for Business Transactions*, 1 N.Y.U. J. L. & Bus. 511 (2005); Symposium, *A New Legal Frontier in the Fight against Global Warming*, 16 Fordham Envt'l L. Rev. 289 (2005).
130. *See*, a general discussion of U.S. sanctions in William Fox, *The United States and Economic Sanctions: One American Perspective*, 15 J. Energy & Nat. Res. L. 387 (1997).
131. A good list of possible offenses and some guidance on avoiding problems is to be found in Bruce Zagaris, *Avoiding Criminal Liability in the Conduct of International Business*, 21 Wm. Mitchell L. Rev. 749 (1996).
132. For a great discussion of some of the early issues of integration, *see*, e.g., Amy Deen & David A. Westbrook, *Return to Europe: Integrating Eastern European Economies into the European Market Through Alliance with the European Community*, 31 Harv. Int'l L.J. 660 (1990).

Some countries have moved toward regional trade initiatives. The United States, Canada, and Mexico ratified the NAFTA in 1993. Some optimists believe that a hemisphere-wide FTA may emerge in the next several years. Regional trade groupings, such as MERCOSUR in South America and the Association of Southeast Asian Nations (ASEAN) group of nations in the Pacific Rim are worthy of attention and concern.[133] Most of the world watches as fifteen European countries try to forge a true Union with a single currency by the end of the century.[134]

§3.7.1 Trade with the EU

Dreamers such as Jean Monnet talked of a politically and economically unified Europe well before World War Two; but it took the destruction and chaos of that war to stimulate realistic plans for integration. In 1951 a number of European nations signed the Treaty of Paris creating the European Coal and Steel Community (ECSC) to help the countries cope with substantial shortages of both commodities caused by the devastation of the war. The ECSC worked so well that by 1957 six nations (Belgium, The Netherlands, Luxembourg, West Germany, Italy, and France) signed the two Treaties of Rome, establishing the European Economic Community (EEC) and the European Atomic Energy Community.[135] Over the last few years of the twentieth century and the first few years of the twenty-first, the membership of the EU has exploded, now consisting of twenty-seven nations with an additional three "candidate" nations.[136] The Union now stretches the length and breadth of Europe, both east and west.

In 1986, the European Community (EC) members signed the Single European Act—a statute that merges the three original treaties, sets out certain objectives of the

133. *See*, e.g., Samuel A. Arieti, *The Role of MERCOSUR as a Vehicle for Latin American Integration*, 6 Chi. J. Int'l L. 761 (2006); Rafael A. Porrata-Doria, *MERCOSUR: The Common Market of the Twenty-First Century?* 32 Ga. J. Int'l & Comp. L. 1 (2004). For a perspective on Pacific Rim trade integration *see*, Alyssa Greenwald, *The ASEAN-China Free Trade Area: A Legal Response to China's Economic Rise?* 16 Duke J. Comp. & Int'l L. 193 (2006); Thomas C. Fischer, *A Commentary on Regional Institutions in the Pacific Rim: Do APEC and ASEAN Still Matter?* 13 Duke J. Comp. & Int'l L. 337 (2003).

134. For a comprehensive description of the EU, *see*, the Union's website: http://europa.eu. For book-length treatment, *see*, John Mccormick, *Understanding the European Union: a Concise Introduction* (2011); Roy H. Ginsberg, *Demystifying the European Union: The Enduring Logic of Regional Integration* (2007); Dick Leonard, *Guide to the European Union* (9th ed., 2005); John Mccormick, *Understanding the European Union: A Concise Introduction* (3d ed., 2005). *See also*, Symposium, *Narrowing the Gap? Law and New Approaches to Governance in the European Union*, 13 Colum. J. Eur. 513 (2007). For a broad discussion of many EU issues relevant to the topics in this book *see*: Thomas C. Fischer, *The United States, the European Union, and the "Globalization" of World Trade: Allies Or Adversaries* (2000); *The Need for a European Contract Law: Empirical and Legal Perspectives* (Jan M. Smits ed., 2005) and Jan M. Smits, *Law Making in the European Union: On Globalization and Contract Law in Divergent Legal Cultures*, 67 La. L. Rev. 1181 (2007).

135. The EEC Treaty is 298 U.N.T.S. 11 (March 25, 1957).

136. Current members (as of late 2017) are: Austria, Belgium, Bulgaria, Croatia, Cyprus, Czech Republic, Denmark, Estonia, Finland, France, Germany, Greece, Hungary, Ireland, Italy, Latvia, Lithuania, Luxembourg, Malta, Netherlands, Poland, Portugal, Romania, Slovakia, Slovenia, Spain, Sweden, and the United Kingdom. In 2016 the United Kingdom voted to leave the EU. The U.K.'s departure to be completed no later than 2019 is discussed below.

EC and provides, most strikingly, for the economic and monetary integration of the entire Community. The notion of a single economic union was embodied in the Treaty of Maastricht in 1992. Ensuring certain human and political rights as well as further implementing the concept of union is the function of the draft Treaty of Amsterdam, whose components were worked out in 1997.[137] When fully accomplished, the economic integration of Europe will result in the creation of a single multi-trillion dollar market consisting of more than 400 million persons. Among the member countries, the Union hopes to achieve virtually barrier-free movement of goods, services, people, and capital.[138]

At the same time, integration has not been a seamless process. In 1990, the European Commission identified a sizable number of impediments to full integration (particularly on the matter of a common agricultural policy and the movement of services and professionals across national boundaries).[139] Germany has encountered many difficulties in integrating the eastern portion of Germany. The integration of the countries of central Europe and some of the former Soviet republics have proved challenging to say the least. In hindsight, the goal of having all the work of integration completed by 1993 was never met and was probably unrealistic to begin with.[140]

The EU consists of three governing bodies, the European Parliament that holds its plenary sessions in Strasbourg, France, the European Commission (located in Brussels) the body that functions as the executive branch of the EU and the European Court of Justice, the high court of the Union.[141] In addition the EU's Council of Ministers meets periodically in order to develop policy for the EU at the highest level of the Union.

[1] The Council of Ministers

The Council of Ministers is comprised of the Heads of State or Heads of Government of each of the Member States. The Council meets at least three times each year either in Brussels or in the capital of the Member State that holds the Council's presidency (the presidency is a six-month term i.e., rotated among Member States). The Council is the highest political body within the EU. Its power is reflected in the fact that its pronouncements do not have to be ratified by the parliaments of the Member States. It

137. *See*, the Single European Act, February 28, 1986, 30 Official Journal European Community (No. L 169) 1 (1987). The three candidate members as of mid-2008 are Croatia, Macedonia, and Turkey.
138. One of the best recent articles on many issues confronting the EU is John P. Flaherty & Maureen E. Lally-Green, *The European Union: Where Is It Now?* 34 Duq. L. Rev. 923 (1996).
139. *See*, e.g., EC Commission, *Fifth Report Concerning the Completion of the Internal Market* (March 1990).
140. There is always some delay in bringing new members in. Two of the additions, Spain and Portugal, took several years for full integration. *See*, e.g., Spanish-Portuguese Accession Treaty, June 12, 1985, 28 O.J. Eur. Comm. (No. L 302) 9 (1985). *See also*, Karl M. Meessen, *Europe en Route to 1992: The Completion of the Internal Market and Its Impact on Non-Europeans*, 23 Int'l Law. 359 (1989); Symposium, *1992: Doing Business in the European Internal Market*, 9 Nw. J. Int'l L. & Bus. 463 (1989).
141. A single commission and a single council were established by what is referred to as the Merger Treaty signed in Brussels in 1965 with an effective date of July 1, 1967. O.J. Eur. Comm. (No. L-152) 2 (1967).

is charged with the task of establishing what might be called the highest law of the Union. Voting on various pronouncements by the Council is taken on the basis of a simple majority, a qualified majority (a complicated methodology for counting votes set out in the Treaty of Rome)[142] and unanimity. Most of the truly monumental pronouncements by the Council have been taken on the basis of unanimous votes. In the past, that has frequently led to a kind of legislative paralysis. However, the Single European Act extends majority voting to certain decisions in the areas of: (i) the completion of the single market; (ii) research and technology; (iii) regional policy formation; and (iv) improvement of the working environment.[143]

The legislation of the Union is set out in a hierarchy of pronouncements as established by Article 189 of the Treaty of Rome.[144] These include:

(1) *Regulations*: these are directly applicable and binding on Member States without the need for enactment of any implementing legislation at the national level by the Member States.
(2) *Directives*: these are binding on the members states in terms of the result commanded by the directive, but each Member State is free to work out its own method of compliance.
(3) *Decisions*: these are pronouncement that can be issued directly to companies and individuals as well as to Member States. They are normally derived from the subject matter of regulations and directives.
(4) *Recommendations and Opinions*: These are, as the terms connote, not binding but rather are exhortations or admonitions that are intended to promote certain practices and activities within the EU without having the force and effect of law.

[2] The European Parliament

The Parliament is comprised of members (currently 518) elected by direct suffrage from within each Member State on the basis of a specific country-by-country apportionment. For example, France, Germany, Italy and the United Kingdom have eighty-one members each while Ireland has fifteen and Luxembourg six. The members of the Parliament sit within the Parliament on the basis of political affiliation rather than national identity. Their loyalty is expected to be to their constituency, rather than to the government of the country from which they come. Because of the structure of the remainder of the EU, the Parliament sits in what is regarded as an essentially consultative role—providing advice on legislation and the EU's budget. The true power of the EU emanates from the Council and filters through the Commission.

142. For a qualified majority, fifty-four votes out of seventy-six are required. Germany, France, Italy and the United Kingdom have ten votes each; Spain has eight votes; Belgium, Greece, the Netherlands, and Portugal have five votes each; Denmark and Ireland have three votes each; and Luxembourg has two votes. EC, *The Institutions of the European Community* 7 (1990).
143. *Id.*
144. A similar discussion is set out in Terry R. Broderick & Arnold B. Calmann, *Introduction to a New Europe: A Primer for 1992*, 20 Int'l Bus. Law. 9 (1992).

[3] The Commission

The European Commission has its headquarters in Brussels and currently consists of 17 members appointed for four-year terms. The Commission is essentially the executive secretariat for the EU. Its members are not permitted to take instruction from their national governments. It performs essentially two tasks: (1) it may propose initiatives to the Council; and (2) it carries out the various promulgations of the Council. It can bring cases in the Court of Justice in the name of the Union, if it believes that any pronouncements have not been complied with. More specifically, under Article 155 of the EEC Treaty it has the following responsibilities:

(1) to monitor and insure compliance with the application of the various treaty provisions and Council initiatives;
(2) to provide recommendations or opinions on matters within the cognizance of the various treaties;
(3) to participate in the preparation of the acts of the Council of Ministers and the European Parliament; and
(4) to implement the pronouncements of the Council.

To use a U.S. analogy, the Commission is the executive branch of the EU and exercises most of the day-to-day functions of the Union.

[4] The Court of Justice

The European Court of Justice at this writing consists of thirteen judges and six advocates-general. Both the judges and advocates-general are appointed for six-year terms with the consent of the Member States. Under various articles of the Treaty of Rome, the Court is empowered to quash, at the request of any EU institution, national government or individual, any measure issued by either the Council, Commission or any national government that is incompatible with the various treaties. In addition, in certain circumstances, the Court is empowered to issue interpretations and preliminary rulings on various points of Union law at the request of a national court.[145]

The Single European Act also created a Court of First Instance that functions as a lower echelon of the Court of Justice. The Court of First Instance took its first cases in October 1989. Persons who come before the Court of First Instance have a right of appeal as to the law to the Court of Justice. Its primary subject-matter jurisdiction concerns the Union's competition rules and certain claims for damage brought by private parties under the treaties.[146]

Everyone interested in world trade eagerly awaits the development of the single market. Perhaps of primary concern to persons outside the Union is the question of

---

145. For a much more comprehensive statement of the European Court *see*, Trevor C. Hartley, *The Foundations of European Community Law* (3d ed., 1994).
146. *See*, e.g., Timothy Millett, *The New European Court of First Instance*, 38 Int'l & Comp. L. Q. 811 (1989).

whether the single market will produce what has been referred to as a "Fortress Europe." Most insiders debunk that particular fear. For example, an EU Commission vice president has stated: "The achievement of the Internal Market will be of economic benefit not only to Union citizens, but also to the world economy as a whole. ... Both Union producers and foreign exporters will benefit directly from operating in an Internal Market with a generally uniform set of regulations, standards, testing, and certification procedures. They will no longer have to face twelve divergent sets of requirements, nor intra-Union border controls."[147]

[5] Brexit

As this edition goes to press in late 2017, the United Kingdom is working on its withdrawal from the EU, a process colloquially referred to as *Brexit*. It is far too early to make grand pronouncements about this event. It will certainly not destroy the EU but it may well severely weaken the institution. The impact on the U.K. is uncertain, but most commentators believe the departure will require the creation of certain trade barriers and other measures between the U.K. and the remaining EU members. Some background may be helpful.

On June 23, 2016, the United Kingdom held a referendum on its membership in the EU. On a close vote (and with the British government opposed to leaving the EU) approximately 52% of the British electorate chose to leave. As of this writing, full implementation of the U.K.'s departure from the EU should be effected as of early 2019.

This is such an important event for the world economy that some speculation is probably necessary. To begin with, it should not have a major impact on the central thrust of this book—the drafting and negotiation of commercial contracts between private-sector business entities. In other words, contracts will likely look much the same whether or not Brexit is concluded. But as many people like to say: "The devil may be in the details." A great deal of the uncertainty is due to the fact that the U.K. referendum was essentially a "yes" or "no" vote with nothing more in terms of guidance on the exit. It is clear that Brexit will affect:

(1) the financial liabilities of the U.K. with regard to the EU;
(2) the status of EU citizens living in the U.K. and British subjects living in Europe;
(3) the economic framework between the two entities following Brexit.

An economist from the United States has speculated that the economic framework would evolve under three possible scenarios:

(a) "[T]he United Kingdom could remain part of the European Union's Single Market by joining Norway, Iceland and Liechtenstein in what is called the European Economic Area."

147. Martin Bangemann, *Fortress Europe: The Myth*, 9 Nw. J. Int'l L. & Bus. 480 (1989).

(b) "[T]he UK and EU could sign a free trade agreement to govern their trade and economic relations."

(c) "If no alternative agreement is reached, the UK and the EU would trade under the most-favored nation terms available to all World Trade Organization member."[148]

There is not much more that can be said at this point.

§3.7.2 The NAFTA

Free trade in the Americas has been an often elusive concept; but in the past thirty years major strides, at least in North America, have been made toward its achievement. Canada and the United States had always had a robust trading arrangement, but in a striking development on March 17, 1985, Saint Patrick's Day, two national leaders of Irish descent, President Brian Mulroney of Canada and President Ronald Reagan shook hands on one of the most important FTAs in the history of international trade, the USCFTA.[149] Reporters sometimes referred to the accord as the "Shamrock Agreement." Its importance, however, goes much farther than mere lip service to Irish traditions. It was in many respects the most ambitious bilateral trade agreement ever completed. The USCFTA envisioned a common market between two of the richest nations on earth, including innovative dispute resolution mechanisms and the gradual erosion of all tariff barriers between the two countries. But even before the USCFTA was fully implemented, the United States, Canada and Mexico negotiated and ratified the even more striking NAFTA or the "Agreement."[150]

NAFTA comprises twenty separate chapters in the main agreement supplement by a substantial number of annexes and two side agreements (on environmental

148. Thomas Sampson, *Brexit: The Economics of International Disintegration*, 31 J. of Econ. Persps. 163, 165 (2017). For a short monograph on the topic of Brexit *see* Philip B. Whyman & Alina I. Petrescu, *The Economics of Brexit: A Cost-Benefit Analysis of the UK's Economic Relationship with the EU* (2017).

149. The treaty is set out at 27 I.L.M. 281 (1988). Implementing legislation in the United States is contained in Pub. L. No. 100-449, 102 Stat. 1851 (1988). Some of the earlier discussion on this topic is taken from William Fox, *The Canada-United States Free Trade Agreement: Implications for Latin America*, a paper delivered to the 27th Conference of the Inter-American Bar Association, Cartagena, Colombia (May 8, 1989). *See also*, J. Johnson & J. Schachter, *The Free Trade Agreement: a Comprehensive Guide* (1988); Kazanjian & Craig, *The Canada-United States Free Trade Agreement*, 16 Int'l Bus. L. 112 (1988).

150. There is a significant body of NAFTA literature. Some representative writings are Michael J. Boskin, NAFTA at 20: The North American Free Trade Agreement's Achievements and Challenges (2014); M. Angeles Intl. Bus. Publications, *NAFTA Handbook: Framework, Implementations, Problems* (2d ed., 2006); Gary Clyde Hufbauer, Jeffrey L. Schott & Paul L.E. Greco, *NAFTA Revisited: Achievements and Challenges* (2005); Sidney Weintraub, *NAFTA's Impact on North America: The First Decade* (2004); Judith Bello, Alan F. Homer & Joseph J. Norton, *NAFTA: A New Frontier in International Trade and Investment in the Americas* (1994). Another distinguished writing that integrates a NAFTA discussion with the World Trade Organization mechanisms is Frederick M. Abbott, *Law and Policy of Regional Integration: The NAFTA and Western Hemispheric Integration in the World Trade Organization System* (1997). *See also*, *Symposium on NAFTA*, 14 Ariz. J. Int'l & Comp. L. 305 (1997).

protection and labor) that are as important as any of the express treaty language. The NAFTA's stated objectives, embodied in the Preamble, and paraphrased here, are both comprehensive and ambitious:

The NAFTA countries commit to:

- strengthen the special bonds of friendship and cooperation between the nations;
- contribute to the harmonious development of world trade;
- create an expanded and secure market in the North Americas;
- reduce distortions to trade and to establish clear trade rules that enhance trade in both goods and services;
- create new employment opportunities and improve working conditions;
- promote sustainable development;
- enhance the development and enforcement of environmental laws and the protection of workers' rights.[151]

NAFTA is most easily understood in terms of its major components: (1) the elimination of tariffs on goods; (2) the rules of national origin; (3) the diminishing of barriers to trade in various services and professional activities; and (4) a number of special dispute resolution mechanisms.

[1] Elimination of Tariffs on Goods

The USCFTA purported to eliminate virtually all tariff barriers between the U.S. and Canada. NAFTA seeks to accomplish virtually the same thing, over time, between the three signatory countries. Indeed, NAFTA includes the scheduled tariff removals originally set out in the USCFTA. Some products, including roughly half of the industrial products shipped by the U.S. to Mexico are on what NAFTA calls the "A List" and were eliminated upon ratification. Certain products on the so-called B List are given five-year treatment; and the final ten-year phaseout is reserved for items on the "C List." Most tariffs on goods whose origins are in North America should be eliminated by 2003; and all tariffs are scheduled for elimination by 2008. These eliminations are to be gradually accomplished by a four phase series of reductions and eliminations that began shortly after ratification.[152]

There are some special categories that are fascinating, but understandable exceptions to the general thrust of eliminating tariff barriers. For example, U.S. exports of beans and corn have a fifteen-year phaseout, rather than the ten-year elimination period. Likewise, Mexico exports to the U.S. of orange juice, peanuts, and sugar are given a fifteen-year period of transition.[153]

151. NAFTA's full text may be found at 32 I.L.M. 296 (1993).
152. NAFTA, Art. 302 and related annexes.
153. NAFTA, Ch. 3(B).

[2] The Rules of Origin

One of the primary concerns of the negotiators of the FTA was to insure that only goods actually produced in the three countries receive the special protections of the agreement. So a table saw manufactured in Taiwan that is shipped through Mexico City on its way to a Baltimore, Maryland purchaser is not supposed to get any protection under NAFTA. As a consequence, the agreement's rules of origin are crucial to a proper understanding of NAFTA and are somewhat different from the rules of origin in the GATT. Under the NAFTA, goods that are produced exclusively in either country are fully covered. If a good is partially the product of some other country, a complicated formula involving customs classifications and the notion of value added is applied to determine the origin of the goods. Generally, products will qualify for a waiver of the NAFTA rules if the nonregional (i.e., from outside Canada, Mexico, or the U.S.) content of the good is no greater than 7% of the total price of the good.[154] Automobiles are subject to some special rules. Automobiles and light trucks must have a North American content of 62.50%.

The concept of *regional value* is a complicated one. The value is to be calculated on the basis of either a *transactional value* or a *net cost* formula.[155] Net cost is defined in part as the total cost of a good less royalties, sales promotion costs (such as advertising), packing, shipping, and allowable interest. The formula for transactional value includes the concept of value of the good adjusted on an F.O.B. basis. Once again, there are special rules for certain energy and petrochemical products.[156]

[3] Trade in Services

One of the most important innovations of the USCFTA was the mechanism for freeing trade in services. Much of this innovation is preserved under NAFTA. For example, all trade in services that cross the borders of the NAFTA region are subject to the Agreement's *national treatment* rules. This means that persons from outside the host country who seek to sell services must be given no less favorable treatment than that offered similarly situated professionals in the host country itself.[157] There is an express prohibition in the Agreement forbidding the host country to require that a person selling services establish or maintain a residence, local office or branch in the host country. But as with most aspects of NAFTA there are many complications. For professional services the most complicated factor is host-country licensing requirements. NAFTA, after two years, eliminates any citizenship or permanent residency requirements for licensed professionals, but only encourages mutual recognition of professional licenses.

In a major departure from the earlier USCFTA (where services were covered by the agreement only if expressly listed in the treaty), NAFTA has taken what is called the

154. NAFTA, Art. 401.
155. NAFTA, Art. 402.
156. NAFTA, Ch. 6.
157. NAFTA, Ch. 12.

"negative listing" approach to the types of services that are covered. Under NAFTA all services are covered unless the NAFTA expressly provides otherwise. So, among lots of other categories, the types of services given NAFTA treatment include: accounting, advertising, architecture, broadcasting, commercial education, construction, consulting, enhanced telecommunications, engineering, environmental science, health care, land transport, legal, publishing and tourism.

[4] The Dispute Resolution Mechanisms

The NAFTA negotiators, much like their USCFTA predecessors, recognized immediately that treaty language is destined to cause problems and raise issues that could not be resolved merely by reviewing the document's language. Continuing on the model of the USCFTA, NAFTA has implemented for the highest levels of the treaty, a trilateral Trade Commission, to be supported by a Secretariat, that would provide treaty oversight. In addition, intergovernmental committees dealing with specific topics such as competition policy will continue to deal with these issues, although the committees are expected to work by consensus with unresolved issued forwarded to the Trade Commission.[158] Certain topical areas are subject to special dispute resolution mechanisms: investment, dumping and subsidy, financial services, environmental, and standards.

The general NAFTA dispute resolution procedure is not terribly complicated. When a particular country believes its rights have been adversely affected by some occurrence under NAFTA, it may invoke its right of *consultation*. The consultations are essentially informal, negotiation-style mechanisms. If the consultation does not produce the desired effect, the country bringing the complaint may convene a meeting of the Trade Commission. If the Trade Commission's work does not produce a resolution, the complaining party may then seek resolution through either the dispute mechanisms of the World Trade Organization or a special panel convened under NAFTA.

The NAFTA panel procedures are essentially a form of arbitration by which a dispute is presented to a panel of five arbitrators (taken from a roster prepared by the Trade Commission and agreed upon by all three countries). The chair is designated first, either by agreement of the disputing parties or by one of the parties which becomes the *selecting* party by casting lots. The chair must be a citizen of one of the NAFTA countries but *not* a citizen of the country that is the selecting party. Each contending party then selects two more panel members who must be citizens of the country on the other side of the dispute.

The panel hears the dispute, renders its decision and, under normal expectations, the losing party simply complies. If the losing party is still aggrieved, the party that is the complainant at this stage may suspend equivalent benefits under NAFTA in

158. NAFTA, Ch. 21.

retaliation. If the country being retaliated against believes that the retaliation is excessive, it may resort to the panel hearing process to test the legitimacy of the retaliation.[159]

[5] Other Aspects of the Agreement

Most readers will recall that NAFTA was not lacking in controversy. Perhaps the most heated discussions surrounded the twin issues of environmental protection and labor rights. Rather than scrap the treaty itself, the NAFTA negotiators developed two crucial side agreements for these two issues that commit each signatory country to developing trilateral commissions to monitor environmental and labor standards in each of the three countries. These side bar agreements, like NAFTA itself, contain a dispute resolution mechanism that is much like the basic panel process in the treaty.

There is no question that the agreement is a monumental one. It may prove to be a model for other agreements, not just in the Western Hemisphere but around the world. NAFTA is unquestionably a powerful economic entity, although it has been subject to recent criticisms by then-candidate and later President Barack H. Obama. But President Obama did not repeal NAFTA and many of the criticisms offered during his administration merely barked at the Agreement's heels. Mexico is now the United State's number three trading partner (after Canada)—one benefit of NAFTA. If NAFTA leads to a comprehensive Western Hemisphere FTA, the consequences will be even more telling.

[6] The Election of President Donald Trump

In early November, 2016 the American electorate voted in favor of Donald Trump to be the forty-fifth president of the United States. Mr. Trump took office in January 2017. He had campaigned for the office on a tragic conglomeration of racist and ethnic comments, many of which were directed to Mexico. The comments ranged from calling people rapists and murderers to demanding and committing to building an actual physical wall between Mexico and the United States. Interestingly, he did not direct similar comments towards Canada. As a part of these diatribes, Mr. Trump promised to do away completely with NAFTA.

As this edition goes to press in late 2017, it remains to be seen what will happen to NAFTA. It could be that the United States will simply withdraw from the treaty. It may be that the United States has sufficient negotiation leverage as compared with Canada and Mexico to force significant changes in the treaty.

Currently, the announced position of the United States government as of November, 2017 comprises, among many other things, the following:[160]

159. NAFTA, Ch. 20.
160. Office of the United States Trade Representative (Executive Office of the President), Summary of Objectives for the NAFTA Renegotiation (November, 2017). The full text of the objectives may be found at www.ustr.gov.

- to improve the U.S. trade balance and reduce its trade deficit with the NAFTA countries;
- to increase transparency in import and export licensing procedures;
- to discipline import and export monopolies to prevent trade distortions;
- to update and strengthen the rules of origin, as necessary to ensure that the benefits of NAFTA go to products genuinely made in the United States and North America;
- to secure commitments not to impose customs duties on digital products (e.g., software, music, video, e-books);
- to ensure that NAFTA investors in the United States are not accorded greater substantive rights than domestic investors;
- to bring the labor provisions in to the core of the Agreement rather than in a side agreement;
- to bring the environmental provisions into the core of the Agreement rather than in a side agreement;
- to secure provisions committing each Party to criminalize government corruption;
- to increase opportunities for U.S. firms to sell U.S. products and services into the NAFTA countries.

These are only a few of a long list of proposals for further negotiation. One striking thing, however, is that nothing in this language suggests abandoning the treaty itself, although the U.S. trade representative has hinted that if the U.S. does not get its way on these proposals, the U.S. will leave NAFTA. We will simply have to await further developments.

§3.7.3 The Trans-Pacific Partnership

For several years, the United States along with eleven other countries worked diligently to create a new trade framework for the Pacific region. It was envisioned as a groundbreaking trade agreement that would create a strong counterweight to the rapidly increasing power of China. The participating countries are the United States, Australia, Brunei, Canada, Chile, Japan, Malaysia, Mexico, New Zealand, Peru, Singapore, and Vietnam. The agreement grew out of an earlier, rudimentary agreement (the Trans-Pacific Strategic Economic Partnership) between Brunei, Chile, New Zealand, and Singapore, signed in 2005.

The TPP's goals are striking:

- to lower both nontariff and tariff barriers (cutting over 18,000 tariffs);
- to create an investor-state dispute resolution mechanism;
- to create a robust environmental protection mechanism, including protections for endangered species, illegal logging and illegal fishing;
- to combat bribery and corruption by requiring all members to join the United Nations Convention Against Corruption;

- to prohibit child and forced labor and to eliminate barriers to trade unions and collective bargaining;
- to develop strong standards for the protection of intellectual property.[161]

During his presidential campaign, Donald Trump spent a great deal of time attacking the "evil" TPP, largely without he himself having even an inkling of what is in it. He promised to take the United States out of the agreement. On January 23, 2017 President Trump signed a presidential memorandum withdrawing the United States from further participation. The other TPP nations have committed to continuing to implement the agreement even in the absence of the United States.[162] On January 23, 2018, Australia, Brunei, Canada, Chile, Japan, Malaysia, Mexico, New Zealand, Peru, Singapore, and Vietnam announced an agreement on a "Comprehensive and Progressive Agreement for Trans-Pacific Partnership." The agreement is expected to be signed in March 2018.[163]

161. A full-text English language version of the TPP may be found on the Australian website: dfat.gov.au/agreements/TPP.
162. *See*, e.g., Alex Ward, *The Trans-Pacific Partnership Has Been Resurrected—and It's Happening Without the United States*, www.vox.com/November 11, 2017.
163. *See* the text of Canada's announcement, www.international.gc.ca.

CHAPTER 4

Drafting International Commercial Agreements

§4.1 INTRODUCTION

Most lawyers talk in terms of "negotiating and drafting" of contracts, suggesting that negotiation always precedes the actual drafting of contract language. That is not necessarily a realistic way to view the process, although in most cases negotiation and drafting go hand in hand. Many agreements are based on standard form contracts that one or the other party has drafted long in advance of the actual transaction. In other cases, negotiation of the agreement's provisions takes place after one party submits a draft agreement to the other party for consideration. There are still other cases in which a letter of intent—a document that has many of the attributes of a contract without necessarily being a binding instrument—is the first meaningful communication between the parties. There are many instances in which an exchange of documents precedes face-to-face negotiation. Submitting a preliminary document such as a draft contract or letter of intent may itself be a powerful negotiating tactic in the same sense that a great deal of power (sometimes referred to as "leverage") accrues to the person who sets the agenda for a meeting. As a consequence, it is frequently more logical to think about what you would like your version of the contract to say, and then to see what occurs during the negotiating sessions.

Often the party who proffers the first draft will carry the day on many of the points of the transaction simply by having been first to suggest written language. Even if the contract is substantially redrafted during the negotiation process, the party who has thought about the wording of various provisions and who has at least tried to put some words on paper before the meeting frequently develops a great deal of negotiation leverage when alternative provisions are discussed and drafted.

For all these reasons, this chapter discusses contract drafting and Chapter 5 takes up negotiating techniques and strategy. There is nothing wrong, however, with a reader beginning with Chapter 5 if he or she does not agree with this analysis. Contract drafting and contract negotiation go together—to use a favorite American expression—like ham and eggs.

§4.2 SOME THRESHOLD CONSIDERATIONS

There are probably as many theories on how to draft contracts as there are drafters of contracts. Anyone who has tried to write anything from a personal letter to a short story to a legal document has a store of pet language, a list of "do's" and "don'ts" and various rules of thumb for everything from the length of sentences to the alignment of paragraphs. If there is any principle that cuts through all these individualized techniques and idiosyncrasies, it is simply this: language is communication, or put a bit more realistically, the use of language is an attempt by two or more persons to communicate with each other.[1] At bottom, any drafting exercise is largely a matter of taking what is in one person's mind and putting that information on paper in a sufficiently precise form to convey that same information into the mind of the other party. But as everyone recognizes, this is easier said than done.

Is writing something that most people do naturally? Is it something that can only be left to the specialists? Are lawyers necessarily the best judge of contract language? The answer to all three of these questions is either "no" or, since lawyers always hedge their bets, "probably not." Is it possible even to discuss contract drafting generally?

1. No American law professor writing about legal drafting can ignore the contributions of probably the foremost scholar in the area, the late Professor F. Reed Dickerson; *see*, e.g., F. Reed Dickerson, *Materials on Legal Drafting* (1981) and his classic treatise on the subject, F. Reed Dickerson, *The Fundamentals of Legal Drafting* (1965). One of the best statements of a growing development in U.S. legal circles known as the Plain English movement is Carl Felsenfeld & Alan Siegel, *Writing Contracts in Plain English* (1981). More recent works that may be profitably consulted are: Kenneth A. Adams, *A Manual of Style for Contract Drafting* (3d ed., 2013); Bryan A. Garner, *Garner's Modern English Usage (2016) and* Bryan A. Garner, *The Elements of Legal Style* (2d ed., 2002); Marcel Fontaine & Filip De Ly, *Drafting International Contracts: An Analysis of Contract Clauses* (2d ed., 2009); Fabio Bortolotti, *Drafting and Negotiating International Commercial Contracts* (2008);Peter Butt & Richard Castle, *Modern Legal Drafting: A Guide to Using Clearer Language* (2006); Edward W. Daigneault, *Drafting International Agreements in Legal English* (2005); A very healthy article on lawyer's passion for absolute precision is Vincent A. Wellman, *The Unfortunate Quest for Magic in Contract Drafting*, 52 Wayne L. Rev. 1101 (2006). For a creative but cautionary approach to international business contracts *see*, Larry DiMatteo, *An International Contract Law Formula: The Informality of International Business Transactions Plus the Internationalization of Contract Law Equals Unexpected Contract Liability*, 23 Syracuse J. Int'l L. & Com. 67 (1997). There are many law journal articles devoted to specific categories of international contracts. *See*, e.g., Karla C. Shippey, *International Contracts: Drafting the International Sales Contract* (2009); James M. Klotz, *International Sales Agreements: An Annotated Drafting and Negotiating Guide* (2d ed., 2008); Mark S. Walter & Harry M. Flechtner, *Drafting Contracts Under the CISG*, (2007); Dena H. Elkhatib, *The ABA Practical Guide to Drafting Basic Islamic Finance Contracts* (2013); Some representative articles include: Klaus Peter Berger, *Renegotiation and Adaptation of International Investment Contracts: The Role of Contract Drafters and Arbitrators*, 36 Vand. J. Transnat'l L. 1347 (2003); John C. Grabow, *Negotiating and Drafting Contracts in International Barter and Countertrade Transactions*, 9 N.C.J. Int'l L. & Com. Reg. 255 (1984); Craig A. Jaslow, *Practical Considerations in Drafting a Joint Venture Agreement with China*, 31 Am. J. Comp. L. 209 (1983); S. John Byington, *Planning & Drafting of International Licensing Agreements*, 6 N.C.J.Int'l L. & Com. Reg. 193 (1982).

This author's firm belief is that it can be discussed and that the best contracts are drafted by people who take some time to review basic concepts of drafting before committing themselves to paper.

If the normal goal of writing is to communicate, the specific goal of a contract is to express the agreement between the parties as clearly and as fully as possible so that there is little need to go beyond the document if later misunderstandings arise between the parties. Recall the twin principles of basic contract law: the parties are generally free to frame whatever agreement they choose (*party autonomy*) and once having agreed, they will be held to the terms of that agreement (*pacta sunt servanda*).[2]

One of the basic dilemmas of contract drafting is that all forms of human communication are subject to misunderstandings and misinterpretation. It is virtually impossible to put anything on paper that is totally free of ambiguity. Even so, a writer can strive for clarity and precision even if no document drafted by mere mortals is going to be perfect.

In diagram form, *see* Figure 4.1, the task of a contract drafter can be viewed as a series of communication steps.

Figure 4.1 Communication in Contract Drafting

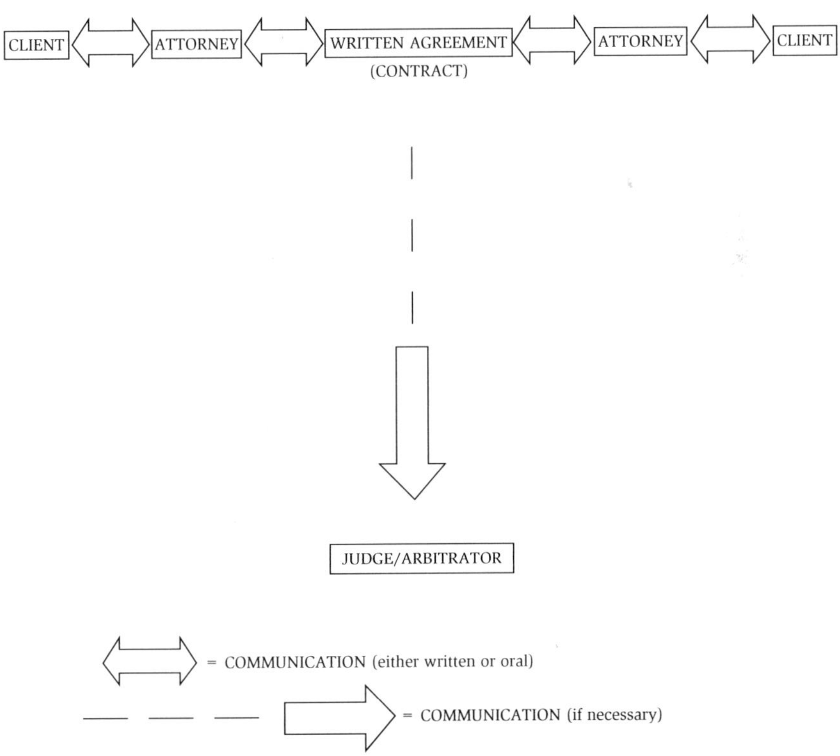

2. *See*, e.g., Maya Mandery, *Party Autonomy in Contractual and Non-Contractual Obligations* (2014).

To begin with, the client must have some sense of what he wants to do. It may be an idea as simple as wanting to market her telescopes in another country without any good sense of how to go about the transaction. By contrast, a contract drafter may encounter a sophisticated client who has a complete understanding of the transaction and simply needs someone to put the words on paper. Whether the client is an experienced business executive or a neophyte, it is vital that the drafter have a solid idea of what the client hopes to accomplish. For this reason, the client/drafter communication must flow *both* ways to be truly effective. For all the same reasons, the party on the other side of the transaction must be dealt with in a similar fashion.

The diagram assumes that it is a lawyer who will serve as contract drafter although the author recognizes that in many countries lawyers are not commonly brought into the transaction at the drafting stage.

Once the two parties and their lawyers have a sense of what each of them hopes to accomplish, the communication then takes place between the two parties, usually in the form of negotiation. That communication can take place in many forms (e-mail, telephone, facsimile, face-to-face) but it is once again vital that virtually everything in the heads of people on one side of the transaction get into the heads of the people on the other side. The communication that takes place during the negotiation must then be transferred to paper so that the written document may be reviewed and eventually signed by the parties.

But a drafter cannot rest on his or her laurels at that point. Too many contract drafters forget that they are not writing merely for the parties. They are, in truth, writing for a possible third-party—that is, an arbitrator or judge who may have to examine the document, decide what the document means, and render a decision on a dispute that arises at some point in the transaction. A good contract drafter always acknowledges the ghostly presence of that judge or arbitrator who was not present at the creation, who may be reading the document years after the agreement was signed, but who must try to understand what the parties were getting at when they first put words to paper.

§4.2.1 Identifying Goals and Objectives

The first step toward clarity and precision is identifying the goals and objectives of the client. There must be a common denominator of understanding between people on the same side of the transaction to create a good document. In many cases, this is very hard work, particularly if the client and the drafter are working together for the first time. A lawyer working with new clients is well advised to spend a substantial amount of time in discussions with that client to make absolutely certain that there is a meeting of the minds between lawyer and client. To make sure that important things are not forgotten, even experienced lawyers often resort to contract drafting outlines and checklists. Checklists of important elements may seem a tool only for beginners, but they can help insure that the final writing covers all of the important components in the transaction.

Most people in business have a good idea of what they want to accomplish from a business standpoint. Understanding the fundamental nature of the transaction in question is the first place to start. A contract's aim may be to sell 20,000 brass fittings on a one-time basis to an Argentine retailer, or to commence a multi-million dollar turnkey construction project in Pakistan. If the drafter is a business executive drafting her own contract, it is likely that she will have a fairly good grasp of the contract's basic goals. Outside the United States, some business executives draft their own contracts. But many business executives will stop at the conception stage and then turn the remainder of the transaction over to the lawyers for the drafting work. Obviously, a lawyer's job is to try and accommodate the wishes of the client. A favorite client of the author's nicely expressed this concept when he said: "I don't want you to tell me no; I want you to tell me how."

Most clients remain involved far longer than the initial consultation with the lawyer and, in any event, American lawyers have an ethical obligation to zealously represent their clients within the bounds of the law.[3] This means that a lawyer engaged in drafting a contract for a client cannot be satisfied with merely learning the client's basic short-term goals. The client may have objectives beyond the specific business deal at hand that will affect the manner in which the contract is drafted and the tone and content of the negotiations. For example, the sale of the 20,000 brass fittings may be viewed by the seller as a pilot project with the additional goal of establishing a long-term business relationship with the buyer. This single fact might prompt the drafter of the contract to include more evenly balanced and conciliatory terms in the document—and to negotiate more gently—than might be the case if the transaction is merely incidental to the seller's domestic business and one in which the seller does not have any long term interests. In the latter case, a contract drafter representing the seller might emphasize speed and security of payment and might write language that makes it very difficult for the buyer to terminate the contract once it is executed.

If the seller regards the sale as merely a sideline and one in which the seller does not want to incur any great expense, the seller's lawyer may decide to rely more heavily on preprinted forms or clauses copied out of form books rather than create a completely new document. Whether lawyers admit it or not, this type of informal cost-benefit analysis (i.e., how much professional time and attention does this deal deserve?) always takes place in the mind of the lawyer, if not in conversations with the client.

But as the diagram shows, communication cannot run only from client to lawyer. The client will articulate both short-term and long-term goals; but it is normally up to the lawyer to identify both problems and opportunities. For example, novice business executives may not appreciate the importance of the parole evidence rule—a legal requirement that severely limits the amount of external evidence a court will consider in construing a contract. In Anglo-American legal systems, the document is supposed to stand or fall on its own terms and normally cannot be altered by oral understandings or extraneous documents.

Other legal systems are more accepting of materials and information outside the written document to evidence the transaction, but even in those systems, most contract

3. *See*, e.g., Canon 7, American Bar Association, Model Code of Professional Responsibility. The language is almost a verbatim quote from Canon 7. The more recent Model Rules of Professional Conduct express similar sentiments using a slightly different vocabulary.

drafters try to craft a writing that sets out all the important understandings of the parties even if certain matters such as equipment specifications or price lists are left to annexes or subsequent agreement.

There can be additional external consequences triggered by the document beyond the transaction itself. For example, certain language in the contract may initiate serious tax or antitrust problems for either buyer or seller. Business executives are not normally experts in these matters. It is a lawyer's job to alert the client to the dangers that arise in a legal context outside the scope of a particular agreement. Developing a sensitivity to *all* the consequences of a contract is frequently left to the lawyer.

A business deal can sometimes become far more complicated than the business executive may suspect when first setting up the transaction. For example, a novice business executive may not know that, in certain countries, it is nearly impossible to deal with retail establishments without going through wholesale entities. A national government may insist on the foreign company's forming a joint venture with some of its own citizens in order to conclude an agreement for a large-scale construction project in that country. These things need to be sorted out as early as possible. It is embarrassing and often professionally dangerous to learn something new about the deal, the client's wishes, or the state of the law only when sitting across from the other side in the final negotiating session. Proper planning and client counseling at the predrafting stage will substantially reduce the number of subsequent problems and surprises.

Remember, finally, that while the primary audience for any contract is the parties and lawyers who are involved in the transactions, there may be yet another set of important readers of the document whose identity is not even known when the contract is drafted. If some dispute arises in the course of the agreement, judges or arbitrators may be brought into the process, asked to read the document and ultimately to resolve the dispute based on what the document says and what the parties testify to. As lawyers and business executives work on their drafts, they should always give an over-the-shoulder glance at those persons who may eventually read and decide.

§4.2.2 Research as a Planning and Drafting Tool

Chapter 5 will constantly remind the reader that in business negotiations knowledge is power. It is axiomatic that the more knowledge negotiators have, the more leverage they will accrue in negotiating the deal. Without question, the more research that can be performed before negotiation, the better will be the negotiation. In many cases, the problem is not so much where to start but rather where to stop.

Business executives often perform a great deal of relevant research long before they focus on a specific transaction. Trade fairs and business publications convey a great deal of information on the climate for doing business in particular countries. Credit reporting services can quickly obtain information on the financial status and the creditworthiness of individual companies in many countries. In the United States, as in other countries, various government entities such as the Department of State, the Department of Commerce, the Export-Import Bank and the OPIC regularly collect and publish an enormous amount of information on international transactions and on targeted countries. Prior to entering into a contract, businesses frequently exchange information on themselves, especially if they do not have an existing relationship. This generic information can often enhance both the drafting and negotiating of individual transactions. These days the Internet is an enormous compendium of information (a lot accurate, some erroneous) that no competent drafter can ignore.

Proper interviewing and counseling of the client is vitally important. An understanding of the legal issues is indispensable. But how far should a lawyer go? Is the question just a matter of economics? In other words, does the lawyer research only as much as the client is willing to pay for? For American attorneys, the problem is not simple. Lawyers have special responsibilities and special difficulties in this area because ethically they are not permitted to handle cases in which they are not competent and they are generally not permitted to educate themselves at the expense of their clients.[4]

There is no easy way to resolve the problem of where to halt one's research or investigation. Obviously, lawyers should not attempt transactions on which they are not at least minimally informed and competent; but even experienced lawyers must grapple with many of these questions. Consider, for example, an issue that is discussed extensively in §4.4 below—choosing the law applicable to that contract for the sale of 20,000 brass fittings by an American manufacturer to an Argentine company. Most international contracts take a very cavalier approach to this problem. Almost as an afterthought the contract drafter will state that the governing law is "the law of the State of New York" if the seller is located in New York. If the buyer does not have enough negotiation leverage to insist on a choice of Argentine law (assuming i.e., his preference), this clause may well find itself in the final contract.

In practice, choice of law can be more complicated than one might assume. Given that New York has adopted the Uniform Commercial Code (UCC), given that Article Two of the UCC expressly covers the sale of goods, and given that almost all U.S. lawyers specializing in commercial transactions have extensive education and training in the UCC, there should be no major problems arising from the choice of law issue from the seller's standpoint. The Argentine buyer might be agreeable, particularly if the buyer is represented in the transaction by New York lawyers. If both sides feel comfortable with the body of law chosen, the transaction should proceed smoothly.

But assume the contrary. The U.S. seller is so desperate to get rid of those brass fittings that he will agree to nearly anything in terms of a choice of law clause. He may, in fact, have instructed his lawyer not to argue over peripheral matters in the contract. The Argentine buyer may insist on Argentine law governing the contract. How deeply does the seller's lawyer have to research Argentine law to protect the seller's interests (and the lawyer's own professional interest in not committing malpractice). If money and time is no object, the New York attorney might perform substantial research on Argentine sales law and possibly even hire a consultant on Argentine commercial law

4. Rule 1.1 ("Competence") of the American Bar Association's Model Rules of Professional Conduct requires U.S. lawyers to do an adequate amount of preparation and research to properly counsel the client. Lawyers in other countries are subject to similar requirements.

to help advise the client. If the fittings contract is to be the first of many such agreements, both seller and the seller's lawyer have a long-term stake in knowing more about Argentina's legal system so a greater initial investment in legal research may be justified.

But if the fittings contract is for a modest amount of money and if it is viewed as a one-time transaction, the research problem becomes stickier. There are a number of options over a wide spectrum. A lawyer might take some minimal comfort from the notion that a contract's choice of law becomes relevant only if the contract is subject to some kind of dispute and only if the person (judge or arbitrator) who has to resolve the dispute believes that it is necessary to refer to principles in an underlying legal system to reach a decision. The seller's lawyer could simply do nothing and hope for the best. It is possible that: (1) even if a dispute arises, the judge or arbitrator may not have to refer to underlying law; and (2) even if the judge or arbitrator makes such a reference it is possible that the decision will be the same irrespective of which law is applied.

But is it proper to leave something this important up for grabs—simply to play the probabilities that choice of law will never be important? There are plenty of disputes in which choice of law is vitally important and someone working on the draft of a contract cannot possibly anticipate all possible disputes or all possible outcomes. A more careful lawyer might want to seek out an attorney knowledgeable in Argentine law for advice on choice of law. But seeking comprehensive legal advice from an outside attorney may cost a lot of money. Many lawyers, and many clients, do not want to pay the underlying costs for a comprehensive analysis of choice of law.

There are some less-costly options. The seller's lawyer could try to personally research Argentine law using resources available in her own law library or by way of online legal research. The lawyer could commission a qualified lawyer to perform research in Argentine law only on a limited number of legal issues that the lawyer anticipates might arise and use that research as a comfort factor. The lawyer could hire an Argentine practitioner solely to review the final contract, rather than to spend all the hours that go into preparing early drafts of the document.

There are no hard, fast answers here. Predrafting and prenegotiation research is not just a matter of business wisdom. For lawyers involved in international contracts, it can become a difficult question of professional responsibility. In any event, the question of "research, how much?" should be given close attention by both lawyers and clients.

§4.2.3 Beginning the Drafting Process

The blank page syndrome that all authors face is equally common in contract drafting. How does a writer begin to fill up the paper? One method used by a large number of contract drafters is to begin from some kind of checklist or standard outline for commercial contracts. Using a typical contract for the sale of goods as an example, most contracts address the substantive matters of the contracts in something like the following order:

(1) Date and place of the agreement.
(2) Description including full names and addresses of the parties.
(3) Definitions, if any.
(4) Description of the subject matter of the contract.
(5) Recitation of offer and acceptance.
(6) Price term.
(7) Payment term.
(8) Security interest, if any.
(9) Delivery term.
(10) Title, risk of loss and insurance.
(11) Specifications and warranties, if any.
(12) Taxes.
(13) Authorizations, permits, and licenses.
(14) Breach, termination, and liquidated damages, if any.
(15) Notices.
(16) Cancellation and rescission.
(17) Applicable law.
(18) Official language.
(19) Dispute resolution.
(20) Force majeure.
(21) Assignment of contract.
(22) Alterations (including a prohibition on oral modifications, if desired).
(23) Annexes, if any.
(24) Signatures and counterpart provision (if necessary).

Most of these clauses are self-explanatory or are discussed more elaborately later in this chapter.

A counterpart provision is a clause in or near the signature lines that provides that each party may sign a copy of the contract in his or her location. Each of these signed copies will be merged into a final single contract, but the date of execution is the date on which all of the parties put their signatures to the document, rather than the date of final merger. A counterpart provision is particularly helpful if the parties are a long distance from each other and if they do not want to spend the time and expense to travel to a central location for a signing ceremony. Counterpart provisions are also helpful if a contract must be executed as of a particular date when the parties cannot all come together for signing on that date. As more and more drafting and negotiation takes place electronically via e-mail, text messages, and the like, counterpart provisions may become more common. The reader should check the law of the applicable jurisdiction to make sure that counterpart clauses are valid.

Contracts for the sale of goods are the most common form of international commercial agreement, but there are many other types of contracts. For example, in the context of international licensing agreements, a contract normally includes clauses on the following as well as most if not all of the clauses in the foregoing list:

(1) Transfer of the license from licensor to license.
(2) Royalty rate.
(3) Place and manner of payment of royalties.
(4) Determination of rates of exchange [a currency fluctuation clause].
(5) Allocation of tax burdens between the parties.
(6) Government approvals.
(7) Registration and recordation of the license.
(8) Compliance with export laws in country of origin.

Contracts for multi-million dollar turnkey construction projects can be even longer and more extensive. The following Tables 4.1–4.12 are an example of an outline for an international construction contract for the construction of offshore oil drilling platforms.

Table 4.1 Chapter One: Introduction

Article 1:	Definitions
Article 2:	Scope of Work
Article 3:	Representatives of the Parties

Table 4.2 Chapter Two: General Obligations of Contractor

Article 4:	Performance of the work
Article 5:	Personnel
Article 6:	Drawings and Specifications
Article 7:	Compliance with Laws and Regulations
Article 8:	Authorizations, Permits and Licenses
Article 9:	Care of Company Provided Items
Article 10:	Independent Contractor Relationship
Article 11:	Publicity
Article 12:	Use of Host Country's Goods and Services
Article 13:	Access to Sites
Article 14:	Taxes

Table 4.3 Chapter Three: General Obligations of Company

Article 15:	Company Provided Items, Drawings, Specifications and sites
Article 16:	Authorizations, Permits and Licenses

Table 4.4 Chapter Four: Progress of the Work

Article 17:	Progress of the Work
Article 18:	Quality Assurance and Quality Control

Table 4.5 Chapter Five: Variations

Article 19:	Company's right to Order Variations
Article 20:	Contractor's Right to Propose Variations
Article 21:	Contractor's Estimate
Article 22:	The Effects of the Variation on the Contract Price, Contract Schedule and Other Terms of the Contract
Article 23:	Variation Order Procedure
Article 24:	Disputed Variations

Table 4.6 Chapter Six: Cancellation and Suspension

Article 25:	Cancellation
Article 26:	Suspension

Table 4.7 Chapter Seven: Delivery and Payment

Article 27:	Delivery and Completion of the Work
Article 28:	Payment, Invoices and Audit
Article 29:	Invoice Retention/Bank Guarantee
Article 30:	Title and Liens
Article 31:	Guarantee and Final Acceptance Certificate

Table 4.8 Chapter Eight: Breach of Contract

Article 32:	Contractor's Delay
Article 33:	Contractor's Liability for Breach of Guarantee
Article 34:	Termination Because of Contractor's Default
Article 35:	Company's Breach of Contract

Table 4.9 Chapter Nine: Risk, Liability, Indemnification, and Insurance

Article 36:	Passing of Risk for Contract Object and Company Provided Items
Article 37:	Liability and Indemnification
Article 38:	Insurance

Table 4.10 Chapter Ten: Proprietary Rights

Article 39:	Ownership of Drawings, Plans and Specifications
Article 40:	Patents and Inventions
Article 41:	Confidential Information
Article 42:	General Competence

Table 4.11 Chapter Eleven: Miscellaneous Clauses

Article 43:	Subcontracting and Assignment
Article 44:	Non-Waiver of Default
Article 45:	Force Majeure
Article 46:	Governing Law and Dispute Resolution
Article 47:	Notices
Article 48:	Alteration of Contract
Article 49:	Signatures

Table 4.12 Annexes and Attachments

Equally interesting is the following outline for a relatively simple joint venture agreement:

Preamble

1. Description of parties
2. Name of joint venture and principal place of business
3. Description of project
4. Relationship between the parties
    a. corporation, partnership or other relationship to be formed
    b. jurisdiction of venture formation
    c. principal structural features
5. Term
    a. commencement
    b. threshold termination if purpose is unattainable
    c. completion of project or early termination
    d. government approvals (if and when required)
6. Obligations of each party to the joint venture
    a. equity (capital) contribution
    b. financial liability for future cash needs (including guarantees)
    c. service and management personnel
    d. research obligations and offer of new developments acquired
    e. property or contracts transferred

- f. positive covenants
  - (1) right to enter agreement
  - (2) right to property
- g. negative covenants
  - (1) not to pledge joint venture credit
  - (2) not to compete in joint venture market

7. Management and control
   - a. board of directors or similar body
     - (1) membership, representation of shares, chairperson
     - (2) meetings (in person, by phone or e-mail, in writing)
     - (3) voting
     - (4) deadlocks
     - (5) major issues
     - (6) language
   - b. Chief Executive Officer
     - (1) responsibilities
     - (2) remuneration
     - (3) appointment of initial CEO/manager
     - (4) dismissal
     - (5) Indemnities
8. Capital interests
   - a. relative shares and voting power
   - b. treatment in books of account; initial balances
   - c. treatment of surpluses and deficits
   - d. allocation of tax benefits
   - e. additional contributions
     - (1) by both parties
     - (2) by one party
   - f. extraordinary majorities required for major decisions
   - g. special procedures for shareholder meetings/votes
9. Use of funds
   - a. use to which initial capital contributions may be put
   - b. budget for first year
   - c. three-year projected budget
   - d. financial delegations
   - e. profits and declarations of dividends
10. Schedule of work (business plan)
    - a. agreed plan at commencement of work
    - b. schedule for first year

c. three-year projected work schedule
d. amendments to business plan

11. Insurance
    a. joint venture activities
    b. officers/directors
    c. integration with parents' plans
12. Information and reporting
    a. description of liaison officers
    b. exchange of information
    c. financial reporting
        (1) scope of needs
        (2) frequency of reports
        (3) fiscal year
        (4) location and access
        (5) Audit
        (6) retention after termination
    d. language of company affairs, records, reports, meetings
13. Patents, trademarks, other intellectual or industrial property
    a. existing
        (1) ownership
        (2) license of parents' rights
        (3) defense of law suits brought by third parties
        (4) prosecution of infringers
        (5) reassignment or termination
    b. future
        (1) ownership
        (2) other issues as above
14. Accountants/counsel
    a. independent of parents
    b. general/special
    c. local/foreign
15. Joint venture opportunities/conflicts of interest
    a. what must be referred for resolution
    b. what each party may retain
16. Disputes
    a. negotiation
    b. cooling off
    c. arbitration
17. Dissolution/buy-out
    a. time
    b. completion

c. early
   (1) for cause
   (2) by agreement
d. distributions on termination
e. survival of covenants
f. disposition or retrieval of inventory, intangibles

18. Admission of new shareholders
19. Excusable delay/force majeure
20. Miscellaneous
   a. entire agreement; no oral representations or modifications
   b. assignments
   c. waiver
   d. severability
   e. validity
   f. clause headings
   g. additional instruments
   h. counterpart
21. Signatures
22. Annexes, if any[5]

Note that the construction contract and the sample joint venture outline are far longer and far more detailed than a typical contract for the sale of goods. There are a number of reasons for this. One is that the dollar amount of large-scale construction and joint venture contracts justify far greater detail in the document. A second reason is the fact that such contracts typically extend over a period of years in a setting in which changed conditions and fresh thinking on the part of the contracting parties is likely to require modifications of the original understanding. A third is that the risks on all sides are far greater in contracts of this scope and dimension. The parties typically do not want to have a great deal of uncertainty or ambiguity in the transaction.

These last two contracts also illustrate another common technique in drafting lengthy contracts. There are plenty of occasions when the parties will want to set out specifications for the goods or services in question in separate annexes or attachments to the basic contract. Simply because the dimensions of a few bolts in the oil platform must be changed is no reason to revisit and redraft the underlying contract. It is far easier to change an annex of specifications. It may also be procedurally dangerous to revisit the basic contract. If one party's mind has changed substantially over time, that party might use the excuse of a change in bolt specifications as an excuse to re-do the entire agreement. For expensive, long-duration contracts, annexes, and attachments play an important role.

5. This outline was provided by and used by two outstanding lecturers, Peter Ehrenhaft and Anita Esslinger, in the now-defunct ALI-ABA program entitled "Fundamentals of International Business."

A contract drafter can find sample outlines and checklists in various form books. A drafter can create an original contract outline by simply considering all the elements that he or she would like to see in the contract. Even though that list is likely to be modified during conversations with the client and with the other side, an outline is a good place to begin and a good way to work around the blank page trauma. Once a drafter has set out most if not all of the ingredients in the contract, she can begin to order these items into an outline and to think about how to fill in the blanks with precise, substantive contract language.

Drafting actual contract language is something that many lawyers find highly intimidating. Traditional contract language is so abstruse and complex that it bears little relation to the way in which people normally communicate with each other. One recourse for the neophyte contract drafter is to borrow from form books. Contract drafting is one form of human activity where the concept of plagiarism simply does not apply. Lawyers in particular borrow constantly from documents that have gone before. One reason for this is simply the innate conservatism of the legal profession. Lawyers hesitate trying anything new if they can adopt something that someone has already used successfully. Another reason is that the doctrine of *stare decisis*—an Anglo-American doctrine concept growing out of litigation that requires courts to abide by previous court decisions—is carried over, often inappropriately, to transactional work. If a lawyer finds a document that seems to have passed muster sometime previously, he is happy to use it for his own transaction. Sometimes that makes sense; other times it is the height of stupidity.

Because lawyers tend to be such large-scale borrowers most law libraries stock numerous form books containing sample contract clauses, checklists for the content of contracts, and often complete contracts. For the easily intimidated somewhat lazy lawyer, these may simply be copied with appropriate changes in the parties' names and other specific details and presented to the client as a newly created legal document.

There are better ways to think about contract drafting. Form books ought to be a drafter's starting point, not her finishing point. When using preexisting language or when creating language of one's own, there are some generic considerations that ought to be applied. If there is a cardinal rule in contract drafting it is that you rely on other people's work at your peril. §4.5 discusses the use of standardized clauses and form agreements in more depth. Most contracts for any substantial amount of money are tailored to the parties' specific situation.

How then does one go about this process of refinement? A contract drafter, whether lawyer or nonlawyer, should not forget everything he has already been taught about the use of language and what constitutes good writing.[6] While there is no single approach to writing of any sort, there is no question that well-written contracts go a long way toward avoiding problems. To be even a little more patronizing, contracts ought to be properly punctuated, verb tenses ought to agree and language ought to be used accurately and with precision.

6. Felsenfeld & Siegel, *supra* n. 1, is a particularly good source of material on these issues. A newer variant on the same theme is Howard Darmstadter, *Hereof, Thereof and Everywhereof: A Contrarian Guide to Legal Drafting* (2002).

In working with form books and other preexisting language, or in drafting original contracts, a drafter should consider three generic problems that occur in contract drafting: the use of superfluous language, the use of ambiguity and the use of legal or industrial terms of art. The modern trend in legal drafting is to eliminate excessive legalisms in contracts while avoiding colloquialisms. Modern contracts do not need terms such as *witnesseth, heretofore*, the excessively used *whereas*, or the particularly disgusting *said* as in "This contract is for the sale of fittings. *Said* fittings. . . ." When these words are strung together in a single clause in a contract they become hilarious.

One clause of similar import from an actual contract reads: "NOW, THEREFORE, in consideration of the premises and of the mutual covenants of the parties hereto to be faithfully performed as hereinafter specified, the parties hereto hereby covenant and agree as follows." What the parties are trying to say is that they have come together to make a contract and the terms of the agreement follow that clause. Is all this language necessary to a valid agreement? Absolutely not.

Terms such as these are archaic; their origins are obscure. If they ever had a special meaning or purpose, such things have been lost in history. They contribute nothing but word count to the contract. Tragically, too many lawyers and not a few clients do not realize this and insist—wholly without justification—that contracts must contain such language to be valid agreements. When the author drafted a contract for a client several years ago, the client rejected the document saying: "It just doesn't look like a contract." When asked why, the client said: "Because it doesn't have any 'witnesseths' in it, like my other lawyer's contracts." After a long-distance hassle as to what a real contract looked like, the client concluded the discussion by saying: "If you don't put those words back in, I'm not going to pay you." The words were put back in. This is the second lesson on superfluous language. Even if it does not contribute anything to a contract, it probably does not destroy the legal integrity of the document either.

Superfluous language has a first cousin—verbosity. Lawyers often try to accomplish too much and wind up saying nothing of consequence. Verbosity and complexity in contract language often causes rather than cures problems. For example, a sales contract might say something such as: "Seller agrees to sell and Buyer agrees to buy 1000 fittings at $1.00 per fitting." There are plenty of other simple variations on this language that are perfectly permissible and that accurately convey the intent of the parties. What is not needed is something such as: "Seller agrees to sell, convey, transfer, assign and otherwise relinquish claim to and otherwise commit into the permanent possession and ownership of buyer 1000 fittings."

Language such as this occurs in contracts for two different reasons, one somewhat commendable and understandable; the other far less so. The less commendable reason simply reflects the drafting process in so many law firms. Each lawyer cannot feel that he or she has made a contribution to the document unless something is added to the contract. Even a few extra words will suffice, but the contract cannot escape the average lawyers' desk without having something else grafted on to it.

The second reason at least has a legitimate purpose behind it even if the purpose is rarely accomplished. In writing clauses such as this, lawyers are trying to cover all bases, to prepare for all possible contingencies. There may have been actual litigated cases long in the past where the absence of one or another synonym caused a court to declare the agreement invalid. Even without close examination of the facts of those early cases, we can now say with certainty that this sort of verbosity is not necessary today. Worse, unlike purely superfluous language, many of the verbs in the quoted price term do not mean the same thing: for example, assignments in the U.S. legal system are somewhat different from pure sales transactions, so *to assign* is not necessarily the same as *to sell*. To the extent that the verbs are completely synonymous, they are superfluous—akin to saying, "Seller seller seller agrees agrees agrees to buy to buy to buy."

Contract drafters should appreciate that all human communication is imprecise and that additional detail does not necessarily constitute additional precision. Business executives are almost always far more realistic. When one executive says "buy" the other executive knows pretty much what is meant. Lawyers ought to be secure enough to accept and utilize this sort of simplicity.

Many contract drafters agonize over the meaning of words. For the most part that is a good trait. In most instances contract drafters should avoid ambiguity and imprecision. For example, a contract that states: "The price of each fitting may be $5.00 per fitting" is simply bad usage. A price term is usually expected to be clear and definite. The use of the verb "may" creates ambiguity where none should exist. In the English language, the mandatory verb is "shall." By contrast, there are times when contract drafters may want to use what is called deliberate or purposeful ambiguity. For example, a contract could specify the actual shipping vessel (SS Hermes, say) on which the fittings are to be shipped. This is the height of precision, but it is probably uncalled for. In all likelihood, other problems may occur if the Hermes is not available. In the alternative, using the device of deliberate ambiguity, the contract might simply state: "Seller agrees to transport the fittings using a mutually acceptable form of surface transportation." Or, "seller agrees to transport the fittings by rail."

Underlying legal systems occasionally invoke deliberate ambiguity. The Uniform Commercial Code in the United States provides that when a contract does not specify price, the price shall be a price that is reasonable at the time of shipment of the goods. Deliberate ambiguity can accomplish two things: it can leave open a contract term on which the parties cannot agree while permitting them to achieve agreement on everything else; and it can leave peripheral matters to the discretion of one or another of the parties without triggering a breach of contract simply because the other party might have done something differently.

The use of terms of art can also shorten the length of contracts or lead to substantial conflict. On this point, there are a few good rules of thumb. Most courts and most people who work with contracts define words by applying the ordinary, dictionary meaning of those terms. So a contract that calls for the sale of 120 "eggs" would generally not be construed as calling for the sale of 120 Scotch eggs (the British pub food). There are, however, some departures from the plain meaning rule. Within specific industries, and among merchants in those industries, it may be permissible to use terms in other than their ordinary meanings on the plausible assumption that "everybody" (i.e., all the parties) knows what the contract talking about. But a contract for the sale of 120 Scotch eggs between two British pub owners might conceivably use only the term "egg" to describe the commodity. Petroleum refineries use a device called a reformer to manufactured lead-free gasoline. A contract for the construction of an oil refinery that calls for the installation of a reformer, without further definition, would probably not cause problems. None of the parties to the oil refinery contract would define the term as "a person who seeks to change things by making them better."

There is another way to deal with terms in a contract. Certain terms may be defined specifically in a separate definition section of the contract. A definitional section has the advantage of explaining the term in the contract itself and thus not leaving a definition to the vagaries of judges or arbitrators. Lawyers know that even so-called everyday definitions can vary from time to time and place to place. A definitional section has the additional advantage of making the body of a contract shorter. For example, two merchants can agree to buy and sell 100 wooden boxes. The definitional section (or conceivably a separate addendum on specifications) can prescribe that each box shall be of top grade walnut and of certain dimensions. Once having set out this definition, the contract may then simply refer to "box" or "boxes" whenever it is necessary to mention the commodity in question without reiterating the boxes' specifications.

These are just a few of the things that contract drafters should consider before setting words down on paper. There are no categorical rules in this regard except perhaps the homily that well-written contracts cause fewer problems than poorly written contracts. The remainder of this chapter considers more specific contract drafting issues.

§4.3 THE USE AND EFFECT OF A LETTER OF INTENT

In complicated undertakings, the parties often need a document that signals that they have "agreed to agree." The drafting of a letter of intent or a memorandum of understanding is often necessary when matters central to the final agreement such as financing and government approval are not yet a certainty. A letter of intent may occasionally be taken to a government official or bank officer in order to get the permissions or funding necessary for the agreement. On other occasions, a letter of intent has the effect of resolving certain preliminary matters while a long-term negotiation hammers out the remaining components of the deal.[7]

The difficulty, of course, is that a letter of intent itself has to be drafted and negotiated. While this is usually not terribly difficult, persons engaged in contract drafting who also draft letters of intent should be aware that these documents can

7. For more commentary on letters of intent generally *see*, Ekaterina Pannebakker, *Letter of Intent in International Contracting* (2016); Ralph B. Lake & Ugo Draetta, *Letters of Intent and Other Precontractual Documents* (2d ed.,1994) and Alan Schwartz & Robert E. Scott, *Precontractual Liability and Preliminary Agreements*, 120 Harv. L. Rev. 661 (2007). *See also*, J. Andrew Holten, *Letters of Intent in Corporate Negotiations: Using Hostage Exchanges and Legal Uncertainty to Promote Compliance*, 162 U. Penn. L.Rev. 1237 (2014); Giuditta Cordero Moss, *The Function of Letters of Intent and Their Recognition in Modern Legal Systems*, in *New Features in Contract Law* (Reiner Schultze ed., 2007).

sometimes take on a life of their own, particularly in jurisdictions where the requirement of a writing allows a contract to be formed by something less than a comprehensive, fully executed agreement.

In most legal systems, letters of intent and memoranda of agreement are viewed as merely preliminary and have virtually no force and effect. In international contracts for the sale of goods that incorporate U.S. law as the contract's choice of law there are particular dangers. Under the U.S. legal doctrine known as the statute of frauds, a preliminary letter or memorandum signed "by the party to be charged" (i.e., the person accused of breaching the agreement) may be sufficient proof of the existence of a contract, and any violation of that document and whatever else is deemed to constitute the agreement, may lead to court-imposed sanctions for breach of contract. A writing that satisfies the statute of frauds can be terribly vague and incomplete.

By contrast, the U.S. UCC merely points out that the required writing need not contain all the material terms of the contract and such material terms as are stated need not be precisely stated. All that is required is that the writing afford a basis for believing that the offered oral evidence rests on a real transaction. It may be written in lead pencil on a scratch pad. It need not indicate which party is the buyer and which the seller. The only term which must appear is the quantity term which need not be accurately stated but recovery is limited to the amount stated. "The price, time and place of payment or delivery, the general quality of the goods, or any particular warranties may all be omitted."[8]

Coping with this problem is often easier said than done. A number of authorities suggest that the letter of intent or memorandum include express language that the document is merely evidence of the parties' "willingness to negotiate and nothing more." One option for the drafter of a letter of intent is to insert into the letter language such as: "This memorandum is not intended to constitute a binding contract" or this letter refers to "the possible formation of a joint venture."[9] Such disclaimers may very well work if the only goal is to eliminate problems with an U.S.-style statute of frauds. But what happens when a government official who is being asked to give permission to export or import the commodities in question or a bank officer who is being asked to approve a multi-million dollar loan reads the letter of intent. The very disclaimers that may keep the document from being construed by a court or arbitrator as a binding agreement may persuade the government or bank that the parties are still so far apart that they should not take the action requested. This often puts contracting parties between the "rock and a hard place" often described by President Abraham Lincoln when the choices he was offered gave him no meaningful way out.

There is another way to view letters of intent and preliminary memoranda—that is, as potentially enforceable documents. In other words, the parties may proceed on the basis that the terms and conditions spelled out in the letter of intent could at some

8. UCC §2-201, comment 1.
9. *See*, e.g., Lawrence M. Solan, *Contract as Agreement*, 81 Notre Dame L. Rev. 353 (2007) (questioning whether letter of intent ever constitutes a contract); Keith E. Witek, *Drafting a More Predictable Letter of Intent—Reducing Risk and Uncertainty in a Risky and Uncertain Transaction*, 9 Tex. Intell. Prop. L.J. 185 (2001).

subsequent time be considered enforceable. However, the letter of intent may still include express language making formation of the actual contract expressly conditional on the happening of later events (in American contract parlance the occurrence of a condition subsequent). This might cause the parties to write into the letter of intent language such as: "This letter may not be viewed as a final contract unless Government X gives final export approval [or unless Bank Y gives final approval to the financing agreement.]"

There are, of course, dangers associated with this action. If those subsequent conditions fall into place, the parties may have an agreement even if one or another is not quite ready to put a signature to the final document. This possibility shows up the dilemma of a letter of intent. If it is too loose, persons external to the agreement may not want to act on the basis of the letter. If it is too detailed and does not contain a sufficient number of disclaiming phrases, the letter of intent itself could be construed as a binding contract. There is probably a moral here, if not a complete answer in the law. Parties should be wary of putting their signatures to any document, however preliminary and no matter what the document's language, if they are not sure they want to enter into the agreement.

§4.4 CHOOSING THE LANGUAGE AND THE LAW OF THE AGREEMENT

§4.4.1 Choosing the Contract's Language

International lawyers to warn of the pitfalls and dangers of negotiating and drafting contracts that cut across cultural and linguistic lines. In even the most innocuous settings language differences can cause severe problems of interpretation. Consider a partial list of terms from Professor George DeLaume's book on transnational contracts to show the enormous contrasts between French and English legal expression (*see* Table 4.13):

Table 4.13 English-French Differences

English	*French*
compromise	transaction
agreement to arbitrate	compromise
execution	signature
performance	execution[10]

These are striking differences and point up the problems that occur even in cultural systems and languages that are somewhat similar and that have common roots. Contemplate what could happen when there are vast differences in culture, legal system, and language.

10. This chart is taken from Georges Delaume, *Transnational Contracts* 231 (1982).

If a contract is between two parties who speak different languages, it is generally conceded that an international commercial contract should have an "official" language as well as be translated into the languages of the various contracting parties. For example, a contract drafted for an English seller and a French buyer might state that while the contract has been translated into both English and French "the English language text is to be regarded as the definitive and official text of the agreement." There are occasions when the parties simply cannot agree on language. In that instance, the contract can simply remain silent on official language, letting a judge or arbitrator fill in the blank.

For the most part, contracting parties should view a choice of language clause as simply another matter to be expressly addressed in the document. Generally, the choice is negotiable; and even when, for various reasons, one party insists on using his native language as the official language, the other party has a simple means of insuring that the choice does not hamper further negotiations or actual performance under the contract. If you are not comfortable with a contract's language, hire a translator—preferably one who is also something of a legal specialist. Courts and arbitrators will not disturb a choice of official language so long as no fraud or undue influence was exercised by one party against the other in making the choice.

The actual wording of a choice of language clause need not be complicated. The traditional samples are excessively cumbersome: "Notwithstanding subsequent translations of this agreement, whether or not said translations are made contemporaneously with the negotiation and execution of said agreement, the English language version of said agreement shall exclusively control." The following wording should suffice: "This contract may be translated into languages other than English. The English language version of this contract is the official version and shall be controlling in any dispute arising under this contract."

§4.4.2 Choosing the Contract's Applicable Law

The discussion in this chapter and in Chapter 2 should give the reader a good understanding why a choice of law clause in a contract is often crucial. As will be seen in §4.6, choosing a system of law applicable to the contract could have the effect of inserting clauses or terms in the contract without the express consent of the parties. In other words, the underlying legal system can provide a gap-filling function for the agreement. This is not necessarily a bad thing. Gap-filling can free the parties from drafting clauses on many peripheral matters. It does, however, require that the parties be alert to how gap-filling may occur.

But even though risks are involved in choosing a body of law applicable to the contract, there are far more dangers associated with executing a document that is silent on choice of law.[11] Silence on applicable law can come back to haunt the parties if any

11. *See* generally, Maria Hook, *The Choice of Law Contract* (2016); Dolly Wu, *Timing the Choice of Law by Contract*, 9 Nw. J. Tech. & Intell. Prop. 401 (2011); Mo Zhang, *Contractual Choice of Law in Contracts of Adhesion and Party Autonomy*, 41 Akron L. Rev. 123 (2008); Andreas Junius, *Issues Surrounding Islamic Law as a Choice of Law under German Conflict of Laws Principles*, 7

dispute arises under the contract. Moreover, it is difficult to negotiate and draft a contract when the parties have no idea which legal system or body of law will govern the undertaking because the constraints of the chosen system will govern many of the provisions in the contract. For these reasons, this subsection will first discuss why most parties go about affirmatively choosing the law of the contract.

[1] Affirmatively Choosing the Law

There are essentially two ways to choose law affirmatively. First, the parties may try to avoid all choice of law problems by spelling out, in intricate detail in the contract itself, all the interpretative and substantive rules necessary to resolve any dispute under the contract. For small transactions in the hands of lawyers and business executives who are both brilliant and psychic, it is conceivable that such a contract could be drafted. However, excessive detail in the written document could lead to the breakdown of negotiations. Companies rarely have an infinite amount of time to spend on any individual agreement; and even assuming all this detail could be plausibly reduced to contract language, the contract itself would be gargantuan. Excessive detail sometimes also hampers efficient dispute resolution. If arbitrators have to plow through hundreds of pages, they may miss the central issues in the dispute.

There is a far more workable alternative. The parties can draft all the clauses that they believe are necessary to a proper agreement and then can choose law that fills in the remaining details. In the past, parties have normally chosen the law of a single country, usually that of either the seller or the buyer or, in some cases, the law of a respected, neutral third country. Swiss law, for example, is frequently chosen by parties who cannot agree on the law of either the seller's or the buyer's country. Since the entering into force of the Convention on the CISG, parties involved in sale of goods transactions may choose the CISG as the applicable law.

One attorney of the author's acquaintance sometimes dispenses with choosing the law of a specific country. When his clients cannot agree on choice of law, he incorporates a clause in the contract requiring arbitrators to apply "generally accepted principles of international trade and commercial practice" (or similar language) to resolve the dispute. Another version of this alternative permits the parties to declare an arbitrator as an *amiable compositeur*, a device that permits the arbitrator to apply fundamental principles of equity, fairness, and common sense to settle the dispute without the necessity of referring to and applying a body of specific municipal law. The selection of an international code of commercial law or the *amiable compositeur*

Chi. J. Int'l L. 537 (2007); Giuditta Cordero Moss, *Tacit Choice of Law, Partial Choice and Closest Connection: The Case of Common Law Contract Models Governed by a Civilian Law*, in *Rett Og Toleranse—Festkrift Helod Johan* (2007); Giesela Ruhl, *Methods and Approaches in Choice of Law: An Economic Perspective*, 24 Berkeley J. Int'l L. 801 (2006); Mo Zhang, *Party Autonomy and Beyond: An International Perspective of Contractual Choice of Law*, 20 Emory Int'l L. Rev. 511 (2006). Friedrich K. Juenger, *Contract Choice of Law in the Americas*, 45 Am. J. Comp. L. 195 (1997); Ian F.G. Baxter, *International Conflict of Laws and International Business*, 34 Int'l & Comp. L.Q. 538 (1985); George A. Zaphiriou, *Choice of Forum and Choice of Law Clauses in International Commercial Agreements*, 3 Int'l Trade L.J. 311 (1978).

alternative could be particularly attractive to negotiating parties who are unwilling to adopt each other's domestic commercial legal system as the choice of law. Under the twin doctrines of party autonomy and *pacta sunt servanda*, there appears to be no reason why such choices would not be honored.[12]

There is some debate as to whether the contracting parties' choice is completely unfettered, however. Classic choice of law doctrine in most of the major trading nations has generally required some connection between the legal system chosen and the contract itself. Under the U.S. UCC's rules for contracts involving the sale of goods, the choice of law must bear some reasonable relation to the contract and the contracting parties.[13] In other contracts in the U.S. and under British law, the parties' choice of law is honored so long as there is some reasonable basis for the choice.[14] For example, in an important choice of law case in the United Kingdom, *Vita Food Products v. Unus Shipping Co.*,[15] the contract for a shipment of goods from Newfoundland, Canada to New York was to be governed by English commercial law. The British court enforced the choice and determined that if contracting parties voluntarily choose a body of law, that choice will be honored irrespective of whether the law chosen has any special connection with the contract.

The United States Supreme Court in the important case, *Scherk v. Alberto-Culver Co.*,[16] concluded that choice of law clauses in contracts promote "the orderliness and predictability essential to any international business transaction" and thus suggested that U.S. courts would honor virtually any reasonable choice. Similarly, the recently promulgated European Communities Convention on the Law Applicable to Contractual Obligations[17] appears to follow the United States Supreme Court in promoting party autonomy and honoring the parties' choice.[18] In a number of other countries whose legal systems are based on civil law doctrine, the courts usually require some fairly close connection between the transaction, the parties, and the system of law chosen. In a few countries, contract drafters must cope with legal principles that provide that contracts that are to be performed within the country are to be governed by that

12. *See*, §4.9 of this chapter and the discussion in Chapter 9.
13. UCC §1-105 states: "when a transaction bears a reasonable relation to this state and also to another state or nation the parties may agree that the law either of this state or of such other state or nation shall govern their rights and duties." This appears to limit a contract's choice of law solely to the country of the seller or the country of the buyer. However, judicial construction of this term has generally permitted the parties to choose the law of a neutral third country.
14. Restatement (Second) of Conflict of Laws §187(2)(a). Readers not familiar with the American system of Restatements of the Law should simply consider that these documents are attempts by groups of law professors, practitioners and judges to gather into a single source, as a kind of private codification, legal principles derived and announced by courts throughout the United States. Principles of law set out in the Restatements are frequently cited by U.S. courts on an advisory basis but they have no controlling effect on the outcome of cases.
15. [1939] A.C. 277.
16. 417 U.S. 506 (1974).
17. 23 O.J. Eur. Comm. (No. L-266) (1980).
18. *See*, e.g., Russel J. Weintraub, *How to Choose the Law and How Not To: The EEC Convention*, 17 Tex. Int'l L.J. 155 (1982).

country's law, irrespective of whether the parties might have made another choice.[19] For example, petroleum agreements with the Kingdom of Saudi Arabia, for example, are to be governed solely by Saudi law.[20]

Making a choice can eliminate a great deal of uncertainty, although parties must be careful in their choice.[21] If a third country is chosen, it should be a country with an easily researched, well-defined body of commercial law. Far out choices—for example choosing the law of Tanzania in a contract between a seller in Iceland and a buyer in Taiwan—would raise eyebrows among arbitrators and reviewing courts. Such a choice is so bizarre and so totally unrelated to the transaction, that a court or arbitrator might feel free to disregard it. Choosing, as a neutral country, the law of one of the major trading nations is the better alternative.

There is a secondary problem in choice of law that bears discussion. When courts or arbitrators apply choice of law, they generally apply those legal principles that are in effect in the chosen country at the time of the arbitration or litigation, rather than those principles that might have existed when the contract was drafted. Usually this is not a major problem. The commercial principles of most countries evolve so slowly that drastic changes are not likely to occur in the life of the average contract. The parties could try to stipulate that the choice of law is the set of legal principles in effect at the time the contract was executed, but it is uncertain whether a court or arbitrator would be bound by such a stipulation.

Once the choice itself is made, there is no trouble drafting the clause itself. The parties may simply state: "This contract shall be governed by and construed in accordance with the laws of ____________." The Japanese External Trade Organization (JETRO) suggests that contracts contain a provision stating: "Governing law: This contract shall be governed in all respects by the laws of Japan." More cumbersome clauses sometimes attempt to show the relation between the choice of law and the contract in the clause itself. The following is an example: "This contract shall be subject to and shall be construed and enforced pursuant to the laws of ____________ (country), which is the location of the headquarters of the Seller [or Buyer]." Lawyers and business executives outside the United States must understand that if U.S. commercial law is chosen, the choice of law clause must specify a particular state in the United States. There is no body of national commercial law that can be chosen for a contract between private parties. The U.S. UCC comes into being only through the sovereignty of the various states. It is national only in the sense that each state's version of the UCC is essentially the same as any other state. It is also possible, although terribly cumbersome, to choose different systems of law for different portions of the contract. This can lead to a lot of confusion when disputes arise, but even here the parties' choices will generally be honored.

19. Chile is an example. *See*, the Chilean Codigo de Comercio, Art. 113.
20. *See*, e.g., Ernest Smith & John S. Dzienkowski, *A Fifty Year Perspective on World Petroleum Arrangements*, 24 Tex. Int'l L.J. 13 (1989).
21. On this issue and several other relevant topics *see*, David Hricik, *Infinite Combinations: Whether the Duty of Competency Requires Lawyers to Include Choice of Law Clauses in Contracts They Draft for Their Clients*, 12 Willamette J. Int'l L. & Disp. Res. 241 (2004).

[2] Choosing the Law When the Contract Is Silent

The question here is why any contracting party would let such an important matter as choice of law be decided at some later date by a decision-maker who may not be fully under the control of the parties. The short answer is that many negotiating parties cannot come to an agreement on choice of law. Rather than forego the deal itself, the parties simply leave that matter for later resolution by a third party such as a court or arbitrator. To a certain extent, silence reflects a hope that no dispute will ever arise under the contract; or, in the alternative, that if a dispute arises, the arbitrators or judge will make an intelligent choice, hoping, obviously, that no dispute will ever arise. As noted earlier, some contracts try to avoid problems by providing that the governing law will be "principles of law common to 'civilized nations'," or that the parties undertake the contract in "mutual good will and good faith" without applying a specific country's legal system. But there is no readily accepted or generally available reference source for these common principles. The practical effect of such clauses is to simply turn over the dispute to the good sense of the judge or arbitrator.

Some of these issues have been the subject of litigation. In an oil concession agreement entered into between a British oil company and the country of Abu Dhabi, the parties recognized that they could not agree as to a specific body of law and inserted a clause providing merely: "[The parties] declare that they base their work in this Agreement on good will and sincerity of belief and on the interpretation of this Agreement in a fashion consistent with reason." In 1951 a dispute arose under the concession and was submitted to arbitration. Lord Asquith, sitting as one of the arbitrators, asked:

What is the "Proper Law" applicable in construing this contract? This is a contract made between Abu Dhabi and wholly to be performed in that country. If any municipal system of law were applicable, it would prima facie be that of Abu Dhabi. But no such law can reasonably be said to exist. The Sheikh administers a purely discretionary justice with the assistance of the Koran; and it would be fanciful to suggest that in this very primitive region there is any settled body of legal principles applicable to the construction of modern commercial instruments. Nor can I see any basis on which the municipal law of England could apply.[22]

Thus, the question faced by Asquith was: Is it possible to construe or interpret a commercial contract without reference to an identifiable system of municipal law? Lord Asquith hit on a Solomonic solution: he invoked certain principles of British commercial law that he deemed "of ecumenical validity" but chose to disregard other rules of British commercial practice that he characterized as excessively "rigid." This was probably not a bad solution for Lord Asquith as arbitrator; he had to come to some decision under the contract. But there is considerable danger in this approach. There is no assurance that every judge or arbitrator will have the stature and brilliance of Lord Asquith. A different arbitrator might well have applied Abu Dhabi law or the whole of British commercial law, however inappropriate, or some melange of commercial

22. *Id.*

principles that did violence to the underlying agreement. When a contract is silent on choice of law many unpredictable things can happen.

There are, of course, certain legal concepts derived from that body of law known as conflict of laws that assist courts and arbitrators in determining which body of municipal law to apply in the absence of an express choice by the parties. A compilation of legal principles in the United States entitled the Restatement (Second) Conflict of Laws suggests that the law to be applied is the law of the country having the "most significant relationship to the transaction and the parties" taking into consideration the place of contracting, the place where the contract was negotiated, the place where the contract is to be performed, the location of the subject matter of the contract and the domicile, residence, nationality, place of incorporation and place of business of the parties.[23] The UCC (now effective in all states except Louisiana) provides that the when the parties have not chosen law, the applicable law is the law of the state bearing the most "appropriate relation" to the commercial agreement.

In other countries the rules vary. In some instances the domestic commercial law provides that the applicable law will be the law of the place where the contract was made. In other instances it is the law of the place where the contract is to be performed; and in yet other countries it is the national law of the contracting parties if they are of common nationality or the law of the country where the contract was made or where it is to be performed if the parties are not of common nationality.[24] But, again, the ultimate choice is not certain and will be made by someone other than a party to the contract.

In 2015, The Hague Conference on Private International Law issued a set of guidelines on choice of law in international commercial agreements: The Principles on Choice of Law in International Commercial Contracts. As with the other Hague Conference materials, these provisions in the words of the Conference, are to be considered a "code of best practice."[25] Set out in a Preamble with twelve articles (and extensive accompanying commentary), they can be briefly summarized as follows:

(1) The parties may choose the law applicable to the whole contract or only parts of the contract and different law may be applied to different parts of the same contract (Article 2). But the choice must be made expressly in the contract (Article 4).

23. Readers who are not lawyers or who are from outside the United States should keep in mind that while the Restatement is prestigious, it is essentially a compilation of legal principles by law professors and, accordingly, is not regarded as controlling law in any jurisdiction in the United States. Restatement principles become binding only when they are formally adopted by the various state courts.

24. *See*, James R. Lowe, *Choice of Law Clauses in International Contracts: A Practical Approach*, 12 Harv. Int'l L.J. 1 (1971); For a discussion of some of the civil law doctrines on choice of law *see*, e.g., Christoph Reithmann, *Internationales Vertragsrecht* 2-17 (2d ed., 1972). For a distinguished but perhaps now somewhat dated statement that civil law requires a reasonable relationship between parties, performance and choice of law (and that discusses the "excesses" of party autonomy) *see*, Niboyet, *Traite De Droit International Prive Francais* 51-60 (1948).

25. The full text of the principles may be found at The Hague Conference website: www.hcch.net.

(2) The choice may be made when the contract is drafted or at any time thereafter.
(3) There is no requirement that there be a connection between the law chosen and the parties to the agreement.[26]

§4.5 USING STANDARDIZED CLAUSES AND FORMS

There are both benefits and dangers in using standard forms in contracts. Chapter 3, §3.4, has warned about certain problems that parties involved in contracts for the sale of goods will encounter if the buyer and seller merely exchange forms. But standard forms save money and for low-value contracts they may be virtually the only way that the companies can do business.

On the international level, contracts tend to be for larger amounts of money and are often performed over longer periods of time. Accordingly, those contracts' provisions tend to be more detailed and intricate. As a result, many international contracts are separately negotiated between the parties and the resulting contract is tailored to the deal at hand. But even these contracts are likely to contain a large amount of standardized language. There is absolutely nothing wrong with this. Using certain standardized clauses promotes efficiency and economy in contract drafting. There is no need, normally, to draft each and every word in a contract from scratch. On occasion, use of standard language will promote agreement and may enhance any dispute resolution since arbitrators and judges are likely to have encountered this standard language previously.

There are many number of sources for standard clauses. Most law libraries contain form books that recite language from earlier contracts. The unfortunate result of using some of these form books is that totally archaic language and syntax tends to be preserved beyond its reasonable life span. There are a number of useful compendiums of sample contracts covering different types of agreements.[27] A number of international bodies now provide stock contract language. For example, the UNCITRAL has recently released a compilation of contract terms applicable to large-scale international construction contracts entitled Legal Guide on Drawing Up International Contracts for Construction of Industrial Works.

Many contracts for the sale of goods include stock language known as trade terms, such as F.O.B., C.I.F., or F.A.S. Trade terms are often familiar to laypersons, but

26. There is some new literature on choice of law under The Hague Principles. *See*, e.g., Andreas Schwartze, *New Trends in Parties' Options to Select the Applicable Law? The Hague Principles on Choice of Law in International Contracts in a Comparative Perspective*, 12 U. St. Thomas L.J. 87 (2015); Marta Pertegas & Brooke Adele Marshall, *Harmonization Through the Draft Hague Principles on Choice of Law in International Contracts*, 39 Brook. J. Int'l L. 975 (2014); Symeon C. Symeneonides, *The Hague Principles on Choice of Law for International Contracts: Some Preliminary Comments*, 61 Am. J. Comp. L. 395 (2013).
27. *See*, e.g., Marcel Fontaine & Filip De Ly, *Drafting International Contracts: An Analysis of Contract Clauses* (2006); Stefan Grundmann, Denis Mazeaud & Martijn W. Hesselink, *General Clauses and Standards in European Contract Law* (2005).

from a legal standpoint they actually fulfill three separate functions in a contract. They function as part of the price term (determining who pays for what portion of the transportation of the goods); they help allocate risk of loss, and they affect the transportation requirements for the goods. Some domestic legal systems contain specific definitions for these terms that would apply if a contract chose that country's law as the applicable law.

For international sales of goods contracts, the ICC has promulgated a set of trade terms, updated in 2010, called *Incoterms*. Incoterms include definitions of ten major trade terms as those terms are believed to be understood in eighteen major trading nations. However, there can be subtle differences when compared with parallel definition in other systems. For example, an earlier version of Incoterms define "FOB" as: "The goods are placed on board a ship by the seller at a port of shipment named in the sales contract. The risk of loss or damage to the goods is transferred from the seller to the buyer when the goods pass the ship's rail."[28] The current Incoterms definition of FOB is: "'Free on Board' means that the seller delivers the goods on board the vessel nominated by the buyer at the named port of shipment ... The risk of loss of or damage to the goods passes when the goods are on board the vessel, and the buyer bears all costs from that moment onwards."[29] A now outdated UCC definition was slightly different: "when the term is FOB the place of shipment, the seller must at that place ship the goods in the manner provided [in this article] and bear the expense and risk of putting them into the possession of the carrier...the seller must in addition at his own expense and risk load the goods on board. ..."[30] Incoterms defines "C & F" as: "The seller delivers the goods on board the vessel or procures the goods already so delivered. The risk of loss of or damage to the goods passes when the goods are on board the vessel. The seller must contract for and pay the costs and freight necessary to bring the goods to the named port of destination."[31] The older version of the UCC defined CIF somewhat differently: "The term CIF means that the price includes in a lump sum the cost of the goods and the insurance and freight to the named destination.[32]

The actions of the I.C.C. in promulgating Incoterms was certainly a good faith effort; but even with these ostensibly uniform definitions, there is little true uniformity. Some countries such as Japan simply do not abide by uniform rules.[33] In England sellers and buyers only infrequently make use of Incoterms.[34] In the United States, for a very long time, the definitions for terms such as "FOB," "CIF," and others were somewhat different from the definitions found in Incoterms. In 1995, after researching the differences and noting that most, if not all, international contracts used Incoterms,

28. Incoterms 2010, International Chamber of Commerce (2010). *See also*, the helpful companion volume, Jan Ramberg, Phillipe Rapatout, Frank Reynolds & Charles Debattista, *ICC Guide to Incoterms 2010* (2010). *See also*, Jan Ramberg, *Incoterms 2010*, 29 Penn. St. Int'l L. Rev. 415 (2011).
29. ICC, Incoterms 2010.
30. UCC §2-319 (Repealed).
31. *Id.*
32. UCC §2-320 (Repealed).
33. *See*, Hishashi Tanikawa, *Risk of Loss in Japanese Sales Transactions*, 42 Wash. L. Rev. 463 (1967).
34. *See*, Frederic Eisemann, *Note, Incoterms and the British Export Trade*, 1965 J. Bus. L. 114.

and that there was no principled reason for preserving the differences in the UCC, the National Conference of Commissioners on Uniform State Laws (the drafters of the UCC) repealed those sections of UCC Article 2 that contained trade term-like definitions.[35]

But the reader should keep in mind that these amendments were only promulgated by the National Conference. To be effective as controlling law, each state must adopt the amendments as positive legislation. Some states have preserved the old UCC definitions for the various trade terms by refusing to accept the National Conference's recommendations. As a result, there may be problems stemming from different legal systems using slightly different definitions. While the definitions may be similar, there could be just enough linguistic differences to pose interpretative problems.

The path of least resistance and risk is simply to refer expressly to Incoterms when including terms such as FOB and CIF. If a contract uses Incoterms or any other set of privately commissioned uniform definitions, a truly cautious drafter will make sure to refer to the particular version of Incoterms used, to insure that if the ICC later changes the terms, a judge or arbitrator will refer to the definitions in force when the contract was drafted. For example, a contract stating a price of fittings to be "$5.00 per fitting, FOB New York" should, if the drafters are using Incoterms, additionally provide: $5.00 per fitting, "FOB (Incoterms 2010) New York."

§4.6 SAMPLE CLAUSES IN INTERNATIONAL COMMERCIAL AGREEMENTS: FORMATION AND PERFORMANCE

However an agreement is reached, the final document will almost always contain, at a minimum, language covering the matters discussed below. While an omission of any particular term (except, possibly, the quantity term) is not necessarily fatal to the formation of a valid and enforceable agreement, careful drafters of contracts do not normally write contracts that are silent on these matters. A provision may be deliberately flexible—as, for example, a price term that turns on the rise or fall of a specified cost of living index—but the term will still be mentioned in the contract. Many contracts begin with a recitation of the purposes of the agreement and contain boilerplate establishing the promises made by each party to the other. The sample clause set out on p. 124, *supra*, is a short example of some of these recitations. In traditional contracts, the recitations are frequently preceded by the term whereas: "Whereas the two parties to this agreement wishing to commence a commercial relationship for the purchase and sale of brass fittings do hereby solemnly and mutually promise and agree to the following. ..." As discussed in §4.2 this is great lawyerese, and conceivably may be indispensable language under the law of some country, but really counts for nothing in the typical commercial agreement.

The best agreements are specific and to the point, including clauses that set out the parties' agreement on all the important aspects of the relationship. Senior partners

35. The amendments to UCC Art. 2 simply eliminated sections 2-319–2-324. The National Conference stated that the old terms were "inconsistent with modern commercial practices." *See*, John Spanogle, *Incoterms and the UCC Article 2—Conflicts and Confusions*, 31 Int'l L. 111 (1997).

in law firms for reasons of tradition rather than rationality also get caught up in these hackneyed expressions and cannot be persuaded that a document that does not contain these recitations can be valid. If the contract drafter is not the person who has to sign the document, he or she may have to knuckle under to traditions which fly in the face of wisdom and efficiency. Nonetheless, all other things being equal, a good contract generally begins with a plain statement describing the parties and the subject matter of the agreement: "This is a contract between Buyer [including full name and address] and Seller [full name and address] for the purchase and sale of brass fittings." The contract then normally sets out definitions, if the drafters have decided to insert a separate definition section.

Following these preliminary items, the contract then moves to those provisions that insure the proper formation of a contract. Subsequent sections will deal with other parts of the contract.

§4.6.1 The Quantity Term

In contracts for the sale of goods a quantity term is indispensable. It can be either a fixed quantity (100 arm chairs) or a flexible term stated in terms of the seller's output or the buyer's requirements in any given period of time, for example, "Buyer shall purchase all Windsor chairs manufactured by Seller between January 1 and June 30, 1992." (an output contract) or "Buyer shall purchase from Seller a quantity of Windsor chairs equal to the total requirements for Windsor chairs incurred by Buyer during the period January 1 through June 30, 1992." (a requirements contract). Other possible arrangements include an exclusive dealing agreement by which a seller agrees to sell only to a single buyer over a specified period of time.

§4.6.2 The Price Term

Specifying price in a contract has always been tricky, particularly in periods of sharp inflationary or deflationary movements.[36] A contract may specify a fixed price, ("$100 per chair"), or may provide a price reference that becomes effective at the time of shipment or the time of receipt of the goods. Petroleum contracts, for example, are rarely fixed price contracts because of the volatility of the price of crude oil. To compensate for this volatility, a typical contract will state the price of the contract with reference to the spot market price for a barrel of crude oil on one of the internationally recognized markets in, say, New York or Rotterdam effective on the day of receipt by the buyer of the actual commodity. In theory, a price term for the sale of any good could be pegged to the price of, for example, a barrel of crude oil. This is a rare practice except in the context of barter and countertrade agreements.

When a contract drafter is writing a flexible price term, the important consideration is to make sure all parties fully understand the reference point for the price. For

36. *See*, e.g., Thomas R. Hurst, *Drafting Contracts in an Inflationary Era*, 28 U. Fla. L. Rev. 884 (1976).

example, many contracts for the sale of goods that are to be performed over a long period of time contain a price escalation clause tied to a cost of living index. The difficulty is that there are a number of cost of living indexes published in the United States. A precise cost of living index will: (1) specify the particular cost of living index—for example, the "Consumer Price Index published monthly by the United States Department of Labor;" and (2) will specify the specific point in time on which the index is to reset prices—for example, "prices under this contract shall increase by the percentage increase of the Consumer Price Index annually on the anniversary date of this contract." Some long-term contracts for both goods and services set fixed prices that increase over time on a particular schedule. The price-increase schedule is sometimes included in the basic price term; more often it is included in an annex to the agreement and the contract's price term simply incorporates the annex by reference. There are any number of variations for all these alternatives that will pass muster with courts and arbitrators.

Buyers typically favor fixed price contracts so that they can predict their future costs of doing business while sellers often prefer flexibility. There are times when both parties want to contract with each other but simply cannot settle on a specific price for the goods. There are other times, particularly in transactions involving the exchange of forms rather than carefully drafted contracts, where the price cannot be ascertained from the documents. In these circumstances some legal systems, for example the U.S.'s UCC, the underlying law will fill in a "reasonable" price term if price is not specified in the contract.[37] More specifically, the Code provides for a reasonable price established by the parties in good faith at the time for delivery if:

(a) nothing is said as to price; or
(b) the price is left to be agreed upon by the parties and they have not agreed; or
(c) the price is to be fixed in terms of some agreed market or other standard;
(d) Other well-known variants in international commercial contracts include cost-plus contracts, often used in contracting with governments (the price is the seller's cost of producing the good plus a fixed percentage increment added to that cost) and gold clauses (the price is a specified number of ounces of gold, even though the ultimate price will fluctuate depending on the sales price of gold).

Price terms in some contracts such as licensing agreements are normally stated in terms of a percentage royalty, rather than a price per unit shipped. Licensing

37. *See*, UCC §2-305. For excellent discussion of many different "incomplete" contract issues *see*, e.g., Scott Baker & Kimberly D. Krawlec, *Incomplete Contracts in a Complete Contract World*, 33 Florida St. U. L. Rev. 725 (2006); Symposium, *Incomplete Contracts: Judicial Responses, Transactional Planning and Litigation Strategies*, 56 Case W. Res. L. Rev. 135 (2005); Juliet P. Kostritsky, *What to Do When Parties Have Not Achieved Bargains or Have Drafted Incomplete Contracts*, 2004 Wis. L. Rev. 323; Omri Ben-Shahar, *Filling Gaps in Deliberately Incomplete Contracts*, 2004 Wis. L. Rev. 389; Steven L. Harris, *Rules for Interpreting Incomplete Contracts: A Cautionary Note*, 61 La. L. Rev. 1279 (2002).

agreements also frequently contain minimum royalty payment requirements that are stated in fixed dollar terms. A typical percentage royalty term is: "Licensee shall pay to Licensor, annually from the date of execution of this agreement, a royalty of 4% of licensee's ex-factory price on each gross of brass fittings manufactured under the license granted in this contract."

However price is stated in the contract, the drafter should not lose sight of the fact that this is one of the central provisions of any transaction. People make commercial agreements to earn a profit; proper pricing is essential to a profit.

§4.6.3 The Payment Term

In most domestic contracts, payment is simply made at a time specified (e.g., "within thirty days following delivery") with an understanding that payment will be made in the legal tender of that country or by way of a recognized negotiable instrument (such as a check). In the United States the bank collection system and sources of financial information are quite efficient. Most businesses in the U.S. have standard courses of dealing with regard to payment that rarely have to be stated in elaborate form.

Such is not the case, however, in international commercial contracts. For international transactions, the payment term is crucial. Many contracts provide expressly for both a time of payment and the currency in which payment is to be made. Some contracts provide for payment in any one of several currencies at the option of one of the parties. Some contracts contain payment terms with currency fluctuation clauses to accommodate drastic changes in the valuation of the specified currency. One way to circumvent most problems associated with currency fluctuation is to call for payment in a highly stable currency—Swiss francs are an international favorite—rather than drafting a complicated fluctuation clause.

If payment is not made in cash, the contract will likely contain a detailed clause calling for the issuance of a letter of credit. Occasionally payment will be made in the form of barter—as, for example, when Boeing exchanges jet aircraft for Saudi Arabian oil. Much like other clauses in the contract, payment terms range from the simple to the highly complicated. The following is an example of a payment term involving a letter of credit: "Payments under this contract shall be made in Swiss francs by the means of an irrevocable and confirmed documentary credit at the date of order issued by a bank acceptable to seller." In construction contracts, progress payments are usually made without the requirement of a letter of credit. A term of payment for a construction contract might state: "Contractor shall, upon reaching of each payment milestone as described in Annex B, submit to Company an invoice covering such payment milestone, with relevant documentation to verify the appropriateness of the invoice. Company shall, within thirty days from receipt of the invoice, pay to a bank account designated by Contractor all undisputed portions of the invoice. Company shall advise contractor promptly of any amount in dispute. Any invoice which is not paid within the period stipulated in this clause shall be subject to interest at the rate set out in Annex B."

§4.6.4 Provisions Allocating Risk of Loss During Shipment

Virtually no contract fails to include some provision for allocating the risk of loss during shipment. Some contracts simply specify which party shall bear the loss at any given time during the transit of goods; other contracts also provide expressly for the passing of title to the goods from seller to buyer. In most contracts, the point in time at which title passes is also the time at which risk of loss shifts from seller to buyer. Like so many other clauses in the typical contract, risk of loss and passing of title provisions are of no consequence. The contract is fully performed and everyone goes away happily. If something goes wrong, however, it a different story. These clauses become crucial to the transaction when the shipment is destroyed. They are also one of the contract provisions that are typically borrowed from external sources such as the ICC's Incoterms. In contracts where the goods are highly perishable—a contract for gasoline, for example—the parties might want to draft a lengthy risk of loss clause that reflects industry practice in shipping gasoline from seller to buyer.

In many contracts, a number of the clauses discussed above are merged into a single paragraph in the contract. The clause— "Buyer shall purchase 100 fittings at a unit price of $5.00 per fitting, FOB (Incoterms) Seattle, payment by check on receipt of goods."—is simultaneously a quantity term, a price term, a payment term and a risk of loss term. By Incoterm definition, risk of loss passes when the goods pass the ship's rail.

§4.6.5 Performance Clauses and Express and Implied Warranties

Most international contracts contain some type of performance or warranty requirement. These clauses can include express promises that the goods or the services will be of adequate quality. Express performance or warranty provisions are more important in international contracts because there is no uniformity as to express or implied warranties under the domestic law of most countries. Particularly in construction contracts, performance is central to the agreement and performance obligations should be spelled out in the document.

If warranties are not spelled out in the contract itself they may not necessarily be filled in by operation of law. While the commercial law of most countries contains some requirement that goods be delivered free of defects the scope and effect of those warranties diverges greatly.[38] The United States UCC, for example, contains some sophisticated warranty provisions that may be disclaimed by sellers only with difficulty.[39] The warranty provisions in the Convention for International Sales of Goods (CISG) differ from those in the UCC. Warranty law in many other countries is not nearly

38. *See*, e.g., Wortley, *Mercantile Usage and Custom*, in *Rabels Zeitschrift Fur Auslandisches Und Internationales Pirvatrech* (1959), 259; D. Jacobson, *International Sales of Goods*, 3 Int'l & Comp. L.Q. 659 (1954).

39. The UCC recognizes express warranties (i.e., those inserted specifically in the contract) and two different forms of implied warranty: (1) a warranty of merchantibility (that the goods are fit for the ordinary purposes for which such goods are used and are of fair average quality); and (2) a

so highly developed, however. Consequently, if parties to international contracts want the special protections that warranties afford, the wisest course of action is to spell out those warranties in the document itself, or to very carefully select a system of underlying law that provides those warranties desired by the parties.

§4.7 SAMPLE CLAUSES: BREACH, REMEDIES, AND MISCELLANEOUS

Some contracts actually spell out some of the acts of either party that will constitute breach of the contract. For example, a contract for the sale of goods under an installment payment agreement might specify: "Buyer's failure to pay any single payment within fifteen days of the date payment is due constitutes breach of this agreement." Another clause might specify that "Any dishonor of buyer's letters of credit constitutes breach of this agreement." There may be occasions when such language is called for, but by and large, such clauses are superfluous. In virtually all legal systems, a contract is breached when one of the parties fails to live up to the terms of the agreement. Put another way, the act of breaching the contract is usually obvious to both parties. Even when breach is more subtly evidenced, it is rare that the contract itself will have anticipated subtle breaches.

There are, of course, numerous cases inquiring into whether the breach is material or whether the party deemed in breach substantially performed even if it did not fully perform; but there is little that a contract drafter can do to cover such situations. As a consequence, many contracts forego such language and concentrate on drafting provisions such as force majeure clauses to identify those circumstances in which performance may be forgiven.

§4.7.1 Force Majeure Clauses

When Professor Andreas Lowenfeld enumerated the special risks of international trade he specifically mentioned "the risk of international turmoil, tension and change."[40] These risks include war, riots, insurrection, invasion, and other matters that may not be totally foreseeable but may certainly be anticipated by appropriate contract language. The inability of human beings to foresee everything that might go wrong in a transaction is a principal reason for force majeure clauses. These clauses typically contemplate natural disasters, although most clauses also extend to political disruptions. Many of the traditional clauses recite a list of different occurrences such as war, fire, flood, embargo, explosion, import or export prohibitions, strikes or other labor troubles, and supply interruptions due to similar causes. In effect, a force majeure

---

warranty of fitness for a particular purpose (which is in effect if the seller knows that the buyer has a particular purpose for the goods and is relying on the seller's skill or judgment to select appropriate goods. UCC §§2-313, 2-314, 2-315.

40. Andreas F. Lowenfeld, *International Private Trade* (1981), 3. *See also*, Joseph M. Perillo, *Force Majeure and Hardship under the UNIDROIT Principles of International Commercial Contracts*, 5 Tul. J. Int'l & Comp. L. 5 (1997).

clause suspends performance without penalty for the party affected by the disruption. The forgiveness is normally only for the period of the disruption.

Some force majeure clauses have included "inflation beyond the expected rate" as a possible ground for invoking force majeure. One legal system, the U.S. UCC, forgives performance that has been made commercially impracticable.[41] Other systems recognize certain changes in government policy as a proper basis for forgiving or suspending performance. Under the fundamental doctrine of party autonomy, parties should be able to include virtually any event of their choosing in the force majeure clause. However, traditional force majeure clauses normally are restricted to events unforeseen at the time of the execution of the contract and typically confined to a physical inability to perform, so-called acts of God.

There are many variations of force majeure clauses. Recall that the central purpose of such clauses is to forgive performance when events occur to dispute performance that were outside the contemplation of the parties when they first signed the agreement. As a result, force majeure clauses may simply state: "A party shall not be considered to be in default in the performance of its obligations to the extent that it proves that such performance has been prevented by force majeure." In the definitional section of the contract, force majeure is defined as: "An occurrence beyond the control of the party affected, provided that such party could not reasonably have foreseen such occurrence at the time of entering into the contract or could not reasonably have avoided or overcome its consequences." This clause may be viewed as a modern form of force majeure clause.

The more traditional clauses tend to be far more verbose, without adding that much more to the parties' understanding of force majeure: "The parties hereto shall not be responsible for failure to perform this contract due to force majeure. Force majeure includes but is not limited to: fires, floods, riots, strikes, labor strife, transportation disruptions, interruptions in the supply of raw materials, Acts of God or other causes that are beyond the reasonable control of the affected party." Force majeure clauses in contracts using the U.S. UCC as the applicable law that do not wish to incorporate the UCC's more flexible concept of commercial impracticability should include an express disclaimer: for example, "Force majeure is limited to a party's physical inability to perform the contract. It does not include disruptions that make the contract's performance merely commercially impracticable."

§4.7.2 Government Approval Clauses

Some private international transactions, particularly those involving transfer of technology, require the approval of one or more governments. The specific approval mechanism may be a registration requirement, the obtaining of export or import permission, or formal approval for a joint venture. If approvals are necessary most contracts simply provide that the contract is not fully effective until the necessary

41. UCC §2-615.

approvals have been obtained. In other words, government approvals are usually treated as a condition precedent to the formation of the contract, rather than a failure that leads to breach of the contract.

In addition, most contracts place the obligation to obtain the permission from the party in the country that must issue the permission. Buyer usually obtains any necessary import permissions; seller obtains permission to export the goods. This is a rational approach to something that can occasionally prove troublesome in practice. The burden of obtaining permission should fall on the person with the best access to the government in question. A typical government permissions clause for a sale of goods contract might read: "Seller shall obtain all necessary permits, licenses or permissions to export the goods. Buyer shall obtain all necessary permits, licenses or permissions necessary to import the goods. This contract is not fully executed and enforceable until all such permissions have been received."

§4.7.3 Penalty and Liquidated Damages Clauses

Contracting parties often wish to have some special protection against the possibility of nonperformance by the other party, particularly in agreements such as construction contracts in which time is of the essence. It is not unusual for an international contract to contain some type of penalty or liquidated damages clause that provides for the payment of a penalty (e.g., "Builder shall pay Purchaser $5000.00 per day for each day the project remains uncompleted after January 1, 1984.") or for liquidated damages (e.g., "The parties agree that in the event of a breach of this contract by either party the breaching party shall pay the amount of $15,000.00 in damages.").

In some legal systems liquidated damages provisions will be honored while provisions deemed penalty clauses will not, even though there is a very thin line between clauses that might constitute penalties and those that appear to be liquidated damages clauses. As a consequence, contract drafters should be aware that not all penalty or liquidated damages clauses will be honored by courts or by arbitrators.[42]

The foregoing discussion was intended to be only an illustrative list of possible contract provisions. Contracts for specific purposes other than the sale of goods such as distributorship and licensing agreements or complex financing contracts require many other provisions to be fully satisfactory. There are numerous sources of information on appropriate clauses for these contracts.[43]

42. For an excellent comparative article *see* Emily Nordin, *The Penalty Clause Bias*, 21 Maastricht J. of Eur. & Comp. L. 162 (2014). *See also*, Jack Graves, *Penalty Clauses and the CISG*, 30 Pitt. J. of L. & Com. 153 (2012); Eric A. Posner, *There Are No Penalty Default Rules in Contract Law*, 33 Fla. St. U. L. Rev. 563 (2006); Aaron S. Edlin & Alan Schwartz, *Optimal Penalties in Contracts*, 78 Chi.-Kent L. Rev. 33 (2003); Peter Benjamin, *Penalties, Liquidated Damage and Penal Clauses*, 9 Int'l & Comp. L.Q. 600 (1960); John Thilmany, *Fonctions et Revisibilite des Clauses Penale en Droit Compare*, 8 Revue Internationale de Droit Compare 17 (1980).

43. *See*, e.g., Harry R. Mayers, *Drafting Patent License Agreements* (3d ed., 1990); Philip Wood, *Law and Practice of International Finance* (1984); T. Johnson, *International Distributor and Agency Agreements* (1967).

§4.8 DRAFTING THE DISPUTE RESOLUTION AND CHOICE OF FORUM CLAUSES

Most international contracts contain some kind of dispute resolution clause. The typical dispute resolution clause provides for arbitration under the rules of some domestic or international arbitration association. Indeed, many of these associations, notably the AAA and the ICC, furnish model arbitration clauses that may be inserted into contracts.[44]

Most of these prototype arbitration clauses also provide for a choice of forum (i.e., "Disputes under this contract shall be subject to the rules of AAA and any arbitration under this clause shall take place in Washington, D.C.") Some commercial contracts provide for dispute resolution by litigation in the domestic courts of one party or the other or for litigation in the domestic courts of a country regarded as neutral by the contracting parties. For the most part, the parties' choices on these issues will be honored. In one important case eventually decided by the United States Supreme Court, a dispute arose between a German shipping company and an American oil company under a contract that provided for the resolution of any disputes by litigation in the High Court of Justice in London. The United States Supreme Court honored that agreement, commenting that international commercial transactions are usually carefully negotiated bargains between sophisticated parties and the agreement of the parties, including their agreement as to choice of forum must be honored to preserve the stability and integrity of international agreements.[45] Within the EC choice of forum clauses are generally honored so long as one of the parties is deemed to be domiciled within the jurisdiction of a signatory state.[46]

It is possible, of course, for the contract to be silent on dispute resolution. For contracts that lack express dispute resolution clauses, the parties may simply negotiate differences that arise during the performance of the contract. They may agree to negotiate in the presence of a third-party mediator or conduct some other type of dispute resolution process without having made special provision for these events in the original document.[47] Alternatively, the parties may execute a subsequent written agreement to arbitrate any grievances that have arisen under the contract; or the parties may simply choose to litigate their differences in some appropriate court.

---

44. Some general considerations and some helpful hints may be found in Paul D. Friedland, *Arbitration Clauses for International Contracts* (2d ed., 2017); Ya-Wei Li, Kasoparas Tolkusinas, *Defective Arbitration Clauses in International Commercial Contracts: Common Mistakes and Proper Drafting Guidelines* (2011); *Dispute Resolution Clauses in International Contracts: An Empirical Study,* 30 Cornell Int'l L.J. 789 (2006); Robert Donald Fischer & Roger S. Haydock, *International Commercial Disputes: Drafting an Enforceable Arbitration Agreement,* 21 Wm. Mitchell L. Rev. 941 (1996). *See also*, William Fox, *How to Think About International Commercial Dispute Resolution*, in *International Trade for the Non-Specialist* (2d ed., 1997).
45. The *Bremen v. Zapata Off-Shore Company,* 407 U.S. 1 (1972).
46. Article 17, EEC Convention on Jurisdiction and Enforcement of Judgments in Civil and Commercial Matters, done, September 27, 1968, reprinted in 8 Int'l Leg. Materials 229 (1969). Choices will not be enforced if a particular court has exclusive jurisdiction or if undue influence or a contract of adhesion (a printed form agreement) is involved.
47. *See* generally, *Adaptation and Renegotiation of Contracts in International Trade and Finance* (Norbert Horn ed., 1985).

Those drafters who prefer to include a dispute resolution clause in their contracts—and most international commercial agreements contain such clauses—should remember that the vast majority of international agreements choose arbitration, even though the author of this book would urge all drafters to at least consider incorporation of some language urging renegotiation, mediation or a minitrial before the parties go to arbitration, because of the expense and procedural complexity now associated with commercial arbitration. Many international contracts simply use a domestic form of arbitration, such as: "All disputes under this agreement shall be settled through arbitration under the commercial arbitration rules of the Stockholm Chamber of Commerce." If the parties are predisposed to sign a simple arbitration clause, the contract drafter should be prepared to brief the client on some of the components of arbitration under that system, including typical fees assessed, the manner of selecting the arbitrator, the rules governing the arbitration hearing, and the mechanisms for either compelling or enforcing arbitration that exist in the host country's domestic courts. One good reference for this type of information is the International Handbook on Commercial Arbitration.[48]

In certain circumstances, the parties may have very little choice. For example, in the past in negotiating contracts with the former Soviet Union, the Soviet negotiators normally insisted on arbitration before a domestic U.S.S.R. tribunal, the Foreign Trade Arbitration Commission. However, if a foreign party objected, the Soviet negotiators usually had no problem agreeing to arbitration in Sweden, with a Stockholm arbitration site using the arbitration rules of the Stockholm Chamber of Commerce.[49] It remains to be seen whether the republics constituting the Commonwealth of Independent States will retain these rigid attitudes toward dispute resolution. The likelihood is that they will not. Given that the republics are so hungry for foreign commerce, they are likelier to adopt modern and far more flexible arbitration techniques than those applied by the Soviet Union. Nonetheless, there are countries, China for example, that are still in existence whose attitude toward dispute resolution is equally rigid. In dealing with those countries, contracting parties may simply have to decide whether they want to do the deal (and thereby concede the matter of dispute resolution) or contract with parties in countries that are more flexible.

In most international commercial negotiations, the choices are broader. The parties may simply elect the arbitration system of either the seller or the buyer's country or choose arbitration under the domestic arbitration laws of a third country. Recall that in most countries, including the United States, when the parties select arbitration they will be held to that choice even if, at some later point in time, they conclude that litigation would be preferable.[50] If the contracting parties believe that all domestic arbitration systems are inappropriate they may choose arbitration under the rules and supervision of one of the international arbitration bodies. A few agreements

48. *International Handbook on Commercial Arbitration: National Reports and Basic Legal Texts* (Jan Paulsson ed., 2017).

49. Thomas Hoya & Daniel Stein, *Drafting Contracts in U.S.-Soviet Trade,* 7 L. & Pol'y Int'l Bus. 1057 (1975). (With the demise of the Soviet Union and the fragmentation of the former Soviet Republics, Mr. Hoya's work is now mainly of historical interest.)

50. *See* the discussion of the U.S. Supreme Court's decision in *Mitsubishi v. Soler,* Chapter 8, §8.2.

provide for ad hoc arbitration, by which the parties concoct (or borrow) their own rules, select the arbitrators and administer the arbitration proceeding completely on their own. While permissible, and while there are some cost savings associated with ad hoc arbitration, it should be elected only by experienced companies accompanied by experienced counsel.

Most disputing parties need the assistance of a recognized arbitral institution. As a result, most dispute resolution clauses in international commercial agreements choose among the major arbitration institutions such as the ICC or among highly experienced national systems of arbitration such as the London Court of Arbitration or the AAA.

Once these preliminary choices have been made, drafting the dispute resolution clause is relatively simple: most contracts adopt the sample clause suggested by the supervising institution and then modify that clause to suit their particular needs and desires. The much harder part of the equation is knowing which body's rules to select. The discussion in Chapter 5 of the different procedural systems for international commercial arbitration should be consulted to determine the advantages and disadvantages of each of the major procedural schemes.

The major arbitration bodies such as the AAA and ICC have drafted standard form arbitration clauses that they believe will suffice as a contract's dispute resolution clause. The AAA suggests: "Any controversy or claim arising out of or relating to this contract, or any breach thereof, shall be settled by arbitration in accordance with the Rules of the AAA, and judgment upon award rendered by the arbitrator(s) may be entered in any court having jurisdiction thereof." The London Court of International Arbitration recommends: "Any dispute arising out of or in connection with this contract, including any question regarding its existence, validity or termination, shall be referred to and finally resolved by arbitration under the Rules of the London Court of International Arbitration, which Rules are deemed to be incorporated by reference into this clause." The sample clause drafted by UNCITRAL states: "Any dispute, controversy or claim arising out of or relating to this contract, or the breach, termination or invalidity thereof, shall be settled by arbitration in accordance with the UNCITRAL Arbitration Rules as are present in force." The ICC suggests: "All disputes arising in connection with the present contract shall be finally settled under the Rules of Conciliation and Arbitration of the ICC by one or more arbitrators appointed in accordance with the Rules."

The World Intellectual Property Organization's arbitration center suggests a much more elaborate clause: "Any dispute, controversy or claim arising under, out of or relating to this contract and any subsequent amendments of this contract, including without limitation, its formation, validity, binding effect, interpretation, performance, breach or termination, as well as noncontractual claims, shall be referred to and finally determined by arbitration in accordance with the WIPO Arbitration Rules. The arbitral tribunal shall consist of [three arbitrators][a sole arbitrator]. The place of the arbitration shall be ____________. The language used in the arbitral proceeding shall be ____________. The dispute, controversy or claim shall be decided in accordance with the law of ____________."[51]

If a contract drafter needs a quick arbitration clause, any of these will suffice because the institution's underlying rules will supply the missing details. However, most experienced international lawyers find those clauses too simplistic, and recommend that the contract set out more of the details of dispute resolution even when the parties agreed to use a supervising institution and that institution's rules.

As a minimum, the dispute resolution clause in a contract electing institutional arbitration (i.e., a proceeding supervised by one of the recognized arbitration institutions) should specify the following:

(1) *The type of dispute resolution to be employed.* If two different devices are to be utilized, such as mediation and arbitration, the clause should make clear that mediation is to take place before arbitration.
(2) *The rules system for the arbitration.* (ICC, AAA, UNCITRAL, etc.) Note that many of the institutions will agree to supervise an arbitration using UNCITRAL rules, rather than the institution's rules. Under normal circumstances, it is advisable to use the rules promulgated by the institution that will be supervising the arbitration.
(3) *The language of the arbitration proceeding and the arbitral award.* The language of the arbitration in most cases will be the same as the official language of the contract. However, there may be instances when the parties want to utilize another language—for example, the language of the country that is the site of the arbitration—to make it easier for any arbitrators who are selected from that country to follow the proceedings.
(4) *The site of arbitration.* There many choices available here. Typical choices include the country of the buyer or the country of the seller. If a neutral site is selected, most parties choose a site such as London, Cairo or Stockholm that has solid experience with arbitration and an ample supply of arbitrators. The arbitrators may be imported for the hearing, of course, but that greatly increases the expense of the arbitration. Most parties choose a site in a country that has signed the New York Convention for the Recognition and Enforcement of Arbitral Awards.[52] Recall that an arbitral award rendered in a country that has signed the New York Convention is enforceable under the terms of the Convention even if one or more of the parties is from a country that has not signed. A final consideration for selecting the arbitration site is the court structure of the host country. Because parties sometimes have to refer prearbitration issues to a court and

51. The WIPO arbitration center and the WIPO rules are discussed more extensively in Chapter 9, §9.5.4.
52. *See* the discussion of the New York Convention in Chapter 10, §10.3.

because the winning party sometimes has to seek enforcement of the arbitral award in court, the host country's court system could figure importantly in the arbitration.

(5) *The number of arbitrators.* In most international commercial arbitration systems, the rules provide for the appointment of a panel of three arbitrators (one selected by each of the two parties with the third selected by the two party-appointed arbitrators; this third arbitrator normally presides over the arbitration as chairman). If the parties want to reduce expenses associated with any arbitration, they must expressly provide for a single arbitrator. Some arbitration clauses also set out the credentials of the arbitrators (e.g., "each arbitrator shall have at least ten years experience in commercial real estate matters"). If there are special reasons for specifying credentials, these choices will normally be honored by the supervising institution. Most arbitration clauses do not go this far.

If institutional arbitration is selected, the parties may still go ahead and specify the nationalities of the arbitrators, specific procedures for the arbitration (including, e.g., whether prehearing discovery is permitted and under what circumstances) and other details. This is probably drafting over-kill. It adds enormous detail to the contract itself when the rules of the supervising institution can fill in most of the details. Obviously, if the parties disagree with the procedures set out in the institution's rules, they need to set out the different procedures either in the contract itself or in a subsequent arbitration agreement.

If the parties want to go ahead on their own without the assistance of a supervising institution, choosing what is known as ad hoc arbitration, the contract—or a subsequent agreement—needs to contain far more detail. Harry Arkin, a U.S. lawyer who is an experienced international arbitrator suggests the following components for a proper ad hoc arbitration clause:[53]

(1) Scope of the arbitration.
(2) Jurisdiction of the arbitrators.
(3) Demand for arbitration and response time.
(4) Representation by counsel.
(5) Selection of arbitrators (including credentials, a party's failure to select, removal and replacement).
(6) Site of arbitration.
(7) Language of arbitration.
(8) Applicable law.
(9) Procedural rules (including hearing procedures, taking of evidence, discovery, provisional remedies).
(10) Issuance of the award (including appeal or vacating the award, modification or correction of the award).

53. Harry G. Arkin, *International Ad Hoc Arbitration: A Practical Alternative,* Int'l Bus. Law. 5 (1987).

(11) Enforcement of the award.
(12) Allocation of costs of arbitration.

It is possible to make both too much and too little of a dispute resolution clause. The author has experienced contract negotiations where the negotiators have resolved the price term in thirty seconds and spent three days on the arbitration clause. There have been other negotiations where the contract drafters casually toss a standard form arbitration clause into the agreement without thirty seconds of thought. Neither approach makes a great deal of sense. No one enters an agreement expecting the contract to be breached, but when breach occurs, dispute resolution becomes a vital component of the transaction.

§4.9 USING INTERNATIONAL TECHNICAL STANDARDS AS CONTRACT CLAUSES

The topic of International technical standards is rarely taught in either law schools or schools of business. Most lawyers and business executives encounter these concepts only when they find themselves on the job dealing with vocabulary and processes that are totally unfamiliar to them. Essentially, technical standards (hereafter we will just use the term "standards") grew out of a need for uniformity in various areas of economic enterprise. The best way to begin thinking of standards is to envision railroads in Germany and Russia around the turn of the twentieth century. The distance between the two rails (the width of the tracks) was different in the two countries. So a train that reached the German-Russian border from either direction could not proceed into the other country because the track width was different. Had the European nations created and imposed a standard track width, the trains could have moved freely in either direction.

Standards began as common measurements for various human activities. The world needs common definitions of weights and measures, of time, of dimensions, of chemical and physical concepts and the like; otherwise businesses, educators, scientists and other professional groups cannot communicate and work effectively with each other. These days standards reach into virtually every important area of economic activity.

§4.9.1 Standards: Some Basic Concepts and Definitions

> The Inch in a standard of measurement. Honey is a standard of exchange. Words are standards of communication. Traffic lights are safety standards. Octane numbers of gasoline are quality standards. "No more than one-inch shrinkage" is a performance standard.[54]

54. Brochure, National Institute of Standards and Technology at 1–2.

Standards affect virtually every human being in virtually every segment of human behavior and activity.[55] Consumers take comfort in knowing that camera film speed notations on the box of film indicates the relative efficiency of the film in various conditions of light and dark. However, very few persons grasp the fact that those labels on the film containers were set by way of standard-setting activities of the International Organization for Standardization. Students returning to school buy paper punched with three-holes without the need to bring along their three-ring binders to ensure that the paper will fit the binder. Private-sector standards determine the size and spacing of those holes to ensure uniformity throughout the United States. Drivers of automobiles quickly learn the differences between the different shapes of traffic signs: octagonal for stop signs and inverted triangles for yield signs. The shape of these signs alone (made to government specifications) has a salutary effect on driving behavior in this country.

A more serious definition of a standard has been issued by the National Standards Policy Advisory Committee: A prescribed set of rules, conditions or requirements concerning definitions of terms; classification of components; specification of materials, performance, or operations; delineation of procedures; or measurement of quantity and quality in describing materials, products, systems, services, or practices."[56]

As noted above, standards enhance public health and safety. They are important components in industry and commerce. They help promote—and indeed may drive—international trade. The National Institute of Standards and Technology estimates that there are approximately 300,000 "voluntary" standards currently in use in the United States that were developed by more than 400 standards development organizations. Moreover, these figures do not include thousands of additional procurement specifications (discussed below under the "military specification" heading) that are imposed through the procurement activities of various levels of government.

While there are numerous classifications for standards, and while the classification vocabulary is not necessarily accepted throughout the world, some basic definitions are offered here to set the stage for the remainder of this paper. Standards may be either *design* or *performance* standards. Design standards comprise specific requirements for the building of a particular product and are often used when the factor of compatibility and interchangeability are the paramount considerations. Performance standards normally say nothing about the precise nature of building a product, but rather focus on the manner in which the product works when it is put to use. Performance standards normally seen as less restrictive and, as such, do not have the same "technology freezing" impact as design standards. Most observers believe that performance standards promote innovation while design standards stifle it.

Another way to classify standards is according to their impact on commercial entities. *Voluntary* standards are standards that are recommended to be used but which are not imposed—or made mandatory—on the various entities that encounter those standards. *Mandatory* standards are those standards that are either set out expressly or incorporated by reference in statutes and regulations promulgated by appropriate bodies of government. Since voluntary standards are often incorporated into

55. The discussion in this section borrows heavily from the NIST brochure.
56. NSPAC Brochure at 4.

government rules and regulations, the distinction in practice between the two is often blurred. As might be expected, there are currently huge struggles in the United States legal system over the question of whether adherence to voluntary or mandatory standards exempts a commercial entity from liability for failures of its products.

Yet another set of classifications breaks standards down into: *testing* standards that measure product performance; *service* standards that impose requirements for performing service, rather than product manufacturing activities; and *interface* standards—requirements that promote connectivity of various products.

In the United States the main governmental coordinating body is the National Institute of Standards and Technology (NIST).[57] NIST, however, does not actually create standards. It merely coordinates many of the activities involved in the use of standards. Standards in the United States come mainly from private-sector organizations including many trade associations. One of the primary creators of standards for the petroleum industry is the American Petroleum Institute, one of the major industry lobbying groups.

§4.9.2 The International Organization for Standardization (ISO)

The international organization somewhat akin to NIST is the International Organization for Standardization (ISO), headquartered in Geneva, Switzerland.[58] ISO is a nongovernmental organization that, unlike NIST, actually creates and sells standards as well as providing a large number of standards coordination activities around the world. The ISO includes 162 national standards bodies and has published (as of late 2017) 21971 international standards in an enormous number of areas. ISO was created in 1946 in London with a meeting of delegates from 25 countries was convened at the Institute of Civil Engineers "to facilitate the international coordination and unification of industrial standards." ISO began operations in February 1947. The first ISO project involved development of standards for screw threads. In broad, general terms, ISO defines a standard as a document "that provides requirements, specifications, guidelines or characteristics that can be used consistently to ensure that materials, products, processes and services are fit for their purpose."

ISO develops standards through the work of technical committees that employ consistent procedures and practices.[59] As you might expect, ISO has standards that govern the creation of standards. ISO has approximately 781 technical committees working in various areas. For example, Technical committee ISO/TC 5 deals with "ferrous metal pipes and metallic fittings." ISO/TC 94 concentrates on "personal safety—protective clothing and equipment." ISO/TC 154 works on "processes, data elements and documents in commerce, industry and administration." ISO/TC 286

57. *See* the NIST website: www.nist.gov.
58. The ISO website is: www.iso.org. A great deal of the information in this section is gleaned from the NIST and ISO websites.
59. A comparison between U.S. and ISO standards practices is beyond the scope of this section. As noted earlier, U.S. standards are developed by the private sector and coordinated by NIST. ISO by contrast actually develops standards. For the remainder of this section, we will concentrate on the work of the ISO.

handles "collaborative business relationship management and ISO/TC 305 covers "sustainable non-sewered sanitation systems." By way of illustration: A few years ago, in 2009, ISO created a technical committee ISO/TC 249 for traditional Chinese medicine. As ISO explains the work of the committee:

> Standardization in the field of medical systems derived from ancient Chinese medicine which shall be able to share one common set of standards. Both traditional and modern aspects of these systems are covered. The committee focuses on quality and safety of raw materials, manufactured products and medical devices and of informatics, including, service standards limited to involving the safe use and delivery of devices and medicine, but not into the clinical practice or application of those products.[60]

One of the standards currently under development is CD 20487: "Test method for acupuncture needles for single use on electrical stimulation." NP 21311 concentrates standards for "astragalus root."

As might be expected, the ISO now has a technical committee (TC 309) for the development of standards governing the operation and organization of standards development committees. TC 309 is currently working on AWI 37000: "Guidance for the governance of organizations."

ISO organization follows the traditional model for international NGOs. The governing body is the General Assembly. Day-to-day governance is in the hands of the ISO Council and the Technical Management Board (TRB). The TRB in turn supervises the work of the technical committees where the vast bulk of the substantive work of the ISO is conducted. The standards themselves are developed on a consensus basis with each technical committee following a detailed procedure.

The work flow within the ISO for developing individual standards is relatively straightforward:

- *Step One*: A technical committee receives a proposal for a "new work item." The proposals can come from industry, academic, or government sources. It is possible for the technical committee itself to generate, internally, new proposals.
- *Step Two*: The committee engages in various types of research and analysis in an attempt to "build expert consensus. Each committee has in its membership various expertise. But typically, the committee will canvas various outside sources of information, scientific data, expert opinion, and the like to produce a "committee draft" of the proposed standard.
- *Step Three*: The committee engages in elaborate consultation and discussion to build a consensus on the standard within the technical committee itself. This involves a great deal of meeting time, electronic debate, etc. This normally results in a technical specification statement or a Technical Report (for non-normative documents).

60. Statement of "Scope" TC 249.

- *Step Four*: The committee works with the ISO secretariat to produce a "draft international standard." This is normally the final text for announcing a "Final Draft International Standard."
- *Step Five*: After a proof check by the ISO secretariat, ISO conducts a formal vote on the Final Draft International Standard that results in the final text of the International Standard.
- *Step Six*: The international standard is published and made available to the relevant industry.

The technical committees work on both new standards and possible revisions for old standards. The ISO goal is a review of each published standard every five years. The review process follows approximately the same process as the procedure for developing new standards. As part of this process, ISO prides itself in consulting with and listening to large numbers of entities from industry, academia, government, developing countries, and the like. To encourage participation from developing countries, ISO has created "twinning relationships" As the ISO describes it:

> Twinning is a partnership between a developing country ISO member and a developed country ISO member. It aims to improve the standardization infrastructure and capacities of the developing country member, to optimize the use of resources through increased cooperation, and to develop long-term strategic partnerships.[61]

Once a standard is issued, the ISO makes its money from selling copies of the standard. These publications are subject to international intellectual property doctrine, mainly copyright law, and are not cheap. For example, a standard long in place from that very first ISO technical committee, ISO/TC 1 (screw threads) is ISO 68-1: 1998 (general purpose screw threads—basic profile—Part 1: Metric screw threads). This standard was last published in 1998 and comprises three pages of text. A customer may purchase the standard in either PDF or paper format for 38 Swiss Francs. Among other things, the standard prescribes a basic profile for metric screw threads, has so-called "normative references" that are drawn from other standards, contains a basic definition section and a detailed mechanical drawing of "the theoretical profile of a screw thread in an axial plane defined by theoretical dimensions and angles common to internal and external threads."[62]

§4.9.3 The Use of Standards in International Commercial Agreements

How does all of this work in "real life." As just one example, ISO has developed more than 600 standards that affect aircraft and space vehicles. The central technical committee for aerospace is TC 20, first established in 1947. TC 20 has ten

61. *See* the ISO pamphlet: *Guidance on Twinning in ISO Standards Development Activities* (2017).
62. The ISO permits customers to examine a partial text of each standard to make sure that the standard satisfies the customers' needs. This description is taken from the ISO's Online Browsing Platform (ISO 68-1: 1998).

subcommittees, including ISO/TC 20/Subcommittee 16 which deals with unmanned aircraft systems (sometimes colloquially referred to as "drones").

There has been a great deal of attention paid to commercial drones that deliver packages to customer's homes and business locations with companies such as the United States' Amazon and China's Alibaba. But there are entirely different and innovative uses of drones to improve farming methods.[63] Drones can be used to fly, survey and photograph agricultural fields with a number of overlapping passes up and down the rows that replicates with far more efficiency, low risk and low cost the tradition of a farmer's "walking the field." The drone can take accurate measurements much faster than the human farmer, can establish parameters for the planting of the crops, use of fertilizer and irrigation, detection of fungus and other threats and produce a "map" of all these things for the farmer's use.

To enhance these technologies, ISO is developing three standards: ISO/AWI 21384-1 (unmanned aircraft systems: general specifications); ISO/AWI 21384-2 (product systems); and ISO/AWI 21384-3 (operational procedures).

Standards can have a substantial impact on drafting and negotiating international commercial agreements by serving as a standard reference. So, for example, a U.S. business executive who wants to engage in the selling of drones to farmers can deal with a Chinese manufacturer of drones by incorporating the ISO standards on unmanned aircraft systems in the contract. Not only does this create uniformity and a common basis of understanding, it also greatly shortens the text of the contract itself because the specific terms of the standard do not have to be repeated in the contract itself. The standards are normally incorporated by reference.

But incorporation by reference can be a bit tricky. The best way to start is by making absolutely sure you want to incorporate a standard. There are plenty of times when contracting parties may want to create their own specifications for the contract rather than incorporating a standard. Among other things, that gives the parties a great deal of autonomy. They are not frozen into a committee-standard that they may find only partially acceptable. Moreover, the parties can change the specifications anytime they wish.

If the parties decide they want to use a standard, it is vital (however simplistic this advice sounds) that they fully understand the standard itself. This almost always involves buying a copy of the standard and reviewing the language of the standard as carefully as they review their own contract language. Many standards are quite detailed and lengthy. For example, the ISO has promulgated a superior standard (the ISO 28000 series) relating to risks of terrorism, piracy and fraud in supply chain management. This is something that should be of enormous interest to parties establishing a long-distance, long-term distribution agreement. The ISO Secretary General has commented: "Threats in the international market-place know no borders. The ISO 28000 series provides a global solution to this global problem. With an internationally

63. This discussion borrows heavily from the ISO publication: Barnaby Lewis, Precision Farming Takes Off (May 9, 2017).

recognized security management system, stakeholders in the supply chain can ensure the safety of cargo and people, while facilitating international trade, thus contributing to the welfare of society as a whole."

The 28000 series comprises four separate standards:

(1) ISO 28000:2007: Specification for security management systems for the supply chain.
(2) ISO 28001:2007: Security management systems for the supply chain—best practices, assessments and plans, requirements and guidance.
(3) ISO 28003:2007: Security management systems—audit and certification requirements.
(4) ISO 28004:2007: Guidelines for implementation of the 28000 series.

It is possible that parties might want to use only one or two of this series, but that would probably be a big mistake because the series was promulgated as a whole. Using only one or two of its constituent parts is probably a recipe for disaster. ISO 28000 is 16 pages long and costs 88 Swiss francs. ISO 28001 is 27 pages long and costs 138 Swiss francs. There is no ISO 28002. ISO 28003 is 43 pages long and sells for 158 Swiss francs. ISO 2004 is 56 pages in length and costs 178 Swiss francs. Accordingly, a contract drafter wanting to incorporate the standard will have to review 142 pages of dense writing and reasoning, having paid 562 Swiss francs for the package.[64]

And do not forget that the standard—to be effective as a contract term—must be *implemented*. That is, the commands and instructions in the standard must be put into actual operation, otherwise the term in the contract is simply meaningless. Implementation of the more complex standards can involve thousands of person-hours and hundreds of thousands (if not more) of dollars. Unless renegotiated, the applicable standard must be enforced for the entire duration of the contract.

Finally, when a contract drafter incorporates a standard, he or she must be careful to specify the date of the standard incorporated. Recall that the ISO tries to review standards every five years. ISO 28000 was originally promulgated in 2007 and its components were reviewed in 2013 and 2014. Standards are not usually static documents, although many of the older standards such as those applying to the construction of machine screws do not change appreciably over time. But a dynamic standard such as 28000 (attempting to cope with all the nuances involved in combatting terrorism, fraud, and piracy over a long period of time) may change frequently and significantly. If you are drafting the contract, do you want the parties to abide only by the standard that is in effect when the contract is signed, or should the parties be obliged to change their practices to confirm with changes in the standard. The contract needs to be clearly drafted to make sure everyone understands *which* version of the standard is applicable to the contract, or whether the parties intend their obligations to change as the standard changes. This latter provision requires someone keeping in touch with the work of the ISO in reviewing the standard.

64. All of this information is taken from the ISO website, www.iso.org (the ISO "Store") as of December 2017.

At the same time, standards are not free of controversy. Standards are frequently incorporated in government regulations where they can have enormous impact on an entire industry and a nation's citizenry without the elaborate public participation and transparent review normally given to the issuance of government regulations. While the work of the ISO is generally known and respected, large numbers of standards are generated by much smaller, private-sector organizations with far less participation and transparency.[65]

§4.10 ARTIFICIAL INTELLIGENCE AND CONTRACT DRAFTING

§4.10.1 Artificial Intelligence: Some Basic Definitions and Concepts

Artificial intelligence is a new concept that many lawyers and business executives find intriguing, challenging and—very often—threatening. The issue for all of us is that it is a concept whose time has come and we need to cope with it and use it to our advantage rather than dismissing it. To start from the beginning, artificial intelligence (sometimes AI) is typically defined as:

> the ability of a digital computer or computer-controlled robot to perform tasks commonly associated with intelligent beings. The term is frequently applied to ... systems endowed with the intellectual processes characteristic of humans, such as the ability to reason, discover meaning, generalize, or learn from past experience.[66]

Most readers have no doubt heard all of the stories of computers beating grand master chess champions or discovering new mathematical proofs. Most of us see it daily in the work of Internet search engines or voice, face, or handwriting recognition. There remains a great deal of controversy even as to the use of the term "artificial intelligence." As some commenters see it: "Artificial intelligence" is a misnomer, an airy and evocative term that can be shaded with whatever notions we might have about what 'intelligence' is in the first place. Researchers today prefer the term 'machine learning', which better describes what makes such algorithms powerful."[67] For the sake of simplicity, this section will stick with the AI terminology.

At the same time, human intelligence is almost impossibly complex and diverse so most AI researchers focus on the traits of: (1) learning; (2) reasoning; (3) problem

65. For additional discussion of these points *see* Donald Purcell, *The Interrelationship of Standardization, Public Policy and Ethics* (2017) (privately published, copy in the author's files); Gregory Tassey, *The Roles and Impacts of Technical Standards on Economic Growth and Implications for Innovation Policy*, 1 Annals of Sci. & Tech. 215 (2017); Jorge L. Contreras, *Technical Standards, Standards-Setting Organizations and Intellectual Property*, 2 Research Handbooks on the Economics of Intellectual Property Law (2017).
66. B.J. Copeland, *Artificial Intelligence*, Encyclopedia Britannica (2017).
67. Cliff Kuang, *Can AI Be Taught to Explain Itself*, The New York Times Magazine (November 21, 2017).

solving; (4) perception; and (5) using language as the components of intelligence to be found in artificial intelligence.[68]

Each of these concepts is distinct: *Learning* can be as simple as rote memorization (a list of names and addresses, e.g.) or as complicated as what researchers call *generalization*. Generalization involves the application of past experience to similar, but new situations.[69] *Reasoning* is the drawing of inferences from any situations that may be either deductive or inductive. Problem solving is "a systematic search through a range of possible actions in order to reach some predefined goal or solution."[70] The term *perception* involves scanning of the environment by way of one's senses to arrive at conclusions as to what it is one is observing. *Language* is a system of signs that give rise to meaning and expression. Artificial intelligence can involve any one of these concepts or all of them together. As we will see, all of them are, in one sense or another, involved in AI as applied to contract drafting.

Development of AI and the search for plausible applications and uses for AI are now being seen in almost every human activity, including such learned professions as medicine and law. Researchers at Stanford University have launched the One Hundred Year Study on AI to produce an annual AI Index.[71] This is a compendium of academic research and other data to try to answer the question of where we are going in AI. As the authors put it: "Artificial intelligence has leapt to the forefront of global discourse, garnering increased attention from practitioners, industry leaders, policy makers and the general public."[72] The AI Index is an attempt to facilitate an informed conversation about AI. One prediction, based on the work of the index suggests: "[AI] can probably do less right now than you think. But it will eventually do more than you probably think, in more cases than you probably think, and will probably evolve faster than powerful technologies have in the past."[73]

What is becoming equally obvious is that AI will not likely replace all human activity. It will merely conduct a great deal of the mundane or routine work, freeing the professionals for the final, human assessment. Moreover, the machines will not necessarily be smarter than the humans. They will simply work much more quickly and much less expensively. Some commentators suggest that as much as 50% or more of the traditional work of law firms could be given over to AI. But whatever is in our future, what is absolutely clear is that AI has now grown to the point where it simply cannot be ignored—or, put a bit differently—is ignored at your peril.

---

68. Copeland, *supra* n. 66.
69. This discussion borrows heavily from the Copeland article, *supra* n. 66.
70. *Id.*
71. The index and a great deal of explanatory material and data can be found at www.aiindex.org. The index was launched in November 2017.
72. *Id.*
73. Steve Lohr, *Will Transform the Economy. But How Much, and How Soon?*. The New York Times (November 30, 2017). *See also*, Erik Brynjolfsson, Daniel Rock & Chad Syverson, *Artificial Intelligence and the Modern Productivity Paradox: A Clash of Expectations and Statistics*, report by the National Bureau of Economic Research (November 2017), available at the NBER website: www.nber.org/papers.

§4.10.2 Artificial Intelligence and the Legal Profession

The practice of law has long been mired in convention and tradition. This chapter speaks of these things in terms of the use, in international commercial agreements, of wholly useless and outmoded expressions such as "said" and "whereas" and "hereinbefore." We have discussed the common tendency of lawyers simply to borrow older language rather than crafting their own. But as we observe this behavior, all of us have seen the enormous strides made in, for example, electronic legal research. The author often sits in beautiful bricks and mortar law libraries to observe the library users. These days, at least based on the author's observations, it is almost unheard of for a library user to actually take a book down from the shelf and read it. Almost all users concentrate on the screens of their laptops while retrieving, electronically, virtually all of their information from one or another of the major legal research providers. And devices that we viewed as dynamic and progressive just a few years ago have yielded to new things. For example, e-mail and texting have totally replaced things such as facsimile machines and telexes.

The newer developments in AI within the legal profession are striking. AI is becoming increasingly used in due diligence reviews. In litigation, at least in the United States, almost all case filing and documentation is electronic. Litigators are now using AI for electronic discovery.[74] The first AI applications involved relatively primitive search engines that simply looked for key words in documents containing megabytes of data. AI was also used to compare and string together large numbers of documents such as e-mails or financial information. But more recently: "AI is now capable of searching documents for context, concepts and tone with what is known as predictive coding, going far beyond simple keyword searches. Predictive coding is even being used as a tool in internal compliance investigations—to sift through mounds of data in minutes or hours."[75] These technics are being used in the drafting of legal documents in far more sophisticated form than in the past.[76]

There are many other AI applications now being used around the world. The form of artificial intelligence known as *litigation analysis* involves the sifting through hundreds or even thousands of previously filed court records such as orders, opinions, jury verdicts and other data to permit lawyers to compare the facts of their current case with previously decided cases to predict an outcome in the current case. Lawyers frequently express this question colloquially as: "what are our chances of winning."[77]

74. Much of this discussion is taken from Sterling Miller, *Part III: Benefits of Artificial Intelligence: What Have You Done for Me Lately?* (2017). This series of articles was also published in the online periodical Above the Law, www.abovethelaw.com.
75. *Id.*
76. The firm Ross Intelligence (www.rossintelligence.com) has created search engines and other devices to compile legal research and write memoranda using a lawyer avatar called "Ross, your new artificially intelligent legal researcher."
77. *Id.*, One such firm, Lex Machina, www.lexmachina.com, "mines litigation data, revealing insights never before available about judges, lawyers, parties, and the subjects of the cases themselves, culled from millions of pages of litigation information, [looking] for the discovery and communication of meaningful patterns in data." *See also* Ravel Law (www.ravellaw.com).

Detection of corporate wrong doing is always of great concern. AI, by way of predictive coding, is being used to examine large numbers of internal corporate documents to discern bad behavior such as fraud and bribery. Using a company's own data and documents, "AI can summarize conversations and the ideas discussed, sniff out the use of code words, note the frequency of the communications, and even identify the mood of the speakers."[78]

§4.10.3 Artificial Intelligence and Contract Drafting

Lawyers who are heavily bound to traditional methods even now disdain any notion that artificial intelligence can be an important tool in contract drafting. But the glimmerings of AI began to appear twenty and thirty years ago when companies such as LegalZoom and Rocket Lawyer began offering electronic versions of contracts, wills, leases and other documents that could be quickly tailored to a specific person's situation. There was an initial outcry by the profession with some lawyers arguing that most of the forms were far too simplistic and, accordingly were erroneous. Not stopping there, lawyers went on to argue that providing these forms to specific individuals constituted the unauthorized practice of law. Most of these battles have been lost and LegalZoom and many other entities seem to be doing just fine.[79]

But LegalZoom-type documents comprise simple agreements—such as a simple will—that may suit only individuals on a budget who just cannot afford anything more. They may or may not suffice given the user's particular situation and do not necessarily capture all the nuances of a well-thought-out agreement that deals will all the nuances of a person's situation. So where do we stand today (early 2018) on AI and contract drafting? On this point, it is helpful to distinguish between contract drafting and contract review.

§4.10.4 Artificial Intelligence and Contract Review and Management

AI already plays a major role in a firm's review and analysis of existing contracts. Among other things, AI systems can scan a firm's contract library, can generate spreadsheets that sort and categorize underlying data. AI can scan a firm's contract files to develop data on deadlines and obligations, including such things as expiration

---

Among other things, Ravel Law is working with Harvard Law School to make American case law open and free. One of its features is a program called "Judge Analytics" that "understands how judges think, write, and rule."

78. *Id.*

79. *See*, e.g., Mary Juetten, *Technology and the Unauthorized Practice of Law*, Law Technology Today (June 12, 2015): "Eight state bar associations have filed actions against LegalZoom for the unauthorized practice of law. Of those, one has been sent to binding arbitration (Arkansas), and one, in North Carolina, is still pending. The other six lawsuits have either been settled or dismissed, and LegalZoom is still providing documents to every state." *Id.* In one instance, a federal court in Texas concluded that certain forms and templates provided by the Quicken organization constituted the unauthorized practice of law (*Unauthorized Practice of Law v. Parsons Tech. Inc.*, 179 F.3d 956 (5th Cir. 1999) only to have the Texas state legislature enact a statute that exempted such forms from the definition of practicing law. *Id.*

dates and intermediate deadlines. If an attorney has spotted a weak or defective clause in a contract, AI can scan all of the firm's contracts for similar language and make—or at least offer—corrective language. AI can scan files and sort contracts by type, currency, language, and location. By analyzing and organizing specific clauses from individual contracts, AI can generate contract outlines on a clause-by-clause basis. These outlines can be used as checklists for future contracts by ensuring that the drafting lawyer does not forget and leave out important clauses. All of these activities can be useful for planning new contracts, for internal audits, for merger and acquisition planning and the like.

AI can be very helpful in monitoring and policing existing contracts (i.e., the *implementation* of the contract), an issue that many law firms and corporations frequently ignore to their detriment. AI can improve tracking and management of specific existing contract obligations such as when notice is required, when confidentiality is promised, and what kind of promises have been made as to insurance coverage and indemnification. Similar data set comparisons can show when a company has an opportunity to reclaim revenue, when certain credits can be claimed and when renewal dates are approaching.

An innovative supplier of computer services, Kira Systems, has pioneered a number of innovative approaches to contract review and management.[80] Kira has software that can perform various aspects of due diligence by, for example, extracting and analyzing key phrases and provisions from a company's entire data base of contracts. Similarly, clients involved in mergers and acquisition activities can identify key phrases and concepts (e.g., "affiliate" or "bankruptcy" or "change of control") that will be located in the entire client data base, including obscure forms, contracts, memos, letters, e-mails and the like that may have previously escaped review. Kira estimates that human review of all these documents will result in approximately 65% accuracy, while human searching assisted by certain e-discovery techniques result in around 75–80% accuracy.[81] Kira asserts that its systems result in more than 90% accuracy—thus, in Kira's words: "allowing you to focus your time on the remaining 10 percent."[82] These developments standing alone warrant close scrutiny. But what about using AI techniques to actually write contracts?

§4.10.5 Artificial Intelligence and Contract Drafting

There likely are a few lawyers left who write their contracts in longhand on yellow legal pads and then hand that draft to a secretary for typing the final document. But these people must now be few and far between. In the past 70 years, the typewriter has been replaced by the word processor which has been replaced by the computer and printer. Word-processing programs and computer hard drives are capable of storing large

80. Kira's URL is www.kirasystems.com.
81. Maura R. Grossman & Gordon V. Cormac, *Technology-Assisted Review in E-Discovery Can be More Effective and More Efficient Than Exhaustive Manual Review*, 17 Rich. J. of L. & Tech. 11 (2011).
82. The U.K. firm, cognitive + , (www.cognitivplus.com) is doing similar things in Europe.

numbers of predrafted clauses and provisions from which an attorney can choose for her contract. The word processor—assisted by spreadsheets and file management software—permitted lawyers to create basic or "master" documents that could be altered to fit a particular client's needs.[83]

From these beginnings lawyers progressed to rudimentary "expert" systems that permitted a lawyer (or the client in certain circumstances) to answer a string of questions, the answers to which could be converted into contract clauses built into the final contract. In a more recent twist on this technique, lawyers now have access to data systems that generate progressively more sophisticated and focused questions based on answers to previous questions. The Thomson-Reuters ContractExpress system, referred to as *document automation* or *document assembly*, is a good example.[84] As the company explains:

> Document automation software abstracts users from the underlying legal language of a document template and instead presents them with a questionnaire that collects data and guides them through the document creation process. A questionnaire might ask, for example, who is the counterparty, what is the effective date, etc. Based on the input provided by the users the appropriate data and clauses from the template are then automatically inserted into the document, which is generated by the system and then returned to them. In addition to building the required text, the system will also apply the appropriate document styles and numbering to give a perfectly formatted document.[85]

But the reader will recognize immediately the shortcomings of this system. It relies on preexisting language and mainly borrows and rearranges already-drafted clauses in a format that appears to conform to the answers in the questionnaire. Some of these programs rely solely on a firm's internal data base. Some, such as those used by LexPredict and the Bloomberg system, Corporate Transactions, will search contracts in a much wider data base—for example, contract samples and contract language that is submitted to the United States Security and Exchange Commission as part of its regulatory processes. These are improvements, concededly, over the old word processors, but what the legal profession is now searching for is a system (a true artificial intelligence system) that can create new things, not merely organize old things. As Betts and Jaep put it: "[T]he available contract drafting software is most useful in practices in which future contracts are going to closely approximate existing contracts.... [T]he available programs are ill-suited for complex commercial deals and more nuanced agreements."[86]

Beyond these defects, Betts and Jaep identify another issue: these drafting programs "are unable to distinguish between high and low-quality language. Because

83. This section borrows very heavily from two exceptional studies: Kathryn D. Betts & Kyle R. Jaep, *The Dawn of Fully Automated Contract Drafting: Machine Learning Breathes New Life into a Decades-Old Promise*, 15 Duke L. & Tech. Rev. 216 (2017) and Irene Ng (Huang Ying), *The Art of Contract Drafting in the Age of Artificial Intelligence: A Comparative Study Based on US, UK, and Austrian Law*, Transatlantic Technology Law Forum Working Paper No. 26 (2017).
84. The website is: www.contractexpress.com.
85. *Id.*
86. Betts and Jaep, *supra* n. 83, at 220.

the public data bases relied on by these programs do not sort contracts based on the *quality* of the drafting, the machines learn from both good and bad drafting without the ability to distinguish between the two"[87]

In other words, we need machines that can both learn from older contracts and create new contracts based on that learning experience. This is true artificial intelligence. We are moving in the right direction, but we are not yet there.

There have been some interesting developments. As identified by Ms. Ng in her report,[88] a software developer, Joe Dewey, has created a program called ContractCode that builds a contract based not on existing clauses but on what he calls "code-based principles." Mr. Dewey believes that contracts can "be constructed using many of the same principles used by software engineers in developing software applications."[89] As he explains it: this will be "a system that permits the integration of the contract code distilled from a traditional 'paper contract' with the blockchain.... These 'smart contracts' will transform the concept of contract performance [by] setting off a host of automated contingencies, requiring significantly less human input and oversight."[90] He envisions "code based contracts [that] are objects that hold all of the material logic of a contractual relationship.... A code based contract, however, would be distilled to the core logic and coded in one or more predefined patterns and syntaxes." Among other things, code based contracts "would be capable of debugging themselves. In other words, a code based legal document platform would spot errors and inconsistencies within a legal document through machine logic."[91]

This is a possible path toward a true AI contract drafting system. But there are additional difficulties. A contract not only must accommodate the wishes of the parties but also conform to the law of the relevant jurisdiction. It may be that an international contract could be governed by more than one jurisdiction's law. Presumably these considerations can be built into a machine based system—possibly through the concept of deep learning used e.g., by Google in its face recognition experiments.

There may be serious ethical problems. The issue raised earlier as to whether fully automated contracts constitute the unauthorized practice of law will continue to be addressed. Could this ethical issue be satisfied simply by having a lawyer touch the contract after it has been generated by a machine? We do not yet have an answer. In addition, as noted earlier by several commentators, there remains the crucial issue of quality control—what lawyers' ethical rules refers to as the doctrine and requirement of "competence." We do not have many answers to this question. Fundamentally, we

87. *Id.*, at 227.
88. Ng, *supra* n. 83, at 18.
89. Joe Dewey, *What If We Developed Legal Contracts Like We Developed Software Applications?*, guest post in MEDIUM (April 6, 2016).
90. *Id.*
91. *Id.* As this edition goes to press, four Harvard Law students announced the creation of a company called "Evisort" that will perform rapid search functions throughout a company's contracts for various information that they describe as the "Google for Contracts." *See*, Elaine McCardle, *HLS Students Harness Artificial Intelligence to Revolutionize How Lawyers Draft and Manage Contracts*, Harvard Law Today (December 20, 2017).

are not yet to the point of having legal systems fully staffed by so-called robot lawyers. We may never get there, but the developments discussed above warrant a very long discussion and close monitoring.

§4.11 SOME CONCLUDING COMMENTS

The drafting of a contract deserves all the time and attention that the parties can afford to devote to it. Care in the planning, negotiation, and drafting stages will prevent disturbances during the life of the agreement. In the final analysis, drafting a contract is no more—or less—than the parties saying what they mean in a way that conveys the same meaning to both persons. If all contracts could accomplish this, there would be far less need for the dispute resolution mechanisms discussed in the later chapters of this book. But before we move to a comprehensive analysis of dispute resolution, some hints on how to negotiate the initial agreement should prove helpful.

CHAPTER 5

Negotiating International Commercial Agreements

§5.1 INTRODUCTION

Some lawyers and business executives may scoff at the subject matter of this chapter. Thirty or forty years ago, the common understanding within these two professions was that negotiation—although always important and frequently crucial to the proper consummation of a commercial agreement—could not be taught, discussed, or even written about in any fashion other than the merely anecdotal. In the past, to the extent that negotiation was discussed as a separate topic, it was generally couched in the form of a simple admonition to the negotiator to know the subject matter (both the commercial and legal aspects) of the deal thoroughly. A few less-than-satisfactory writings on negotiation dealt with the topic in terms of psychological intimidation or under-the-table manipulation. Thus, the prevailing view has long been that negotiation is purely a matter of experience. People learn to negotiate simply by doing negotiations. It was often suggested that every negotiation is so unique that no systematic evaluation of negotiating is possible. At best, certain hints on negotiation technique can be related in case history or "war story" form but nothing more could be said.

There is something to this viewpoint. All things being equal, an experienced negotiator who knows the subject matter thoroughly will probably prevail over an ignorant neophyte. But that is not all there is to consider about negotiation, whether it is negotiation between two spouses trying to agree on tonight's restaurant or between two business executives trying to reach agreement on the sale of USD 100 million worth of telecommunications equipment.

Fortunately, as this book goes into its sixth edition, there is an established body of high-quality negotiation literature that is helpful to persons just entering the field. Best of all, many of these readings have made it possible to systematically evaluate actual negotiations and thus to provide a framework by which even experienced negotiators can evaluate their behavior. This chapter describes and analyzes some of the contemporary approaches to negotiation. This chapter begins with some basic considerations on negotiating generally and then moves to a comprehensive discussion of cross-cultural negotiation, a matter vital to international business agreements. This chapter concludes with a little-discussed topic—the ethics of negotiation—too frequently ignored by professionals in many fields, but one that can have pragmatic as well as moral repercussions.

§5.2 ESTABLISHING A BASIC FRAMEWORK FOR NEGOTIATION: A SHORT EXCURSUS IN NEGOTIATION THEORY

The best place to begin a discussion of negotiation theory and practice is with the proposition that there are many different negotiation settings and countless different styles and techniques of negotiating. Moreover, things that work in one setting might be terribly inefficient or downright counterproductive in another. For example, the negotiation between husband and wife about where to have dinner is going to be far different in tone and content from a multilateral negotiation to resolve problems of cross-boundary air pollution. A multilateral environmental negotiation is, in turn, going to differ substantially from negotiations between two lawyers in a divorce proceeding. Although certain factors are common to all negotiations, this chapter concentrates on negotiating commercial agreements between businesses in two or more countries.

This assumption—that we are dealing with a commercial arrangement—provides a solid foundation for analyzing some of the more sophisticated issues in negotiation. Thus, for the most part, this chapter will assume a two-party negotiation between business people who *want* to reach an agreement and who also may want to use the current negotiation as a precursor for future business dealings. This makes the discussion in this chapter more efficient, but does not necessarily make the actual negotiations any easier. Virtually all negotiations are characterized by uncertainty; and, in many instances, the two parties are not compelled to do business with each other—that is, each can find willing buyers and sellers elsewhere if an agreement cannot be reached. All persons approaching negotiation should keep in mind a few fundamentals.

§5.2.1 Diagramming a Negotiation

The first principle to keep in mind is that all negotiations are characterized by a negotiating range developed in confidence by each of the parties prior to the actual negotiation. In other words, in a contract for the sale of goods, the parties normally establish in their own minds prices below which they will refuse to sell or above which they will refuse to buy. Thus, the price becomes not a fixed point, but rather a range of potential prices that each party may find acceptable. These ranges are usually established through business decisions based on costs of materials or services, labor, shipping, risk of loss and the like. In most business negotiations, the price of the contract is usually the most important component of the agreement, while in noncommercial negotiations such as multilateral treaty negotiations, price is often not an issue or serves a secondary role to such considerations as national honor and domestic politics. Although the psychological or emotional dynamic is present in all negotiations, it is usually less intrusive in commercial negotiations than it might be in, say, a divorce negotiation. Recall the fundamental precept of this chapter: in normal business negotiations the parties want to agree because they both want to make money. It is that simple even if such is not the case in many divorces.

To understand how price ranges affect a commercial contract, assume that Party A (seller) and Party B (buyer) come together to try to work out an arrangement for the buying and selling of 100 telescopes. Both A and B want to do business, but being good executives, A does not want to sell at a loss nor does B want to buy at such a high price that he cannot resell the product for some profit. Assume further that A and B are knowledgeable generally about pricing conditions in their industry, but have no idea how the telescopes will sell in the country of destination.

Prenegotiation preparation by each party leads to the following preliminary conclusion by each. A would like to sell the telescopes for USD 100 per unit (resulting in a fairly large profit) but can make a 5% profit if the telescopes are sold for USD 50 each. He will break even at USD 40 per telescope. Assume, however, that B is so uncertain about the demand for telescopes in her country that she is willing to risk no more than USD 35 per telescope and had hoped to pay as low as USD 10 for each telescope. Further assume that these prices represent what Americans like to call the "bottom line"—that is, no other factors, however nicely stated, will budge the parties away from these numbers.

The parties' prenegotiation posture is illustrated by the following Figure 5.1.

Figure 5.1 A Diagram of Possible Negotiating Positions

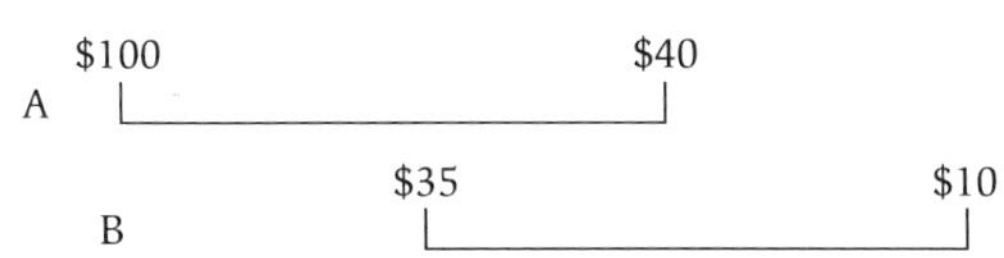

Unless B changes her mind and is willing to take more of a risk, or unless A is willing to sell at a loss, no agreement is possible no matter how skilled the negotiators are or how much time they spend negotiating.

By contrast, consider the potential result if A's range is USD 100–USD 25 and B's range is USD 75–USD 15, *see* Figure 5.2:

Figure 5.2 Probable Agreement

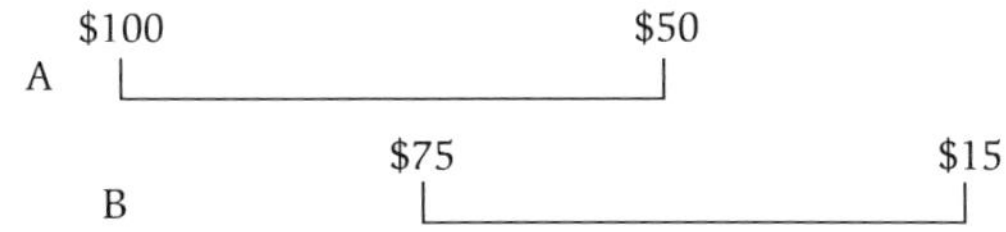

In this case, even the most inept negotiators are probably going to be able to conclude an agreement satisfactory to both sides because the overlap of prices is substantial. This analysis suggests that while studying the theory and technique of negotiation is important, most commercial agreements stand or fall on whether there is overlap between the pricing determinations made by each party.

There are other cases in which there is not nearly so much overlap. Consider, for example, the following Figure 5.3:

Figure 5.3 Possible Agreement

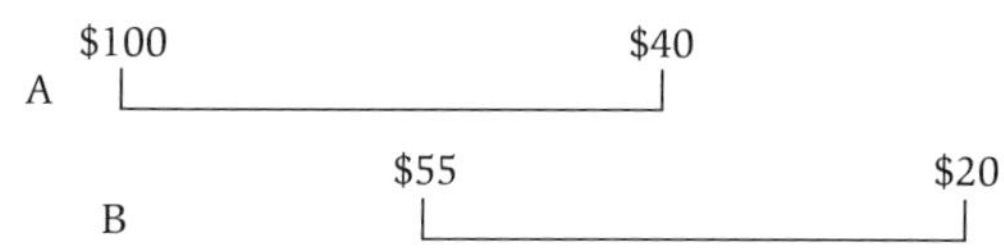

In this case, skilled negotiation on both sides may save the transaction, while ineptness may result in both parties not only walking away from the deal but walking away with such distaste that they never again seek to do business with each other. For these reasons, it makes sense to examine the theory of negotiation in greater depth.

The literature of negotiation runs from highly quantitative studies by social scientists to rudimentary rules-of-thumb proffered by lawyers who are self-styled expert negotiators. The social science literature tends to be nearly impenetrable for lay persons and so esoteric that even when it can be understood, the information conveyed has virtually no practical value. On the other hand, much of the literature generated by people in the legal and business communities tends to be so purely anecdotal (a sort of "great-negotiations-in-which-I-have-prevailed" approach) and so personalized that it provides virtually no useful framework for others. If the reader is searching this chapter only for a single useful rule-of-thumb for negotiators, consider the wisdom of a lawyer of the author's acquaintance who once stated: "My favorite negotiating position is my foot on the other guy's neck."

Fortunately, there is now something of a middle ground. Negotiation can be studied systematically with good results. Much that grows out of these studies can be effectively communicated to layperson negotiators. Indeed, the literature has grown significantly since the first edition of this book, although it is also becoming somewhat repetitive and overlapping.[1] With this profusion of literature, we may have come full

1. Any list of solid negotiation literature would likely include: Roger Fisher, William Ury & Bruce Patton, *Getting to Yes: Negotiating Agreement Without Giving In* (3d ed., 2011); *International Business Negotiations (International Business and Management Series)* (Pervez N. Ghauri & Jean-Claude Usunier eds., 1996); *ABA Guide to International Business Negotiations: A Comparison of Cross-Cultural Issues and Successful Approaches* (James R. Silkenat & Jeffrey M. Aresty eds., 1994); *Managing Cultural Differences: High Performance Strategies for a New World of Business* (Philip R. Harris & Robert T. Moran eds., 3d ed., 1991); Philip Sperber, *Attorney's Practice Guide to Negotiations* (1985); Howard Raiffa, *The Art and Science of Negotiation* (1982); Gerald Williams, *Legal Negotiation and Settlement* (1983); Gary Bellow & Bea Moulton, *Negotiation* (1979); Harry T. Edwards & James J. White, *The Lawyer as Negotiator* (1977); Gerard I.

circle. There may be a limit to what one can say about negotiation in an analytical context, perhaps thereby confirming, at least in part, what those older negotiators would have us believe—that good negotiation is *still* mainly a matter of experience and not a matter of theory.

Nonetheless, to understand theory, there are some good starting points. One place to begin to search for a theory of negotiation is in the rather arcane mathematical field, the theory of games, an area of inquiry derived from probability theory. Games theory is at bottom a set of concepts that mathematicians developed to try to explain the behavior of persons involved in conflict.[2] It is based on the following premises:

(a) the participation of two (or more) persons or entities in the transaction;
(b) the availability of more than one course of action available to each party (sometimes referred to as strategies);
(c) the existence of one or more points of congruence between or among the various strategies (i.e., there must exist at least one point at which the participants can agree);
(d) the existence of some set of conditions that form boundaries for each party's behavior (i.e., the parties' behavior cannot be simply random; it must be limited by, e.g., commercial legal principles, the laws of physics as might govern, say, the operation of ballistic missiles), or existing world economic conditions.[3]

There are in essence two types of matrices that can be drawn on this basis. The first, commonly referred to as a win/lose situation, is one in which one party must lose if another wins. Examples include a criminal trial where either the prosecutor or the defendant wins—an outcome that automatically means that the other loses. Trading in stock options is another illustration, albeit outside the context of negotiation. In normal options trading, a deal is struck because one person believes that the underlying stock is going to go down while the other believes that the stock is going to go up. Obviously, both cannot be right; thus, one wins and the other must lose. This type of game, sometimes referred to as distributional bargaining is diagrammed very simply as:

- In a criminal prosecution, the defendant is found either guilty or not guilty. In a divorce in which the wife wants the divorce and the husband does not, the divorce is either granted or not granted—thus, one of the two *must* lose.

Nierenberg, *Fundamentals of Negotiating* (1973); Carrie L. Menkel-Meadow, *Toward Another View of Legal Negotiation: The Structure of Problem-Solving*, 31 U.C.L.A. L. Rev. 754 (1984); Carrie L. Menkel-Meadow, *Legal Negotiation: A Study of Strategies in Search of a Theory*, 1983 Am. Bar. Fdn. Res. J. 905 [cited as "Study of Strategies"]. To add a few more references, the following may be profitably consulted: Damien Ward, *Contract Negotiation Handbook: Getting the Most Out of Commercial Deals* (2012); Jeffrey Edmund Curry, *International Negotiating Planning and Conducting International Commercial Negotiations* (2009); Sophie Meunier, *Trading Voices: The European Union in International Commercial Negotiation* (2007); Frank Adoranti, *The Manager's Guide to Understanding Commercial Contract Negotiation* (2006).

2. *See*, e.g., Erving Goffman, *Strategic Interaction* (1969).
3. Bellow & Moulton, *supra* n. 1, at 40.

Fortunately, there are few international commercial relationships that are appropriately characterized as win/lose situations. Most commercial dealings permit both parties to conclude a transaction reasonably satisfactory to both. But in most such transactions it is highly unlikely that either party will be able to prevail so completely that the other side gets nothing (the expression in the United States is "getting taken to the cleaners"). Accordingly, international commercial negotiation is almost always "win/win" negotiation; and "win/win" negotiation requires, among many other things, an assessment of probabilities.

- In a commercial context, calculating probabilities is almost never as complicated as it might be in, say, a multilateral negotiation on air pollution or even bilateral arms reduction negotiations. It involves mainly the assignment of probabilities based on some kind of estimate as to how the other party will behave. Assigning probabilities is largely a matter of experience, judgment, and research. Consider a very simple example. Assume that a U.S. seller wishes to sell stainless steel fittings for a particular manufacturing operation. A potential buyer, a French company, has purchased only aluminum fittings in the past.

Research on the French buyer's previous behavior may reveal that the buyer has never paid more than USD 10 per unit for aluminum fittings. However, the seller may conclude, as a matter of business judgment and experience in domestic sales, that stainless steel fittings are far superior in quality to aluminum, but not so superior that any previous buyer has been willing to double the price. In addition, the engineering information available suggests that while stainless steel is superior, it is not indispensable to the French manufacturing operation. As a result, it is clear that the French company will not be *compelled* to do business with the American seller, although it is obvious that the French will have some interest in replacing aluminum with stainless steel.

This analysis suggests that there is a virtual certainty that the French buyer will not be willing to pay USD 20 per fitting (double the price the French are currently paying for aluminum fittings). Analyzing the prospective negotiation along the lines of games theory, the American seller might assign a probability of close to 95% against the buyer being willing to buy at USD 19. At the same time, the French buyer should be willing to pay more than USD 10 for stainless steel fittings that are clearly superior in quality to the aluminum fittings it currently purchases.

Looking at the other side of the equation, the American seller might then assess the probability of the French purchaser insisting on a sale price of USD 12 or below to be less than 5%. The stainless steel fittings are significantly superior to aluminum so a price that is close to the price for aluminum is unrealistic. The whole of this analysis suggests that there is a substantial probability, perhaps around 90%, that the final contract price will be between USD 12.50 per unit and USD 18.50 per unit.

This example is of course very simplistic. When buyers and sellers extend their analysis to issues such as risk of loss, risk of expropriation, possible cancellation of export or import permissions, and other uncertainties that are frequently encountered in international transactions, the combinations and permutations of agreement increase dramatically.

Consider, for example, a situation in which a buyer might be willing to buy at a higher unit price if the seller does not insist on a letter of credit. Consider a negotiation in which the seller might be willing to accept a far lower unit price if the buyer were willing to sign a *requirements* contract (one in which the buyer purchases all of his required parts from the same seller).

Are there any advantages to this type of analysis even if a negotiator is not a mathematician? Two prominent American writers on negotiation, Professors Gary Bellow and Bea Moulton, suggest that thinking about probability forces negotiators to develop a structure for the negotiation and further helps negotiators to think through the possible range of choices and the manner in which each party might influence the final agreement. Put another way: "For many inexperienced negotiators, the major problem in framing bargaining strategy seems to be in their inability to envision the bargaining situation as a complex of intersecting choices and perceptions; for some, games theory may provide a useful way to begin to think systematically about the relationships involved."[4]

Readers who recoil from overly quantified approaches to negotiation may be put off by the esoterica of games theory. Unfortunately, for many years, the only body of literature was derived from social science data on the behavior of individuals and of groups. There were also those purely anecdotal writings that taught negotiation by relating "war stories." The literature has often been faulted because so much writing on negotiation fails to develop a comprehensive theory of negotiation that fits both adversarial negotiation (prosecutor versus defense attorney, for example) and the win/win negotiation that typifies much of commercial negotiations. In other words, most of the literature focuses on "competitive gain" when "[w]ork on the purpose and evaluation of goals and outcomes much precede any consideration of strategy and tactics."[5]

Notwithstanding the absence of a truly unifying theory, virtually all of the literature recognizes essentially three points:

(1) negotiation is a function of *leverage* (leverage is the allocation of power or control between the two sides);
(2) negotiation can often turn as much on the personalities and behavior of the negotiators as on the relative merits of the parties' positions; and
(3) in a commercial setting, as well as many other settings, requirements of law and regulation frequently shape the outcome irrespective of the wishes of the individual parties.

Now consider these concepts in a little more depth. First, all bargaining is a function of leverage. People come together to bargain because they want something (in

4. *Id.*, at 44–45. *See also*, David Sally, *Game Theory Behaves*, 87 Marq. L. Rev. 783 (2004).
5. Study of Strategies, *supra* n. 1, at 922.

either the affirmative or negative sense of the term) and because they do not have the power to conclude the transaction entirely on their own. In other words, if a party can do something completely on his or her own, there is no need to bargain with anyone else. By contrast, anyone who is completely lacking in leverage is totally at the mercy of the other side. Such parties have no reason to negotiate. The strong party imposes her will on the weak. The weak party must simply "grin and bear it."

Beyond this, all negotiation is purposeful. Merchants want to buy and sell telescopes, not for the mere doing of the transaction, but to make either short-run or long-term profits. Divorcing spouses frequently want not only a monetary benefit from the dissolution of the marriage, but also possibly some kind of psychological vindication or even some type of retribution. Leverage is the ingredient that forces people to bargain.

Leverage is almost always present in commercial dealings because commercial relationships are normally characterized by:

(1) parties who *want* to do business together;
(2) a range of possible outcomes that will be generally satisfactory to both parties (note the diagrams set out above); and
(3) a fairly dispassionate approach to the deal making itself.

While emotions occasionally intrude into commercial decision-making and while vindication and retribution are not totally foreign to the behavior of business people, these ingredients are not commonplace.

Instead, leverage in business dealings is derived mainly from the acquisition of information. A party may acquire data on the transaction from openly held information or through confidential sources. This information will include such things as the identity and history of both the seller and buyer, on the nature and quality of the goods or services offered for sale, on the organization and structure of foreign markets, trends in government regulation, the status of various currencies, anticipated consumer behavior, and the like.

To establish a nonquantitative analytical framework for negotiation, many dispute resolution professionals now use the classic work by Roger Fisher and William Ury, *Getting to Yes,* as a starting point. *Getting to Yes* is probably the most popular book ever written on negotiation and has attracted both praise and criticism from a vast spectrum of readers.[6] Fisher and Ury believe that there is virtually no conflict that cannot be negotiated if the parties engage in what they refer to as *principled* negotiation. Principled negotiation begins when both parties appreciate and began to

6. The book is now in its third edition with an additional author: Roger Fisher, William Ury & Bruce Patton, *Getting to Yes* (3d ed., 2011). These authors have published a number of other books that are helpful for negotiators in various fields. *See*, e.g., William Ury, *Getting to Peace: Transforming Conflict at Home, at Work and in the World* (1999); William Ury, *Getting Past No: Negotiating Your Way from Confrontation to Cooperation* (1993); Roger Fisher & Scott Brown, *Getting Together: Building Relationships as We Negotiate* (1988). There is now a companion workbook for *Getting to Yes*: Roger Fisher & Danny Ertel, *Getting Ready to Negotiate: A Step-by-Step Guide to Preparing for Any Negotiation* (1995).

accommodate the fact that each party has both conflicting and compatible interests. Building on the identification of compatible interests, it becomes far easier for the parties to reach some kind of reconciliation on the conflicting issues. Indeed, even when interests directly collide and seem totally irreconcilable, there may be, at the very least, a shared interest in preserving the negotiation as a dispute resolution device rather than resorting to more costly and cumbersome forms of conflict resolution.

From these basic premises, *Getting to Yes* moves to a series of what looks suspiciously like anecdotal rules-of-thumb for negotiators but which are, in actual practice, good general principles applicable to virtually any negotiation.[7] Since these guidelines have a great deal of applicability to the relatively harmonious, nonbelligerent discussions of people in business, they bear close analysis by persons interested in succeeding in international commercial negotiations.

The *Getting to Yes* guidelines are:

(a) Separate the people from the problem.
(b) Focus on interests, not positions.
(c) Invent options for mutual gain.
(d) Insist on objective criteria.
(e) Know your "best alternative to a negotiated agreement" (hereafter "BATNA").[8]

§5.2.2 Separating the People from the Problem

When initially set out, the Fisher and Ury guidelines sound intriguing, but they are not easily understood without putting them into a more practical setting. Assume that two people in business, a seller in the United States and a buyer in Japan, wish to negotiate a contract for the sale of telecommunications equipment. While thinking through the negotiation beforehand, a negotiator (or the parties themselves as is often the case) may wish to begin by understanding that there is a great difference between the problem (executing an equipment contract) and the people who are going to be negotiating that contract (the lawyers, e.g.) or the people (buyer and seller themselves) who are standing behind that contract. A negotiator can over generalize by simply deciding that profit is the single motivating force in the transaction and may try to hammer through a deal on that basis. However, a more careful, more sophisticated negotiator will recognize that business executives, like all other human beings, are an amalgam of personal needs and professional goals.

7. *See*, e.g., the debate between Professor James White, a University of Michigan law professor who likes to be regarded as a hard-nosed traditional negotiator and Roger Fisher, one of the authors of *Getting to Yes*, in an academic law journal. Professor White believes that *Getting to Yes* is excessively soft, concentrating on win/win negotiation to the almost total exclusion of win/lose negotiation—a setting that is far more difficult to deal with. Compare James J. White, *The Pros and Cons of Getting to Yes*, 34 J. Leg. Educ. 115–116 (1984) with Roger Fisher, *Comment [in response to White]*, 34 J. Leg. Educ. 120 (1984) (Professor Fisher believes that even win/lose bargaining can profit from a Getting to Yes-type analysis).
8. Fisher & Ury, *supra* n. 1, at 10.

For example, a U.S. negotiator may be put off by the personal desire of the Japanese to begin the project with some social amenities or by the inclination of Japanese to bow rather than shake hands. The U.S. party may, conceivably, harbor some residual dislike of Japanese for that country's role in World War Two. But those things are not the problem; they are the people. The problem is mainly to consummate a purchase and sale agreement within the instructions given the negotiator by the client, not to refight World War Two or muse over the relative wisdom of shaking hands or bowing as a greeting.

This may seem like such a commonplace that it is not worth mentioning; but when one considers some of the horror stories set out below in §5.5 on cross-cultural negotiation, it is obvious that this is one of the first lessons forgotten by negotiators. Merely recognizing this does not necessarily tell a negotiator what to do in a specific situation. This guideline and those that follow provide assistance in developing a structure for analyzing the negotiation. The next section of this chapter contains some practical hints on handling specific negotiation problems.

§5.2.3 Focus on Interests, Not Positions

This is another concept that frequently gets lost in the negotiation process. Inexperienced negotiators may hear a statement from the other side to the effect that "I will not agree to a letter of credit" and automatically turn on the heat, deciding that this is obviously a time to get tough. The parties' positions then become hardened and a shouting match ensues that frequently leads to a total breakdown in the negotiation. There is another way to view such a statement, however.

In an international commercial setting, a buyer may enter a negotiation with the announced position that he will simply not execute a letter of credit. It could be that he was hurt in an earlier unrelated transaction in which a seller shipped nonconforming goods—a defect that may have taken years to resolve—yet the seller received instant payment in full under the letter of credit. Even if the seller ultimately has to reimburse the buyer for the nonconforming goods, it frequently happens in international transactions that the reimbursement is made with inflated funds, so the buyer is never made fully whole. A seller may take the position that she absolutely demands a letter of credit because she shipped goods to another buyer and was years collecting on the invoice. However the buyer may hear the demand for a letter of credit as an accusation that his credit is no good.

Note that the position of the buyer is flatly: "No letter of credit." Yet his interest is much different: he really wants protection against the risk of having to receive and contend with nonconforming goods while the seller walks away with all the money due under the contract. Simply recognizing this difference may make all the difference between a successful and unsuccessful negotiation because recognition will permit the parties to work with the third Fisher/Ury guideline.

§5.2.4 Create Options for Mutual Gain

This factor is nearly self-explanatory. But as Fisher and Ury explain, it is not so easily factored into an ongoing negotiation. They recognize that there is more than a little tension and pressure associated with even the smoothest and friendliest negotiations: "Trying to decide in the presence of an adversary narrows your vision. Having a lot at stake inhibits creativity. So does searching for the one right solution."[9] This is, nonetheless, a factor that marks a good negotiation.

Take the letter of credit imbroglio. Buyer and seller could simply butt heads forever on this and eventually walk away from what could be a very lucrative deal simply because of mutual stubbornness. A wise negotiator will take a step back and ask: "Is there any reasonable alternative to the letter of credit?" It could be that some other payment device would sufficiently protect the seller's interest. Not every international sale of goods is accompanied by a letter of credit. If seller suspects the buyer's creditworthiness, some kind of credit check such as a Dun & Bradstreet report might provide the assurances she needs to let the deal go forward on an open account basis. She might be willing to accept a partial payment on the goods before shipment in lieu of a letter of credit.

Granting that none of these alternative forms of payment provide the absolute security of a letter of credit, the seller might be persuaded to accept a less-secure form of payment in order to consummate the transaction. On the buyer's part, his interest in obtaining conforming goods (the underlying reason for his reluctance to execute the letter of credit) may be satisfied by having some right to inspect the goods prior to payment; for example, the letter of credit might be made payable only after he has had an opportunity to inspect. In the alternative, the buyer could appoint a third-party inspector who inspects the goods at the seller's factory immediately prior to shipment, releasing for shipment only those goods which are truly conforming. In commercial transactions, there are usually a myriad of options available for any situation. Creativity, rather than intransigence, ought to be the hallmark of commercial negotiators.

§5.2.5 Insist on Objective Criteria

This factor ties in with the previous factor. It recommends that crucial evaluations be measured by devices that are outside the control of either party. The public international law prototype is the use of United Nations military peacekeeping forces composed of personnel from wholly uninvolved nations to monitor and keep separate belligerent forces. Consider again the problem with the letter of credit. Assume that the seller will agree to on-site inspection of goods prior to shipment. Seller may say something such as: "We'll inspect the goods before we crate them up and make sure

9. *Id.*, at 12.

they're okay." Buyer may like the idea of inspection before shipment as one part of a quality control protocol, but will likely object to the seller's employees performing that crucial inspection.

At the same time, buyer may not have the financial wherewithal to station an employee at the seller's factory; and even if she could afford it, seller may worry that an employee of the buyer's would object to the tiniest discrepancy, however insignificant. One way to incorporate objective criteria into this agreement is to have that final preshipment inspection performed by a third party who is trusted by both seller and buyer. The presence and reputation of this third person will frequently provide all the objectivity required by the contracting parties.

§5.2.6 Know Your "BATNA"

This guideline urges negotiators to understand what may take place if the negotiations prove unsuccessful. For lawyers negotiating settlement agreements in ongoing litigation, the alternative is usually a return to the court for final resolution. Thus, the parties give over their dispute to a judge or jury for resolution. A parallel alternative in international commercial dispute resolution is to hand the matter over to an arbitrator. As a result, parties engaged in renegotiation or mediation following some breach of contract should always consider how an arbitrator might dispose of the issues as part of their evaluation of BATNA.

However, in precontractual international negotiation BATNA has only limited applicability. A breakdown in negotiations in a commercial setting means simply that the parties do not do business with each other. As a result, precontractual BATNA means either that a party does no deal at all or that a party does the deal with someone else. An Indonesian entrepreneur whose negotiation to purchase and operate a McDonald's hamburger franchise in Jakarta falls through may have to consider a deal with Burger King or may look for some other business opportunity. In initial contract negotiations a BATNA is sometimes useful as leverage ("If you don't sign, I'll take my business to Microsoft") but is rarely as important a factor as it is in negotiations prior to litigation.

To some readers, the Fisher/Ury guidelines may seem not much more than simplistic rules of thumb that may or may not work in any particular setting. They are much more than that. For example, they can serve as an analytical framework that may be applied either before the fact or after the fact to virtually any negotiation. This permits observers and participants to evaluate a number of different negotiations from the same perspective. To that extent, the criteria constitute an attempt to develop a unified theory of negotiation. They represent a quantum leap beyond the merely anecdotal approach to negotiation. Moreover, they are not merely suggestions of specific negotiation techniques. The following two sections show how the Fisher/Ury criteria differ from negotiation strategy and tactics.

§5.3 THE STAGES OF COMMERCIAL NEGOTIATION

Every negotiation goes through several stages. Understanding the different stages and thinking though the stages of your particular negotiation is one secret of success. One striking study of legal negotiation performed by Professor Gerald Williams and discussed in his book, *Legal Negotiation and Settlement*, identifies four stages:

(a) Orientation and Positioning.
(b) Argumentation.
(c) Emergence and Crisis.
(d) Agreement or Final Breakdown.[10]

Much like the Fisher/Ury criteria, this framework appears simplistic and commonsensical at first glance but when analyzed and applied it becomes, as Professor Williams puts it, "a surprisingly powerful tool for the practicing lawyer. Inexperienced attorneys often misperceive which stage of the process the case is in and use tactics that are unnecessary or even harmful to the dynamics of the negotiation."[11] While Professor Williams based most of his conclusions on negotiations in other than an international commercial context, the stages prove quite useful in that setting as well.

§5.3.1 Orientation and Positioning

At this point, the parties first come into contact with each other. In international commercial transactions, these first points of contact may be by a personal, on-site visit, regular mail, e-mail, or telephone; but however they are made they become crucial to everything that follows. In contracts for the purchase and sale of goods, the initial contact may be made by the seller searching for new markets for his goods. The seller will typically identify potential buyers and then, either directly or indirectly, initiate contact with those persons. Those first contacts are likely to comprise a description of the seller's company, an explanation of the goods offered by the seller and a suggestion for further discussions that may lead to a sale. Buyers may initiate the contact by seeking a provider of the goods or services that they seek. Whether the seller or the buyer initiates the contact, this first approach may include a statement of the price of the goods. The statement of price may be direct or may be set out in a catalog of products or a separate price list. In more complicated international transactions, there may be an elaborate dance of protocol even before the first face-to-face meeting. In certain cultures, a direct approach is not favored and the initial contact may take place quietly through the actions of intermediaries. Outside the United States the use of agents or brokers as a conduit for business information is quite common. In Williams'

10. Williams, *supra* n. 1, at 70–72.
11. *Id.*, at 72.

parlance, these activities comprise the orientation stage. Orientation provides those crucial first impressions by which the tone and process of the entire negotiation is often set.

Positioning begins only when one or both of the parties sets out an opening position. In commercial transactions, it is frequently the first offering of a quantity of goods at a particular price, or the initial letter inviting the other side to bargain with specificity. Williams speculates that there are essentially three categories of positions: First, many negotiators attempt what he calls the maximalist position—by which a party states almost an outrageous position from which she secretly realizes she will have to retreat. Recall the earlier hypothetical involving the sale of stainless steel fittings. A seller might ask USD 30 per unit knowing full well that no buyer has ever paid more than USD 20 and fully expecting that the price will inevitably come down from USD 30 to, say, USD 20 per unit. But USD 20 represents an extremely high price for the fittings—indeed, it is the highest price others have paid. If the buyer and seller agree on USD 20, the seller will be very happy. Even so, the maximalist position can have palpable disadvantages. What happens if the buyer has done his research and knows that the highest price ever paid is USD 20? A well-informed buyer may react with outrage to a USD 30 price and walk away from the table. At the very least, the seller may severely damage her credibility at a crucial point in the negotiation.

Professor Williams has identified a second tactic. His research shows that many negotiators stake out what he calls an equitable position—one that is intended at the outset to be fair and equitable for both sides. Note that this has advantages, particularly in international commercial negotiations between sophisticated sellers and buyers. For example, the seller sends an early letter to the buyer detailing the specifications of the fittings, the labor costs, and the other components of the final price. She then asks for USD 18 per unit. The buyer, being familiar with these products, recognizes instantly that this is a fair price, although clearly one at the high end of what we might call the zone of reasonableness. Taking an equitable position may result in a quickly consummated transaction; but, at the same time, it eliminates the possibility of the seller's realizing a price of USD 20 per unit.

A third possible position is developed by Professor Williams by taking a page out of the Fisher/Ury book. Williams describes the matter of integrative positioning—initial bargaining characterized by one or the other party's setting forth a number of possible options to be considered by the other side. For example, the seller of fittings might offer a unit price of USD 22 with freight and insurance prepaid to buyer's place of business or, in the alternative, a unit price of USD 17 on an FOB ("freight on board" the buyer pays the transportation costs) basis. There are other possibilities: the seller might reduce the price by USD 1 per unit if the buyer pays cash prior to delivery. In his empirical study of students who take part in simulated negotiations, Williams observed that integrative positioning was frequently adopted by those student negotiators who were ultimately rated as "effective" by the observers of the negotiations. But like the other positioning techniques, it has its drawbacks. If the seller sets out a number of pricing possibilities at the outset of the negotiation, the buyer may require a much longer time to evaluate and compare all the alternatives. The statement of multiple possibilities by one side may trigger multiple counteroffers by the other side, increasing the complexity of the negotiation itself. If the parties begin jumping around among the various options during the negotiations, their discussions are likely to take a long time and increase the frustration level for the negotiators to the point that one party walks away.

Williams' evaluation of the various positions shows that there is no single permissible approach to the orientation and positioning stage. Whatever the techniques used, orientation and positioning is likely to encompass more time than all the other stages of negotiation put together.[12]

§5.3.2 Argumentation

This stage is characterized by a defining of issues—attempts by the parties to discover the true positions of the other side and a stage in which at least a few concessions are made by each side. Put a little more colloquially, this is the "back and forth" part of negotiation. For example, a buyer might agree to a letter of credit but ask for a USD 1 per unit discount because of the letter of credit. The seller might counter with a price reduction of USD 50 per unit if the buyer agrees to use a particular bank for the letter of credit. The parties can go around and around at this stage, but at some point they will move to stage number three.

§5.3.3 Emergence and Crisis

However long the argumentation takes, at some point the parties will begin to see the final shape of the bargain or to identify those points on which agreement is simply not possible. Professor Williams refers to this stage as emergence and crisis. This is the point at which Fisher/Ury's suggestions for the development of options often come into play. As Williams sees the negotiation process, a crisis can occur when each side believes it has conceded all it can and is still without an agreement, or when a psychological sense of being exploited begins to form in the minds of one or another of the negotiators. If there is a rigid chronological deadline for the negotiations, or if a deadline is imposed by rapidly changing business conditions, this step in the negotiation process can take on an almost frantic quality. For example, in negotiations for the sale of oil drilling equipment, fluctuations in the price of crude oil may have a substantial effect on the buyer's willingness to purchase the equipment. If the bottom appears to be dropping out of the market, the negotiations may be terminated long before the contract is drafted and signed.

§5.3.4 Agreement or Breakdown

Here the parties either reach an agreement or postpone or completely break off negotiations. This is not to say that every last detail needs to be worked out at this

12. *Id.*, at 78.

stage. The actual agreement can be stated in general terms, leaving the details to be fleshed out later. By contrast, some parties may need a comprehensive agreement before they leave the table. In some circumstances, the negotiations may be concluded with a handshake and the final contract will be drafted at a later date. In others, the parties may not leave until all the contract language has been agreed upon and the document signed. There are many models for completing a transaction. Professor Williams' contribution to an understanding of this stage is an important one. Note that he uses the term agreement or final breakdown.

Parties must understand that many negotiations fail, even when the parties come to the table wanting to do business with each other. A breakdown can occur simply by the passage of time when the parties cannot reach an agreement within the deadline. It can occur because of an outright failure to agree—for example, when a seller will take no less than USD 15 per unit and a buyer is willing to offer no more than USD 13. The harder question is whether breakdown should be regarded as a failure. This analysis may turn on the precise issue under negotiation.

The breakdown of settlement negotiations in litigation mean that the parties simply let the judge or jury decide who wins. The dispute will somehow be resolved whether or not the parties do it themselves. Breakdown in a precontractual negotiation may simply mean that the parties do business with someone else. If A cannot buy shoes from B, he can still deal with C. It is possible, of course, for inept negotiators to poison a negotiation that would have been successful but for their ineptness. That might properly be classified as failure. In another sense, true failure probably occurs only when a negotiator fails to carry out the wishes and instructions of the client. That is the final evaluation of any negotiation.

§5.4 NEGOTIATING STYLES, STRATEGY, AND TACTICS

Many books on negotiation begin with a discussion of these issues and never provide any unified framework for analyzing negotiations. Many negotiators never get beyond the rule-of-thumb approach to negotiations and frequently establish inflexible principles when perhaps the hallmark of successful negotiation is flexibility. For example, a lawyer of the author's acquaintance absolutely refuses to negotiate in the offices of opposing counsel, no matter how much inefficiency, ill-will, and consternation he creates by such a refusal. It seems that he was told in law school that one should never negotiate on the turf of the opposition. Another lawyer counsels new associates that one should never be the first to mention a price in a commercial negotiation. She believes that stating price is regarded as a sign of weakness. While there may be a grain of truth in each homily, each can quickly become counterproductive. What happens in a commercial negotiation if no party ever mentions price? People do not have endless amounts of time to dance around the central issues at hand. Is it possible that agreeing to meet in the other party's office could trigger some beneficial concession on the part of the person in whose office the parties are meeting? While Fisher and Ury are quick to remind us that being nice is not the answer, most successful negotiations are characterized by civility, if not cordiality. In reality, if there is any kind of axiom for successful negotiation, it might well be: "Don't artificially hamper yourself as a negotiator by establishing inflexible axioms of negotiation."

Still, so many people believe that tactics and strategy are the stuff of negotiation that no discussion of negotiation can ignore them completely. Fisher and Ury, for example, have a chart of "hard/soft" negotiation styles. An example of a soft negotiator is one who changes her position easily; a hard negotiator sticks to his position. "Soft" is characterized by an attempt to be "friends" with the other party; "hard" negotiating posits that the parties are adversaries and must treat each other as such.[13]

There are lots of other examples. Virtually everyone recognizes the classic technique sometimes referred to as the "Mutt and Jeff" or "good cop/bad cop" tactic in which one negotiator in a team of negotiators constantly takes hard positions while another member of the team takes ostensibly soft positions seeming to protect the other side from the "bad" guy on his own team. Another negotiating tactic, Boulwarism, is now named after Lemuel Boulware, a corporate vice president in charge of labor relations who pioneered it. Mr. Boulware had a standard tactic: he simply announced the corporation's position in detail to the newspapers, stated that the company's position was a "take-it-or-leave it" offer and then refused to participate in any further discussions at the bargaining table. Ultimately, the United States National Labor Relations Board denounced this tactic as an unfair labor practice because it effectively destroyed any meaningful collective bargaining. Tactics such as this may work at one point or another in some negotiations. Unfortunately, because Boulwarism is seen by so many as a tough negotiation tactic (and who in his or her right mind ever wants to be perceived as a "weak" negotiator) it has gotten much more attention than it deserves. Properly analyzed, Boulwarism is most often stupid rather than tough.

There are other detrimental side effects in approaching negotiation in this manner. Experienced negotiators almost always have a tactic or strategy worked out to counter any ploy by the other side. A seller who engages in a lot of Boulwarism may soon find himself without customers. Most commercial negotiations are characterized by calm, rational bargaining, rather than by stunts and shams—contrary to the convictions of novice negotiators who insist that negotiation is nothing more than a matter of ploy and counter ploy. If there is a central theme to this chapter, it is this: For the most part, people in business are neither fools, children nor charlatans. They should not be dealt with as such.

Moreover, most of these cracker-barrel homilies and ill-considered stunts are detrimental to effective negotiation. Business negotiations are characterized by people who normally want to do business with each other and who may want to preserve the elements of a long-lasting relationship. These elements dictate a lot of a negotiator's style and behavior. Think of how much damage is done to a business relationship by an overly aggressive negotiator who saws off the legs of his counterpart's chair so that he can appear taller or more in control? How long will an executive want to continue a relationship when she finds out that your good cop/bad cop act was all

13. Fisher & Ury, *supra* n. 1, at 9.

gamesmanship? What happens if a third company inquires of a negotiator (whom you have just devastated and ridiculed) as to the prospects of doing business with your company? These are important points to ponder.

Is there a place for consideration of tactics and strategy? There is, but only if a negotiator fits individual tactics and strategic moves into a principled framework. The important thing to remember is that most good negotiation tactics are simply a matter of common sense. The best first move is almost too obvious for comment. *Prepare* for the negotiation. Preparation can run the gamut from investigating the business behavior of the other party, to market and price surveys, to developing an understanding of the character and personality of the person who will be sitting on the other side of the table, to understanding human behavior in general, to actual rehearsals of the negotiations before entering into the negotiation itself. Remember that knowledge is power and power is leverage. Knowledge should include a thorough grasp of one's product and company, of the other company and its negotiators and of oneself.

In commercial negotiations when the negotiator is someone different from the principal, the first order of business is to have an absolutely clear understanding of the instructions and positions of the client. For lawyer/negotiators, this understanding is crucial because, as the discussion in §5.7 shows, a failure to accommodate a client's instructions may lead to ethical abuses and issues of professional liability. Even after the most elaborate briefings, conditions in the actual negotiation may change so drastically that the client must be consulted further. Good preparation requires that the parties allow ample private time for consultation with the respective clients when this occurs. One of the worst possible mistakes in negotiating on behalf of others is to blunder through to an unsatisfactory agreement when a quick telephone call or an e-mail could have alleviated a misunderstanding. For these same reasons, careful negotiators instruct clients to stand by during negotiations for these consultations. Many negotiations break down when clients cannot be reached for further instructions.

How much time should be spent on matters peripheral to negotiation and how important are these matters? No one knows for sure. The negotiators of the Paris Peace Accords, by which the Vietnam War was ended, devoted a substantial percentage of the entire negotiating process to the shape of the table. Some experienced negotiators refuse to sit, as a matter of principle, at a square table—insisting that only a round table can create the psychological climate necessary to reach an agreement. In recent discussions between Israel and other countries in the Middle East, the geographical setting of the negotiations is of primary importance to many of the parties. Peripheral matters may be merely minor impediments on the road to a final agreement or may become as important as any other issue under discussion.

These questions are best analyzed in terms of relative costs and benefits. If the negotiation is extremely important and if your client agrees to spare no expense to reach an agreement—and if time is not a factor—resolving the shape of the table might be productive in the long run because it contributes to the sense of comfort felt by all the parties throughout the negotiations. By contrast, arguing over the shape of the table simply to show yourself as a strong, aggressive negotiator when that behavior is viewed as ridiculous and childish by the other side is highly counterproductive.

Most negotiation is verbal. The negotiators talk to each other throughout the negotiation. The ultimate work product is a written document that expresses the parties' understanding in words. At the same time, a sophisticated negotiator may want to inquire thoroughly into so-called body language—a concept that assumes that a great deal of human communication is nonverbal (surely an unassailable proposition). Negotiators should be observant and sensitive to such things as physical stiffness on the other side of the table and facial expressions of discomfort or disbelief. But much like the negotiation ploys discussed earlier, some proponents of body language carry their theories to the extreme by listing all sorts of physical behavior and by trying to correlate precise aspects of that behavior with a person's mental state or with what it might reveal about a party's secret negotiation positions.

Professionals who know a lot about human behavior caution about generalizing too much on this topic. One book on negotiating written by a lawyer who ought to know better insists that a person who puts his hands together in the form of a church steeple (both hands touching with the fingers pointed up) is signaling that he feels "confident" and that the opposing party should quickly calculate whether too much is being conceded.[14] Maybe it does, and maybe it does not. Individual physical movements are too idiosyncratic to be used as a basis for generalized comments on human behavior.

There are other negotiation ploys that go well beyond even an artificial analysis of body language. One lawyer describes at length how an office ought to be set up to facilitate a negotiation—and to enhance the influence of the office holder. He talks about the color of the carpeting, whether one uses fluorescent lights or table lamps, the tone set by various wall colorings and the like. His basic point is unassailable: the physical setting of a negotiation can often have an effect on the substantive outcome. But he carries this much too far. What happens when one party goes to such great lengths to arrange an office setting and then discovers that he is up against one of those negotiators who refuses to negotiate on the other side's turf?

In international commercial negotiations, the parties often have very little choice in terms of physical location, and it is rare that one side or the other can artificially manipulate the setting. These days lots of international negotiation takes place by e-mail, on the telephone and, less frequently, by an exchange of facsimile transmissions. Many companies use agents rather than negotiating directly with each other. Even when the parties' engage in face-to-face negotiation those sessions take place in sterile hotel suites and borrowed offices. No competent negotiator should put much stock in ploys and trickery, particularly if the planning of tricks and ploys takes away preparation time from the truly important issues. The best negotiators spend time investigating far more productive matters such as the nature of the client's product and the reasons why another company might want to purchase it.

Other commentators on negotiation like to talk about "power" negotiating techniques such as threats, ridicule, intransigence, and the like. Some work on these

14. I hope my readers will forgive me if I do not cite to the actual work. All that needs to be said is that far too many books on negotiation follow this approach. Heaven only knows what violence they are doing to rational bargaining and to the proper study of negotiation.

topics is productive mainly because a negotiator should always be aware that the other side may try to manipulate him. After all, no one goes into a negotiation wanting to lose; and these tactics may be frequently encountered in win/lose bargaining. But, commercial transactions are rarely win/lose propositions and most people in business prefer to build rather than destroy relationships.

Consequently, much of this discussion is out of place in a book devoted to successfully managing international commercial transactions. Even if these platitudes are accurate, they are designed for negotiation within the American culture and are totally inapplicable and may have a devastating impact when negotiating on a cross-cultural basis. Even the use of humor can have a negative impact on cross-cultural negotiations. One of the author's frequent guest lecturers, a career U.S. State Department employee with ambassadorial status who has managed a number of important multilateral negotiations, frequently tells the students to avoid making jokes in multilateral discussions because, in his view, "there is no joke, however well-intended, that can survive translation into five or six languages." Commercial negotiators should keep his admonition in mind and consider one thing more: if you are new to negotiation, keep in mind that games are for children; games are not for negotiators.

§5.5 CROSS-CULTURAL NEGOTIATION

Successful cross-cultural negotiation begins by keeping in mind the fact that different people have different backgrounds, attitudes and beliefs. Most commercial negotiators normally take into account their counterpart's gender, racial and ethnic background whether they are negotiating a domestic or international transaction. This is usually done not out of any ulterior motive but simply out of a recognition that we do not all spring from the same roots. In domestic commercial negotiation, many of these things are taken for granted and if adjustments are made, they are generally only slight, almost imperceptible shifts in behavior or tactics.

It is more complicated when a transaction cuts across national boundaries.[15] Differences in language, behavior, and attitude are instantly apparent and successful negotiators must normally accommodate those differences. This is not to say that all of one's personal beliefs and attitudes must be sacrificed for the sake of negotiation. It is quite difficult for businesses in the United States to cater to parties who categorically refuse to deal with blacks or women. Indeed, U.S. companies could get themselves into serious trouble under the domestic civil rights laws if they did cater to these attitudes. And no one should forget that commercial negotiation is always a two-way street. In other words, both sides presumably want to reach an agreement and will normally be willing to curb many personal idiosyncrasies for the sake of the agreement.

15. Three excellent books on general aspects of cross-cultural business dealings are: Jeanne M. Brett, *Negotiating Globally: How to Negotiate Deals, Resolve Disputes and Make Decisions across Cultural Boundaries* (2001); Dean Allen Foster, *Bargaining Across Borders: How to Negotiate Business Successfully Anywhere in the World* (1995) and Philip D. Curtin, *Cross-Cultural Trade in World History* (1984).

Many companies try to minimize any problems that might arise due to differences in cultural background by conducting the negotiation through agents who have a common background.[16] It is not unusual for Third World countries to employ an American agent in the United States to conduct their commercial negotiation with domestic U.S. companies. Companies in the United States seeking to do business abroad often deal through agents and employees who are nationals of the target country rather than sending in a U.S.-based negotiation team. Each approach has advantages and disadvantages. A company that deals exclusively through agents loses a great deal of control over the outcome of the transaction. Conversely, many negotiations that might otherwise succeed have been destroyed by the ineptness and lack of sensitivity of a poorly briefed and badly prepared foreign negotiator.

It is also possible to overemphasize cultural differences in a commercial setting. Normally the party that is most anxious to consummate the transaction will also be the party most likely to submerge any sense of injury over perceived slights or offenses. A lawyer of the author's acquaintance dealt with a Latin American colleague on a daily basis for well over a year. Nearly fourteen months after their first meeting, the U.S. lawyer could not properly pronounce his colleague's last name. The lawyer got away with this lapse because the Latin American representative desperately needed the lawyer's assistance. Most business executives are not quite so desperate.

There is an acceptable middle ground. Even if a company prefers to use national agents for on-site negotiations and even if a company perceives itself as being the stronger of the two parties, all persons involved in the deal should make some attempt to come to terms with cultural differences because those differences are likely to penetrate to the marrow of the agreement. Personal slights that may not have an effect on a one-time transaction may destroy the possibility of establishing a long-term business relationship.

There are additional considerations to keep in mind. No one should assume that cultural differences are superficial or that cultural differences can be accommodated by doing only trite things. For example, one of the suggestions often found in U.S. business literature dealing with negotiation with Japanese companies urges U.S. business executives to have their business cards printed in Japanese. Elsewhere in the literature can be found hints on bowing rather than shaking hands, comments on the need to put up with a large-scale social event before getting down to business, and developing a taste for raw fish.

There is nothing intrinsically wrong with these admonitions. Japanese-language business cards can be very helpful. Japanese executives frequently enjoy and prefer a social gathering prior to beginning the negotiation. But suggestions such as this can be taken too far and may lead to serious problems because they fool people into thinking that a person's culture can be understood as a series of platitudes, clichés, or generalizations. For example, one of the common generalizations made in the case of Latin American business people is that they have less of a sense of time and urgency than do North American executives. One book on business negotiation recommends

16. *See*, e.g., Trevor C.W. Farrow, *The Negotiator as Professional: Understanding the Competing Interests of a Representative Negotiator*, 7 Pepp. Disp. Resol. L.J. 373 (2007).

that North American negotiators not expect their Latin counterparts to be on time for appointments or to scrupulously follow a chronological agenda. This homily may have come from someone's actual experience. It is conceivable that some Latin American business person involved in some deal was perpetually tardy for appointments. It is also entirely possible that this notion is derived from nothing more than the ugliest sort of ethnic stereotype; and any negotiator who bases his conduct on such things—who, for example, indicates that his counterpart is not likely to be on time for any future activities—is likely to find himself dealing with an exceptionally hostile counterpart.

The best place to start is not with the platitudes and homilies but with serious research into the backgrounds of the people who are going to be involved in the negotiation.[17] Here again, cost-benefit analysis is likely to play a major role. A company entering into a USD 10,000 transaction may not do very much in terms of exploring the culture of the opposite party; the dollar amount of the contract—particularly if the contract is seen as a one-time deal—simply does not justify the expense and effort of a full-blown cultural analysis. By contrast, companies negotiating multi-million dollar contracts may wish to conduct a thorough investigation into the host country's culture.

Obtaining solid information on other cultures is often difficult. For the most part, the information is not to be found in the literature on negotiation although a few reasonably well-written books exist.[18] Fortunately, there are some readily available sources of information in the United States which can provide good information. The U.S. State Department publishes one-volume area manuals on different regions and on individual countries that provide a quick grasp of a country's history, society, and economy. These are cheap and normally accurate; but on occasion they do not track the most recent developments in the target country. Even when they are a little out of date, they can provide a basis for understanding current events. For example, the area manual on Iran goes into some detail on the Shah's accession to power, pointing out

17. *See*, e.g., Liangguang Huang, *Cross-Cultural Communication in Business Negotiations*, 2 Int'l J. Econ. & Finance (2010); Kevin Avruch, *Culture as Context, Culture as Communication: Considerations for Humanitarian Negotiators*, 9 Harv. Negotiation L. Rev. 391 (2004).

18. *See*, e.g., Jeanne M. Brett, *Negotiating Globally: How to Negotiate Deals, Resolve Disputes, and Make Decisions Across Cultural Boundaries* (3d ed., 2014); Jeswald W. Salacuse, *Making Global Deals: What Every Executive Should Know about Negotiating Abroad* (2d ed., 2002) (This book emerged from several columns on international business negotiation written by Professor Salacuse for the Harvard Negotiation Journal. It is written mainly for U.S. business executives. Readers from outside the United States may have problems with Professor Salacuse's frequent use of U.S. colloquialisms.); Pierre Casse & Surinder Deol, *Managing Intercultural Negotiations: Guidelines for Trainers and Negotiators* (1985) (This book is more a syllabus for a negotiations training program than a book on theory); *International Negotiation: Art & Science* (Diane Bendamane & John Mcdonald eds., 1983) (This is a collection of papers delivered at a conference on negotiation sponsored by the U.S. Foreign Service Institute. While its focus is on country-to-country negotiation, many of the individual papers provide good insight into private-sector international negotiation); Ashok Kapoor, *Planning for International Business Negotiation* (1985). Professor Kapoor's book is based on a series of case histories. He does, however, try to derive some general insights from those case histories which can be beneficial particularly for those who have to deal both with a host government and with a private company. *See also*, Raymond Cohen, *Negotiating Across Cultures: International Communication in an Interdependent World* (rev. ed., 1997); Susan C. *Schneider & Jean-Louis Barsoux, Managing Across Cultures* (1997); *Professional Cultures in International Negotiation: Bridge Or Rift?* (Gunnar Sjostedt ed., 2003); Anselm Strauss, *Negotiations: Varieties, Contexts, Processes and Social Order* (1978).

that the Shah, while claiming an historic lineage, in fact derived his title from his father who acquired it just after World War Two. That fact provides some understanding of the rise of Islamic fundamentalism in Iran even when that edition of the handbook on Iran made no mention of the Ayatollah Khomeni. The historical discussion in the area manual on the Philippines gives much insight into the fall of Ferdinand Marcos and the rise of Corazon Acquino even though it was written before Mrs. Acquino attained the presidency.

There are other sources of information. In one of the few readable, yet scholarly treatments of private, cross-cultural negotiation, Professor Ashok Kapoor of New York University School of Business describes four case histories of transnational negotiations and has developed some criteria for analyzing such negotiations.[19] His central principle should not be forgotten. Major cross-cultural business negotiations normally involve heavy negotiation not only with a company in the host country, but also with the host government. This intrusion by the government is a factor that businesses in the United States do not always have to contend with. As Professor Kapoor points out, the success with which a negotiator deals with the host government is likely to determine the success of the business negotiation.

Professor Kapoor has identified four typical defects—what he calls *failures*—in coping with commercial negotiations that provide a good framework for analysis of any agreement. Failure One is a lack of empathy with the people and government of the host country. This goes much deeper than merely having one's business cards printed in the host country's language. It extends to a lack of knowledge and appreciation for the totality of that country's existence, including—when dealing with former colonies—an understanding of their recently acquired independence. Negotiators must take into consideration the entire fabric of the host country.

Failures Two and Three are characterized by a lack of appreciation for and understanding of a country's governmental system and the manner in which decisions are made. Overcoming these failures requires knowing which people at what level of government are likely to make decisions. In the case of Japan it would include some sensitivity for the unique relationship between Japanese corporations, the Ministry of International Trade and Industry (MITI) and other government agencies, and the University of Tokyo—the educational institution from which virtually all the important Japanese actors graduate. Failure Four is the absence of planning and organization when entering into these negotiations. This lapse may include an inability to make decisions on the spot due to a negotiator's constantly having to communicate with headquarters; an inability to adjust to crucial, on-the-spot-shifts in the negotiation; and poor communication and training among the negotiators themselves.

Professor Kapoor's failures should not be taken as a panacea. They do not answer all questions; but they can be used profitably as a checklist when planning for cross-cultural negotiation. At bottom, of course, is the central theme of this entire chapter: knowledge is power.[20]

---

19. Kapoor, *supra* n. 18.
20. For some additional reading on a country-by-country basis: Richard H. Solomon & Charles W. Freeman Jr., *Chinese Negotiating Behavior: Pursuing Interests Through "Old Friends"* (2016);

§5.6 NEGOTIATION WHEN DISPUTES ARISE UNDER AN EXISTING AGREEMENT

This aspect of negotiation is treated more extensively in Chapter 6 under the heading renegotiation. It is both a process of reaching an agreement and an identifiable form of dispute resolution. Contracts in China, by statute, require disputing parties to first engage in "friendly discussions" and only later to engage in the more adversarial forms of dispute resolution. In certain contacts executed by the Boeing Corporation, renegotiation by specific corporate officers in the two contracting companies is required under the contract's dispute resolution clause.

When the parties are trying to adjust a contract to unanticipated circumstances in a friendly, nonconfrontational manner, renegotiation does not differ materially from the initial negotiation. However, when renegotiation is conducted under the threat of litigation or arbitration because one side believes the other breached the contract, it takes on many of the characteristics of win/lose (distributional) negotiation. In that setting the negotiators are usually attorneys who are negotiating in the shadow of the court. While actual negotiating behavior would not necessarily change, the atmosphere of the renegotiation may be far more adversarial than that of the initial discussions. As a consequence, persons engaged in renegotiation should be prepared to deal with a great deal more hostility.

§5.7 THE ETHICS OF NEGOTIATION

§5.7.1 Ethics Generally

There are three ethical dimensions in negotiation. The first is simply the normal duty one human being owes to another human being. In this context, the term ethics is used in its dictionary sense of morality: as the Oxford English Dictionary puts it—a set of principles that "direct men's actions to the production of the greatest possible quantity of happiness." All negotiators are subject to certain constraints on their behavior as human beings wholly apart from the subject matter of the negotiation. While cultures differ greatly in their approach to and definition of morality, some minimal ethical conditions apply to virtually all negotiations.

Consider, for example, the issue of lying in negotiation.[21] While defining "lie" is never easy, most people will probably concede that telling an outright

Richard H. Solomon & Nigel Quinney, *American Negotiating Behavior: Wheeler-Dealers, Legal Eagles, Bullies and Preachers* (2011); Charles Cogan, *French Negotiating Behavior: Dealing with La Grande Nation* (2003); W. R. Snyder, *How Germans Negotiate: Logical Goals, Practical Solutions* (2002).

21. It is something of an indictment of the American legal profession that one of the best books on lying has been written by a nonlawyer, albeit a person married to the former dean of the Harvard Law School. *See* generally, Sissela Bok, *Lying* (1979). A more recent look at the topic is: *What's Fair: Ethics for Negotiators* (Carrie Menkel-Meadow & Michael Wheeler eds., 2004). There is some very good writing in the law journals: Art Hinshaw, Peter Reilly & Andrea Kupfer Schneider, *Attorneys and Negotiation Ethics: A Material Misunderstanding?*, 29 Negot. J. 265

misrepresentation on which the other side is expected to rely is a lie. In the negotiation hypothetical involving stainless steel fittings that was discussed extensively in preceding sections of this chapter, a seller-negotiator who describes his fittings as being able to bear a stress of 100 pounds per square inch when he knows for a fact that they will bear only 50 pounds is clearly lying. The lie is compounded if the negotiator knows for certain that stress-bearing capacity is an important factor in the buyer's purchasing decision and further knows that the buyer is not likely to have instrumentation capable of measuring stress-bearing capacity. Virtually no culture or legal system excuses this kind of affirmative misrepresentation.

The harder question is whether simply remaining silent in negotiation is also a lie. For example, if the buyer acts as if he believes that the fittings can bear a stress of 100 foot pounds and the seller says nothing to disabuse him of that notion, is the seller's inaction a lie? Would the definition turn on the specific context of the nondisclosure; as, for example, when the seller knows that the buyer's processes will never expose the fitting to a stress greater than 10 pounds. Would nondisclosure constitute a lie if the seller knows that the fittings are to be a part of, say, an aircraft wing exposed to varying stresses?

Ethicists may debate these questions at length. A number of legal systems have attempted to deal with such issues. The Anglo-American legal system centuries ago established the doctrine of caveat emptor (let the buyer beware). This doctrine places virtually all risks on the buyer and imposes virtually no duties of disclosure on the seller. But it is an exceptionally harsh doctrine, particularly when it is imposed in a setting where most of the knowledge and information is in the hands of the seller. In the United States, the harsher aspects of caveat emptor—particularly in consumer transactions—have been modified by legislation. Most countries now have legal principles that place some burden of disclosure on the party who is in the best position to know of defects or limitations in a product.

At the same time, there is a thin line between the sort of misrepresentation or nondisclosure discussed above and the more innocuous statements that takes place in most negotiations. Is it ethically impermissible for the seller to tell buyer: "our fittings are the best in the world?" Probably not. This type of behavior, commonly referred to as puffing, is age-old business conduct and has almost never led to either official or unofficial sanctions. Most people, whether they are consumers or business executives automatically discount such comments as soon as they are offered.

A purely philosophical discussion of these issues may make many business executives uncomfortable. In the United States it is a commonplace that morality bears

(2013); Tu Yu-Te, *The Relationships Between Trust and Unethical Negotiation*, 3 Int'l J. Bus., Humanities & Tech. 45 (2013); Van M. Pounds, *Promoting Truthfulness in Negotiation: A Mindful Approach*, 40 Willamette L. Rev. 181 (2004); Brian C. Haussmann, *The ABA Ethical Guidelines for Settlement Negotiations: Exceeding the Limits of the Adversarial Ethic*, 89 Cornell L. Rev. 1218 (2004); Jonathan R. Cohen, *The Ethics of Respect in Negotiation*, 18 Negot. J. 115 (2002); Charles B. Craver, *Negotiation Ethics: How to Be Deceptive Without Being Dishonest/How to Be Assertive Without Being Offensive*, 38 S.Tex. L. Rev. 713 (1997); Thomas L. Shaffer, *On Lying for Clients*, 71 Notre Dame L. Rev. 195 (1996); Gerard Wetlaufer, *The Ethics of Lying in Negotiation*, 75 Iowa L. Rev. 1219 (1990).

very little relation to business practices. For readers who find the philosophical dimension unproductive, it is entirely possible to address these questions from a pragmatic standpoint. Setting philosophy aside, a negotiator should simply ask the question: "what may happen if the other side finds out I'm lying?" This analysis forces a negotiator to consider the risks of lying (whether affirmative misrepresentation or nondisclosure) in a practical context. There could be legal ramifications involved in a negotiator's misleading the other side on the stress-bearing capacity of fittings used in an airplane wing. If the aircraft crashes, a product liability lawsuit may implicate the seller as well as the buyer. But even in a nonlife-threatening context, truth-telling has a lot of advantages. For example, assume a negotiator who comes into the room with instructions from her client to do two things: make the best deal possible on the transaction at hand and do everything you can to build toward a long-term business relationship. In normal circumstances, a negotiator armed with these instructions would likely not commit an affirmative misrepresentation, but would probably go out of her way to make full disclosure even when she might not be faced with a specific request for information. Buyers who are lied to are unlikely to want to continue the business enterprise. Can there be any doubt, for example, that a stainless steel fitting negotiator armed with these instructions would have an obligation to disclose stress capacity even if the buyer forgot to ask the question? When the risk of lying is the possible destruction of the long-term business relationship, the negotiator has very little alternative but to tell the truth.

There are other issues that a good negotiator should consider. In the examples discussed above, the misrepresentation or nondisclosure involved the capability of the good to be sold—what the lawyers would call the heart of the bargain. Now assume a situation in which a fitting negotiator needs some time to think during the actual negotiation and obtains this thinking time by implying that he cannot set the price when in fact his price-setting authority runs from USD 0 to USD 45 per unit (i.e., encompasses virtually the entire range of possible price outcomes). Is it a lie for the negotiator to leave the room pretending to make a telephone call to the client when he already has all possible authority to agree? While there may be a misrepresentation here, the misrepresentation does not relate to the quality of the goods. A price for the fittings is eventually going to be established if the parties are to have a contract at all. The actions of the negotiator here are more in the nature of a delaying ploy, rather than a lie that goes to the heart of the bargain. Second, the risk of some adverse reaction by the other side if the buyer finds out that the negotiator did have price-setting authority is likely to be minimal. Many negotiators use such techniques, and it is virtually certain that the other negotiator is engaged in similar activities. The end product of lying on one's price-setting authority may make the other side a little more skeptical in later negotiations but is not likely to drive them away from the bargaining table. It is doubtful that such a ploy would damage long-term relationships or in any way affect the health or safety of the ultimate users of the product.

The issue might be resolved differently, however, if the negotiator gets a direct question from the other side: "Do you have independent authority to set the price of this contract?" A negative response to such a direct question would be, by definition, be an affirmative misrepresentation, and might lead to future hostility between the parties. In this instance, a negotiator might permissibly choose either not to answer the question or to give an evasive response if she believes that concealing her price-setting authority is important to the negotiation. It is highly unlikely that concealment in this setting will poison the business relationship.

Many commentators on negotiation go even further. If negotiation is viewed as a game then it is axiomatic that good gamesmanship will pay results. It is something of a conundrum, at least as seen by Professor James White, who has written:

> On the one hand the negotiator must be fair and truthful; on the other he must mislead his opponent. Like the poker player, a negotiator hopes that his opponent will overestimate the value of his hand. Like the poker player, in a variety of ways he must facilitate his opponent's inaccurate assessment. The critical difference between those who are successful negotiators, and those who are not, lies in this capacity both to mislead and not to be misled.[22]

Readers should not be misled. Professor White is mainly concerned with win/lose bargaining where winner takes all, while most business negotiation is a matter of win/win bargaining, permitting both sides to gain advantages from the deal.

There are no easy answers here. Cynical readers of this book can point to large numbers of ethical abuses on the part of negotiators who seem to be highly successful. But at least in win/win negotiation, ethical issues can best be handled by application of the famous golden rule: "Do unto others as you would have them do unto you."

§5.7.2 Ethical Constraints on U.S. Lawyer-Negotiators

Lawyers in the United States and in many other countries are subject not only to general constraints on their behavior but also to express principles governing their professional behavior. Violations of a lawyers' code of ethics can lead to disciplinary action against the lawyer irrespective of whatever effect the ethical abuses have on the client. One U.S. code of ethics, the Model Code of Professional Responsibility, addresses dishonesty (including the matter of lying to others) mainly in generalities. The Code admonishes a lawyer to "represent his client zealously within the bounds of the law."[23] In so doing, however, a lawyer is not to "engage in conduct involving dishonesty, fraud, deceit, or misrepresentation."[24] The Code contains some other restrictions on lying, but those restrictions essentially prohibit lying to a court—as contrasted to lying to another lawyer or to a third person. A more recent statement of ethical behavior, the Model Rules of Professional Conduct, has been adopted by a majority of the states in the U.S. and, for the first time, contains some specific admonitions on lying in a negotiation context. Rule 4.1 requires that a lawyer "shall not knowingly: (a) make a false statement of material fact or law to a third person; or (b) fail to disclose a material fact to a third person when disclosure is necessary to avoid assisting a criminal or fraudulent act by a client [unless, however, the matter is covered

22. James J. White, *Machiavelli and the Bar: Ethical Limitations on Lying in Negotiation*, Am. B. Fdn. Res. J. 926, 927 (1980).
23. Canon 7, Model Code of Professional Responsibility ("MCPR").
24. Disciplinary Rule 1-102(A)(4), MCPR.

by attorney-client privilege]." This principle is limited by a comment to the rule that states: "whether a particular statement should be regarded as one of fact can depend on the circumstances. Under generally accepted conventions in negotiation, certain types of statements ordinarily are not taken as statements of material fact. Estimates of price or value placed on the subject of a transaction and a party's intentions as to an acceptable settlement of a claim are in this category."[25]

These express constraints may not be terribly helpful in raising the level of the typical lawyer/negotiator's conduct. There are virtually no reported instances involving sanctions imposed on a U.S. lawyer for violating Rule 4.1, for example. Nonetheless, Rule 4.1 is one of the first instances of a lawyer-drafted code of conduct that specifically refer to conduct in a negotiation and that attempt to establish at least some principle of minimally acceptable behavior. If effective enforcement of Rule 4.1 is not forthcoming, its requirements will remain largely a platitude.

§5.7.3 Statutory Controls on Negotiator Conduct

There are other restrictions on the negotiating behavior of both lawyers and nonlawyer negotiators imposed by U.S. law. Article One of the U.S. Uniform Commercial Code provides expressly that: "Every contract or duty within this Act imposes an obligation of good faith in its performance or enforcement."[26] Good faith is further defined as "honesty in fact and the observance of reasonable commercial standards of fair dealing in the trade."[27] But it remains unclear whether this provision governs precontract negotiations. In the United States the controversial Foreign Corrupt Practices Act (FCPA),[28] places severe constraints on the giving of certain gratuities to foreign agents in order to obtain business. While there are no constraints in the act specifically devoted to the negotiation process, the FCPA may constrain negotiating behavior that in the past has been regarded as normal and permissible. Even so, the FCPA, discussed at length in Chapter 3, §3.6.5, is mainly a constraint on the paying of bribes to foreign government officials, rather than a specific constraint on international business negotiations.

25. MRPC, Comment to Rule 4.1.
26. UCC §1-203.
27. UCC §2-103(b).
28. 15 U.S.C. §78a note.

CHAPTER 6

International Electronic Commerce

§6.1 INTRODUCTION AND SOME BASIC DEFINITIONS

The lifeblood of international commerce has always been communication. The first forms of communication involved physical travel by human beings—i.e., people going from place to place and communicating by word-of-mouth. Later, as early societies mastered the art of writing, pieces of paper that contained important information were conveyed from one location to another. The benefit of the piece of paper is that it could be transported by a messenger who did not necessarily have to know the contents of the paper. More recently, those pieces of paper could be transported rapidly over long distances by such things as train, automobile, ship, or airplane. Beyond the physical transportation of a message, many societies developed other forms of communication: African tribes communicated with drums; American Indian tribes sometimes communicated with smoke signals. An early form of military communication, the heliograph, involved the transmission of messages by flashing mirrors and was used by the Roman legions.

Approximately 150 years ago, as society gained better knowledge of electricity and all those things that derive from the use of electrical power, new forms of data transmission were invented—for example, the telegraph, the telephone, the radio, and the facsimile. The invention of television and its increasing use by the midpoint of the twentieth century constituted yet another form of communication. These forms of communication are based on the availability of electricity and grow out of electronic concepts. They permit the transmission of large amounts of data over long distances with great rapidity and relatively inexpensively without the need for the physical transportation of pieces of paper. But even these new forms of electronic communication almost always began as a piece of paper at one end and, after transmission, were converted to a piece of paper at the receiving end. Until very recently when communication of data served a legal purpose, such as the formation of a contract, it was understood that even if some of the communication took place in electronic form, the crucial item was the final piece of paper that constituted the final, enforceable agreement.

But in the last decades of the twentieth century, something new emerged—a form of communication that was accomplished solely through electronic means, that did not have to be reduced to paper, and that frequently had legal consequences. This new form of communication is accomplished by the electronic transmission of computer-generated content. The medium for most of this communication is through a network of communication and computer devices known as the *Internet* using the protocols developed for the *World Wide Web.*[1] When this new form of communication results in the doing of business, we frequently refer to that communication as *electronic commerce.* The legal principles that are derived from the use of the Internet for electronic commerce is sometimes called *cyberlaw.*

Electronic commerce has now become a large, and growing, component of international commerce. As international electronic commerce has grown, a significant number of lawyers, judges and law professors concluded that entirely new legal principles must be created to accommodate this new form of commerce. There is some truth to that proposition. Electronic commerce, particularly international electronic commerce, has led to some thorny jurisdictional issues. The use of the Internet has fostered the development of new forms intellectual property such as domain names. The volume of business now done over the Internet and the difficulties in ascertaining a fixed geographical location for Internet activities has created some singular problems with regard to national taxation of Internet-based business activity. The relative ease with which electronic communications can be penetrated and observed by outsiders causes many within the legal community to worry about personal privacy issues.

Nonetheless, as we watch the development of international electronic commerce and cyber law, what we see is that most of the principles previously established for bricks-and-mortar companies and for paper-based legal transactions work reasonably well for Internet-based transactions. So for example, an enforceable contract still requires offer and acceptance, even if the offer and the acceptance are communicated electronically. A bill of lading or a letter of credit may be initiated in electronic form but still must contain all the previously established requirements for a valid bill of lading or letter of credit. To warrant protection under national or international intellectual

1. There is occasional confusion between the term *Internet* and the term *World Wide Web.* The electronic encyclopedia, Wikipedia, defines the "Internet" as "a global system of interconnected computer networks that interchange data by packet switching using the standardized Internet Protocol Suite (TCP/IP). It is a 'network of networks' that consists of millions of private and public, academic, business, and government networks of local to global scope that are linked by copper wires, fiber-optic cables, wireless connections and other technologies." Wikipedia defines "World Wide Web" as "a system of interlinked hypertext documents accessed via the Internet....The World Wide Web enabled the spread of information over the Internet through an easy-to-use and flexible format. It thus played an important role in popularising use of the Internet to the extent that the World Wide Web has become a synonym for Internet, with the two being conflated in popular use." For simplicity's sake, this chapter will simply refer to this system of communication as the Internet.

property laws, a piece of intellectual property must still satisfy all the requirements for, say, a patent, copyright, or trademark even if that property was created and exists only in electronic form.

This means that the vast bulk of traditional legal principles that regulate and enhance the doing of business around the world are still fully valid in electronic commerce and, at least so far, appear to work quite well. As a result, almost everything discussed elsewhere in this book remains valid for agreements that are concluded electronically. In the view of the author, it is not so much that we need a lot of new legal rules in cyberspace but rather that the old rules are properly understood and enforced by those who work with electronic commerce. Accordingly, this chapter concentrates mainly on those relatively few areas of the law where the growth of electronic commerce has fostered debate and discussion that lead to new rules for doing business electronically.

Electronic commerce is having a profound, if not transformative effect on business operations. To begin to understand its impact, it is helpful to establish a few basic definitions while accepting the fact that because of the newness of electronic commerce, there are not necessarily a lot of commonly accepted definitions currently in force. In the United States, a component of the government's legislative branch, the Government Accountability Office, has commented:

> Different institutions use the term 'electronic commerce' to describe different things. For example, some definitions imply use of the Internet, while others define electronic commerce more broadly to include transactions that involve devices such as facsimile machines, telephones, and computer-based systems. However, for measurement purposes, there is general agreement that the on-line commitment to sell a good or service is necessary for any transaction to be categorized as electronic commerce. International electronic commerce, as a subset of total electronic commerce, generally involves an on-line commitment to sell that results in the import or export of goods and services.[2]

This is a good starting point although as this chapter proceeds, other definitions will be suggested in specific contexts. Moreover, it is important not to define electronic commerce too broadly. For example, should the mere exchange of a few e-mail messages to deal with certain peripheral issues between the parties to a traditional contract—that is, a contract that is written on paper and executed with traditional pen-and-ink signatures constitute electronic commerce. Probably not. By contrast, a transaction that is fully set out and fully consummated solely in electronic form would certainly qualify. But this example is probably too narrow. Even if a transaction eventually results in the acquisition of a tangible (as contrasted with a purely electronic) good, if virtually the entire transaction was initiated and completed electronically, such a transaction should qualify.

Looking in Wikipedia, we find the following definition: "Electronic commerce...consists of the buying and selling of products or services over electronic

---

2. United States General Accounting Office, *International Electronic Commerce: Definitions and Policy Implications* 1 (GAO-02-404 2002) (The Government Accountability Office was formerly known as the General Accounting Office).

systems such as the Internet and other computer networks." The Organization of Economic Cooperation and Development (OECD) takes a two-part approach, proposing both a broad and a narrow definition. The *broad* definition is: "The sale or purchase of goods or services, whether between businesses, households, individuals, governments, and other public or private organizations, conducted over computer-mediated networks. The goods and services are ordered over those networks, but the payment and the ultimate delivery of the good or service may be conducted on or off-line."[3] The OECD *narrow* definition is: "The sale or purchase of goods or services, whether between businesses, households, individuals, governments, and other public or private organizations, conducted over the Internet. The goods and services are ordered over those networks but the payment and ultimate delivery of the good or service may be conducted on or off-line."[4]

The United Nations Commission on International Trade Law has done a substantial amount of work on electronic transactions. The UNCITRAL Model Law on Electronic Commerce covers transactions involving "any kind of information in the form of a data message used in the context of commercial activities." "Data message is defined as 'information sent, received or stored by electronic, optical or similar means including, but not limited to, electronic data exchange (EDI), electronic mail, telegram, telex or telecopy'."[5]

There is yet another way to view international electronic transactions. In this instance, a vocabulary has already been created that is in general use. We can distinguish transactions by looking at the identity of the participants. There are electronic transactions between consumers that we now refer to as "C2C" (consumer-to-consumer) transactions. An example is an individual seller of a camera on eBay who sells that camera to an individual buyer. By contrast, an individual buyer who buys a book from Amazon.com would be placed in the category of business-to-consumer or "B2C." A third category is the primary focus of this book—that is, two businesses consummating an international transaction or "B2B."[6]

3. OECD, Measuring the Information Economy (2002) at Annex 4, p. 29. This definition includes: "orders received or placed on any online application used in automated transactions such as Internet applications, EDI, Minitel or interactive telephone systems."
4. *Id.* This definition includes: "orders received or placed on any Internet application used in automated transactions such as Web pages, Extranets and other applications that run over the Internet...regardless of how the Internet is accessed...[but excluding] orders received or placed by telephone, facsimile or conventional e-mail."
5. Article I, UNCITRAL Model Law on Electronic Commerce (1996).
6. There is another type of transaction that is becoming more and more important and can, on occasion, give rise to some type of economic activity. In the United States and in a number of other countries, a large part of the interaction between the population of a country and its government is now taking place on the Internet. In the United States, virtually all levels of government have websites. These websites are used to provide and collect information and also used for certain financial transactions such as the payment of taxes, fees for government permits, and the like. This component of Internet activity is sometimes referred to as "G2C" or "government-to-citizen." While outside the scope of this book, it is fascinating and worthy of close attention.

These definitions are helpful for setting the stage.[7] For the purposes of this chapter, we will consider an electronic commerce transaction to be a transaction in which the substantial portion of the information exchanged is conducted electronically. This will permit the examination of contracts that are developed through e-mail exchanges between merchants as well as commercial sales that originate through vendor's websites. At this juncture, there is very little need to agonize over a definition. This may be a situation where anyone will recognize an electronic transaction when he or she sees it.

§6.2 A BRIEF HISTORY OF THE INTERNET

No one interested in international electronic commerce should jump into it without some basic understanding of how the Internet got started. The Internet is not, as one United States senator said recently, a "collection of electronic tubes," even though it does rely very heavily on various electronic devices. The Internet is far more than a mere sum of all the computers connected to it. In truth, it is a peculiar, perhaps unique, confluence of electronic devices and human thought and interaction. It is a significant achievement in human culture and in international business. We can probably say, with some certainty, that most predictions as to where the Internet is going and how it will grow will probably prove to be too modest.

Even so, the Internet had modest beginnings in both the United Kingdom and the United States.[8] To understand the development of the Internet, we must first have an understanding of how computers began. It is generally conceded that one of the earliest concepts of a computer was developed by a British inventor named Charles Babbage. In 1833 Mr. Babbage, in an attempt to create more sophisticated astronomical tables, described an invention that he called the Difference Engine to do various mathematical calculations. Babbage's Difference Engine led him to propose an even more sophisticated device powered by steam engine called the Analytical Engine which he claimed would be capable of performing a vast number of mathematical calculations even though the machine was never actually manufactured.[9] One of the striking features of Babbage's inventions was the ability of people using the machine to program the machine by way of giving the machine directions to perform specific calculations.

Babbage's work was followed, in 1854, by the publication of a work by the British mathematician, George Boole. This contribution, now known as Boolean logic, developed the conceptual basis for the digital analytical process that now drives Internet search systems. At roughly the same time, the United States and Great Britain were

7. For additional discussion *see*, Jeffrey B. Ritter, *Defining International Electronic Commerce*, 13 NW J. Int'l L. & Bus. 3 (1992).
8. Most of the discussion in this section comes from Christos J.P. Moschovitis, Hilary Poole, Tami Schuyler and Theresa M. Senft, *History of the Internet: A Chronology, 1843 to the Present* (1999) and John Naughton, *A Brief History of the Future: From Radio Days to Internet Years in a Lifetime* (1999).
9. More than 100 years later, a team of British scientists and engineers took Babbage's blueprints and descriptions and actually constructed an Analytical Engine to find that it did very much what Babbage claimed. Moschovitis, *supra* n. 8, at 96.

collaborating on the laying of a transatlantic telegraph cable providing the first basis for truly global electronic communication. At roughly the same time, Alexander Graham Bell invented the telephone which triggered the laying of a transatlantic telephone cable. Marconi's invention of the radio led to the vast network of wireless communication that now affects almost everyone. In the 1930s another British mathematician named Alan Turing, one of the moving forces behind Britain's cracking of the German enigma code during World War Two, published the theoretical basis for digital computing in a paper entitled "On Computable Numbers."

The United States followed a slightly different path over the same time period but eventually reached essentially the same point in computing science as that of the British. Shortly after World War One, an American physicist, Vannevar Bush, took up an academic appointment at the Massachusetts Institute of Technology. Both a laboratory scientist and a theoretician, Dr. Bush, worked on a number of experiments and theoretical proposals that led to substantial advances in information processing. Among other things, he invented a machine that had the capability of reading microfilm and selecting items on each piece of microfilm. In the 1930s, Dr. Bush constructed one of the earliest true computers, a device known as the Differential Analyzer. The Analyzer was prompted by a commercial need—the electricity industry wanted to develop a properly functioning electricity network. People understood the basic physics of electricity but needed much more information on questions involving electric surges, line failures, and the manner in which electricity could be efficiently transmitted over long distances. Solving these problems proved to be more a matter of mathematics than of physics. Dr. Bush, among others, realized that the solution was going to involve the application of complex differential equations. Working with those equations required something more than simply having a single mathematician sit at a table and work out the answers with pencil and paper. Underlying Bush's thinking was and understanding of certain work by British scientists who created a theory for a machine called an Integrator which could solve relatively simple mathematical equations.

Bush's Differential Analyzer, while theoretically adept, was in fact a very large, unwieldy *analog* computer. The machine was capable of solving a number of differential equations but took up huge amounts of space and used large resources of energy and time. Worse, it had to be reconfigured to solve each new equation, and, of course, the entire concept was going down the wrong road. The better road proved to be work involving *digital* computers. But Bush was clearly inspirational. A few years later, an MIT colleague of Dr. Bush's, Norbert Wiener, did some preliminary work on the nature and theory of digital computers just before both he and Dr. Bush joined that incredible team of scientists and engineers that comprised the Manhattan Project, the venture that developed the atomic bomb.

While Bush and Wiener were doing their work at MIT a number of companies including the American Telephone and Telegraph Company and its subsidiary, Bell Labs, were engaged in parallel work in a crucial area of telephony that was primarily concerned with extraneous noise and static over telephone lines. The International Business Machines company, now known as IBM, was engaged in various research activities to enhance the processing power and the speed of business calculators and adding machines. After the United States entered World War Two, a great deal of the scientific work in corporations and universities was redirected to assist the war effort.

Toward the end of World War Two and the start of the Cold War, a great deal of civilian scientific effort was launched to help the military cope with increasingly complex science and technology. For example, near the end of the war a joint venture between IBM and Harvard University led to the creation of a computer called the Mark One, also known as the IBM Sequence Controlled Calculator. In 1946 in very large complex and powerful computer named ENIAC was constructed at the University of Pennsylvania. In 1951, the United States Bureau of the Census acquired what is regarded as the first true data processing computer known as UNIVAC, a creation of the Remington Rand Corporation. These machines were powerful and innovative but extraordinarily large because they relied essentially on vacuum tubes—the same devices then found in radios and television sets. The computers often occupied entire rooms that technicians walked into. But the size of these devices meant that space and energy consumption became major limiting factors. Fortunately, about this same time, another electronic component, the transistor, was invented and placed in commercial service. As a result, as computers became more and more powerful they also became smaller and smaller.

The technological advances stemming from World War Two made an additional contribution to information technology. Particularly in the United States, inventions and acquisitions for defense purposes were heavily funded. Many of these developments also proved to have important applications in the private sector. As a result, the growth in computer and information technology sprang from the twin streams of commercial innovation and military acquisition.

There were other events that sparked IT development. In 1957, the launching of a small satellite by the Soviet Union called Sputnik, had a profound, almost traumatic, effect on the United States and other Western countries with repercussions in many different areas of Western society and government. Among other things, Sputnik led to a national debate on whether students in the United States were being properly educated in mathematics, engineering, and science. Sputnik provoked a vastly expanded race to outer space culminating in the United States' putting men on the moon twelve years later. Because Sputnik was regarded as having as a scientific achievement with important military consequences, President Eisenhower ordered the United States Department of Defense to create the Advanced Research Projects Agency (ARPA) to engage in long-range, open-ended scientific research that hopefully would have substantial military application. Among many other projects, ARPA investigated the possibility of a national military communication system that would survive a nuclear attack. In a separate inquiry, because of a significant shortage of computers among the ARPA scientists, ARPA administrators commissioned a project to link together the various ARPA computers that stretched across the United States. By late 1969, ARPA connected computers among four separate ARPA research sites. An additional twenty research sites were added to the ARPA network by 1970.

Coinciding with these developments, which were predominantly military, came the development of the computer modem, the integrated circuit, the creation of a standard character recognition computer language called the American Standard Code for Information Interchange (ASCII), and invention of concepts such as hypertext, hyperlink, and the hypertext editing system. And perhaps most importantly of all, by the late 1970s the world profited from the development and commercial success of the personal computer, the mechanism that lies at the heart of today's Internet. Simultaneously with the emergence of the PC came with the creation of a common, standardized computer languages by such people as Bill Gates and Paul Allen, the founders of Microsoft.

The military continued to play a large part in all of this. By the end of the 1970s, ARPA had become the Defense Advanced Research Projects Agency (DARPA), a Defense Department component that developed some of the basic concepts for a nationwide computer network linked by common standards. DARPA wisely made many U.S. universities a partner in these ventures and the universities quickly saw the advantages of this computer network for civilian research and education. These undertakings, in turn, led to the development of the Internet protocol standards and ultimately to the creation of domain names. In 1990 two Swiss scientists, Tim Berners-Lee and Robert Caillau, announced the name World Wide Web for a hypertext system used at the CERN nuclear research facility near Geneva. A year later CERN scientists developed a hypertext transfer protocol (HTTP), hypertext markup language (HTML), and the Universal Resource Locator (URL). As all these innovations began to take hold, others were developing web browsers, Internet directories, and search engines. By the end of the 1980s millions of flowers were blooming. Within another two decades the world began to reap the benefits of this phenomenal, revolutionary system of communication and information that we now know as the Internet.

But as important as the Internet is, this chapter takes up some narrower issues. Does the Internet, with all of its innovation, require completely revamped and reconfigured legal principles? As the following discussion makes clear, the answer is "probably not."

§6.3 THE SIZE AND SCOPE OF INTERNATIONAL ELECTRONIC COMMERCE

The definitions of electronic commerce set out in §6.2 are helpful in trying to determine the size and scope of international electronic commerce. Information gathering for this component of international business is a bit elusive but we are now beginning to understand how large and how important it is.

In the United States, the United States Census Bureau develops various statistical profiles for electronic commerce by distinguishing between B2B and B2C commerce.[10] Within the U.S. manufacturing sector, electronic commerce comprise USD 1,568 billion for the year 2006, an increase of 16.7% from 2005 when that sector saw electronic transactions amounting to USD 1,344 billion. These electronic transactions amounted to 31.2% of all manufacturing transactions in 2006. In the economic sector referred to

10. The figures in this paragraph are taken from United States Census Bureau, E-Stats, May 16, 2008. Updated information may be found at www.census.gov/stats.

as "merchant wholesale trade" e-commerce sales were USD 1,148 billion in 2006, up from 1,049 billion in 2005, an increase of 9.4%. In the merchant wholesale trade, electronic transactions amount to 11.3% of total sales. In the retail sector, B2C, electronic commerce appears to be growing at better than 10% per year. As of 2006, electronic retail sales comprised 2.7% of total annual retail sales.

It is instructive to look at even more recent Census Bureau figures. The Bureau released figures for 2015 on May 24, 2017 that confirm the impact of e-commerce on the U.S. economy.[11] In 2015, e-commerce shipments comprised 63.2% of all manufacturing shipments with a total USD value of 3,506.9 billion. Total e-commerce sales for merchant wholesalers were USD 2,198.8 billon, comprising 30.2% of all wholesale transactions. E-commerce retail sales were USD 340.4 billion, an increase of 14% over 2014. E-commerce retail sales comprised 7.2% of all retail sales. E-commerce revenues in the service industries were USD 549.7 billion, an increase of 7.4% over 2014. E-commerce transactions in services comprised 3.9% of total revenues.[12]

International electronic commerce statistics are more difficult to obtain. One of the best sources of international information is the Organization for Economic Cooperation and Development.[13] OECD collects a substantial amount of statistical information on a large number of factors. The OECD tells us that in 2007 businesses in OECD countries with ten or more employees used the Internet for 33% of their purchase transactions and 17% of their sales transactions. The OECD estimates that electronic transactions in the B2B context increased five to seven times between the late 1990s and the mid-2000s.

In 2016, in cooperation with the OECD, the World Trade Organization (WTO) and others, the United Nations Conference on Trade and Development launched an initiative to develop more and better data on international e-commerce. The UNCTAD technical notes point out: "[O]fficial and market research data on cross-border B2C e-commerce trade are starting to emerge. However, the quality, methodology and transparency differ, inhibiting cross-country benchmarking."[14] Using somewhat anecdotal information, the Economist Magazine states:

> Over the past decade global e-commerce has been expanding at an average rate of 20% a year as bricks-and-mortar shops have languished. Yet its share of total retail trade last year [2016], at 8.5% worldwide, was still modest. Even in South Korea, the country with the highest percentage of retail sales online, it amounted to only 18% ... In America, the world's biggest consumer market, it made up about 10% of the total. And in many middle-income countries its share was much lower: less than 5% in India and Brazil...[15]

---

11. E-Stats 2015—Measuring the Electronic Economy (May 24, 2017). *See* www.census.gov/E-Stats 2015.
12. *Id.*
13. OECD information may be found at its website: www.oecd.org. The statistics in this paragraph are taken from OECD, *The Future of the Internet Economy: A Statistical Profile* (June 2008). As of mid-2013, the OECD continues its significant body of work on vital issues in electronic commerce. All of those reports, symposium proceedings and the like are too numerous to list here but may be found on the OECD website: www.oecd.org.
14. UNCTAD, In Search of Cross-Border E-Commerce Trade Data Technical Note No. 6, April 2016.
15. Economist Magazine, Special Report on E-Commerce, October 28, 2017.

Even so, virtually all statistical analyzes show significant annual growth in Internet usage. There is no question that these trends will continue as we move into the third decade of the twenty-first century.

§6.4 CONTRACT FORMATION AND DIGITAL SIGNATURES

The heart of any international electronic transaction is the formation of the contract. As discussed above, there are any number of methods for sellers getting in touch and negotiating with buyers. Between two merchants who already know each other, a lot of the negotiation dialogue might take place via e-mail. Merchants who are seeking new business opportunities may receive inquiries to their own website or seek out the websites of potential purchasers. Given that there are still large numbers of hard-copy information resources such as magazines and newspapers, information might first be gleaned from a printed advertisement with a website address that is followed up by an electronic inquiry directed to that website.

Once initial contact is made and the two parties decide that they would like to do business with each other, further negotiations might involve lengthy e-mail exchanges, possibly interspersed with telephone conversations, the exchange of facsimile transmissions and the like. In other situations, a merchant-buyer might simply review the list of products on the seller's website, look at the price list and make a purchase decision on the spot without further conversation. The central issue leading to an enforceable contract is when and how the contract is created and signed. Contract formation can take place in a number of different contexts. The question of signature often involves the matter of digital signatures.

§6.4.1 Contract Formation Generally

This issue is not nearly as complicated as some pundits would have us believe.[16] We can start with some simple scenarios that will illustrate most of the possibilities for

16. For an extensive general analysis of many of the issues discussed in this section *see*, Raymond T. Nimmer, *The Legal Landscape of E-commerce: Redefining Contract Law in an Information Era*, 23 J. Contract L. 1 (2007); John M. Norwood, *A Summary of Statutory and Case Law Associated with Contracting in the Electronic Universe*, 4 DePaul Bus. & Comm. L.J. 415 (2006) and Joseph Savirimuthu, *Online Contract Formation: Taking Technological Infrastructure Seriously*, 2 Ottawa L. & Tech. J. 105 (2005). For an interesting discussion of these issues in the context of an emerging Eastern European economy *see*, Stephen E. Blythe, *Bulgaria's Electronic Document and Electronic Signature Law: Enhancing E-Commerce with Secure Cyber-Transactions*, 17 Transnat'l & Contemp. Probs. 361 (2008). For a similar study of an Asian economy *see*, Stephen E. Blythe, *On Top of the World and Wired: A Critique of Nepal's E-Commerce Law*, 8 J. High Tech. L. 1 (2008). For a study of some of the special problems faced by China *see*, Jane K. Winn & Song Yuping, *Can China Promote Electronic Commerce Through Law Reform? Some Preliminary Case Study Evidence*, 20 Colum. J. Asian L. 415 (2007). A recent book with solid information and analysis of electronic commerce and consumer contracts is: Lorna E. Gillies, *Electronic Commerce and International Private Law: A Study of Electronic Consumer Contracts* (Ashgate, 2008). *See also*, Amelia H. Boss, *The Evolution of Commercial Law Norms: Lessons to be Learned from Electronic Commerce*, 34 Brook. J. Int'l L. 673 (2009); Amelia Rawls, *Contract Formation in an Internet Age*, 10 Columbia Science & Tech. L. Rev. 200 (2009). For a European perspective, *see*

contract formation that occur in electronic commerce. Each scenario will be followed by an annotated discussion making reference to some of the more prominent legal provisions on contract formation in electronic commerce.

Scenario One: Merchant A, a manufacturer of woodworking equipment located in Wellington, New Zealand, sends an e-mail, dated January 4, 2009, to Merchant B, a wholesale dealer in woodworking machines located in Chicago, Illinois, USA. The e-mail states: "We have 500 new woodworking lathes that are available for immediate delivery. We are offering the 500 lathes as a package deal for a total price of USD 475,000 (US), F.O.B. Wellington. Specifications for the lathes are contained in Attachment One, attached to this e-mail. We warrant that each lathe complies with all of the stated specifications. This offer will remain in effect until January 20, 2009. Payment shall be either wire transfer for the full amount of the transaction received by us prior to shipment or by letter of credit issued by Bank of America, Chicago, Illinois." Following this text, there is a block of type on the e-mail: "John H. Jones, Sales Manager."

Merchant B reviews the e-mail and the attachment containing the specifications. Concluding that the lathes can be resold in the United States for approximately USD 1,500 each, B believes this is a sound transaction and sends the following e-mail to Merchant A. "We accept your offer so long as shipping can be arranged to ensure that the lathes arrive in Chicago no later than April 30, 2009. We will provide you with all necessary information with regard to the letter of credit that we have arranged with Bank of America, Chicago, Illinois." Following this text, there is a block of type on the e-mail: "Susan Smith, Director of Purchasing."

Merchant A responds with an e-mail that states: "We hereby confirm receipt of your acceptance. Upon further receipt of the details of the letter of credit which details are to be received by us no later than January 15, 2009, we will tender the lathes to ABC Shipping Company, Wellington, New Zealand. ABC Shipping informs us that they can arrange transportation for the lathes to Chicago to arrive no later than April 10, 2009."

Merchant B responds with a very simple e-mail: "The additional terms you propose are satisfactory to us. The details for the Bank of America letter of credit are attached to this e-mail. We will expect receipt of the lathes in Chicago no later than April 10, 2009." Each of these e-mails contains the same "signature" blocks as the first two e-mails.

For our analysis, first assume that each of these communications was reduced to a piece of paper and each piece of paper, with original "pen-and-ink" signatures, was sent to the respective parties via air courier. Do these hard-copy documents comprise an enforceable contract? Note that the communications are silent on choice of law. But recall that the Convention on Contracts for the International Sale of Goods (CISG) entered into force in the United States in 1988 and in New Zealand in 1995. When a

---

Esperanza Gomez Valenzuela, *Regulation of Electronic Contracts in the European Community: New Challenges*, 2 Eur. Int'l J. of Sci. & Tech. 209 (2013).

contract is silent on choice of law but the two merchants are located in countries that subscribe to the CISG, CISG becomes the applicable law.[17]

Reviewing the appropriate provisions in CISG, we find Article 14(1): "A proposal for concluding a contract addressed to one or more specific persons constitutes an offer if it is sufficiently definite and indicates the intention of the offeror to be bound in case of acceptance. A proposal is sufficiently definite if indicates the goods and expressly or implicitly fixes or makes provision for determining the quantity and the price." Merchant A's first e-mail is clearly an offer under CISG. Article 15(1) states: "An offer becomes effective when it reaches the offeree." There is no question that Merchant A's e-mail has "reached" Merchant B so A's offer is "effective."

Has there been acceptance of the offer by Merchant B? The answer is "yes." CISG Article 18(1) provides that "a statement made by or other conduct of the offeree indicating assent to an offer is an acceptance." Article 18(2) provides that "An acceptance of an offer becomes effective at the moment the indication of assent reaches the offeror." A close look at the full text of each of the e-mails suggests, perhaps, a bit of "battle of the forms" as the parties exchange proposals for shipment, but it would appear that the final exchange of e-mails between A and B l resolve any problem with regard to shipment.[18] So if this entire transaction were evidenced by hard-copy documents with original signatures there is very little question that we have an enforceable contract. The result would surely be the same if New Zealand's law of contract or the American Uniform Commercial Code were applied.

But recall that scenario one involves only the exchange of e-mails between the companies and there are no "original" signatures. This is a contract that has been concluded, except for the actual shipment and receipt of the goods themselves, electronically. Does that make a difference? The answer is "no." The contract remains fully valid and enforceable under CISG. We know this because the CISG Advisory Council has promulgated Opinion No. 1: Electronic Communications under CISG.[19] Opinion No. 1 begins its analysis by citing and quoting CISG Article 11: "A contract of sale need not be concluded in or evidenced by writing and is not subject to any other requirement as to form. It may be proved by any means, including witnesses." While conceding that the original CISG did not contemplate electronic transactions, Article 11 fully supports electronic contracts: "A contract may be concluded or evidenced by electronic communications." Beyond this, Opinion No. 1 states that an electronic offer is received by the offeree "when an electronic communication has entered the offeree's server."

17. CISG Art. I(1): "This Convention applies to contracts of sale of goods between parties whose places of business are in different States; (a) when the states are Contracting States." For some good commentary on the intersection of electronic contracts and the CISG, *see* Charles H. Martin, *The Electronic Contracts Convention, the CISG and New Sources of E-Commerce Law*, 16 Tulane J. of Int'l & Comp. L. 467 (2007).
18. For some excellent, insightful comments on why the battle of the forms may be irrelevant to electronic transactions *see*, Francis J. Mootz III, *After the Battle of the Forms: Commercial Contracting in the Electronic Age*, Info. Socy. J. L. & Pol'y 271 (2008). *See also*, Esperanza Gomez Valenzuela, *International Electronic Contracting: Offer and Acceptance*, 8 Euro. Scientific J. 266 (2012).
19. The Advisory Opinions may be found in full text at www.cisg.law.pace.edu.

The issue of acceptance is handled a bit differently but to the same effect.[20] Opinion No. 1 provides that under CISG Article 18: "An acceptance becomes effective when an electronic indication of assent has entered the offeror's server, provided that the offeror has consented, expressly or impliedly, to receiving electronic communications of that type, in that format, and to that address."

Indeed, the letter of credit mentioned in the e-mails might be substantially concluded by electronic means. The International Chamber of Commerce (ICC) promoted and encouraged the use of electronic letters of credit by promulgating an addendum to the Uniform Customs and Practices (UCP) 500, called "eUCP."[21] The eUCP delineates a framework within which electronic records may be presented and reviewed, discusses the bank's obligations when it is unable to receive an electronic record and covers other details that are important in an electronic exchange.[22] Some of the shipping documents might also be created and transmitted, at least in part, by electronic means although the international shipping industry, unlike other segments of the international economy, is very traditional and hidebound and has not yet fully grasped the utility and convenience of electronic documents.[23]

Would the result be any different under some other systems of law? Probably not. In 1996, UNCITRAL promulgated a Model Law on Electronic Commerce.[24] Using language that differs slightly from the CISG, Article 5 provides: "Information shall not be denied legal effect, validity or enforcement solely on the grounds that it is in the form of a data message."[25] Even if a "writing" is required for an enforceable contract, "that requirement is met by a data message if the information contained therein is accessible so as to be usable for subsequent reference."[26]

Article 9 of The European Directive on Electronic Transactions provides:

> Member States shall ensure that their legal system allows contracts to be concluded by electronic means. Member states shall in particular ensure that the legal requirements applicable to the contractual process neither create obstacles for the

20. *See* generally, Anjanette H. Raymond, *Manner, Method, Receipt or Dispatch: The Use of Electronic Media Is Nothing New to the Law,* 52 Loy. L. Rev. 1 (2006).
21. International Chamber of Commerce Pub. No. 500/3, UCP Supplement for Electronic Presentation (2002). The ICC makes clear that the eUCP supplements and does not supplant the UCP itself.
22. *See,* e.g., Janet Koven Levit, *A Bottom-Up Approach to International Lawmaking: The Tale of Three Trade Finance Instruments,* 30 Yale Int'l L.J. 125 (2005); Gao Xiang & Ross P. Buckley, *The Unique Jurisprudence of Letters of Credit: Its Origin and Sources,* 4 San Diego Int'l L.J. 91 (2003).
23. *See,* e.g., Marek Dubovec, *The Problems and Possibilities for Using Electronic Bills of Lading as Collateral,* 23 Ariz. J. Int'l & Comp. L. 437 (2006).
24. *See* generally, Charles H. Martin, *The Electronic Contracts Convention, the CISG, and New Sources of E-Commerce Law,* 16 Tul. J. Int'l & Comp. L. 467 (2007).
25. Recall that the Model Law defines "data message" quite broadly. Art. 1 applies the model law "to any kind of information in the form of a data message used in the context of commercial activities." Art. 1(a) defines "data message" as "information generated, sent, received or stored by electronic, optical or similar means including, but not limited to, electronic data interchange (EDI), electronic mail, telegram, telex or telecopy."
26. Virtually identical language is used in the United Nations Convention on the Use of Electronic Communications in International Contracts. *See,* e.g., Henry D. Gabriel, *United Nations Convention on the Use of Electronic Communications in International Contracts and Compatibility with the American Domestic Law of Electronic Commerce,* 7 Loy. L. & Tech. Ann. 1 (2007).

use of electronic contracts nor result in such contracts being deprived of legal effectiveness and validity on account of their having been made by electronic means.

However, the EU directive adds an important supplemental requirement for valid contract formation. The Directive requires not only the basic requirements of offer and acceptance but also requires what the Directive refers to as *confirmation*. When the recipient of a service places the order through an electronic medium, the seller of the service must "acknowledge the receipt of the recipient's order without undue delay and by electronic means."[27] However, a subsequent provision does not apply the confirmation requirement to contracts that are "concluded exclusively by exchange of electronic mail or by equivalent individual communications." So, in the case of our scenario No. 1, no confirmation would appear to be necessary since the entire dialogue took place through the exchange of e-mails. The confirmation requirement appears to be mainly applicable to persons who order goods or services from a vendor's website.[28]

In the United States, the individual states have the authority to make law governing private contracts. As seen in preceding chapters, the predominant body of law for commercial transactions is the Uniform Commercial Code. For electronic transactions, a group called the National Conference on Uniform State Law (the same entity that produces the Uniform Commercial Code) has created the Uniform Electronic Transaction Act (UETA) to govern electronic agreements. When the National Conference promulgates a uniform act, it urges the individual state legislatures to adopt the act by way of a state legislative enactment. At the moment, 48 states in the United States have adopted the UETA.

The UETA follows the same model as the provisions discussed above. The act begins by describing as its primary goal the "validating and effectuating electronic records and signatures" on which contracts may be based. It then provides in two separate subsections: "A record or signature may not be denied legal effect or enforceability solely because it is in electronic form" and "A contract may not be denied legal effect or enforceability solely because an electronic record was used in its formation."

Accordingly, it seems that Scenario One has created a perfectly acceptable and enforceable contract. Would there be any difference if a buyer purchased goods or services from a seller's website. Consider Scenario No. 2.

Scenario Two: Seller A sells aircraft parts for small aircraft. Seller A has created a website that provides a substantial amount of information on the seller's equipment, prices, shipping costs and policies and the like. Buyer B owns and operates a small aircraft maintenance and repair facility. B finds A's website through an Internet search engine and after reviewing the site finds a number of parts that she wishes to purchase. B reviews those pages on A's website that provide photographs of the parts, the parts'

27. EU Directive Art. 11. *See also*, J.E. Bassett, *Unanswered Arguments after the Pirate Bay Trial: Dropping Sail in the Safe Harbors of the EU Electronic Commerce Directive*, 12 N.C. J. L. & Tech. 67 (2010).
28. *See*, e.g., Sylvia Mercado Kierkegaard, *E-Contract Formation: US and EU Perspective*, 3 Shidler J. L. Com. & Tech. 12 (2007).

specifications and prices. After B conducts this review, the website asks the buyer to identify each part (and the total number of each part) that she wishes to purchase. Once these selections have been made, the buyer is then directed to a series of pages called "checkout." At the checkout stage, buyer reviews the terms of the agreement (payment and return policies, etc.), provides her bricks-and-mortar address and telephone number, furnishes a credit card number and other payment information, selects a shipping method (and the price for the shipping) and concludes by clicking on a box called "purchase." Prior to clicking the buyer is warned by the website that the buyer should review all of the purchase information including payment and shipping information and that a click on the "purchase" box will result in her credit card being charged and the shipment of the goods.

Anyone who has engaged in a web-based purchase transaction will recognize this scenario. Is it a valid transaction? The answer is "yes." Scenario Two is, in essence, a model of Internet-based commercial transactions. There is full disclosure by the seller as to the nature and quality of the goods, the payment terms, and shipment information. There is certainly no undue influence on the buyer. The buyer can simply walk away from the transaction at any point prior to clicking on that "purchase" box by exiting the website just a buyer in a bricks-and-mortar store can leave the store without completing the purchase at any point before she puts the money on the counter and pushes it over to the seller.

Apply all the same language that we reviewed in resolving Scenario One. It would seem that the website itself with all of the information and content that it contains constitutes the "offer." The offer is certainly intelligible and definite. It contains product descriptions and specifications, payment terms and shipping information. Clearly, the terms are not truly negotiable in the sense that Scenario One provides an opportunity for negotiation through the exchange of e-mails. It is essentially a contract of adhesion, but are contracts of adhesion automatically invalid? The answer is "no."[29] While there may be a need for some special protections for consumers, remember that we are working with transactions between merchants.[30] Recall the model for all of these provisions. A contract shall *not* be denied validity or enforceability *merely* because it is concluded through some electronic medium. But it still makes sense to take our analysis a bit further and to look at the manner in which contracts can be authenticated through a signature. This has been a significant issue in so-called clickwrap contracts which will be discussed in the following subsection.

29. *See* generally, Clayton P. Gillette, *Pre-approved Contracts for Internet Commerce*, 42 Hous. L. Rev. 975 (2005); Robert L. Oakley, *Fairness in Electronic Contracting: Minimum Standards for Non-negotiated Contracts*, 42 Hous. L. Rev. 1041 (2005).

30. The EU has been particularly concerned about electronic transactions involving consumers and has included in the E-Commerce Directive and other EU pronouncements special protection for consumers that seem not to be required for "between merchant" transactions. For example, the EU has promulgated the "Unfair Terms in Consumer Contracts Directive" for consumer transactions. The full text of all of these directives may be found on the EU website: www.europa.eu.int. For a lengthy article that looks at all these issues from a consumer's perspective *see*, Ty Tasker & Daryn Pakcyk, *Cyber-Surfing on the High Seas of Legalese: Law and Technology of Internet Agreements*, 18 Alb. L.J. Sci. & Tech. 79 (2008).

§6.4.2 The Matter of Digital Signatures

When parties come to an agreement on a transaction that is evidenced by pieces of paper, they typically write their names in the form of a pen-and-ink signature at the bottom of the page. This is not a casual step. It has traditionally been required under general contract doctrine because it signifies a number of things. Because the signature block is almost always at the end of the document, a party's signature suggests that the signer has read the entire contract from first page to last. Because a signature is not normally coerced, it is an indication that the signer is putting ink to paper on a voluntary, knowing basis. Because it is an affirmative action on the part of the signer, it clearly connotes assent to the transaction. If the signer is the buyer, the signature unquestionably indicates acceptance of the seller's offer. Finally, and perhaps most importantly, under traditional legal principles a person's signature is truly personal so it is regarded as a device of authentication. In other words, when John Jones signs a document, his signature is proof that it is actually John Jones who is the contracting (and signing) party. So signatures bear considerable weight in the traditional law of contract.

When the world first encountered electronic contracts, the issue of signature was of great importance. These days, of course, there are computer programs that permit an individual to place in an electronic communication a facsimile of his or her signature so that a document that is purely electronic can still contain what looks like a party's actual signature. But most parties to an electronic transaction do not go this far. Neither does the law.

The UNCITRAL Model Law on Electronic Commerce is a good place to start. Article 7(1) (Signature) of the Model Law provides:

> Where the law requires a signature of a person, that requirement is met in relation to a data message if: (a) a method is used to identify that person and to indicate that person's approval of the information contained in the data message; and (b) that method is as reliable as was appropriate for the purpose for which the data message was generated or communicated, in the light of all the circumstances, including any relevant agreement.

So UNCITRAL does not require anything specific by way of a signature. It is, of course, impossible to put a pen-and-ink signature to an electronic document. What then might suffice? A number of other statutes illustrate the breadth of what constitutes a valid signature. In the United States, the Uniform Electronic Transactions Act (enacted by 48 states) authorizes the use of electronic signatures and goes on to provide that "An electronic record or electronic signature is attributable to a person if it was the act of the person. The act of the person may be shown in any manner, including a showing of the efficacy of any security procedure applied to determine the person to which the electronic record or electronic signature was attributable." Beyond this, UETA provides that the effect of a person's electronic signature "is determined from the context and surrounding circumstances at the time of its creation, execution or adoption."[31]

The United States Congress got into this issue by passing a statute called the "The Electronic Signatures in Global and National Commerce Act" (sometimes referred to as the "E-Sign Act").[32] The E-Sign Act, much like the other acts discussed immediately above, does not require any particular thing as a signature. Indeed, it approves as a signature: "an electronic sound, symbol, or process, attached to or logically associated with a contract or other record and executed or adopted by a person with the intent to sign the record."[33] So almost anything seems to work as a digital signature—for example, typing one's name in an e-mail, clicking the "purchase" box on a vendor's website, and the like.

There have been some attempts to develop standards for digital signatures that involve encryption and other sophisticated techniques mainly to try to ensure the authenticity of a party's signature. The ICC promulgated some standards for digital signatures in 2001: The General Usage for International Digitally Ensured Commerce (GUIDEC) Principles.[34] The GUIDEC principles urge the use of techniques that derive from cryptography to produce almost perfect authentication and security for digital signatures. Briefly stated, one party creates a message (or just a signature) in plain text that is then encrypted and sent to the other party in encrypted form. Encryption involves the use of "keys" by which the message is scrambled and thus made unintelligible to unauthorized persons who may intercept the message. Using a private key, the proper recipient can unscramble the message and make use of it. Initially, these techniques were seen as vital to ensuring a healthy system of international electronic commerce. They may be necessary in certain instances such as the transmission of financial information through, for example, the international banking systems use of the Society for Worldwide Interbank Financial Telecommunciations ("SWIFT") protocol. But there seems to be little interest in, or need for, elaborate encryption techniques for run-of-the-mill electronic transactions. In Scenario Two, authentication is provided by submitting the buyer's personal information (name, address, telephone number, e-mail address) coupled with a legitimate credit card number. If the credit card has been purloined, the credit card company typically bears most if not all of the risk of nonauthentication.

In a number of consumer transactions, so-called clickwrap or shrinkwrap contracts have been attacked as invalid. In the typical transaction, a vendor sells an end-user license for software to a consumer. The consumer cannot load and use that software until he or she views a page where the text of the license appears and then uses the computer mouse to click on a "yes" or an "I accept" box. Payment to the vendor has already been made by the purchaser. Such techniques have been attacked

31. UETA, §9.
32. 15 U.S.C. §§7001–7903. This statue is imposed on the individual states unless a state has separately enacted the Uniform Electronic Transactions Act.
33. *Id.*, §7006(5).
34. *See*, William F. Fox, *The International Chamber of Commerce's GUIDEC Principles: Private-Sector Rules for Digital Signatures*, 35 Int'l L. 71 (2001).

as unconscionable, the use of undue influence, failure to fully disclose, and the like. Nonetheless, at least in the United States, the use of a mouse click to signal assent—and thereby to "sign" the agreement—have been uniformly upheld in U.S. courts.[35]

This does not appear to be a major issue in transactions between merchants. Accordingly, a party has any number of ways to affix a "signature" to an electronic agreement.

§6.4.3 The Requirement of an "Original" Agreement

Another issue that occasionally arises in the context of electronic transactions is the need for an "original" version of the agreement. Recall that under traditional contract law, the only version of the contract that is truly enforceable is the original version with the actual pen-and-ink signatures. This is an important device for avoiding agreements that have been altered or tampered with by one of the parties after execution of the document. Indeed, in the United States a principle of evidence law known as the *best evidence rule* insists on the production of the original document unless a plausible argument may be made as to why the original cannot be produced.[36]

In electronic transactions, there is really nothing that could be said to be the "original" of a document. Nonetheless, there may be times when the integrity and authenticity of the agreement is at stake. The UNCITRAL Model Law takes up this issue by providing that when "the law requires information to be presented or retained in its original form, that requirement is met by a data message if: (a) there exists a reliable assurance as to the integrity of the information from the time when it was first generated in its final form as a data message or otherwise; and (b) where it is required that information be presented, that information is capable of being displayed to the person to whom it is to be presented."[37] The article goes on to provide that "the criteria for assessing integrity shall be whether the information has remained complete and unaltered, apart from the addition of any endorsement and any change which arises in the normal course of communication, storage and display ..."[38]

In actual practice, most parties appear to preserve in their own electronic files copies of the final documents that can be compared with the document under review. Those file copies typically contain date and time information indicating when the copies were created. Forensic computer specialists can often reproduce material contained on computer hard drives. Perhaps best of all—even though it harks back to

35. *See*, Nathan J. Davis, *Presumed Assent: The Judicial Acceptance of Clickwrap*, 22 Berkeley Tech. L.J. 577 (2007). Other articles that make good contributions to the dialogue on "clickwrap" are: Cheryl B. Preston & Eli W. McCann, *Unwrapping Shrinkwraps, Clickwraps, and Browsewraps: How the Law Went Wrong from Horse Traders to the Law of the Horse*, 26 B.Y.U. L. Rev. 1 (2011); Paul J. Morrow, *The Unconscionability/Unenforceability of Contracts (Shrink-Wrap, Clickwrap, and Browse-wrap) on the Internet: A Multijurisdictional Analysis Showing the Need for Oversight*, 11 Pitt. J. Tech. & Policy 1 (2011).
36. Federal Rule of Evidence 1002 (Requirement of Original) provides: "To prove the content of a writing, recording, or photograph, the original of the writing, recording, or photograph is required except as provided in these rules."
37. UNCITRAL Model Law, Art. 8(1).
38. *Id.*, Art. 8(2) and (3).

the horse and buggy days—almost all parties to an electronic agreement print out and file a hard-copy of the agreement itself. Indeed, a large number of web-based vendors strongly urge purchasers to print a hard-copy of the transaction for their records. As important as an original might be in traditional dispute resolution, this issue does not seem to have generated much controversy in the context of electronic transactions.

§6.5 JURISDICTION OVER E-COMMERCE TRANSACTIONS

§6.5.1 Jurisdiction Generally

The issue of jurisdiction over e-commerce activities is one of the thorniest and most difficult of all the e-commerce problems.[39] The primary difficulty springs from the traditional assumptions that legal systems make with regard to jurisdiction. The traditional assumptions are built around the concept of physical presence. A human being can be in only one place at one time. For jurisdiction over human persons we assume that a court may exercise jurisdiction over a human being if that person is found within the geographical limits of the court. So a human being who is in France is subject to French court jurisdiction. A human being physically present in the state of New York in the United States is subject to the jurisdiction of New York courts. A human being can, of course, move around. So that person in New York who travels to California is subject to the jurisdiction of the state of California once he crosses into California. Similarly, a bricks-and-mortar company has at least one physical location—say, Munich, Germany. But companies can move as well as humans. If the Munich company opens an office in Birmingham, Alabama, in the United States, it will be subject to the jurisdiction of the State of Alabama.

The two components for traditional jurisdiction are: (1) physical location; and (2) political (geographical) boundaries and virtually all of our jurisdictional rules are tailored accordingly. But where is an e-commerce business "located"? The palpable effect—the "reach" of an e-commerce business—is global. Anyone, anywhere, who

39. There is now a substantial body of literature on this issue. Some representative articles are David R. Johnson & David Post, *Law and Borders: The Rise of Law in Cyberspace,* 48 Stan. L. Rev. 1367 (1996); Dan L. Burk, *Jurisdiction in a World Without Borders,* 1 Va. J. L. & Tech. 3 (1997); Henry H. Perritt, Jr., *The Internet Is Changing the Public International Legal System,* 88 Ky. L.J. 885 (2000); Andrea M. Matwyshyn, *Of Nodes and Power Laws: A Network Theory Approach to Internet Jurisdiction Through Data Privacy,* 98 Nw. U. L. Rev. 493 (2004); Joel R. Reidenberg, *Technology and Internet Jurisdiction,* 153 U. Pa. L. Rev. 1951 (2005); Yulia A. Timofeeva, *Worldwide Prescriptive Jurisdiction in Internet Content Controversies: A Comparative Analysis,* 20 Conn. J. Int'l L. 199 (2005); Kevin A. Meehan, *The Continuing Conundrum of International Internet Jurisdiction,* 31 B.C. Int'l & Comp. L. Rev. 345 (2008). *See also,* Uta Kohl, Jurisdiction and the Internet: Regulatory Competence Over Online Activity (2004). Additional contributions to this literature are: Joshua Beldner, *How Technologically Savvy Do You Have to Be to Apply Zippo?: An Approach to Internet Personal Jurisdiction after Fancaster and Edvisors,* 17 B.U. J. Sci. & Tech. L. 318 (2011); Kevin F. King, *Personal Jurisdiction, Internet Commerce and Privacy: The Pervasive Legal Consequences of Modern Geolocation Technologies,* 21 Alb. L.J. Sci. & Tech. 61 (2011); Anne McCafferty, *Internet Contracting and E-Commerce Disputes: International and U.S. Personal Jurisdiction,* 2 Global. Bus. L. Rev. 95 (2011); Burke T. Ward, Janice C. Sipior & Linda Volonino, *Internet Jurisdiction for E-commerce,* 15 J. Internet Com. 1 (2016).

owns a computer and has access to the Internet can do business with that entity. So our business in Munich through its website, or e-mail, can make contact and ultimately do business with a company in Jakarta, Indonesia. But we have seen such things before. In the past, businesses mailed out catalogs and advertised on television and in magazines and newspapers—all of which media can have a global reach. In the not too distant past, there was a great deal of business done via telegraph, telephone, and facsimile. Still, we could always trace and locate the physical location of both the seller and the buyer.

With an Internet business, physical location is much more elusive. Where does the business *reside*? Is it where the company's server is located? Is it where the human being who functions as the company's webmaster live? Is it the residence of the company's chief executive officer? Might it be where the company is registered to do business? Would it be possible to exercise jurisdiction over the seller in the place where the *buyer* is found? All of these are possibilities. At one time or another in various countries each has been considered as a basis for jurisdiction. None has been found fully satisfactory.

There is another question that must be addressed at the outset. It is possible that we will have different tests and different solutions for jurisdiction depending on why we wish to litigate a matter in a particular country's judicial system. We may get one answer if the Internet company (or that company's product) caused some kind of injury to a purchaser. The answer may be different if we wish to sue an Internet company because it breached a contract or violated a rule of intellectual property.

These are difficult but not necessarily insoluble issues. In the context of B2B transactions, there are less-drastic means to resolve these problems. Under concepts known in the United States as *private ordering*, the parties themselves might agree to a forum in the underlying contract—either through a forum selection clause or by way of an arbitration clause that provides a site for any dispute resolution that might arise.[40] If something such as this were attempted in business-to-consumer contracts, it might be seen as overreaching or even unconscionable, but between merchants (the focus of this book), forum selection in the contract should be viewed as a reasonable solution to a nearly intractable problem. It may also possible to write a treaty, something analogous to the New York Convention on the Recognition and Enforcement of Foreign Arbitral Awards (*see* Chapter 10). There have been a number of treaty proposals that will be discussed below.

§6.5.2 Jurisdiction over Internet Transactions in the United States

As discussed above, jurisdiction in virtually all countries is based on a party's physical presence (its location) and political boundaries between states. If a person or a company is located within the geographical boundaries serviced by a particular court there is usually no further problem. But a number of countries recognize certain

40. *See*, e.g., Haitham A. Haloush, *Jurisdictional Dilemma in Online Disputes: Rethinking Traditional Approaches*, 42 Int'l L. 1129 (2008).

concepts of extraterritorial jurisdiction in which a particular country might reach into another country to assert jurisdiction over an actor in that second country. In the United States, the Due Process Clause of the U.S. Constitution places limits on a court's ability to reach beyond its borders to get at a party in another jurisdiction. The primary test for determining whether a nonresident party can be brought into court in a particular state is whether that party has "minimum contacts" with that state sufficient, within the boundaries of fairness and sovereignty, to justify jurisdiction. But as discussed earlier, Internet transactions do not fit easily in the traditional categories. A number of courts in the United States have recognized some of these differences. For example, an early case involving child pornography on the Internet set out the following "unique" characteristics of Internet transactions:

(1) The Internet is wholly insensitive to geographical distinctions. Indeed, Internet protocols were designed expressly to ignore geographical location.
(2) Web-based entities have digital addresses on an electronic network rather than a physical location address. Moreover, Internet addresses almost never contain geographical information. Because Internet data is often moved through a number of different networks, it is almost impossible to trace the path of that information from sender to recipient.
(3) Further, recipients of Internet content may be anywhere. The sender of Internet content will have no idea where that content is ultimately received or by whom and there is no practical way to restrict receipt of Internet content either in terms of the identity of the recipient or that recipient's geographical location. Similarly, a recipient may have no firm understanding of the location of the sender of the information.[41]

Because of all these difficulties, a number of countries have taken different approaches to Internet jurisdiction. In one of the more prominent cases in the United States involving the name "Zippo" the Pennsylvania-based manufacturer of the cigarette lighter called Zippo brought an action for trademark infringement and dilution against a California news gathering service called "Zippo Dot Com" who registered Internet domain names such as "zippo.net," "zippo.com" and "zipponews.com." Zippo Dot Com had no offices in Pennsylvania but the company, using the Internet, had registered around 3,000 residents of Pennsylvania as subscribers of the news service. The news service had also contracted with a number of Internet service providers for access to the Zippo Dot Com site and two of those service providers were located in Pennsylvania. The federal court, located in Pennsylvania, determined that it could exercise personal jurisdiction over the California news service because of the extent of the service's activities in the state of Pennsylvania.[42] This is not an unsupportable conclusion and can easily be accepted by anyone familiar with jurisdictional concepts in U.S. law. However, the case has taken on a life of its own because the court, in concluding that it had jurisdiction, set out the so-called Zippo continuum

41. *Cyberspace Communications, Inc. v. Engler*, 55 F.Supp. 2d 737, 744–745 (E.D. Mich. 1999).
42. *Zippo Manufacturing Co. v. Zippo Dot Com, Inc.*, 952 F. Supp. 1119 (W.D. Pa. 1997).

for analyzing jurisdictional issues involving Internet transactions. The continuum is relatively easily stated as three separate but connected points of analysis. An Internet company may engage in "active" activities within a particular state when, for example, the out-of-state company repeatedly and deliberately sends packets of information to a particular party in the state. The far end of the continuum is merely "passive" activity, when an out-of-state company merely provides information on its website but takes no action whatsoever to interact with persons in another state. The center of the continuum is what the court refers to as "interactive"—that is, when a website invites and permits a visitor to the site to exchange information with the website.

A number of courts in the United States and elsewhere have used the Zippo tests to make jurisdictional rulings. In a prominent case involving a Web-based retailer in the state of Maine, L.L. Bean, and a California consumer, a California court determined that the L.L. Bean website activities were "the functional equivalent of a store" and that a bricks-and-mortar facility was not required so long as the website engaged in substantial commercial activity.[43] Other courts in the United States have adopted an "effects" test for jurisdiction, determining that jurisdiction will exist only when a website purposefully targets people or companies in a particular jurisdiction by: (1) engaging in electronic activity that is directed to a particular state; and (2) with the intent to do business in that state; and (3) with the result that someone in the destination state is actually harmed by the website's activity.[44]

§6.5.3 Internet Jurisdiction in the EU and Elsewhere

Under international law, jurisdiction over companies or individuals turns on the application of a number of different concepts.[45] Perhaps the strongest and most often utilized concept is *territoriality*. Put simply, a sovereign nation has jurisdiction over virtually anything that occurs within its borders. This answers most questions for anything that occurs within a particular country. So, for example, there is no question that Germany can exercise jurisdiction over a German Internet company that does business with another German business or with a German consumer.

The reach of a nation beyond its borders is less settled. The doctrine of *nationality* permits a country to reach outside its territory to control the behavior of its own citizens. The doctrine of *passive personality* is sometimes used to exert jurisdiction over a nonresident party when the "victim" of that party's misconduct resides in the forum nation. Within generally accepted principles of international law, many countries

43. *Gator.com v. L.L. Bean, Inc.*, 341 F.3d 1072 (9th Cir. 2003).

44. *In Young v. New Haven Advocate*, 315 F.3d 256 (4th Cir. 2002) a resident of Virginia asked a Virginia court to exercise jurisdiction over a Connecticut newspaper because the resident said he had been defamed, in Virginia, by an article published on the newspaper's website. The court concluded that there was no jurisdiction because there was no targeting of individuals in Virginia by the Connecticut-based website. For a good overall analysis of the issue of tortious conduct on the Internet *see*, Holger P. Hestermeyer, *Personal Jurisdiction for Internet Torts: Towards an International Solution?* 26 Nw. J. Int'l L. & Bus. 267 (2006).

45. An excellent discussion of virtually all of these basic concepts can be found in I. Brownlie, *Principles of Public International Law* (5th ed., 1998).

recognize an *effects* doctrine that permits the exercise of jurisdiction in a country where a nonresident's actions have palpable consequences. One of the most prominent recent cases invoking the effects doctrine occurred when the United States-based Internet company, Yahoo, permitted the sale of Nazi paraphernalia to residents of France—a country where such sales constitute a criminal offense.[46] The French courts directed Yahoo to restrict access to its site by French nationals, an order that a United States court refused to enforce. The case is a striking example of the differences in approaches to Internet jurisdiction and regulation between many European countries and the United States. The French court determined that the result of the Yahoo auction, the "damages" or harm, as it were, was suffered in France. The French court directed Yahoo to inform its web surfers that displays or sales of Nazi materials was prohibited and a criminal act in France, to demonstrate to the court that Yahoo had complied with this order, and to pay the French plaintiffs EUR 10,000.

By contrast, the federal court in the United States was far less sympathetic to the plaintiffs. The court cited the United State Constitution's protection of free speech as the principal ground on which enforcement of the French court order would be refused, but also concluded that it (the U.S. court) had personal jurisdiction in California because the French plaintiffs had sent the "cease and desist" orders to California, that the actions to be taken by Yahoo set out in the French directive would be implemented in California. Urged by the French plaintiffs to extend the doctrine of comity to the French decision, the U.S. court refused, again on First Amendment grounds.[47]

The EU has taken a much different approach to jurisdiction over Internet activities than has the United States. The starting point for EU jurisdiction is the 1968 Brussels Convention on Jurisdiction and the Enforcement of Judgments in Civil and Commercial Matters. Under the Convention, there are two places where jurisdiction may attach for disputes arising out of commercial dealings: (1) the "place of performance of the obligation in question;"[48] or (2) the place where the transaction is or should have been completed.[49] The Brussels Convention has different rules for business-to-consumer transactions, giving consumers a choice of forum of either the seller's place of domicile or the consumer's domicile.[50]

A subsequent action by the EU Council of Ministers resulted in the promulgation of Council Regulation No. 44/2001 on December 22, 2000. Often referred to as "Brussels I," this regulation takes a consumer-friendly approach to jurisdiction in B2C cases by adopting the "country of destination" concept for jurisdiction. The Council

46. For a comprehensive analysis of this controversy, *see*, the report of the U.S. portion of the litigation: *Yahoo!, Inc. v. La Ligue Contre le Racisme et L'Antisemitisme*, 160 F.Supp. 2d 1181 (N.D. Calif. 2001).
47. On appeal in the United States, the federal Court of Appeals eventually upheld the lower court's exercise of jurisdiction. *See*, *Yahoo! Inc. v. La Ligue le Racisme et L'Antisemitiseme*, 379 F.3d 1120 (9th Cir. 2004).
48. Brussels Convention, Art. 5(1).
49. *Id.*
50. *Id.*, Art. 13 (definition of a consumer contract) and Art. 14 (jurisdictional choices for consumer transactions). *See*, e.g., Michael Cordera, *E-Consumer Protection: A Comparative Analysis of EU and US Consumer Protection on the Internet*, 27 Rutgers Computer & Tech. L.J. 231 (2001).

reasoned that consumers need to build confidence in Internet transactions and would be highly disadvantaged if they had to go to the country of origin for recourse in Internet consumer transactions.[51]

But keep in mind that Brussels I is devoted entirely to B2C transactions. In addition, to use an American football expression, the EU Electronic Commerce Directive "punted" when it came to jurisdiction, providing that the Directive "does not establish additional rules on private international law nor does it deal with the jurisdiction of Courts."[52] Once again, persons involved in B2B transactions would be well advised to include either a forum selection clause or an arbitration clause that provides for a site for the arbitration hearing (which, in turn, triggers jurisdiction by the courts in the country in which the hearing is held).

§6.5.4 The Prospect of an Internet Jurisdiction Treaty

Over the past several years, a number of proposals for a treaty approach to Internet jurisdiction issues have been suggested. There are suggestions that the Internet, much like other global resources such as ocean resources and historical sites, represents a component of the "Common Heritage of Mankind."[53] Accordingly, an international treaty similar, perhaps to the Law of the Sea Treaty, could be drafted and implement. Such a treaty would determine that all the world's population should be given reasonable access to the Internet and that the wealthier countries have an obligation to help poorer countries develop this access. This treaty could also provide rules for Internet jurisdiction that supplant national rules and as principles of international law, have a true cross-border impact.

It is at least theoretically possible that certain international organizations that concern themselves with international trade and business, such as the WTO or the OECD, could fashion an acceptable jurisdictional treaty. The WTO could do this through the General Agreement on Tariffs and Trade. The OECD might develop an Internet jurisdiction treaty analogous to its recent Convention on Bribery and Corruption.

Yet another proposal has been to revive the now-stalled negotiations on The Hague Convention on Jurisdiction and Foreign Judgments in Civil and Commercial Matters.[54] The revived venture would include provisions on jurisdiction over Internet issues. But as we move into the second decade of the twenty-first Century, none of these proposals have been anything more than mere discussion vehicles. An international treaty on Internet jurisdiction may be far in our futures.

---

51. Additional and helpful analysis and commentary may be found in Aurelio Lopez-Tarruella, *Cross-Border Disputes in Online Consumer Contracts in the European Union: The Brussels Convention, the Brussels Regulation and the Role of Alternative Dispute Resolution Systems,* 2 J. Network Indus. 231 (2001).
52. Article 1(4).
53. *See*, e.g., Kevin A. Meehan, *The Continuing Conundrum of International Internet Jurisdiction,* 31 B.C. Int'l & Comp. L. Rev. 345 (2008).
54. *See*, e.g., Moriz Keller, *Lessons for The Hague: Internet Jurisdiction in Contract and Tort Cases in the European Community and the United States,* 23 Marshall J. Computer & Info. L. 1 (2004).

§6.6 TAXATION

International electronic commerce is a money-making activity if done right. This tells us that governments all over the world will be interested in getting their share of the business revenues through some form of taxation. Of course, there are some related dangers. Excessive taxation at the beginning of an innovative economic activity might kill it. On the other hand, it is not fair to have bricks-and-mortar businesses subject to taxation while Internet-based businesses bear no tax burden whatsoever. Many governments, including that of the United States have not yet resolved this problem, and taxation of international electronic commerce remains uncertain and somewhat ad hoc.[55]

There are a number of different tax vehicles that might be used in e-commerce. The first is the sales tax. This is a tax imposed on the dollar amount of sales made by Internet-based companies to other companies or to individuals. In the United States, most states impose a sales tax at the point of purchase stated as a percentage (normally a relatively small percentage, say, 2%–6%) on the amount of the sale. In a number of countries this type of tax is known as a value added tax or VAT. In virtually all situations, the seller is the entity that is expected to calculate and collect the tax from the purchaser.

Another form of taxation is a tax imposed on business income. Corporations in the United States are subject to income taxation in the same way that individuals pay tax on their personal incomes. In the United States, most states also claim to impose a "use" tax which is a sales tax that springs from purchases made from a remote location (e.g., a purchase made by telephone from a company in an adjoining state) on which the purchaser is expected to pay a tax equivalent to the same tax that would have been imposed on an in-state transaction of the same kind. Unfortunately, because these purchases are very difficult for a government to police, the use tax is rarely effective. This is not to say that these issues are unfamiliar to governments. Mail-order trade, either from state-to-state within the United States or between different countries have posed some of the same problems for government.

All of these questions make for important public policy issues. They are also closely tied with the issue of jurisdiction over Internet-based companies so the section in this chapter on jurisdiction should be read in tandem with this section. Because it is often difficult for a particular country to effectively tax international electronic commerce a number of proposals have surfaced to appoint some international body as a tax agent, assessing and collecting taxes from e-commerce businesses and remitting a proper share of that tax to individual countries.

---

55. For lengthy discussions of all of these issues *see*, Subhajit Basu, *Global Perspectives on E-Commerce Taxation Law* (2007); Richard A. Westin, *International Taxation of Electronic Commerce* (2d ed., 2007); and Richard L. Doernberg, Walter Hellerstein, Jinyan Li & Luc Hinnekens, *Electronic Commerce and Multijurisdictional Taxation* (2001). A very good report issued by the United States government is: Congressional Research Service, *State Taxation of Internet Transactions* (June 2011).

§6.6.1 Internet Taxation in the United States

Since the Internet's inception, governments in the United States have not imposed direct taxes on e-commerce businesses.[56] In 1998, the United States Congress decided to exempt e-commerce from all taxation for a period of three years through a statute called the Internet Tax Freedom Act. This legislative moratorium on Internet taxation was extended several times, most recently in 2007.[57] The current moratorium now extends until November 1, 2014. While a number of people have argued for a permanent moratorium, the initial intent was to establish a temporary period of breathing room for a new technology that could have been decimated by taxation. So the original tax freedom legislation also established a study commission to look at e-commerce, relate it to existing bricks-and-mortar businesses and recommend an appropriate tax system for the technology. The commission was duly appointed but for various reasons could never achieve a consensus on an appropriate tax policy.[58]

§6.6.2 Internet Taxation in Other Countries

Taxation of international business transactions is nothing new. Individual countries and regional associations have struggled with these issues for years. When cross-border transactions take place, both the country in which a business resides (sometimes referred to as the *residence* country) and the country in which the transaction is implemented (sometimes referred to as the *source* country) have an interest on imposing taxes. The Organization for Economic Cooperation and Development (OECD) has set out some basic principles that effectively address many of these issues. If and when the OECD proposals become the law of a particular nation, these pronouncements will become governing law on taxation.[59] Under the OECD's Model Convention on Taxes on Income and on Capital:

> The profits of an enterprise of a Contracting State shall be taxable only in that State unless the enterprise carries on business in the other Contracting State through a permanent establishment situated therein. If the enterprise carries on business as

56. This is not to say that individuals who earn money from the doing of Internet business are not taxed. The subject of taxation of individuals is beyond the scope of this chapter. Suffice it to say that persons who have income derived from e-commerce activities are subject to the income tax laws of the United States. For a book-length treatise on Internet taxation, *see*, e.g., Albert Tokin, *Internet Taxation* (2004). At least one writer predicts the end of the U.S. tax moratorium: David H. Gershel, *COMMENT: The Day of Reckoning: The Inevitable Application of State Sales Tax to Electronic Commerce*, 14 Tul. J. Tech. & Intell. Prop. 335 (2011).
57. Pub. L. 110-108.
58. A discussion of the work of this commission can be found in Alan E. Wiseman, *The Internet Economy: Access, Taxes, and Market Structure* 89–92 (2000). For some proposals for a post-moratorium tax policy *see*, Pamela Swidler, *The Beginning of the End to a Tax-Free Internet: Developing an E-Commerce Clause*, 28 Cardozo L. Rev. 541 (2006).
59. *See*, e.g., Arthur J. Cockfield, *The Rise of the OECD as Informal World Tax Organization Through National Responses to E-Commerce Tax Challenges*, 9 Yale J. L. & Tech. 59 (2006).

> aforesaid, the profits of the enterprise may be taxed in the other State but only so much of them as is attributable to that permanent establishment.[60]

Article 5 of the Model Convention defines *permanent establishment* with a great deal of precision and explanation. To begin with, a permanent establishment has a fixed place of business and may, when appropriate, include: (1) a place where management activities take place; (2) a branch or office maintained by the company; or (3) a factory or workshop.[61] But the Convention does not stop at these basic definitions. In a somewhat unusual technique of legislative drafting, the Convention goes on, with a great deal of elaboration, to specify what a permanent establishment is *not*. For example, it does not include a facility that is set up solely for the purpose of storage, display, or delivery of goods or merchandise belonging to the enterprise. It does not include a facility that exists solely for the purpose of purchasing goods or merchandise or of collecting information for the company. And, importantly for this discussion of Internet taxation, a permanent establishment does not include any facility that is created to carry on a business activity that is merely in the nature of "preparatory or auxiliary" activities.

More recently, the OECD has taken a very close look at a large number of Internet activities and issues and recently added an elaborate commentary to Article 5 of the Model Convention to address expressly the matter of taxation of Internet activities. As we work through these concepts, keep firmly in mind that the OECD is attempting to deal with a definition of permanent establishment. Having a permanent establishment in a particular country obviously permits that country to tax the entity, regardless of the type of tax that might be imposed. This commentary comprises one of the most thorough statements on the issues of taxation and builds its positions by focusing mainly on servers and ISPs.

The OECD begins by noting correctly that an Internet website is only an intangible amalgam of software and electronic data that "does not have a location that can constitute a place of business." A website typically carries on its functions and is hosted by a server provided by an Internet Service Provider (ISP). A server is a tangible piece of equipment that does have a physical location. But the company (OECD uses the term *enterprise*, rather than company) that owns the website does not have total control over the ISP even though it may have a contract for a certain amount of storage space on the ISP's server and even though the company may know which server contains the website's data, the ISP typically does not guarantee that the data will be on a particular server at a particular location. Accordingly, it cannot be said that a company operating a website acquires a place of business (a permanent establishment) merely because of the ISP's hosting agreement. The situation might be different if the

---

60. The Model Convention may be found in full text on the OECD website: www.oecd.org, under the subheading marked "treaties."
61. Because the Convention addresses, in some parts, taxation of natural resources, a permanent establishment may also include a mining, and oil or gas well, make where he or any other place of extraction of natural resources.

company wholly owns or leases the server and maintains that server at a particular location for a lengthy period of time (the concept of a location being *fixed*, in the parlance of the Model Convention).

There are other points of analysis to determine an e-commerce permanent establishment. The manner in which the company makes use of the computer equipment at a particular location is to be examined on a case-by-case basis to determine the extent of the control of the company over the equipment. But even if a company maintains certain personnel at a location does not necessarily confirm a permanent establishment if "no personnel are in fact required to carry on business activities at that location." Here, the OECD relates e-commerce activities to, for example, extraction equipment (automatic pumping equipment) in the natural resources industry.

The company's e-commerce activities in a particular place may be merely "preparatory or auxiliary." Here, the OECD recommends a case-by-case analysis but suggests that certain activities would clearly be preparatory or auxiliary. Some examples: (1) merely providing a communications link between suppliers and customers in the same sense that a company might have earlier provided a telephone link; (2) simply advertising goods or services; (3) "relaying information through a mirror server for security and efficiency purposes;" (4) acquiring market data; or (5) merely supplying information. By contrast, a company may use the computer equipment for "essential and significant" or "core" functions and thereby might be considered a permanent establishment.

There could easily be a completely different answer if the tax authorities were examining the activities of the ISP, rather than the activities of only one website hosted by the ISP. An ISP is likely to use its equipment for many core purposes as an "essential part of [its] commercial activity." A server that is used to conclude the contract with the customer and to process the customer's payment are significant. In these instances, the activities would not be merely preparatory or auxiliary.

There are, as noted above, different types of taxes that might be imposed on an Internet business. Many countries, including those of the EU, place a great deal of reliance on the form of taxation knows as or VAT. While there can be country-by-country differences in VAT, within the EU, VAT is applied to: (a) the supply of goods or services within a particular country; (b) the acquisition of goods or services from other Member States; or (c) the importation of goods and services from outside the EU. An income tax might be levied against a corporation or individual based on the amount of money the company or individual makes from the Internet business activities. It is possible to regard customs duties as a form of taxation. Each of these vehicles has been proposed at one time or another as a basis for a country's obtaining revenue from e-commerce activities.[62]

62. For an excellent discussion of many of these vehicles in the dual contexts of e-commerce and a developing nation's economy *see, Scott* Budnick, *Internet Taxation and Burkina Faso: A Case Study,* 10 I.L.S.A. J. Int'l & Comp. L. 549 (2004).

§6.7 INTELLECTUAL PROPERTY

There are a number of intellectual property issues that spring from e-commerce activities.[63] Many of these issues can be resolved by applying traditional concepts of intellectual property. So if someone creates a new software that enhances Internet business, that software is likely to be copyrighted in the same manner that all other software is protected. Similarly, if one were to invent, say, a new form of computer modem or network device that had application for e-commerce, that invention could be patented. Similarly, a trademark used in e-commerce is subject to the same constraints and protections that are afforded trademarks in other areas of international business. As we work through some of these issues, it may be helpful to review some of the basic concepts of intellectual property and to see how those concepts might relate to some specific Internet activities.

§6.7.1 Copyright

Ideas, standing alone, cannot be copyrighted. The basis for a claim of copyright must grow out of the expression of an idea in the context of an "original" work that is expressed in some tangible form. One early Internet copyright controversy involved the work of Yahoo! in developing an early web site directory by collecting and listing a substantial number of individual URLs. The URLs are, without question, "mere" facts that are not subject to copyright. But in this instance, Yahoo! made some decisions on the selection of the URLs and arranged them in a certain fashion that had never been done before. Most intellectual property experts would probably conclude that Yahoo! could seek copyright protection for its efforts although this Yahoo!'s index did give rise to some fierce litigation in the United States many years ago.

Most web pages are protected by copyright law because the websites arrange those pages (a combination of words, graphics and HTML tags) in a creative way that results in an "original" work, albeit an original work that exists in electronic, rather than paper form. But a great deal of difficulty in copyright on the web stems from the fact that when a recipient accesses a particular website, some or all of the content of that website then exists (is copied to) the recipient's computer from the website's server. People are permitted to work with copyrighted material to the extent that their work involves the *fair use* of that material. What is or is not fair use in an Internet context can lead to serious disagreements. Fair use can include using portions of the copyrighted material for any number of purposes such as criticism, comment, news reporting, teaching, scholarship, or research. The breadth and ambiguity of the fair use concept has resulted in a number of controversies involving the copying (or

63. For a fascinating article that proposes an entirely new form of property expressly designed for computer technology and the Internet, *see*, Joshua A.T. Fairfield, *Virtual Property*, 85 B.U. L. Rev. 1047 (2005). Professor Fairfield proposes that this new form of property supplant the old concepts of intellectual property because the older concepts simply do not fit the new technology.

downloading) of music from the Web. The digitization of the music and the subsequent downloading is not only a completely accurate reproduction of the music but also a copying of the entire musical work.

A number of years ago, the U.S. Internet company, Napster, established a website that permitted the downloading of literally millions of musical works and performances that other people had copied to their computers from CDs, tape recordings and broadcast media. As might be expected, Napster was sued by the copyright holders of this music. Napster defended the law suit by claiming that it (Napster) had only facilitated the copying and downloading—that it had not itself infringed the copyright. Napster invoked the analogy of a video recording machine. Just because a purchaser of a Sony VCR records a copyrighted broadcast and then, impermissibly, sells copies of that broadcast to others this does not mean that Sony is liable for copyright infringement. The dispute was resolved in U.S. courts with a finding that Napster's role was significant. It had engaged in what amounts to secondary copyright infringement and had garnered a substantial financial benefit from that activity.[64]

§6.7.2 Patents

A patent is an exclusive right granted by the government to an individual to make, use, and sell an invention. To be patentable, an invention must be genuine, novel, useful, and not obvious given the current state of technology. In the early years of the Internet and the development of computer software, a number of software developers sought patent protection for the software. It is permissible to do so, but in truth the computer industry and the life span of software proved inappropriate for protection under the patent laws. Patents are expensive to obtain and the patent application is very lengthy. Changes in the computer and Internet sector come so rapidly that a patent on software may be useless because the software has become obsolete or superseded long before the patent is issued. On the other end of the time spectrum, a patent lasts for only twenty years, making the huge investment of time and expense in obtaining the patent not terribly cost-beneficial.

There are, of course, some exceptions. Amazon.com obtained a patent for its "one-click" purchasing method that was initially approved by a U.S. federal district court but eventually overturned by the United States Court of Appeals for the Federal Circuit because the "one-click" method was obvious in view of the prior art of computer technology and Internet business.[65] There have been numerous other attempts to develop and obtain patents involving Internet technologies under the *business method* patent concept, that permits conferring patent protection on what

64. For a very good discussion of many Internet-related international copyright issues *see*, Christian A. Camarce, *Harmonization of International Copyright Protection in the Internet Age*, 19 Pac. McGeorge Global. Bus. & Dev. L.J. 435 (2007). *See also* Daniel Gervais & Susy Frankel, *The Internet and the Emerging Importance of New Forms of Intellectual Property* (2016); Neville Del Cordell. *Intellectual Property and the Internet: A Global Guide to Protecting Intellectual Property Online* (2014).
65. *Amazon.com, Inc. v. Barnesandnoble.com, Inc.*, 73 F. Supp. 2d 1228 (W.D. Wash. 1999), *reversed*, 239 F.3d 1343 (Fed. Cir. 2001).

amounts to a process for doing a certain type of business. These attempts have met with mixed results in the U.S. Patent and Trademark Office and have encountered a great deal of criticism among academics.[66]

§6.7.3 Trademarks and Trade Names

A trademark is a distinctive mark, device, model, or implement that a company places on the goods it manufacturers to identify and distinguish those goods from similar goods manufactured by a company's competitors. The parallel concept, a service mark, is used to identify and distinguish individual services. A business's trade name can also derive protection from trademark concepts if the trade name and the trademark are virtually the same. Trade names are sometimes afforded separate protection under the common law. A trademark is registered in the United States at the federal level with the United States Patent and Trademark Office. A trademark in the United States may also be registered with an individual state government. A trademark is normally protected from infringement so long as it is actively used by the trademark holder who has an obligation to prevent the trademark from slipping into common usage. The growth and worldwide scope of the Internet has led to a number of thorny issues regarding the extraterritorial or international scope of trademark protection.[67]

Part of the problem with trademarks is that the concept of "use" in a bricks-and-mortar context does not necessarily fit within similar concepts of use on the Internet. Trademark issues have arisen in the application for domain names and in the use of "metatags" and hyperlinks. The domain name controversy also factors into the now-prohibited practice of cybersquatting. Metatags are pieces of information that are embedded in a webpage but not necessarily visible to the viewers of that webpage. The best analogy is to the concept of "key words" in a data base search. Metatags sit hidden on a webpage but are identified and retrieved by various search engines. There have been a number of instances when a particular website used metatags that contained the registered trademarks of a competitor with the result that searchers were led to the infringers website rather than to the proper website of the competitor. These issues were taken up in at least two major cases decided by federal appellate courts in the United States. In *Promatek Industries, Ltd. v. Equitrac Corp.*,[68] the two companies were competitors in the sale of cost-recovery equipment. Working with its webdesigner, Equitrac set up a number of meta tags on the website, one of which was the term "Copitrak." Apparently, Equitrac was authorized to maintain and service Copitrak equipment but it was Promatek that held the trademark for Copitrak. Promatek sued Equitrac for trademark infringement and dilution after Equitrac refused to remove the metatag from its website. The appellate court authorized an injunction against Equitrac on two separate grounds. First, there was a strong likelihood of consumer confusion, in

66. *See*, e.g., John H. Allison & Emerson H. Tiller, *The Business Method Patent Myth*, 18 Berkeley Tech. L.J. 987 (2003); Eugene R. Quinn, Jr., *The Proliferation of Electronic Commerce Patents: Don't Blame the PTO*, 28 Rutgers Computer & Tech. L.J. 121 (2002).
67. *See*, e.g., Ryan Isenberg, *Trademarks and the Internet*, 32 U. West. L.A. L. Rev. 229 (2001).
68. 300 F.3d 808 (7th Cir. 2002).

this case what is called *initial interest confusion*, even if the consumer ultimately learns the true nature of the trademark and its owner before any transaction is consummated. Second, the metatag was, in essence, a misappropriation of Promatek's goodwill and thus a violation of the trademark laws.

In *Brookfield Communications, Inc. v. West Coast Entertainment, Corp.*,[69] the Brookfield company registered the words "MovieBuff" as both a trademark and a service mark. Brookfield developed various computer software and searchable databases containing entertainment industry information. Somewhat earlier, West Coast Entertainment had registered the website, "moviebuff.com" with the organization then in charge of URL registration, Network Solutions, Inc. Eventually, Brookfield went to court to enjoin West Coast from using the name "MovieBuff" either overtly or as a metatag on its website. During the course of the lawsuit, West Coast argued that it was the "senior user" for the Moviebuff term because it had registered the name with Network Solutions. In a lengthy decision in which the appellate court educated itself on many of the internal workings of the Internet, the court pointed out that "using another's trademark in one's metatags is much like posting a sign with another's trademark in front of one's own store."[70] While the court noted some shortcomings in some of the other arguments made by Brookfield, it ultimately approved an injunction prohibiting West Coast from inserting the MovieBuff metatag on its website.

The problem of hyperlinks is somewhat analogous to the issues surrounding meta tags. Hyperlinks are not hidden. They are deliberate insertions on a particular website that, when clicked, send the viewer to another website. While not yet a heavily litigated area of trademark law, a number of commentators have identified possible infringement issues arising out of the use of links as possible false or misleading advertising.[71]

Another issue is the matter of "framing"—a technique by which a website shows information pertaining to another website but in a setting where that information is "framed" by various other things such as advertisements, links and the like that do not directly pertain to the website whose information is being featured.

§6.7.4 Domain Names and Cybersquatting

On the Internet, the matter of a website's domain name may be crucial to its financial success. Domain names clearly deserve protection in the same fashion that a trademark or trade name in traditional commerce was given protection. The term *cybersquatting* involves someone registering a domain name that is identical with or very similar to the trade name of an existing bricks-and-mortar company. As the Internet began to grow, some enterprising individuals sought to register these names wholly apart from the existing trade name in the hope that the holder of the trade name would pay large sums of money to buy the domain name from the cybersquatter. Cybersquatting because

69. 174 F.3d 1036 (9th Cir. 1999).
70. *Id.*, at 1064.
71. *Id.*

such an abusive activity that many countries determined to stop the practice either as a matter of internal governance or by way of an international mechanism.

In the United States, the United States Congress enacted the Anti-Cybersquatting Consumer Protection Act.[72] The Act recognizes the abuses of cybersquatting and permits owners of registered trademarks to bring action in court against anyone who attempts, in bad faith, to register a domain name that infringes or dilutes a registered trademark.

In 1999, the World Intellectual Property Organization (WIPO) began registering domain names on an international basis. Functioning with the framework of the Internet Corporation for Assigned Names and Numbers (ICANN), WIPO has developed a process (described at length in §6.7.4, below, for dealing with international cyber-squatting.[73]

§6.8 PAYMENT SYSTEMS

As more and more international commercial transactions took place over the Internet, vendors and purchasers were compelled to develop new and reliable electronic payment devices. This section will examine a number of the more innovative payment vehicles, but we should not forget that many traditional mechanisms for payment are perfectly acceptable for electronic commerce transactions. For example, even though a transaction might be set up electronically, it is possible to have payment made by cash. But given the distances between parties in the typical international electronic contract, payment in cash is unrealistic and very rare. But a number of other traditional mechanisms are frequently used.

§6.8.1 Payment by Check

It is entirely possible to pay for an Internet transaction using a bank check. A check is a simple document, an actual piece of paper, that is made out by the account holder in favor of the payee for a specified monetary amount. The check is an order to the account holder's bank to pay the specified amount to the payee from the funds available in the account holder's account. There are a number of ways that the payee can receive the money. The simplest form of payment is what the bankers call *direct presentment*. In this instance the payee simply presents herself at the account holder's bank and hands the check to a teller and receives payment—typically in cash. But for international transactions direct presentment is rarely convenient. An alternative for the payee is simply to deposit the check in her bank. Her bank will then credit the amount to her account and initiate the process known as *indirect collection*. The bank that initially receives the check, the *depository bank*, communicates the information on the check to the account holder's bank. Frequently, the depository bank will actually

72. 15 U.S.C. §1125(d).
73. For a comprehensive discussion of these issues *see, Domain Name Law and Practice* (Torsten Bettiger ed., 2007).

send the hard-copy check itself to the *payor bank*. The payor bank is the bank in which the person who wrote the check has an account (i.e., is a customer in that bank). The payor bank takes the amount of the check out of the customer's account and remits it to the depositary bank. This process is referred to as *direct send*.

There are alternatives to direct send. In many countries, the bankers have created *clearing houses* to handle checks for a large number of banks in a particular area. In the United States the Federal Reserve Bank has established a process for clearing checks on a national basis. Central banks in a number of other countries have implemented a similar process.

But transporting huge numbers of hard-copy checks over long distances is time-consuming, expensive, and very inefficient. In many countries including the United States, the banking systems have begun to work with a process called *truncation* to eliminate the need to transport the checks themselves. Truncation is relatively simple. The depositary bank reviews and records the information on the paper check and then either retains the paper check or destroys it. The information on the check that is crucial for proper payment of the check by the payor bank is then transmitted electronically to the payor bank. The system certainly sounds both simple and efficient, but in the past, tradition has sometimes gotten in the way of truncation. Many account holders want to take possession of the hard-copy check. Still, depositors' resistance to truncation seems to be weakening in recent years.

There are a number of varieties of truncation but in the typical system, the depositary bank makes a copy of the check that is usually stored in electronic format. The information on the check that crucial for final payment is then forwarded electronically to the payor bank for final payment.

§6.8.2 Electronic Checks

Paper checks are efficient in that they can be used in virtually any situation (at least any situation in which the recipient is willing to take a check) for any type of transaction. Paper checks are inefficient in that they take up space and have to be moved physically from place to place for final payment and storage. There is also a worldwide system of well-known and well-established rules for checks that provides considerable protection for all parties involved.

Recently, the banking system has begun to experiment with electronic checks. One relatively simple system has been created by the Financial Services Technology Consortium and is called the *eCheck*. Using patented eCheck software a user calls up a template on a computer screen that is virtually identical to a paper check. Using the computer keyboard, the check is filled out and can be sent electronically (frequently by e-mail) to the payee who can, in turn, send the check to his account in a depositary bank.[74]

Another banking consortium in the United States, the Automated Clearing House (ACH) has pioneered a form of electronic funds transfer that is widely used for

74. Further information may be obtained at the FSTC website: www.fstc.org.

interbank money transfers and for the benefit of depositors who wish to authorize their banks to make regular and repetitive payments for such things as home mortgages and car payments. Utilizing the Federal Reserve System and authorized by the Electronic Funds Transfer Act,[75] the system transfers trillions of dollars each year with few problems. The electronic transfer funds eliminate the paper check and does away with the requirement that the check be physically conveyed from place to place. The Electronic Funds Transfer Act provides protection for the various parties involved. There are parallel systems in Japan and many European countries.

§6.8.3 Credit Cards and Debit Cards

In the United States, credit cards are ubiquitous. They are used by consumers and businesses for virtually any kind of payment, including, recently, the payment of government fees and tax assessments. Credit card transactions comprise trillions of dollars in value and are the single most-used form of payment for Internet transactions. The system is remarkably simple. The holder of a credit card presents it to a merchant for payment of the goods. This presentment can be physical, as when a credit card holder gives over his card to a waiter in a restaurant in payment for his meal. The presentment can be done electronically by sending all the relevant credit card information (name, billing address, credit card number, and the like) to an Internet vendor. Once the transaction has been completed, the payment is credited to the vendor and a charge is placed on the credit card holder's account. Typically, the credit card holder pays all or a portion of the amounts charged to her credit card on a monthly basis. In recent years, an analogous form of payment, the debit card, has emerged. The debit card is virtually indistinguishable in appearance from the credit card but rather than permitting the card holder to build up a balance in an account which is paid off gradually the debit card removes the amount charged immediately from the card holder's bank account.[76] While not quite as common as in the United States, credit cards and debit cards are being used more and more in other countries both for conventional transactions and for Internet purchases.

---

75. 15 U.S.C. §1693.
76. A great deal of additional information on payment systems can be found in Horst Treiblmaier, Andreas Pinterits & Arne Floh, *Success Factors of Internet Payment Systems*, 6 Int'l J. Electronic Bus. 369 (2008); Ronald J. Mann, *Making Sense of Payments Policy in the Information Age*, 93 Geo. L.J. 633 (2005) and Ronald J. Mann, *Regulating Internet Payment Intermediaries*, 82 Tex. L. Rev. 681 (2004). Additional insights may be gleaned from Stephen L. Harris & Stephanie Heller, *A Proposal for Consideration of a Unified Payments Law*, 83 Chi.-Kent L. Rev. 477 (2008) and Robert G. Ballen & Thomas A. Fox, *The Role of Private Sector Payment Rules and a Proposed Approach for Evaluating Future Changes to Payments Law*, 83 Chi.-Kent L. Rev. 937 (2008). Three excellent book-length treatments of many of these issues are Ronald J. Mann, *Charging Ahead: The Growth and Regulation of Payment Card Markets around the World* (2006); Weidong Kou, *Payment Technologies for E-Commerce* (2003) and Donal O'mahony, Michael A. Pierce & Hitesh Tewari, *Electronic Payment Systems for E-Commerce* (2001). *See also*, Jayaram Kondabagil, *Risk Management in Electronic Banking: Concepts and Best Practices* (2007).

In most countries with significant credit and debit card usage, the governments have worked out rules for payment, for "reversability" (i.e., whether or not a credit card holder can cancel or revise the credit card payment) and for unauthorized usage and dispute resolution.[77]

§6.8.4 Innovative Electronic Payment Systems

The growth of Internet transactions has led to the development of a number of innovative payment systems tailored specifically for certain types of activity. For example, the remarkable growth of eBay as a private sector, electronic auction house led to a problem with payment. In an eBay transaction, a buyer agrees to purchase a good from a seller but because the parties are typically a long distance away from each other, there is no easy way for the buyer to inspect the good prior to tendering the purchase price. Also, individuals (as opposed to companies) do not normally have the authority to accept credit card payments. Similarly, sellers are reluctant to accept checks from buyers when the seller might ship the good but later find that the buyer's check has been dishonored.

To cope with these problems, eBay fostered the development of an innovative payment system known as PayPal.[78] The system itself is both simple and ingenious. Buyer and seller agree to the purchase and sale of a good. Buyer sends a payment (typically, but not always, by credit card) to PayPal, rather than to the seller. PayPal informs the seller that the payment is authentic and seller ships the good to the buyer. Buyer has the opportunity to inspect the good upon receipt and then to authorize PayPal to make the payment to the seller. The transaction has taken place. Neither buyer nor seller need be apprised of confidential information (such as credit card numbers or bank account information) of the other party. The buyer is protected by being able to inspect the good in advance of final payment. The seller does not ship the good until and unless PayPal informs him that the buyer's payment is valid. PayPal is beginning to make inroads in various foreign markets as well as in the United States.

There are other payment systems with various techniques and attributes that might prove useful such as CyberCash, First Virtual, and CheckFree. Most of these systems are not widely used because of the utility and convenience of a party using either a recognized credit card system or PayPal. What is certain is that merchants who wish to engage in electronic transactions are now able to use a number of devices to ensure safe, secure, speedy payment. While initially a huge worry for merchants doing business on the Internet, these days payment is not a major problem.

§6.8.5 The Phenomenon Known as "Bitcoin"

One of the most striking developments in electronic commerce is the creation of the new currency and payment system known as *bitcoin*. The need for something such as

77. Mann, *Making Sense of Payments Policy, supra* n. 76, at 642.
78. Details on PayPal can be found at the PayPal website: www.paypal.com.

bitcoin was anticipated by the noted economist, Milton Freedman, who in 1999 commented: "One thing that's missing [from electronic commerce] but will soon be developed is a reliable e-cash, a method whereby on the Internet you can transfer funds from A to B without A knowing B or B knowing A—the way I can take a $20 bill and hand it over to you, and you may get that without knowing who I am."[79]

But bitcoin's origins are among its most puzzling and mysterious characteristics. The concept of bitcoin and the first use of the name appeared in a strange article authored by someone claiming to be "Satoshi Nakamoto."[80] Apparently Nakamoto has never surfaced as a human being, but the article itself has had enormous impact. As Nakamoto proposed: bitcoin is an anonymous currency not connected with any political jurisdiction that is digital and decentralized. Bitcoin derives its integrity and continued existence from peer-to-peer networking and cryptography. It is both a currency and a payment system.[81] It was developed as open source software that permits users to deal with each other directly without any intermediary.

Bitcoin transactions get their verification from network nodes and are recorded in a form of ledger known as a *blockchain*. If the bitcoin system has a heart, it is probably the blockchain—essentially a ledger that serves as a recordation device for all bitcoins. Explained in more detail:

> The essential power of blockchain technology is its ability to distribute information. Because it is distributed across all of the nodes, or individual computers, that make up the system, the term "blockchain technology" is often swapped with "distributed ledger technology." A blockchain's database isn't held in a single location, which could be infiltrated by a single party, but rather it is hosted by numerous (in the case of bitcoin, tens of thousands of) computers all at once.[82]

An early debate raised the question of whether bitcoin is a true currency. But as of the end of 2017, that question seems to be answered in the affirmative, not so much by doctrine, but by acceptance. As of 2017, bitcoin has a market cap of more than USD 40 billion, is used around the world by millions of people and is accepted by hundreds of thousands merchants. A short, partial list of merchants who now accept bitcoin

---

79. Freedman is quoted in an article by Mark Andreessen, *Why Bitcoin Matters*, New York Times (January 21, 2014).
80. Satoshi Nakamoto, *Bitcoin: A Peer-to-Peer Electronic Cash System*, Bitcoin Project, http://bitcoin.org (2011).
81. The discussion in this section is taken from an amalgam of the following: Pierluigi Cuccuru, *Beyond Bitcoin: An Early Overview on Smart Contracts*, 25 Int'l J. of L. & Info. Tech. 179 (2017); Trevor I. Kiviat, *Beyond Bitcoin: Issues in Regulating Blockchain Transactions*, 65 Duke L.J. 569 (2015); Tara Mandjee, *Bitcoin, Its Legal Classification and Its Regulatory Framework*, 15 J. Bus. & Sec. L. 157 (2015); Hongki Kim, *Bitcoin Regulation: Legal and Regulatory Issues of the Virtual Currency System*, 15 Korean J. of Sec. L. 377 (2014); Reuben Grinberg, Bitcoin: An Innovative Alternative Digital Currency, 4 Hastings Sci. & Tech. L.J. 159 (2011). There is a steadily growing list of book-length treatments of Bitcoin. *See*, e.g., Andreas M. Antonopoulos, *Mastering Bitcoin: Programming the Open Blockchain* (2017); Ikuya Takashima, *Bitcoin: The Ultimate Guide to the World of Bitcoin, Bitcoin Mining, Bitcoin Investing, Blockchain Technology, Cryptocurrency* (2d ed., 2017); Nathaniel Popper, *Digital Gold: Bitcoin and the Inside Story of the Misfits and Millionaires Trying to Reinvent Money* (2016); Paul Vigna & Michael J. Casey, *The Age of Cryptocurrency: How Bitcoin and Digital Money Are Challenging the Global Economic Order* (2015).
82. *See* www.bitcoinmagazine.com.

includes: Expedia, Microsoft, Virgin Galactic, Whole Foods, and LOT Polish Airlines. As this chapter goes to press, a single bitcoin is worth more than USD 9,000, but merchants and consumers can acquire portions of a bitcoin—the smallest denomination of which is a "satoshi" (in honor of the putative creator of bitcoin). But neophytes should not be misled by a bitcoin valuation. The price of a bitcoin can fluctuate wildly even over short periods of time. Worse, bitcoin has many detractors and is not universally accepted because it is not directly connected with or backed by any particular country and thus vulnerable to use by the criminal element.

To get started in bitcoin, an individual is permitted to run a bitcoin protocol on his or her personal computer or may create an account established by a business entity that deals in bitcoin. The individual creates a bitcoin "wallet" that stores the bitcoin value and is protected by various levels of passwords and encryption. There are various types of bitcoin wallets. A *desktop* wallet permits a user to create an address to send and receive bitcoins as from, for example, a desktop computer. A mobile wallet permits a user to engage in bitcoin transactions on the move, such as buying books at a bookstore and using one's mobile telephone to complete the transaction. There are also *paper* wallets that actually translate the bitcoin into a piece of paper with a bar code. *Hardware* wallets are essentially bitcoin data and access on usb sticks or external hard drives.

The individual then uses the values within the wallet to complete various financial transactions. In November 2017, the Chicago Board Options Exchange (CBOE) announced the creation of a bitcoin futures exchange.

There are a number of large questions associated with bitcoin that require some consideration. First, from what source(s) does bitcoin derive its value? The short answer is that bitcoin has value only insofar as individuals who deal with bitcoin trust the system to create and preserve value. Recall that traditional currencies are supported (as, e.g., in the United States) by the "full faith and credit" of the national government and by stores of tangible objects things such as gold and silver. Bitcoin is supported by neither of these, but rather exists in what commentators refer to as its own "ecosystem." One bitcoin website captures this as follows:

> Bitcoin derives its unique value from the fact that despite its lack of official backing or wide acceptance, it has generated an ecosystem in which many people are willing to trade and accept it. In fact, some perceive bitcoin to be more valuable, or more useful, than other currencies in that it is a better option for certain purposes, such as seamless digital transfers and use across borders. Also, because there is a cap set on the total number of bitcoins that will ever exist, the currency cannot be devalued through inflation as others can. Finally, a key benefit of bitcoin is known as "censorship resistance," its ability to be used for transactions that could normally be censored by other payment networks.[83]

It would appear that international business is engaged in a number of truly innovative and ground-shifting changes. Bitcoin is among the most important.

83. This quote is from www.bitcoinmagazine.com.

§6.9 PRIVACY

The issue of Internet privacy has been of major concern for many national governments because of the difficulty of policing Internet activities. Around the world, as more and more activities take place in electronic form, more and more personal information is subject to unauthorized disclosure. There has been an additional concern, directly related to the concept of privacy, as to protection of children from inappropriate information on the Internet. The United States responded with the Children's Online Privacy Protection Act[84] to address the issues of websites that target children in the collection and use of personal information. In Europe, privacy protection rules are set out in the EU Data Protection Directive that directs EU Member States to take concerted action to protect private information from unauthorized disclosure. The OECD has published its Guidelines on the Protection of Privacy and Transborder Flows of Personal Data. Additional information on each of these can be obtained from the respective websites. The OECD Guidelines are worthy of note because a number of countries around the world have implemented some or all of the guidelines through national legislation.[85]

§6.10 THE FUTURE OF INTERNATIONAL ELECTRONIC COMMERCE

We have already seen the future. International electronic commerce will continue to grow. It is now a relatively small percentage of total world commerce but will become a significantly larger percentage over the near term. As more and more countries develop more and more broad band capacity and as more and more merchants acquire sophisticated computer technology, more trade will be accomplished via the Internet. But the Internet, like the telegraph, telephone, and facsimile machine will remain, predominantly, a facilitator of international commerce rather than the commerce itself. We can buy a book or a pair of shoes using our computers to set up the transaction but the transaction itself will not be concluded until that book or those shoes are actually delivered to a human being at a bricks-and-mortar location.

---

84. 15 U.S.C. §§6501–6506.
85. There is now a growing body of literature on various Internet privacy issues. For some book-length publications, *see*, e.g., Lothar Determann, *Determann's Field Guide to Data Privacy Law: International Corporate Compliance* (3d ed., 2017); Michael Bazzell, *The Complete Privacy and Security Desk Reference* (2016); Paul Bernal, *Internet Privacy Rights: Rights to Protect Autonomy (Cambridge Intellectual Property and Information Law)* (2014); Martha C. Nussbaum & Saul Levmore, *The Offensive Internet: Speech, Privacy, and Reputation* (2012). For a number of journal articles, *see*, e.g., Nokhbeh Zaeem, *A Study of Web Privacy Policies Across Industries*, 13 J. Info. Privacy & Sec. 1 (2017); Jonathan D. Frieden, Charity M. Price & Leigh M. Murray, *Putting the Genie Back in the Bottle: Leveraging Private Enforcement to Improve Internet Privacy*, 37 Wm. Mitchell L. Rev. 1666 (2011); Rolf H. Weber, *Internet of Things—New Security and Privacy Challenges*, 26 Computer L. & Sec. Rev. 23 (2010); James P. Nehf, *The FTC's Proposed Framework for Privacy Protection Online: A Move Toward Substantive Controls or Just More Notice and Choice?* 37 Wm. Mitchell L. Rev. 1727 (2011).

The OECD recently issued a striking pronouncement on the Internet that is worthy of quotation:

> The Internet is transforming our economies and societies. It provides an open, decentralized platform for communication, collaboration, innovation, productivity improvement and economic growth. Along with information and communication technologies, it promotes closer integration of the global economy and interactions that increase general well-being. As the services it supports become pervasive, ubiquitous and more essential in everyday life, the economy is increasingly the Internet economy....Promoting the Internet economy is a way to improve our ability to boost economic performance and social well-being, and to strengthen societies' capacity to improve the quality of life for citizens worldwide.[86]

What is absolutely certain is that the final words on the issues raised in this chapter have not yet been written.

86. OECD, *Digital Economy Outlook 2017*; OECD, *Shaping Policies for the Future of the Internet Economy* (2008). Some additional predictions may be found in David Satola & Henry L. Judy, *Towards a Dynamic Approach to Enhancing International Cooperation and Collaboration in Cybersecurity Frameworks: Reflections on the Proceedings of the Workshop on Cybersecurity Legal Issues at the 2010 United Nations Internet Governance Forum*, 37 Wm. Mitchell L. Rev. 1745 (2011).

CHAPTER 7

International Intellectual Property and Licensing Agreements

Licensing is a process by which the owner of some form of intellectual property (*licensor*) such as a patent, copyright, or trademark—each of which is a form of intellectual property that requires formal registration with an appropriate government body—or unpatented trade secrets and commercial processes (sometimes referred to as *know-how*) gives permission to another person (*licensee*) to make use of the property. The license is normally stated for a term of years or, in certain instances, for the life span of the underlying intellectual property. In return, the licensee uses the intellectual property and pays the licensor royalties for that use. Because licensing agreements are of increasing importance in international trade, this book now devotes an entire chapter to intellectual property and licensing agreements.

§7.1 CHOOSING A LICENSING AGREEMENT

Business people have entered into licensing agreements for as long as governments have recognized and protected intellectual property. Indeed, the best way, conceptually, to view a licensing agreement is as an exception to the standard doctrine that owners of intellectual property have the *exclusive* right to use that intellectual property. This chapter concentrates on the nature and characteristics of licensing agreements although for readers who are not familiar with basic intellectual property concepts, §7.2 will provide ample basic information.

There are a large number of reasons for selecting the license agreement as a device for expanding business operations into foreign countries.[1] The country of origin

1. For some excellent and lengthy readings on all these topics *see*, e.g., Cynthia Cannady, *Technology Licensing and Development Agreements* (2015); Raymond T. Nimmer & Jeff Dodd, *Modern Licensing Law* (2005); Noel Byrne, *Licensing Technology* (2d ed., 1998); Michael Z. Brooke & John M. Skilbeck, *Licensing: The International Sale of Patents and Technical Knowhow* (1994); *Antitrust, Technology Transfer and Joint Ventures in International Trade* (B. Hawk ed.,

may have established trade or tax barriers that make the export of the finished product cost prohibitive. The holder of the license may not have the financial wherewithal to establish an elaborate manufacturing operation in the country of destination. The government of the country of destination may have established barriers of its own to foreign-owned manufacturing ventures. At the same time, that country may want access to new devices and new technology so long as the manufacture and marketing of those devices are carefully constrained by the government—and, for the most part, in the hands of that country's nationals.

Of course, there can be considerable risk in a licensing agreement. Patents and trade secrets are valuable because of their uniqueness and are normally given a great deal of protection within the country of origin by conferring exclusive control over the patent or secret on the person who developed it. Western nations and particularly the United States have stringent controls on patent infringement. Because these protections are not always available in the country to which the patent is to be exported, secrecy clauses are a prime ingredient of licensing contracts. Even so, loose and casual policing of intellectual property and trade secrets rights by government agencies and courts in the host country can lead to the leaking of the secret to persons who are not licensees.

There are other pitfalls, as well. The country where the license originated may not want the license exported if that country's government believes that the technology represented by the license is a matter of national security. The United States, for example, implementing the Export Administration Act, has in the past placed stringent limitations on export of certain types of technology as an outgrowth of the government's national security concerns, although many of these controls are being lifted.[2]

Even though a license is regarded as an exception to antitrust constraints, an attempt on the part of the licensor to control the activities of the licensee too tightly, or to insist on the licensee's purchasing (tie-ins) or refraining from purchasing (tie-outs) goods or processes other than the license can trigger antitrust problems. Countries with hard currency problems quite often object to large royalty payments flowing out of the country and thereby make it extremely difficult to obtain government approval for the importation of the license without the imposition of stringent controls on royalty amount and royalty collection.

These problems have led to a surprising number of regional and country-by-country initiatives to control licensing and technology transfer. The European Union

1983); L. Eckstrom, *Licensing in Foreign and Domestic Operations* (1983). There is a vast amount of information on licensing to be found in legal periodicals. Some representative articles are: Symposium, *The Licensing of Intellectual Property*, 78 U. Chi. L. Rev. 1 (2012); Symposium, *Issues in Licensing*, 42 Hous. L. Rev. 941 (2005); Symposium, *The Transfer of Technology in the International Marketplace*, 7 B.C. Int'l & Comp. L. Rev. 235 (1984); S. John Byington, *Planning and Drafting of International Licensing Agreements*, 6 N.C. J. Int'l L. & Com. Reg. 193 (1984). Dennis Unkovic, *Negotiating and Preparing an International Licensing Agreement*, 25 Prac. Law. 77 (1979). For a comparative view *see*, *The Know How Contract in Germany, Japan and the United States* (1984). For some alternative proposals *see*, Keith E. Maskus, *Using the International Trading System to Foster Technology Transfer for Economic Development*, 2005 Mich. St. L. Rev. 219 (2005). For a fresh look at some intriguing European issues, *see* Anastasios Kaburakis, Johan Lindholm & Ryan Rodenberg, *British Pubs, Decoder Cards and the Future of Intellectual Property Licensing after Murphy*, 18 Colum. J. Eur. L. 307 (2012).

2. 50 U.S.C. app.

(EU) has paid close attention to licensing within the EU, especially insofar as licensing affects EU antitrust policy.[3] A number of Latin American countries have begun to develop tight controls on licensing. The countries that are now part of the Andean Group (Bolivia, Columbia, Ecuador, and Peru) have developed joint, uniform licensing rules in an attempt to protect host countries and individuals in the host countries and to prevent internecine bidding wars between Andean members.[4] Some of the abuses associated with the licensing process that have had a particularly detrimental effect on developing countries prompted the United Nations Conference and Trade and Development (UNCTAD) to draw up a code of conduct (discussed in Chapter 5) attempting to regulate technology transfer between developed and developing countries by placing constraints on the negotiating process. Most of these issues will be discussed at greater length in the following sections.[5]

§7.2 THE FORMS OF INTELLECTUAL PROPERTY: PATENTS

As noted at the beginning of this chapter, licensing agreements are contracts that convey the right to use some form of intellectual property from the licensor (the owner of the property) to the licensee (the user). So at the heart of any licensing agreement will be a presumably valuable piece of intellectual property.

Intellectual property is recognized throughout the world by virtually all governments and all systems of law. Indeed, these forms of property have been regarded historically as so valuable that many countries, including the United States, provide for protection in the country's constitution.[6] As will be discussed below, there are now a significant number of international treaties and agreements that provide protection for intellectual property that crosses international boundaries.

Perhaps the best place to begin an analysis of intellectual property is to confirm the basic goals of intellectual property protection. Intellectual property is presumably valuable. To provide incentives for creative people to continue to create and innovate, governments have decided that the creators of such valuable things should be permitted to profit from that creativity and that the things that are created should be protected from the intrusions and unauthorized uses by others (typically referred to as *infringement*). Accordingly, the creator of a piece of intellectual property is given the

3. *See*, e.g., Francois Dessemontet, *Transfer of Technology Under UNCTAD and EEC Draft Codifications,* 12 J. Int'l L & Econ. 1 (1979); David J. Noonan, *Technology Licensing: Common Market Competition Implications,* 19 N.C. J. Int'l L & Com'l Reg. 439 (1984).
4. *See*, e.g., Celso Furtado, *Economic Development of Latin America* (1976); Frank M. Lacey, *Technology and Industrial Property Licensing in Latin America,* 6 Int'l Law. 388 (1972).
5. For a close look at a number of important issues relating to intellectual property in developing countries, *see* Sunil Kanwar, *Intellectual Property Protection and Technology Licensing: The Case of Developing Countries*, 55 J. L. & Econ. 539 (2012).
6. *See*, e.g., Art. I, §8, cl. 8 of the United States Constitution: "To promote the progress of science and useful arts by securing for limited times to authors and inventors the exclusive right to their respective writings and discoveries." This clause was part of the original United States Constitution, drafted in 1787 and ratified by the states in 1791—a good indication that intellectual property was respected and valued more than 200 years ago. Indeed, a number of intellectual property historians report that The City of Venice enacted a patent protection law in 1474.

exclusive use of that property. The right of exclusive use is, in some forms of intellectual property (such as patents and copyrights), limited by a term of years. In other instances, the exclusive use may not be limited in time (e.g., trademarks) so long as the creator continues to use the property.

Protections for intellectual property do not spring up automatically. In every instance, the creator must take certain steps to initiate and protect his or her creation. In some instances, such as protecting patents, the process is lengthy and cumbersome. In other instances, such as registering a copyright or trademark the process, within a particular country, is typically simpler. When a creator wishes international protection for the intellectual property certain additional steps must be taken. All of these considerations differ as to the form of the intellectual property.

As noted above, intellectual property is governed by both the domestic ("municipal") law of various countries and international law. In normal circumstances, the process of registration is begun in a particular country and then carried into international effect through one or another of the applicable treaties and agreements. In the context of this book, it is impossible to set out and analyze all the various municipal law doctrines for registration. Accordingly, we will discuss the manner in which the intellectual property is registered and protected in the United States (with some references to other countries) and then describe some of the applicable international controls.

§7.2.1 Patents in the United States

In the United States the form of intellectual property known as a *patent* may be granted by the U.S. Patent and Trademark Office to someone who has invented a device or object. The granting of the patent confers the right on the owner of the patent to exclude others for a limited time from producing or copying the device or object within the United States its territories and its possessions.

In the United States, patent law is always a matter of what is called federal law (i.e., the law made by the national government). The various states in the United States are not permitted to have independent patent legislation or regulation. The law of patents is established by the United States Congress through legislation. There is no common law of patents.

The United States Patent Act of 1953,[7] identifies and protects three different categories of invention: *utility* patents, *design* patents, and a relatively recently added protection for asexually reproduced plant matter. Of these categories, the utility patent is, by far, the most frequently utilized category. To obtain a patent, an inventor must file an application with the U.S. patent and trademark office that describes the patent fully enough to allow a patent examiner that is someone in the patent office was skilled in his art and science of this particular type of patent to produce the invention.

7. 35 U.S.C. §§1-376.

described in the scope of the invention defined currently U.S. patents run for a term of twenty years from the date they are granted for so-called utility patents and fourteen years for design patents.

Looking at some specific language of the Patent Act is instructive. Section 101 provides that any person who "invents or discovers any new and useful process, machine, manufacture, or composition of matter, or any new and useful improvement thereof, may obtain a patent." Accordingly, section 101 establishes the first element necessary for the grant of a patent: an invention, in order to be given patent protection must be useful, or it is more commonly expressed, a patent must have *utility*.

In very elaborate language, most of which is reproduced here, section 102 provides:

> An applicant may obtain a patent unless prior to his or her invention, the same device "(a) was known or used by others in this country, or patented or described in a printed publication in this or a foreign country, before the invention thereof by the applicant for the patent, or (b) the invention was patented or described in a printed publication in this or a foreign country or in public use or on sale in this country, more than one year prior to the date of the application for patent in the United States, or (c) he has abandoned the invention, or (d) the invention was first patented or caused to be patented, or was the subject of an inventor certificate, by the applicant or his legal representative or assigns in a foreign country prior to the date of the application for patent in this country...(e) the invention was described in a patent granted on an application for patent by another filed in the United States before the invention thereof by the applicant for patent...or (f) he did not himself invent the subject matter sought to be patented...."

Section 102 sets out the requirement that a patent be a new development. In patent parlance, this is normally stated as the requirement of *novelty*. In the words of the statute, "A person shall not be entitled to a patent unless—(1) the claimed invention was patented, described in a printed publication, or in public use, on sale, or otherwise available to the public before the effective filing date of the claimed invention, or (2) the claimed invention was described in a patent issued under section 151 ..."

Traditionally, the United States has followed a "first to invent" policy with regard to patent protection. However, in 2011, with a March, 2013 effective date, the United States changed its patent policy to "first to file" in order to conform to standard international practice.[8] As will be discussed below, in virtually all other countries, priority is given to the person who first *files* the application for patent. In similarly turgid language, section 103(a) provides: "A patent may not be obtained through the invention if not identically disclosed or described as set forth in section 102 of this title, if the differences between the subject matter sought to be patented in the prior art are such that the subject matter as a whole would have been obvious at the time the invention was made to a person having ordinary skill in the area to which the said matter pertains." This section establishes the requirement of *nonobviousness*. Accordingly, the patent act requires that an invention be useful, novel and nonobvious.

---

8. 35 U.S.C. §102.

The concept of utility is, generally, the easiest of the three requirements to satisfy. The applicant must show that the invention can *do* something—can perform some task—that it is not merely a fanciful notion. The U.S. Patent Office, in attempting to illustrate utility, excludes such things as perpetual motion machines. It also excludes mere ideas or suggestions for devices. In other words, the device must not only do something, it must have been reduced to some tangible state in order to demonstrate that it actually works. This requirement of functionality has two prongs: the device must actually work (sometimes referred to as *general* utility) and in working must actually perform the task for which it is identified (sometimes referred to as *specific* utility). Finally, the Patent Act builds into the concept of utility some moral values. The device must have a proper purpose. This is the concept of *moral* or *beneficial* utility—that is, the invention cannot be something that, for example, involves "poison" or "debauchery" or "facilitates private assassination."[9] In other countries usefulness or utility appears not to be an express requirement for granting a patent, but the idea of utility is certainly incorporated into the basic concept of patentability. For example, the European Patent Office (EPO) (the patent arm of the EU) requires that an invention demonstrate what the EPO calls "industrial applicability."

The concept of novelty or what might be called "newness" requires that the invention cannot have previously been known to others. This is essentially a negative construct. The Patent Act, as quoted above, contains elaborate language setting out this requirement. The concept of novelty ties in closely with the third concept of "nonobviousness" (discussed immediately below). As part of this requirement, there are a number of obligations placed on an inventor who seeks a patent. For example, under the U.S. Patent Act, no patent will issue if the inventor has previously permitted others to use the invention. A patent cannot issue if the invention or discovery was known or used by others in the United States and those persons have not abandoned the invention. A patent will not be granted if the invention or discovery was described in a publication in the United States or a foreign country or if the invention or discovery was set out in an earlier patent application filed by another person. It is sometimes said that novelty refers to novelty of conception rather than novelty of use.

The third concept—that of nonobviousness—is perhaps the most difficult of these concepts to define and to work with. It has been described by the United States Supreme Court in the seminal case of *Graham v. John Deere Company*,[10] as an issue "of inquiry, not quality."[11] Nonobviousness is determined in the United States by way of a three-part test involving an examination of the invention under consideration as

9. The quoted language is taken from a federal case in the United States that is nearly 200 years old: *Lowell v. Lewis*, 15 F.Cas. 1018 (C.C.D. Mass. 1817).
10. *Graham v. John Deere Co.*, 383 U.S. 1 (1966). The Graham opinion is a fine compendium of many basic patent concepts as well as an excellent excursus into the philosophical and constitutional underpinnings of U.S. patent law. The Court, in its excursus, delves deeply into the writings of Thomas Jefferson, the third president of the United States and a masterful inventor in his own right. Jefferson was sympathetic to the idea of patents but generally favored the notion that the law should not protect or promote exclusive rights or exclusive use of things that are beneficial to society. For a fresh look at some similar concepts, *see* Jonathan S. Masur, *Patent Liability Rules as Search Rules*, 78 U. Chi. L. Rev. 187 (2011).
11. *Id.*

compared with everything that has gone before. This examination, generally referred to as a prior art inquiry, is conducted by patent examiners in the U.S. Patent and Trademark Office who search data bases, existing literature, prior patent applications and the like to determine both novelty and nonobviousness.

The Supreme Court's opinion in *Graham* set out a three-part test for nonobviousness: first, there must be an inquiry into the "scope and content of the prior art." Second, the Patent Office must analyze the differences between the prior art and the claims made in the current patent application. Third, the PTO must consider "the level of ordinary skill in the pertinent art." Making this analysis, it is permissible for the PTO to examine what the Supreme Court calls the secondary considerations of "commercial success, long felt but unsolved needs, [and] failure of others." In other words, the new invention must be sufficiently different from what came before and this difference has to involve the application of "skill and ingenuity" rather than being, for example, mere changes in color or size of the object or substitution of materials where the underlying object stays essentially the same.

Much the same analysis is performed by the PTO for design patents and patents for certain plant life. The PTO and the Patent Act define a design patent as "a new, original, and ornamental design for an article of manufacture." For design patents, the component of "ornamentality" substitutes for the basic concept of utility imposed on utility patents.[12] Patents for plant life must involve the invention or discovery of "asexually reproduced" plants that are new and distinct varieties of plant.[13]

In the United States, a patent is granted only after the submission of a written application using rules and forms promulgated by the PTO.[14] Normally, only the inventor himself or herself may apply for a patent. Applications for patents by persons other than the inventor are normally invalid. There are some limited exceptions that permit applications to be filed by the estate of a deceased inventor or the guardian of a mentally incompetent inventor.

The application itself must include information on three separate matters. The application must contain a description of the invention and formal claims of utility, novelty, and nonobviousness. An accurate drawing of the invention must be included when appropriate. The applicant must pay the necessary fees which include searching and examination fees. Applications are accepted by the PTO on a first come first serve basis and when received are assigned to individual technical divisions within the PTO

12. For a discussion of design patents, *see*, §171 of the Patent Act, 35 U.S.C. §171 and *Black & Decker Inc., v. Pittway Corp.*, 636 F. Supp. 1193 (N.D. Ill. 1986).
13. The full statutory language is: "Whoever invents or discovers and asexually reproduces any distinct and new variety of plant, including cultivated sports, mutants, hybrids, and newly found seedlings, other than an tuberpropagated plant, or a plant found in an uncultivated state, may obtain a patent therefor...." For a discussion of plant patents, *see*, e.g., *Yoder Brothers, Inc. v. California-Florida Plant Corp.*, 537 F.2d 1347 (5th Cir.1976) (a battle of two different varieties of chrysanthemums).
14. All of these requirements and relevant forms may be found on the PTO's website: www.uspto.gov. Other helpful hints may be found in Anne Kelley, *Practicing in the Patent Marketplace*, 78 U. Chi. L. Rev. 115 (2011).

where the application is closely scrutinized by skilled patent examiners. After this lengthy and detailed review, a patent is either granted or denied.[15]

§7.2.2 Patents under the European Patent Convention

While a detailed examination of a large number of individual patent practices is not feasible, it is instructive to consider some differences between the United States patent practices and those of the EU. The European patent system, which the EU is careful to note, does not spring from a formal EU "legal instrument."[16] Nonetheless, only EU countries may participate in the European Patent Convention (EPC) which entered into force in 1977. The EPC created the EPO which administers the system. In essence, an inventor may file a single patent application that will trigger the grant of a European patent, but that patent is still subject to the national laws of the various participating countries.[17] This somewhat complicated jurisdictional scheme permits someone seeking patent protection in European countries to follow one of three different paths.[18] The inventor may file an application in the individual countries of the EU. The inventor may file an application under the Patent Cooperation Treaty (PCT) which is discussed below. The inventor may file an application under the EPC. Each of these alternatives has advantages and disadvantages that must be closely scrutinized.

The basic provision is Article 52 of the EPC. A European patent may be issued "for any inventions, in all fields of technology, provided that they are new, involve an inventive step and are susceptible of industrial application." Excluded from this very broad definition are: discoveries, mathematical methods, scientific theories, aesthetic creations and schemes for performing mental acts, playing games, presentations of information and programs for computers.

Thus, one can discern many of the same concepts that underlie U.S. patent policy, albeit using slightly different language. The concept of utility is included in the phrase "susceptible of industrial application." Article 57 further defines this phrase as an invention that "can be made or used in any kind of industry, including agriculture." The notion of moral utility is captured by Article 53 (exceptions to patentability), which provides that no patent may be granted for things that contravene the "'ordre public' or morality." The European practice recognizes "industrial design" as a proper basis for a normal patent while the United States would give such an invention only a design patent which carries only a fourteen-year life span.

15. This is a very cryptic and abbreviated description of what is, in fact, an elaborate, lengthy, and complicated process. More elaboration on the process of application and consideration may be found on the PTO's website.
16. Much of this information may be found on the European Union and related websites. *See*, e.g., www.europa.eu/invest-in-research/policy/ipr_en.htm. For an excellent and lengthy work on the EPC, *see*, Stephan Luginbuehl, *European Patent Law: Toward a Uniform Interpretation* (2011); Guy Tritton, *Intellectual Property in Europe* (1996). *See also*, Paul England, *Novelty of Patents in Europe and the UPC*, 12 J. of Intell. Prop. L. & Prac. 739 (2017); Vincenzo Di Cataldo, *From the European Patent to a Community Patent*, 8 Colum. J. Eur. L. 19 (2002).
17. *EU website, supra* n. 16.
18. Tritton, *supra* n. 16, at §§2.217–2.218.

The concept of novelty is covered by the EPC's term "new." Article 54 elaborates on novelty by pointing out that something will be considered new "if it does not form part of the state of the art." State of the art is "everything made available to the public by means or a written or oral description, by use, or in any other way, before the date of filing of the European patent application." There are some important difference, however, with regard to ascertaining novelty. The United States uses the concept of national geography. If something is novel with regard to the United States, a U.S. patent may issue even if the invention is known outside the United States. The EPC, by contrast, provides that the term new is to be determined on a worldwide basis.

Nonobviousness is largely put into effect by the notion of "an inventive step." Article 56 fleshes out this term by providing: "An invention shall be considered as involving an inventive step if, having regard to the state of the art, it is not obvious to a person skilled in the art. If the state of the art also includes documents within the meaning of Article 54, paragraph 3 [prior filed EPC patent applications] these documents shall not be considered in deciding whether there has been an inventive step."

Under the EPC, priority is determined by date of filing of the patent application rather than the U.S. practice of granting priority based on the date of invention. Once an EPC patent has been granted, the EPC provides in Article 64 that the patent is to be treated as if it had been granted as a national patent in each designated country.

§7.2.3 The International Regime for Patent Protection

There are number of different juridical vehicles for the international protection of patents. In many cases, individual multilateral or bilateral investment treaties contain express language on patents and other forms of intellectual property. This section will discuss three international agreements: the Paris Patent Convention, the Patent Cooperation Treaty, and the agreement developed under the auspices of the World Trade Organization (WTO) and the General Agreement on Tariffs and Trade (GATT) known as the Trade-Related Aspects of Intellectual Property Rights (TRIPS).

[1] The Paris Convention

This treaty is the first comprehensive agreement for the international protection of intellectual property rights. It extends to both patents and trademarks. It was first signed in Paris in 1883. The United States joined soon after (in contrast to the lengthy delay in the United States' acceding to the Berne Copyright convention which is discussed below). There are now around 172 contracting states.[19] The convention has been amended a number of times. The 1967 amendments were accompanied by the formation of the World Intellectual Property Organization (WIPO). The Convention was most recently amended in 1979.

19. The full text and a narrative description of the Convention may be found on the website of the World Intellectual Property Organization (WIPO): www.wipo.org. The website also tracks the list of current contracting states.

While highly detailed, the Paris convention has three major components that are relevant here. The first is the doctrine of national treatment, the second is the right of priority (different from the right of priority in the United States), the third is a compendium of what are known as the "common rules." National treatment is not a complicated doctrine. Under the convention, contracting states are obliged to give the same patent protections to persons in contracting states that the country affords to its own residents. The common rules are highly detailed and may be best understood by examining the express language of the convention. Among other things, the common rules provide that an inventor has the right to be named as the inventor in the patent. Patents granted in individual contracting states are independent of each other. In other words, a contracting state is not obliged to issue a patent to an inventor simply because another contracting state has done so.

Probably the main contribution of the Paris convention is the provision on priority. This right, frequently referred to as the "Convention priority right" is established by Article 4 of the Convention and is essentially a right based on the "first to file" principle. Article 4(A)(1) provides: "Any person who has duly filed an application for a patent...in one of the countries of the [Paris Convention] Union...shall enjoy, for the purpose of filing in the other countries, a right of priority during the periods hereafter fixed." Section C of Article 4 establishes a period of twelve months for patents and six months for design patents and trademarks. This right of priority does not absolve the inventor of filing in various countries but does give the inventor a date of filing, applicable in all contracting states, of the date of the first filing so long as the inventor files properly in those other countries within the twelve or six-month period.

[2] The Patent Cooperation Treaty

The PCT is closely coupled with the Paris Convention.[20] It provides an extremely complicated administrative mechanism for filing in many countries that also gives the inventor the Paris priority protection. Under the PCT an inventor may file an international application that establishes a priority date or may file in a contracting state to establish priority. The international application may then be filed within twelve months of the initial filing. The inventor may then request, under the PCT, procedures through an international search authority (ISA). Patent offices in a number of countries, including the United States, the EU, and Japan, are commissioned as ISAs. Within various time periods after that, the ISAs commence an international search report and various other investigations. Eventually, the data accumulated by the ISAs helps an inventor decide where to file subsequent applications even though the PCT does not, in and of itself, constitute or authorize the issuance of a patent.

20. The full text of the PCT may also be found on the WIPO website.

[3] *The Agreement on Trade-Related Aspects of Intellectual Property Rights (TRIPS)*

Since 1994 and the international trade negotiations known as the Uruguay Round, the WTO, which incorporates the earlier GATT, has provided important processes and protections for intellectual property. Now involving more than 140 signatory nations, the TRIPS agreement now exerts enormous influence in the area of international intellectual property.[21]

The TRIPS agreement is not an independent mechanism for enforcing rules with regard to intellectual property. Rather, TRIPS, working through a Council of members, provides an international supervisory mechanism that examines the national laws of the contracting nations to assure that each country's domestic intellectual property laws are consistent with TRIPS requirements. TRIPS affects both patents and copyrights. While far too detailed to set out here, some examples are instructive. For example, TRIPS requires that countries grant patents in all "fields of technology." Patents must be given at least a twenty-year duration. TRIPS requires national treatment: no benefits may be given to a country's own citizens that are not extended to citizens of other TRIPS nations. The TRIPS mechanisms contain special provisions for developing countries that may find full compliance difficult.

§7.3 COPYRIGHT

The intellectual property right known as copyright is assuming greater and greater importance as people publish more and more data and as such entities as the Internet continue to grow in international importance. Simply put, a copyright is a bundle of rights granted to persons who engage in creative expression in various forms such as books, articles, paintings, sculpture, and the like that permit those persons to enjoy the exclusive use of their creations. Copyright has now been extended to such things as the creation of computer software, conferring even more importance on copyright law. These days, copyrights provide the basis for large numbers of licensing agreements.

§7.3.1 Copyright in the United States

The original United States copyright act, enacted in 1790, establishes protections for authors and other creators. By its own terms, it is "an act for the encouragement of learning, by securing the copies of maps, charts, and books, to the authors and proprietors of such copies, during times therein mentioned." The first copyright act gave the author "sole right and liberty of printing, reprinting, publishing and vending"

21. The TRIPS agreement and a large number of accompanying documents and information may be found on the website of the World Trade Organization: www.wto.org. One of the best book-length works on the WTO is Mitsuo Matsushita, Thomas J. Schoenbaum & Petros Mavroidis, *The World Trade Organization: Law, Practice and Policy* (2d ed., 2006). *See also*, Donald Harris, *TRIPS After Fifteen Years: Success or Failure as Measured by Compulsory Licensing*, 18 J. Intell. Prop. L. 367 (2011).

for a period of fourteen years, with the possibility of another subsequent period of fourteen years.[22] As with patents, copyright law in the United States springs directly from the U.S. Constitution. The Constitution's Copyright and Patent Clause authorizes the United States Congress "to promote the Progress of Science and useful Arts by securing for limited Times to Authors and Inventors the exclusive Right to their respective Writings and Discoveries."[23]

The current U.S. copyright act was enacted in 1976 and is far broader in scope and more detailed in terms than the original act. In present terms, copyright protection extends to "all original works fixed in a tangible medium of expression."[24] The act expressly mentions but is not limited to the following: (1) literary works; (2) musical works, including words that accompany the music; (3) dramatic works including any possible music; (4) pantomime and choreography; (5) pictorial, graphic and sculptural works; (6) motion pictures and other audiovisual works; (7) sound recordings; and (8) architectural works.[25]

Under the statute there are three basic requirements for obtaining a copyright. The work must be "original." The original work must be "fixed." The original fixed work must be "in a tangible medium of expression." So, much like patents, a mere idea or mere facts cannot be copyrighted. Nor can a work that exists solely in the author's head be subject to copyright. However, an idea that is eventually written up as a book chapter is copyrightable as is a compilation of facts into a new "whole."

The hurdle of originality is relatively easy to overcome. The United States Supreme Court has described originality as the *sine qua non* of copyright law. It is essentially a statement of minimum requirements. In the Supreme Court's view, "original, as the term is used in copyright means only that the work was independently created by the author (as opposed to copied from other works), and that it possesses at least some minimal degree of creativity."[26] The Court did not impose a stringent test. It made clear, for example, that "originality" is not the same as "novelty." Different from the requirement for a patent, an original work for copyright purposes can resemble things that have gone before. Nor does "originality" mean brilliant. As the Court notes, "the requisite level of creativity is extremely low; even a slight amount will suffice. The vast majority of works make the grade quite easily, as they possess some creative spark, no matter how crude, humble, or obvious it might be."[27]

The Copyright Act itself defines "fixation" in broad terms. Readers should also be aware that fixation is closely tied (perhaps inextricably) to the third requirement of "tangible medium of expression." A work will satisfy the fixation requirement so long

22. Act of May 31, 1790, 1 Stat. 124. Archaic capitalization in the original act has been removed from the quoted section.
23. U.S. Const. Art. I, §8, cl. 8.
24. 17 U.S.C. §§101 et seq.
25. 17 U.S.C. §102. In the United States, the classic treatise is David Nimmer, *Nimmer on Copyright* (2007). *See also*, Craig Joyce, Marshall Leaffer, Peter Jaszi, & Tyler Ochoa, *Copyright Law* (10th ed., 2016).
26. *Feist Publications, Inc. v. Rural Telephone Service Co.*, 499 U.S. 340 (1991) (the *Feist* case involved a compilation of telephone numbers in special telephone directories).
27. *Id.* The Court did make clear, however, that originality is a requirement set out in the Constitution itself and not one that may be dispense with by Congress.

as the work is captured in some form "sufficiently permanent or stable to permit it to be perceived, reproduced, or otherwise communicated for a period of more than transitory duration." This suggests that even a poem written on a paper napkin accommodates the fixation requirement. Courts in the United States have determined, for example, that sights and sounds that are generated by a computer program are fixated.[28] A tangible means of expression simply suggests that the creative work must be something that can be seen, heard, or touched—that is, books, photographs, musical scores.

Unlike a large number of other countries, in the United States a copyright springs into being at the time the work is created. The "right" of copyright is automatic. There are, however, some advantages even in the United States, to registering the creative work with the United States Copyright Office, which is part of the Library of Congress.[29] Any holder of a copyright who wishes to bring an infringement lawsuit must first register the work, although the registration may take place immediately before the launching of the litigation.[30]

The "author" of the work is the owner for copyright purposes. If the work is co-authored the co-authors are deemed to own the work jointly and anything written for an employer places the copyright in the employer's hands, rather than the employee-writer.[31] Even though this chapter concentrates on the use of intellectual property in the context of a licensing agreement, it is especially important to remember that a copyright can be conveyed to another by way of sale or other type of transfer as is the case with other forms of property. The duration of the copyright was extended a few years ago by Congress to bring U.S. copyright practice in line with the international conventions. Currently, a copyright extends for the life of the author plus seventy years.[32] For jointly created works, the terms is seventy years after the life of the last surviving author. Works for hire provide a copyright duration of either ninety-five years from the date of publication or 120 years from the date of creation, whichever period expires first.

Copyright gives the creator of the work a large number of rights and prerogatives with regard to the work, but those rights are not absolute. For example, in certain limited circumstances, libraries may reproduce portions of the work. The Copyright Act also provides for so-called *fair use* of the work by others. Fair use is a somewhat ambiguous concept that is determined by reviewing courts under four separate criteria: (1) the purpose and character of the use, including whether such use is of a commercial nature or is for nonprofit educational purposes; (2) the nature of the copyrighted work;

28. *See*, e.g., Stern Electronics, *Inc. v. Harold Kaufman*, 669 F.2d 852 (2d Cir. 1982).
29. The Copyright Office website, www.copyright.gov, is a compendium of useful information on U.S. copyright. Also helpful is David Tollen, *The Tech Contracts Handbook: Software Licenses and Technology Services Agreements for Lawyers and Businesspeople* (2011).
30. 17 U.S.C. §411.
31. 17 U.S.C. §201.
32. 17 U.S.C. §302.

(3) the amount and substantiality of the portion used in relation to the copyrighted work as a whole; and (4) the effect of the use upon the potential market for or value of the copyrighted work.[33]

§7.3.2 Copyright in International Law and Practice

As with other forms of intellectual property, copyright grows out of the municipal law of the various countries.[34] Virtually all of the major trading nations have had laws affecting copyright for quite a number of years. For example, the British Parliament enacted the Statute of Anne in 1710 to accomplish two things: (1) to dislodge the monopoly created by the Stationers groups; and (2) to give authors rights in their created works for fourteen years with a subsequent fourteen-year renewal period. The Statute of Anne had a major impact on the United States' first copyright act. France promulgated a copyright law shortly after the French Revolution reflecting certain assumptions regarding intellectual property in continental Europe which assumptions were different from those of Britain. The notion of "moral rights," for example, (discussed below) grows out of the French tradition. In a number of countries, the traditional approach appears to favor written works such as books to the detriment of other types of creativity such as sound recordings.

There have been serious initiatives to try to harmonize copyright law around the world. The three discussed in this section are the Berne Convention and the TRIPS agreement. This section makes mention of some other intellectual property treaties of lesser importance such as the Rome Convention and the WIPO Copyright Treaty and the WIPO Performances and Phonograms Treaty[35] and the Rome Convention. Each of these three instruments may have a significant effect on copyrights that move into international waters.

[1] The Berne Convention

The Berne Convention was first signed in 1886 with the purpose of establishing minimum standards for international copyright in the face of significant differences among the domestic law of various countries.[36] The Convention was largely an undertaking of the larger European nations, particularly France and England (which

33. 17 U.S.C. §107. A fresh view of many of these issues is provided in Guy A. Rub, *Contracting Around Copyright: The Uneasy Case for Unbundling of Rights of Creative Works*, 78 U. Chi. L. Rev. 257 (2011).
34. For general reading on this topic, *see*, e.g., Paul Goldstein & P. Bernt Hugenholtz, *International Copyright: Principles, Law, and Practice* (2012); Silke Von Lewinski, *International Copyright Law and Policy* (Oxford, 2008); J. L. Sterling, *World Copyright Law* (2003); Roberto G. Barbosa, *Revisiting International Copyright Law,* 8 Barry L. Rev. 43 (2007). For some interesting commentary on a number of copyright and intellectual property issues *see*, *Intellectual Property: The Many Faces of the Public Domain* (Charlotte Waelde & Hector Macqueen eds., 2007). For a special perspective on copyright in China, *see* Ge Chen, *Copyright and International Negotiations: An Engine of Free Expression in China?* (2017).
35. The full text of these two treaties may be found at the WIPO website: www.wipo.int.
36. The full text of the Berne Convention may be found at the WIPO website.

countries were also then the largest producers of literary and artistic works).[37] The United States, for various reasons, did not get around to signing the Berne Convention until nearly the end of the twentieth century. Since 1886, the Convention has been put through five revisions and two additional acts. Most of these revisions have had the effect of broadening the rights of authors.[38]

The Convention may best be understood through a brief review of some of its major provisions. Article 2 contains an exceptionally broad definition of "literary and artistic works:" they "include every production in the literary, scientific and artistic domain, whatever may be the mode or form of its expression."[39] Article 2(5), while not using the word "originality" provides protection for a product involving "intellectual creation" at least with regard to compilations of materials.[40] The Convention (Article 2(2)) leaves to the contracting states the issue of whether to insist on fixation as a requirement for copyright.

Article 3 extends Berne Convention protections to authors who are nationals of contracting states, or those who have their work first published in a signatory nation, or authors who have their "habitual residence" in a contracting state even if that particular author is not a national of that country.

The heart of the Convention is Article 5(1) which provides for national treatment, is similar to the national treatment requirement in the Paris Patent Convention. The Convention is explicit on this point: "Authors shall enjoy, in respect of works for which they are protected under this Convention, in countries of the [Berne Convention] Union other than the country of origin, the rights which their respective laws do now or may hereafter grant to their nationals, as well as the rights specially granted by this Convention."

Article 5(2) expressly rejects any formalities necessary to procure a copyright. This was one of the reasons that the United States, between 1886 and 1989, refused to sign the treaty. Since then, the United States, as discussed above, has abandoned any formalities for the formation of a copyright, although as noted, registration with the U.S. Copyright Office is still necessary before an infringement suit may be brought in the United States. Article 10 permits a certain amount of "fair use" of copyrighted material. Someone other than the author is permitted to "make quotations" or utilize "by way of illustration in publications, broadcasts or sound or visual recordings for

37. *See*, e.g., Peter Burger, *The Berne Convention: Its History and Its Key Role in the Future*, 3 J. L. & Tech. 1 (1988).
38. *Id.*
39. Article 2 goes on to expressly set out: "books, pamphlets and other writings, lectures, addresses, sermons and other works of the same nature; dramatic or dramatico-musical works; choreographic works and entertainments in dumb show; musical compositions with or without words; cinematographic works to which are assimilated works expressed by a process analogous to cinematography; works of drawing, painting, architecture, sculpture, engraving and lithography; photographic works to which are assimilated works expressed by a process analogous to photography; works of applied art; illustrations, maps, plans, sketches and three-dimensional works relative to geography, topography, architecture or science."
40. *See*, e.g., Daniel J. Gervais, *Feist Goes Global: A Comparative Analysis of the Notion of Originality in Copyright Law*, 49 J. Copy. Soc'y USA 949 (2002).

teaching, provided such utilization is compatible with fair practice." But even fair use requires that the work be identified and the author named.

The Berne Convention contains important provisions on moral rights—another reason why the United States was so slow in signing the treaty. In Article 6*bis*, the Convention recognizes a number of economic rights possessed by the author and also extends to the author the right "to object to any distortion, mutilation or other modification of, or other derogatory action in relation to said work, which would be prejudicial to his honor or reputation."

[2] The TRIPS Agreement

As discussed in the sections on patents, the Agreement on TRIPS was promulgated in 1994 after negotiations during the Uruguay Round of the GATT. It now constitutes one of the most important international controls on intellectual property including copyright. TRIPS sets out minimum standards that all members of the WTO must adhere to in dispensing and sorting out intellectual property rights. The TRIPS was launched to provide more or less uniform protections for intellectual property throughout the WTO.

While TRIPS affects most forms of intellectual property including patents and trademarks, its provision on copyright are essentially borrowed from the Berne Convention. Indeed, TRIPS expressly incorporates most of the articles of the Convention. So a reader will find a minimum copyright term of fifty years after the death of the author, automatic grants of copyrights with a prohibition on any formalities for obtaining copyright. Computer programs are expressly defined as "literary works" and subject to the same protections as other forms of expression. National treatment for copyrights is central to TRIPS as it is to the Berne Convention. The agreement also contains some provisions specially crafted for developing countries. Among many other things, TRIPS finally resolved the question of how to protect computer software. Since 1994, under Article 10 of the TRIPS agreement, "Computer programs, whether in source code or object code, shall be protected as literary works under the Berne Convention." Earlier, in the United States, a controversy emerged as to whether computer software was subject to patent or copyright protection. The U.S. courts determined that computer software was best protected under the copyright laws.[41]

Different from the Berne Convention, TRIPS covers sound recordings and broadcasts. The intellectual property rights encompassed in recordings and broadcasts are labeled *neighboring* or *related* rights. Neighboring rights are subject to slightly different rules and given somewhat less protection than conventional creative works. Because Berne was silent on recordings and broadcasts, many European nations negotiated the Rome Convention to protect, among other things, the rights of performers. The Rome Convention requires national treatment and minimum standards for recordings and broadcast media.[42]

---

41. *See*, e.g., *Apple Computer Inc. v. Franklin Computer Corp.*, 714 F.2d 1240 (3d Cir. 1983).
42. The full text of the Rome Convention along with a summary of the treaty and a list of contracting states may be found at the WIPO website.

§7.4 TRADEMARKS

§7.4.1 Trademark in the United States

All business wish to distinguish themselves from their competitors. A business may make claim to an innovative product, a manufacturing process, a chemical formula that is superior and that is attractive to purchasers of the product. In business, one of the ways that companies make these distinctions is by giving the product, process or formula a unique name. The name can be simply a word, or, as in the case of probably the most famous trademark, the logo for the Coca Cola Company, the words may be unique and also set up in a special typeface. Thus, a company may create a special name for their product that promotes product identification and that distinguishes their product from that of their competitors.[43] Moreover, certain unscrupulous companies may wish to use the same name or mark as their more successful competitors deliberately to generate confusion on the part of purchasers. To deal with this phenomenon, an effective name or mark ought to be assigned to the exclusive use of the company that created the name or mark.

In the United States, trademarks were initially dealt with through the common law, growing out of the so-called business torts and legal concepts of unfair competition. The state legislatures and the United States Congress entered the fray relatively late in U.S. history when it became apparent that the common law was not fully equipped to deal with intense business competition and the regulatory aspects of trademark usage. In trademark parlance, there are two basic concepts: *trademark* and *service mark*. A trademark is defined as "a word, phrase, symbol or design, or a combination of words, phrases, symbols or designs, that identifies and distinguishes the source of the goods of one party from those of others."[44] A service mark is defined as: "the same as a trademark, except that it identifies and distinguishes the source of a service rather than a product."[45] For the rest of this discussion, mainly for simplicity, we will refer to a trademark or mark to illustrate the various concepts.

There are plenty of trademarks that are in use for conventional business purposes—for example, the name of a building supply store such as Home Depot—without being directly attached to another form of intellectual property. However, most of the truly valuable trademarks are connected to (perhaps inextricably) a piece of intellectual property such as a patent or trade secret. Trademarks have occasionally been used to protect something that might not be subject to the protection of other forms of intellectual property. As noted in the section on copyright, a book's title is not copyrightable. Nonetheless, a distinguished U.S. author, Theodore White, now deceased, set out to write a series of books the first of which was titled, "Making

43. For general discussion of this topic *see*, e.g., Graeme B. Dinwoodie & Mark D. Janis, *Trademark Law and Theory: A Handbook of Contemporary Research* (3d ed., 2010); Siegrun D. Kane, *Kane on Trademark Law: A Practitioner's Guide* (5th ed., 2007).
44. This is the definition suggested by the United States Patent and Trademark Office (PTO). The definition and many other things pertaining to federal trademarks may be found at the PTO's website: www.uspto.gov.
45. *Id.*

of the President, 1960." Author White wanted to write a series of books on a twenty-year span of U.S. presidential elections running from the 1960 election through the 1980 election. While he could not copyright the title, he was able to register "Making of the President ____________" as a trademark. So trademark law was able to give him protection where copyright law did not work.

The rapid increase in commerce conducted over the Internet has given rise to a number of intellectual property issues. Perhaps the major issue is the issue of trademark registration and infringement that grow out of the nature of the Internet—a truly worldwide basis for doing business. Some of these issues are dealt with in Chapter 7 Electronic Commerce. While it remains unsettled whether purely domestic statutes such as the U.S. Lanham Act have true extraterritorial application, the emergence of such international procedures as established, for example, by the Madrid Protocol have lessened the problems that were initially perceived.[46]

In the United States, different from the matter of a patent or copyright, the various states may register trade and service marks. The federal government, working through the United States Patent and Trademark Office (PTO) may also register trademarks. To avoid a lot of confusion, the remainder of this section will concentrate on federal trademarks.

Under the federal trademark law, a trademark or service mark is broadly defined and is typically identified as such when it is "used by a person." However, a mark may be given certain protection even before actual use so long as the creator of the trademark has a "bona fide intention" to use the mark in commerce and proceeds to register it.[47] Registration is not required for the trademark to confer legal rights in the mark so long as the mark is actually used, but registration does give the registrant some additional and important rights and prerogatives. For example, registration with the PTO does the following:

(1) it gives constructive notice to the public of the registrant's claim of ownership in the mark;
(2) it establishes a nationwide legal presumption of the user/registrant's ownership of the mark and the right of the owner of the mark to use it on a nationwide basis;
(3) it establishes the owner's right to bring a legal action involving the mark in a federal court;
(4) it permits the owner to use registration as the basis for seeking registration of the mark in foreign countries; and
(5) it may be filed with the U.S. customs services to prevent importation of foreign goods that infringe on the U.S. mark.[48]

46. *See*, e.g., Joshua Clowers, *On International Trademark and the Internet: The Lanham Act's Long Arms*, 13 Rich. J. L. & Tech. 4 (2006); Dan L. Burk, *Trademark Doctrines for Global Electronic Commerce*, 49 S.C.L. Rev. 695 (1998).
47. 15 U.S.C. §1127.
48. This list is taken from the PTO's website and from the language of the trademark statute (the Lanham Act), 15 U.S.C. §§1057, 1124.

These days the registration process is relatively simple and most applications for registration are handled electronically. Using the PTO's website, an owner fills out a detailed application and pays the requisite fees. The application system is referred to as the Trademark Electronic Application System (TEAS) and is available twenty-four hours a day online. Once the application is completed and the basic fees paid, the PTO conducts a search for conflicting, preexisting marks and if the Office deems the application satisfactory, the registration of the mark is accepted. Under United States law, any person claiming ownership of a mark may use the symbol™ even if the mark is not registered. For service marks, the letter "s" is substituted for the letter "t." However, only owners of marks who have completed the PTO registration process are permitted to use the symbol®.[49] The proposed trademark is published for comment. Persons objecting to the mark are permitted to enter their objections before a final decision is made. The law provides a five-year window after initial registration in which an objecting party can enter objections. After five years, the mark is normally not contestable.

There are a number of rules governing the selection of a trademark. The first set of decisions lie in the hands of the business seeking a trademark. In all likelihood, no business in the United States would want to develop a trademark and trade name that was off-putting to potential purchasers. We do not see products with brand names such as "White Elephant Vacuum Cleaner" or "Average Refrigerator." So in the first instance, the business will seek a catchy, memorable name or phrase that is distinctive to that company or product and that fits within all the cultural assumptions that go into doing business in the United States. As with the Coca Cola brand, the trademark might be a combination of an interesting name plus a particular design for the name's typeface.

As noted above, trademarks are the *exclusive* property of the owner. So the new mark cannot be one that has already been designed and used by another company, although there is maneuvering room even within this basic construct. For example, if two different companies are both named Antelope Spring where one company operates an amusement park and the other bottles designer water, the PTO may well be willing to register separately a trademark for "Antelope Spring Pure Water" and another mark for "Antelope Spring Amusement Park."[50]

There are other considerations. Under the U.S. trademark statutes and trademark case law, there are essentially four categorizations for proposed trademarks: (1) generic; (2) descriptive; (3) suggestive; and (4) arbitrary or fanciful.[51] The Lanham Act provides expressly that a trademark that starts out as a generic expression may not be

49. *See*, PTO website, www.pto.gov.
50. The Lanham Act contains some prohibitions as well. The following may not registered as trademarks: "immoral, deceptive or scandalous matter," trademarks that "disparage or falsely suggest a connection with persons, living or dead, institutions, beliefs, or national symbols," "the flag or coat of arms or other insignia of the United States, a state or municipality, or a foreign nation," or a trademark that "consists of or comprises a name, portrait, or signature identifying a particular living individual except by his written consent. ..." 15 U.S.C. §1052.
51. This discussion is taken largely from a seminal judicial opinion authored by the late federal judge Henry Friendly (one of the most distinguished jurists in U.S. legal history), *Abercrombie & Fitch Co. v. Hunting World Inc.*, 537 F.2d 4 (2d Cir. 1976).

registered and a trademark that eventually becomes generic must have its registration cancelled.[52] Each of these terms is dealt with on a case-by-case basis. One federal court has pointed out that the term "Ivory" is generic with regard to products made from the tusks of elephants but not generic as the name of a soap.[53] A term may be descriptive in one setting and appropriately registered in another. A "gold ring" is merely descriptive. The term "gold tequila" can probably be registered. Suggestive or fanciful words are usually within the parameters of a permissible trademark. The courts have considered that a "suggestive" mark is one that "requires imagination, thought and perception to reach a conclusion as to the nature of the goods."[54] A fanciful word is one that is made up entirely for that product—for example, "Normentonic scissors." For this illustration, the author simply made up a word. Inventing a completely new word is not all that easy. He was forced to make several tries at a completely new word. A Google search for his first try, "Normento," came up with a proper noun involved with the Spanish martyr, San Feliciano. A separate search for his second variation, "Normentony," uncovered an ancient family name in Britain. Blessedly, Google was unable to come up with anything under "Normentonic."

Under U.S. law, there is no express life span for a trademark. Although trademark owners are obliged to renew their registration with the PTO at regular (usually ten year) intervals, the mark itself survives with appropriate protection so long as the owner continues to use the mark consistently and so long as the owner aggressively polices the mark so that competitors and the general public are not permitted to dilute the mark such that the mark becomes a "generic" expression. One early example of a trademark becoming generic came around the 1920s when the word "aspirin" that had been used as a trademark by the Bayer Aspirin Company was deemed to have become generic by a federal court in the United States.[55] The Coca Cola trademark has remained firmly in the hands of the Coca Cola Company for roughly 100 years. The Coca Cola Company is among the most aggressive in the world at policing infringement and fighting the slide toward generic treatment.[56]

§7.4.2 Trademark in the EU

In Europe, a person seeking a trade or service mark may simply register in the individual countries of the EU. But there are two the routes for obtaining protection for a trademark. One, discussed in the next section, is registration through the procedures of the international agreement known as the Madrid protocol. The third, discussed here, is the use of the EU's Community Trade Mark (CTM) process. CTM registration is enforceable in all of the EU countries and extends even to new countries as they join

52. 15 U.S.C. §1057.
53. Abercrombie & Fitch, *supra* n. 51, n. 34.
54. *Id.*
55. *Bayer Co. v. United Drug Co.*, 272 Fed. 505 (S.D.N.Y. 1921). Quite a few years later, the trade name "Bayer" was subject to litigation in United States courts, *Sterling Drug, Inc. v. Bayer AG, Bayer USA Inc. & Miles, Inc.*, 14 F.3d 733 (2d Cir. 1994).
56. *See*, among many other things, the company's website: www.thecoca-colacompany.com.

the Union.[57] A uniform, single process for trademark registration was proposed in 1964 for what was then called the European Economic Community. Those proposals bore final fruit in 1994 with the establishment of the CTM.

The CTM process is administered by the EU's Office for Harmonization in the Internal Market, section of Trade Marks & Designs (OHIM), located in Alicante, Spain. OHIM was created by the same set of EU regulations that set up the CTM itself. Application for CTM registration may be filed directly in the Alicante office or given to a national registration body in one of the EU countries which will forward the application to Alicante. The list of possible applicants is quite broad and includes nationals and companies within the EU, nationals of countries that are signatories of the Paris Convention for the Protection of Industrial Property or the TRIPS agreement and nationals from countries that do not adhere to the Paris Convention or TRIPS but who are domiciled or have a business in either the EU or a country that is a participant in the Paris Convention.

The OHIM examines the application to determine whether the proposed trademark is appropriate for registration. This examination, referred to as grounds for *absolute* refusal, concerns only the trademark itself involves issues of generic language and descriptive language but does not include a search for preexisting trademarks that conflict with the proposal. Once the initial examination is complete, the OHIM publishes the proposed mark in the CTM Journal and any adversely affected parties may file an opposition to the registration. It is the opposing parties, if any, who can base their objections on conflicts with existing marks, an objection referred to as *relative* refusal.

Under Article 4 of EU regulation (EC) 49/94 a trademark may be registered if it can be depicted in graphic form, which includes the following specific things: words (either invented or of a known language), collections of words, graphic elements and complex signs, names, signatures, numbers, logos, designs, figures, pictographs, portraits of people, colors or color combinations and sounds.

Registration and the payment of fees confers protection for ten years with the prerogative of renewing the registration so long as the owner can show continuous use of the mark. Registration also permits the owner to bring infringement actions in EU countries.

57. A great deal of information may be found on the European Union's website: www.europa.int. *See also*, Martin Senftleben & Annette Kur, *European Trade Mark Law* (2017); Tobias Cohen Jehoram, Constant Van Nispen & Tony Huydecoper, *European Trademark Law: Community Trademark Law and Harmonized National Trademark Law* (2010); Lars Meyer, *Much Ado About Nothing?: Characteristics, Benefits, and Practical Implications of the European Community Trademark*, 5 Chi-Kent J. Intell. Prop. 158 (2006); Justin A. Horwitz, Note: *Conflicting Marks: Embracing the Consequences of the European Community and Its Unitary Trademark Regime*, 18 Ariz. J. Int'l & Comp. L. 245 (2001); Soyoung Yook, *Trademark Dilution in the European Union*, 11 Int'l Leg. Persp. 223 (2001). For a comparative approach that looks at EU and German trademark law, *see*, Bernd Stegmaier, *Trademarks in the International Arena: German and European Trademark Law*, 12 J. Contemp. Leg. Issues 433 (2001).

§7.4.3 International Protection for Trademarks

There are a number of international mechanisms that provide protection for trademarks.[58] The Paris Convention for the Protection of Industrial Property covers both patents and trademarks. As more elaborately discussed in §7.2.3., above, it establishes requirements of national treatment and provides for rights of priority based on the person who is first to file, rather first to use the mark. However, there is no centralized filing or registration system. The holder of a mark must first file in a country that participates in the Paris Convention. As with other forms of intellectual property, the TRIPS Agreement, administered by the WTO and discussed elaborately above, deals with trademarks and mandates national treatment.

But for international registration, probably the most utilized agreement is the treaty known as the Madrid Protocol, which currently has more than fifty signatory countries, and which the United States joined in 2003. The Madrid Protocol, effective in 1996, continues many of the policies and procedures first set out in the Madrid Agreement of 1891 and is administered by the WIPO.[59] The United States initially had little confidence in the Protocol but now appears to be fully supportive. Briefly stated, the Protocol establishes a procedure by which the owner of a trademark will obtain international protection for the mark (in the countries that adhere to the Protocol) by filing a single application in a single place, referred to in the Protocol as the *office of origin* and which can be the owner's national registration office. The registrant pays a single fee and gets a single registration number with a single renewal date. As part of the registration and fee-paying process, the registrant must specify those countries in which he or she wishes registration. The owner pays an administrative fee and then an additional fee for each country. The initial registration period is for ten years with the prerogative of subsequent ten-year renewals so long as the owner has continuously used the mark.

§7.5 TRADE SECRETS

Trade secrets are frequently combined with other forms of intellectual property such as a patent, but trade secrets (also sometimes referred to as *know-how*)[60] can stand alone as a form of intellectual property. However, one vital characteristic of trade secrets is that they are protected by private contractual agreements, rather than national or international protocols of the sort that protect patents, copyrights and trademarks. Although recently some of the international protocols have been amended or

58. *See* generally, Gustavo Bravo, *Trademarks in the International Arena: From the Paris Convention to TRIPS, A Brief History*, 12 J. Contemp. Leg. Issues 445 (2001). For a good discussion of the 2014 Chinese trademark law *see* Paul Kossof, *Chinese Trademark Law: The New Chinese Trademark Law of 2014* (2014).
59. The full text of the Madrid Protocol may be found on the WIPO website: www.wipo.int. The USPTO website has a great deal of information on the Protocol. www.uspto.gov.
60. Some of the intellectual property literature appears to try to distinguish between trade secrets and "know-how." There seems to be no good reason to do so, and this section does not even try. For the purposes of this chapter, we will treat trade secrets and know-how as the same concept.

interpreted to provide some trade secret protection but these agreements essentially require each country to develop a system for the protection of trade secrets rather than providing the protections themselves.

Another important characteristic of trade secrets is that they do not have an expiration date. A trade secret will have legal viability so long as the secret is preserved. It is for this reason that a number of companies opt to use the trade secret device rather than a patent or copyright. Perhaps the best known, and one of the longest lasting, trade secrets is the chemical formula used to produce Coca Cola. The Coca Cola Company chose not to patent the formula because after a number of years the patent would have expired and the formula would have become part of the public domain. As a trade secret, the formula for Coke has been preserved for more than 100 years.

Apart from the lack of an expiration date for trade secrets, there are some other advantages. Trade secret doctrine can be used to protect information from disclosure that might not qualify for protection under the strict definitions of patent or copyright. Trade secrets can include such things as customer lists and business strategies that would never qualify for the more formal types of intellectual property. Since secrecy is the hallmark of a trade secret, there are no registration requirements that attach so there are normally no "formalities" attached to the creation and protection of a trade secret. Finally, even when a trade secret is compromised, it may be possible in the context of either litigation or arbitration to keep the trade secret confidential even while disputing with the person who compromised the information. In litigation, this is typically accomplished through the device of judicial seals and protective orders. An arbitration can be structured so that the entire proceeding takes place outside the public's view. Accordingly, trade secrets are in constant use and comprise a valuable form of intellectual property so long as they are protected from disclosure.

§7.5.1 Trade Secrets Generally

In the United States, trade secrets grew out of the common law and to the extent that they are protected by statute were protected by state statutes rather than federal legislation. Until recently flawed trade secrets in the United States was governed solely by state law under a statute, enacted in more than 40 states, known as the Uniform Trade Secrets Act. A number of years ago, the United States Congress enacted a federal trade secrets measure that now has a great deal of utility within the U.S.

Because the concept of trade secret is both broad and somewhat amorphous, it is best to start with a definition. Under U.S. federal law—the Economic Espionage Act of 1996—a trade secret is defined as:

> all forms and types of financial, business, scientific, technical, economic, or engineering information, including patterns, plans, compilations, procedures, programs, or codes...if the owner thereof has taken reasonable measures to keep such information secret, and the information derives independent economic value,

actual or potential, from not being generally known to, and not being readily ascertainable through the proper means by, the public....[61]

Parsing the statutory language, we can see that the definition is exceptionally broad in scope. When one looks at the "all forms and types of...information" it is difficult to see what might be excluded as a type of information. But the reader cannot stop there. A particular piece of information is a trade secret only if two other elements are confirmed: (1) the owner of the trade secret must take affirmative steps to make sure that the trade secret remains a secret; and (2) the information must be such that the public does not know it and cannot easily obtain it. The definition of trade secret under state law (the Uniform Trade Secrets Act) is nearly identical with the federal definition.[62]

The Economic Espionage Act goes on to make the theft of trade secrets a crime. The criminal activity, as might be expected, is broadly defined to include a person who steals a secret or obtains it by fraud or deception or who copies or duplicates such information or who receives or possesses trade secrets for the economic benefit of one other than the proper owner of the secret. Such acts can trigger large fines or imprisonment up to ten years or both.[63] By contrast, the Uniform Trade Secrets Act, a civil law, permits courts to issue injunctions to prevent theft and to award money damages for unauthorized disclosure.[64] Reflecting the noncriminal underpinnings of a great deal of U.S. trade secret law, the Restatement Torts (a compendium of rules of law gleaned mainly from judicial opinions) provides:

One who discloses or uses another's trade secret, without a privilege to do so, is liable to the other if:

(a) he discovered the trade secret by improper means; or
(b) his disclosure or use constitutes a breach of confidence reposed in him by the other in disclosing the secret to him; or

61. 18 U.S.C. §1839. Some suggestions for additional, in-depth reading on trade secrets law and practice: David W. Quinto & Stuart H. Singer, *Trade Secrets: Law and Practice* (2012); C.D. Freedman, *Global Secrets: Global Trade Secret Protection* (2008); Henry H. Perritt, Jr., *Trade Secrets: A Practitioner's Guide* (2005); Roger Milgrim, *Milgrim on Trade Secrets* (2004); Jerry Cohen & Alan S. Gutterman, *Trade Secrets Protection and Exploitation* (1998). *See also*, Charles Tait Graves, *Trade Secrets As Property: Theory and Consequences*, 15 J. Intell. Prop. L. 39 (2007); Sharon K. Sandeen, *A Contract By Any Other Name Is Still a Contract: Examining the Effectiveness of Trade Secret Clauses to Protect Databases*, 45 IDEA 119 (2005). For some interesting new comments *see* David S. Almeling, *Seven Reasons Why Trade Secrets Are Increasingly Important*, 27 Berkeley Tech. L.J. 1091 (2012) and Matthew Edward Cavanaugh, *Contract + Tort = Property: The Trade Secret Illustration*, 16 Marq. Intell. Prop. L. Rev. 427 (2012).
62. The full text of the Uniform Trade Secrets Act with accompanying documents and explanation may be found on the website of the National Conference of Commissioners on Uniform State Laws, www.nccusl.org. As noted, it is also the law in the more than forty states that have adopted it through state legislation.
63. 18 U.S.C. 1832(a).
64. UTSA §§2 and 3.

(c) he learned the secret from a third person with notice of the facts that it was a secret and that the third person discovered it by improper means or that the third person's disclosure of it was otherwise a breach of his duty to the other; or

(d) he learned the secret with notice of the facts that it was a secret and that its disclosure was made to him by mistake.[65]

Because they are not subject to the more formal protections given to patents and copyrights, trade secrets are normally protected by contract. The owner of the trade secret typically has his or her employees sign nondisclosure and confidentiality agreements and, frequently covenants not to compete if the employee chooses to leave the employment. It is typical that when businesses negotiate with each other in transactions that may implicate trade secrets the negotiators sign nondisclosure agreements. Licensing agreements that involve trade secrets typically include confidentiality and nondisclosure requirements that are imposed on the licensor and may also include requirements that the licensee's employees and agents sign individual confidentiality and nondisclosure agreements.

On May 11, 2016 President Barak Obama signed into law the Defend Trade Secrets Act of 2016 which creates a basis for federal court jurisdiction for litigation involving the theft of trade secrets.[66] The act gives litigants an election of going into federal court or state court for trade secret actions while essentially preserving the substance of the Uniform Trade Secrets Act.

A number of other countries have specific provisions in law for protection of trade secrets. For example, China has some trade secret provisions imbedded in its unfair competition law.[67] Other countries, such as the United Kingdom, have stayed away from express provisions of statutory law with the expectation that owners of trade secrets will litigate when the secret has been compromised.[68]

Since protection of trade secrets is grounded largely in contractual provisions, it is helpful to set out and examine a prototype confidentiality clause. In this discussion, we will use the terms "nondisclosure" and "confidentiality" interchangeably. Keep in mind that when such clauses govern the activities of current employees, they are typically embedded in a larger contract that includes "noncompete" language if and when the employee leaves his or her current employer. Licensing agreements frequently contain nondisclosure clauses in the licensing agreement.

---

65. Restatement Torts, §757.
66. 18 U.S.C. §§1836 et seq. For more commentary on the act, *see* Patrick J. Manion, *Two Steps Forward, One Step Back: The Defend Trade Secrets Act of 2016 and Why the Computer Fraud and Abuse Act of 1984 Still Matters for Trade Secret Appropriation*, 43 J. Legis. 289 (2016).
67. Unfair Competition Law, Peoples Republic of China, §84. *See also*, Daniel C.K. Chow, *Navigating the Minefield of Trade Secrets Protection in China*, 47 Vand. J. Transnatl L. 1007 (2014); Ping Xiong & Philip Griffith, *Protecting Trade Secrets in China: History and Context*, 4 Queen Mary J. of Intell. Prop. 30 (2014) Nathan Greene, *Enforceability of the Peoples' Republic of China's Trade Secret Law: Impact on Technology Transfer in the PRC and Preparing for Successful Licensing*, 44 IDEA 437 (2004).
68. *See*, e.g., Aidan Robertson and Audrey Horton, *Does the United Kingdom or the European Community Need an Unfair Competition Law?* 17 Eur. Intell. Prop. Rev. 568 (1995).

A typical clause defines "confidential information," expressly prohibits disclosure to either outsiders or to others within the company who are not authorized to have such information, and often provides for remedies and dispute resolution. The following is a list of items that are usually set out in a nondisclosure agreement:

(1) *Identification of the parties.* If the nondisclosure agreement grows out of an employment setting, the parties are normally referred to as "employer" and "employee." If the parties to the agreement are not in an employment relationship, the parties may be described as "discloser" and "recipient."
(2) *Nature of the contract.* The agreement should set out the reason for the nondisclosure requirement. What kind of a contract does the nondisclosure requirement grow out of—a licensing agreement, a sublicense, an employment contract, an agent, an independent contractor, etc.? Early in the contract's recitals, it is important to give readers of the contract some sense of why it is so important to safeguard this information.
(3) *Definition of "confidential information."* This provision is crucial. It is the heart of the agreement. As with so many other issues in contract drafting, there are a number of ways to approach the task. If there is only a single piece of confidential information (e.g., the formula for Coca Cola) that needs to be guarded, it is probably sufficient for the agreement to identify that one thing and not go into other things. An excessively broad clause can strike judges and arbitrators as overreaching on the part of the discloser. But the usual nondisclosure setting involves many types of confidential business information: customer lists, advertising plans, business strategy, etc. In these circumstances, the agreement will probably first write a generic definition of "confidential information" and then follow that with some specific illustrations. So the confidentiality clause might start by reciting:

> The term "confidential information" includes any forms and types of financial, business, scientific, technical, economic, or engineering information, including patterns, plans, compilations, procedures, programs, and codes not generally known and not readily ascertainable to persons outside the company. This information specifically includes but is not limited to accounting and personnel information, marketing plans, business strategy, proprietary data, formulas, internal management systems, product development, customer lists, and the like.

Note several things here. The basic definition is taken from some of the statutory material on trade secrets—in this case from the U.S. Economic Espionage Act. In many circumstances, a contract drafter might just stop at that point. But in the typical corporate setting, it is not all that difficult to identify a number of specific things that should remain confidential. Customer lists is just one example of something that very few companies would like to reveal to their competitors. So a more specific laundry list following the generic terms is probably a good idea. Even so, because no one can likely list all the types of data that should be kept secret, this portion of the clause should include the standard "includes but is not limited to" language.

(4) *Definition of nonconfidential information.* Some agreements go a step further by setting out an additional description of what is *not* confidential. These definitions are usually taken directly from the statutory language (e.g., "information in the hands of and generally known to the public"). This is probably not necessary. The crucial thing in a nondisclosure agreement is to prevent the release of confidential information. What happens to nonconfidential material is irrelevant.

(5) *Determination of confidential information.* This is a point that the author recommends putting into the agreement although most nondisclosure agreement seem not to cover it. Particularly in an employment situation, there are times when what constitutes confidential information is a close call, or new information may come into the company that may warrant protection. The agreement should identify someone in the company with whom an employee may consult for a determination as to what is protected and what is not. The conscientious employee, knowing with whom he or she can consult will likely do so. Similarly, even if the data is given to someone outside the company, the recipient should be given a contact person much like the employee.

(6) *Permissible disclosure.* Even when information is highly confidential, to be effective that information must be shared with someone. A nondisclosure agreement should specify with whom the recipient can share protected data. The typical clause mentions directors, officers and other employees who have a "need to know" the information. As in the case with item number 5, the author normally specifies a person within the company who can answer questions on permissible disclosure and the need to know. Some agreements specify the purposes to which the recipient can put the confidential agreement (e.g., "only for the purpose of seeking a joint venture partner in the countries of France and Germany").

(7) *Injunctive relief.* When a discloser learns of a potential breach or a breach that may be continuing, one recourse is to rush into an appropriate court for an injunction prohibiting the disclosure (or the continuing disclosure). Many confidentiality agreements expressly provide that the discloser has no adequate remedy at law and may seek injunctive relief.

(8) *Dispute resolution.* In the United States, the normal understanding is that a discloser will go to court to protect the information. Some agreements set out a forum selection clause for this reason. There is probably no reason why the agreement could not specify arbitration but arbitrators do not have independent authority to issue injunctions (they must seek injunctive relief in an appropriate court) and the difficulties and amount of time it takes to find an arbitrator when speed is of the essence probably militates against arbitration. However, if the data is compromised and the discloser seeks monetary remedies, there is no reason why the dispute over money damages could not be subject to arbitration.

(9) *Other provisions*. Keep in mind that a nondisclosure agreement is, at bottom, a contract. The drafter of the agreement may want to make provisions for choice of law, warranties and disclaimers (the typical disclaimer provides that the confidentiality agreement by itself does not constitute a license of the intellectual property). Many agreements provide that the agreement may not be subject to oral modifications and that the writing constitutes the entire agreement. Do not forget things such as notice provisions.

These are some of the more important provisions for an effective confidentiality agreement. But the single most important thing to keep in mind is the simple fact that even the best-crafted agreement is almost entirely dependent on the good faith and proper behavior of the recipient. Once secrets are disclosed, they cannot easily be taken back. So if there is a single, vitally important, consideration it is this: THE BEST NONDISCLOSURE AGREEMENT IS ONLY AS GOOD AS THE PERSON WHO SIGNS IT!

§7.5.2 International Protection of Trade Secrets

The international intellectual property treaties, conventions and agreements provide fewer protections for trade secrets than for other forms of intellectual property. The Paris Convention on Industrial Property prohibits unfair methods of competition in Article 10*bis*. This clause, while silent on trade secrets, may arguably prevent unauthorized trade secret disclosure.

Article 39 of TRIPS uses the term "unfair competition" and cites to the Paris Convention and then goes on to provide that "Members shall protect undisclosed information...[and] natural and legal persons shall have the possibility of preventing information lawfully within their control from being disclosed to, or acquired by, or used by others without their consent in a manner contrary to honest commercial practices. ..."

But beyond these provisions, there is not much else. Once again, if trade secrets are to be protected they will be protected in virtually all circumstances by private contractual arrangements.

§7.6 COMPONENTS OF A LICENSING AGREEMENT

Licensing agreements tend to have a number of common characteristics.[69] First, they are normally for a long period of time. Indeed, the more complex technology requires a longer start-up time. This means that royalties and other forms of remuneration do not begin to flow back to the licensor for months and even years. Moreover, licensees and host countries normally do not wish to enter into short-term agreements because setting up licensed projects often consume a vast amount of time and effort on the part of both private parties and the government itself.

69. These points are covered in different form in Byington, *supra* n. 1, at 196–200.

Second, the secrecy clause is the heart of the licensing agreement. Licensors normally insist on strict confidentiality and on elaborate mechanisms for policing confidentiality. This need for secrecy also has a palpable effect on any assignment of the license or on sublicensing agreements. Frequently, a licensing agreement will flatly prohibit either assignment or sublicensing entirely.

Third, a licensor's business reputation is often at stake because people know that the licensor is behind the product ultimately manufactured. To that extent, licensors look as carefully at quality control provisions in a contract as they do at the secrecy clause.

Beyond these matters, the amount and timeliness of the royalty payments is of great concern to both parties as are the termination provisions in the contract. Host governments do not take lightly to licensors withdrawing a license on spurious or arbitrary grounds after large investments have been made. At the same time, licensors have a legitimate interest in being able to extricate themselves from a deal gone sour since their worldwide reputation and good will may be at stake.

All these components when put together along with a large number of other conventional contract provisions (dispute resolution, force majeure, etc.) comprise a proper licensing agreement. What follows is a more intense discussion of the major individual components of a typical licensing agreement with some suggested language for each clause. This segment begins with a sample outline of a typical licensing agreement.

§7.6.1 An Outline of a Typical Licensing Agreement

As with all other contracts, there are wide variations in the scope, organization, and language of licensing agreements. The following outline is simply a suggestion of the sort of provisions that one might find in a typical licensing agreement:

- Identification and Description of the Parties and the Purpose of the Agreement.
- The Granting Clause (exclusive or nonexclusive and territory).
- Licensor's Duties and Representations.
- Licensee's Duties and Representations.
- Fees and Royalty Payments.
- Sublicenses (if any).
- Books and Records (accounting, recordkeeping, and reporting).
- Modifications and Improvements.
- Permits and Government Permissions.
- Best Efforts.
- Termination.
- Noncompete Following Termination.
- Confidentiality (both during performance and after termination).
- Dispute Resolution.
- Choice of Law (sometimes included in dispute resolution clause).
- Force Majeure.

- Prohibition of Assignment by Licensee.
- Successors and Assigns.
- Severability.
- Duration and/or Renewal.
- "Entire Agreement" clause (prohibition of oral modifications; modifications must be in writing).
- Notices.
- Signatures.

§7.6.2 An Analysis of Licensing Agreement Clauses

A large amount of the language in a licensing agreement is similar to language in all other contracts. Almost all international contracts have a force majeure clause and a choice of law clause. Most contracts have provisions on severability, "entire agreement," and successors and assigns. This section will not spend any time on those matters, many of which are covered in earlier chapters of the book. But there are a number of provisions that are either specific for licensing agreements or so important that they bear some further discussion.

[1] The Granting Clause

This is the central provision in a licensing agreement. It is the clause that conveys the right to use the intellectual property from the licensor to the licensee: "Licensor hereby grants to Licensee ...." As such, it normally contains a description of the specific intellectual property conveyed—for example, "Patent No. 11445 relating to enhancements for automatic breaking systems on four-wheel drive sport utility vehicles." Some agreements specifically identify the intellectual property in the definitions clause of the contract and then for the rest of the agreement simply refer to "The Mark" or "The Patent." As the reader continues with this review, he or she should remember that almost everything discussed is subject to negotiation between the parties. There are very few absolutes or nonnegotiable elements in licensing agreements.

All granting clauses must specify whether the license is an *exclusive* or *nonexclusive* license. While central to the agreement, it is self-explanatory. An *exclusive* license gives the licensee the right to the license to the exclusion of all others in the territory specified and for the term specified. A nonexclusive license may be given to any number of licensees in that same territory and over the same period of time.

The granting clause frequently specifies the duration of the agreement and the territory within which the licensee may use the intellectual property: "for a period of twenty years from the date of this agreement in the country of Indonesia." Duration can be less than the life span of the intellectual property but is almost never longer than the property's life span. There is simply no reason to license a patent for more than twenty years since the invention falls into the public domain after twenty years and can be used by anyone. Many license agreements prescribe a relatively short initial period for the license but with the possibility of renewal of the license after that. This gives the licensor time to observe the licensee's behavior without committing to the full life span of the intellectual property.

Territory is one of those things that is subject to negotiation. It can be almost anything: Germany, Austria and the Czech Republic or the State of New York, or the City of Edinburgh, Scotland. The important thing about territory is that the agreement refer precisely to some geographical area (normally using accepted maps and boundaries) so that neither of the parties is unsure where the license applies. Some agreements put these provisions elsewhere in the contract but it is normally simple and helpful to combine them with the grant itself.

Sublicenses are a related issue. Usually, the licensor gives only the licensee the permission to use the intellectual property. However, there are plenty of instances when the licensor has such faith and trust in the initial licensee that the licensee is given authority to grant licenses to others. This is frequently seen in franchise agreements where the initial licensee gets an "umbrella" license under which he or she may grant sublicenses to others without seeking additional permission from the licensor.

Also directly related to the basic grant of the license is the question of whether the licensee is free to make improvements or modifications to the intellectual property. Sometimes the answer is "no." Most licensors do not want their licensees tinkering with the product. There are, however, some instances when the licensor has no such objection. A number of license agreements provide that the licensee may make improvements or modifications only with the separate, subsequent permission of the licensor.

[2] Duties and Representations

Some lawyers consider this section of the agreement to be mere boilerplate but this language is still important. This is the part of the contract where, for example, the licensor warrants that he or she owns the intellectual property at issue. The licensee will typically warrant that he or she will use the property subject to all the terms and conditions in the agreement.

[3] Fees and Royalty Payments

This clause comprises the economic heart of the agreement. The licensor expects to earn money from the licensee; the licensee hopes to make profits from the downstream use of the property. When licensors have a lot of negotiation leverage, they may impose two different types of payments from the licensee. The first payment, frequently referred to as an administrative fee (or sometimes a "license fee") is simply an up-front payment by the licensee that is usually paid at the time the contract is signed. It is normally a one-time payment.

The more important payment term for a licensing agreement is the royalty clause. There are any number of ways to calculate and state royalties. A royalty may be a simple percentage of the licensee's gross downstream revenues. Royalties may be calculated on a profit-sharing basis. If the licensor wants to give the licensee some time to get up and fully running with the transaction, royalty payments might be waived for, say, the first year of the agreement. Payment of the royalties may be periodic (quarterly, semi-annually or annually) or, in certain rare instances, a lump-sum payment.

In most transactions, the parties are free to negotiate whatever they wish for the percentage royalty. But keep in mind that the percentage must be struck against some other financial calculation. For example, a licensor might be happiest with a 12% royalty against gross sales while the licensee (happy with the percentage) might ask for the royalty to be calculated against net sales.

Directly related to the calculation and payment of royalties is the concept of best efforts. Note that the licensor assumes that the licensee will be vigorous in seeking sales and profits. If the licensee proves more passive than the licensor prefers it may be possible to use the best efforts clause to trigger a termination of the agreement. Also related to royalty calculation and payments is the recordkeeping and reporting clause. These clauses spell out what types of records the licensee must keep, when and how the licensee must report to the licensor and whether the licensor has the prerogative of making his or her own inspection of the licensee's books and records.

[4] Termination and Noncompete

A lot of licensing agreements expire quietly without much need to engage in a lot of efforts to smooth out the termination. Nonetheless, virtually all agreements include some events that may trigger termination prior to the normal expiration of the contract such as the licensee's permitting others to infringe on the intellectual property. If the licensing undertaking is complicated—for example involving large-scale manufacturing processes and the like—there may be a need for the licensee to return such things as equipment, blueprints, formulas and the like to the licensor. This is akin to the winding-up of a dissolved corporation. Once the agreement is terminated, many licensors do not wish the licensee to be able to continue in this line of work and negotiate a noncompete clause for the licensee by which the licensee agrees, for a specified period of time, not to engage in activities that compete with the licensor.

Termination may come as a result of dispute resolution. Most courts and all the major arbitration institutions have experience with licensing agreements. A number of years ago, noting that people were sometimes unhappy with licensing dispute resolution, the WIPO established an arbitration center specifically for the resolution of licensing disputes. It has had particular success in the resolution of disputes involving Internet domain names.[70]

70. *See*, the WIPO website, www.wipo.org. for more details on WIPO arbitration.

CHAPTER 8

The Less-Drastic Forms of Commercial Dispute Resolution

§8.1 INTRODUCTION

Lawyers and business executives occasionally lose sight of the fact that inserting terms in a contract that promote flexibility, or drafting a clause that calls for renegotiation when the deal becomes unstuck can solve a lot of problems that otherwise would have to be dealt with through the vastly more expensive processes of arbitration or litigation. Flexibility, particularly in long-term contracts, should be a matter of concern both when a contract is initially drafted and when disputes arise during the life of a contract.

The language of the contract can alleviate many problems. Express provisions that work to resolve disputes can be inserted in many contracts. Even when the contract is silent on some of these matters, many legal systems have created rules of law that permit contracts to be adjusted without breach (1) over the life of the contract either automatically (e.g., a contract whose price term increases a fixed percentage each year) or at the insistence of one or another of the parties (e.g., when one party is allowed to adjust quantity or quality requirements unilaterally), or (2) on the occurrence of certain specific events, such as war, strikes or currency devaluations.

Most international contracts contain some of these provisions as a matter of course;[1] but even if a contract is totally inflexible when it is initially drafted, renegotiation of the entire contract or portions of the contract is always a possibility.[2] Occasionally, renegotiation takes place in the presence of a third-party mediator/conciliator who attempts to assist the parties in reaching a satisfactory solution.

1. *See*, the discussion of typical contract provisions in Ch. 4, *supra*.
2. The first portion of this chapter owes a great debt to two of the principle works on contract adaptation and renegotiation: *Adaptation and Renegotiation of Contracts in International Trade and Finance* (Norbert Horn ed., 1985) [hereinafter *Contract Adaptation*] and Martin Bartels, *Contractual Adaptation and Conflict Resolution* (1985). *See also* Giorgio Zanarone, *Contract Adaptation under Legal Constraints*, 29 J. L. Econ. & Org. 799 (2012).

Finally, there is a new device on the horizon, the minitrial, not yet fully accepted by international business executives but which shows great promise as an alternative to formal arbitration or litigation. Each of these options is discussed in depth below, but one thing should be kept firmly in mind: all of these options are far less disruptive to the underlying business relationship and far less costly than either litigation or arbitration. In some cultures, notably many of the Pacific Rim countries, these devices are preferred over the more traditional methods of arbitration or litigation. While none of these techniques is the perfect dispute resolution device, they may be profitably explored before a party commences a lawsuit or triggers the contract's arbitration clause.

§8.2 CONTRACT ADAPTATION

The term contract adaptation generally refers to the incorporation of certain terms and conditions in a contract that promote flexibility and that permit the contract to conform to certain changes in conditions without automatic termination or without the need for renegotiation. Adaptation is most important in those contracts that are expected to be of long duration. Contracts calling for a one-time sale of goods transaction or a single service activity to be performed over a short period of time immediately after signing normally do not require adaptation provisions. Similarly, contracts executed by parties who have no expectation of ever seeing each other again or ever doing business again usually have little or no interest in adaptation provisions.

Short-term contracts can be safely drafted with a view toward only the conditions existing at the time of the transaction or at the anticipated time of performance. By contrast, contracts of longer duration require more thought and planning and generally include a number of clauses that are specifically designed to promote flexibility over the life of the contract. Even contracts involving single sales transactions in which the parties want to continue to do business in the future will often contain clauses promoting flexibility because both parties wish not to antagonize each other. An easy way to antagonize someone is to accuse him of breach of contract.

The longer the duration of the contract the more interest the parties are going to have in proper adaptation clauses because the parties are rarely able to predict internal or external conditions over the long run. On the international scene, at least in the twentieth and twenty-first centuries, change in circumstances rather than stability has been the rule. In exceptionally long contracts such as petroleum sharing contracts and other natural resource production agreements—which often have a duration of thirty years—the drafters of the original contract will of necessity include a sizable number of adaptation provisions.

There are a number of ways to categorize adaptation provisions. Professor Norbert Horn, for example, has developed a classification that makes a great deal of sense: "[Adaptation] clauses are designed either to specify details of contractual obligations (gap-filling) or to slightly modify the contents of these obligations (adjustment, adaptation)."[3] Clauses such as force majeure clauses are normally referred to as automatic adaptation clauses. In other words, the happening of certain events external to the contract—such as strikes, political insurrection, or war—automatically suspends or, in certain cases, alters one or both parties' performance obligations.

Sometimes, adaptation can be triggered unilaterally by one of the parties. For example, a contract may contain a "most-favored" clause that requires a contract to receive the same treatment as a contract subsequently negotiated with another party, even though the first party may have absolutely nothing to do with the later agreement.[4] The concept is akin to the idea of most-favored nation: when one country is extended certain trade benefits, all other countries with most-favored nation status must be given the same treatment. In other circumstances a contract may provide that a party may unilaterally assign all rights under the contract or may terminate the contract on the occurrence or nonoccurrence of certain conditions. So, for example, if a contract calls for the buyer to purchase all his requirements from a seller and the contract contains a provision that provides for a minimum amount of requirements that never materialize, the contract might permit the buyer to terminate, irrespective of the wishes of the seller, because the buyer's actual requirements never reach the amounts specified in the contract.

In many cases, conditions may change to the point where both parties see the need for adaptation. Occasionally, bilateral adaptation may occur simply by minor adjustments in the manner of performance by one or both parties that do not trigger an objection by the other side. For example, a contract may call for payment in the currency of a specific currency, say, Swiss francs. If that currency for some reason cannot be utilized, the buyer may simply proffer payment in a substitute currency, say U.S. dollars, that the seller then accepts without protest. Usually, however, bilateral adaptation follows some intense renegotiation between the parties. Many long-term contracts provide an express mechanism for bringing the parties together to work out appropriate adaptation clauses.

There are a number of other ways to categorize adaptation provisions. Professor Horn has developed four different groups. In his view, contracts may be divided into: (a) "open" contracts such as turnkey construction projects or complex technology transfer projects in which the parties concede that all the details cannot be anticipated and written into the basic document; (b) "flexible" contracts in which certain of the details underlying the basic agreement such as the price of a vital natural resource is expected to change over time and thus cannot be specified in the original document; (c) contracts involving "special risks" which the parties did not specifically anticipate but for which they incorporated a special risk clause; and (d) contracts with force majeure provisions.

3. Norbert Horn, *Standard Clauses on Contract Adaptation in International Commerce,* in Contract Adaptation, *supra* n. 2, at 112. *See also,* Klaus Peter Berger, *Renegotiation and Adaptation of International Investment Contracts: The Role of Contract Drafters and Arbitrators,* 36 Vand. J. Transnat'l L. 1347 (2003); John Y. Gotanda, *Renegotiation and Adaptation Clauses in Investment Contracts Revisited,* 36 Vand. J. Transnat'l L. 1461 (2003).
4. Mr. Bartels notes that "most-favored" clauses are not very common. Bartels, *supra* n. 2, at 35.

The first two categories are self-explanatory. With regard to the latter two categories, there is not a great deal of difference between a special risk clause and a force majeure clause in actual operation. The effect of both is to forgive or suspend performance, or, in certain instances, to alter performance requirements. A special risk clause is usually inserted in a contract when the parties believe a certain event might happen—such as a change of government that might lead to nationalization of a certain industry. The special risk clause will make specific adjustments in the contract to accommodate that occurrence. A force majeure clause, by contrast, is inserted in virtually every commercial contract, whether or not of international scope, and provides for relief from the occurrence of unanticipated events of a more general nature such as earthquakes, floods, and war.

Another way to look at adaptation issues is with regard to the ultimate effect of the change in circumstances. Some changes can be so drastic that they totally prevent further performance under the contract. Other changes can have a somewhat milder effect in that they merely make the contract more difficult or more burdensome to perform. For example, British commercial law recognizes the doctrine of "frustration" and may occasionally apply the doctrine to forgive performance, but the British courts have almost always applied the doctrine narrowly to mean that performance has become technically impossible, not merely difficult.[5] For example, a change in a government regulation may make performance of the contract unlawful. A contract between a Scottish distillery and a United States liquor dealer to sell single malt whisky in the United States would have been deemed "frustrated" and performance thereby forgiven when the United States government made the sale of liquor illegal in 1919.

The United States' Uniform Commercial Code (UCC) is considerably more flexible on this point. The UCC recognizes through its doctrine of "commercial impracticability," that excessively burdened performance may require forgiveness. While the burden of increased costs is usually never a proper excuse (as the Code points out: "that is exactly the type of business risk which business contracts made at fixed prices are intended to cover"), such matters as severe shortages of raw materials or unforeseen shutdowns of major sources of supply may excuse performance or at least permit delayed performance.[6] Other countries deal with these issues of difficult or impossible performance on a case-by-case basis by construing the force majeure clause in individual contracts.

In drafting contracts, there are essentially two ways in which parties can cope with changed conditions: they can let the contract remain silent on these matters with the expectation that the law underlying the contract will fill in the necessary gaps; or they can address them specifically in the contract by drafting clauses which provide the necessary flexibility to accommodate the changes.

5. *See*, e.g., *Ford & Sons, Ltd. v. Henry Leetham & Sons, Ltd.*, 21 Com. Cas. 55 (1915, K.B.D.).
6. For some excellent discussion and analysis of commercial impracticability, *see* Jennifer Camero, *Mission Impracticable: The Impossibility of Commercial Impracticability*, 13 U.N.H.L. Rev. 28 (2014); Paula Walter, *Commercial Impracticability in Contracts*, 61 St. John's L. Rev. 225 (2012).

§8.2.1 Gap-Filling Mechanisms in the Underlying Law

To understand this topic, it is important to have some understanding as to the manner in which the law underlying the contract is ascertained. As discussed in Chapter 2, the applicable law may be expressly stated in the contract by way of a choice of law clause. If the contract contains no express choice of law clause, virtually all mature legal systems provide rules and mechanisms by which a court may determine which law to apply.[7] These court- or arbitrator-imposed rules can be complex; but for the purposes of the following discussion it is enough to realize that if the parties become engaged in a dispute under the contract the entity charged with resolving the dispute will choose a body of law to apply to that contract if the parties have not made their own choice of law.

Frequently, a choice made by a judge or arbitrator satisfies neither party. That is, a court or an arbitrator choosing a body of law may not make the same choice the parties might have made had they chosen the law when the contract was drafted. Nonetheless, when a body of law is chosen, that law will frequently impose certain gap-filling mechanisms on the parties. These mechanisms will apply in addition to whatever is expressed in the contract.

Leaving the choice of law to others is dangerous. It greatly lessens both predictability and stability under the contract. It can have consequences never intended by the parties; and, if the contract becomes the subject of an intense dispute culminating in arbitration or litigation, the lack of an express choice of law provision in the contract often prolongs the dispute because parties then have to fight over which law to apply as well as fighting over the substantive parts of the contract. Most international contracts contain a carefully considered choice of law provision even if the remainder of the contract is less detailed. When the negotiators cannot agree on a choice of law, some contract drafters invoke "commonly accepted principles of commercial behavior" as a kind of choice of law that avoids tying the contract to any particular country's system of contract law.

By and large, the parties' choice of law will be honored by courts and arbitrators. In a few instances, the choice will not be honored for reasons of public policy. The court or arbitrator is then empowered to impose a choice of its own. This is a rare

7. An intense discussion of choice of law rules in various jurisdictions is beyond the scope of this chapter. For additional information on this topic *see*, Ian F.G. Baxter, *International Conflict of Laws and International Business*, 34 Int'l and Comp. L.Q. 538 (1985); Russell Weintraub, *How to Choose Law for Contracts, and How Not To: The EEC Convention*, 17 Tex. Int'l L. J. 155 (1982); Georges R. Delaume, *The European Convention on the Law Applicable to Contractual Obligations: Why a Convention?* 22 Va. J. Int'l L. 107 (1981); and George A. Zaphiriou, *Choice of Forum and Choice of Law Clauses in International Commercial Agreements*, 3 Int'l Trade L. J. 311 (1978). The reader should also review the lengthy section on choice of law in Chapter 4. There is some new literature on choice of law under The Hague Principles. *See*, e.g., Andreas Schwartze, *New Trends in Parties' Options to Select the Applicable Law? The Hague Principles on Choice of Law in International Contracts in a Comparative Perspective*, 12 U. St. Thomas L.J. 87 (2015); Marta Pertegas & Brooke Adele Marshall, *Harmonization Through the Draft Hague Principles on Choice of Law in International Contracts*, 39 Brook. J. Int'l L. 975 (2014); Symeon C. Symeneonides, *The Hague Principles on Choice of Law for International Contracts: Some Preliminary Comments*, 61 Am. J. Comp. L. 395 (2013).

occurrence, of course, and to avoid it, contract drafters should simply insure that there is a reasonable relation between the law chosen for the contract, the identity of the parties and the place of performance. A contract between a Swiss seller and a Mexican buyer that chooses either Swiss or Mexican law will virtually never have its choice of law disturbed. By contrast, a contract between a United States seller and a Ghanian buyer that chooses Icelandic law will be automatically suspect and possibly not honored. When parties, for whatever reason, make a rather exotic choice of law, they should probably explain their reasons for doing so in the contract itself or in some contemporaneous sidebar document. Even an exotic choice of law properly explained by the contracting parties will normally be accepted by the court or arbitrator when a dispute occurs.

Some legal systems are better equipped to fill gaps than others. Under the United States' UCC, many details of a contract may permissibly be left open with the expectation that the general legal principles applicable under the UCC will fill in many of the gaps. For example, in the United States, a contract for the sale of goods governed by Article 2 of the UCC can be silent on a number of important matters and still remain enforceable. Under the UCC, an offer that does not specify a time during which it may be accepted is deemed to remain open "a reasonable time, but in no event [in excess of] three months."[8] A contract that leaves the price term open will require the payment of "a reasonable price at the time of delivery."[9] In other circumstances, as discussed above, the UCC forgives performance in cases in which performance becomes "commercially impracticable" due to unforeseen supervening circumstances not within the contemplation of the parties at the time of contracting.[10]

Accordingly, an international commercial contract that incorporates the UCC as its substantive legal framework could in theory dispense with a substantial amount of detail, could leave out a large number of specific terms, and might still be an enforceable document. But even a contract that chooses the UCC that leaves too many things out exposes the parties to some risks. Most of the gap-filling of the UCC turns on the concept of "reasonableness"—a term that may be readily understood by two parties in the United States who are used to functioning in the same commercial atmosphere, but that may be very difficult to ascertain by business executives from other cultures whose concepts of acceptable commercial behavior (what is frequently called the "course of dealing" or "course of performance") may be radically different from practices in the United States. Moreover, even U.S. contract drafters find themselves extremely uncomfortable leaving open all the terms permissibly left open under the UCC. In international contracts, especially between two parties who have not had prior dealings and who come from different cultural and legal backgrounds, leaving open such crucial items such as price and delivery is almost never done.

Virtually no other legal system provides for the breadth of gap-filling permitted under the UCC. Under the French law, the basic concept of force majeure excuses performance only when an event occurs that is totally beyond the control of one of the

8. UCC §2-205.
9. *Id.*, §2-305.
10. *Id.*, §2-615.

parties. In limited circumstances involving contractual dealings between private parties and the state, the doctrine of imprevision permits a court to forgive performance when conditions change such that performance becomes extremely burdensome for one of the parties. However, Professor Horn notes that those French courts that have recognized the principle of imprevision have also required, apparently as a condition precedent, that the parties attempt to renegotiate the terms before seeking forgiveness of performance in court.[11]

Under German law the doctrine of impossibility of performance may be used to excuse performance when the nonperforming party is not negligent and when the event which inhibits performance is found to be beyond that party's control. Under British common law, performance under a contract is virtually never excused unless the nonperforming party can show "frustration" of performance—that is, that performance was absolutely impossible due to an event beyond that party's control.

A number of recent commentators have suggested that to the extent there exists an international law of contract—and most observers seem to have concluded that in practice there is really no such thing because virtually all contracts which cross national boundaries remain tied in some fashion to some nation's domestic substantive law—it may be possible to ascertain gap-filling provisions in these principles of international law. For example, Professor Horn points to Article 62 of the Vienna Convention on the Law of Treaties[12] and its language on fundamental change of circumstances as an instance of international recognition of the doctrine of impossibility or frustration. Similarly, Article 79 of the United Nations Convention on Contracts for the International Sale of Goods (CISG) contains a forgiveness provision that operates essentially as a force majeure clause: "A party is not liable for a failure to perform any of his obligations if he proved that the failure was due to an impediment beyond his control and that he could not reasonably be expected to have taken the impediment into account at the time of the conclusion of the contract or to have avoided or overcome it or its consequences." As more and more countries accept the CISG, and as more and more parties choose the CISG as the law applicable to their contract, Article 79 may be used more frequently as a gap-filling device.

§8.2.2 Coping with Uncertainty Through Express Contractual Provisions: Some Typical Adaptation Clauses

Most contracting parties will probably not wish to leave important details in the contract to the mercy of gap-filling mechanisms derived from the underlying substantive legal system. Instead, they will likely wish to deal with as many uncertainties and create as much flexibility as possible through express provisions in the contract itself. Although express contractual language will not totally eliminate risk—there is virtually nothing that can accomplish this—it does give a great deal of control over most of the important matters to the parties themselves; because in virtually all instances, whether

11. Norbert Horn, *Changes in Circumstances and the Revision of Contracts in Some European Laws and in International Law,* in Contract Adaptation, *supra* n. 2, at 18.
12. This is the so-called treaty on treaties and is reprinted in 8 *Int'l Leg. Materials* 679 (1969).

the contract is simply performed, whether it is litigated or whether it goes to arbitration, the contract language will be honored and enforced in the dispute resolution process.[13]

There are essentially two ways that contracting parties can incorporate adaptation clauses in the contract. On the one hand, the parties may simply search the literature for standard form clauses and write those clauses into the document with perhaps slight changes. A number of organizations provide such clauses. For example, for international construction contracts, two organizations, the Federation Internationale des Ingenieurs-Consiels (FIDIC) and the United Nations International Development Organization (UNIDO), have developed standard form clauses covering a variety of matters including alterations, delays, cost overruns, special risks and other issues.

The FIDIC clauses have been frequently used even though many of the clauses have internal defects and are not universally appropriate. As Professor Horn puts it: the clauses "do not display much consistency with regard to [their] terminology or scope ... and, as an offspring of British contractual practice, are hardly compatible with [the legal systems] of civil law countries."[14] The UNIDO clauses are often useful for only very narrow specific purposes, because they have been drafted in the context of specific model construction contracts, such as turnkey fertilizer plant construction projects. Many domestic commercial organizations such as trade associations and chambers of commerce also provide model contracts or standard form clauses.

Models and standard forms are cheap and quick; but they contain a number of pitfalls and hazards. First, they may not fit precisely the commercial dealing in question, just as clothing off the rack rarely fits as well as custom-made clothing. Second, it is virtually impossible to draft a single model contract or standard clause that meets the legal requirements of all the world's legal systems. It is always possible, of course, to alter a standard form to meet the requirements of a specific transaction; but it is sometimes more difficult and time consuming to change a standard clause than it is simply to draft an original clause that satisfies the desires of the parties.

At the same time, striving for complete originality is rarely called for or even possible in most circumstances. Given that so many contracts are drafted by or with the assistance of lawyers, and that lawyers in all countries tend to be inordinately conservative when it comes to breaking new linguistic ground, most contracts are based on preexisting, traditional language. Also, standard form clauses and model contracts may contain a great deal of language that is suitable for the transaction in question; and, at the very least, may provide a checklist of issues and phrases that the parties should consider for incorporation in their document.

13. The reader should be aware that there are instances in which courts have refused to honor contractual provisions that somehow violate a nation's "public policy" or which are so unfair or biased as to be deemed "unconscionable"; but such rulings are relatively rare. Most courts and arbitrators insist that the parties live with language that they have previously agreed to.
14. Norbert Horn, *Standard Clauses on Contract Adaptation in International Commerce* in Contract Adaptation, *supra* n. 2, at 113–114.

If the parties choose to draft their own language, they are well advised to consider—as gap-filling or adaptation provisions—the following checklist of possible clauses:[15]

(1) *Variation and change clauses.* These clauses, often incorporated in construction contracts, permit the parties to alter materials specifications, techniques of construction and the like so that excessive rigidity in the original contract does not prevent the completion of the project.

(2) *Price escalation clauses.* These clauses cope with price uncertainty and permit the seller to maintain his profit margins even if costs begin to escalate. As one might expect, there are virtually no fixed price contracts in, for example, the international petroleum industry. Almost all natural resource contracts provide for some type of automatic price escalation (or in certain cases, price reduction) based on the prices set at the source.

(3) *Stabilization and tax clauses.* These clauses help protect against changes in government and government policy. They typically excuse performance when government policy changes to the extent that contract performance is impaired. Tax clauses address expressly the prospect of changes in a nation's tax policy that may impair the economic worth of the contract.

(4) *Review clauses.* Review clauses are essentially renegotiation clauses and obligate the parties to discuss unanticipated changes in circumstances with a view toward amending the contract language to cope with those changes. However, as noted in the next section, renegotiation may take place without a specific contractual provision obligating the parties to do so.

§8.3 RENEGOTIATION

To a certain extent, this section restates the obvious. In most instances when a contract begins to cause trouble, the parties voluntarily get together to see what can be done to preserve the business relationship. People in business, pragmatists that they are, rarely jump immediately into court merely because something troublesome occurs.

The obligation to renegotiate can also be built into the contract and conceivably enforced as any other provision in the document. Renegotiation clauses are not a panacea, of course. On occasion, uncooperative parties who are forced to renegotiate simply because a contract clause demands that they renegotiate will probably make sure that the negotiation fails and that the contract is put through some more formal—and adversarial—type of dispute resolution mechanism. Readers about to enter a renegotiation session should refresh their recollection of the basic negotiation principles set out in Chapter 5. Renegotiation is distinct from initial contract

15. Space limitations do not permit a comprehensive discussion of all these clauses. Readers who wish specific illustrative language for these clauses should consult two of the preeminent multivolume treatises in the area. *The International Law of International Commercial Transactions* (Norbert Horn & Clive M. Schmitthoff eds., 1983) and Georges R. Delaume, *Transnational Contracts* (1982).

negotiation in only one sense: it is negotiation as Professor Horn puts it, "in the shadow of the court." When an initial negotiation fails, the parties simply do not execute the contract; when a renegotiation fails, the parties generally resort to some more structured type of dispute resolution mechanism such as arbitration or litigation. But even at this point parties should seriously consider the two other mechanisms discussed in this chapter—mediation/conciliation and the minitrial before resorting to either arbitration or litigation.

§8.4 FACT FINDING AND EARLY NEUTRAL EVALUATION

There are additional processes that are recognized as forms of alternative dispute resolution (ADR) that might prove efficient and effective for international commercial disputes. One such procedure is known as *fact finding*.[16] In this instance, a neutral person (i.e., one with no relationship to the parties) conducts an investigation of the dispute and, mainly, determines what the facts of the matter are and gives a report of that fact finding to the parties. This process has a great deal to commend it because it is fast and relatively inexpensive. It deals with a component of a dispute (i.e., what the facts really are) in the same way that a judge or jury might find the facts. Often, when the parties are confronted by a report of a neutral third party setting out the facts as that third party sees the dispute, there are strong pressures to settle the dispute realistically.

In yet another type of ADR that stands, in the taxonomy of ADR, somewhere between fact finding and mediation known as *early neutral evaluation*.[17] In this instance, as in fact finding, the parties select a neutral third person to engage in both fact finding and a broader evaluation of the dispute that may, conceivably, include an analysis and evaluation of legal and economic issues apart from the facts themselves. As in fact finding, the neutral issues a report to the parties for their consideration. The process is typically speedy and relatively cheap and often provides just enough objectivity that the parties are able to resolve the dispute armed with the neutral's report. Persons experienced with early neutral evaluation often note that the report of the evaluator differs little from the view of the dispute that arbitrators or mediators might take. For this reason, it is yet another form of less-drastic dispute resolution that parties may wish to consider. In both fact finding and early neutral evaluation, the parties have a great deal of control over the process and confidentiality is rarely compromised.

16. *See*, e.g., Tim K. Klintworth, *The Enforceabiity of an Agreement to Submit to a Non-Arbitral Form of Dispute Resolution: The Rise of Mediation and Neutral Fact Finding*, 1995 J. Disp. Resol. 181 (1995).
17. *See*, e.g., Norman Zakiyy & Kamal Halili Hassan, *Prospects of Using Early Neutral Evaluation in Case Management of Complex Civil Cases in Malaysia*, 3 Eur. J. Econ. & Bus. Stud. 9 (2015); Karen Engro & Lisa Pupo Lenihan, *Understanding Early Neutral Evaluation in the Western District of Pennsylvania*, 10 Laws. J. 3 (2008).

§8.5 MEDIATION AND CONCILIATION

§8.5.1 Mediation and Conciliation Generally

Mediation as a commercial dispute resolution process has been with us probably as long as there have been people doing business. Conceptually, it is not much more than negotiation in the presence of, and facilitated by, a third person or persons. It can be informal, as for example, when two disputing shop owners ask a third shop owner to help resolve their conflict, or it can be relatively structured with the application of rules of procedures, the exchange of written memoranda prior to the mediation, the formal appointment of a mediator, a final written agreement and the like. There is even a lack of consensus on the basic terminology. A number of writers on the topic, particularly some of the European commentators, appear to distinguish sharply between mediation and conciliation, viewing mediation as the use of a third party facilitator who, both literally and figuratively, sits between the contesting parties and helps them come to terms and conciliation as a process by which each party designates a conciliator for his or her side who then, on their own, meet to hammer out some kind of resolution that is then presented to the actual parties for their confirmation.

This distinction is probably not necessary in most circumstances since there are any number of successful models for mediation/conciliation that have been worked out over the years. Accordingly, for the purposes of this section, the term mediation will be used as the generic term for this type of dispute resolution.

§8.5.2 A General Theory of Mediation

Mediation is a device for resolving disputes that attempts to defuse a great deal of hostility and anguish between the parties by using a third party as a go-between.[18] And

18. The basic mediation literature is growing, but the mediation writings specifically addressed to international business disputes remains relatively sparse. For some basic works *see*, e.g., Alexia Georgakopoulos, *The Mediation Handbook: Research, Theory & Practice* (2017); Eileen Carroll & Karl Mackie, *International Mediation: Breaking Business Deadlock* (2016); Klaus Peter Berger, *Private International Dispute Resolution in International Business: Negotiation, Mediation, Arbitration* (2015); Nadja Alexander, *International Comparative Mediation: Legal Perspectives* (2009); Christian Buhring-Uhle, *Arbitration and Mediation in International Business: Designing Procedures for Effective Conflict Management* (1996); Jay Folberg & Alison Taylor, *Mediation* (1984) [hereinafter *Folberg*]; Roger Fisher & William Ury, *International Mediation: A Working Guide* (1978) (emphasizing diplomatic mediation rather than private commercial mediation). For more general, but helpful, reading on mediation *see*: Robert A. Baruch Bush & Joseph P. Folger, *The Promise of Mediation: The Transformative Approach to Conflict* (2004); Christopher W. Moore, *The Mediation Process: Practical Strategies for Resolving Conflict* (2003); Jay Folberg, Dwight Golann, Thomas J. Stipanowich & Lisa Kloppenberg, *Resolving Disputes: Theory, Practice and Law* (2d ed., 2010). For some articles *see*, the classic jurisprudential work by Professor Lon Fuller, *Mediation—Its Forms and Functions*, 44 S. Calif. L. Rev. 305 (1971). Also helpful are: Penny Booker & Anthony Lavers, *Lawyers' Experience with Commercial and Construction Mediation in the United Kingdom*, 5 Pepp. Disp. Resol. L. J. 161 (2005); Judd Epstein, *The Use of Comparative Law in Commercial International Arbitration and Commercial Mediation*, 75 Tul. L. Rev. 913 (2001); Symposium, *International Commercial Dispute Resolution: Courts, Arbitration, and Mediation*, 15 B.U. L. Rev. 175 (1997); Julie Barker, *International*

while it places enormous (sometimes excessive) importance on the role of the mediator has a number of characteristics that commend it for commercial disputes. For example, mediation is relatively inexpensive and compared with some of the more adversarial forms of dispute resolution, not very time consuming. It is normally confidential—thus sparing the parties the prospect of a fight in open court—and it is normally not burdened by such things as rigid rules of procedure and evidence. Best of all, it is a superior device for preserving the underlying business relationship while permitting the parties to resolve the dispute at hand because it is not nearly as confrontational as litigation. A skillful mediator can sometimes preserve a spirit of good feeling between the parties even as they work through the specific problem at hand.

In theory, mediation is not that different from negotiation, so many of the concepts and issues discussed in Chapter 5 are relevant here. The insertion of the third party mediator, however, lends a slightly different atmosphere to mediation. For this reason, much of the theory of mediation revolves around the behavior of the mediator. Professors Jay Folberg and Allison Taylor postulate seven stages for mediation that now serve as a model for much mediation research. The Folberg-Taylor stages are almost self-explanatory and bear a distinct and understandable relation to the Fisher and Urey stages of negotiation. They are:

(1) Introduction—creating trust and structure.
(2) Fact finding and isolation of issues.
(3) Creation of options and alternatives.
(4) Negotiation and decision-making.
(5) Clarification and writing of a plan.
(6) Legal review and processing.
(7) Implementation, review, and revision.

Set in an international commercial context, the stages might work in the following manner. In the beginning, the mediator works with the parties to defuse whatever hostility and distrust has arisen from the dispute so far. This may be merely a matter of getting the parties to talk quietly with each other in some neutral setting such as a hotel suite. If tempers are too hot for this, a mediator might begin the mediation by some kind of shuttle diplomacy, by which the mediator keeps the parties in their respective rooms and moves back and forth between the two sides, conveying information, clarifying positions and discussing issues. There are additional complications of linguistic and cultural differences in international contracts. A mediator who is sensitive to these nuances can make all the difference in the world between success and breakdown.

Mediation: A Better Alternative for the Resolution of Commercial Disputes, 19 Loy. L.A. Int'l & Comp. L. J. 1 (1996); Walter A. Wright, *Mediation of Private United States-Mexico Commercial Disputes: Will It Work?* 26 N.M. L. Rev. 57 (1996); Joseph B. Stulberg, *The Theory and Practice of Mediation: A Reply to Professor Susskind,* 6 Vt. L. Rev. 85 (1981); and Lawrence Perlman & Steven Nelson, *New Approaches to the Resolution of International Commercial Disputes,* 17 Int'l L. 215 (1983).

Stages 2 and 3 in an international commercial setting are frequently crucial to a successful outcome. Often the parties come together knowing only their side of the story because so much of the business transaction has been conducted over long distances. A mere appreciation of the difficulties faced by the other party is sometimes enough to provoke an amicable resolution. Mediators can play a crucial role in developing creative options. The two parties frequently become what the psychologists call field dependent and can see only their own point of view filtered through all their own prejudices. They lose sight of other possibilities that are not within their limited field of vision. A mediator who knows something about international transactions can suggest possibilities that would never occur to the two disputants.

Stages 4 and 5 are inevitable in any mediation or negotiation. A decision that is acceptable to both parties must be reached to have a successful conclusion. In a commercial setting that decision is almost always committed to paper. The paper may be a wholly new contract or a mere addendum to the existing contract. Occasionally, it is signed on the spot by the parties' representatives, if they have been given that power, or it is drafted, initialed, and returned to corporate headquarters for ratification.

Folberg and Taylor's Stage 6 (legal review and processing) is a stage more important to disputes in the area of domestic relations or community grievances and is rarely a factor in international commercial disputes unless those disputes are already in some form of litigation and the mediation is used in an attempt to settle the litigation. By contrast, Stage 7 (implementation and review) is highly important and sometimes ignored. It is vital that two parties dealing at long distance develop some process by which the mediated agreement can be properly monitored.

The monitoring can be by third parties or by a requirement of periodic reporting between the parties; but it must occur in some fashion if only to avoid the reoccurrence of the problems that lead to the initial dispute. One common deficiency in renegotiated or mediated agreements is a lack of some kind of policing mechanism to insure that the new agreement is being fully performed. Another common defect is falling into the trap of thinking that renegotiation or mediation need occur only once, thus failing to establish some mechanism by which the parties can reconvene if any problems arise. The mechanism need not be elaborate. It can be something as simple as a letter notification process by which one party notifies the other that a problem has occurred and that invites the other party to participate in a mediation.

There are inherent problems with mediation, of course. No one should consider it a panacea for all commercial disputes. One of the problems with the rush toward mediation in the United States is that its proponents emphasize its positive attributes but are generally blind to its defects. Mediation is often unsuccessful when there is disproportionate power or leverage on one side or another. In contrast, the formal procedures of litigation can go a long way toward equalizing leverage. Like negotiation, mediation is normally useless when one party insists on acting in a confrontational, take-it-or-leave it manner. While the mediation itself is usually fairly quick—speed is one of its distinct advantages—a mediation failure means that the parties must resort to some more formal mechanism such as arbitration or litigation when they could have begun with that process. So it can waste a lot of time and expense for the parties and leave them no better off than they were at the beginning.

Even the benefit of confidentiality can sometimes be a two-edged sword. Parties who first try to mediate may be forced to reveal a great deal of their case in a forum that cannot finally resolve the dispute and thus find all their arguments in court fully anticipated and countered by their opponent.

Perhaps the most glaring defect of mediation is that its result is not truly enforceable in the same way that a court decision or arbitral award is enforceable. Obviously, a mediation that results in a new written agreement signed by the parties has created a new contract that can be enforced in the same fashion as any other contract, through arbitration or litigation. But note that this merely moves the dispute back into a forum that, presumably, the mediating parties were seeking to avoid.

Moreover, it is unclear whether a provision in the original contract by which the parties agree to mediate is enforceable. This is in sharp contrast to numerous decisions holding arbitration clauses in contracts fully enforceable.[19] But, here again, compulsory mediation is both superfluous and probably a contradiction in terms. A party who does not want to mediate will simply poison the mediation at the first possible opportunity and go on to the more adversarial forms of dispute resolution.

§8.5.3 Procedures for International Commercial Mediation

If rules making activity is any indication, it appears that international commercial mediation is a dispute resolution technique whose time is coming. The International Chamber of Commerce (ICC), the United Nations Commission on International Trade Law (UNCITRAL) and the American Arbitration Association (AAA), as well as many other national arbitration institutions have promulgated specific procedures for mediation.

Each of these procedural systems is characterized by brevity and simplicity. For example, the UNCITRAL procedures (referred to as conciliation rules) comprise only twenty separate rules.[20] Under the UNCITRAL system, the following steps are mandated:

(1) The party initiating mediation sends a notice to the other party describing the matter in dispute and inviting mediation under the UNCITRAL rules. If the other party objects, that is where the process stops. There is simply no mediation.[21]

(2) The parties may agree on a single mediator, or if they wish to have a three-person mediation panel, they may each appoint one mediator and those two mediators choose the third.[22]

19. *See*, e.g., a United States Supreme Court decision, *Mitsubishi v. Soler*, 473 U.S. 614 (1985) in which the Court demanded that parties abide by an agreement to arbitrate even when many of the issues involved antitrust claims—an issue in the United States that normally is taken directly into the court system.
20. The seminal work of UNCITRAL in both arbitration and mediation is described in considerable detail in Pieter Sanders, *The Work of UNCITRAL on Arbitration and Conciliation* (2d ed., 2004).
21. UNCITRAL Conciliation Rules, Art. 2.
22. *Id.*, Art. 4.

(3) The mediator has the parties write up their statement of the claim and of the issues involved for submission to the mediator and to the other party.[23]

(4) Once these papers are exchanged and examined, the mediator convenes a mediation session "in such a manner as he considers appropriate" and is expected to "be guided by principles of objectivity, fairness and justice, giving consideration to, among other things, the rights and obligations of the parties, the usages of the trade concerned and the circumstances surrounding the dispute, including any previous business practices between the parties."[24]

(5) The proceedings are terminated by either the signing of a written agreement between the parties or by a declaration by one or both of the parties that further proceedings would be futile.[25]

Note that the rules are deliberately relaxed and somewhat ambiguous, vesting enormous discretion in the mediator as to the conduct of the proceedings. The parties themselves also carry a substantial burden. They may propose possible points of settlement; they may take the lead in drafting the final agreement; and they may terminate the process unilaterally. This does not, of course, do great violence to the process. When the UNCITRAL procedures were initially drafted, they were intended to be voluntary, nonbinding, and simple.[26]

The procedures for the ICC are similar, although they use a different vocabulary. The ICC process is set out in a 2014 pamphlet ("Mediation Rules"). The Rules establish a process by which, separate from arbitration, the parties submit the dispute to a mediator or mediators who listen to the parties, examine the record and submit proposed terms of settlement to the parties. The parties are free, of course, to accept, modify, or reject the terms.

In 2003, UNCITRAL took many of these concepts a step further to promulgate a Model Law on International Commercial Conciliation. This body of work represents some of the freshest thinking on the international stage and is, finally, a concession to the idea that mediation/conciliation can stand on its own two feet and is not merely an adjunct (or perhaps a poor stepchild) to arbitration or litigation. The model law essentially merges the concepts of mediation and conciliation by defining the process (irrespective of label) as one "whereby parties request a third person or persons to assist them in their attempt to reach an amicable settlement of their dispute arising out of ... a contractual or other legal relationship."[27] Beyond this, the law permits the use of one or more conciliators as the parties wish.[28] The parties may develop their own rules for the proceeding or the conciliator may set up rules.[29] The model law deals with

23. *Id.*, Art. 5.
24. *Id.*, Art. 7.
25. *Id.*, Art. 15.
26. Issak I. Dore, *Peaceful Settlement of International Trade Disputes: Analysis of the Scope of Application of the UNCITRAL Conciliation Rules*, 21 Colum. J. Int'l L. 339 (1983).
27. UNCITRAL Model Law on International Commercial Conciliation, Art. 1(3). The full text of the model law may be found on the UNCITRAL website: www.uncitral.org.
28. Article 5(1).
29. Article 6.

the crucial issue of confidentiality by providing that "all information relating to the conciliation proceedings shall be kept confidential, except where disclosure is required under the law or for the purposes of implementation or enforcement of a settlement agreement."[30] Among other things, the law provides that any settlement agreement that emerges from such a proceeding is itself fully enforceable.[31]

§8.5.4 Mediation in the Future

The fact that mediation has not yet caught on in the international commercial community is something of a disappointment. Mediation, even when it is used, is rarely reported in the legal or business literature. For persons as conservative as lawyers and business executives, this lack of a track record for mediation severely inhibits its use. Few lawyers want to be attacked by their clients or to get a reputation among other lawyers for engaging in costly, futile actions. This fear of failure probably stifles a lot of innovative dispute resolution techniques. But while the process has both advantages and disadvantages, it is a process that bears more attention and consideration than it is now getting. Some disputes—especially those involving certain Pacific Rim cultures who abhor the adversarial nature of arbitration and litigation—simply cry out for mediation. It would be a shame if the innate conservatism of international commercial lawyers was the only thing standing in the way of increased use of these techniques.

§8.6 THE MINITRIAL

§8.6.1 The Minitrial Generally

Although mediation has been with us practically since time immemorial, the minitrial device is newly developed and just beginning to be appreciated. No one knows precisely when or where the idea was first developed. One of the first articles describing a minitrial was written in 1978 by Professor Eric Green who may remain the device's strongest and most articulate proponent.[32] Recently, the Canton of Zurich promulgated minitrial rules that may catch on in Europe and elsewhere. The AAA has now gotten into the act with minitrial rules, and it appears as if a number of other arbitral bodies may follow suit.

The process is relatively simple. The disputing parties convene for a short period of time, usually for not more than two days. The lawyers for each side make summary

---

30. Article 9.
31. Article 14. For some explanation of the history and negotiating context of the model law *see*, Robert N. Dobbins, *UNCITRAL Model Law on International Commercial Conciliation: From a Topic of Possible Discussion to Approval by the General Assembly*, 3 Pepp. Disp. Resol. L.J. 529 (2003).
32. Eric D. Green, *Settling Large Case Litigation: An Alternative Approach*, 11 Loyola L.A. L. Rev. 493 (1978). *See also*, Thomas J. Klitgaard & William E. Mussman III, *High Technology Disputes: The Minitrial as the Emerging Solution*, 8 Santa Clara High Tech. L. J. 1 (1992); Lewis D. Barr, *Whose Dispute Is This Anyway: The Propriety of the Mini-Trial in Promoting Corporate Dispute Resolution*, 1987 J. Disp. Resol. 133.

presentations of the cases to a senior executive from each of the companies involved. Under normal ground rules, that executive attends on condition that he/she have full settlement authority in the dispute. In other words, the executives present must be capable of coming to an agreement on the spot when the minitrial concludes. Frequently, the executives will enlist the help of some third party such as a retired judge who is commonly referred to as a "neutral advisor," to help them understand and evaluate the factual presentations and the legal issues involved. The proceeding is conducted in a private setting (i.e., confidentiality is enforced), without a record, under informal rules of procedure and without rules of evidence, and is nonbinding. Once the presentations are concluded, the executives sit down together either by themselves or in the presence of the neutral advisor and negotiate a settlement of the dispute.

Note the advantages to this procedure. The delay factor caused by court congestion is eliminated. The parties work out their own schedule. The expense and agony of a lengthy trial is eliminated by three components of the minitrial procedure: the summary presentations, the lack of an excessive number of formal rules of procedure, and the absence of rules of evidence. To the extent that the executives have to be educated on the legal issues of the case, they are educated by the neutral adviser, presumably a person with some degree of expertise and prestige. Confidentiality is usually assured, and if things blow up in the parties' faces, they may move into binding arbitration or litigation without having made any damaging formal and public concessions on any of the issues. Most importantly, the presentations are made to, and the ultimate decision made by, two persons with the requisite authority to commit their companies to the settlement. In other words, a draft agreement does not have to be cleared through successive echelons of a corporate structure long after the minitrial has been completed.

§8.6.2 Specific Minitrial Rules

For persons interested in utilizing the minitrial, a short description of two typical rules systems may be helpful. One of the first sets of minitrial rules was promulgated by the Zurich Chamber of Commerce (Switzerland) in October 1984. Described by the Chamber as an "attractive fourth route," the rules were: (a) compared with arbitration which was explained as being perhaps too "cumbersome and expensive;" (b) were seen as preferable to mere negotiations by senior executives who may be insufficiently briefed when they enter a conventional negotiation; and (c) as an improvement over mediation which the Chamber of Commerce drafters believed is too "unstructured and unpredictable."

A Zurich minitrial is commenced in much the same way as an UNCITRAL mediation. One of the parties to a dispute files a petition with the Zurich Chamber of Commerce and sends a copy of the petition to the opposing party.[33] Once the opposing party is notified and has consented to the procedure, the two parties designate "a member of their senior management" as associate members of the minitrial panel. The

33. Zurich Mini-Trial Rules, Rule 3.

two associate members either agree on the appointment of one "neutral person" as an umpire for the proceeding or the Zurich Chamber of Commerce will appoint an umpire.[34] After the minitrial panel is fully constituted the umpire directs the parties (who may be represented by lawyers, although lawyers are not obligatory) to file written statements of their claims in a document not to exceed twenty-five typewritten pages. These statements are exchanged, and one reply document for each party is permitted in response to the statement of claims.[35]

Once the paperwork is exchanged, usually under a thirty-day deadline, the panel convenes and essentially works out its own rules of procedure. As Rule 11 states: "[The panel] may invite the parties to plead orally, to attend meetings or to clarify the facts further in writing. It may also request information from knowledgeable third parties." Then the panel discusses the dispute with the parties orally at what the rule describes as "meetings," which may take more than one day.

After these presentations, the panel may simply assist the parties in drafting a settlement agreement or may recommend the terms of an agreement if the panel is unanimous. If the panel is not unanimous, the umpire is permitted to draft and recommend an agreement. The rules further provide that all information is to be confidential and most importantly, "[f]or the duration of the Minitrial the parties shall be deemed to have waived their rights to submit the ... dispute to the ordinary courts or to an arbitral tribunal or to continue judicial or arbitral proceedings ... unless, in their opinion, the taking of such action is critical in order to avoid applicable limitation statutes or in order to preserve rights which would otherwise be endangered."[36]

The AAA rules are patterned closely on the Zurich rules with only slight shifts in vocabulary. For example, the presiding officer is called the "neutral advisor" rather than the umpire, and rules of evidence are expressly prohibited. If the senior executives on the panel cannot agree, the neutral advisor is required to "render an advisory opinion as to the likely outcome of the case if it were litigated in a court of law. The neutral advisor's opinion shall identify the issues of law and fact which are critical to the disposition of the case and give the reasons for the opinion is offered."[37]

§8.6.3 Minitrials in the Future

The proponents of minitrials view the process as one that is particularly suited for breaking a negotiation impasse. Note that the presence of the senior executives is crucial to a successful outcome. At least some cost savings are realized through the element of speed and the relaxation of rules of judicial procedure and evidence. Among other things, a minitrial directs the panel's attention to crucial issues of law and fact that lie at the heart of the dispute rather than spending endless amounts of time arguing about and briefing issues on the periphery of the problem.

34. *Id.*, Rule 5.
35. *Id.*, Rule 9.
36. *Id.*, Rule 13.
37. AAA Mini-Trial Rules, Rule 12.

At the same time, not all commercial disputes are suitable for a minitrial. Some recent experience in the United States suggests that a minitrial might be most efficient after litigation has commenced—that is, after the parties have developed a fair amount of the factual basis for the case and after the legal issues have been carefully identified. This, of course, makes the minitrial a kind of court-annexed dispute resolution process, a development that does not appear to have been envisioned by the drafters of the Zurich and AAA rules. Further, minitrials are not necessarily cheap. While none of the rules systems require the presence of lawyers it is clear, at least in the United States, that lawyers will drive the system even if the executives make the final decision. If a minitrial is used mainly as an intermediate step in litigation, parties will not be able to avoid many of the costs associated with such things as discovery and pretrial motions. Finally, much like all the other less-drastic dispute resolution devices if a minitrial breaks down, the parties must still resort to some other forum, thus duplicating a fair amount of time and effort.

At the same time, the device has a distinct appeal for commercial disputes. In the words of Professor Green, "the minitrial process [reconverts] into a business problem what has often been transformed by the litigation process into a technical, lawyers' fight."[38] Most importantly, the dispute is in the hands of executives who are experienced at cutting through chaff, at making difficult decisions and "who often are better able than the legal representatives to assess the strategic risks and overall importance of the case to the client."[39] All of these characteristics make it an exceptionally inviting form of dispute resolution, but one whose future is not yet assured.

38. Eric D. Green, *The CPR Mini-Trial Handbook*, in *Corporate Dispute Management* (1982).
39. *Id.*

CHAPTER 9

Commencing Arbitration, the Arbitration Hearing, and the Arbitral Award

§9.1 INTRODUCTION

Arbitration is almost always the dispute resolution device of choice among parties entering into international commercial agreements. Unfortunately, many contracting parties blithely drop a standard form arbitration clause into an agreement without paying much attention to its consequences and frequently without understanding fully the nature of international commercial arbitration. To begin with, arbitration is voluntary in nature; the parties must agree to arbitrate.[1] That agreement must be found either in the original contract or in a subsequent agreement. An agreement to submit a commercial dispute to arbitration puts the resolution of the dispute into the hands of a third party, either a single arbitrator or a panel of three arbitrators. Arbitration is similar to litigation in that it contains many elements of the adversary process—particularly as orchestrated by lawyers from the United States and it is, at least in theory, final and binding on the parties.[2] In this last respect, it differs materially from the less-drastic forms of dispute resolution such as mediation/conciliation, minitrial, and renegotiation.

1. The traditional assumption has always been that arbitration is purely voluntary and requires consent of both parties. But that assumption may be changing. *See* Gilles Cuniberti, *Rethinking International Commercial Arbitration: Towards Default Arbitration* (2017).
2. The list of superb book-length studies of international commercial arbitration continues to grow as we move toward the third decade of the twenty-first century. Among these are: Margaret L. Moses, *The Principles and Practice of International Commercial Arbitration* (3d ed.,2017); Giudetta Cordero-Moss, *International Commercial Arbitration: Different Forms and Their Features* (2013); William W. Park, *Arbitration of International Business Disputes: Studies in Law and Practice* (2012); Gary B. Born, *International Arbitration: Law and Practices* (2015); Julian D.M. Lew, *Comparative International Commercial Arbitration* (2003); Constantine Partasides & Nigel Blackaby, Redfern & Hunteron *International Arbitration* (6th ed., 2015). For a slightly different, albeit American viewpoint *see*, Jack J. Coe, Jr., *International Commercial Arbitration: American*

The arbitration process has some singular advantages. Because arbitration avoids the courts and court congestion, it can sometimes be speedier than litigation. Arbitration is normally confidential, so two disputing companies do not have to worry about revealing important trade secrets in a public courtroom. The arbitrator is usually an expert in the industry or the transaction concerned, a factor that not only increases the speed of the decisional process since the arbitrator usually does not need nearly as much educating as a judge, but also promotes a technically sound decision. For international commercial transactions, an arbitration hearing held in a neutral country before unbiased arbitrators goes a long way toward alleviating the problems of prejudice and unfairness occasionally encountered in local courts. Finally, because of a treaty—The New York Convention on the Recognition and Enforcement of Foreign Arbitral Awards—an arbitral award issued in one country can often be enforced against the losing party in many other countries.[3] There is no transnational equivalent for litigation outcomes.

Although arbitration is not subject to the myriad technical rules of litigation, it is nevertheless a rules-based decisional process. While simpler in text and direction than typical rules of litigation, arbitration rules can be cumbersome. Because arbitration can be difficult to administer, international commercial arbitrations are usually subject to the supervision of one of the major arbitration institutions such as the International Chamber of Commerce (ICC), the London Court of Arbitration, or the American Arbitration Association (AAA). Because governments recognize arbitration as a good device for resolving disputes, virtually all countries have established some form of underlying law that guides arbitration and permits the use of that country's courts to deal with certain prearbitral problems, to compel arbitration, or to enforce arbitral awards. Through various treaties, principally the New York Convention on the Recognition and Enforcement of Arbitral Awards (*see* Chapter 10) many countries have agreed to honor arbitral awards even when the arbitral award is made in another country.

Moreover, the United Nations takes arbitration quite seriously. Over twenty years ago, the United Nations Commission on International Trade Law (UNCITRAL) promulgated a first-rate set of procedural rules for arbitration. In 1985, in one of the most promising developments on the international scene, UNCITRAL adopted a Model Law on International Commercial Arbitration—which, if adopted by all or most of the members of the UN, is proving to be the one of most significant developments in the history of international commercial dispute resolution.

Arbitration is not free of defects, however. For many disputing parties, it may be far less satisfactory from a procedural standpoint (there is very little discovery permitted in arbitration, e.g.) and far less final than litigation (disgruntled parties to arbitration occasionally try to string things out in court after the arbitration is

Principles and Practice in a Global Context (1997). Other distinguished works that are well worth consulting are: Christian Buhring-Uhe, *Arbitration and Mediation in International Business* (1996); Yves Dezalay & Bryant G. Garth, *Dealing in Virtue: International Commercial Arbitration and the Construction of a Transnational Legal Order* (1996).

3. *See* the discussion in Chapter 10, *infra*.

concluded). For example, one prominent arbitration proceeding in the United States involved a complicated contract for the construction by Condec Corporation of aluminum liquefied natural gas containers for Kaiser Aluminum. The parties had signed an agreement containing what has been described as a "limited" arbitration clause that attempted to identify only a small number of issues that would be subject to arbitration. Any issues not specified in the arbitration clause were to be disposed of only in court. In theory, it is permissible for parties to segregate issues into two separate categories: arbitration and court. But in practice, segregation of issues is extremely difficult. In the Condec arbitration the haggling over the issues proved to be almost endless. Condec eventually won a USD 25.5 million award (USD 12 million of which was interest). However, that victory came only after Condec spent eight years in both arbitration and court; after the record grew to more than 30,000 pages of transcript, 5,000 exhibits, 2,500 hearing days and a 600-page final opinion; and after Condec had incurred around USD 350,000 in arbitration costs and paid around USD 5 million in legal fees. Satirizing an earlier AAA announcement boosting arbitration as a "speedy" and "economical" alternative to litigation (no longer the AAA's position), one writer described Condec-style arbitration as, "the slower, more expensive alternative."[4]

The absence of a lot of procedural detail in typical arbitration rules often cause problems for lawyers schooled in litigation techniques. Lawyers in the United States who are comfortable in the highly structured and highly proceduralized setting of U.S.-style litigation often find international commercial arbitration highly disconcerting. In one case involving a protracted arbitration under the much looser rules of the ICC, an American lawyer lamented:

> There was no transcript, and the arbitrators resisted any sort of transcript. There was really no record of the proceedings that had gone before, even though there had been well over one hundred hearing days. There were little blue books, like we use for [law school] exams here in the States, in which the [previous counsel, British] barristers had taken notes in a microscopic script that was indecipherable by anyone I knew of, including the barristers [themselves]....Our predecessors had not prepared any witnesses for our case, and the first problem I was confronted with was the need to cross-examine [the opposing party's] last two witnesses for approximately 30 days each.[5]

These two horror stories are not necessarily typical of all international commercial arbitration, but they do serve to illustrate some of the disadvantages of arbitration. Arbitration is a good device for resolving disputes; but it is not a panacea, and it is definitely not free of defects.

4. John Lyons, *Arbitration: The Slower, More Expensive Alternative?* Am. Law. (January/February 1985), 107.
5. Statement of Robert Wallace, Esq., in the District Lawyer (publication of the Washington, D.C. bar) (November/December 1985) at 49–50. For a more academic discussion of a number of problems associated with international commercial arbitration *see*, James M. Rhodes & Lisa Sloan, *The Pitfalls of International Commercial Arbitration*, 17 Vand. J. Transnat'l L. 19 (1984). For an excellent guide to many of the issues of advocacy that arise in arbitration *see* R. Doak Bishop & Edward G. Kehoe, *The Art of Advocacy in International Arbitration* (2d ed., 2010).

Of course, one cannot ignore the continuing discussion of whether arbitration has now become too much like court. Concerns are constantly raised without a lot of definitive answers. Many now worry about the "judicialization" of arbitration.[6] One reaction to this has been the development of "expedited" arbitration processes (discussed below) and there is fresh discussion of the use of artificial intelligence (AI) techniques in arbitration (discussed below). The arbitral institutions themselves are beginning to take a pro-active approach to some of these criticisms.[7] But most commentators, as we near the third decade of the twenty-first century, believe as do Professors Trakman and Montgomery:

> [B]alancing party autonomy, accountability, efficiency, and fairness in [international commercial arbitration] can help resolve these growing criticisms of "judicialization." Ultimately, the reform of international arbitration should take place within a framework of 'international best practice' that is both analytical in nature and functional in operation. As such, [international commercial arbitration] should not only be affordable and expeditious, it should serve as a legitimate and effective method of resolving international commercial disputes. In addition, it should balance the virtue of transparent proceedings against the need to respect the confidences of the parties.... [A]ttempts to address the cost and length of arbitration proceedings ought not to undermine the value of finely reasoned arbitral decisions grounded in law and justice.[8]

On these broad, conceptual issues, the reader may profitably review this chapter and others and come to his or her own conclusions.

This chapter concentrates on the major international commercial arbitration rules systems and on the arbitration hearing process including an examination of how arbitral awards are drafted. Chapter 10 is an intensive examination of the role of the courts in arbitration and Chapter 11 analyzes some important regional and national peculiarities of commercial arbitration for those readers whose interest focuses on, say, Latin America or the Pacific Rim. Chapter 11 should not be reviewed closely because in some countries a private agreement to arbitrate may not be honored. For example, Saudi Arabian contracts involving petroleum may not be arbitrated outside Saudi Arabia. When contracts involving China mention arbitration, the Chinese parties normally require some type of mediation before any arbitration takes place in part because the Chinese find arbitration too adversarial in nature. Readers who are reading this chapter and Chapters 10 and 11 prior to drafting an international commercial agreement should also review Chapter 4.

---

6. *See*, e.g., Leon Trakman & Hugh Montgomery, *The "Judicialization" of International Commercial Arbitration: Pitfall or Virtue?* 30 Leiden J. Int'l L. 405 (2017); Remy Gerbay, *Is the End Nigh Again? An Empirical Assessment of the "Judicialization" of International Arbitration*, 25 Am. Rev. of Int'l Arb. 223 (2014); W. Matti & Thomas Dietz, *International Arbitration and Global Governance: Contending Theories and Evidence* (2014); Thomas Stipanowich, *Reflections on the State and Future of Arbitration: Challenges, Opportunities, Proposals*, Legal Studies Research Papers No. 29 (2014); Thomas Stipanowich, *Arbitration: The "New" Litigation*, 49 U. Ill. L. Rev. 1 (2010); Christopher R. Drahozal, *Disenchanted? Business Satisfaction with International Arbitration*, 2 World Arb. & Med. Rev. 5 (2008).
7. *See*, e.g., International Chamber of Commerce, *Techniques for Controlling Time and Costs in Arbitration*, ICC Pub. No. 861-1 (2015).
8. Trakman & Montgomery, *supra* n. 6, abstract.

For readers new to arbitration as a dispute resolution process, a brief overview and an introduction to some basic arbitration vocabulary may be helpful. Arbitration is normally triggered when parties to a commercial agreement encounter a dispute that they cannot resolve by less-drastic means. Arbitration is not permissible unless both parties have agreed to arbitrate. That agreement is set out either as an arbitration clause in the original contract or in the form of a subsequent agreement to arbitrate signed by the parties. On occasion, parties agree to arbitrate after a dispute arises and when other, less-drastic means have failed to resolve their differences.

The language of the arbitration clause establishes many of the terms and conditions of the arbitration. Although some traditional arbitration clauses are excessively wordy, there are certain minimum requirements for an acceptable clause. The simplest form of arbitration clause provides that any dispute arising under the contract will be subject to arbitration under the rules and supervision of some institution (such as the AAA or ICC) in a particular place (the forum or site of the arbitration hearing). Parties are always free to administer their own arbitration, thus avoiding the fees and administrative delays involved in dealing with one of the arbitral institutions. If the parties conduct the proceeding on their own, the process is called *ad hoc arbitration*. If the parties elect to have one of the arbitration organizations such as the AAA or the Japan Commercial Arbitration Association supervise the arbitration, the process is referred to as *institutional arbitration*.

However, ad hoc arbitration is not for beginners; it should be elected only by parties who have previous experience with arbitration who feel confident of their own ability to manage a procedure that can become extraordinarily complicated. The major arbitral institutions contribute a large administrative staff, preprinted forms, long and carefully screened lists of potential arbitrators and a lengthy institutional memory that can frequently be invoked to help the parties avoid many problems.

While some contracting parties may simply insert a standard form arbitration clause and then rely on the rules of the supervising arbitral institution to flesh out the terms and conditions of the arbitration, large-scale contracts between sophisticated companies usually set out additional details in the arbitration clause such as: the number of arbitrators, the credentials of the arbitrators, the manner in which the arbitrators are to be appointed, the language of the arbitration, whether the arbitrators can use equitable decisional principles to resolve the dispute (the concept of *amiable compositeur*), the courts to which the parties will resort for either compelling arbitration or enforcing the award and other matters.

When a dispute arises, the party who wishes to arbitrate will send a notice to that effect to the opposing party. This document was traditionally referred to as the "demand" for arbitration. Most contemporary arbitration systems now refer to the document as the "request" for arbitration. If the other party agrees to arbitrate, it usually files a written reply, the answer, and may append a counterclaim to the answer. As soon as this initial paperwork is exchanged, the remainder of the arbitration process can go forward. These papers are usually short and simple declarations. Many of the arbitration institutions such as the AAA provide preprinted, fill-in-the-blank forms for both request, answer and counterclaim. The ICC does not provide preprinted forms for the request, but suggests that at a minimum the request include the full names, descriptions and addresses of the parties, the statement of the claimant's case, copies of the relevant agreements, information on the number of arbitrators and proposals for the appointment of particular arbitrators. The ICC request for arbitration must be accompanied by a payment of money as an advance on the ICC's administrative costs; otherwise, the ICC will not begin processing the arbitration.[9]

If the other party resists the request, the party seeking arbitration may be forced into an appropriate court for a court order to compel arbitration. Similarly, the responding party may attempt to block the arbitration by filing, with an appropriate court, a request to stay the arbitration. The possibility of having to bring an action to compel or to respond to an action to stay is one of the Achilles heels of arbitration. Long after the parties have agreed to arbitration by signing a contract containing an arbitration clause, a resisting party may be able to delay the proceedings by forcing an action to compel or bringing an action to stay. In most jurisdictions the courts will act quickly to order the parties to arbitrate, but such an order can occasionally be taken up on appeal, delaying matters even further. Many parties who thought an arbitration clause would let them arbitrate their dispute quickly and efficiently find themselves involved in protracted litigation in court merely to determine whether the arbitration should commence.

If the parties have selected an institution to assist with the arbitration, many of the details of the proceeding will be taken care of by that institution including, for example, providing forms for the request identifying and, on occasion, selecting arbitrators, and transmitting various documents between the parties. This work is not free, of course. The arbitration institutions perform their administrative functions only after the party initiating the arbitration pays the proper administrative fee.

The jurisprudence of arbitration is beyond the scope of this book. But any analysis of the underpinnings of arbitration should begin with an analysis of a number of theories, sometimes referred to as juridical bases for arbitration that have been described by a preeminent European arbitrator, Julian Lew. Professor Lew identifies four theories, or juridical bases, for arbitration that provide a good understanding of the jurisprudential roots of arbitration: (1) the jurisdictional theory (arbitration springs from the sovereignty of nations and their authority to prescribe methods of dispute resolution within their boundaries) exemplified by arbitration legislation in the various countries; (2) the contractual theory (arbitration springs from the freedom of contract established for private parties in many countries) demonstrated by the fact that arbitration is largely a matter of agreement between private parties under the umbrella of a nation's legal system; (3) the hybrid theory (arbitration really has elements of both sovereignty and contract); and (4) the autonomous theory (a relatively new idea that arbitration is really a creature unto itself and fits squarely within none of the older theories).[10]

9. ICC, Rules of Arbitration, Appendix III, Art. 1(1). The ICCs rules are available either for purchase or on the ICC's website: www.iccwbo.org.
10. Julian D.M. Lew, *The Applicable Law in International Commercial Arbitration* 51–61 (1978). For additional guidance on the jurisprudence of arbitration *see*, e.g., George A. Bermann, *International Arbitration and Private International Law (Hague Academy of International Law* (2017); Emmanuel Gaillard, *Legal Theory of International Arbitration* (2010).

The arbitration process has five stages: (1) the exchange of the initial paperwork (request and answer); (2) the selection of the arbitrator or arbitrators; (3) preparation for the arbitration hearing (a process that may involve the gathering of facts and documents as well as the preparation of witnesses); (4) the arbitration hearing; and (5) the issuing of the arbitrator's decision—a document called the *arbitral award*. If the losing party abides by the terms of the award, the dispute is concluded when the losing party pays the amount of the award to the winning party. However, if the award is ignored by the losing party, the winning party may be forced to enter a court of law to have the award implemented through the judicial process of recognition and enforcement. The enforcement of arbitral awards in some jurisdictions may involve the process of confirmation—a judicial procedure by which the award is effectively converted into a court judgment. If a court agrees to enforce the award, the losing party usually complies because a refusal to abide by a court judgment exposes the losing party to various types of judicial sanctions such as contempt of court.

§9.2 A BRIEF HISTORY OF COMMERCIAL ARBITRATION

Some form of the arbitration process may be found even in the earliest societies. Professor Peter Stein has noted a rudimentary form of arbitration in ancient Athens, with commercial arbitration in disputes involving large sums of money subject to institutional arbitration as early as 403 B.C.[11] The process he describes is even now instantly recognizable as what we might call a form of "mediation/arbitration" with only a limited opportunity for judicial review: "[A]ll civil cases involving substantial sums were sent first to an arbitrator. If he was unable to bring the parties to a settlement [a rudimentary form of mediation], he heard witnesses and tried the case [arbitration]. His decision could be appealed to the popular court [judicial review], but only on the basis of the arbitrator's record, and new evidence could not be admitted [on judicial review]."[12]

Some of the modern trappings of arbitration spring from an exceptionally harsh principle of Roman law that in the first instance did not recognize freedom of contract and in the second instance gave no legal force or effect to the decision of an arbitrator. However, as Professor Rene David notes, private parties in Rome were able to circumvent some these difficulties by framing a double promise (eventually known as a *com-promissum*) by which the parties mutually agreed to arbitrate and to pay a penalty if the arbitration were not honored. A reviewing court would then examine not the arbitration, but only the existence of the double promise.[13]

11. Peter Stein, *Legal Institutions: The Development of Dispute Settlement* (1984), 17.
12. *Id.*, at 17–18.
13. Rene David, *Arbitration in International Trade* (1985), 84. The English version of Professor David's book is a translation of *Arbitrage dans le Commerce International*. For additional guidance, *see*, e.g., Alec Stone Sweet & Florian Grisel, *The Evolution of International Arbitration: Judicialization, Governance, Legitimacy* (2017); Leon Trakman, *From the Medieval to the Twenty First Century Law Merchant*, 28 Am. Bus. L.J. 775 (2011); Leon Trakman, *Legal Traditions and International Commercial Arbitration*, 17 Am. Rev. of Int'l Arb. 1 (2007).

Those same Renaissance merchants who gave the world the substantive law that we now refer to as *lex mercatoria* (the law merchant) because their trade crossed international boundaries and required uniform principles of commercial dealing also worked out forms of arbitration because their transnational dealings could not be suitably dealt with in domestic courts. Court procedures were rudimentary; justice was frequently arbitrary; the judges were not particularly skilled in commercial disputes; and prejudice in favor of the local party was commonplace. Additionally, workable principles of commercial law did not exist in many countries. For all these reasons, the merchants simply did not trust the courts to render reasonable decisions. The merchants set up their own system of arbitration as an alternative to the courts.

In addition, the merchants took an important concept of commercial arbitration, the doctrine of *amiable compositeur*, and grafted it onto the process of arbitration. When the parties have agreed to the principle of *amiable compositeur*, the arbitrator is permitted either to render a decision within established legal principles, or—growing out of his role as a mediator (in Latin, *amicabilis compositor*)—to work out a just and equitable solution (sometimes referred to as Solomonic justice) and to impose that decision on the parties.[14]

In the United States, arbitration caught on quickly in the business community. Even before the turn of the century, business people in New York City developed sophisticated arbitration schemes because the courts were crowded and because arbitration institutionalized under the auspices of the New York Chamber of Commerce gave them more control over the process (and over their consumer opponents) than they might have had in court.[15]

These developments were not without their detractors, of course. English courts, in particular, exhibited a significant degree of hostility to arbitration as did certain courts in the United States. This hostility—usually exhibited as a disdain for arbitration and an inclination simply to ignore arbitral awards—was based on the idea that a court was not obligated to recognize any dispute resolution mechanism that ousted the courts of jurisdiction over that dispute. The overt hostility of the judiciary severely weakened both domestic and international arbitration. As a consequence, many legislatures began to get into the act. One of the major developments in modern international commercial arbitration has been the enactment of statutes and the ratification of treaties that make arbitration a recognized and legitimate process and

14. David, *supra* n. 13, at 87. For some good recent discussion of *lex mercatoria* and *amiable compositeur see*, Christopher R. Drahozal, *Contracting Out of the Uniform Commercial Code: Is Arbitration Lawless?* 40 Loy. L.A. L. Rev. 187 (2006); Christopher R. Drahozal, *An Empirical Look at the New Law Merchant*, 80 Notre Dame L. Rev. 523 (2005); Ning Jin, *The Status of Lex Mercatoria in International Commercial Arbitration*, 7 Am. Rev. Int'l Arb. 163 (1996); Karyn S. Weinberg, *Equity in International Arbitration: How Fair is "Fair"? A Study of Lex Mercatoria and Amiable Composition*, 12 B.U. Int'l L.J. 227 (1994). For additional commentary *see* Regis Bonnan, *Different Conceptions of Amiable Composition in International Commercial Arbitration: A Comparison in Space and Time*, 6 J. Int'l Dis. Settle. 522 (2015); Leon Trakman, *Ex Aequo et Bono: De-mystifying an Ancient Concept*, 8 Chi. J. Int'l L. 621 (2008); A.F.M. Maniruzzaman, *The Arbitrator's Prudence in Lex Mercatoria: Amiable Composition and Ex Aequo Et Bono in Decision Making*, 18 Mealey's Int'l Arb. Report 1 (2003).
15. Jerold S. Auerbach, *Justice without Law? Resolving Disputes without Lawyers* 101–102 (1983).

that minimize interference and second-guessing on the part of the courts. For example, in the United States, all fifty states have an arbitration act and Congress has enacted the Federal Arbitration Act.[16] In the United Kingdom one of the major recent breakthroughs in arbitration was Parliament's enactment of the 1979 Arbitration Act—a statute that "drastically reduced the supervisory powers of the English courts over arbitrations."[17] In 1981, France enacted a powerful statute limiting the manner in which a French court may interfere with an international commercial arbitration award.[18] Virtually all of the major trading nations have similar provisions and in most instances arbitration is fairly well insulated from judicial intervention.

Even the courts are beginning to recognize the legitimacy of the arbitration process. In two striking decisions by the United States Supreme Court issued slightly over ten years apart, the Court has moved from something of an interventionist court historically to a court that lets arbitration alone. In the first case, *Scherk v. Alberto-Culver Co.*,[19] a U.S. company bought several businesses and certain trademark rights from a German citizen. The contract, signed in Austria, contained a standard form arbitration clause providing for arbitration in Paris under the rules of the ICC. The U.S. purchaser disputed some of the trademark rights and brought an action in a United States federal court alleging that the seller had violated U.S. securities law and arguing that such securities violations were not arbitrable in the United States.

However, the Supreme Court disagreed with this proposition. The Court issued an opinion ordering the U.S. buyer to arbitrate under the terms of the arbitration clause. The Court reasoned that the sanctity of arbitration clauses must be preserved because a substantial degree of certainty and predictability in international contracts is important for American business. In the 1985 decision, *Mitsubishi v. Soler*,[20] the Supreme Court decided that a standard form arbitration clause encompasses even disputes under a contract involving potential violations of U.S. antitrust laws. There the parties had signed an agreement calling for arbitration in Tokyo under the rules of the Japan Commercial Arbitration Association. The Court concluded that it would not be impossible to find arbitrators in Japan who knew something about U.S. antitrust law; and, if enforcement of an award were ever sought in the United States, a U.S. court could review the award to insure that it did not do violence to U.S. antitrust doctrine. In *Vimar Seguros y Reseguros v. M/V Sky Reefer*,[21] the U.S. Supreme Court applied the *Mitsubishi* doctrine to a standard form bill of lading (what is normally referred to as a *contract of adhesion*) that contained an arbitration clause requiring arbitration in Tokyo under the rules of the Japan Maritime Arbitration Commission.

---

16. 9 U.S.C. §§1–14.
17. Johan Steyn, *Arbitration in England*, in *International Handbook on Commercial Arbitration: National Reports, Basic Legal Texts* (P. Sanders ed., 1984).
18. Decree of May 12, 1981, Noveau Code de Procedure Civile; for an authoritative commentary on this statute *see*, Georges R. Delaume, *International Arbitration Under French Law: The Decree of May 12, 1981*, 37 Arb. J. 38 (1982).
19. 417 U.S. 506 (1974).
20. 473 U.S. 614 (1985).
21. 515 U.S. 528 (1995).

Mitsubishi and its progeny have been read by many as making the U.S. Supreme Court almost totally noninterventionist in matters subject to arbitration.[22] At the moment, possibly the only large category of issues that may not be subject to arbitration are certain violations of U.S. civil rights laws—a matter rarely encountered in international commercial contracts. Many other national courts take similar positions.[23] *Mitsubishi* has prompted some contract drafters to attempt drafting elaborate arbitration clauses that try to distinguish between arbitrable and nonarbitrable issues; but these maneuvers are highly dangerous and almost always lead to more problems and delays. The basic message of *Mitsubishi* is plain and should not be disregarded. When a U.S. party signs a contract containing a standard arbitration clause, any dispute under that contract will be subject to arbitration.

§9.3 THE STATUTORY BASIS FOR ARBITRATION

The difficulty of looking to courts for support and assistance in conducting arbitration is that courts move slowly and without a great deal of predictability—that is, there is no special guarantee that a particular national court system will not continue to be hostile to the idea of arbitration. Consequently, there is more wisdom and efficiency in the use of legislation to tidy up international commercial arbitration.

It is impossible in a book of this length to analyze or even discuss every piece of arbitration legislation, but there is some merit in briefly examining three different statutes, the United States' Federal Arbitration Act, the relatively new 1996 Arbitration Act in Great Britain and, one of the most important recent developments in the entire area of international commercial arbitration, the United Nations Model Law on International Commercial Arbitration.

§9.3.1 The Federal Arbitration Act

The Federal Arbitration Act,[24] enacted in 1924, governs interstate and maritime transactions in the United States and provides a solid statutory base that clearly

22. *See*, e.g., William Fox, *Mitsubishi v. Soler and Its Impact on International Commercial Arbitration*, 19 J. World Trade L. 579 (1985).
23. Professor Carbonneau believes that the French courts take a noninterventionist position regarding international commercial transactions while remaining somewhat interventionist when it comes to domestic arbitration. *See*, Thomas E. Carbonneau, *The Elaboration of a French Court Doctrine on International Commercial Arbitration: A Study in Liberal Civilian Judicial Creativity*, 55 Tul. L. Rev. 1 (1980); *see also*, Arthur T. von Mehren, *International Commercial Arbitration: The Contribution of the French Jurisprudence*, 46 La. L. Rev. 1045 (1986).
24. 9 U.S.C. §§1-14. Readers should be aware that this edition goes to press in 2017, the Federal Arbitration Act has been proposed for extensive revision but so far Congess has not accomplished much of anything. In the United States, the principal issue is whether arbitration can properly protect the interests of consumers, employees and others who must sign contracts of adhesion containing mandatory arbitration clauses—and the derivative issue of whether arbitration supplants class-action litigation for small amount consumer disputes. These issues are beyond the scope of this book but a great deal of insight can be gleaned from, for example, Jeremy McManus, *A Motion to Compel Changes to Federal Arbitration Law: How to Remedy the Abuses Consumers Face When Arbitrating Disputes*, 37 B.C. J.L. & Soc. Just. 177 (2017).

establishes the legitimacy of arbitration. Indeed, the United States Supreme Court in cases such as *Mitsubishi v. Soler* invoke it frequently as a statement from the United States Congress that arbitration is a proper and respected form of dispute resolution. The act begins by making arbitration clauses in contracts generally enforceable and irrevocable "save upon such grounds as exist at law or in equity for the revocation of any contract."[25] It then permits the federal courts to stay any attempt by a party to litigate the dispute when an arbitration clause is applicable and permits the federal courts to compel arbitration in appropriate cases.[26] The *Mitsubishi* case, for example, went up to the Supreme Court as an action brought by Mitsubishi in federal court to compel Soler to arbitrate the dispute. In instances of ad hoc arbitration in the United States, the act permits a court to appoint an arbitrator, provides the arbitrator with subpoena power to "summon in writing any person to attend before [the arbitrator]...as a witness and in a proper case to bring with him...any [documents]...which may be deemed material as evidence in the case." Any failure to abide by an arbitrator's subpoena may be litigated in federal court and the person failing to honor the subpoena may be subject to contempt of court proceedings.[27]

The act goes on to provide for the recognition and confirmation of arbitral awards in court and to severely limit the grounds on which a reviewing court may overturn an award. The grounds for overturning an award are interpreted narrowly (i.e., a court has very little authority to vacate awards) and include: (a) when the award was procured by fraud or undue influence; (b) when the arbitrator was guilty of various types of misconduct such as refusal to hear pertinent evidence; and (c) when the arbitrator exceeded his power or wrote an incomplete award.[28]

Simply reciting the act's provisions conceals many of the major contributions made by the statute to the arbitration process in general. First, note that the statute was enacted in 1924, long before the alternative dispute bandwagon began rolling. Second, it minimizes—at least in theory—the manner in which a court may interrupt or interfere with the arbitration process. In an important U.S. Supreme Court decision, *Moses H. Cone Memorial Hospital v. Mercury Construction Corp.*,[29] the Court noted that the enactment of the federal act "is a congressional declaration of a liberal federal policy favoring arbitration agreements, notwithstanding any state substantive or procedural policies to the contrary....[Moreover, under the act] any doubts concerning the scope of arbitrable issues should be resolved in favor of arbitration, whether the problem at hand is the construction of the contract language itself or an allegation of waiver, delay or a like defense to arbitrability."[30] Thus, the act has assisted the

25. *Id.*, §2.
26. *Id.*, §§3, 4.
27. *Id.*, §7.
28. *Id.*, §§9, 10.
29. 460 U.S. 1 (1983).
30. *Id.*, at 19. Since the decision in Cone, the Supreme Court has continued to reaffirm the legitimacy of arbitration as an alternative to the courts. *Dean Witter Reynolds v. Byrd*, 470 U.S. 213 (1985) (the Federal Arbitration Act creates a presumption in favor of arbitration); *Shearson/American Express v. McMahon*, 482 U.S. 220 (1987) (domestic securities disputes are subject to arbitration clauses in the same fashion as the international contract at issue in Mitsubishi).

Supreme Court in its recent moves to enhance the credibility of arbitration and to urge disputing parties to try some dispute resolution mechanism apart from litigation.[31]

§9.3.2 The English Arbitration Act

As a major center of international commerce, London has had long experience with arbitration, but the history of arbitration in England for a long time was a pattern of unwarranted judicial intervention and, on occasion outright hostility to arbitral awards.[32] However, by the middle of the twentieth century, Parliament recognized that the arbitration process required modernization and enacted the Arbitration Act of 1950, a statute that codified and consolidated various legislation and that attempted to rationalize the entire process of arbitration. For example, section 1 of the 1950 Act made an arbitration clause irrevocable. Subsequent sections permitted a court to stay litigation if arbitration has been agreed to and to appoint arbitrators if the parties cannot agree. The arbitrator was given various powers to conduct the hearing and to fashion an award. In addition, the act permitted the arbitrator to issue subpoenas and to frame interim awards. Merely reading the 1950 Act, one might come away with the feeling that arbitral awards are generally free from judicial scrutiny.

Unfortunately, according to most observers, the Act contained two defects that made it far too easy for British courts to interfere in arbitration proceedings and to set aside arbitral awards. Indeed, one observer of the European arbitration scene determined while the 1950 Act was in place that the number of ICC arbitrations taking place in England was less than half the number sited in Switzerland and roughly one-third the number of arbitrations held in France.[33] A distinguished British jurist, Lord Hacking, was told by a lawyer from New York that New York firms believe that any lawyer who permits his client to sign a contract with an arbitration clause calling for arbitration in England was committing an act of professional malpractice.[34]

The perceived defects grew out of two practices under the 1950 Act: (i) the special case procedure (sometimes referred to as the stated case) by which arbitrators could be

---

31. For additional general commentary on arbitration in the U.S. *see*, Eric Bergsten, *The Americanization of International Arbitration*, 18 Pace Int'l L. Rev. 289 (2006); Christopher R. Drahozal, *New Experiences of International Arbitration in the United States*, 54 Am. J. Comp. L. 233 (2006); Kenneth F. Dunham, *International Arbitration Is Not Your Father's Oldsmobile*, 2005 J. Disp. Resol. 323 (2005); Alan Scott Rau, *The Culture of American Arbitration and the Lessons of ADR*, 40 Tex. Int'l L.J. 449 (2005); Hans Smit, *Elements of International Arbitration in the United States*, 1 Am. Rev. Int'l Arb. 64 (1990). For a somewhat leary view of international commercial arbitration *see*, Kevin T. Jacobs & Matthew G. Paulson, *The Convergence of Renewed Nationalization, Rising Commodities, and "Americanization" in International Arbitration and the Need for More Rigorous Legal and Procedural Defenses*, 43 Tex. Int'l L.J. 359 (2008).
32. International Handbook, *supra* n. 17, at 1 (England). Two fine compendia on English arbitration practice that include substantial information on the current posture of English arbitration are Julian D.M. Lew, H. Bor, G. Fullelove & Joanne Greenaway, *Arbitration in England Including Chapters on Scotland and the Republic of Ireland* (2013) and Andrew Tweeddale & Karen Tweeddale, *Arbitration Of Commercial Disputes: International And English Law And Practice* (2007).
33. Sigvard Jarvin, *London as a Place for International Arbitration*, 1 J.Int'l Arb. 59 (1985).
34. Lord Hacking, *Where We Are Now: Trends and Developments since the Arbitration Act (1979)*, 1 J.Int'l Arb. 9 (1985).

compelled by the High Court to submit various questions of law to the court for resolution; and (ii) the provision in the act that permitted the court to set aside an arbitral award for errors of law or fact apparent on the face of the award. The upshot of these two provisions gave England a reputation for being an exceptionally strong interventionist state, in which courts commonly set aside arbitral awards.

To counter this reputation and to strengthen the arbitration process generally, Parliament enacted the Arbitration Act of 1979, a statute that abolished both the stated case procedure and the prerogative of a court to overturn an award for factual and legal errors. The 1979 Act substituted a much simpler provision permitting an appeal to the High Court with leave of the Court, on questions of law.[35]

But even the 1979 Act was found lacking in many respects. Nearly twenty years later, the British Parliament enacted the Arbitration Act of 1996 to correct a number of deficiencies in the 1979 Act and to reinforce the idea that arbitration in England, Wales, and Northern Ireland has its own identify and reason for being separate from litigation and the judicial system. While too elaborate to set out here, a quick review of the "mandatory" provisions in the act reveals the underpinnings of a modern arbitration statute. Among many other things, the provisions cover immunity of arbitrators (section 29), the general duty of the arbitral tribunal (section 33), the general duty of the parties (section 40), obtaining the presence of witnesses (section 43), and enforcement of the award (section 66).[36] It is now clear that the 1996 arbitration act has given England a modern system of arbitration, largely free of arbitrary interference by the courts.

There is now a great deal of debate as the United Kingdom prepares to leave the European Union—a process colloquially referred to as *Brexit*. Some recent commentary suggests: "The full implications of Brexit for arbitration in the U.K. are being closely monitored by the industry, but it does not appear to have had any immediate impact. For a number of reasons, London remains a very attractive venue for parties to choose as a seat for arbitration. The London Court of Arbitration (LCIA) reported that non-UK parties accounted for more than 80% of its users in 2016."[37]

§9.3.3 The UNCITRAL Model Law on International Commercial Arbitration

The difficulties created by wide variances in the domestic arbitration law of various countries prompted UNCITRAL in the early 1970s to commence drafting a model law on arbitration that is probably one of the most important developments in the history of international commercial arbitration—the Model Law on International Commercial

35. Adam Samuel, *The 1979 Arbitration Act—Judicial Review of Arbitration Awards on the Merits in England,* 1 J.Int'l Arb. 53 (1985).
36. *See*, Okezie Chukwumerije, *English Arbitration Act 1966: Reform and Consolidation of English Arbitration Law,* 8 Am. Rev. Int'l Arb. 21 (1997). For an analysis of the manner in which English courts interpret and apply the New York Convention, *see*, May Lu, *The New York Convention on the Recognition and Enforcement of Foreign Arbitral Awards: Analysis of the Seven Defenses to Oppose Enforcement in the United States and England,* 23 Ariz. J. Int'l & Comp. L. 747 (2006).
37. Justin Williams, Hanmish Lal & Richard Hornshaw, *Arbitration Procedures and Practice in the UK: Overview* in *Thomas Reuters Practical Law* (2017).

Arbitration (discussed more fully in Chapter 11). The Model Law has become the domestic law of many countries. In recent years, it has even become the law of a number of states in the United States, including California, Florida, Connecticut, and Texas, each of which has aspirations to become a major site of international commercial arbitration.[38] The Model Law establishes a comprehensive framework for international commercial arbitration that preserves a substantial degree of party autonomy along with a modicum of sensitivity for a country's own institutions and legal system.

The Model Law is restricted on its terms to international commercial agreements but when we review the language of the individual provisions there seems to be no reason why most of its terms could not be used as the basis for a domestic arbitration law. The Model Law preserves party autonomy, insures fairness in the arbitration process, and seeks to minimize judicial intervention. There is occasional confusion on the part of first-time readers of the Model Law because any of its provisions are similar to the UNCITRAL rules on arbitration discussed below. The similarities are deliberate. The Model Law is intended to serve as the basis for national legislation in countries that have only rudimentary provisions governing arbitration. The UNCITRAL rules of arbitration may be applied at the election of the parties to a dispute even in countries with modern arbitration legislation.

The primary contribution of the Model Law is uniformity and equality of treatment. As it is adopted by more and more countries it has begun to legitimize arbitration as a premier international commercial dispute resolution mechanism. But even with the promulgation of the Model Law, many international commercial arbitration proceedings will be processed under domestic arbitration statutes that sometimes vary widely and trigger inconsistent results. On many occasions, inconsistencies and incongruities in domestic arbitration statutes can be smoothed out by the use of an international arbitration institution, using the institution's rules of procedure.[39]

§9.4 THE LEX LOCI ARBITRI AND "AD HOC" VERSUS "INSTITUTIONAL" ARBITRATION

One factor that all parties to an international commercial agreement must consider is the manner in which an arbitration will proceed and under whose body of law the arbitration will be administered. There are actually three issues here: (1) what body of substantive law will apply to the contract under dispute (this is *choice of law*, discussed

---

38. *See* the list of states and appropriate statutory citations in Jack Garvey & Tottob Heffelfinger, *Towards Federalizing U.S. International Commercial Arbitration Law*, 25 Int'l L. 209 (1991). For specific commentary on California's adoption of the Model Law *see*, Kenneth B. Wright, *California's International Commercial Arbitration Act*, 17 Int'l Bus. L. 45 (1989).

39. For excellent guidance on the UNCITRAL Model Law and the 2006 amendments *see*, e.g., Howard M. Holtzman & Joseph E. Neuhaus, *A Guide to the 2006 Amendments to the UNCITRAL Model Law on International Commercial Arbitration* (2015); Frederic Bachand & Fabien Gelinas, *The UNCITRAL Model Law After Twenty Five Years: Global Perspectives on International Commercial Arbitration* (2013).

extensively in Chapter 4); (2) which country's judicial system will supervise the arbitration and the enforcement of the arbitral award; and (3) which system of arbitration procedure will apply.

Choice of law is mainly a matter of party autonomy and is often stated expressly in the contract. One can find a choice of law clause as a free-standing provision in a contract or, on occasion, as a component of the dispute resolution clause. If the parties cannot themselves agree to a choice of law for the arbitration, the arbitrator has the power to impose a choice following internationally accepted choice of law rules.

Disputing parties must also confront issues two and three. Although a debate is currently in progress as to whether an arbitral award can survive if divorced from the law of the country in which it is made, most arbitration scholars concede that an arbitration needs a juridical "home." If an arbitration does not have such a home, crucial questions such as which courts supervise the arbitration or which judicial system might recognize and confirm the award may be very difficult to resolve and may hamper the entire proceeding because of these difficulties. There are times when parties to an arbitration must turn to an appropriate court for various types of interim relief, asking for, say, an injunction when one of the parties shows signs of transferring assets subject to the arbitration. An arbitrator may have the nominal power to grant interim relief, but *effective* enforcement of that relief may have to come only from a court order. When an arbitrator's subpoena is ignored, a party must resort to a court for subpoena enforcement. On occasion, when the parties cannot agree on the identity of the arbitrators, they must seek court appointment of the arbitration panel. As Professor William Park has put it, very succinctly: "Some legal system, therefore, must legitimize the arbitrator's authority. Otherwise, the award remains an unenforceable conciliation attempt that the parties are free to treat as mere foreplay to litigation."[40] Professor Park's frequent co-author, Jan Paulsson disagrees, arguing that an international commercial arbitral award may exist "without a specific legal system serving as its foundation."[41] The debate is fascinating and suitable for tomes on the jurisprudence of international commercial arbitration, but a safer, more conservative view is simply to concede that, generally speaking, an arbitration proceeding needs a juridical base and that base will be normally be the courts of the country in which the arbitration hearing takes place and in which the award is issued, even though the award may ultimately be enforced elsewhere.

The second major question is whether the parties are obliged to have the arbitration supervised by an arbitration institution such as the ICC or the AAA. These days, there is little question that the parties may proceed entirely on their own under a form of dispute resolution known as ad hoc *arbitration*. In ad hoc arbitration, the parties themselves work out the entire process and administer the arbitration without

40. William W. Park, *The Lex Loci Arbitri and International Commercial Arbitration*, 32 Int'l & Comp. L.Q. 21 (1983). For some wise commentary on many arbitration issues *see*, William W. Park, *Text and Context in International Dispute Resolution*, 15 B.U. Int'l L.J. 191 (1997). For some additional insights into this and related issues *see*, Loukas Mistelis, *Reality Test: Current State of Affairs in Theory and Practice Relating to "Lex Arbitri,"* 17 Am. Rev. Int'l Arb. 155 (2006).
41. Jan Paulsson, *Arbitration Unbound: An Award Detached from the Law of the Country of Origin*, 30 Int'l & Comp. L.Q. 358 (1981).

the assistance of an outside body. In ad hoc arbitration, the parties select the arbitrator, and choose the location of the arbitration, the language of the arbitration, the rules applicable to the proceeding, the applicable law and the arbitrator's fees and costs. They also resolve between themselves the administrative expenses associated with the dispute.[42] There are certain advantages to ad hoc arbitration: the fees and costs are likely to be less; the parties retain virtually complete control over all aspects of the arbitration—permitting them to provide for things such as prearbitration discovery of information (something not normally countenanced under traditional arbitration rules). Since no institution's bureaucracy is involved, the arbitration may well proceed in a more timely fashion.[43]

However, there are certain disadvantages, as well. If the dispute is a sizable one, the parties may be taking on an enormous task in an area in which they have very little expertise. What may have seemed to be a full and complete ad hoc arbitration agreement may turn out to be full of holes and ambiguities when the parties actually arrive at the dispute resolution stage. They may have a difficult time even identifying appropriate persons to serve as arbitrator. Or, they may disagree on the appointment of an arbitrator. To avoid many of these problems, most contracting parties provide for, or subsequently agree to, institutional arbitration, a process by which some institution such as the ICC or London Court of Arbitration administers and supervises the arbitration under prescribed rules.

There are a number of arbitration institutions that deal with most international commercial arbitrations: the ICC, the AAA, the London Court of Arbitration and to a lesser extent, the Zurich Chamber of Commerce, The Japan Commercial Arbitration Association and, particular in the case of East-West arbitration (at least for China and for the former Soviet Union), arbitration under the supervision of the Stockholm Chamber of Commerce. Recently, other centers of commerce, such as Brussels, Cairo, Hong Kong, and Kuala Lumpur have begun to hold themselves out as proper sites for international commercial arbitration.[44] When seeking a site for arbitration, factors such as ease of access, good telecommunications, a corps of well-educated potential arbitrators and a nonhostile judiciary are of primary importance.

Each of the major arbitration institutions has promulgated rules for commercial arbitration that control the major aspects of the arbitration process. In addition, these entities help administer individual arbitrations by transmitting documents between the parties; providing interpretations of ambiguous rules or procedures; and assisting in

42. *See*, e.g., Harry L. Arkin, *International Ad Hoc Arbitration: A Practical Alternative*, 15 Int'l Bus. L. 5 (1987). Another good commentary on the topic of ad hoc versus institutional arbitration is William K. Slate II, *International Arbitration: Do Institutions Make a Difference?* 31 Wake Forest L. Rev. 41 (1996). For a fascinating excursus on ad hoc arbitration in China *see* Tietie Zhang, *Enforceability of Ad Hoc Arbitration Agreements in China: China's Incomplete Ad Hoc Arbitration System*, 46 Cornell Int'l L.J. 362 (2013).

43. Arkin, *supra* n. 42.

44. For details on most of these centers *see*, AAA, *Handbook on International Arbitration and ADR* (2d ed., 2010); Paul Friedland & Loukas Mistelis, *2010 Arbitration Survey: Choices in International Arbitration*. For a more comprehensive treatment of virtually all possible arbitration sites *see*, the Kluwer compilation, *International Handbook on Commercial Arbitration: National Reports and Basic Legal Texts* (Jan Paulsson, ed., 2017).

the selection and replacement of the arbitrator, in the proper recordation of the arbitral award, including assistance in obtaining judicial recognition if necessary. For parties new to arbitration or simply unwilling to burden themselves with all the administrative burdens of an arbitration, institutional arbitration makes a lot of sense.

§9.5 A DESCRIPTION OF THE MAJOR INTERNATIONAL ARBITRAL INSTITUTIONS INCLUDING A BRIEF SUMMARY OF THEIR RULES

Just a few years ago, parties drafting an arbitration clause in an international commercial agreement would probably call for arbitration in Paris under the rules of the ICC. The ICC was then—and remains—the preeminent international arbitral body. Other agreements, particularly if one of the parties was from the United States might call for arbitration in New York under the rules of the AAA and other contracts might specify a London forum under the rules of the London Court of Arbitration. But these days there is a great deal of ferment in the area of institutional arbitration. The World Bank set up within the Bank a specialized arbitration body, the International Center for the Settlement of Investment Disputes (ICSID) established specifically to resolve—in an arbitral forum—investment disputes between private companies and banks in the developed countries and sovereign entities in the developing countries. More recently, UNCITRAL promulgated rules for international commercial arbitration without providing an institutional framework—thus enabling parties who choose the UNCITRAL rules to select some established arbitration institution such as the AAA to administer the arbitration under UNCITRAL procedures. Unique forms of arbitration have sometimes been created to defuse an otherwise totally hostile environment between nations. For example, an innovative arbitration process sited at The Hague was set up specifically to permit the United States and the government of Iran to resolve numerous commercial disputes that grew out of the fall of the Shah of Iran and the seizure of the American embassy.

This book does not attempt to work through each of the arbitral systems on a rule-by-rule basis. Rather, by way of illustration, this section will select three rules systems, the ICC, the AAA, and UNCITRAL as examples of the process of international institutional commercial arbitration. Any reader interested in institutional arbitration under other systems should carefully review the specific procedures established for those systems. While there are many similarities under all the systems, the nuances of the arbitration process in each system are sufficiently different that over-generalization is dangerous.[45]

In addition, in 1996 the World Intellectual Property Organization (WIPO) established an arbitration center with headquarters in Geneva, Switzerland to deal with

45. A very good book-length comparison of the major arbitration rules systems is Simpson, *Thacher and Bartlett, LLP, Comparison of International Arbitration Rules* (4th ed., 2013). Two good comparative articles are: David J. Branson & W. Michael Tupman, *Selecting an Arbitral Forum: A Guide to Cost-Effective International Arbitration*, 24 Va. J. Int'l L. 917 (1984); Steven J. Stein & Daniel R. Wolman, *International Commercial Arbitration in the 1980s: A Comparison of the Major Arbitral Systems and Rules*, 38 Bus. L. 1685 (1983).

international commercial disputes that involve some type of intellectual property. The WIPO rules are clear and straightforward; the WIPO recommended arbitration clause, mentioned earlier in Chapter 4, has been well received. WIPO is well on the way to creating a prestigious list of arbitrators. Lawyers and business executives who deal with licensing agreements would do well to consider a WIPO arbitration clause.[46]

§9.5.1 The International Chamber of Commerce

The ICC administers international commercial arbitration under the auspices of its Court of Arbitration, located in Paris.[47] The Court—actually an administrative secretariat composed of a Secretary General, a General Counsel, and five Counsel (who take an active role in administering each ICC arbitration)—is responsible for the promulgation of the ICC's Rules of Conciliation and Arbitration as well as responsible for administering individual arbitrations. As of late 2017, the ICC had administered more than 25,000 requests for ICC arbitration.[48] The ICC rules of arbitration are regarded as the one of the world standards for international commercial arbitration. The ICC also administers separate rules of conciliation that initially entered into force in 1988 and "remain entirely optional unless the parties have otherwise agreed. The ICC Rules of Arbitration recommend that parties carefully consider both mediation and arbitration as dispute resolution vehicles, but parties are not required to do both.[49]

The ICC's current rules were promulgated in 2012 with some revisions in 2017. The 2017 iteration of the rules includes for the first time extensive provisions for "expedited arbitration," that can be particularly useful for small amount disputes. This section covers only the basic ICC arbitration rules. Under the rules, an arbitration is commenced by one party's (the *claimant*) filing a *request for arbitration* that describes the parties, states the claimant's case, appends relevant documents, including, of course, the basic contractual document, and identifies the party's choice of arbitrator. The ICC's Secretariat sends a copy of this request to the opposing party.[50] The opposing

46. The WIPO rules and related information may be found at the WIPO website: www.wipo.int. For some commentary on the WIPO rules from a lawyer who worked as a WIPO consultant *see*, William Grantham, *The Arbitrability of International Intellectual Property Disputes*, 14 Berk. J. Int'l L. 173 (1996). *See also*, Thomas D. Halket, *Arbitration of Intellectual Property Disputes* (2012).
47. The definitive work on ICC arbitration is William Craig, William W. Park & Jan Paulsson, *International Chamber of Commerce Arbitration* (4th ed., 2018). Two other excellent works are Yves Derains, *A Guide to the ICC Rules of Arbitration* (2d ed., 2005) and Erik Schafer, Herman Verbist & Christophe Imhoos, *ICC Arbitration in Practice* (2004). The ICC rules may be found at its website: www.iccarbitration.org. For some additional general commentary on the ICC *see*, J. Gillis Wetter, *The Present Status of the International Court of Arbitration of the ICC: An Appraisal*, 1 Am. Rev. Int'l Arb. 91 (1990) and the rejoinder by an ICC official, Stephen R. Bond, *A Comment on an Appraisal*, 1 Am Rev. Int'l Arb. 108 (1990).
48. ICC International Court of Arbitration Bulletin 4 (December 1990).
49. Foreword to the 2012 ICC Arbitration Rules.
50. ICC Arbitration Rules, Art. 4.

party, referred to as the *respondent*, must respond in thirty days with his *answer* setting out his defenses and any counterclaims and with his comments on the number and selection of the arbitrators.[51]

Under normal circumstances, it is up to the parties to agree on the number and identity of the arbitrators. Only when the parties disagree will the Court step in and appoint a sole arbitrator, although either by contract language or in exceptional cases by decision of the Court, the Court will appoint a panel of three arbitrators, designating one as the chairman). If the Court makes the appointment, the ICC rules provide that the arbitrator is to "be chosen from a country other than those of which the parties are nationals," although in certain circumstances, and if the parties do not object, an arbitrator may come from one of the parties' countries. The Court rules on any challenges to the arbitrators and replaces arbitrators who are unable to carry on their duties.[52] The ICC's rules require that an arbitrator "be and remain independent of the parties."[53] If the parties have not agreed to a hearing site, the Court determines an appropriate site.[54]

Once the arbitration is initiated, the Request is responded to by the defendant, and the arbitrator selected. The arbitrator then draws up the terms of reference, a crucial document under the ICC's rules. The terms of reference identify and describe the parties and the arbitrator, provide addresses for the giving of notice, establish the arbitration site, summarize the parties' claims and set out the issues in the dispute.[55] One commentator has described the function of terms of reference as "bringing clarity and safety to the arbitration process...an educational value to the parties [and] a protection of awards against attack."[56] The ICC's Rules expressly provide that the parties may choose the applicable law. The law governing the dispute will be established by the arbitrator if no choice has been made in the contract. Moreover, the arbitrator is expressly permitted to act as an *amiable compositeur* (permitting the arbitrator to apply his own concepts of fairness and equity, in addition to principles of law) if the parties so agree.[57] The terms of reference are signed by both the parties and the arbitrator.[58]

Shortly after the terms of reference are completed and signed the arbitrator commences the arbitration hearing—a proceeding almost entirely within her control and of her own construction. The ICC's rules do not expressly provide for prehearing discovery, rules of evidence, or a precise order of presentation in the hearing. The arbitrator may call experts on his own initiative, may hear from the parties or their representatives and may entertain additional claims or counterclaims so long as those

51. *Id.*, Art. 5.
52. *Id.*, Arts. 7, 8 and 9.
53. *Id.*, Art. 7.1.
54. *Id.*, Art. 14.1.
55. *Id.*, Art. 18.
56. Jean-Claude Goldsmith, *How to Draft Terms of Reference,* 3 Arb. Int'l 298 (1987).
57. *Id.*, Art. 17.
58. *Id.*, Arts. 20 and 21.

new matters are within the terms of reference.[59] Under the rules, the arbitrator may grant "any interim or conservatory measure it deems appropriate."[60]

After the hearing concludes, the arbitrator, in his discretion, may permit the parties to try to reach an award by settlement. If she decides that settlement is not a possibility or if the parties refuse her invitation or cannot reach a negotiated agreement, the arbitrator must then write the award which is then submitted in draft form to the ICC's Court of Arbitration before it becomes final. This is a time-consuming but mainly ministerial step; the Court's review is normally a matter of reviewing the award for form, rather than for substance. It is rare for the Court to tamper with the arbitrator's decision regarding the merits of the controversy although the rules expressly provide that the Court "without affecting the [arbitrator's] liberty of decision, may also draw its attention to points of substance."[61] Once the Court has performed its review, the parties are notified and the award is automatically made final—that is, there is no appeals process within the ICC.[62] A party that objects to the arbitral award has recourse only to an appropriate court for corrective action.

The ICC's rules are brief and relatively simply stated. The brevity has triggered a number of criticisms. Early versions of the ICC rules, for example, contained no express provision for any kind of interim relief to be awarded by of the arbitrator, such as conferring authority on the arbitrator to attach property to insure that the award will be honored. The parties are free, of course, to request such prehearing attachment from a competent court, but such petitions often prolong the arbitration process indefinitely.[63] Sensing this weakness in its rules, the ICC provides for "Emergency Arbitrator Rules" by which a neutral referee may: "order any conservatory measures or any measures of restoration that are urgently necessary either to prevent immediate damage or irreparable loss" and to take other interim steps (e.g., to preserve evidence) that may be necessary even before the parties can launch a full-blown arbitration proceeding.[64] That language was, in greatly modified form, added to the 1998 rules.[65]

Second, even though the US dollar amounts in the ICC's fee schedule have recently been reduced, the fees turn on the amount in controversy, not on the work actually performed in the arbitration. However, the Court does have the authority to reduce the arbitrator's fee and the administrative fee in exceptional circumstances.[66] In the absence of such circumstances, the fee schedule as of March 1, 2017, based on U.S. dollars, is:

59. *Id.*, Arts. 14–16.
60. *Id.*, Art. 23.
61. *Id.*, Arts. 25, 26 and 27.
62. *Id.*, Art. 28.
63. *Id.*, Art. 8(5).
64. ICC Emergency Arbitrator Rules (Appendix V). For some commentary on an earlier framework *see*, Jan Paulsson, *A Better Mousetrap: 1990 ICC Rules for a Pre-arbitral Referee Procedure*, 18 Int'l Bus. L. 214 (1990).
65. ICC Emergency Arbitrator Rules, Appendix V.
66. *Id.*

Table 9.1 ICC Fee Schedule

A. Administrative Expenses				
Sum in Dispute (In U.S. Dollars)		*Administrative Expenses* (*)		
Up to	50,000		100,000	USD 5,000
From	50,001	To	200,000	1.53%
From	100,001	To	500,000	2.72%
From	200.001	To	1,000,000	2.25%
From	500,001	to	2,000,000	1.62%
From	1,000,001	to	5,000,000	0.788%
From	2,000,001	to	10,000,000	0.46%
from	5,000,001	to	30,000,000	0.25%
from	10,000,001	to	50,000,000	0.10%
from	30,000,001	to	80,000,000	0.09%
from	50,000,001	to		0.01%
from 80,000,00 to 500,000,000 over 500,000,000	0.0123% USD 150,000			

B. Arbitrator's Fees					
Sum in Dispute (In U.S. Dollars)			*Fees* (**)		
				Minimum	*Maximum*
Up to	50,000			USD 3,000	18.0200%
From	50,001	to	100,000	2.65%	13.5680%
From	100,001	to	200,000	1.4310%	7.6850%
From	200,001	to	500,000	1.3670%	6.8370%
From	500,001	to	1,000,000	0.9540%	4.0280%
From	1,000,001	to	2,000,000	0.6890%	3.6040%
From	2,000,001	to	5,000,000	0.3750%	1.3910%
From	5,000,001	to	10,000,000	0.1280%	0.9100%
From	10,000,001	to	30,000,000	0.0640%	0.2410%
From	30,000,001	to	50,000,000	0.0590%	0.2280%
From	50,000,001	to	80,000,000	0.0330%	0.1570%

B. Arbitrator's Fees					
Sum in Dispute (In U.S. Dollars)				*Fees* (**)	
				Minimum	*Maximum*
from	80,000,001	to	100,000,000	0.0210%	0.1150%
from	100,000,000	to	500,000,000	0.0110%	0.0580%
over 500,000,000—(min) 0.0100% to (max) 0.0400%					

* For illustrative purposes only, the table on the following page indicates the resulting administrative expenses in U.S. Dollar when the proper calculations have been made.

** For illustrative purposes only, the table on the following page indicates the resulting administrative expenses in U.S. Dollar when the proper calculations have been made.

When one considers that these figures do not include attorneys' fees, ICC arbitration can be expensive indeed. Final costs for the arbitration including arbitrators' fees and expenses, administrative expenses, expert fees and expenses and the parties' "normal legal costs" are fixed by the Court of Arbitration.[67]

§9.5.2 AAA Procedures

Most attorneys in the United States who are familiar with arbitration are usually familiar with the AAA's commercial arbitration rules.[68] The current set of AAA rules for international commercial arbitrations were promulgated in 2014. These rules establish the International Center for Dispute Resolution in New York, an office that now administers all AAA international arbitrations irrespective of the AAA regional office in which the arbitration was initially filed. The current rules bring AAA procedure more in line with existing international practice and expectations. The AAA has also tailored special sets of rules for specific disputes involving commercial, patent, and construction matters that parties may find suitable for international disputes arising in those subject areas.

The AAA's rules are somewhat more detailed than those of the ICC and are closer in scope and concept to American litigation practice, although they are, of course, nowhere nearly as detailed and complex as U.S. litigation procedures. There is, for example, more of an adversary flavor to the rules and more emphasis on the arbitration hearing as the place in which things are resolved. The current rules include provisions for dispute mediation and for "international expedited procedures (Articles E-1 through E-10).

Under the AAA rules, an arbitration under the AAA's supervision is commenced by a party's (the "Claimant") filing a written notice of its intention to commence arbitration accompanied by relevant papers, such as the underlying contract, with the

67. *Id.*
68. The AAA's web site where much of this information is available is: www.adr.org.

AAA and the opposing party (the "Respondent"). The notice of arbitration may be filed in hard-copy form (the traditional method) or now via the AAA's online filing system (www.icdr.org). The notice of arbitration must contain:

(1) a demand that the dispute be referred to arbitration;
(2) the names, addresses, fax numbers, telephone numbers and email addresses of the parties; and if known to the parties' representatives;
(3) a copy of the entire arbitration clause or the agreement that is the subject of the arbitration; reference either to the relevant arbitration clause or to the agreement that is invoked as providing the basis for arbitration;
(4) a reference to the contract out of which the dispute arises;
(5) a description of the claim and of the facts supporting the claim; and
(6) a statement of the relief or remedy sought and the amount claimed.[69]

The Claimant must enclose the appropriate filing fee. The date on which the AAA receives the notice becomes the date of commencement for the arbitration proceeding. The AAA then confirms receipt of the notice to all parties. The Respondent has thirty days to prepare and submit a response (deemed an "Answer" in AAA parlance) along with any counterclaim.[70] The parties may agree on an arbitrator or a panel of arbitrators; if the parties cannot agree the AAA will appoint the arbitrator or the panel.[71] The rules provide expressly: "if the parties have not agreed on the number of arbitrators, one arbitrator shall be appointed unless the [AAA] determines in its discretion that three arbitrators are appropriate because of the large size, complexity or other circumstances of the case."[72] If the parties cannot agree on the identity of the arbitrator(s), the AAA may make the appointment and may, at the request of either of the parties, appoint nationals of countries other than the countries of the contending parties.[73]

Unlike the ICC's rules, the AAA "may invite the parties to mediate" and the mediation (conducted by a separate mediator) may proceed simultaneously with the arbitration itself.[74] The rules permit the arbitrator to hold a preliminary meeting, called

69. This initial notice may also make reference to the manner of designating the arbitrator(s) and the number of arbitrators and the place and language of the arbitration hearing. AAA, International Commercial Arbitration Rules, Art. 2. An important companion for the rules themselves is the AAA's separate publication on international arbitration: AAA, *ICDR Handbook on International Arbitration Practice* (2d ed., 2017). For a book-length work on virtually all of the AAA's arbitration rules *see, AAA Handbook on Commercial Arbitration* (3d., 2016). The AAA also publishes an extremely helpful practice handbook: AAA, *Handbook on Arbitration Practice* (2d ed., 2016). *See also*, College of Commercial Arbitrators, *Guide to Best Practices in Commercial Arbitration* (4th ed., 2017) and Jay E. Grenig & Rocco M. Scanza, *Case Preparation and Presentation: A Guide for Arbitration Advocates and Arbitrators* (2013). This library, part of what the AAA calls its *Arbitration Law Database* is a marvelous compendium of arbitration information, relevant to all arbitrations and all arbitrators, not merely AAA international arbitration.
70. Articles 2 and 3.
71. Article 12.
72. *Id.*, Art. 11.
73. *Id.*, Art. 12.
74. *Id.*, Art. 5.

a *preparatory conference* in the rules, to organize the hearing process by identifying witnesses to be called, arranging for the exchange of documents and establishing the final hearing schedule.[75] To a large extent, the preparatory conference reflects American trial practice and as such at least partially substitute for the ICC's terms of reference—a procedure conducted almost entirely on paper.

In conducting the hearing, the arbitrator has a great deal of discretion in terms of hearing witnesses, ruling on issues of evidence, ordering the presentations and conducting site inspections and investigations. Again conforming somewhat to American practice, the AAA's rules tilt in favor of oral testimony and oral presentations. Unlike the ICC's rules, the arbitrator is given express authority to sequester or conserve the property at issue in the dispute during the course of the arbitration "including injunctive relief and measures for the protection or conservation of property."[76]

After the hearing is concluded, the arbitrator is obliged to make the award in writing "promptly;" but there is no review of any draft under AAA rules as there is under ICC rules. In some instances in purely domestic arbitration there is no obligation for an American arbitrator to produce an elaborate written award setting out the grounds and reasoning of the award. The typical domestic AAA award simply identifies the parties and the dispute and specifies the winning party and the amount of the award. Recognizing that this is usually not the case on the international level, the early versions of AAA's rules for international arbitrations provided: "Parties in international cases often expect arbitrators to provide a written opinion explaining the reasons for their award. The AAA will make arrangements for such an opinion in consultation with the parties and the arbitrators." This was the original posture of the AAA. The current rules simply require: "The tribunal shall state the reasons upon which the award is based, unless the parties have agreed that no reasons need be given."[77]

There are other possible options for AAA arbitrations. For example, the AAA's rules now incorporate the possibility of "expedited" procedures for smaller controversies. The expedited rules provide that the expedited procedures "shall apply in any case in which no disclosed claim or counterclaim exceeds USD 250,000 exclusive of interests and the costs of arbitration."[78] Those rules speed up the arbitration time frame and cut down on expenses incorporating the following features:

- Abbreviated filing requirements.
- Expedited appointment of arbitrators from a list of experienced arbitrators "ready to serve on an expedited basis.
- Early preparatory conference with the arbitrator requiring participation of the parties and their representatives.

75. *Id.*, Art. 20-2.
76. *Id.*, Arts. 20 through 27.
77. *Id.*, Art. 30-1. The preceding quotation is taken from the commentary to Art. 28 of the original AAA international rules.
78. *Id.*, Introduction. In addition, parties to an arbitration of any size may agree to use the expedited procedures in lieu of the normal procedures. The full text of the expedited arbitration rules is set out as Arts. E-1 through E-10 in the ICDR rules pamphlet.

- A presumption that cases of a value of up to USD 100,000 will be decided on documents only.
- An expedited schedule and limited hearing days (if a hearing is to be held).
- An award within 30 calendar days of the close of the hearing or the date established for the receipt of the parties' final statements and proofs.

Second, the AAA's fee schedule provides some flexibility with regard to payment and structure. As of October 1, 2017 the "standard fee" schedule is as follows:[79]

Table 9.2 AAA Fee Schedule

Amount of Claim	*Initial Filing Fee*	*Final Fee*
Less than USD 75,000	USD 1000	USD 1000
USD 75,000 to less than USD 150,000	USD2,025	USD 1,450
USD 150,000 to less than USD 300,000	USD 3,050	USD 2,300
USD 300,000 to less than USD 500,000	USD 4,600	USD 4,025
USD 500,000 to less than USD 1,000,000	USD 5,750	USD 72,125
USD 1,000,000 to less than USD 10,000,000	USD 8,625	USD 10,350
USD 10,000,000 and above	USD 12,650 plus .015 of the claim above USD 10 million	USD 16,100
Undetermined Monetary Claims	USD 8,625	USD 10,350
Nonmonetary Claims	USD 3,750	USD 2,875

The AAA gives the parties the option of a "flexible fee schedule" that has lower initial filing fees and permits the payments to be spread out in three payments over the lifetime of the arbitration proceeding.[80]

These fees do not, of course, include the arbitrator's fee. Arbitrators' fees are set in the following manner: "The fees and expenses of the arbitrators shall be reasonable in amount, taking into account the time spent by the arbitrators, the size and complexity of the case, and any other relevant circumstances." The AAA designates an appropriate hourly or daily fee for the arbitrators. The AAA resolves any disputes as to fees or expenses.[81]

79. At www.adr.org/international arbitration fee schedule.
80. *Id.*
81. *AAA Rules*, Art. 35.

§9.5.3 The UNCITRAL Procedures

The most recent set of comprehensive, generally applicable rules for international commercial arbitration have been promulgated by UNCITRAL in an attempt to develop some uniformity among arbitral bodies around the world. The UNCITRAL rules were revised in 2010, and the full text of the rules are to be found on the UNCITRAL website. Many national and international arbitral bodies, including the AAA and the ICC, will supervise arbitrations conducted under the UNCITRAL rules. The United States—Iranian Claims Tribunal at The Hague adopted the UNCITRAL rules with only a few minor modifications.[82] The former Soviet Union was generally agreeable to the use of UNCITRAL procedures in commercial arbitration with Western firms in Stockholm; it may be expected that most if not all of the republics of the Commonwealth of Independent States will be similarly agreeable.[83]

The UNCITRAL rules are expressly designed to work among business from all over the world and to help alleviate the inevitable differences of culture, language and legal systems that frequently impede dispute resolution. In the words of Pieter Sanders, who had a large hand in drafting them, "[The rules] offer a well balanced and modern set of arbitration rules, prepared with the assistance of arbitration experts from all parts of the world. They may also be particularly welcomed by developing countries, which were vigorously represented in [their] drafting and...preparation. ..."[84] One international body, the Inter-American Commercial Arbitration Commission, headquartered in Rio de Janiero, Brazil has adopted the UNCITRAL rules as the Commission's rules virtually without change.[85] Initially promulgated in 1976, the rules are frequently used in ad hoc arbitration, as well as institutional arbitration.

Briefly summarized, the UNCITRAL rules require a party commencing arbitration, the claimant, to provide the opposing party, the respondent, with a notice of arbitration.[86] Arbitrators may be appointed by the parties, but if there is no agreement, the supervising institution (if there is one) may make the appointment. Illustrating the UNCITRAL rules' adaptability, if there is no supervising institution, the parties are permitted to apply to the Secretary-General of the Permanent Court of Arbitration at The Hague to designate the appointing authority.[87] The rules contain extensive provisions on the challenge of arbitrators by one or both of the parties.[88]

While the arbitration may include an oral hearing at the request of the parties or the discretion of the arbitrator, it is obvious that a great deal of the dispute is to be

---

82. *See*, e.g., Jamison M. Selby & David P. Stewart, *Practical Aspects of Arbitrating Claims Before the Iran-United States Claims Tribunal*, 18 Int'l L. 211 (1984).
83. *See*, e.g., Thomas W. Hoya, *East West Trade: Comecon Law, American Soviet Trade* 326 (1984).
84. Pieter Sanders, *Procedures and Practices Under the UNCITRAL Rules*, 27 Am. J. Comp. L. 453 (1979). Anyone interested in UNCITRAL arbitration may profitably consult: Clyde Croft, Christopher Lee & Jeff Waincymer, *A Guide to the UNCITRAL Arbitration Rules* (2013); David D. Caron & Lee M. Caplan, *The UNCITRAL Arbitration Rules: A Commentary* (2013) and Sophie Nappert, *Commentary on the UNCITRAL Arbitration Rules: A Practitioner's Guide* (2012).
85. Rules of Procedure of the Inter-American Commercial Arbitration Commission.
86. UNCITRAL Arbitration Rules, Art. 3.
87. *Id.*, Arts. 6–8.
88. *Id.*, Arts. 9–12.

handled on the basis of the paper record. In a direct parallel to the ICC's terms of reference, the claimant (and the respondent if any counterclaim is filed) is expected to state the claim, the points at issue, and the relief sought in writing. That writing is submitted to the respondent and to the arbitrators. The respondent is then, within a period of time specified by the arbitrators but generally not to exceed forty-five days, to submit a statement of defenses to the claim.[89] The rules authorize the arbitrator to take interim measures "including measures for the conservation of the goods forming the subject matter in dispute, such as ordering their deposit with a third person or the sale of perishable goods."[90]

A written award is required and the arbitrators are permitted to sit as *amiable compositeurs* or in *ex aequo et bono* only if the contract—or subsequent party agreement—expressly authorizes them to do so.[91] Because the UNCITRAL rules were developed outside the context of a specific supervising institution, they are vague on fees. Costs comprise only the fees of the arbitrators, including their travel and living expenses, the costs associated with expert advice provided the arbitrators and witness costs, "the costs for legal representation and assistance of the successful party if such costs were claimed during the arbitral proceeding and only to the extent that the arbitral tribunal determines that the amount of such costs is reasonable" and any fees and expenses incurred by the appointing authority.[92] The rules contemplate that the costs of the arbitration be borne by the losing party unless the arbitrator decides to apportion all or part of the costs.[93] The arbitrator may require the parties to make a deposit against costs either before or during the arbitration.[94]

However, since there is no continuing supervising body, costs are merely to be "reasonable" and are not set expressly with reference to a fixed schedule unless a selected supervising authority has a schedule of fees. In other words, the arbitration will merely incorporate a fee schedule of, say, the ICC or the AAA, depending on which institution is the appointing authority.

Do the UNCITRAL rules work? The short answer appears to be yes. They have been accepted by virtually all the major international arbitration bodies and by a large number of developing countries. They appear to have been a large factor in keeping the U.S.—Iranian Claims Tribunal functioning smoothly over the past several years. Granted that the rules make no major breakthroughs—they are very similar in language, content, and thrust to the AAA's rules—they are one of the most recent attempts to develop workable yet flexible rules of procedure, and for that reason alone they deserve considerable attention.

89. *Id.*, Arts. 18 and 23.
90. *Id.*, Art. 26.
91. *Id.*, Arts. 31–33.
92. *Id.*, Art. 38.
93. *Id.*, Art. 40(1).
94. *Id.*, Art. 41.

§9.5.4 The WIPO Rules

As noted above, the WIPO is relatively new to the matter of international commercial arbitration. WIPO itself is a specialized agency of the United Nations system of organizations and is responsible for the "promotion of the protection of intellectual property throughout the world."[95] The WIPO arbitration center began operations in 1994 and administers four separate dispute resolution procedures: mediation, arbitration, expedited arbitration and a combination of mediation and arbitration. The center has promulgated rules for each of these procedures. Within the center are maintained a number of different groupings and divisions: the arbitration council, comprised of a number of prominent practitioners and academics, public and private sectors persons, who make recommendations on policy and planning for the center. The arbitration consultative commission is comprised of leading experts in the areas of both intellectual property and arbitration and provide opinions and advice on nonroutine issues that come before the center. In addition the center maintains an administrative staff to deal with the day-to-day issues that arise in the context of supervising arbitrations.

The WIPO rules are straightforward and, in many instances, either borrow from or improve upon the rules of some of the older institutions.[96] The current rules were effective as of June 1, 2014. Some of the vocabulary has changed. For example, an entity commencing WIPO arbitration files a request for arbitration that must contain appropriate names and addresses of the parties, a copy of the arbitration agreement, a "brief description of the nature and circumstances of the dispute," and a "statement of the relief sought."[97] The responding party then submits an answer which may also contain a set-off or counterclaim.[98]

The arbitration tribunal is comprised of whatever number of persons has been specified in the parties' arbitration clause; or if no such number has been specified, "the Tribunal shall consist of a sole arbitrator, except where the Center in its discretion determines that, in view of all the circumstances of the case, a Tribunal composed of three members is appropriate."[99] If there is a sole arbitrator the parties may appoint the arbitrator or failing to so appoint, the Center may make the appointment through Article 19s *default appointment process.*[100] In the instance of a default appointment, the center presents a list of at least three arbitrators to the parties. The parties may strike any of the names, but if there is no name remaining on the list that has not been struck by one party or the other, the center may then make the appointment without further reference to the parties.[101]

95. Virtually all of this discussion is taken from the WIPO website and an earlier pamphlet, The Services of the WIPO Arbitration Center (1994).
96. For additional commentary *see*, Camille A. Laturno, *International Arbitration of the Creative: A Look at the World Intellectual Property Organization's New Arbitration Rules,* 9 Transnat'l L. 357 (1996).
97. WIPO Arbitration Rules, Art. 9.
98. *Id.*, Art. 11.
99. *Id.*, Art. 14.
100. *Id.*, Arts. 16 and 19.
101. *Id.*, Art. 19.

The rules go on to provide for the conduct of the hearing, the admission of evidence, the testimony of experts, site visits, protection of trade secrets and the like. The award may include an assessment of interest against the losing party.[102] However, the WIPO rules appear to be silent on the matter of punitive damages. The arbitrator(s) are required to give reasons for the award.[103] The center sets a registration fee that normally must be paid to commence arbitration in the following manner: If the amount of claim is up to and including USD 2.5 million, the fee is USD 2,000; for claims over USD 2.5 million and up to USD 10 million the fee is USD 10,000; for claims over USD 10 million, the fee is USD 10,000, plus 0.05% of the amount over USD 10 million up to a maximum fee of USD 25,000. In addition, the WIPO Arbitration Center requires a separate administration fee, again calculated upon the amount of the claim. Arbitrators' fees are subject to a complicated formula that has certain fixed amounts depending on whether there is a sole or a panel of arbitrators, plus a percentage of the amount of the claim. When fixing the amount of the claim for these purposes, any counterclaim is added to the amount of the initial claim.[104]

§9.6 COMMENCING THE ARBITRATION

The preceding sections have provided an overview of the arbitration process and the major rules systems. But how does arbitration work in practice? For some helpful insights it makes sense to step away from most of the international literature, much of which tends to be more theoretical than practical[105] and to examine some of the advice provided by lawyers whose primary experience is domestic commercial arbitration.[106] The guidance and advice provided by these experts will prove highly useful in any arbitration setting. The following subsections are essentially a distillation of the comments of a large number of expert arbitrators and commenters.

Most arbitrations involve only two parties: the party that makes a claim and the party that responds to the claim.[107] The reason for this is that traditionally most international commercial arbitrations grew out of bilateral contracts. Modern

102. *Id.*, Art. 60(b).
103. *Id.*, Art. 62(c).
104. WIPO Arbitration rules, Schedule of Fees.
105. This statement should specifically exclude the Craig, Park, Paulsson book on ICC arbitration, *supra* n. 47, which is filled with helpful, practical hints.
106. There are a number of substantial treatises now on the market. Gary B. Born, *International Commercial Arbitration* (4th ed., 2017); Margaret L. Moses, *The Principles and Practice of International Commercial Arbitration* (3d ed., 2017); Gary B. Born, *International Arbitration and Forum Selection Agreements: Drafting and Enforcing* (5th ed., 2016). For many years, Martin Domke's classic, Commercial Arbitration, most recently edited by Professor Gerard Wilner, was the standard. Domke is now out of print. One of the best small books, is George Goldberg, *A Lawyer's Guide to Commercial Arbitration* (2d ed., 1983). Also useful are: Craig A. Peterson & Claire McCarthy, *Arbitration Strategy and Technique* (1986) and Robert M. Rodman, *Commercial Arbitration with Forms* (1984). A very good treatise covering many of the important issues faced by the advocate is R. Doak Bishop & Edward G. Kehoe, *The Art of Advocacy in International Arbitration* (2d ed., 2010).
107. *See*, Carolyn B. Lamm & Jocelyn Aqua, *Defining the Party: Who Is a Proper Party in an International Arbitration before the American Arbitration Association and Other International Institutions*, 34 Geo. Wash. Int'l L. Rev. 711 (2003).

arbitration, especially in matters such as construction project and joint venture disputes, can become much more complex and may require even more creativity on the part of the lawyers and business executives who seek to resolve their grievances through arbitration.[108] Multiparty disputes are the Achilles Heel of dispute resolution devices such as arbitration. It is extremely difficult in normal circumstances to arbitrate between more than two parties and to entertain a multiplicity of claims. The major arbitration institutions are just now beginning to deal with multiple-party, multiple claims proceedings. There are now some rules on joinder of parties and consolidation of disputes.[109]

It is very difficult to discuss and understand arbitration issues in the abstract. The remainder of this chapter poses a hypothetical fact pattern involving two companies that have a dispute subject to an arbitration clause that, hopefully, will assist the reader in appreciating and analyzing all the things that come up when one is involved in international commercial arbitration. Consider a purchase and sale transaction between a manufacturer-seller in Los Angeles, California, Tangerine Corporation, and a purchaser, Parthenon Ltd. in Athens, Greece. The contract is for 100 computers to be shipped in five installments of twenty computers each and contains all the common elements including a choice of language clause (English), a choice of law clause (the Uniform Commercial Code (UCC) of the State of New York), and a conventional arbitration clause that requires the arbitration of any dispute arising under the contract to be conducted in New York City under AAA supervision using only one ("sole") arbitrator and applying the UNCITRAL arbitration rules.

Further assume that Parthenon received four of the five shipments of computers all of which were fully satisfactory. The last shipment arrived two months ago but consisted of computers that did not meet the contract specifications. The Greek buyer intends to use these computers for highly detailed accounting matters and business projections and thus the speed with which the computer processes the data is extremely important. The final shipment consisted of computers that contained a slower mechanism ("chip") than the computers in the first four shipments. The defective computers are currently in a warehouse in Athens where the storage charges are USD 150 per day (the computers have to be kept in a temperature controlled

108. For some advice on managing complex commercial disputes *see*, *Handling the Complex Commercial Case*, 46 Arb. J. 6 (1991).

109. There may now be some possibilities to reconsider the two-party limitation in international commercial arbitration. *See*, e.g., R. Doak Bishop, *Multiple Party Actions in International Arbitration* (2009); Belinda MacMahon (ed.), *Multiple Party Actions in International Arbitration: Consent, Procedure and Enforcement* (2009); Michael P. Daly, *Come One, Come All: The New and Developing World of Nonsignatory Arbitration and Class Arbitration*, 62 U. Miami L. Rev. 95 (2007); J. Gillis Wetter, *A Multi-Party Arbitration Scheme for International Joint Ventures*, 3 Arb. Int'l 2 (1987). For some discussion on consolidating a number of disputes into a single arbitration, *see*, Lara M. Pair & Paul Frankenstein, *The New ICC Rule on Consolidation: Progress or Change?* 25 Emory Int'l L.J. 1061 (2011); F.B. MacKellar, *To Consolidate or Not to Consolidate: A Study of Federal Court Decisions*, 44 Arb. J. 15 (December 1989). For a discussion of the contract doctrine of privity as it may or may not control parties to an arbitration *see*, Olagoke O. Olatawura, *The "Privy to Arbitration" Doctrine: The Withering of the Common-Law Privity of Contract Doctrine in Arbitration Law*, 16 Am. Rev. Int'l Arb. 429 (2005).

building that also has with good security because of their value). Parthenon's staff productivity is not what it should be because the company does not have all the fast computers it needs.

Parthenon executives have corresponded with Tangerine officers, notifying them of the defect and requesting that Tangerine cure the defects or refund 20% of the contract price, that is, USD 125,000. Tangerine has not responded to any of these letters; and accordingly, Parthenon's attorney recommends that the company trigger the arbitration clause in the contract by filing a request for arbitration. The threshold question to be addressed is whether the issues presented by this dispute are arbitrable. These days, at least in the United States, the answer to that question will almost always be "yes."

§9.6.1 Determining the Issues to Be Arbitrated

Since the 1985 United States Supreme Court decision in *Mitsubishi v. Soler,*[110] there was some question as to whether certain issues such as violations of securities laws or antitrust complaints were subject to arbitration or whether those issues could only be resolved by a court. In *Mitsubishi* the Supreme Court wrote an exceptionally broad decision holding that even a general arbitration clause encompasses, and thus makes arbitrable, virtually all issues that might spring up under an international commercial agreement. There are precious few exceptions. For example, a party claiming that he was fraudulently induced into entering into a contract that contained an arbitration clause will probably not be permitted to take that issue directly to court. In *Prima Paint Corp. v. Flood & Conklin Manufacturing Co.*,[111] the U.S. Supreme Court determined that such claims would be subject to arbitration unless the claim of fraud went directly to the arbitration clause itself. In other words, a party would have to arbitrate even a claim of fraud in the inducement unless he could show a court that he was specifically induced to agree to arbitration.

Thus, the lawyers' traditional dilemma—which issues are arbitrable and which are not—seems to be no longer a major question in the United States. Most of the major trading nations now also approach this question in similar fashion. There is now considerable discussion of whether certain issues that used to be considered flatly nonarbitrable—such as bribery and corruption—can be raised in the context of arbitration.[112] As a consequence, the question faced by a party trying to decide on how to structure an arbitration is which issues to press before the arbitrator. Here, an attorney will proceed in the same fashion as he or she would get ready for court. Obviously, both the facts and the law need to be researched to determine what is truly

---

110. 473 U.S. 614 (1985).
111. 388 U.S. 395 (1967).
112. *See* Kathrin Betz, *Proving Bribery, Fraud and Money Laundering in International Arbitration on Applicable Criminal Law and Evidence* (2017); William Fox, *Adjudicating Issues of Corruption and Bribery in International Commercial Arbitration*, 27 J. Energy & Nat. Resources L. 487 (2009).

at issue in the case. The arbitration clause—as noted so often in the preceding chapters—is crucial to this investigation. Properly drafted, it will provide the answers to a number of questions including:

(1) The law applicable to the arbitration.
(2) The site of the arbitration.
(3) The procedural rules applicable to the arbitration.

In the *Parthenon v. Tangerine* controversy, there is nothing that suggests there was fraud in the inducement to agree to the arbitration clause, so it is beyond dispute that the issues presented in this case will be subject to arbitration. Moreover, the contract resolves forum selection, choice of law, the applicable system of procedure and gives supervisory authority to the AAA. Parthenon attorneys investigate further and, in consultation with their experts, determine that there was, in their experts' view, a breach of the contract specifications concerning the computers' processing speed.

§9.6.2 Drafting the Request for Arbitration

Once this preliminary analysis is complete, the complaining party will prepare the request for arbitration. This is be a crucial document and must be drafted with extraordinary care since amendments to the request are permitted only in the discretion of the arbitrator. Attorneys used to the virtually unfettered possibilities of amending pleadings under the United States' Federal Rules of Civil Procedure need to understand that a request for arbitration normally requires more precision. Arbitrators are not nearly as lenient in permitting changes as are U.S. federal judges.

The specific contents of the request for arbitration are fixed by the applicable rules. For example, under the UNCITRAL rules the request for arbitration includes, at a minimum:

(1) The names and addresses of the parties.
(2) The demand for arbitration.
(3) A reference to either the arbitration clause or any separate agreement between the parties requiring that disputes be submitted to arbitration.
(4) A reference to the contract in question.
(5) The general nature of the claim, including an indication of the amount of money involved.
(6) The relief or remedy sought.
(7) A proposal as to the number of arbitrators if the number is not contained in the arbitration clause.

Lawyers who do not want to create a document from scratch may choose to use some of the standard forms available. For example, the AAA has a request form that might be used effectively even when the AAA is not the supervising body. However, most of the supervising institutions do not offer—and really do not recommend the use of a preprinted form. In our hypothetical, counsel for Parthenon may simply send a letter to Tangerine through AAA. Recall that the supervising institution has traditionally served as a collection point and clearing house for all documents exchanged between the parties. The newer rules systems sometimes permit the parties to exchange documents directly, although the supervising institution is almost always given a copy, as are the arbitrators when the arbitrators are identified. The use of an institution to forward documents used to be a singular disadvantage of institutional as opposed to ad hoc arbitration; but easily accessible air courier services, facsimile machines, and email attachments have reduced what used to be nearly intolerable delays. Moreover, there is an advantage to clearing the documents through the institution. Their expertise may help avoid a lot of beginner's mistakes for parties who are new to the arbitration process. It might be helpful, of course, to secure an agreement between the parties either in the contract or in the initial stages of the arbitration that all documents shall be sent air courier.

A common question is the amount of detail to be put into the original request for arbitration. George Goldberg suggests that the claimant simply make out a prima facie case in the request (showing only that a contract exists, that defective goods were shipped and some kind of request for a remedy); and "[t]o the extent the claimant can avoid discussion of quality claims, laboratory tests, and the like, so much the better."[113] Other authorities on arbitration suggest that the request be fairly detailed—at least in terms of the issues—to make sure that the claimant does not have to file an extensive amendment of claim later on, because amended arbitration claims may be denied by an arbitrator more readily than a U.S. federal judge might be able to deny permission to amend a court pleading. In court, a judge must permit amendments freely and in the interests of justice[114] while an arbitrator under the UNCITRAL rules and in most other systems, may deny amendments in his discretion if "the arbitral tribunal considers it inappropriate to allow such amendment having regard to the delay in making it or prejudice to the other party or any other circumstances."[115] The UNCITRAL arbitration rules recognize some of the difficulties a claimant faces at this point and permit the claimant to file a skeletal initial request for arbitration, so long as a more comprehensive "statement of the claim" is filed prior to the hearing. Under ICC rules, the terms of reference are more important as an outline of the arbitration than is the arbitration request; but even parties employing ICC rules should not take the drafting of the request lightly. Almost all requests for arbitration in modern international commercial arbitration are highly detailed.

Once the request is drafted and served on the responding party, the respondent may reply with an answer and a counterclaim, or in certain systems may remain silent, simply waiting to see what the complaining party can prove at the arbitration hearing.

113. Goldberg, *supra* n. 106, at 31. An excellent new book on working with monetary amounts in international commercial arbitration is Irmgard Marboe, *Calculation of Compensation and Damages in International Investment Law* (2017). *See also* Herfried Woss & Adriana San Roman Rivera, *Damages in International Arbitration under Complex Long-Term Contracts* (2014); Mark Kantor, *Valuation for Arbitration* (2008).
114. Federal Rule of Civil Procedure 15(a).
115. UNCITRAL Arbitration Rules, Art. 20.

Under the UNCITRAL rules, the respondent is required to file a "response to the notice of arbitration" after the claimant files the statement of claim. In certain cases, if the responding party believes that the issues are not properly subject to arbitration, he or she may ignore all of these matters and simply wait for the complaining party to move into court for an order compelling arbitration or, in the alternative, might move into court for a declaration that the subject matter is not legally fit for arbitration. As discussed above, there is very little hope these days—at least in the context of international commercial agreements—that the court will agree to hear the case in lieu of the arbitration. But it is a tactic, nonetheless, that might buy a little time—understanding, of course, that interposing such a defense solely for the purposes of delay might create ethical problems for the attorney, both in the United States and abroad. The response is generally more detailed than the original demand, although it can be a simple categorical denial of all the assertions made by the claimant—a signal that the respondent is simply willing to wait and see what develops at the hearing. Once these preliminary papers have been exchanged, the next order of business is selection of the arbitrator, one of the most important stages in the entire process.

§9.6.3 Selecting the Arbitrator

Once again, a wisely drafted arbitration clause may take care of much of this problem. An arbitration clause may specify, for example, the number of arbitrators and the arbitrator's credentials.[116] At the same time, it is extremely rare for a contract's arbitration clause to specify an arbitrator by name, so the parties need to identify a specific individual who will serve as the arbitrator. There are two common models for arbitrator selection. If the contract calls for a sole arbitrator, the parties may simply agree on the arbitrator. Some contracts provide for a detailed selection process. For example, the party seeking arbitration could be required to produce a list of five acceptable arbitrators; and the responding party would be permitted to strike four of the names. When an arbitration panel is required under the contract, the parties

116. There is a growing body of literature on arbitrators. *See*, e.g., Dolores Bentolita, *Arbitrators as Lawmakers* (2017); Sherlin Tung & Patricia Shaughnessy, *The Power and Duties of an Arbitrator: Liber Amicorum Pierre A. Karrer* (2017); Julio Cesar Betancourt, *Defining Issues in International Arbitration: Celebrating 100 Years of the Chartered Institute of Arbitrators* (2016); Lawrence W. Newman & Richard D. Hill, *Leading Arbitrators' Guide to International Arbitration* (3d ed., 2014); Thomas J. Stipanovich & Zacary P. Ulrich, *Commercial Arbitration and Settlement: Empirical Insights into the Roles Arbitrators Play*, 6 Yb. on Arb. & Med. 1 (2014); Emilia Onyema, *International Commercial Arbitration and the Arbitrator's Contract* (2012); Ilhung Lee, *Practice and Predicament: The Nationality of the International Arbitrator (with Survey Results)*, 31 Fordham Int'l L.J. 603 (2008); Susan D. Franck, *International Arbitrators: Civil Servants?; Sub Rosa Advocates?; Men of Affairs?: The Role of International Arbitrators*, 12 I.L.S.A. J. Int'l & Comp. L. 499 (2006); Henry Gabriel & Anjanette H. Raymond, *Ethics for Commercial Arbitrators: Basic Principles and Emerging Standards*, 5 Wyo. L. Rev. 453 (2005); Catherine A. Rogers, *Regulating International Arbitrators: A Functional Approach to Developing Standards of Conduct*, 41 Stan. J. Int'l L. 53 (2005); Catherine A. Rogers, *The Vocation of the International Arbitrator*, 20 Am. U. Int'l L. Rev. 957 (2005). For a book-length work written from an American perspective and not focused on international arbitration but helpful nonetheless, *see* John W. Cooley, *The Arbitrator's Handbook* (2d rev. ed., 2010).

typically appoint their own arbitrator (referred to as *party-appointed* arbitrators) who then appoint a third, neutral panel member who usually presides at the hearing. On occasion, the parties will not be able to reach an agreement as to the arbitrator. Under all of the major arbitration rules systems, an appointing authority will simply choose an arbitrator if the parties are unable to agree. In ad hoc arbitration conducted under an arbitration statute, the parties may apply to the court to appoint the arbitrator if they themselves cannot agree.

Selection of the arbitrator is an important step, perhaps the most important in the entire process. The major factors to look for in selecting an arbitrator are: (1) experience in and knowledge of both the subject matter of the contract and the arbitral process itself; (2) an ability to converse and read and write in the language of the arbitration, unless the parties are agreeable to providing on-site translation services; (3) availability over the time chosen by the parties for the arbitration; and (4) for so-called neutral arbitrators, lack of personal connection with either of the parties.[117] There is a recent emphasis on the ability of the arbitrator to manage the entire arbitration process rather than simply being capable of conducting a hearing and writing a reward.[118] Some research and commentary is beginning to inquire into the psychology of the arbitrator.[119]

This last point gets to the issue of bias and is sometimes difficult to penetrate. Obviously, it would be a fine thing to find an experienced arbitrator skilled in the subject matter of the dispute who had never had any contact, however slight, with any of the parties. However, this is not always possible. Arbitrators tend to specialize in a particular subject matter. Companies who arbitrate frequently may see the same arbitrator more than once. There are procedures in all the major rules systems for moving to disqualify an arbitrator but such disqualification is always easier said than done. For example, an arbitrator's merely knowing one or another of the parties is not sufficient. Having a social relationship with one of the parties is probably not enough. The AAA has promulgated a Code of Ethics for Commercial Arbitrators which requires an arbitrator to "disclose any interest or relationship likely to affect impartiality or which might create an appearance of partiality or bias" but normally this disclosure requirement is limited to:

---

117. *See*, e.g., Catherine A. Rogers, *A Window into the Soul of International Arbitration: Arbitrator Selection, Transparency and Stakeholder Interests*, 46 Wictoria U. Wellington L. Rev. 1179 (2015); Fernando Dias Simoes, *Powered by Expertise: Selecting Arbitrators in Energy Disputes*, 8 J. World Energy L. & Bus. 501 (2015); Carlos A. Matheus Lopez, *Practical Criteria for Selecting International Arbitrators*, 31 J. Int'l Arb. 795 (2014); Charles J. Moxley, Jr., *Selecting the Ideal Arbitrator*, 60 Dis. Res. J. 25 (2005). For arbitrator selection from a particular viewpoint, *see* Chung Yongkyun, *Arbitrator Acceptability in International Commercial Arbitration: The Trading Firm Perspective*, 27 Int'l J. Conflict Mgt. 379 (2016).

118. *See*, e.g., Thomas Schultz & Robert Kovacs, *The Rise of as Third Generation of Arbitrators? Fifteen Years after Dezalay and Garth*, 28 Arb. Int'l 161 (2012).

119. *See*, e.g., Tony Cole (ed.), *The Roles of Psychology in International Arbitration* (2017); Rebecca K. Helm, *Are Arbitrators Human?* 13 J. Emp. Leg. Stud. 666 (2016); Edna Sussman, *Arbitrator Decision-Making: Unconscious Psychological Influences and What You Can Do About Them*, 24 Am. Rev. Int'l Arb. 487 (2013).

(1) any direct or indirect financial or personal interest in the outcome of the arbitration; or
(2) any existing or past financial, business, professional, family or social relationships which would affect impartiality or create an appearance of partiality or bias.[120]

The International Bar Association (IBA) has promulgated a parallel set of ethical rules for international arbitrators that also deserves attention.[121] Under the IBA rules, the arbitrator has similar disclosure obligations even if he or she is party-appointed (this is in contrast to the AAA's relatively relaxed approach to party-appointed arbitrators). The IBA's rules also strictly limit unilateral contacts between the arbitrators and the parties and prohibit unilateral agreements on fees or expenses between one of the parties and the arbitrators.

Irrespective of which set of rules one refers to, most of the ethical constructs involve concededly ambiguous language. No one ever knows with certainty what circumstances will require disqualification. Pecuniary bias, a situation in which the arbitrator has a financial stake in the outcome of the case (as, e.g., owning shares in one of the companies) is surely a disqualifying factor. Seeing a party's chief executive officer at a party is probably not sufficient to disqualify; but a long-standing personal relationship even if it is only a relationship founded in friendship may be sufficient to disqualify. Arbitration systems tend to require arbitrators to make the fullest disclosure and then to permit the parties to challenge the arbitrator if grounds for disqualification exist.[122] For lawyers involved in arbitration, perhaps the best advice is to investigate an arbitrator as thoroughly as possible, make the objection as early as possible and be sure of the grounds offered for disqualification. Probably no tactic can more quickly rebound against a party and with such devastating results as a request for disqualification that fails.

§9.7 PREPARING FOR AND CONDUCTING THE HEARING

Most practitioners approach an arbitration in the same way that they approach litigation. Experienced lawyers gather all the facts available, thoroughly analyze the underlying contractual documents and the various legal issues presented by the controversy, interview and prepare both lay witnesses and expert witnesses and, in general, try to ensure that there are no surprises when everyone gets into the hearing. In the case of *Parthenon v. Tangerine*, counsel for each party would analyze the contract, discuss the controversy thoroughly with the client, identify and consult with experts (who may also give testimony at the hearing) and probably inspect all the goods or at least one of the defective computers.

---

120. AAA, Code of Ethics for Arbitrators in Commercial Disputes, Canon II.
121. *See*, e.g., Rules of Ethics for International Arbitrators, 15 Int'l Bus. Law. 336 (September 1987). David J. Branson, *Commentary on Ethics for International Arbitrators,* 3 Arb. Int'l 72 (1987).
122. *Id. See also*, Karel Daele, *Challenge and Disqualification of Arbitrators in International Arbitration* (2011).

All of this is frequently easier said than done. As this chapter has continually reiterated, arbitration is different from litigation, particularly litigation as it is practiced in the United States. There are few devices available by which an attorney may compel production of evidence; there is usually only a limited subpoena power (calling for witnesses or the production of documents at the hearing) available to parties in arbitration. There are usually few or no meetings between the parties and the arbitrator prior to the arbitration hearing itself. Finally, the hearing, because it depends so much on the discretion of the arbitrator, is not always the predictable carefully staged event that litigation often is.

But no lawyer can use any of this as an excuse for being casual about arbitration. As has been discussed and as will be seen with even greater clarity in Chapter 10, the decision of an arbitrator—that is, the outcome of an arbitration hearing—is normally final. Thus, a client's interests are usually conclusively determined in the arbitration just as they would be in court. Too many lawyers seem to take arbitration less seriously than they do litigation—a tragic mistake in many instances. This section discusses some of the ways that a lawyer can turn the prehearing stage to his or her advantage even if all the tools available to a litigator are not present.

§9.7.1 Discovery

Perhaps the best place to begin an analysis of the discovery issue is to restate the normal rule—there is usually no discovery in arbitration cases. There are two primary reasons for this. First, arbitration is intended to be less formal and time consuming than litigation. Indeed, one reason why lawyers outside the United States tend to be somewhat skittish about U.S.-based arbitration is because they fear becoming entangled in endless pretrial discovery. Massive, interminable discovery is not the rule even in American arbitration, but it is sometimes difficult to convince others of that fact. Second, one of the premises of arbitration is that most if not all of the dispute will be predicated on matters either already committed to paper or readily reduced to documentary form, and that most of the documents will be exchanged by the parties in the ordinary course. The contract is normally on paper. The demand for arbitration and the response to the demand along with any counterclaims will similarly be on paper, accompanied by other documents of relevance to the controversy. Thus, extensive prehearing discovery in the form of, for example, depositions (in which a witness orally answers questions put to him by the opposing counsel) are rarely necessary.

There are other ways to work around the absence of elaborate discovery rules. Discovery may be handled informally by agreement among the parties using, if necessary, the leverage that an arbitrator has to grant postponements and to admit or exclude evidence. For totally recalcitrant parties, many arbitration statutes, including for example, the United States' Federal Arbitration Act, permit the arbitrator to issue subpoenas for witnesses who are to give oral testimony (traditionally referred to as a *subpoena ad testificandum*) or for witnesses who are expected to bring documents (*subpoena duces tecum*). However, under normal circumstances, the subpoena may compel only attendance at the hearing or documents to be produced at the hearing. If the subpoenaed party refuses to comply, the arbitrator may resort to the domestic court system in which the hearing is taking place country for sanctions against the uncooperative party so long as that country's arbitration act recognizes and enforces subpoenas.[123]

In many instances, likely including the Parthenon/Tangerine case, extensive discovery is probably not needed. The basic document, the contract, is in the hands of both parties and will be appended to the statement of the claim. Documents supporting the location and storage fees for the defective computers will be submitted by the claimant. It is possible, of course, that an expert witness will have examined the computers, run tests on the computers and reduced his findings to paper, and then not be called for hearing, thus suggesting that the other party could request the arbitrator to issue a subpoena duces tecum. But there is probably no need for such action. The dispute is not that complicated and the amount in controversy is probably not sufficient to justify massive efforts to secure prehearing information.

§9.7.2 The Prehearing Conference

Although many systems of arbitration procedure do not allow for either prehearing conferences or preliminary hearings, in virtually every system, the arbitrator probably has the inherent discretion to order some kind of prehearing procedure by which the issues are narrowed, stipulations are proffered and accepted, and the hearing process clarified. Granting that international commercial arbitrations that involve parties separated by long distances may find such a procedure inefficient and counterproductive, many of these things can be taken care of through correspondence and modern telecommunications. However, there may be instances, particularly in the case of complex arbitration when there is a real need for a "hearing before the hearing" to expedite matters.

Consider how beneficial a prehearing conference might be even in the relatively small Parthenon/Tangerine dispute. The hearing is to take place in New York City. The defective computers are in a warehouse in Athens. Assume that the final shipment consists of 30 individual computers. It is arguable that the claimant would have to present each of the 30 computers for the inspection of Tangerine's experts and for the arbitrator. A prehearing conference could result in a stipulation by both parties that all 30 computers are identical, irrespective of whether they are truly defective, and a single computer could be shipped from Athens to New York for inspection during hearing as representative of all the others in that Athens warehouse. Or, even better, the parties

123. *See*, e.g., U.S. Arbitration Act §7. For more extensive commentary on discovery in U.S. arbitration, *see*, Nathan D. O'Malley & Shawn C. Conway, *Document Discovery in International Arbitration—Getting the Documents You Need,* 18 Transnat'l L. 371 (2005); Wendy Ho, *Discovery in Commercial Arbitration Proceedings,* 34 Hous. L. Rev. 199 (1997); Charles S. Baldwin, IV, *Protecting Confidential and Proprietary Commercial Information in International Arbitration,* 31 Tex. Int'l L.J. 451 (1996); W. Michael Tupman, *Discovery and Evidence in U.S. Arbitration: The Prevailing Views,* 44 Arb. J. 27 (March 1989). For some commentary on discovery in an English and continental context *see*, W.G.O. Morgan, *Discovery in Arbitration,* 3 J. Int'l Arb. 9 (1986).

might be able to agree to present for inspection a prototype computer from Tangerine's U.S. factory as representative of that final shipment now residing in Athens. All in all a significant saving of time and money and one of the major contributions that a prehearing conference can make. Again, there are a number of creative ways to deal with some of the inherent procedural limitations in arbitration.

§9.7.3 Interim Relief Pending the Hearing

In some cases, there is a need for a party to seek interim relief to prevent the other party from taking actions that have the effect of undercutting the arbitration. For example, the party seeking monetary relief in an arbitration may fear that the other side will conceal or transfer assets or do something with the property at issue that will make it impossible to satisfy any award that may come out of the arbitration. That relief is usually sought first before the arbitrator but may also, in certain circumstances, be sought in an appropriate court. Virtually all the rules make provision for interim relief. The ICC's rules provide:

> Unless the parties have otherwise agreed, as soon as the file has been transmitted to it, the Arbitral Tribunal may, at the request of a party, order any interim or conservatory measure it deems appropriate. The Arbitral Tribunal may make the granting of any such measure subject to appropriate security being furnished by the requesting party. Any such measure shall take the form of an order, giving reasons, or of an Award, as the Arbitral Tribunal considers appropriate.[124]

The AAA rules are almost identical, providing: "(1)At the request of any party, the arbitral tribunal may order or award any interim or conservatory measures it deems necessary, including injunctive relief and measures for the conservation of property. (2) Such interim measures may take the form of an interim award, and the tribunal may require security for the costs of such measures."[125]

However, just as in the case of arbitrator-issued subpoenas, the party against whom one of these orders is issued may choose not to pay attention. In that case, a party is free to seek judicial intervention. The ICC's rules state: "[T]he parties may apply to any competent judicial authority for interim or conservatory measures."[126] The AAA provides: "A request for interim measures addressed by a party to a judicial authority shall not be deemed incompatible with the agreement to arbitrate or a waiver of the right to arbitrate."[127]

Virtually all modern arbitration acts give that country's courts the power to issue interim or conservation relief in the context of an arbitration. The UNCITRAL Model Law provides: "It is not incompatible with an arbitration agreement for a party to

124. ICC Rules, Art. 28(1). Art. 28(2) permits the parties to "apply to any competent judicial authority for interim or conservatory measures.
125. AAA Rules, Art. 24.
126. ICC Rules, Art. 23(2).
127. AAA Rules, Art. 21(3).

request, before or during arbitral proceedings, from a court an interim measure of protection and for a court to grant such measure."[128]

§9.7.4 The Hearing

The comparative absence of an elaborate scheme of prehearing devices makes the arbitration hearing all the more important to the parties. It is the central device for making each party's presentation, for the direct and cross-examination of witnesses and the production and examination of documents. It is frequently one of the first points of face-to-face contact between the parties and the arbitrators. It is at the hearing that the arbitrator becomes completely familiar with the evidence.[129]

[1] Order of Presentation

The arbitrator has virtually unfettered discretion to conduct the hearing. To that extent, a hearing may be highly structured or thoroughly relaxed depending on the personal preferences of the arbitrator. European hearings tend to be very relaxed, reflecting the differences in lawyer behavior and litigation style in those countries. In most instances in the United States, however, arbitration hearings tend to be highly adversarial and contentious. There is a relatively fixed order of presentation similar to the order of presentation in courts in the United States:

(1) Opening statement by the claimant (the party who demanded arbitration (opening statement by respondent at this point is usually optional.
(2) Presentation of claimant's case and cross-examination of claimant's witnesses by respondent.
(3) Opening statement (if reserved) by respondent.
(4) Presentation of respondent's case.
(5) Rebuttal evidence and witnesses by claimant.
(6) Closing arguments.

Documents are typically introduced and marked as exhibits. However, under most arbitration systems, testimony is not under oath and a verbatim transcript of the proceeding is taken only if one of the parties requests and is willing to pay for a stenographer.[130]

---

128. UNCITRAL Model Law, Art. 9. For further clarification on these issues *see*, Ali Yesilirmak, *Provisional Measures in International Commercial Arbitration* (2005); Stephen M. Ferguson, *Interim Measures of Protection in International Commercial Arbitration: Problems, Proposed Solutions and Anticipated Results*, 12 Currents Int'l Trade L.J. 55 (2003).
129. For an excellent discussion of many important procedural issues, including the taking of evidence in arbitral proceedings, *see* Jeffrey Waincymer, *Procedure and Evidence in International Arbitration* (2012).
130. *See*, e.g., AAA Rule 23: "Any party wishing a stenographic record shall make such arrangements directly with the stenographer and shall notify the other parties in advance of the hearing. The requesting party or parties shall pay the cost of such record."

Most of the remainder of the proceeding is subject to the wishes of the arbitrator. A litigation format is frequently used because this type of presentation makes for a relatively orderly and rational hearing; but arbitrators always have the discretion to depart from any fixed format. Because one of the hallmarks of arbitration is its confidential nature, the arbitration hearing usually takes place behind closed doors with the parties, their representatives and the arbitrator the only people in continuous attendance during the hearing.[131]

[2] *Rules of Evidence*

One of the singular characteristics of arbitration is that there are no formal rules of evidence. But what this statement really means is that there are no elaborate rules of evidence applicable by rule in commercial arbitrations. This does not mean that there are no boundaries placed on evidentiary matters, however. The UNCITRAL rules, for example, provide that "Each party shall have the burden of proving the facts relied on to support his claim or defense."[132] The AAA rules are a little more explicit: "The parties may offer such evidence as is pertinent and material to the controversy...The Arbitrator shall be the judge of the relevancy and materiality of the evidence offered."[133] So there are some limits: The evidence must be relevant and the parties share the burden of proof.

Other dimensions to rules of evidence sometimes escape persons new to the arbitration process.[134] Consider that many rules of evidence have a logical, rational basis. In this regard three concepts of evidence need not be codified to be applied in arbitrations. First, the concept of relevance is, as Justice Oliver Wendell Holmes was frequently heard to say, "a concession to the shortness of life." Arbitration hearings should not be dragged out because one of the parties insists on presenting evidence on things that have nothing to do with the controversy at hand. In any arbitral system, the arbitrator must always have the discretion to halt presentations on irrelevant matters even if the rules system does not contain a formal rule of relevance. Second, the evidentiary doctrine of competence is intended to ensure that witnesses testify only as to matters on which they have some knowledge. If a witness in the Parthenon/Tangerine arbitration who has never even seen a computer attempts to give testimony

131. *See*, e.g., UNCITRAL Rules, Art. 25(4): "Hearings shall be held in camera unless the parties agree otherwise." There is now some emerging literature arguing for more publication of arbitral awards in the name of transparency and public interest. *See*, e.g., Anjanette H. Raymond, *Confidentiality in a Forum of Last Resort: Is the Use of Confidential Arbitration a Good Idea for Business and Society?* 16 Am. Rev. Int'l Arb. 479 (2005); Cindy G. Buys, *The Tensions Between Confidentiality and Transparency in International Arbitration*, 14 Am. Rev. Int'l Arb. 121 (2003); Dora Marta Gruner, *Accounting for the Public Interest in International Arbitration: The Need for Procedural and Structural Reform*, 41 Colum. J. Transnat'l L. 923 (2003); Alexis C. Brown, *Presumption Meets Reality: An Exploration of the Confidentiality Obligation in International Commercial Arbitration*, 16 Am. U. Int'l L. Rev. 969 (2001).
132. UNCITRAL Rules of Arbitration, Art. 24.
133. AAA Commercial Arbitration Rules, Rule 31.
134. For an excellent commentary on all the nuances of taking evidence *see* Peter Ashford, *The IBA Rules on the Taking of Evidence in International Arbitration: A Guide* (2013).

on computer processing speed, he should not be listened to. As a corollary to this, the counsel putting that witness on the stand should have an obligation to show the witness's competence, before the witness begins his testimony on the specific issue of the Tangerine computers' speed.

Third, the notion of foundation has some applicability to arbitration hearings. Not only must a competent witness give relevant testimony, but also there should be some demonstration that the witness knows what he is talking about. A witness who is otherwise a qualified computer expert but who has never seen and tested the Tangerine computers that are the subject of this dispute should probably not be permitted to give testimony as to their processing speed. Again, the party introducing this witness should be required to develop the basis for the expert's testimony; and if that party does not, the testimony may be properly excluded.

In many instances, the arbitrator is a lawyer and the parties' representatives are lawyers. Sometimes, all concerned are products of the same legal system. Recall that in arbitration no formal rules of evidence are mandated. But that does not mean that evidence cannot be objected to or that the arbitrator cannot rule on these objections. Sometimes too much is made of the fact that the rules do not provide for the application of principles of evidence. The better practice in an arbitration hearing is that if a party has an objection on any ground, however formal, he should make it and simply see what the arbitrator says.

Of course, some caution is required. Arbitrators do not consider themselves judges and tend to become uncomfortable in the presence of counsel who constantly raise objections on the most tenuous of grounds. Moreover, the arbitrator is both an expert and the person who will make the decision. There is no special reason for an attorney to "put on a show" to impress a jury of lay persons. One of the theories of arbitration is that the arbitrator should receive as much information as possible and, because he is something of an expert, should use his own discretion in sorting it out. In addition, although there appear to be no reported cases on this point, it is arguable that an arbitrator who insists on applying strict rules of evidence when the parties have not previously agreed to their use may be guilty of misconduct and his award overturned on that ground.

§9.8 DRAFTING THE ARBITRAL AWARD

The status and prerogatives of the arbitrator have been established by the preceding sections. The arbitrator is thoroughly in control of the process, and his basic task through the conclusion of the hearing is to see that the parties are dealt with fairly and evenhandedly and that enough information is gathered so that he can render a proper award. As the UNCITRAL rules put it: an arbitral panel "may conduct the arbitration in such manner as it considers appropriate, provided that the parties are treated with equality and that at any stage of the proceedings each party is given a full opportunity of presenting his case."[135] At the conclusion of the hearing, the arbitrator closes the record and proceeds to draft the award. The closing of the hearing is a formal event that no lawyer should disregard. It means that no further testimony will be permitted and no additional documents or argumentation introduced. If an attorney representing a party has some additional matters to be addressed, she should not permit the arbitrator to close the proceeding.

If the arbitration is heard by a sole arbitrator, that person fashions the award. When the arbitration is presided over by a panel of three arbitrators, the various rules systems generally provide that the decision will be made by a majority of the arbitrators.[136]

The actual writing of the award is sometimes a difficult task; but here again, there are rarely any formal requirements; and in some systems an arbitral award simply states which party won—that is, there is no need for the arbitrator even to state reasons for her decision. However, in international commercial practice, it is customary for the arbitrator to give reasons for the decisions unless the parties specifically agree not to request reasons; and many arbitral awards wind up looking much the same as decisions rendered by a court, complete with citations to statutes and cases, elaborate recapitulations of the facts and nearly endless explanations of the arbitrator's findings and conclusions.

A few of the rules systems provide some guidance for the arbitrator. For example, the UNCITRAL rules require the arbitrator to decide the case on the basis of the law chosen by the parties or in the absence of a choice of law to "apply the law determined by the conflict of laws rules which it considers applicable."[137] If the parties have expressly authorized the arbitrator to do so, he may apply concepts of fairness and equity (*amiable compositeur/ex aequo et bono*) to the case, in addition to the law specifically applicable, giving the arbitrator some discretion to depart from rules of law that might otherwise produce an unusually harsh result. But, as the UNCITRAL rules provide, "[i]n all cases, the arbitral tribunal shall decide in accordance with the terms of the contract and shall take into account the usages of the trade applicable to the transaction."[138]

Beyond stating some obvious points, it is very difficult to describe narratively an arbitral award. One U.S. expert on arbitration, the former President of the AAA, Robert Coulson, suggests that this is a profound gap in the scholarship of arbitration. Mr. Coulson urges, among other things, that parties and arbitrators look to certain axioms of psychology and human behavior to get at the process of framing an arbitral award. One of his suggestions is that "[a]n arbitrator will tend to recall evidence that has not

135. UNCITRAL Rules, Art. 15. *See also*, Stacy I. Strong, *Reasoned Awards in International Commercial Arbitration: Embracing and Exceeding the Common Law-Civil Law Dichotomy*, 37 Mich. Int'l L.J. 1 (2015); Lawrence W. Newman & Richard D. Hill, *The Leading Arbitrator's Guide to International Arbitration* (2d ed., 2008).
136. *Id.*, Art. 31.
137. *Id.*, Art. 33(1).
138. *Id.*, Art. 33(3).

become stale [the concept of heuristic memory]. Advocates who request additional time to file [post-hearing] briefs may be losing the advantage of this fundamental heuristic tendency."[139]

But even suggestions such as this are essentially generalizations that no writer on the topic of arbitration should be allowed to get away with. Although there is virtually nothing in the literature on the process of deciding an arbitration, there are ways to try to penetrate the mind of an arbitrator without lapsing into that age-old English language joke that "arbitrator" is very close to "arbitrary."

How might an arbitrator go about fashioning an award? This question needs to be put in a specific context such as the Parthenon/Tangerine dispute. Consider that the arbitrator has conducted the hearing, read the contract and all other relevant documents, listened to each sides' experts and made his own inspection of the prototype computer submitted by Tangerine. As he or she actually begins to put words on paper, the thought of avoiding jargon is particularly attractive. The best arbitral awards tend to be written in plain language.[140]

While arbitrators are never required to write formal judicial-style decisions in which they frame specific findings of fact and conclusions of law, it is very helpful for an arbitrator to consider these two concepts as he proceeds to decide the case. Findings of fact are simply the "who," "what," "where," "when" questions that must be determined in any instance of human conflict. For example, in the Parthenon/Tangerine case an arbitrator will want to know something about the nature of the two companies, possibly something about the manner in which Tangerine manufacturers the computers, the precise technical specifications of the computers at issue, and why the computers need to be kept in such an expensive storage facility? By contrast, conclusions of law spring from the specific legal principles that are to be applied to the dispute. In this instance, an arbitrator would review those portions of the New York UCC that address contract specifications such as the UCC's provisions on warranties of fitness and merchantability.

If the contract permits the arbitrator to decide the case applying *amiable compositeur* principles, he might consider where and under what circumstances he is willing to depart from the UCC's specific commands to do justice in this particular case. For example, the UCC has some very strict rules on disclaimer of warranties. The arbitrator could examine these rules and might conclude that a foreign buyer, even one who has agreed to a New York UCC choice of law provision, had only an incomplete understanding of these provisions. He could then decide, using his authority as *amiable compositeur*, either not to apply the disclaimer rules or to apply them much more gently than the UCC calls for.

The arbitrator's ultimate conclusion of law is, of course, his determination of who wins. There is no bright line between findings of fact and conclusions of law but it is a very healthy way for a judge or arbitrator to get started in writing the award. The following example puts much of this in a specific context.

139. Robert Coulson, *The Decisionmaking Process in Arbitration*, 45 Arb. J. 37 (September 1990).
140. David Elliott, *Writing Arbitral Awards in Plain Language*, 46 Arb. J. 53 (December 1991).

Assume that in the Parthenon/Tangerine case the arbitrator reviews the record and ascertains that there is simply no dispute as to:

(1) the computer speed specified in the contract;
(2) the computer speed of the conforming goods shipped in the first four installments;
(3) the storage charges in the Athens warehouse for the arguably nonconforming computers;
(4) the applicability of the New York UCC.

This data can be immediately incorporated into his thinking (if not into the actual written award) without further consideration.

But the arbitrator must cope with many other things in the record. Assume that Tangerine introduced documentary evidence and testimony on a computer manufactured by a subsidiary company, Pepper Computers, that Tangerine counsel claimed was exactly like the Tangerine computers shipped to Parthenon. This evidence came onto the record because the arbitrator decided to be as lenient as possible in letting the parties make their presentations—and because Parthenon's counsel did not want to be seen to be constantly objecting to Tangerine's presentation, there was no objection from the opposing counsel. Irrespective of how this evidence came in, an arbitrator would likely be justified in disregarding all of this information because it appears clearly to be irrelevant. The issue is the performance specifications of the Tangerine computers, not the performance of some computers that seemed to be similar but that were not actually shipped to Parthenon.

On a more crucial point, the arbitrator heard from Tangerine's expert witness who testified that the computer speed conformed to or exceeded the specifications set out in the contract; and he also heard from Parthenon's expert who testified that the computer speed was substantially lower than the contract specified. This "battle of the experts" is a common phenomenon in commercial litigation and arbitration, and there are a number of ways for an arbitrator to resolve the matter. On the one hand, the arbitrator can simply make a finding of credibility. In other words, he may determine that Tangerine's expert is the more believable based on the expert's previous experience with similar computers, the scientific soundness of the tests that the expert made on the prototype computer, and even the expert's educational and professional background. On the other hand, if the arbitrator finds both witnesses equally credible and if his own expertise does not prompt him to tilt in one direction or another, he can dispose of the matter on the basis of burden of proof, another one of those concepts of evidence that may not be expressly stated in the rules but is applied nonetheless. On that basis, he could determine that the evidence is equally balanced and that the claimant (Parthenon, the firm i.e., claiming that the computers' performance is faulty) did not meet its burden of proof.

Assume that the arbitrator decides that the Parthenon expert is the person to believe. Given that virtually nothing else of importance—the contract language, the applicable law, and other matters—is truly in dispute, he would be justified in deciding in favor of Parthenon. However, an arbitral award is not complete merely because the arbitrator has decided who wins. He must take the additional step of fashioning a remedy. In the Parthenon/Tangerine case, if Parthenon prevails, he might simply award Parthenon normal breach of contract damages, including as is permissible under the UCC, additional incidental and consequential damages such as Parthenon's storage expenses. It is not impossible for an arbitrator to award specific performance. So the arbitrator could conceivably order Tangerine to provide Parthenon with computers which perform up to specifications and to take the defective computers back. In some jurisdictions, it may even be possible for an arbitrator to award punitive or exemplary damage in cases in which the respondent's actions are particularly abhorrent.[141]

Once the award is drafted and signed by the arbitrator, it is given to the parties and, if necessary, filed, or registered with an appropriate governmental entity, although the terms of the award remain confidential unless the parties agree to the award being released to the public. Some rules systems permit the parties to review the award and to request elaboration or clarification by the arbitrator. The UNCITRAL rules permit a party to request both an interpretation of the award and a correction (of clerical errors in) the award.[142] Each of these requests is in the nature of a motion for reconsideration, rather than an appeal of the award.

While there is normally no appeal of an arbitral award within the system of arbitration itself (although under the ICC's rules the ICC as supervising authority requires that the arbitrator give a draft to the ICC's Court of Arbitration for their review), a losing party does have the right to challenge the award in court by refusing to abide by the decision. The prevailing party then must bring some kind of court action either in the country of origin or some other country asking the courts of that country to recognize and confirm the award. That action (a topic addressed in Chapter 10) results in the award's becoming the functional equivalent of a court decision that will be enforced on the same terms as a judgment of a court.

Accordingly, an arbitral award should be considered final for two reasons. First, while not always clearly identified there is a concept of res judicata and collateral estoppel that attaches (or should attach) to an award, thus prohibiting losing party from attempting to readjudicate the award either in a subsequent arbitration or a fresh attempt at litigation.[143] Second, even though there is a path for judicial review of arbitral awards, most reviewing courts are obliged to simply confirm the award as written because of the narrowness of the scope of review provisions in the various domestic arbitration acts and in the New York Convention for the Recognition and

---

141. Compare the following law review articles: John Y. Gotanda, *Awarding Interest in International Commercial Arbitrations in the Wake of Mastrobuono v. Shearson Lehman Hutton, Inc.*, 32 Harv. Int'l L.J. 59 (1997); Robert T. Jones, *Punitive Damages as an Arbitration Remedy*, 4 J. Int'l Arb. 35 (1987); Note, *An Argument Against the Availability of Punitive Damages in Commercial Arbitration*, 62 St. John's L. Rev. 270 (1988). For a related topic *see*, John Y. Gotanda, *Awarding Interest in International Arbitration*, 90 Am. J. Int'l L. 40 (1996).
142. UNCITRAL Arbitration Rules, Arts. 35, 36. *See also*, James M. Gatis, *The Need for a Rule Providing a Limited Opportunity for Arbitral Reconsideration of Reasoned Awards*, 15 Am. Rev. Int'l Arb. 9 (2004).
143. *See*, e.g., Randy D. Gordon, *Only One Kick at the Cat: A Contextual Rubric for Evaluating Res Judicata and Collateral Estoppel in International Commercial Arbitration*, 18 Fla. J. Int'l L. 549 (2006).

Enforcement of Foreign Arbitral Awards. A wise losing party will need to carefully consider whether the time, effort and expense of challenging an award is worth it.

§9.9 AI AND ARBITRATION

In recent years there has been increasing discussion of AI and its impact on the practice of law and business. Chapter 4 (§4.10) deals with the impact of AI on the drafting of contracts. These days, it is entirely conceivable that AI will have an impact of the work of judges and arbitrators even though virtually all arbitrators schooled in the traditional methods scoff at such things. Many of the traditionalists use the pejorative term "robot arbitrator" to signal their discomfort with these issues.

AI is usually defined as intelligence that is found in a machine of some sort, rather than natural intelligence that is found in human beings. It is a relatively new phenomenon because up until just a few years ago there were virtually no machines that could replicate human thinking. Chapter 4 (§4.10) contains a much longer summary of the history and basis for AI. This section concentrates on the use of AI in the context of making decisions that have up until now been made by judges or arbitrators. It is clear that we have a long way to go, but the glimmerings of AI as a valid tool for making arbitration decisions is now known if not fully accepted and will likely only increase in importance.[144]

AI is now capable of producing software that finds patterns in complex decisions. One example is the way Amazon tracks a person's purchasing decisions in order to predict future purchases, and to recommend appropriate purchases based on those decisions. In computer speak, the machine applies an algorithm toward a particular decisional result. "Algorithm" in this instance is normally defined as "a finite set of unambiguous instructions performed in a prescribed sequence to achieve a goal, especially a mathematical rule or procedure used to compute a desired result."[145] At the same time, AI is much more than mere algorithms. Wikipedia suggests that AI includes as a long-range goal "general intelligence" whose components include "reasoning, knowledge, planning, learning, natural language processing, perception and the ability to move and manipulate objects."

Some of the pioneering work in this area has focused on the United States Supreme Court and has attempted to develop a tool (an algorithm, so to speak) that permits a computer to predict the votes of the justices in future cases based on their views, opinions and votes in prior cases. One researcher has posed the problem this way: "Could we replace a justice of the U.S. Supreme Court by an algorithm that does not know anything about the law or the case at hand but has access to the remaining

144. *See*, e.g., Erik Brynjolfsson & Andrew McAfee, *The Second Machine Age: Work Progress and Prosperity in a Time of Brilliant Technologies* (2014).
145. Dictionary.com definition of algorithm. Algorithms predate modern computers, but now comprise the basis for most computer operations.

justices' votes and the voting record of the court? Surely, the algorithm would not be able to hear the case or write an opinion, but would it be able to mimic the vote of the missing judge?"[146]

This analysis has its basis in both the mathematical topic of decision theory and in concepts and doctrines of legal studies and political science. Two researchers in Spain looked at decisions in the United States Supreme Court between 1953 and 2004 that resulted in full opinions. They began by assuming that on an "ideal" court, would be uncorrelated—that is, the fact that any two justices agreed or disagreed in one case gave no information on their agreement in later cases.[147] They justified their research and computations as: "Predicting [the behavior of justices] is a way to test hypotheses about how justices make decisions. Their conclusion involved the development of a stochastic block model, while not uniformly accepted within the legal community, is striking:

> For real courts [versus "ideal" courts], the block model algorithm correctly predicts 83% of the individual justices' decisions, and is therefore consistently more accurate than the majority rule. Although direct comparison with previous forecasting attempts is not straightforward, it is remarkable that our algorithm based on hidden associations between justices is more accurate at predicting justice votes than forecasts made by legal experts as well as those made by algorithms that take into consideration the content of the cases. Indeed, while we correctly predict 83% of the votes, legal experts predicted 67.9% and content-based algorithms correctly predicted 66.7%.[148]

Concededly, mere predictions, no matter how accurate they may seem, would be permitted to form the basis for actually deciding future cases, but what we seem to be seeing is the development of tools that deciders such as judges or arbitrators could conceivable apply as they work toward a decision in their own cases.

This type of thinking is becoming more and more prominent. Caleb Watney, writing in a publication of the Brookings Institution, believes that AI can be very helpful particularly in the criminal justice system. As he puts it: "Liberal democracies long have struggled to minimize or eliminate elements of bias in their systems of criminal justice. Maybe justice is just too difficult for humans to administer alone. Thankfully, new advances in AI could help balance the scales."[149]

Watney points out that various court systems already use AI-type techniques to assess such risks as whether a defendant will skip bail or a parolee will commit a new offense. He points out that these tools can alleviate the enormous congestion in the U.S. criminal system and promote fairness and safety by eliminating a great deal of the bias

146. Roger Guimera & Marta Sales-Pardo, *Justice Blocks and Predictability of U.S. Supreme Court Votes*, PLOS ONE 6(11), retrievable at http://journals.plos.org.
147. *Id.*, at 3. Their research acknowledged the contributions of many others, such as: C.F. Camerer, *Behavioral Game Theory: Predicting Human Behavior in Strategic Situations* in *Advances in Behavioral Economics* (C.F. Camerer, et al., eds, 2004); T.W.Ruger, et al., *The Supreme Court Forecasting Project: Legal and Political Science Approaches to Predicting Supreme Court Decisionmaking*, 104 Colum. L.Rev. 1150 (2004); Richard A. Posner, *How Judges Think* (2010).
148. *Id.*, at 4.
149. Caleb Watney, *It's Time for Our Justice System to Embrace Artificial Intelligence* (2017), www.brookings.edu/blog/techtank.

inherent in the determinations of individual judges. "While humans rely on inherently biased personal experience to guide their judgments, empirically grounded questions of predictive risk analysis play to the strengths of machine learning, automated reasoning and other forms of AI."[150] But as he concedes: "Humans would still need to guide the process."[151]

In a similar study, AI researchers at University College, London created a process by which a computer analyzed decisions of the European Court of Human Rights based on data from 584 cases already decided by the court. "The AI judge was able to analyze existing case law and deliver the same verdict as the ECHR 79 percent of the time, and it found that the ECHR judgments actually depended more on non-legal facts around issues of torture, privacy, fair trials and degrading treatment than on legal arguments."[152] This same author notes, however, that the European Union has just promulgated a General Data Protection Regulation (effective in 2018) that provides: "Every person has the right not to be subject to a decision biased solely on automated processing."

One commentator on a list serve of prominent international arbitrators suggests several positive developments from AI techniques in arbitration and a number of negative attributes. On the positive side are:

(1) making attempted bribery of arbitrators irrelevant;
(2) making conflict of interest irrelevant;
(3) thereby making codes of conduct irrelevant;
(4) making a process of review (appeal) irrelevant;
(5) making the process more dispassionate.

On the negative side are these questions: (1) does AI just displace the problem from arbitrator elites to "coding" elites; (2) how do we develop transparency in algorithms and AI; and (3) is a dispassionate (e.g., AI) system automatically a "fairer" system?

There is a great deal more to be discussed on this topic, but it clearly will not go away. A reader who is searching for some "real world" examples of how these things might work is directed to a system of "smart contracts" developed by the French insurance organization, AXA.

The process is relatively simple. An AXA customer buys flight-delay insurance on the AXA "Fizzy" platform (a blockchain system). The purchase transaction is recorded in an electronic ledger and a smart contract created on the blockchain. The smart contract is automatically linked to global air traffic data bases that identify any flight delays of over two hours. Those delays are automatically entered on the ledger and compensation to the traveler is triggered. The traveler is told when he or she buys the insurance what will be the level of compensation based on predetermined parameters.

---

150. *Id.*, at 2.
151. *Id.*
152. Ziyaad Bhorat, *Do We Still Need Human Judges in the Age of Artificial Intelligence? Transformation* (August 8, 2017) at www.opendemocracy.net/transformation.

The need for the traveler to file a claim is eliminated and the final amount of compensation is determined by an "automated arbitrator" whose actions do away with any potential dispute between the insurance company and the policy holder. Once the automated arbitrator makes a decision (presumably very quickly after the various parameters are satisfied), the claim is paid directly to the policyholder.[153]

This is a small example of how modern businesses may choose to deal with a large number of matters that have in the past been given over to traditional arbitration processes. We have not yet seen the last word on these issues.

153. This discussion is taken from Maria Terkhova, *AXA Turns to Smart Contracts for Flight-Delay Insurance*, Business Insider (September 15, 2017).

CHAPTER 10

International Commercial Arbitration: Arbitration in the Courts

§10.1 INTRODUCTION

In theory, courts should have very little impact on arbitration because commercial arbitration is normally viewed as an alternative rather than a precursor to litigation. International commercial arbitration in particular ought to be immune from court interference because so many contracting parties deliberately choose arbitration *to avoid* the domestic courts of certain countries. But in practice, the relationship between arbitration and courts is far more complex and tangled and is likely to remain so for the foreseeable future because arbitration systems are not self-effectuating and must rely heavily on an existing judicial system to implement many of actions taken during arbitration and, when necessary, to enforce the arbitral award itself. In other words, if a party chooses not to participate in an arbitration or refuses to honor an arbitral award, the other side has no recourse but to go to court either (1) to compel the other side to engage in arbitration or (2) to restrain (stay) any judicial proceedings until the arbitration is completed, or, finally, to force the losing party to honor the award by recognizing and confirming the arbitral award. There are, of course, instances when a party who does not wish to arbitrate will petition the court to stay any arbitration proceeding.

The limitations of arbitration are characteristic of all arbitration systems and are in part, the reason for so much of the cynical commentary on arbitration. Because courts are permitted to get involved in the arbitration process, many observers contend that arbitration is nothing more than a precursor of litigation, a trial run so to speak, that merely sets the stage for the proper and far more legitimate proceeding in court. Until recently, this cynicism was probably justified; but in recent years, a number of countries including the United States and England have taken steps—either through statutes or court decisions, or both—to severely restrict the opportunities for courts to interfere with arbitration. In the United States, the Supreme Court has played a major role in insulating the arbitration process from judicial interference. In a number of major decisions between 1972 and 1990, the Court not only shored up the doctrine of party autonomy and sanctity of contract (*pacta sunt servanda*) but also instructed federal courts to let arbitral awards alone unless the court had proper grounds for stepping into the controversy—and such grounds are now very few and far between.

To be more specific, in 1972 the Court decided *The Bremen v. Zapata Off-Shore Oil Company*,[1] a case involving an international contract for towing of oil rigs in which the contract specified that the dispute resolution forum should be the High Court of Justice in London, by compelling the parties to live up to that agreement, even though the parties might otherwise have been able to litigate in federal court in the United States. Among other things, the Court noted:

> The choice of that forum [the forum selection clause in the contract] was made in an arms-length negotiation by experienced and sophisticated businessmen, and absent some compelling and countervailing reason it should be honored by the parties and enforced by the courts.... [Moreover, the contract was an] international commercial transaction...[and] selection of a London forum was clearly a reasonable effort to bring vital certainty to this international transaction and to provide a neutral forum experienced and capable in the resolution of admiralty jurisdiction.[2]

At least in the United States, *The Bremen* set the stage for everything that followed. In a 1974 case, *Scherk v. Alberto-Culver Co.*,[3] the Court honored a general arbitration clause that provided for arbitration in Paris under the rules of the International Chamber of Commerce (ICC) even though the disputes in question involved violations of United States securities laws. In *Scherk*, for possibly the first but certainly not the last time, the Court noted the existence of the New York Convention on the Recognition and Enforcement of Arbitral Awards (discussed extensively in §10.4 below) and pointed out that the parties could always come into court under the New York Convention—but only after they completed the arbitration.

Approximately ten years later, in quick succession, the Court decided two cases involving purely domestic arbitration which have had an important impact on the U.S.' view of international commercial arbitration. In *Moses H. Cone Memorial Hospital v. Mercury Construction Co.*,[4] the Court read the federal arbitration act to create a statutory presumption in favor of arbitration; and in *Dean Witter Reynolds Inc. v. Byrd*,[5] the Court ordered the parties to engage in arbitration even when that process would resolve only a part of the dispute. The Court reasoned that concepts of judicial efficiency and economy must give way to the federal arbitration act's implied command that arbitration is to be permitted when the parties have previously agreed to arbitrate.

1. 407 U.S. 1 (1972).
2. *Id.*, at 13.
3. 407 U.S. 506 (1974).
4. 460 U.S. 1 (1983).
5. 470 U.S. 213 (1985).

With these cases as background, the Supreme Court, in the crucial 1985 decision of *Mitsubishi v. Soler*,[6] held that a general arbitration clause calling for arbitration in Tokyo under the rules of the Japan Chamber of Commerce included even claims arising under the U.S. antitrust laws—laws which have traditionally been resolved through litigation in U.S. federal court. The Court, coming full circle, reiterated much of its support for the integrity of international commercial arbitration expressed in *The Bremen*, pointing out that "where the international cast of a transaction would otherwise add an element of uncertainty to dispute resolution, the prospective litigant may provide in advance for a mutually agreeable procedure whereby he would seek his antitrust recovery as well as settle other controversies ... [In addition,] there is no reason to assume at the outset of a dispute that international arbitration will not provide an adequate mechanism" even for the resolution of U.S. antitrust claims. The Court, as it did in *Scherk*, went on to note the existence of the New York Convention and the fact that the Convention contains a provision permitting a reviewing court to set aside an arbitral award on public policy grounds if it determines that the arbitral tribunal did serious violence to the substance of the antitrust statutes.

Mitsubishi has been a watershed case for international commercial arbitration in the United States. It has resolved conclusively the scope of general arbitration clauses in international commercial agreements (the clause encompasses virtually all issues arising under the contract) and signaled, to both courts and lawyers, the Supreme Court's special sensitivity to the needs and integrity of the international commercial arbitration process.

Since the *Mitsubishi* decision, the Supreme Court has gone on to hold that even arbitration clauses in contracts that are so-called contracts of adhesion bind the parties to proceed by arbitration.[7] In the 1995 case of *Vimar Seguros y Reseguros S.A. v. M/V Sky Reefer*,[8] one of the parties to a contract for the sale of fruit transported from Africa to New York had signed a standard form bill of lading (the contract for the transportation of the fruit) with a carrier that was owned by a Japanese company. The contract called for arbitration in Tokyo under the Japanese maritime arbitration commission's rules. The party resisting arbitration argued that arbitration clauses in contract of adhesion such as bills of lading were not freely negotiated and thus not enforceable. The Supreme Court disagreed sharply and ordered enforcement of the arbitration clause.

6. 473 U.S. 614 (1985). Mitsubishi has been the subject of both praise and criticism: Compare Thomas E. Carbonneau, *Mitsubishi: The Folly of Quixotic Internationalism*, 2 Arb. Int'l 116 (1986) with Andreas F. Lowenfeld, *The Mitsubishi Case: Another View*, 2 Arb. Int'l 178 (1986). *See also*, William F. Fox, *Mitsubishi v. Soler and Its Impact on International Commercial Arbitration*, 19 J. World Trade L. 579 (1985). For a recent book-length analysis of these issues *see* Gary B. Born, *International Arbitration and Forum Selection Agreements: Drafting and Enforcing* (5th ed., 2016).
7. *Rodriguez de Quijas v. Shearson/American Express*, 490 U.S. 477 (1989).
8. 515 U.S. 528 (1995).

Vimar Seguros answers what few questions might have remained under *Mitsubishi*. When parties sign papers that contain arbitration clauses they must arbitrate in accordance with the terms of the arbitration agreement.[9]

England has taken a slightly different road. There, the courts had been regarded as strongly interventionist (and even as being hostile to arbitration) due to two provisions in the 1950 Arbitration Act which were used by the English courts to review and occasionally overturn arbitral awards or to interfere with ongoing arbitrations. The first of these, the special (or stated) case procedure, required the High Court of Justice to review issues of law growing out of controversies then in arbitration. This procedure had the effect of taking a whole panoply of issues out of the arbitrators' hands. Because it is frequently not difficult to convert any issue into a question of law, the stated case procedure severely undercut the integrity and continuity of the English arbitration process.

The second bone of contention in the 1950 Arbitration Act was a provision permitting the courts to set aside arbitral awards for errors of fact or law apparent on the face of the arbitral award. This provision, operating in tandem with the stated case procedure, permitted courts to review virtually any issue arising out of an arbitration—thereby destroying any finality in the arbitration process. English lawyers came to understand that arbitration was often nothing more than a rehearsal for a proceeding in court.

In 1979, the British Parliament enacted the 1979 Arbitration Act in large part to eliminate these two provisions and, presumably, to make the English courts somewhat less interventionist. While there seems to be some controversy on this point, most of the commentary on the 1979 Act supports the proposition that Parliament took this legislative action to make London a more hospitable place for international commercial dispute resolution.[10]

France appears to have created exceptional insulation from court interference in international commercial arbitrations both by case law and by statute. Professor Arthur T. von Mehren believes that French case law squarely establishes the proposition that doctrines of law which the French courts might apply to domestic arbitrations "do not apply to arbitrations which involve the interests of international commerce. The jurisprudence further intimates that certain of the rules and principles governing the regime applicable to international commercial arbitrations need not flow from rules and principles found in a national law."[11]

In addition, there has been legislative action in France that buttresses the integrity of the international arbitration process. In 1981, the French promulgated

9. There are a number of recent articles confirming these assertions that may be profitably consulted. *See*, e.g., Thomas E. Carbonneau, *The Revolution in Law Through Arbitration*, 56 Clev. St. L. Rev. 233 (2008); Peter B. Rutledge, *Whither Arbitration?* 6 Geo. J. L. & Pub. Pol'y 549 (2008); Susan L. Karamanian, *The Road to the Tribunal and Beyond: International Commercial Arbitration and United States Courts*, 34 Geo. Wash. Int'l L. Rev. 17 (2002).
10. *See*, e.g., Sigvard Jarvin, *London as a Place for International Arbitration*, 1 J. Int'l Arb. 59 (1985).
11. Arthur T. von Mehren, *International Commercial Arbitration: The Contribution of the French Jurisprudence*, 46 La. L. Rev. 1045 (1986).

Article 1496 of Title 6, Book 4 ("L'Arbitrage") which greatly enhances party autonomy in specifying principles of law to govern the dispute irrespective of whether those principles are the applicable law in the country of the award's origin. This appears to effectively insulate international arbitral awards from any reversals in French court on substantive legal grounds.[12]

These three examples should provide some notion of the dimensions of the relationships between courts and arbitrators. The following sections take up some of the more specific issues involving judicial action. Each of the following sections also involves the basic process of litigation—that is, irrespective of the label of the particular proceeding (action to stay, action to compel, action to enforce) the process a court proceeding and thus is to be disposed of under traditional concepts of subject-matter jurisdiction, personal jurisdiction, service of process and venue. For these reasons, it is advisable to take a close look at all the preliminary concepts discussed in Chapter 7 before working through the remaining sections in this chapter.

§10.2 ACTIONS TO COMPEL OR STAY ARBITRATION

There are essentially four instances in which a court can become enmeshed in commercial arbitration prior to the issuance of the arbitral award:

(1) Party A begins a judicial proceeding against Party B; Party B believes that an arbitration clause in the underlying contract must be honored; Party B files a request (normally in the form of a motion) to stay the litigation pending the outcome of the arbitration.
(2) Party A commences an arbitration; Party B believes that arbitration is impermissible; Party B files a court action to stay the arbitration.
(3) Party A sends Party B a demand for arbitration; Party B simply ignores the demand; Party A then goes to court and files a motion to compel arbitration.
(4) A party or a witness ignores an arbitrator's subpoena; the arbitrator goes to court to enforce the subpoena.

Scenario number 4 was discussed in Chapter 9. Recall that both the American Arbitration Association (AAA) and the United Nations Commission on International Trade Law (UNCITRAL) arbitration rules permit the arbitrator to issue subpoenas and to apply to an appropriate court for enforcement of those subpoenas if they are disregarded by the persons to whom they are addressed. Anyone who disregards the court's order is subject to a contempt of court citation.

The first three scenarios are really just different sides of the same coin. For the sake of simplicity and clarity, there will be no attempt here to analyze a large number

12. *Id.*, at 1058, citing Pierre Bellet & Edmunc Mezger, *L'arbitrage international dans le nouveau code de procedure civile,* 70 Revue Critique de Droit International Prive 611 (1981) and Philippe Fouchard, *L'arbitrage en France Apres le decret du 12 Mai 1981,* 109 J.de Droit International 394 (1982).

of different arbitration statutes. Instead, we will use the United States' Federal Arbitration Act[13] as a prototype arbitration statute along with some illustrative court decisions that construe the Act.

Under the Federal Arbitration Act, a federal court has the authority either to stay judicial proceedings or to compel arbitration. The statute is not ambiguous on this point: in an action to stay judicial proceedings "the court in which such suit is pending, upon being satisfied that the issue involved in such suit or proceeding is referable to arbitration under such an agreement, shall on application of one of the parties stay the trial of the [court] action until such arbitration has been had. ... "[14] This is a good place to recall the *Mitsubishi* decision: there are now virtually no issues that are not comprehended under a standard form arbitration clause, so a court is now normally bound to stay the judicial action. While the language of this section suggests that a court might retry the controversy after the arbitration is concluded, such is not the case. Once the arbitration is concluded and the award issued, the only thing a court may do is review the award under the recognition and confirmation principles discussed in §10.3.

Similar concepts govern actions to compel arbitration. Under the Act, a party may apply for an order compelling the other party to participate in the arbitration when that party fails to respond to a demand for arbitration. After a court hearing and after the court satisfies itself that "the making of the agreement for arbitration ... is not the issue ... the court shall make an order directing the parties to proceed to arbitration in accordance with the agreement."[15] Recall again that the *Mitsubishi* case was in federal court on a motion to compel arbitration filed by the Mitsubishi Company. The Supreme Court determined that the motion to compel should have been granted.

There is another provision in the Federal Arbitration Act that can provide a party with some leverage in an international commercial dispute. In a separate section of the Arbitration Act that was intended to bring the United States in compliance with the New York Convention on the Recognition and Enforcement of Arbitral Awards, a federal court is authorized to issue an order compelling a party to arbitrate, under the terms of the agreement, "whether that place [for arbitration] is within or without the United States."[16]

This provision works in the following manner. Assume that seller in the United States and a buyer in Costa Rica have signed an agreement for the purchase of telecommunications equipment. The contract contains a standard form arbitration clause by which the parties agree to arbitrate their grievances in Mexico City under UNCITRAL arbitration rules. After receipt of the goods, the Costa Rican purchaser decides that some of the equipment is defective and properly serves a demand for arbitration on the seller. The seller simply ignores the demand. On investigation, it appears that the seller has no presence and no assets in Mexico so it is impossible for

13. 9 U.S.C. §§1–14, 201–208. For an interesting discussion of many of these issues in a country-specific setting, *see* Sandra Synkova, *Courts' Inquiry into Arbitral Jurisdiction at the Pre-Award Stage: A Comparative Analysis of the English, German, and Swiss Legal Order* (2013).
14. *Id.*, §3.
15. *Id.*, §4.
16. *Id.*, §206.

the Mexican courts to obtain personal jurisdiction over the seller. In this hypothetical there is very little if anything the Mexican courts can do because they lack judicial power over either the person or the assets of the nonresponding party.

The Costa Rican buyer has essentially two choices: first, he can proceed unilaterally with the arbitration and get an award based in his favor even if the nonresponding party does not appear at the hearing. This works somewhat like a default judgment in court except that the arbitrator is required to pass on the merits of the claim even if the respondent is not present to make his presentation.

The arbitral award can then be taken to the United States where the buyer can ask a federal court to recognize and enforce the award against the American seller. This approach is a bit risky, however. An American court may be very suspicious of an award rendered in a Mexico City arbitration in which the U.S. party has not appeared and may refuse to recognize it even though both Mexico and the United States are parties to the New York Convention. U.S. courts tend not to support adversarial proceedings in which one of the adversaries has not appeared. While the award may be presumptively enforceable under the New York Convention, a U.S. court might still refuse enforcement on one ground or another. In any event, this approach has a number of disadvantages.

Fortunately, the Costa Rican buyer has another alternative which, when completed, is virtually foolproof. The buyer can travel to an appropriate U.S. federal court where the seller is located. There, the buyer may invoke §206 of the Act to file a motion to compel arbitration. The Federal Arbitration Act empowers the court to order the seller to engage in arbitration even if the arbitration is to be held outside the United States. Given Mitsubishi, there is no reason why a U.S. court would not order the U.S. seller into a Mexico City arbitration, unless the buyer could show some special defect in the process or the underlying contract. On the facts of the hypothetical, such a showing would be virtually impossible. If the court issues an order compelling arbitration, a failure of the seller to abide by the court's order would expose the seller to contempt of court proceedings. Disregarding a court's order compelling arbitration is a very dangerous tactic. Virtually everyone obeys such orders.

The upshot of these statutory provisions is that courts generally stay out of ongoing arbitrations or issue only those orders necessary to continue the arbitration such as subpoena enforcement orders and orders compelling arbitration. The only other role for courts in the arbitration process is in enforcing the arbitral award. At the same time, the potential role of a court is sufficiently important that virtually all lawyers setting up an international arbitration try to insure that an arbitration has a juridical "home" in the sense the parties to the arbitration must always have a court to which they may refer questions and issues that cannot be resolved within the arbitration.

§10.3 RECOGNITION AND ENFORCEMENT OF ARBITRAL AWARDS

Once an arbitral award is made final, many losing parties simply comply voluntarily with the terms of the award. There are any number of reasons for voluntary compliance. A party who loses in arbitration may want to continue the underlying business relationship, recognizing that noncompliance with the award will surely jeopardize that relationship. Some losing parties take a realistic look at what happened in the arbitration and may conclude that nothing is likely to change even if the award is taken to court since, as we shall see, the grounds on which a court may overturn an arbitral award are exceptionally narrow. In a statistical sense, arbitration is a "final" proceeding given that very few arbitral awards are ever overturned in court. Nonetheless, there is always the theoretical possibility that a court may overturn an award. For this reason, lawyers working in the arbitration setting try to make sure that the arbitration itself is as free of error as possible; but even when they have prevailed during the arbitration, they must consider the possibilities in court if the loser does not comply.

There are a number of different procedural routes available for obtaining judicial review of an arbitral award. A losing party may ask a court to vacate or modify the award. Under the Federal Arbitration Act, this must be done within three months after the award is filed or delivered and, as would be expected, the moving party must give proper notice of the court proceeding to the other side.[17] If the losing party does not voluntarily abide by the award, the arbitration winner may ask a court to confirm the award, an action that has the functional effect of converting the arbitral award to a court judgment, which is then enforced in the same manner as judicial decrees are enforced in the jurisdiction. Actions to confirm under the Federal Act must be brought within one year after the award is made.[18]

Under the Federal Arbitration Act, the grounds on which a court may review an arbitral award—irrespective of whether the action is to confirm, vacate, or modify—are exceptionally narrow. They are:

(1) where the award was procured by corruption, fraud, or undue means;
(2) where there was evident partiality or corruption in the arbitrators, or either of them;
(3) where the arbitrators were guilty of misconduct in refusing to postpone the hearing, upon sufficient cause shown, or in refusing to hear evidence pertinent and material to the controversy; or of any other misbehavior by which the rights of any party have been prejudiced;
(4) where the arbitrators exceeded their powers, or so imperfectly executed them that a mutual, final, and definite award upon the subject matter submitted was not made;
(5) where an award is vacated and the time within the agreement required the award to be made has not expired the court may, in its discretion, direct a rehearing by the arbitrators.[19]

17. *Id.*, §§10 and 11.
18. *Id.*, §9.
19. This is verbatim language from the Federal Arbitration Act, *id.*, §10.

The grounds for judicial review under the UNCITRAL Model Law on International Commercial Arbitration are similar. An arbitral award may be set aside by a court only if:

> (a) (i) a party to the arbitration agreement...was under some incapacity; or the said agreement is not valid under the law to which the parties have subjected it or, failing any indication thereon, under the law of this State; or
> (ii) the party [challenging the award]...was not given proper notice of the appointment of an arbitrator or of the arbitral proceedings or was otherwise unable to present his case; or
> (iii) the award deals with a dispute not contemplated by or not falling within the terms of submission to arbitration, or contains decisions on matters beyond the scope of the submission to arbitration, provided that, if the decisions on matters submitted to arbitration can be separated from those not so submitted, only that part of the award which contains decisions on the matters not submitted...may be set aside; or
> (iv) the composition of the arbitral tribunal or the arbitral procedure was not in accordance with the agreement of the parties, unless such agreement was in conflict with a provision of this [the Model] Law from which the parties cannot derogate, or, failing such agreement, was not in accordance with this law, or
>
> (b) (i) the subject matter of the dispute is not capable of settlement by arbitration under the law of this State; or
> (ii) the award is in conflict with the public policy of this State.[20]

At first glance, these grounds seem to give the court extraordinarily broad powers of review, but the language of the Federal Arbitration Act as interpreted by the federal courts since 1925 and the legislative history of the Model Law require that reviewing courts construe these grounds as narrowly as possible. The AAA believes:

> Courts considering arbitral awards will resolve doubts in favor of confirming the award as rendered. The statutory grounds for modifying or correcting an award are exclusive; failure to plead any of the specified grounds is fatal to a request for modification. In addition, judicial power to correct an award is limited to clearly discernible errors.[21]

Additionally, courts in the United States have occasionally invalidated arbitral awards on public policy grounds even though public policy is not an enumerated ground in the Federal Arbitration Act. This is a power that springs from a court's general common law authority to invalidate contractual arrangements after a finding that a particular contract violates a jurisdiction's public policy. To give a specific

20. UNCITRAL Model Law, Ch. VII, Art. 34.
21. AAA, International Commercial Arbitration in New York at 134 (1986).

example, an arbitral award that divides the proceeds of an illegal narcotics sale between person A and person B would not have to be honored by a reviewing court even though none of the defects set out in the Act provide a ground for overturning the award.

In the past, one might be able to argue that the public policy exception was on the verge of swallowing the general rule that courts should let arbitral awards alone. Fortunately, the courts have construed the term narrowly. For example, the United States Court of Appeals for the District of Columbia Circuit stated that the public policy ground is "not available for every party who manages to find some generally accepted principle which is transgressed by the award. Rather, the award must be so misconceived that it compels the violation of law or conduct contrary to accepted public policy."[22] On occasion, U.S. courts have overturned awards of punitive damages on grounds that punitive damages are not an appropriate sanction in arbitration.[23]

As noted above, public policy is an express ground for review in the UNCITRAL Model Law. The public policy ground as it effects enforcement of international arbitral awards is briefly discussed in the following section.

In the United States, a confirmed arbitral award is a very powerful document. In the first place, it generally precludes any new arbitration or litigation on the subject matter of the initial arbitration under those firmly established principles of preclusion known as res judicata and collateral estoppel (these concepts are now discussed in the literature under their new labels: claim preclusion and issue preclusion).[24] Stated very briefly, the principle of res judicata (or claim preclusion) prevents a party from relitigating (or in our case rearbitrating) a dispute that has already been litigated. Recall the lengthy hypothetical used in Chapter 8 involving the arbitration of a dispute over defective computer equipment in New York City between an American seller, Tangerine, and a Greek buyer, Parthenon. If the Greek buyer prevails on the arbitration and confirms the award in federal court in New York (or, for that matter, confirms the award in New York State court), Tangerine cannot sometime thereafter ask a court to try the same dispute all over again.

Collateral estoppel is a first cousin of res judicata and normally prevents a party from relitigating individual issues already decided in one case in a subsequent proceeding. While collateral estoppel is a slightly more elusive concept, assume that the Greek company has a Spanish subsidiary that encounters the same problem with the Tangerine computers and initiates an arbitration in New York against Tangerine. Assume that the first arbitration included a finding that Tangerine's principal place of business is Los Angeles, California. If Tangerine wants to relitigate the issue of its principal place of business in the arbitration with the Spanish subsidiary, it may be precluded from doing so under the doctrine of collateral estoppel. It had the chance to fully litigate that issue in the previous arbitration involving Parthenon and may now be

22. *Revere Copper & Brass, Inc. v. Overseas Private Investment Corp.*, 628 F.2d 81, 83 (D.C.Cir. 1980).
23. *See*, e.g., *Domke on Commercial Arbitration* (George. Wilner ed., 1984), §33.03; *United States Fidelity and Guaranty Co. v. DeFluiter*, 456 N.E.2d 429 (Ind., 1983) (punitive damages not available in arbitrations involving contractual relationships).
24. *See*, e.g., Domke, *supra* n. 23, at §39:04.

barred from going over the same ground in the second arbitration. Even though the two doctrines are somewhat selectively applied, they both spring from a homily in U.S. law—that a person gets one day in court, not two.

Confirmation confers other benefits on an arbitral award. In the United States, an award confirmed in one state (including awards confirmed in federal court within that state) are given the same force and effect as a judgment in the court of that state. Having the status of a court judgment makes the award enforceable in any other state under the U.S. Constitution's full faith and credit clause.[25] These two concepts (the process of confirmation and the doctrine of full faith and credit) make an arbitral award just as effective a pronouncement as anything handed down in court. Establishing an arbitral award's legitimacy by confirmation contributes substantially to the security and predictability of arbitral awards in general. Consider that Parthenon won the arbitral award in New York City but Tangerine does not pay up. Parthenon's lawyers would then likely search for assets belonging to Tangerine in the State of New York from which to satisfy the award. Assume further that no such assets can be found. It turns out that the siting of the arbitration in New York was simply a matter of mutual convenience for the parties. It happens, however, that Tangerine has lots of assets in California. All Parthenon has to do is take the confirmed New York award to California and ask the California courts to enforce it against Tangerine in that state. Under the full faith and credit clause, California courts must enforce the award as if it had been rendered and confirmed in California.

Furthermore, in the United States under the Full Faith and Credit clause, there is no requirement of double exequatur,[26] which parties sometimes encounter on the international level. The concept of double exequatur asks whether an award won and confirmed in State A must be confirmed for a second time in State B. Under the U.S. Constitution, the answer is no; but the proposition is best illustrated by a diagram, *see* Figure 10.1.[27]

25. *Id.*, at §41:01.
26. For an excellent discussion of double exequatur and other issues *see*, W. Laurence Craig, *Uses and Abuses of Appeal from Awards*, 4 Arb. Int'l 174 (1988). *See also*, Radu Lelutiu, *Managing Requests for Enforcement of Vacated Awards under the New York Convention*, 14 Am. Rev. Int'l Arb. 345 (2003).
27. This diagram was provided by David Stewart, Esq., who has been a guest lecturer in the author's dispute resolution seminar.

Figure 10.1 A Double Exequatur Diagram

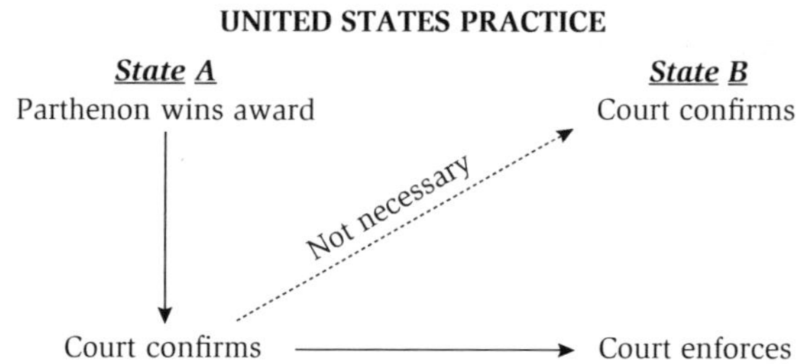

Thus, in the United States, there is no double exequatur requirement so long as the court in State A confirms. Parthenon simply presents the confirmed award from State A to the court in State B and obtains enforcement.

On the international level, however, the concept of double exequatur works in a slightly different fashion. Consider the following hypothetical under the United Nations Convention on the Recognition and Enforcement of Foreign Arbitral Awards (New York Convention) (discussed at length in the following section). Tangerine (a California company) and Parthenon (a Greek company) conduct their arbitration in London. Parthenon wins an award of USD 150,000 but can find no assets belonging to Tangerine in the United Kingdom (again, the forum selection was simply a matter of mutual convenience—effectively splitting the distance between Greece and California). Under the New York Convention, the holder of a valid, binding arbitral award does not need to seek confirmation in the country where the award was made, but may simply take the arbitral award itself to another signatory country where it will be enforced under the Convention. Under the New York Convention, the process is illustrated by the following diagram Figure 10.2.

Figure 10.2 New York Enforcement Process

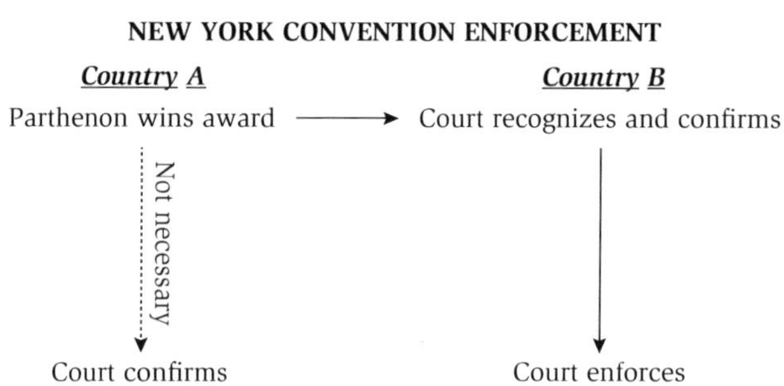

§10.4 INTERNATIONAL RECOGNITION AND ENFORCEMENT OF ARBITRAL AWARDS

The United States Constitution makes the U.S. a single economic unit. Arbitral awards made in one state may be confirmed and enforced in another state with relative ease. That is not the case on the international level, however. International recognition and enforcement of arbitral awards present a range of different problems that typically are dealt with by treaty.

Chapter 7 points out that there is no special principle of international law that requires the courts in one nation to abide by the judgments of the courts of another nation. At the present time, the only multilateral treaty currently in effect that requires courts in one country to abide by the decisions of courts in another country governs the EC under provisions of the Brussels Convention. Arbitration is accorded a different status, however. Since 1958, the United Nations Convention on the Recognition and Enforcement of Foreign Arbitral Awards (New York Convention) has been accepted by over seventy countries and makes recognition and enforcement of foreign arbitral awards a relatively painless and speedy process. There are other instances in which bilateral treaties contain provisions on the enforcement of arbitral awards in the two signatory countries. On occasion even when no treaty governs enforcement, a prevailing party seeking enforcement may use the domestic courts of a country as an appropriate enforcement vehicle.

§10.4.1 The New York Convention

The growth of international business following World War One prompted a number of countries to draft and sign the Geneva Protocol on Arbitration Clauses of 1923 and the Geneva Convention of the Execution of Foreign Arbitral Awards of 1927.[28] These two agreements, negotiated under the auspices of the League of Nations, were a good beginning but they included so many reservations and exemptions that they were not very effective on their terms. Possibly reflecting the same suspicion that prompted it not to join the League of Nations, the United States—then rapidly becoming one of the world's major trading nations—refused to sign either of the two agreements.

Another multilateral attempt to provide some international predictability in this area was initiated by the United Nations just after World War Two. The culmination of those efforts was New York Convention.[29] This time the United States participated in all

28. 27 L.N.T.S. 158, adopted September 24, 1923 and 92 L.N.T.S. 301, adopted September 26, 1927, respectively.
29. 330 U.N.T.S. 38 (1959); 21 U.S.T. 2517; T.I.A.S. No. 6997 (1970). For book-length treatments of the New York Convention, *see* George A. Bermann (ed.), *Recognition and Enforcement of Foreign Arbitral Awards: The Interpretation and Application of the New York Convention by National Courts* (2017); Reinmarr Wolff, *The New York Convention: Commentary* (2012).

of the negotiations and eventually fully ratified the treaty on February 1, 1971.[30] Fundamentally, the New York Convention is an attempt to make arbitral awards rendered in one country fully effective in any other signatory country.

While virtually all of the major trading nations have accepted the Convention, over time there have been some notable geographical gaps in the Convention's application. Latin America was historically underrepresented. Initially, this lack of participation in the New York Convention led a number of Latin American countries to negotiate and sign a separate treaty with much the same impact, the 1975 Panama Convention on International Commercial Arbitration (discussed in Chapter 10).[31] The Panama Convention did not attract all the countries of Latin America. This problem has probably been corrected by the increasing number of Latin American countries that have joined the New York Convention. Some countries—China is a prime example—have accepted the New York Convention as a signal that they wish to join the community of trading nations. There are some recent suggestions that if countries wish to become regarded as acceptable international trading partners they should accede to the Convention.[32]

In the United States, the New York Convention has been elevated to major importance by such Supreme Court decisions as *Mitsubishi v. Soler.*[33] In *Mitsubishi*, the Court cited U.S. participation in the New York Convention as a signal from Congress and the President that international commercial agreements were a special form of commercial transaction to be given special treatment.

Described briefly, the Convention applies to arbitral awards made in any country adopting the Convention that the prevailing party wishes to have recognized and enforced in any other adopting country.[34] The Convention also covers arbitral awards made in nonsignatory countries when the arbitrating parties are from signatory countries. For example, the New York Convention will govern an arbitral award between a seller and a buyer (both from nonsignatory nations) if the award was made in London because the United Kingdom, the place where the award was made, is a signatory. Similarly, the New York Convention will apply to an arbitral award made in a nonsignatory state between a British and a U.S. party.

Basically, the Convention requires each country to recognize and enforce arbitral awards based on agreements "in writing" which "include an arbitral clause in a contract or arbitration agreement, signed by the parties or contained in an exchange of

30. *See*, e.g., Gerald Aksen, *American Arbitration Accession Arrives in the Age of Aquarius: United States Implements United Nations Convention on the Recognition and Enforcement of Foreign Arbitral Awards,* 3 S.W. L. Rev. 1 (1971).
31. *See*, e.g., Pieter Sanders, *A Twenty Years' Review of the Convention on the Recognition and Enforcement of Foreign Arbitral Awards,* 18 Int'l Law. 269 (1978). For an excellent analysis of enforcement in China *see* Roger P. Alford, Julian G. Ku & Bei Xiao, *Perceptions and Reality: The Enforcement of Foreign Arbitral Awards in China,* 33 Pac. Basin L. J. 1 (2016).
32. *See*, e.g., Jennifer L. Amundsen, *Membership Has Its Privileges: The Confidence-Building Potential of the New York Convention Can Boost Commerce in Developing Countries,* 21 Wis. Int'l L.J. 383 (2003).
33. 473 U.S. 614 (1985).
34. New York Convention, Art. I.

letters or telegrams."[35] There are very few instances in which a contracting state may refuse recognition and enforcement.[36] These are:

(1) the parties to the agreement were under the law applicable to them under some incapacity, or the agreement is not valid under the law to which the parties have subjected it, or under the law of the country in which the award was made;
(2) the party against whom the award is invoked was not given proper notice of the appointment of the arbitrator or of the arbitration proceedings or was otherwise unable to present his case;
(3) the award deals with a difference not contemplated by or not falling within the terms of the submission to arbitration, or it contains decisions on matters beyond the scope of the submission to arbitration;
(4) the composition of the arbitral authority or the arbitral procedure was not in accordance with the agreement of the parties or, if there is no such agreement, with the law of the country where the arbitration took place;
(5) the award has not yet become binding on the parties or has otherwise been stayed or set aside by a court in that country;
(6) the subject matter of the award is not capable of settlement by arbitration under the law of that country; or
(7) the recognition or enforcement of the award would be contrary to the public policy of that country.[37]

Very much like the grounds for vacating or modifying an arbitral award discussed in the preceding section, these grounds are intended to be construed narrowly.[38] Indeed, the reader will note that the grounds in the New York Convention are almost identical to the grounds for judicial review of arbitral awards promulgated in

35. *Id.*, Arts. II and III. There is some recent scholarship suggesting that oral agreements might be made the subject of a New York Convention enforcement proceeding, *see*, e.g., Peter Kucherepa, *Reviewing Trends and Proposals to Recognize Oral Agreements to Arbitrate in International Arbitration Law,* 16 Am. Rev. Int'l Arb. 409 (2005).
36. Just recently, there has been a flurry of commentary on a number of decisions out of United States courts asserting that those courts are applying domestically derived concepts of personal jurisdiction to avoid enforcement of foreign arbitral awards under the New York Convention. *See*, e.g., William W. Park & Alexander A. Yanos, *Treaty Obligations and National Law: Emerging Conflicts in International Arbitration,* 58 Hastings L.J. 251 (2006).
37. This language is a paraphrase of New York Convention Art. V. For some interesting scholarship on grounds for vacating awards, *see*, e.g., Amina Dammann, *Vacating Arbitration Awards for Mistakes of Fact,* 27 Rev. Lit. 441 (2008); Kenneth R. Davis, *Unconventional Wisdom: A New Look at Articles V and VII of the Convention on the Recognition and Enforcement of Foreign Arbitral Awards,* 37 Tex. Int'l L.J. 43 (2002). For some practical suggestions on enforcing awards under the Convention, *see* Jane L. Volz & Roger S. Haydock, *Foreign Arbitral Awards: Enforcing the Award Against the Recalcitrant Loser,* 21 Wm. Mitchell L. Rev. 867 (1996).
38. One open issue is whether the contracting parties may, by language in the contract, expand the issues that may be reviewed by a court. *See*, e.g., Lee Goldman, *Contractually Expanded Review of Arbitration Awards,* 8 Harv. Negot. L. Rev. 171 (2003); Dan C. Hulea, *Contracting to Expand the Scope of Review of Foreign Arbitral Awards: An American Perspective,* 29 Brook. J. Int'l L. 313 (2003).

UNCITRAL's Model Law of Arbitration. One of the perceived loopholes, the public policy ground, has not materialized as a major barrier to enforcement and recognition. When courts examine the public policy ground, they generally separate the issues into two categories: (1) questions of procedural due process; and (2) questions of the arbitrability of certain issues. Due process is rarely a viable argument so long as the party objecting to recognition and enforcement has received adequate notice of the arbitration. If an arbitration has taken place under established procedural rules such as the ICC, AAA or UNCITRAL arbitration rules, there can be few complaints about the procedural aspects of the arbitration.[39]

The other component of the public policy ground—nonarbitrability of certain issues—appears to be shrinking as a basis for refusing recognition and enforcement. For example, in *Mitsubishi v. Soler*,[40] the Supreme Court of the United States held squarely that issues of competition arising under the U.S. antitrust laws were properly the subject of arbitration in Tokyo under the arbitration rules of the Japan Arbitration Association. The Court expressly left open the possibility of a U.S. court reviewing the outcome of the arbitration under the New York Convention and possibly holding the arbitration void as against public policy, but did not lend any great encouragement to this tactic. Essentially, the Court viewed such review as a kind of safety valve, permitting a U.S. court to refuse recognition only if the arbitration did immense violence to U.S. antitrust concepts and policies. The remainder of the Court's decision focused on determining that it was highly probably that the arbitrators would make reasonable decisions on the antitrust issues.

Even as early as 1977, eight years prior to *Mitsubishi* and only six years after U.S. ratification of the Convention, at least one writer felt comfortable with this comment:

> The attitude of the United States courts towards the [New York Convention's] public policy defense is not one which recognizes the defense as a "catch-all" to protect the integrity of arbitration. Rather, the courts have considered the defense mainly as a means by which a forum might escape binding arbitration. Consequently, the courts have given the public policy defense so narrow a construction that it now must be characterized as a defense without meaningful definition.[41]

How does the Convention work in practice? One of the author's first encounters with an international commercial arbitration involved a Greek ship repair company located in Piraeus that contracted to make some repairs on an oil tanker owned by a private oil company doing business in the Middle East. The contract contained a

39. *See*, e.g., Robert A.J. Barry, *Application of the Public Policy Exception to the Enforcement of Foreign Arbitral Awards under the New York Convention: A Modest Proposal*, 51 Temp. L. Q. 832 (1978).

40. 473 U.S. 614 (1985).

41. Joel R. Junker, *Note, The Public Policy Defense to Recognition and Enforcement of Foreign Arbitral Awards*, 7 Calif. W. Int'l L.J. 228 (1977). *See also*, Homayoon Arfazadeh, *In the Shadow of the Unruly Horse: International Arbitration and the Public Policy Exception*, 13 Am. Rev. Int'l Arb. 43 (2002). *See also*, Robert French, *Arbitration and Public Policy*, 24 Asia-Pacific L. Rev. 1 (2016); Haoqian Chen, Haiklin Bao & Tianyi Zhang, *Piercing the Veil of Public Policy in the Recognition and Enforcement of Foreign-Related Awards in China*, 7 Beijing L. Rev. 23 (2016); *Langang Fei, Public Policy as a Bar to Enforcement of International Arbitral Awards: A Review of the Chinese Approach*,26 Arb. Int'l 301 (2014).

bare-bones arbitration clause requiring that any disputes be arbitrated in Switzerland under ICC rules. Indeed, the arbitration clause was contained in small type text on the obverse of a preprinted work order.

The oil company reneged on payment of the repair bill; and the matter went to arbitration in Switzerland where the Greek company prevailed, winning an award for the full amount of the repair bill plus certain costs. The loser did not pay voluntarily, and when the Greek company looked for ways to satisfy the award, it encountered another difficulty. The tanker itself had been secretly moved back to the Middle East (recall that obtaining prearbitration attachment of property is not easy, particularly outside the United States) where the ship's engine and navigational gear was removed. The hull was then turned into a floating oil storage tank anchored within the territorial waters of a country not a signatory to the New York Convention. So the losing company had no property in Greece (where the repair work was done), no property in Switzerland (where the award was made) and even if the hull could have been seized and sold to satisfy the award (a highly doubtful proposition in the judgment of counsel), its new value as a floating oil tank might not have covered the amount of the award.

The winner came to the author with a request for some suggestions on how to satisfy the award. Put more colloquially, the winner wanted to know where to find some money. Fortunately for the winner, the New York Convention governs arbitral awards made in contracting countries, even if one or both of the parties are not nationals of contracting countries. Switzerland is a contracting country so the award was subject to recognition and enforcement in any other contracting state where the losing party might be found or where the losing party had property. After a quick but fruitful investigation, it became apparent that the oil company, albeit using as part of its title the name of a middle eastern country, was in fact a private corporation and a wholly owned subsidiary of a major U.S. oil company with its corporate headquarters in Delaware. This revelation made the rest of the process relatively simple.

In the United States, actions for recognition and enforcement are commenced in federal court under the authority of a part of the Federal Arbitration Act specifically enacted by Congress to implement the New York Convention.[42] This meant that counsel for the party seeking enforcement had merely to go to federal court in Wilmington, Delaware, where he filed a copy of the arbitral award along with a request for recognition and enforcement. After a short courtroom proceeding, the award was recognized and thus converted into an enforceable federal court judgment. Recall again that the New York Convention does not require a double exequatur—that is, the party seeking enforcement does not first have to seek confirmation or enforcement in the country where the award is made, but can go immediately to a contracting country where the losing party has property. Recall further that there are virtually no viable defenses to recognition and enforcement. The U.S. court properly gave short shrift to certain arguments from opposing counsel about the procedural primitiveness of arbitration in Switzerland under the ICC's rules.

42. 9 U.S.C. §§201–208.

After a few hours of negotiation, the losing company gave up any pretense of a defense and shortly thereafter, the client got his check for the full amount of the award. There are few better illustrations of the powerful contributions the New York Convention has made to international commercial dispute resolution.[43] This explains as well as anything why arbitration is usually the dispute resolution device of choice in international commercial transactions.

§10.4.2 Enforcing Awards Not Subject to the New York Convention

One of the problems with the New York Convention is that it has not been accepted by every country in the world. Earlier it was noted that Latin American countries, in particular, have failed to ratify it. As of January 1, 1991, less than eighty countries have become contracting states; and while this list includes virtually all of the major trading nations of the world, there are almost an equal number of United Nations members who have not agreed to the Convention. What is to be done when an arbitral award must be enforced in a country that is not a contracting state within the New York Convention?

There are two viable paths to enforcement. First, many countries have signed bilateral treaties of friendship, commerce and navigation (so-called FCN treaties) that may contain language sufficient to persuade a court in one country to recognize and enforce the arbitral awards made in the other country. FCN treaties should be thoroughly explored when a prevailing party is seeking enforcement in a non-New York Convention country.

The second route to be explored is simply the internal arbitration law of the country in question. Just because a country has not signed the New York Convention does not mean that it has a primitive legal system or that it is hostile to arbitral awards. Its internal law may be all the authority necessary to have the award enforced on its terms.[44]

The fundamental point to be kept in mind is that arbitration is becoming accepted around the world. Many countries, including many who have not joined the New York convention are modernizing their domestic arbitration laws and executing FCN treaties with each other. Merely because the New York Convention does not apply is no reason to give up on trying to enforce an arbitral award.

---

43. There is some commentary to the effect that the New York Convention might be used as a basis for enforcing settlement agreements that emerge from international commercial mediation. *See*, Brette L. Steele, *Enforcing International Commercial Mediation Agreements as Arbitral Awards under the New York Convention*, 54 UCLA L. Rev. 1385 (2007).
44. For a discussion of these points *see*, e.g., Domke, *supra* n. 23, Chs. 45 and 46 and Lionel Kennedy, *Note, Enforcing International Commercial Arbitration Agreements and Awards Not Subject to the New York Convention*, 23 Va. J. Int'l L. 75 (1982).

CHAPTER 11

International Commercial Arbitration: Special Regional Considerations

§11.1 INTRODUCTION

The two preceding chapters discussed international commercial arbitration generally and concentrated on those instances in which two parties are generally free to write whatever agreement they choose and to agree on any of a number of dispute resolution alternatives. Faced with a lot of possibilities, parties to international contracts usually agree on a conventional arbitration clause with appropriate choices of applicable law and site of arbitration. However, in some situations, the parties' choice of dispute resolution is constrained by the requirements of the particular country in which they are doing business. Some countries impose limitations on private dispute resolution that override choices that the parties might elect. This chapter is a survey of some of the special considerations that apply in certain instances. It is not an exhaustive treatment of any particular country or region nor a comprehensive list of those settings in which special problems may occur. It is simply intended to be a representative sample of some of the limitations faced by business executives and lawyers in different parts of the world.

§11.2 THE INTERNATIONAL CENTRE FOR THE SETTLEMENT OF INVESTMENT DISPUTES (ICSID)

One of the world's most sophisticated systems of commercial arbitration has been developed by the World Bank's International Centre for the Settlement of Investment Disputes (ICSID). However, the ICSID process has severe jurisdictional limitations (it is essentially limited to disputes between private parties and the governments of developing countries) that place it out of reach of the conventional private-party-versus-private-party dispute that is the focal point of this book. Nonetheless, the ICSID procedures warrant attention because of their sophistication and because the readers of this book may encounter a few commercial disputes that may be processed under the auspices of ICSID.

Most systems of international commercial arbitration are based on procedures that are developed by essentially private (i.e., nongovernmental) organizations such as the AAA and the International Chamber of Commerce (ICC). Because arbitration normally must have a juridical and geographic base, domestic legislation in the country in which the arbitration is held provides the remaining legal framework. In sharp contrast, ICSID was created by treaty—the Convention on the Settlement of Investment Disputes between States and Nationals of Other States[1]—and is a component of the World Bank, an organization that is essentially a financial agency that administers loans made by private banks in the developed countries to governments in the developing countries. As of late 2017, the ICSID Convention has been signed by 161 countries, of which 153 countries have deposited with the World Bank their documents of ratification, acceptance or agreement.[2] ICSID derives its importance from the status of the World Bank in international finance. In its early years, the ICSID arbitration process was not a numerically significant system of international commercial arbitration. In the first twenty years of its existence, ICSID processed fewer than thirty individual cases and put fewer than twenty cases through its full-blown arbitration process.[3] The pace has picked up somewhat but still does not come close to the caseload of the private-sector arbitration institutions such as AAA or ICC.[4] ICSID reports 48 cases registered in the calendar year 2016, 52 cases in 2015, 38 in 2014 and 40 in 2013.[5]

1. Opened for signature March 18, 1965, 17 U.S.T. 1270, T.I.A.S. No. 6090, 575 U.N.T.S. 159. ICSID decisions may be found on the ICSID website: http://icsid.worldbank.org/. For an excellent overall analysis of ICSID, past and present, *see*, Christopher H. Schreuer, *The ICSID Convention: A Commentary* (2001). Several recent book-length publications contribute to our understanding of ICSID and its processes: Crina Baltag, *ICSID Convention after 50 Years: Unsettled Issues* (2017); Antonio R. Parra, *The History of ICSID* (2d ed., 2017); Meg Kinnear & Geraldine Fischer, *Buildng International Investment Law: The First 50 Years of ICSID* (2015); Hege Elizabeth Kjos, *Applicable Law in Investor-State Arbitration: The Interplay Between National and International Law* (2013) and Katia Yannaca, *Small, Arbitrtion under International Investment Agreements: A Guide to the Key Issues* (2010). This edition be remiss if it did not also cite a very well-written, insightful and practical guide to ICSID arbitration: Jan Paulsson, Nigel Rawding & Lucy Reed, *Guide to ICSID Arbitration* (2d rev. ed., 2010). There is continuing debate as to the true consequence and contributions of ICSID. *See*, e.g., Ibironke T. Odumosu, *The Antinomies of the (Continued) Relevance of ICSID to the Third World*, 8 San Diego Int'l L.J. 345 (2007).
2. *See*, ICSID website—member countries.
3. *See*, News from ICSID (Winter, 1984); and Georges R. Delaume, *ICSID Arbitration in Practice*, 2 Int'l Tax & Bus. L. 58 (1984). *See also*, W. Michael Reisman, *The Breakdown of the Control Mechanism in ICSID Arbitration*, 1989 Duke L.J. 739 (1989).
4. *See*, e.g., David R. Sedlak, *ICSID's Resurgence in International Investment Arbitration: Can the Momentum Hold?* 23 Penn. St. Int'l L. Rev. 147 (2004). *See also*, Julian Davis Mortenson, *The Meaning of "Investment": ICSID's Travaux and the Domain of International Investment Law*, 51 Harv. Int'l L.J. 257 (2010).
5. ICSID website (cases registered by ICSID). ICSID distinguishes among: (1) ICSID Convention Arbitration cases (approximately 87% of its caseload); (2) ICSID Convention Conciliation cases (2%); (3) ICSID Additional Facility Arbitration cases (10%); and (4) ICSID Additional Facility Conciliation cases (1%). ICSID reports a total (from its beginning) of 419 cases registered under its Convention and Additional Facility Rules, http://www.icsid.worldbank.icsid.

Nonetheless, ICSID is a prestigious organization with a well-thought out process of arbitration that bears further examination. Three basic criteria, set out in Article 25 of the ICSID Convention, are used for determining ICSID's jurisdiction: (1) whether the case is a dispute arising out of an investment agreement; (2) whether the dispute is between a contracting state (or an entity or component with authority to contract in the name of the country) and a national of another contracting state; and (3) whether the parties have consented to ICSID arbitration by way of a written agreement.[6] Most commentators believe that while these jurisdictional terms are to be construed as broadly as possible, they severely limit the total number of disputes that may be brought before ICSID.[7] This is the primary reason why there have been so few arbitrations actually conducted by ICSID. However, once jurisdiction attaches, a number of other consequences flow: first, once having given its consent to ICSID jurisdiction a party cannot later withdraw that consent; second, no domestic court in a contracting country may interfere with the ICSID arbitration process; third, courts in all the contracting nations are obliged by the terms of the treaty to give "prompt and effective recognition" to any ICSID award.[8]

ICSID has developed some exceptionally sophisticated dispute resolution processes. Its procedures in the past have been viewed as models by many scholars of dispute resolution although it has attracted some critics over the years and in 2006 made some significant revisions to its rules.[9] As a threshold matter, the parties may choose one of the two dispute resolution processes—conciliation or arbitration. They initiate either process by filing a request in either of the three official ICSID languages (English, French, or Spanish) for either conciliation or arbitration with the ICSID Secretary General at World Bank Headquarters in Washington, D.C.[10] The ICSID Secretary General registers the request for dispute resolution "unless he finds, on the basis of the information contained in the request, that the dispute is manifestly outside

6. William Rand, Hornick & Friedland, *ICSID's Emerging Jurisprudence: The Scope of ICSID's Jurisdiction,* 19 Int'l L. & Politics 33 (1986). *See also,* Alex Grabowski, *The Definition of Investment under the ICSID Convention: A Defense of Salini,* 15 Chi. J. Int'l L. 287 (2014); Julian Davis Mortenson, *The Meaning of "Investment": ICSID's Travaux and the Domain of International Investment Law,* 51 Harv. Int'l L. J. 257 (2010).
7. *See,* e.g., Yuval Shany, *Contract Claims v. Treaty Claims: Mapping Conflicts Between ICSID Decisions on Multisourced Investment Claims,* 99 Am. J. Int'l L. 835 (2005) and Rand, *supra* n. 6.
8. There are a number of different schools of thought on the true effectiveness of the enforcement of ICSID's awards. *See,* e.g., Lawrence W. Newman & David Zaslowsky, *An Update on Enforcing ICSID Arbitration Awards,* N.Y. L. J. (September 28, 2017); Giuliana Cane, *The Enforcement of ICSID Awards: Revolutionary or Ineffective?* 15 Am. Rev. Int'l Arb. 439 (2004); Vincent O. Orlu Nmehielle, *Enforcing Arbitration Awards under the International Convention for the Settlement of Investment Disputes,* 7 Ann. Surv. Int'l & Comp. L. 21 (2001).
9. *See,* e.g., the discussion in Andrew P. Tuck, *Investor-State Arbitration Revisited: A Critical Analysis of the Revisions and Proposed Reforms to the ICSID and UNCITRAL Arbitration Rules,* 13 L. & Bus. Rev. Am. 885 (2007); Thomas W. Walsh, *Substantive Review of ICSID Awards: Is the Desire for Accuracy Sufficient to Compromise Finality?* 24 Berkeley J. Int'l L. 444 (2006).
10. Articles 28 and 36 of the ICSID Convention.

the jurisdiction of the Centre."[11] The act of registration is the equivalent of a court is docketing a case; and ICSID's supervision of the dispute commences from the date of registration.

If the parties seek conciliation, the ICSID Conciliation Rules provide for either a sole conciliator or an uneven number of conciliators appointed as agreed between the parties. The ICSID Conciliation Rules, although highly detailed, are essentially an informal process by which the conciliator requests the basic documents underlying the dispute, receives written statements of the case and other evidence from the parties, and conducts, if necessary, a hearing attended by the parties. At that hearing, the conciliator may also hear experts or other witnesses produced by the parties.[12] The assumption under the conciliation rules is that the conciliation process will result in a settlement agreement between the parties and that the conciliator will simply prepare a report to that effect that is submitted to the parties and the ICSID Secretary General. If the conciliation process fails, a report recounting the failure is prepared for both the parties and the Secretary General and the parties may then resort to arbitration under the ICSID rules.

Arbitration under the ICSID rules may be resorted to after conciliation fails or directly without going through the conciliation process. Once a request for arbitration is filed with the Secretary General and the arbitral tribunal is appointed (generally the number and the identity of the arbitrators will be agreed on by the parties, or failing an agreement, will be determined by ICSID), the arbitral process begins under a format that the ICSID rules describe as "two distinct phases: a written procedure followed by an oral one."[13] The written procedure requires the drafting and submission of a memorial by the party requesting arbitration, a counter-memorial submitted by the responding party and, if the parties request or if the arbitrator wishes, the filing of a reply by the requesting party and a rejoinder by the responding party.[14]

The oral hearing is a conventional arbitration hearing in which much of the conduct of the proceeding and the submission and consideration of evidence is under the control of the arbitration tribunal. Following the close of the hearing the tribunal is expected to frame an award within sixty days that addresses all the important issues adduced during the proceeding and gives reasons for the tribunal's decision. The award is filed with the Secretary General and transmitted to the parties.[15] In appropriate circumstances, the tribunal may fashion interim relief to preserve the rights of the parties.[16] Arbitration hearings may be held in any location agreed upon by the parties, subject to the approval of ICSID, although ICSID apparently prefers that hearings be

11. *Id.*, Art. 36(3). *See also*, Anoosha Boralessa, *The Limitations of Party Autonomy in ICSID Arbitration*, 15 Am. Rev. Int'l Arb. 253 (2004).
12. ICSID Conciliation Rules 22–29.
13. ICSID Arbitration Rules, Rule 29. For a very good overview of the ICSID process, *see* World Bank Group, *Overview of an Arbitration under the ICSID Convention*, www.ICSID.org.
14. *Id.*, Rule 31.
15. *Id.*, Rules 33 through 48.
16. *Id.*, Rule 39.

held in either Washington, D.C., Cairo, Kuala Lumpur, or The Hague.[17] If the parties cannot agree on a location, ICSID requires that the hearing be held at its headquarters in Washington, D.C.

A limited appeal, by which a party requests annulment of the award, may be taken to the Secretary General.[18] Once the award becomes final, the winning party may seek recognition and enforcement of the award if the losing party does not voluntarily abide by the decision of the arbitrators. The ICSID Convention requires each contracting state to recognize and enforce ICSID arbitral awards "as binding and enforce the pecuniary obligations imposed by that award within its territories as if it were a final judgment of a court in that state."[19] Note that this is somewhat different from the recognition and enforcement mechanisms built into the New York Convention on the Recognition and Enforcement of Foreign Arbitral Awards. Under the New York Convention a reviewing court has authority, albeit limited, to set aside the award (*see* the discussion of the New York Convention in Chapter 9), as for example when an award is contrary to that country's "public policy." Under the ICSID Convention, there seems to be no such power. An ICSID arbitral award is to be treated as a final court judgment in each contracting state.

The ICSID dispute resolution process has been described as "a considerable advance in the progressive development of international law."[20] While that description may include a bit of hyperbole, there is no doubt that the existence of ICSID has enhanced international trade by providing a dispute resolution process that is both intrinsically rational and acceptable to both the investing nations and the developing countries. The knowledge that any dispute arising out of the investment agreement will be handled through an effective international arbitration process provides that necessary margin of comfort that investors normally require. At the same time, the ICSID procedures, while sophisticated, are very much like the United Nations Commission on International Trade Law (UNCITRAL) arbitration and conciliation procedures. Anyone already experienced in other forms of international commercial arbitration should be able to function effectively in an ICSID proceeding.

§11.3 THE EUROPEAN UNION (EU)

Since so many of the members of the EU are major trading nations, commercial arbitration is a well-known and frequently utilized dispute resolution device. Moreover, many of the countries of Europe are beginning to experiment with the more innovative devices such as mediation/conciliation and minitrial. The commercial arbitration systems of England and France have been used frequently throughout this book to illustrate many fundamental concepts. London and Paris have traditionally

17. ICSID Pamphlet No. 12, at p. 9. *See also*, Thomas W. Walsh, *Substantive Review of ICSID Awards: Is the Desire for Accuracy Sufficient to Compromise Finality*, 24 Berkeley J. Int'l L. 444 (2006).
18. ICSID Convention, Art. 52.
19. *Id.*, Art. 54(1).
20. P.F. Sutherland, *The World Bank Convention on the Settlement of Investment Disputes*, 28 Int'l & Comp.L.Q. 367 (1979).

been centers for international commercial arbitration. More recently, because of a 1985 Belgian statute that almost completely prohibits domestic courts from setting aside either domestic or international arbitral awards, Brussels may become what the drafter of that new statute calls, "a paradise for international commercial arbitration."[21]

Thus, the current issues in the EU are not so much a matter of promoting interest in commercial arbitration but rather are matters associated with uniformity of application among members of the Union since the EU has an express provision (Article 177 of the Treaty of Rome) which emphasizes the need for uniformity of law among the EC countries.[22] In one instance, *Nordsee v. Reederei Mond,*[23] the EU Court of Justice noted:

> Community law must be observed in its entirety throughout the territory of all the Member States; parties to a contract are not, therefore, free to create exceptions to it. In that context attention must be drawn to the fact that if questions of Community law are raised in an arbitration resorted to by agreement the ordinary courts may be called upon to examine them [perhaps under the authority of Article 177] either in the context of their collaboration with arbitration tribunals...or in the course of a review of an arbitration award....[24]

Noting that arbitration takes place in private and is generally confidential, William Brown succinctly puts the issue: "The problem therefore arises as to whether, and if so, to what extent, the EC [judicial policy will] ensure the uniform interpretation and application of Community law by commercial arbitrators as well as by national courts."[25] Mr. Brown hints that one solution might be to permit arbitrators to refer certain questions of law to the EU Court of Justice much in the same fashion that certain questions of law have been referred to English courts by arbitrators in that country under the now significantly-altered "stated case" procedure (*see* the discussion on the stated or special case procedure in Chapter 9). However, the Court of Justice has steadfastly refused to permit such reference.

The British House of Lords has decided two important cases since the 1979 Act was passed that seem to promote additional stability in arbitral awards. In the *Nema*, the Lords recommended that judicial review of arbitral awards ought to be permitted only when a review of the award on its face shows that the arbitrator "is obviously wrong."[26] The subsequent decision by the House of Lords in the *Antaios* case reiterated

21. A.N. Cole et al., *Legal Instruments and Practice of Arbitration in the EU*, 6 TDM J. (2015); George A. Bermann, *Reconciling European Union Law Demands with the Demands of International Arbitration*, 34 Fordham Int'l L. J. 1193 (2011); Rainer Lukits, *Private Arbitration and European Union Law*, 3 Y.B. on Int'l Arb. 91 (2013); Marcel Storme, *Belgium: A Paradise for International Commercial Arbitration,* 1986 Int'l Law. 294. *See also*, Giuseppe De Palo & Linda Costabile, *Promotion of International Commercial Arbitration and Other Alternative Dispute Resolution Techniques in Ten Southern Mediterranean Countries*, 7 Cardozo J. Conflict Res. 303 (2006). For an analysis of the impact of EU law on arbitration, *see* Franco Ferrari (ed.), *The Impact of EU Law on International Commercial Arbitration* (2017).
22. Most of the discussion in this section is taken from William Brown, *Commercial Arbitration and the European Economic Community*, 2 J. Int'l Arb. 21 (1985).
23. 1982 E.C.R. 1095.
24. *Id.*
25. *Id.*
26. *See*, the discussion of the *Nema* case in A.L. Marriott, *Arbitrating International Commercial Disputes in the United Kingdom*, 44 Arb. J. 3 (1989).

the concepts of finality of arbitral awards expressed in the *Nema* decision while providing for some additional standards of review when British judges refuse to review an award. The two cases have been viewed by one British commentator as making it "clear that judicial review for errors of law by arbitrators will take place only in exceptional circumstances."[27] As discussed in Chapter 9, §9.3.2, the more recent English Arbitration Act of 1996 goes even further in promoting the integrity of the English arbitration process.

Thus, among the EU nations there exists the continuing possibility that country-by-country differences in substantive law may emerge from individual arbitrations even though Article 177 promotes uniformity in the substantive law with regard to domestic court decisions.[28] Looking at the situation somewhat differently, uniformity may be a dispensable requirement—that is, a requirement that individual business executives and lawyers may be willing to forego—for the benefits speed, confidentiality, and finality provided by commercial arbitration. Of course, one prominent commentator, Professor Clive Schmitthoff takes a slightly different view. He acknowledges that the EU "has done virtually nothing for the harmonization and unification of the law of arbitration of the Member States of the Community[; and][t]his is not due to any lack of powers."[29] But this does not trouble him. He believes—and many of the actions of the EU seem to echo his views—that uniformity in international commercial arbitration is properly a global matter rather than a regional problem. So, for example, any EU pronouncement on the enforcement of foreign arbitral awards would in all likelihood simply duplicate the requirements of the New York Convention on the Recognition and Enforcement of Foreign Arbitral Awards. Moreover, if decisional uniformity is the only problem posed by commercial arbitration with the EU, the Union ought to be considered well off.

Even one of the members of the EC, Spain, is beginning to develop a modern system of commercial arbitration fully compatible with those of the other EU countries and with the major trading nations.[30] All other indications suggest that commercial arbitration in concert with some of the less-drastic means of commercial dispute resolution will continue to thrive within the EU.

Within Europe but not part of the EU, Switzerland may be poised to regain its previous reputation as a good site for international commercial dispute resolution. The Zurich Chamber of Commerce was among the first to promulgate minitrial rules (*see*

27. *Id.*, at 8. For a much lengthier excursus on U.K arbitration *see*, Michael J. Mustill & Steward C. Boyd, *The Law and Practice of Commercial Arbitration in England* (2d ed., 1988).
28. There is a growing body of country-specific arbitration literature. For book-length studies *see*: Guido Carducci, *Arbitration in France: Law and Practice* (2013); Karl Bocksteigel, Stefan Kroll & Patricia Nacimiento, *Arbitration in Germany: The Model Law in Practice* (2008); Roman Khodyin, *Arbitration Law of Russia: Practice and Procedure* (2013); Giuseppe De Palo & Mary B. Trevor, *Arbitration and Mediation in the Southern Mediterranean Countries* (2007) and *Association for International Arbitration, Arbitration in Cis Countries: Current Issues* (2012).
29. Clive M. Schmitthoff, *Arbitration and EEC Law,* Com. Mkt. L. Rev. 143 (1987).
30. *See*, e.g., Evilio Verdera y Tuells, *International Commercial Arbitration and the Spanish Court of Arbitration,* 3 J. Int'l Arb. 47 (March 1986).

Chapter 6, §6.5). In 1989 the Swiss confederation promulgated a modern law of arbitration that appears to remove much of the danger of excessive judicial interference with arbitration.[31]

§11.4 THE IRAN-UNITED STATES CLAIMS TRIBUNAL

The Iran-United States Claims Tribunal ("Tribunal") is a unique commercial dispute resolution body that derived its entire identity and reason for being from the seizure and holding as hostage of a number of the members of the staff of the United States embassy in Teheran in 1979. With the subsequent release of the hostages under a negotiated agreement usually referred to as the Algiers Accords, the United States and Iran agreed to submit a large number of commercial claims growing out of contracts made during the regime of the deposed Shah of Iran.[32] The claims settlement aspects of the Accords were unique in that the two contending parties, the United States and Iran, had no diplomatic relations with each other; the claims grow out of the Islamic Revolution in Iran, rather than as the result of a war between the parties; and the vast bulk of the claims are invariably arbitrated between private companies in the United States and the Government of Iran, rather than between two private parties in a traditional arbitration setting.[33]

In this last sense, the arbitration process is perhaps closer to the ICSID model (discussed above) than to the models of private arbitration discussed elsewhere in this chapter and the preceding chapters. As of late-2017, the Tribunal is still in existence but appears to be nearly at the end of its work. It will go out of business when all pending claims are resolved. The discussion of the Tribunal is preserved in the sixth edition of

31. Philip D. O'Neill, Jr., *Has Switzerland Solved Its Problems as a Site for Arbitration?* 45 Arb. J. 16 (1990). Mr. O'Neill comments: "On balance, the new Swiss law on international arbitration is a very positive step forward in aiding Switzerland to solidify its place as a highly favored neutral site by Americans." *Id.*, at 22.
32. The full title of the Accords is: The Declaration of the Government of the Democratic and Popular Republic of Algeria Concerning the Settlement of Claims by the Government of the United States of America and the Government of the Islamic Republic of Iran. It is reprinted in 20 Int'l Leg. Materials 230 (1981).
33. Jamison M. Selby & David P. Stewart, *Practical Aspects of Arbitrating Claims Before the Iran-United States Claims Tribunal,* 18 Int'l L. 211 (1984). Mr. Stewart has served as Assistant Legal Adviser for International Claims and Administrator for Iranian Claims in the United States Department of State. A portion of the following discussion is taken from this article and his earlier article, David P. Stewart & Laura B. Sherman, *Developments at the Iran-United States Claims Tribunal: 1981-1983,* 24 Va. J. Int'l L. 1 (1983). Other helpful and provocative articles on this topic include: David Lloyd Jones, *The Iran-United States Claims Tribunal: Private Rights and State Responsibility,* 24 Va. J. Int'l L. 259 (1984) (Mr. Jones, an English barrister, provides a healthy non-U.S. view of the Tribunal); and Andreas F. Lowenfeld, *The Iran-U.S. Claims Tribunal: An Interim Appraisal,* 38 Arb. J. 14 (1983). For the views of an American practitioner who has appeared before the Tribunal, *see,* Stanton P. Belland, *The Iran-United States Claims Tribunal: Some Reflections on Trying a Claim,* 1 J. Int'l Arb. 237 (1984). The website for the Tribunal is: www.iusct.org. There is not much new literature available on the Tribunal. *See,* e.g., Casey J. College, *The Iran-United States Claims Tribunal: The Effect of Future Awards on International Terrorism,* 9 Arb. L. Rev. 305 (2017); Aniruddha Rajput, *Problems with the Jurisprudence of the Iran—US Claims Tribunal on Indirect Expropriation,* 30 ICSID Review-Foreign Investment L.J. 589 (2015).

this book because it provides a very good example of how arbitration, properly structured and organized, can serve as a helpful bridge between two countries who otherwise find very little to agree upon. Also, because the Tribunal uses the UNCITRAL arbitration rules, its decisions are a fine compendium of awards made pursuant to the UNCITRAL rules that may profitably be consulted in other arbitration settings.

The Tribunal's jurisdiction included a gamut of issues: claims against Iran by private companies in the United States, claims by individuals and companies in Iran against the United States, and certain claims between the two governments themselves. The claims were paid out of monies formerly held by banks, mainly in the United States, that were sequestered by the President of the United States shortly after the United States embassy was taken over and the hostages seized. Under the Accords, these deposits were placed in a Security Account, originally funded at the level of USD 1 billion which the Iranian government has agreed to maintain at the level of no less than USD 500 million. In other words, as claims are satisfied from the Security Account, the Iranian government takes steps to insure that the amount remaining never drops below USD 500 million.

The Tribunal, whose make-up was part of the original negotiation of the Accords, consists of nine members selected in a traditional arbitration style: Iran appointed three, the United States appointed three and those six chose the remaining three. In certain circumstances, the Tribunal sits as a nine member board, but normally the Tribunal hears individual cases in panels (the Tribunal term is chambers) of three arbitrators each. The procedural rules used for the individual cases are the UNCITRAL rules modified slightly to meet the conditions of the Accords.

One significant modification, imposed early on by agreement between the parties and the Tribunal was the institution of regular prehearing conferences for virtually all individual cases, even though the prehearing conference is not expressly contemplated by the UNCITRAL rules.[34] Other modifications of the UNCITRAL rules were necessary because of the sizable number of cases with which the Tribunal must contend over its lifetime. Even though there was a short cut off date of January 19, 1982 on the submission of all claims (claims could be filed no earlier than October 20, 1981), a total of 3,835 claims were eventually filed, over 2,700 of which were designated as small claims (amounts in controversy of less than USD 250,000).[35] As of mid-2006, the Tribunal had issued over 800 awards and decisions in resolving more than 3,000 individual claims. A relatively small number of claims remain on the Tribunal's docket as of mid-2013.

The Tribunal gets generally high marks from persons who have observed or participated in its work.[36] Professor Andreas Lowenfeld believes the Tribunal has done "moderately well" in accomplishing its goals, even though he faults the Tribunal for not developing "full collegiality among the arbitrators, the process that makes so many proponents of international arbitration associate the process with development of the

34. Selby & Stewart, *supra* n. 33, at 222.
35. *Id.*, at 215.
36. *See*, e.g., Christopher S. Gibson & Christopher R. Drahozal, *The Iran-U.S. Claims Tribunal at* 25 (2007).

conditions for peace."[37] Of course, given the history of the Tribunal, its required membership and the fact that both countries are estranged if not actually hostile over ten years after the Accords were signed, a lack of collegiality is certainly understandable. Indeed, the Tribunal's work is even more impressive given the ostensible lack of collegiality.

There are other complaints. A British barrister, David Lloyd Jones, faults the Tribunal for what he sees as the failure of the Tribunal to address and properly resolve "[a] number of important questions as to the nature and function of the ... Tribunal and the standards and rules it is to apply [in individual cases]. ..."[38] But his qualms seem relatively insignificant ten years later. All in all, a unique experiment appears to have worked. Although it is unlikely that the precise circumstances leading to the Algiers Accords will ever be repeated, the Iran-United States Claims Tribunal could serve as a model for resolving other large-scale monetary disputes between nations that remain hostile toward each other. Indeed, the Tribunal's greatest contribution to international commercial arbitration generally is the large body of case law developed by the Tribunal under the UNCITRAL arbitration rules. This body of law is a major reference work for all other parties who elect the UNCITRAL rules for their arbitrations. As the third edition of this book goes to press, the tribunal appears to be winding up its affairs, but it has produced such a deep body of arbitral jurisprudence under the UNCITRAL rules that dispute resolution specialists will refer to the tribunal's work for years to come.[39]

§11.5 LATIN AMERICA

Among the regions of the world, Latin America—and particularly the countries of South America—had a history of unusual hostility to the idea of international commercial arbitration generally and to the idea of recognition and enforcement of arbitral awards through multinational treaties. Most of the countries of Latin America initially refused to sign the 1958 New York Convention on the Recognition and Enforcement of Foreign Arbitral Awards. Only twelve countries originally ratified a substitute convention, the Inter-American Convention on International Commercial Arbitration. Even the United States, the country that spearheaded the effort to draft the Convention has been a little laggard; full U.S. implementation occurred only in September 1990.[40]

37. Lowenfeld, *supra* n. 33, at 23.
38. Jones, *supra* n. 33, at 285.
39. *See*, e.g., *The Iran-United States Claims Tribunal: Its Contribution to the Law of State Responsibility* (Richard B. Lillich & Daniel B. Magraw eds., 1998); *The Jurisprudence of the Iran-United States Claims Tribunal* (George H. Aldrich ed., 1996); Steward A. Baker & Mark D. Davis, *The UNCITRAL Arbitration Rules in Practice: The Experience of the Iran-United States Claims Tribunal* (1992).
40. *See*, e.g., Jan Kleinheisterkamp, *International Commercial Arbitration in Latin America* (2005); Juan M. Alcala & Joseph Briones, *Arbitration in Latin America: A First Look at the Impact of Legislative Reforms,* 13 L. & Bus. Rev. Am. 995 (2007); Charles D. Norberg, *United States Implements Inter-American Convention on Commercial Arbitration,* 45 Arb. J. 23 (1990). The text of the Convention may be found in the appendix to Title 9, United States Code. As of the second decade of the twenty-first century, we are benefitting from the publication of a number

The reasons for this hostility vary from country to country, but the region's historical reluctance to engage in arbitration or enforcement of arbitral awards apparently stemmed from their fear of foreign economic and political domination. As recently as 1984, one commentator asserted: "Arbitration is little practiced, statistical information on the use of arbitration cannot be found, legal commentaries and treaties on the law of arbitration are rarely published, and reported decisions on the enforcement of foreign arbitral awards are almost nonexistent."[41] By contrast, companies and individuals outside the region are suspicious of domestic courts in the region as a proper dispute resolution forum. One of the reactions of the Latin American countries to these fears of foreign domination has been the development of the Calvo doctrine (sometimes referred to as the Calvo Clause) which is commonly inserted in investment contracts, particularly concession agreements, between Latin American countries and foreign companies.[42] Basically, the doctrine requires investing companies to waive any opportunity to resolve any commercial dispute growing out of the agreement through diplomatic means and to consent to resolution of the dispute in the domestic courts of the host country. There are normally four components in any Calvo clause:

(1) Submission of any disputes to an appropriate domestic court.
(2) A choice of law clause that chooses the domestic law of the host country.
(3) A waiver of any diplomatic protection for the foreign participant.
(4) The surrender of any rights that might be provided under international law.[43]

It is clear that the underlying rationale for the Calvo clause is protection against foreign economic domination through improperly balanced concession agreements that disfavor the host country and that force that country to engage in dispute resolution outside its own boundaries or under the supervision of some international arbitration institution. The seeds for these fears of economic domination were sown over several centuries of rapacious behavior on the part of some of the major trading nations. However, the current problem is far different. Concession agreements, while not totally unknown these days, are not regarded as an acceptable form of modern international commercial agreement. Yet the Calvo clause was traditionally inserted in conventional commercial agreements between private parties. What had been a device

of book-length works on arbitration in Latin America. Among these are: Nigel Blackaby, *International Arbitration in Latin America* (2013) and Joao Bosco Lee, Eduardo Damio Goncalves & Clavio De Melio, *Arbitration in Brazil: Law and Practice* (2013). *See also*, Thomas E. Carbonneau & Mary H. Mourra, *Latin American Investment Treaty Arbitration: The Controversies and Conflicts* (2008). For a shorter, but fascinating inquiry into arbitration in Cuba, *see* Lucy V. Katz, *Arbitration as a Bridge to Global Market in Transitional Economies: The Republic of Cuba*, 13 Willamette J. Int'l L. & Dis. Res. 109 (2005). *See also* M.J. Stoppi, *Commercial Arbitration in the Caribbean: A Practical Guide* (2012); Alejandro Lopez Ortiz & Gustavo Fernandes, *A Year of Legal Developments for International Arbitration in Latin America*, Kuwer Arbitration Blog (2016).

41. Alejandro M. Garro, *Enforcement of Arbitration Agreements and Jurisdiction of Arbitral Tribunals in Latin America*, 1 J. Int'l Arb. 293 (1984).
42. But *see*, Wenhua Shan, *Is Calvo Dead?* 55 Am. J. Comp. L. 123 (2007).
43. Roger C. Wesley, *The Procedural Malaise of Foreign Investment Disputes in Latin America: From Local Tribunals to Factfinding*, 7 L. & Pol'y Int'l Bus. 813, 818 (1975).

intended to provide some protection for the host country in a concession agreement engender distrust on the part of the investing party, particularly in those commercial transactions that bore no relation whatsoever to a concession agreement. It is unquestioned that in the past the existence of the Calvo doctrine has inhibited business relations between the major trading nations and the countries of Latin America.

There are ways to work around the Calvo doctrine. Virtually all Latin American countries have established conventional systems of commercial arbitration within their boundaries with normal limitations on judicial review of arbitral awards.[44] Domestic commercial arbitration is now seen as an increasingly attractive dispute resolution mechanism in Latin America,[45] although a number of countries appear to remain hostile to any kind of arbitration, domestic or international. The prevailing view in those countries is that the only acceptable form of dispute resolution is litigation in that country's courts.[46] It has proved difficult to persuade many of the countries of Latin America to adopt either the UNCITRAL Model Law on International Commercial Arbitration (*see* Chapter 14) or to agree to effective international enforcement of awards once those awards are rendered.

The picture is not completely bleak, however. In 1975 a number of countries including the United States gathered in Panama City, Panama to draft the Inter-American Convention on International Commercial Arbitration, a treaty that has two functions: "(1) to make agreements to arbitrate enforceable—offensively by being eligible for a judicial order to compel arbitration, and defensively by being used to avoid or postpone judicial action in respect to the dispute; and (2) to recognize and enforce arbitral awards—offensively to collect sums payable under an award, and defensively as res judicata if a party attempts to litigate the same dispute in another forum."[47] In other words, the Inter-American Convention has essentially the same scope and effect among its signatories as does the New York Convention. Currently (i.e., as of early 1992), Chile, Colombia, Costa Rica, El Salvador, Guatemala, Honduras, Mexico, Panama, Paraguay, Peru, the United States, Uruguay, and Venezuela have become contracting states under the Convention. More countries may join in the near future.

Under the Convention, parties may agree to arbitration of commercial agreements and the arbitral award is insulated from most forms of judicial interference. Party autonomy is well protected, and the parties may choose either ad hoc or

44. Matthew Heaphy, *The Intricacies of Commercial Arbitration in the United States and Brazil: A Comparison of Two National Arbitration Statutes*, 37 U.S.F. L. Rev. 441 (2003); Alden F. Abbott, *Latin America and International Arbitration Conventions: The Quandary of Non-Ratification*, 17 Harv. J. Int'l L. 131–132 (1976).
45. *See*, e.g., the recent reports of the Inter-American Commercial Arbitration Commission. *See also*, Alexia Brunet & Juan Agustin Lentini, *Arbitration of International Oil, Gas, & Energy Disputes in Latin America*, 27 NW. J. Int'l L. & Bus. 591 (2007).
46. For an exceptionally hostile view *see*, Roberto Ramirez, *Arbitraje Comercial Internacional*, 11 Revista de Law Facultad de Derecho de Mexico 477 (1961), but for a more modern view *see*, Bernardo Malamud, *El Arbitraje Comercial y el Nuevo Codigo de Procedimientos*, 4 Jurisprudencia Argentina 823 (1968).
47. Statement of Michael F. Hoellering, American Arbitration Association, before the Senate Foreign Relations Committee as quoted in AAA, The Inter-American Convention on International Commercial Arbitration, Lawyer's Arbitration Letter (December 1986).

institutional arbitration. In addition, if the parties do not designate a procedural system for their arbitration, the Convention provides that the Inter-American Commercial Arbitration Commission's rules will apply. These rules are virtually indistinguishable from the UNCITRAL rules discussed in Chapter 8.

There are ways to deal with some of the problems in the region. First, virtually all Latin American countries recognize domestic arbitration. A foreign company might want to agree to domestic arbitration—in lieu of litigation—even though it may be doing business in a Latin American country that refuses to join any of the multinational recognition and enforcement conventions. Obviously, this means that the company gives up many of the possibilities of international enforcement of the award, but the award should remain enforceable within the host country.[48] Second, the promulgation of the Inter-American Convention on Arbitration (IACA) is an indication of growing regional interest in international commercial arbitration.

Third, no one doing business in Latin America should forget that as of late-2017 a significant number of Latin American and Caribbean countries have signed the 1958 New York Convention on Recognition and Enforcement of Foreign Arbitral Awards: Argentina, Barbados, Bolivia, Canada, Chile, Colombia, Costa Rica, Cuba, Dominica, Dominican Republic, Ecuador, El Salvador, Guatemala, Haiti, Honduras, Jamaica, Mexico, Nicaragua, Panama, Paraguay, Peru, St. Vincent & Grenadines, Trinidad and Tobago, the United States, Uruguay and Venezuela.[49] Fourth, for those limited instances in which the ICSID process is relevant, that Convention has been signed by Barbados, Costa Rica, El Salvador, Guyana, Haiti, Jamaica, Paraguay, St. Lucia, Trinidad and Tobago, and the United States. Fifth, contracting parties should consider some of those dispute resolution devices that do not require governmental intervention such as mediation/conciliation or the minitrial.[50] Sixth, there are some important breakthroughs on a country-by-country basis. Brazil, for example, has enacted legislation that enhances and promotes arbitration in commercial disputes in that country after decades of intense hostility to the process. Among other things, the country has created the Brazilian Arbitration Centre and is considering the implementation of a Latin American Arbitration Court with its headquarters in Brazil.[51]

---

48. For a country-by-country breakdown *see*, *International Handbook on Commercial Arbitration* (P. Sanders ed., 1985 and updates); for one view on Argentine views on international commercial arbitration *see*, Grigera Naon, *Public Policy and International Commercial Arbitration: The Argentine Perspective*, 3 J. Int'l Arb. 7 (June 1986). For the Brazilian perspective *see*, Keith Rosenn, *Enforcement of Foreign Arbitral Awards in Brazil*, 28 Am. J. Comp. L. 498 (1980). For an excellent analysis of many of the problems *see* Catherine Titi, *Investment Arbitration in Latin America: The Uncertain Veracity of Preconceived Ideas*, 30 Arb. Int'l 357 (2014); Jonathan C. Hamilton, *Three Decades of Latin American Commercial Arbitration*, 30 Penn. J. Int'l L. 1099 (2014); Joshua Briones & Ana Tagvoryan, *Is International Arbitration in Latin America in Danger*, 16 L. & Bus. Rev. Am. 131 (2010).
49. A list of the signatory nations may be found on the UNCITRAL website: www.uncitral.org. *See also*, Hernando Otero & Omar Garcia-Bolivar, *Recognition and Enforcement of International Commercial Arbitral Awards in Latin America: Law, Practice and Leading Cases* (2014).
50. *See*, e.g., William F. Fox, *Innovative Commercial Dispute Resolution Mechanisms: The Benefits for North and South America*, paper presented to the XVI Meeting of the Inter-American Bar Association, Buenos Aires, Argentina (May 13, 1987).
51. *See*, e.g., Heaphy, *supra* n. 44; Joan Ulrich Pestalozzi, *Arbitration and Its New Prospects in Brazil*, 4 J. Int'l Arb. 131 (September 1987).

There is yet another impressive initiative in Latin American arbitration.[52] In 1996 a group of North and Latin American arbitration institutions (the American Arbitration Association, the British Columbia International Commercial Arbitration Centre, the Mexico city National Chamber of Commerce and the Quebec National and International Arbitration Centre) created the Commercial Arbitration and Mediation Center for the Americas (CAMCA).[53] This center is closely integrated with North American Free Trade Agreement (NAFTA). Indeed, its self-described reason for being is to provide the forum for NAFTA's Article 2022—the article that encourages the use of alternative dispute resolution mechanisms as the desirable means of resolving controversies. CAMCA, whose rules are very similar to those of the AAA, sees itself as "an efficient, international forum for the resolution of private commercial disputes" that will inevitably arise under NAFTA.[54] While the Center is just getting off the ground, its reach may be greatly extended if the recent Summit of the Americas held in Santiago, Chile results in a true hemispheric free trade area.

§11.6 THE MIDDLE EAST AND AFRICA

The legal systems and the systems of commercial arbitration in a number of countries in the Middle East and in Africa are significantly affected by the tenets of the Islamic religion.[55] This section will examine mainly the commercial dispute resolution system in Saudi Arabia as an example of a religiously influenced system. As shall be seen, this does not mean that these dispute resolution systems are unacceptable under Western standards. Indeed, the new Saudi system of commercial arbitration is quite sophisticated if one approaches it with the understanding that Saudi Arabia, like many developing countries, has been quite suspicious of Western systems of dispute resolution since those systems frequently assisted foreign countries in the unconscionable exploitation of Saudi natural resources. In reaction, the Saudis have promulgated some protective devices: for example, arbitration of commercial disputes in foreign countries arising out of contracts to be performed in Saudi Arabia is normally forbidden by the Saudi government. A 1963 decree (Decree No. 58) prohibits Saudi agencies from entering into a contract with foreign corporations if that contract contains an arbitration clause calling for arbitration outside Saudi Arabia.[56]

There are essentially five formal dispute resolution mechanisms in Saudi Arabia: (i) the Shari'a Courts which are normally limited to domestic relations, real estate and criminal matters; (ii) the Board of Grievances (Diwan-Al-Mazalem), which hears

52. *See* Nigel Blackaby & Sylvia Noury, *International Arbitration in the MERCOSUR—Is Harmonization the Solution?* 9 L. & Bus. Rev. Am. 445 (2003).
53. The CAMCA website, where its rules and other documents may be found, is www.camca.org.
54. Preamble to the CAMCA rules.
55. Faisal Kutty, *The Shari'a Factor in International Commercial Arbitration*, 28 Loy. L.A. Int'l & Comp. L. Rev. 565 (2006).
56. *See*, e.g., Samir Saleh, *Commercial Arbitration in the Arab Middle East* (2d ed., 2006); Joseph T. McLaughlin, *Arbitration and Developing Countries*, 12 Int'l L. 211 (1980). *See also* Abdul Hamid El-Ahdab, *Arbitration with the Arab Countries* (3d ed., 2011) and Essam Al Tamimi, *The Practitioner's Guide to Arbitration in the Middle East and North Africa* (2009). *See also*, Ali Yesilrmak & Ismail Esin, *Arbitration in Turkey* (2014).

disputes between Saudi government agencies and private parties; (iii) the Committee for the Settlement of Commercial Disputes, which is used for resolving disputes between private parties; (iv) the Commercial Papers Committee, for disputes involving negotiable instruments and other documents of finance; and (v) the Committee for the Resolution of Labor Disputes.[57]

In 1983, to help modernize its system of commercial arbitration (a system which, quite frankly, was nearly nonexistent prior to 1983), the Saudi Government issued Royal Decree M/46, a legal instrument that permits the appropriate Saudi court, described above, to supervise arbitration. In practice, this means that the courts supervise a procedure which has been described as something "between the Western concept of arbitration and the concept of conciliation in the Far East [in that] ... Saudi arbitrators [who normally must be Saudi] ... generally conceive their task to be to reach a compromise which is either brought about between the parties (settlement) or reflected in their decision. ... Also, some Ministries prefer an informal mediation by a Saudi of high reputation over a formal arbitration."[58]

Since arbitrations involving Saudi governmental entities must be conducted in Saudi Arabia under Saudi law, a number of observers have asked whether such arbitrations may be governed by rules of procedure established by international bodies such as the ICC or UNCITRAL. On the one hand, this may no longer be a major problem. Dr. Abdul Hamid El-Ahdab's description of the 1983 Saudi Arbitration Act and the rules promulgated in 1985 under the Act suggest that the arbitration procedures in Saudi Arabia under its new act are not terribly different—in a procedural sense—from those of the international bodies. Those rules provide for notice of the arbitration, the convening of an arbitral tribunal, the conducting of a hearing in which evidence and argument is received, the construction of a hearing record and the issuing of an award upon close of the record.[59] At the same time, there apparently have been a number of construction contract arbitrations carried out in Saudi Arabia using the UNCITRAL rules, although there is a serious question as to whether use of the UNCITRAL rules is permissible since the promulgation of the 1983 Arbitration Act.[60]

Since all arbitration in Saudi Arabia is automatically under the supervision of one of the courts enumerated above, there is normally no problem with enforcement of the award domestically. International enforcement, however, may be more of a problem. At the moment, Saudi Arabia is not a signatory of the 1958 New York Convention on the Recognition and Enforcement of Arbitral Awards, although it has ratified the ICSID Convention, the Agreement on Enforcement of Awards of the Charter of the United

57. Jan van den Berg, *Saudi Arabia*, in *International Handbook on Commercial Arbitration* (Pieter Sanders ed., 1984) and Abdul Hamid El-Ahdab, *Arbitration in Saudi Arabia under the New Arbitration Act, 1983 and Its Implementation Rules of 1985*, Part I in 3 J. Int'l Arb. 47 (September 1986) and Part II in 3 J. Int'l Arb. 23 (December 1986). *See also*, S. Breckenridge Thomas, *International Arbitration: A Historical Perspective and Practice Guide Connecting Four Emerging World Cultures: China, Mexico, Nigeria and Saudi Arabia*, 17 Am. Rev. Int'l Arb. 183 (2006).
58. Jan van den Berg, *supra* n. 57, at 3.
59. El-Ahdab, *supra* n. 57, at 24–51.
60. Jan van den Berg, *supra* n. 57, at 4.

Nations and the Agreement with the American Institute for Guarantee of American Investments (this last is not a treaty but merely an agreement with a private association in the United States).[61]

Outside of Saudi Arabia there have been some attempts to develop modern regional approaches to international commercial dispute resolution. For example, the Asian-African Legal Consultative Committee has begun to push for more commercial arbitration in the Middle East and Africa using Cairo as a regional arbitration center.[62] In 1987 the Council of Arab Ministers of Justice meeting in Amman, Jordan, promulgated the Amman Arab Convention on Commercial Arbitration to provide uniformity among the Arab world in commercial arbitration. The Convention is based on, but not identical with, the ICSID Convention.[63] The Egyptian Civil Code, a statute that contains ingredients found in both the UNCITRAL commercial arbitration rules and the new UNCITRAL Model Law on International Commercial Arbitration, recognizes arbitration as a legitimate form of dispute resolution, permits arbitration under the Civil Code to take place outside Egypt; and, unlike a number of other countries in Africa and the Middle East, Egypt is a signatory of the 1958 New York Convention. In 1994, Egypt adopted a Law, Number 27 of 1994, that is largely based on the UNCITRAL Model Act. The new law repeals a prior requirement in Egypt that arbitrators be named in an agreement. It also restricts the grounds on which arbitral awards may be overturned by the Egyptian courts.[64]

Prior to the 1990–1991 Gulf War the government of Kuwait had taken steps to develop a modern arbitration systems that should remain in effect following Kuwait's liberation from Iraqi occupation.[65] There appears to be little recent activity, however.

In parts of Africa, arbitration may be a perfectly workable device for resolving commercial disputes since most of the Sub-Saharan countries have arbitration statutes. If there is a gap in African practice, it is probably in the lack of institutional bodies such as Chambers of Commerce that might supervise domestic arbitration. Two Ghanian scholars suggest that one entity that might be able to fill such as role is a restructured Commission of Mediation, Conciliation and Arbitration of the Organization of African Unity (OAU).[66] Of course, that suggestion was made over ten years ago, and there seems to be absolutely no movement since then for implementing such a suggestion.

61. El-Ahdab, *supra* n. 57, at 53. For problems and questions associated with enforcing an arbitral award on behalf of a foreign private party against a private party in Oman, *see*, Sigvard Javin, *Enforcement of An Arbitration Award in Oman*, 2 J. Int'l Arb. 81 (1985).
62. *See*, e.g., Aboul Enein, *Arbitration under the Auspices of the Cairo Regional Centre for Commercial Arbitration*, 1 J. Int'l Arb. 23 (1984); J.C. Wall, *The Asian-African Legal Consultative Committee and International Commercial Arbitration*, Canadian Y.B. Int'l L. 324 (1979) (This journal simply uses the year of publication as its volume number).
63. Mahir Jahil, *Amman Arab Convention on Commercial Arbitration*, 7 J. Int'l Arb. 139 (1990).
64. Jannette Hasan & John Bentley, *New Law Vastly Improves Arbitration Framework*, Middle East Executive Rep. (September 1994).
65. Ibraham Huneidi, *Arbitration under Kuwaiti Law*, 6 J. Int'l Arb. 75 (1989).
66. Sylvanus Azadon Tiewul & Francis A. Tsegah, *Arbitration and the Settlement of Commercial Disputes: A Selective Survey of African Practice*, 24 Int'l & Comp. L.Q. 393 (1975). *See also*, L. Bosman, *Handbook on Arbitration in Africa: A Practitioner's Guide* (2013); *Arbitration in Africa* (*London Court of International Arbitration Series*, 2) (Eugene Cotran & Austin Amissah eds., 1996).

The politically charged atmosphere in which the OAU has functioned may frighten away normally conservative Western lawyers and business executives. Nonetheless, as many African countries seek to improve their international trade posture there may be a real need in the future for a regional center for commercial arbitration somewhere in Sub-Saharan Africa.

§11.7 THE PACIFIC RIM

International trade between Japan and many of the countries of the Pacific Rim such as Korea, Taiwan, Hong Kong and Singapore and the Western nations is booming. But as this book has recognized throughout, increased international trading opportunities also increase the number of international commercial disputes. While no city or country on the Pacific Rim has yet developed into a major center of commercial arbitration, many governments are beginning to become aware of the advantages of resolving important commercial disputes at some location in the region and it appears that dispute resolution possibilities will grow in the future.[67]

As the second largest trading nation on the Pacific Rim, Japan generates most of the discussion on dispute resolution. American lawyers became increasingly aware of the possibilities of arbitration in Japan in mid-1985 when the United States Supreme Court, in the case of *Mitsubishi v. Soler*,[68] determined that parties who sign a general arbitration clause with a choice of forum in Japan under arbitration rules promulgated by the Japan Commercial Arbitration Association may have to arbitrate even antitrust claims which may arise under U.S. law.

While one Japanese writer suggests that commercial arbitration is neither common nor popular in Japan,[69] Japan does have an established system of commercial arbitration and is a signatory of the 1958 New York Convention on the Recognition and Enforcement of Foreign Arbitral Awards. There are some possible complications, of course. The rules of the Japanese Commercial Arbitration Association require the arbitration to take place in Japan using the Japanese language unless the parties have agreed to the contrary. But at the same time, the Japanese courts normally let arbitral awards alone and an award is enforced in Japan on the same terms as a court judgment. As a major trading nation, there is normally no shortage in Japan of experienced and expert commercial arbitrators.[70] Indeed, in *Mitsubishi*, the United States Supreme

67. *See*, e.g., Philip J. Mcconnaughay & Thomas B. Ginsburg, *International Commercial Arbitration in Asia* (2d ed., 2007); *Commercial Arbitration Law in Asia and the Pacific* (Kenneth R. Simmonds & Brian H.W. Hill eds., 1987); Ardis McClelland, *A Survey of Pacific Rim Commercial Arbitration*, 40 Arb. J. 4 (March 1985).
68. 473 U.S. 614 (1985).
69. Kazuyoshi Yamane, *Resolving Disputes in U.S.—Japan Trade: The Japanese Perspective*, 39 Arb. J. 3 (December 1984). A fresher look at these issues is to be found in Tony Cole, *Commercial Arbitration in Japan: Contributions to the Debate on "Japanese Non-Litigiousness,"* 40 N.Y.U.J. Int'l L. & Pol'y 29 (2007); Norman T. Braslow, *Contractual Stipulation for Judicial Review and Discovery in United States—Japan Arbitration Contracts*, 27 Seattle U. L. Rev. 659 (2004); Andrew M. Pardieck, *Virtuous Ways and Beautiful Customs: The Role of Alternative Dispute Resolution in Japan*, 11 Temp. Int'l & Comp. L.J. 31 (1997).
70. Doi, *Arbitration in Japan*, in 4 Yearbook of Commercial Arbitration (P. Sanders ed., 1979).

Court was quite sanguine about the ability of Japanese arbitrators to deal with complicated questions of U.S. antitrust law. Apparently, many Japanese businesses are now fully amenable to writing international commercial arbitration clauses in their international contracts.[71] After a period of intense research, legislation modernizing Japan's concededly archaic arbitration law was proposed. It appears that the draft legislation is based heavily on the UNCITRAL Model Arbitration Law and prospects for passage appear good.[72]

The other countries on the Pacific Rim vary in their views of international commercial arbitration.[73] India (perhaps technically not a "Pacific Rim" country) has a modern system of commercial arbitration patterned on but not identical with the English model.[74] It appears that India has a good track record on the enforcement of foreign arbitral awards under the New York Convention.[75] Many of the other countries of the Far East are much more primitive in their approach to commercial dispute resolution; but at least one observer, Arden McClelland, believes that more and more of the countries are beginning to take a sophisticated approach to the process.[76] As he sees it, while no international arbitration center has yet emerged for the region, Hong Kong and Singapore seem to be good possibilities for the establishment of such a center given that they are becoming major centers of trade, that the predominant language of business in the countries is English and that there are sizable numbers of well-educated potential arbitrators. Of these two possibilities, Hong Kong may have the superior claim to becoming a regional center since it recently promulgated a modern arbitration statute patterned on the English Arbitration Act of 1979 and because it exists in close proximity to, and in 1997 became a part of China.[77] There may be some special problems involving the practice of arbitration in Singapore for foreign counsel. Professor Andreas Lowenfeld a number of years ago reported on a decision of the High Court of the Republic of Singapore in which counsel not admitted to the local bar were enjoined from representing clients who had chosen to arbitrate their dispute in Singapore. As Professor Lowenfeld comments: "In my experience, membership of the bar of the state where the arbitration takes place is purely coincidental. Parties choose their counsel based on long time association, or special expertise in arbitrations, or expertise in the industry involved ... or familiarity with the language or languages of

71. Yamane, *supra* n. 69, at 8.
72. Hideki Ogawa, *Proposed Draft of Japan's New Arbitration Law,* 7 J. Int'l Arb. 33 (June 1990).
73. One book with a regional focus is Simon Greenberg, Christopher Kee & J. Romesh Weeramantry, *International Commercial Arbitration: An Asian-Pacific Perspective* (2011).
74. *See,* V.S. Deshpande, *The India Council of Arbitration and the Practice of Arbitration in India,* 1 J. Int'l Arb. 255 (1984); V.S. Deshpande, *International Commercial Arbitration and Domestic Courts in India,* 2 J. Int'l Arb. 45 (1985). *See also,* Pravin Anand, *Arbitration in the Context of Technology Transfer Agreements: The Case of India,* 7 J. Int'l Arb. 87 (June 1990).
75. Fali S. Nariman, *Foreign Arbitral Awards in India: Problems, Pitfalls, and Progress,* 6 J. Int'l Arb. 25 (March 1989).
76. McClelland, *supra* n. 67, at 17.
77. *See,* Neil Kaplan, *Arbitration in Hong Kong,* 3 J. Int'l Arb. 7 (December 1986); Michael D. Thomas, *Arbitration in Hong Kong,* Int'l Bus. L. 142 (May 1986). *See also,* Stephen D. Mau, *Hong Kong's Experience with the New York Convention: An Introduction,* 9 Transnat'l Law. 393 (1996). *See also,* Michael Moser, *Arbitration in Hong Kong* (2d ed., 2009).

the arbitration, not on the basis of the situs of the arbitration."[78] There is some question, however, whether this is an indication of a firm, long-term position by the Singapore High Court or some kind of aberrant decision that may be quickly corrected.[79] Other Pacific Rim countries such as Indonesia may be making progress toward a rational system of commercial arbitration.[80]

§11.8 CHINA

Trade and commerce with China has increased so significantly over the past dozen years that many people are now quite familiar with the spirit if not the language of that old Chinese proverb: "It is better to enter a tiger's mouth than a court of law."[81] This little homily tells a great deal about Chinese attitudes toward dispute resolution. Those attitudes have been shaped by centuries of tradition and philosophy. Confrontation and the adversary process seem never to have been particularly attractive to the Chinese.[82] In developing a legal system, virtually all observers of the Chinese scene report constant tension between the concept of li—essentially an ethical construct that places primary emphasis on harmony among human beings and with the universe—that discourages conflict and adversarial behavior and the concept of fa—the idea of a formal codified legal system that finds its principles not in Confucian ethics but rather in the country's law books and government regulations.[83] It is clear that a legal system based solely on the concept of li could find little place for something as disruptive to harmony as litigation and conventional commercial arbitration. By contrast, fa may encourage some kind of formal dispute resolution mechanisms in

78. Andreas F. Lowenfeld, *Singapore and the Local Bar: Aberration or Ill Omen?* 5 J. Int'l Arb. 71, 73 (September 1989).
79. *Id.*
80. *See,* Noah Rubins, *The Enforcement and Annulment of International Arbitration Awards in Indonesia,* 20 Am. U. Int'l L. Rev. 359 (2005).
81. A Chinese proverb attributed to the Analects of Confucius and first brought to the author's attention by Steven Robinson, Esq. Mr. Robinson's comments on dispute resolution in China are now contained in Steven N. Robinson & George R.A. Doumar, *"It is Better to Enter a Tiger's Mouth Than a Court of Law"—Dispute Resolution Alternatives in U.S.—China Trade,* 2 Dick. J. Int'l L. 1 (1987). The discussion in this section relies heavily on the Robinson-Doumar article. A fresh perspective on the general issues of ADR in China is provided by Jun Ge, *Mediation, Arbitration and Litigation: Dispute Resolution in the People's Republic of China,* 15 UCLA Pac. Basin L.J. 122 (1996). The book-length literature on arbitration in China is now substantial. *See,* e.g., Lea Murphy & Giovanni Pisacane, *Arbitration in China: Rules and Perspectives* (2016); Sun Wei & Melanie Willems, *Arbitration in China, A Practitioner's Guide* (2015); Fan Yang, *Foreign-Related Arbitration in China: Commentary and Cases* (two volumes) (2016); Kun Fan, *Arbitration in China: A Legal and Cultural Analysis* (2013) and Jingzhou Tao, *Arbitration Law and Practice in China* (2008). For a forthcoming book-length analysis of ADR in China, *see* Weixia Gu, *Dispute Resolution in China: Litigation, Arbitration, Mediation and Their Cross-Interactions* (2018). For an excellent, general law journal article *see* Jerome A. Cohen, *Settling International Business Disputes with China: Then and Now,* 47 Cornell Int'l L.J. 555 (2014).
82. *See* generally, Jerome Alan Cohen & H. Ungdah Chiu, *The People's Republic of China and International Law* (1974).
83. For a general discussion *see,* Hyung I. Kim, *Fundamental Legal Concepts of China and the West: A Comparative Study* (1980). For a similar discussion in the pragmatic setting of international trade *see,* Sally Lord Ellis & Laura Shea, *Foreign Commercial Dispute Settlement in the People's Republic of China,* 10 Int'l Trade L.J. 155 (1987).

which the rule of law, rather than the rule of ethics, is paramount. Moreover, in the case of modern China, Marxist thought further complicates matters by imposing a philosophical model developed in the West on traditional attitudes toward the legal system; and the ten-year vacuum in Chinese legal and commercial education caused by the Cultural Revolution deprived China of a decade of potential progress in many of these matters.

While it is clear that the Chinese legal system has not resolved these basic tensions, China's recent nearly phenomenal progress in fostering international trade seems also to have affected the country's view of international commercial dispute resolution.[84] There is now a great deal of stability in Chinese foreign transactions although, most trade is filtered through state-controlled trading bodies. The general rule in China has been that individuals may not execute international contracts,[85] although even that rule is being altered as China puts more emphasis on the New Economic Zones adjacent to Hong Kong.

Most of the recent transactional stability has been contributed by two actions on the part of the Chinese government: the development of modern trading statutes, most significantly the new Joint Venture law (discussed at some length in Chapter 3, §3.3) but also including statutes on protection of intellectual property, investment and trade; and the execution of bilateral commercial agreements such as the United States-Sino Trade Agreement in 1979.[86] The Chinese institutions primarily concerned with international commercial agreements are the commodity-based foreign trade corporations which are contained within the Ministry of Foreign Trade and Economic Relations. The Ministry also interacts with the China Council for the Promotion of International Trade (a nominally private institution) which in turn contains two formal arbitral bodies, the Foreign Economic Trade Arbitration Commission (FETAC) and the Maritime Arbitration Commission.

Most standard form contracts executed by the foreign trade corporations call for a two-step dispute resolution process: first the parties are required to renegotiate the issue and failing a successful renegotiation, the dispute is to be submitted to either FETAC or the Maritime Arbitration Commission in Beijing. In the Chinese Joint Venture Law, the process is actually a three-step process: first the parties are required to engage in "friendly discussion."[87] Next, the parties must engage in conciliation supervised by a Chinese arbitral body. FETAC may supervise the conciliation under existing rules or it may use the new conciliation rules promulgated by UNCITRAL.

84. *See*, e.g., Randall Peerenboom, *Arbitration in China: A Practical Guide* (2004); Ellen Reinstein, *Finding a Happy Ending for Foreign Investors: The Enforcement of Arbitration Awards in the People's Republic of China*, 16 Ind. Int'l & Comp. L. Rev. 37 (2005); Christopher Shen, *International Arbitration and Enforcement in China: Historical Perspectives and Current Trends*, 14 Currents Int'l Trade L.J. 69 (2005).

85. *See*, e.g., P. Theroux, *Technology Sales to China*, 14 J. Int'l L. & Econ. 185 (1980).

86. July 7, 1979, T.I.A.S. 9630, reported in 79 Dep't State Bull. No. 2033-34, 18 Int'l Legal Mat. 1041 (1979).

87. Thomas J. Klitgaard, *People's Republic of China Joint Venture Dispute Resolution Procedures*, 1 U.C.L.A. Pac. Basin L.J. 1 (1982). There is now a short book that translates into English many of the important Chinese legal documents. *See*, Eric Lee, *Commercial Disputes Settlement in China* (1985).

If conciliation fails, the parties generally must resort to binding arbitration—a process which in the past has apparently always meant arbitration in Beijing under the FETAC's rules but which now may call for arbitration outside of China under some of the internationally recognized rules systems such as the rules of the Stockholm Chamber of Commerce or the ICC or even, perhaps, ad hoc arbitration using the UNCITRAL rules.[88] In 1988, FETAC's name was changed to "China International Economic and Trade Arbitration Commission" (CIETAC) and the Maritime Arbitration Commission was renamed the China Maritime Arbitration Commission (CMAC).[89] The new arbitration rules promulgated by CIETAC and CMAC are considerably modernized, providing the form for demands for arbitration, hearing procedures, and a fee schedule.[90]

There have not yet been a sufficient number of commercial disputes involving China to develop firm conclusions on these various mechanisms. One American law professor, Pat Chew, who has studied a large number of Soviet and Chinese commercial arbitrations, believes: "First, the [Chinese] arbitrators appear to be fair toward foreign parties. Chinese arbitrators may even show a bias in favor of non-Chinese parties. Second, the Chinese are developing a hybrid model of arbitration that clearly incorporates a distinctive Chinese approach to the resolution of disputes. ... It is a process that considers the perspective of both sides, including their respective commercial and economic positions, and reaches a result that yields the highest net benefit in the long term for both parties. In addition, the [Chinese process of commercial dispute resolution] encourages amicable and constructive ongoing relationships between the parties, even after the dispute is resolved."[91]

As is characteristic of most countries, there is no trouble enforcing an arbitral award within China. Such awards are binding and have the force and effect of court judgments.[92] Moreover, in January 1987, China became a contracting state under the New York Convention on Recognition and Enforcement of Foreign Arbitral Awards, so it is now possible to obtain extraterritorial enforcement of Chinese arbitration awards in the proper circumstances. Enforcement through China's numerous bilateral treaties of friendship, commerce and navigation may also be possible. For example, the 1974 China-U.S. Trade Agreement contains express language to the effect: "both signatory countries are held responsible for the execution of arbitration rulings by concerned organs under terms provided for under the laws of the country being sought to make the ruling (e.g., the country in which enforcement is sought)."[93]

World trade with China entered the doldrums after the 1989 incidents of violence in Tienamen Square in Beijing, but it shows some signs of reviving as the United States ponders granting most-favored nation status to the Peoples Republic.

88. Robinson & Doumar, *supra* n. 81, at 18.
89. Volker Triebel & Xu Guojian, *International Economic, Trade and Maritime Arbitration in the People's Republic of China: New Developments*, 6 J. Int'l Arb. 13, 14 (June 1989).
90. *Id.*, at 17–30.
91. Pat K. Chew, *A Procedural and Substantive Analysis of the Fairness of Chinese and Soviet Foreign Trade Arbitrations*, 21 Tex. Int'l L.J. 291 (1986).
92. Klitgaard, *supra* n. 87, at 31.
93. 13 Int'l Leg. Mat. 872, 874 (1974).

§11.9 THE FORMER SOVIET UNION

(Note: This section has been preserved for the reader even though the Soviet Union as a political entity no longer exists. The Soviet Union had a fascinating system of arbitration. There are still glimmerings of this system in the current system of Russian arbitration.[94] It is expected that a number of the arbitration institutions discussed below will be preserved at least in the Russian Federation for some time to come. Even so, all the language has been changed to the past tense. The reader should monitor closely future developments in this part of the world.)

International commercial arbitration in the former Soviet Union was affected by two aspects of Soviet governance. First, arbitration was well known within the Soviet Union as a dispute resolution technique. There were essentially three types of arbitration recognized by the Soviet system: (i) state arbitration (which is very close in operation and concept to litigation in Western countries and which is frequently referred to as arbitrazh involves the use of expert tribunals to resolve questions that arise between and among the various economic units of the government); (ii) third-party arbitration (a device that would probably be called "court annexed" arbitration in the United States and is used for citizen disputes and permits people who would ordinarily be litigants in the regular court system to voluntarily submit their dispute to a third-party arbitrator who renders a decision); and (iii) the third form of commercial dispute resolution, foreign trade arbitration (the topic of this section).[95]

In the past all trade with the former Soviet Union was conducted through state-run organizations called Foreign Trade Organizations (FTO). The FTO's conducted business with the West under standard form contracts that called for arbitration in Moscow under the rules of the USSR's Foreign Trade Arbitration Commission (FTAC), a body within the Chamber of Commerce and Industry.[96] This take-it-or-leave-it approach probably reflects many of the Socialist countries' aversion to commercial arbitration as being too much under the control of the capitalist systems—and of the lawyers in those capitalist systems, although it is equally clear that the Socialist countries prefer international commercial arbitration to litigation in a capitalist country.[97]

In 1972 the United States and the Soviet Union signed a trade agreement that, for apparently the first time, permitted the FTOs to sign contracts containing arbitration

94. For an analysis of current arbitration in Russia *see*, Neil F. O'Donnell & Kirill Y. Ratnikov, *Dispute Resolution in the Commercial Law Tribunals of the Russian Federation: Law and Practice*, 22 N.C.J. Int'l L. & Com. Reg. 795 (1997); Kaj Hober, *Enforcing Foreign Arbitral Awards against Russian Entities* (1994). William R. Spiegelberger, *The Enforcement of Foreign Arbitral Awards in Russia: An Analysis of the Relevant Treaties, Laws and Cases*, 16 Am. Rev. Int'l Arb. 261 (2005).

95. 1 *Encyclopedia of Soviet Law* 53 (F. Feldbrugge ed., 1973); *see also*, Olimpiad Ioffe & Peter B. Maggs, *Soviet Law in Theory and Practice* 306 (1983).

96. Thomas F. Hoya, *East-West Trade: Comecon Law and American-Soviet Trade* (1984). For an explanation of a parallel Soviet arbitral body *see*, Robert M. Jarvis, *The Soviet Maritime Arbitration Commission: A Practitioner's Perspective*, 21 Tex. Int'l L.J. 341 (1986).

97. *See*, e.g., Svetozer Hanak, *The Experience of Socialist Lawyers in Arbitration Held in Non-Socialist Countries*, Int'l Bus. L. 145 (March 1982).

clauses that permitted arbitration in a third country—invariably Sweden—under rules other than those of the FTAC.[98] While many of these details were worked out between the American Arbitration Association and the Soviet Union's Chamber of Commerce and Industry, the policies were relatively rigid. The FTOs were permitted to agree to one of the only two alternatives: conventional arbitration in Moscow under FTAC rules or the so-called optional arbitration clause calling for arbitration under Stockholm under the UNCITRAL rules or the rules of the Stockholm Chamber of Commerce.

Most Western businesses elected the optional clause. The UNCITRAL rules are quite sophisticated, and the FTOs apparently rarely protested the insertion of the optional clause.[99] Moreover, Stockholm contains all the support mechanisms necessary for a proper international commercial arbitration. It was not necessarily a bad or defective process. After studying hundreds of FTAC awards, Julian Lew was able to conclude:

> [D]espite the undoubted control which the socialist States have over their arbitration tribunals, [the governments] do not interfere with the arbitrators and are particularly anxious not only to be impartial but also to be seen to be impartial. Indeed, some commentators have argued that if anything, socialist arbitration tribunals are biased in favour of a western party. To prove their impartiality the socialist tribunals generally publish their awards...a practice which is generally opposed in the West.[100]

However, a much more detailed statistical study of FTAC awards conducted by Pat Chew is far more troubling. Having analyzed 68 arbitral awards made by FTAC, he was able to conclude: (i) generally there appeared to be no tendency on the part of FTAC to favor either the claimant or the respondent; and (ii) when the claimant was another Soviet-bloc country (included in the study were Czechoslovakia, East Germany, Hungary, and Poland) FTAC arbitrations appeared to be relatively evenhanded. However, when the arbitration involved an industrial country (in Chew's study the countries were Belgium, Denmark, Finland, France, West Germany, Italy, and the United Kingdom), it was found that FTAC favored the Soviet party 81% of the time.[101]

Of course, these figures are only statistical developments. There was no attempt to correlate the data on the basis of the type of case, the claims made, and the more intimate aspects of the dispute; so the 81% figure should be taken with a large grain of salt. Another lengthy article on Soviet commercial arbitration suggested that "Soviet arbitrators are careful to avoid decisions that might be interpreted by the international arena as being politically-motivated ... [since the USSR wishes to demonstrate] to trading partners that the USSR abides by its bargains in spite of international exigencies and that a Soviet court [sic] can provide an impartial forum for settling disputes."[102] If

98. *See*, Howard M. Holtzmann, *Dispute Resolution Procedures in East-West Trade*, 20 Int'l L. 233 (1978); J. Gillis Wetter, *East Meets West in Sweden*, 20 Int'l L. 261 (1978).
99. Susan E. Samuels, *Note, The Soviet Position on International Arbitration: A Wealth of Choices or Choices for the Wealthy*, 26 Va. J. Int'l L. 417 (1986).
100. Julian D.M. Lew, *Applicable Law in International Commercial Arbitration* 30–31 (1978).
101. Chew, *supra* n. 91, at 325–330.
102. Samuels, *supra* n. 98, at 423, quoting George M. Armstrong, Jr., *The Problem of Autonomy in Soviet International Contract Law*, 31 Am. J. Comp. L. 63, 77 (1983).

the figure is correct, however, Western parties would be ill advised ever to opt for FTAC arbitration if they can avail themselves of the optional clause.

When an award is made either in the former Soviet Union or in Sweden, it is fully enforceable both domestically and on an international basis. Presumably such is now the case at least with regard to the Russian Federation since the Russian Federation has essentially succeeded to all Soviet treaty obligations. The United States, the Soviet Union, and Sweden all accepted the 1958 New York Convention. While there is apparently some question as to the precise legal nature of FTAC awards since a number of commentators view them as more like court judgments than arbitral awards, there are virtually no reports of a refusal on the part of the Soviet Union to honor those awards itself.

On balance, arbitration involving the former Soviet Union seems to have been a relatively successful enterprise. Other Eastern European countries have worked out other arrangements. For example, in 1984 Hungary and the United States, working through the Hungarian Chamber of Commerce and the American Arbitration Association, signed an agreement permitting Hungarian state trading organizations and U.S. companies to sign contracts containing an arbitration clause that calls for arbitration in Vienna under the UNCITRAL rules.[103]

In the years since these several paragraphs were written, there has been a political and economic revolution in Eastern Europe that has now moved into the former Soviet Union. As the countries of Eastern Europe move toward a market mechanism, they also have rejected the concept of state trading company, in most instances. In Poland and Hungary, as well as Czech Republic and a number of other central and eastern European countries, the governments now permit individual businesses to negotiate and sign international commercial agreements.[104] This means that the dispute resolution procedures adapted for the state trading companies no longer control those transactions. In each instance, the private companies appear to have independent authority to engage in private dispute resolution such as commercial arbitration. Some of the state trading companies have not yet been completely abandoned, but there appears to be a strong inclination to abolish them and permit private concerns to do their own trading—and, by definition, their own dispute resolution.

103. AAA, *USA-Hungarian Trade Assisted by New Arrangements for Arbitration in Vienna*, 40 Arb. J. 34 (March 1985).

104. *See*, e.g., Adam J. Sulkowski, *Through the Looking Glass: What a Comparison with the New Polish Legal Framework of Arbitration Reveals about the U.S. Legal Framework of Arbitration*, 7 Wash. U. Global. Stud. L. Rev. 87 (2008); Jerzy Slupinski, *Foreign Investment in the Banking Sector and Emergence of the Financial Market in Poland*, 25 Int'l L. 127 (1991).

CHAPTER 12

Litigation

§12.1 INTRODUCTION

Litigation is almost always the most costly dispute resolution technique available to resolve international commercial disputes. Most lawyers in the United States instinctively consider litigation whenever their clients get into any kind of trouble. That kind of reaction is understandable given the system of law and the structure of legal education in the United States. There is great emphasis (some might argue overemphasis) on litigation throughout the U.S. system. But litigation is important for other reasons. It is the benchmark from which we test all forms of alternative dispute resolution. While subject to a lot of deserved criticism, litigation has advantages and disadvantages that require discussion and consideration when seeking the best form of dispute resolution for our clients.

Litigating a dispute means going to court.[1] People new to international business transactions sometimes think that they can litigate before the International Court of Justice (ICJ) at The Hague. They are mistaken. While the ICJ occasionally deals with commercial issues only national governments may invoke the ICJ's jurisdiction, and the Court spends the vast bulk of its time on questions of public international law. Since this book concentrates on contractual relationships between private parties, the term *litigation* is defined as the resolving of commercial disputes through the processes of the domestic court system of an appropriate country.

1. For some good general reading on many of the topics covered in this chapter a reader might well start with two provocative articles: Anibal Sabater, *National Courts, Supranational Courts and Arbitral Tribunals in International Litigation,* 14 Currents Int'l Trade L.J. 3 (2005) and Cesare P.R. Romano, *The Americanization of International Litigation,* 19 Ohio St. J. Disp. Resol. 89 (2003). *See also*, Symposium, *A Guide to International Civil Practice,* 17 Vand. J. Transnat'l L. 1 (1984); Symposium, *Transnational Litigation,* 18 Int'l Law. 522 (1984); Arthur T. von Mehren, *Transnational Litigation in American Courts: An Overview of Problems and Issues,* 3 Dick. J. Int'l L. 43 (1984).

Although court procedures differ markedly from country to country, litigation has certain general characteristics irrespective of where it actually takes place. Almost everywhere, litigation is slow, cumbersome, costly, and usually administered through a monopoly of lawyers. With the exception of the European Union (EU), many domestic court decisions are unenforceable outside the country in which the litigation took place. By contrast, litigation's singular advantage is that it is normally final and enforceable within that country. The twin characteristics of finality and enforceability often warrant the litigation of many commercial disputes even when alternatives are available. Lawyers frequently resort to litigation simply because they are comfortable with the process and unfamiliar or uncomfortable with the alternatives. Clients often lack the sophistication necessary to steer their lawyers to other less costly and less time-consuming techniques. Moreover, as discussed in Chapters 6 and 9, the other forms of dispute resolution frequently require parties to go into court even after they have mediated or arbitrated the dispute because the party losing the mediation or arbitration does not voluntarily concede. There are cases when going directly to court may be the most cost-beneficial solution for all concerned.

§12.2 LITIGATION: GENERALLY

It is difficult to generalize about litigation because domestic court systems around the world differ significantly. A judicial proceeding in Zaire is different from one in Singapore and both are substantially different from a trial in the United States. However, similarities and common concepts do exist; so it is possible to discuss litigation in general terms irrespective of the country in which it occurs. Litigation is a proceeding in a properly constituted domestic court before a judge or magistrate with the parties normally represented by their own counsel. The court conducts either an investigation or an adversarial hearing, witnesses frequently testify, relevant documents are examined, and some type of formal decision is rendered by the presiding officer. In most countries, this decision usually may be appealed to a higher authority, and once the appeals are exhausted, the parties have a final judicial decision, enforceable at least within that country.[2]

In order to properly litigate a dispute, a court must have jurisdiction over the subject matter of the dispute. In other words, the court must be authorized to hear

2. For practitioners facing international litigation problems in U.S. courts one of the best and most comprehensive references is Gary B. Born & Peter B. Rutledge, *International Civil Litigation in United States Courts* (5th ed., 2011). Other book-length works include: Barton Legum & Theodore Edelman (eds.), *International Litigation Strategies and Practice* (2015); Richard Fentiman, *International Commercial Litigation* (2008); Barton Legum, *International Litigation Strategies and Practice* (2006); Colin Y.C. Ong, *Cross-Border Litigation within ASEAN: The Prospects for Harmonization of Civil and Commercial Litigation within ASEAN* (1997); *Transnational Litigation: A Practitioner's Guide* (Richard H. Kreindler ed., 1997); *Access to Civil Procedure Abroad* (Henricus Joseph Snijders ed., 1996); Lawrence W. Newman & David Zaslowsky, *Litigating International Commercial Disputes* (1996); Louise Ellen Teitz, *Transnational Litigation* (1996); David Epstein & Jeffrey L. Snyder, *International Litigation: A Guide to Jurisdiction, Practice and Strategy* (2d ed., 1994); Russel J. Weintraub, *International Litigation and Arbitration: Practice and Planning* (1994); Andreas F. Lowenfeld, *International Litigation and Arbitration* (1993).

cases of this type. Some courts have limitations based on the monetary amount of the controversy presented (so-called small claims courts are an example of a monetary limitation). After the court assures itself that it has subject-matter jurisdiction, it will also determine whether both parties are subject to the power of the court (the concept of personal jurisdiction). Once these two threshold considerations are satisfied, the controversy evolves under the court's procedural framework. In virtually all judicial systems there is some mechanism enabling either the court or the parties themselves to find out the relevant facts and to gather evidence that can be used at trial. This type of pretrial fact gathering is referred to in many systems as the process of discovery. In United States practice, the party bringing the lawsuit is normally referred to as the plaintiff and the person responding to the lawsuit is the defendant. The remainder of this chapter will use that terminology solely as a matter of convenience for the reader.

Many of these concepts prove difficult to work with when parties to a commercial agreement have a dispute that cuts across national boundaries. Moreover, much more so than any other type of dispute resolution technique discussed in this book, litigation is a matter that must be left in the hands of the experts. No matter where the case is brought, it requires handling by someone sophisticated not just in the broad-brush aspects of litigation, but thoroughly schooled in the local courts. In most countries, only lawyers licensed to practice in a particular court are permitted to appear in those courts on behalf of clients. Thus, in considering litigation as a possibility for resolving a dispute, contracting parties should take into account, among other things, the following:

(1) Does the intended court have jurisdiction over both the subject matter of the dispute and the parties?
(2) Is any resulting judgment fully enforceable in the country of issue?
(3) Might the judgment be enforceable in other countries?
(4) Will the procedures used by the court lead to a fair result?
(5) Are foreign parties treated fairly in that particular court?
(6) Are properly trained and instructed counsel available?
(7) How long will it take to get a final decision and what will everything cost?[3]

The sections that follow will assist the reader in answering most of these questions.

§12.3 SUBJECT-MATTER JURISDICTION

Subject-matter jurisdiction is a question of whether a particular court has the power to adjudicate the issues presented in the case. It is a concept that looks simply to the nature of the issues (or subject matter) in controversy rather than to the parties who are involved in the action. In many other systems, these same doctrines are discussed in

3. These questions were suggested by a similar checklist in Detlev F. Vagts, *Transnational Business Problems* (1986), 158–159.

terms of a court's competence (to hear the dispute) rather than a court's jurisdiction. For example, in the United States, and certain other jurisdictions, small claims courts may hear disputes involving claims of, say, less than USD 5,000. A small claims court by definition will not have subject-matter jurisdiction over a breach of contract claim in which USD 1 million in damages is sought. In countries with bifurcated court systems—those, for example, that divide their courts into law or equity courts—claims of breach of contract are often heard in one court while cases seeking relief against a government agency are heard in a wholly separate court.

As a consequence, it is usually crucial to have the case filed in the proper court. In some legal systems, a party that files in the wrong court will not be permitted to refile the action in the proper court. In the United States' system of federal courts, limitations imposed by the U.S. Constitution permit the raising of subject matter defects even when the case is on appeal. For most breach of contract actions, the U.S. federal courts require that the amount in controversy be over USD 75,000 and that the plaintiff and defendant be citizens of different states, or that the suit be one between a citizen of some U.S. state and a citizen of a foreign country.[4] However, state courts in the United States are normally courts of general jurisdiction; these courts have the power to dispose of virtually any case. In England, most important commercial disputes are tried in the High Court of Justice. Commercial disputes in France may be heard initially in the *Tribunaux de premiere* instance, or in certain cases in courts staffed by merchants, the *Tribunaux de commerce*. In Germany, a lawsuit will likely begin in one of the Landgericht or, if the parties choose, in a commercial chamber (*Handelssachen*) annexed to the Landgericht.[5] In China, commercial disputes are normally heard in the Economic Division of an appropriate level of the Peoples' Courts.[6] In Japan, many international commercial disputes are filed in the Tokyo District Court, a development that reflects Tokyo's prominence among Japanese cities, but there seems to be no special reason why international matters could not be heard elsewhere in Japan.[7]

In virtually every country, some court will be available for the lawsuit. The task is simply to identify the proper court and then to commence the litigation. Once again, an experienced litigator will be able to provide the proper guidance.

§12.4 FOREIGN SOVEREIGN IMMUNITY AND THE ACT OF STATE DOCTRINE

§12.4.1 Sovereign Immunity

A number of issues frequently arise in international commerce that affect a court's ability to take up the dispute. These barriers to litigation are probably best discussed under the concept of subject-matter jurisdiction because the underlying legal doctrines

4. 28 U.S.C. §1332.
5. Arthur T. von Mehren, *The Civil Law System* (1958), 82, 86.
6. Thomas M. Haney, *The Trial of a Contract Dispute in China,* 22 Int'l L. 475 (1988).
7. *See,* Tasuku Matsuo, *Jurisdiction in Transnational Cases in Japan,* 23 Int'l L. 6 (1989).

affect all such cases. In other words, principles of sovereign immunity and the act of state doctrine may block a lawsuit categorically, no matter what the particular merits of the dispute may be.

In commercial contracts between two private parties, sovereign immunity (commonly referred to as state immunity outside the United States) is rarely a factor. However, when one of the parties to a contract is a private person and the other is a government—or some entity such as a state trading company closely associated with a national government—, a serious question arises as to whether the governmental entity may be sued because the doctrine of sovereign immunity holds squarely that a sovereign cannot be sued unless it consents to be sued.[8] The doctrine derives from the concept, nicely put by Justice Oliver Wendell Holmes, that: "there can be no legal right as against the authority that makes the law on which the right depends."[9]

There are now two conflicting schools of thought on the topic of sovereign immunity in international matters. The so-called classical or absolute theory concludes simply that a sovereign cannot, without its consent, be forced to be a defendant in the court of another sovereign.[10] The other school of thought, generally referred to as the restrictive theory, contends that a sovereign may be immune when it comes to public acts of state (*jure imperii*) but is not immune when it engages in essentially private acts (*jure gestionis*) such as entering into commercial contracts, committing personal injury and the like. In these latter instances, there is less interest in protecting the juridical integrity of the state. Thus, a state may be amenable to suit when it functions like a private person.

As might be expected, a number of countries in what was formerly known as the Soviet bloc and the Soviet Union followed the absolute school while the restrictive school has gained a number of adherents in Western Europe. Moreover, a number of countries have voluntarily relaxed the doctrine by treaties such as the Brussels Convention of 1926 in which a large number of signatories waive sovereign immunity in the case of vessels owned by the government.

Many of the problems in this area are definitional. How does one distinguish between *jure imperii* and *jure gestionis*? Occasionally, courts conclude that *jure imperii* involve only acts that an individual simply cannot do, such as declare war, establish national boundaries, or conduct diplomatic relations. However, these distinctions break down when a national government contracts to purchase armaments from a private manufacturer for the purpose of waging war, when state-run industries send air

8. One good discussion of sovereign immunity is: Pierre Lalive, *L'immunite de jurisdiction des Etats et des Organizations Internationales*, 3 Recueil des Cours 285 (Hague Academy of Int'l Law, 1953). *See also*, Georges R. Delaume, *The State Immunity Act of the United Kingdom*, 73 Am. J. Int'l L. 185 (1979).
9. *Kawananakow v. Polybank*, 205 U.S. 349 (1907).
10. This sentence is a paraphrase from the famous "Tate Letter" written by a member of the United States Department of State commenting on foreign sovereign immunity, 26 Dep't State Bull. 984 (1952). *See also*, William R. Dorsey, *III, Reflections on the FSIA after Twenty Years*, 28 J. Mar. L & Com. 257 (1997); Mark B. Feldman, *The United States FSIA of 1976 in Perspective: A Founder's View*, 35 Int'l & Comp. L. Q. 302 (1986); Lakshman Marasinghe, *A Reassessment of Sovereign Immunity*, 9 Ottowa L. Rev. 474 (1977).

pollution over international boundaries or when a country contracts to purchase an office in a foreign country to be used as its consulate.

Some countries have attempted to deal with these problems by statute. For example, in 1976 the United States enacted the Foreign Sovereign Immunities Act,[11] (FSIA) a statute that establishes as a general rule the proposition that "a foreign state shall be immune from the jurisdiction of the courts of the United States and the States." The FSIA has a few narrowly drawn exceptions such as when a nation gives its express consent to be sued and when a treat requires the waiving of immunity. The FSIA also attempts to create a commercial activity exception and defines commercial activity as: "either a regular course of commercial conduct or a particular commercial transaction or act. The commercial character of an activity shall be determined by reference to the nature of the course of conduct ... rather than by reference to its purpose."

What this definition tries to do is relax sovereign immunity in those cases, among others, in which a country buys an airplane from an American manufacturer that it intends to use in its air force. The purpose of the transaction may be to assist the country's war making, but the nature of the transaction is the mere purchase and sale of a piece of merchandise. Of course, even this attempt at a definition has not pleased everyone; the courts still struggle with it.[12]

The United Kingdom has enacted a similar statute, the State Immunity Act of 1978, which defines commercial transaction more specifically as:

> (a) any contract for the supply of goods or services;
> (b) any loan or other transaction for the provision of finance and any guarantee or indemnity in respect of (the loan or guarantee); and
> (c) any other transaction or activity (whether of a commercial, industrial, financial, professional or other similar character) into which a State enters or in which it engages otherwise than in the exercise of sovereign authority.

A number of other countries such as Canada, Australia, Singapore, and Pakistan have addressed the issue by enacting statutes delineating their understanding of sovereign immunity.[13] Of these, perhaps the most important is the promulgation of the Council of Europe: The European Convention on State Immunity and Additional

11. 28 U.S.C. §§1602–11. For additional reading on the FSIA, *see*, Erin Nelson, *Does an Individual Foreign Official Qualify as a Foreign State for Purposes of the Foreign Sovereign Immunities Act?*, 57 Cath. U. L. Rev. 853 (2008); American Bar Ass'n, *Reforming the Foreign Sovereign Immunities Act*, 40 Colum. J. Transnat'l L. 489 (2002).
12. *See*, e.g., Joseph F. Morrissey, *Simplifying the Foreign Sovereign Immunities Act: If a Sovereign Acts Like a Private Party, Treat It Like One*, 5 Chi. J. Int'l L. 675 (2005); John L. McCormack, *The Commercial Activity Exception to Foreign Sovereign Immunity*, 16 L. & Pol'y Int'l Bus. 477 (1984); Beverly May Carl, *Suing Foreign Governments in American Courts: The United States Foreign Sovereign Immunities Act in Practice*, 33 Sw. L.J. 1009 (1979).
13. *See*, e.g., H.L. Molot & M.L. Jewett, *The State Immunity Act of Canada*, 20 Can. Y.B. Int'l L. 79 (1982).

Protocol. The European Convention is essentially a restrictive doctrine formulation. It carries special weight emanating as it does from the Council of Europe.[14]

These concepts set the stage, but it is never easy to work with sovereign immunity concepts in a practical setting. Governments do not like to be sued; and they particularly do not like to be hampered in their conduct of foreign affairs. Many international commercial transactions are closely connected with diplomacy. Sovereign immunity issues generally arise anytime one does business with either the state itself or with a state-owned or state-run entity. There is no sharp, bright line that permits us to distinguish between commercial activity and "other than commercial activity;" so it is obvious that a large part of these conflicts are going to be resolved either in court on a case-by-case basis or by diplomatic means.

§12.4.2 The Act of State Doctrine

A concept closely related to sovereign immunity is the Act of State doctrine, a legal principle that typically affects individual issues in a case rather than, necessarily, the case as a whole. It most commonly occurs in cases involving expropriation of private property by a national government. While sovereign immunity comes into play only when a private party is attempting to sue a state or a state-owned enterprise, the Act of State doctrine can affect even lawsuits purely between private parties.[15]

In essence, the doctrine prevents a court from setting aside a decision made by a foreign sovereign dealing with property in that country. Once the decision—for example, a decision to expropriate property—is made, the decision may not be questioned in court.[16] As explained in a German case in which Chilean expropriation of its copper mines was at issue:

> an expropriation which has been effected abroad must in principle be recognized as being formally valid, since in accordance with the internationally recognized principle of territoriality, measures of expropriation cover without limitation the property which was subject to the [country's] sovereignty...This means that an

14. *See*, e.g., I.M. Sinclair, *The European Convention on State Immunity*, 22 Int'l & Comp. L.Q. 254 (1973).
15. For some general reading on the Act of State doctrine, *see* John Harrison, *The American Act of State Doctrine*, 47 Geo. J. Int'l L. 507 (2016); Andrew D. Patterson, *The Act of State Doctrine Is Alive and Well: Why Critics of the Doctrine Are Wrong*, 15 U.C. Davis J. Int'l L. & Pol'y 111 (2008); Patrick W. Pearsall, *Means/Ends Reciprocity in the Act of State Doctrine*, 43 Colum. J. Transnat'l L. 999 (2005); David Lloyd Jones, *Act of State in English Law*, 22 Va. J. Int'l L. 433 (1982); Michael Singer, *The Act of State Doctrine of the United Kingdom: An Analysis with Comparisons to United States Practice*, 75 Am. J. Int'l L. 283 (1981); A.B. Conant, Jr., *The Act of State Doctrine and Its Exceptions*, 12 Vand. J. Transnat'l L. 259 (1979).
16. That peculiar phenomenon of U.S. law, the American Law Institute's Restatement (Third) Foreign Relations Law of the United States at section 443 defines act of state as:

> In the absence of a treaty or other unambiguous agreement regarding controlling legal principles, courts in the United States will generally refrain from examining the validity of a taking by a foreign state of property within its own territory, or from sitting in judgment on other acts of a governmental character done by a foreign state within its own territory and applicable there.

> expropriation effected in the course of nationalization or socialization measures remains an internal matter of the foreign state as long as it does not cover property located outside of its boundaries....[17]

In the United States, the Act of State doctrine factored prominently in the Supreme Court decision in *Banco Nacional de Cuba v. Sabbatino*,[18] a case involving the Cuban government's nationalization of the Cuban sugar industry. The company argued that the government's taking of the property without any kind of indemnification was contrary to public policy and thus the actions of the Cuban government were not exempt from review under the Act of State doctrine. The Supreme Court restated the doctrine: "Every sovereign state is bound to respect the independence of every other sovereign state, and the courts of one country will not sit in judgment on the acts of the government another, done within its own territory;" and thus confirmed that the action could not be challenged in an American court. As the Court put it: "However offensive to the public policy of this country ... an expropriation of this kind may be, we conclude that both the national interest and progress toward the goal of establishing the rule of law among nations are best served by maintaining intact the act of state doctrine in this realm of its application."[19]

Somewhat alarmed at the *Sabbatino* rationale, Congress has tried to modify the result somewhat by stating in the FSIA that disputes over "rights in property taken in violation of international law" are not subject to sovereign immunity and thus may be litigated in U.S. courts. There are other statutory provisions attempting to narrow *Sabbatino* elsewhere in the U.S. statutes; but the basic principle appears to remain intact. Sovereign acts taken by a state on its own territory may not be questioned in the courts of another country.

Twenty years ago, the international debt crisis provoked some new case law on the act of state doctrine. For example, Costa Rica attempted unilaterally to restructure its international financial obligations in a manner which caused a number of Costa Rican banks to default on their obligations to a number of banks in the United States. One of the arguments mustered in the ensuing litigation by the defaulting Costa Rican banks was that the decision of the Costa Rican government to restructure the country's debt constituted a nonreviewable act of state.

In *Allied Bank International v. Banco Credito Agricola*,[20] a U.S. Court of Appeals dealt with this argument by examining not only the debt restructuring, but also International Monetary Fund policy (which generally enforces obligations to pay the debts while permitting certain restructuring) and the nature of the particular indebtedness at issue in the case. The court concluded that the obligations to pay were in the nature of private contracts, that those private contractual obligations had been incurred in New York and not in Costa Rica and that:

> while Costa Rica has a legitimate concern in overseeing the debt situation of state-owned banks...its interest in the contracts at issue is essentially limited to the

17. Decision in Hamburg District Court in *In re: Kennecott Copper*, 12 Int'l Leg. Materials 251 (1973).
18. 376 U.S. 398 (1964).
19. *Id.*
20. 757 F.2d 516 (2d Cir. 1985).

> extent to which it can unilaterally alter the payment terms. Costa Rica's potential jurisdiction over the debt is not sufficient to locate the debt there for the purposes of the act of state doctrine...The act of state doctrine is, therefore, inapplicable.[21]

It is difficult to tell from some of these cases whether the doctrine is in true ferment or whether it is simply being narrowly confined to traditional settings of expropriation. Only time will tell. For most private contracts, the doctrine has limited applicability.

§12.5 PERSONAL JURISDICTION OVER PRIVATE PARTIES

Sovereign immunity and act of state problems rarely surface in litigation between private parties. The much more difficult problem posed in litigating private international commercial agreements is the matter of whether a court has jurisdiction—judicial power—over all of the parties. Indeed, this is the Achilles heel of litigation because most parties live at great distances from one another and are normally not to be found in the same country.

Consider the following hypothetical. A, a small shoe manufacturer resident in Singapore, contracts to sell 100,000 industrial safety shoes to B, a wholesaler in the United States. B has a contract with several manufacturing companies for the shoes which are of unique grade and quality. The shoes are shipped to the United States and after inspection are found to be defective. The shoes were designed to very narrow specifications and while they could eventually be replaced, there is no way that B can order replacements within the time she is expected to perform on her contract.

Assume further that B has lost a USD 500,000 contract because of A's breach. All of B's attempts at negotiation fail miserably. A will not even respond to B's telexes or telephone calls so B is probably justified in concluding that the less-drastic dispute resolution techniques simply will not work. There is no arbitration clause in the contract.

On these facts, B and her lawyers may conclude that the only meaningful option is to litigate. The question then becomes: "litigate where?" One clear-cut solution to any question of personal jurisdiction is simply to track down the party in breach (the defendant in U.S. practice) and sue him where you find him. Under normal circumstances, a domestic court has power over its own nationals within that country's boundaries. Within the United States, this is often the preferred solution because courts throughout the country are similar in terms of procedure, power, and outlook. It is more complicated, however, when one moves across national boundaries because domestic courts in a particular country may be hostile to foreigners suing its own nationals, may follow only the most rudimentary procedures, may have a reputation for arbitrariness, and, at bottom, may simply be unpleasant sites for litigation.

Of course, Singapore's legal system is essentially British, has highly trained and very sophisticated judges and lawyers, and is quite capable and experienced in dealing with complex commercial matters. There is probably no reason on these facts to avoid

21. *Id.*

Singapore as a reasonable forum for the lawsuit. And, at the very least, suing in a Singapore court will totally alleviate any personal jurisdiction problems since that jurisdiction is where the defendant is to be found. There is virtually no question that Singapore courts have jurisdiction over a business executive found within Singapore's boundaries.

Assume, however, that B strongly prefers to bring the lawsuit in the United States. Such a decision is not totally implausible. All of the defective shoes are there. They may be useful as evidence. Presumably, B will call a number of experts to testify as to the precise defects in the shoes. These experts may well be located in the United States. Transporting evidence and experts to Singapore is expensive. There may be some evidence of fraud in the case. In many U.S. jurisdictions, an act of fraud that induces someone to enter into a business relationship (so-called fraud in the inducement) may be a ground for recovering exemplary damages, sometimes referred to as punitive damages. Consider the plaintiff's choice of forum if we assume that the Singapore courts have no power to award exemplary damages in this type of breach of contract suit, or that proof of fraud is much more difficult under Singapore law.

Is it possible for a United States court to obtain personal jurisdiction over the Singapore manufacturer, who is, in personal jurisdiction parlance, a nonresident defendant? Under U.S. law, there are some possibilities for doing so, although under the facts we hypothesized, it will be difficult. Questions of personal jurisdiction in the United States in garden-variety commercial matters turn on the power of the state courts, rather than the power of the federal courts, since in these cases, the federal courts normally have no greater powers over nonresident defendants than do the state courts.[22]

As a consequence, plaintiffs in the United States who wish to sue a nonresident defendant must examine two different issues. First, each state has what is called a long-arm statute which authorizes its courts to exert personal jurisdiction over defendants who are not physically present in the state if those persons have committed various acts within the state such as causing personal injury or engaging in a commercial transaction within the state. In the shoe case, let us assume for the sake of simplicity that B's state has an appropriate long-arm statute.

Unfortunately, the question is not resolved at that point. The United States Constitution requires that all persons, including nonresident defendants, be afforded due process by courts, so the United States Supreme Court has required that every case be examined to determine whether the nonresident defendant has the necessary minimum contacts with the state before permitting a plaintiff to sue a nonresident

22. For persons wishing more depth on personal jurisdiction issues in the United States, *see*, e.g., Jack Friedenthal Mary Ann Kane & Arthur R. Miller, *Civil Procedure* (Chapter Three) (5th ed., 2015). The U.S. doctrine of personal jurisdiction is somewhat in flux. *See* Cassandra Burke Robertson & Charles W. Rhodes, *The Business of Personal Jurisdiction*, 68 Case W. L. Rev. 775 (2017); Daniel M. Klerman, *Rethinking Personal Jurisdiction*, 6 J. Leg. Analysis 245 (2014); Joann K. Coston, *Embrace the New, But Don't Forget About the Old: Asserting Personal Jurisdiction over the New Internet Age*, 34 S.U. L. Rev. 249 (2007); Glen B. Manishin, *Note, Federalism, Due Process and Minimum Contacts*, 80 Colum. L. Rev. 1341 (1980).

defendant.[23] While the nuances of the minimum contacts doctrine are sometimes difficult to parse, the U.S. Supreme Court has just decided a case which, albeit somewhat muddled and confused, may resolve many of these issues. Indeed, the case may tell us a great deal about how American courts will deal with questions of personal jurisdiction involving foreign defendants in the future.

In *Asahi Metal Industry Co. v. Superior Court of California*,[24] Asahi, a Japanese company, manufactured tire valve assemblies that were sold to Cheng Shin Rubber Industrial Company, a Taiwanese tire manufacturing company. The tires were then sold around the world including the United States. Approximately 20% of the Taiwanese company's American sales took place in the state of California. In September 1978, a California resident and his wife were riding on a motorcycle that collided with a farm tractor. The husband was severely injured and the wife was killed. The husband filed a lawsuit making various claims and allegations, including a claim that the tire was defectively manufactured. Consequently, the husband's lawyer sued Cheng Shin and Cheng Shin, in turn, filed a claim against Asahi, alleging that if the tire was defective, the defect lay in the valve manufactured by Asahi.

In affidavits filed in the lawsuit, Asahi executives admitted that they knew that the valve assemblies were placed in tires that were later sold in the United States, but indicated that they never expected that their activities would subject them to product liability lawsuits in various American state courts. Nonetheless, the California state courts ruled that Asahi knew that tire sales took place in California, that Asahi intentionally put the valves "in the stream of commerce," and that Asahi earned substantial revenues from Cheng Shin's California sales.

After review by the U.S. Supreme Court, Asahi was let off the hook. The Court determined that mere awareness of the fact that goods manufactured by another which contain goods manufactured by Asahi are sold in the United States does not provide the requisite minimum contacts between Asahi and the state of California. Unfortunately, the Court's opinion is considerably blurred by a series of separate opinions in the case.

While the Court was unanimous in concluding that Asahi was not amenable to suit in California, there was no unanimity on the rationale for the case. For example, Justice O'Connor, who authored the lead opinion in the case, concluded that a company's merely placing goods into the stream of commerce was not sufficient. In this case, Asahi had no direct sales in California, maintained no offices or agents there, did not solicit tire valve business in the state and had no control over the tire distribution system which brought Cheng Shin's tires into California. Four other justices, however, rejected Justice O'Connor's use of the stream of commerce approach

---

23. The minimum contacts doctrine was first articulated in a 1945 decision, *International Shoe Co. v. State of Washington*, 326 U.S. 310 (1945). For two good articles on the minimum contacts doctrine in international transactions *see*, Raymond Paretsky, *A New Approach to Jurisdictional Questions in Transnational Litigation in U.S. Courts*, 10 U. Pa. J. Int'l Bus. L. 663 (1998); Gary Born, *Reflections on Judicial Jurisdiction in International Cases*, 17 Ga. J. Int'l & Comp. L. 1 (1987); Graham C. Lilly, *Jurisdiction Over Domestic and Alien Defendants*, 69 Va. L. Rev. 85 (1983).
24. 480 U.S. 102 (1987).

and were willing to conclude only that hauling Asahi into a California court in these circumstances would offend "traditional notions of fair play and justice."

With regard to U.S. court jurisdiction over foreign defendants, the Court was unanimous on the following point:

> [U.S. courts should] consider the procedural and substantive policies of other nations whose interests are affected by the assertion of jurisdiction by the California court. The procedural and substantive interests of other nations in a state court's assertion of jurisdiction over an alien defendant will differ from case to case. In every case, however, those interests, as well as the Federal [national] interest in its foreign relations policies, will be best served by a careful inquiry into the reasonableness of the assertion of jurisdiction in the particular case, and an unwillingness to find the serious burdens on an alien defendant outweighed by minimal interests on the part of the plaintiff or the forum state. Great care and reserve should be exercised when extending our notions of personal jurisdiction into the international field.[25]

Asahi suggests that our company in Singapore might not be amenable to suit in a U.S. court; but one should not be too sanguine on this point. Note the essential differences. Asahi was one step removed from the actual U.S. sales and apparently conducted no other direct activities in the U.S. By contrast our hypothetical Singapore company dealt individually and directly with the U.S. buyer and shipped the goods directly to the United States. The amount in controversy in our case, something in excess of one-half million dollars, is not an insignificant transaction. So it might be possible for a U.S. court to conclude that A is amenable to suit even given the Supreme Court's admonition to the contrary.

Not too many years ago it was sufficient to find some property in the United States, such as a bank account, some real estate or perhaps even an account receivable that could be seized. That property then could be used to obtain personal jurisdiction over the nonresident defendant; and if he failed to appear and defend the lawsuit, the plaintiff could at least take the property seized in partial fulfillment of the obligation (occasionally referred to as *quasi-in-rem jurisdiction*). However, the Supreme Court in *Shaffer v. Heitner*,[26] decided that even in those instances, a court must apply a minimum contacts analysis. So merely finding out that A has a USD 5,000 bank account in a New York bank may not be sufficient to make him amenable to suit in the U.S., particularly if the USD 5,000 has nothing to do with the transaction sued upon.

But what about other countries? Are they quite as expansive as the United States in determining that their courts can exert personal jurisdiction over nonresident defendants? English courts are generally reluctant to entertain suits over persons not served with process within the United Kingdom, but Order 11 of the Rules of the Supreme Court of Judicature[27] allows a plaintiff, after getting a court's permission, to sue a nonresident in certain actions for breach of contract. Article 14 of the French Civil Code provides that an "alien, even one not residing in France, may be summoned

25. *Id.*, at 134 (first emphasis in the original, second emphasis added, quotation marks and citations deleted).
26. 433 U.S. 186 (1977).
27. 3 Stat. Instr. 2529 (No. 2145) (1962).

before the French courts for the fulfillment of obligations contracted by him in France with a French person [or] may be brought before the French courts for obligations contracted by him in a foreign country towards French persons."

By contrast, the German legal system appears to have a fairly broad notion of *quasi-in-rem jurisdiction*, articulated in section 23 of the German civil procedure code (*Zivilprozessordnung*): "For complaints asserting pecuniary claims against a person who has no domicile within the country, the court of the district within which this person has property, or within which is found the object claimed by the complaint, has jurisdiction ..." Sometimes the smallest piece of property—an abandoned undershirt in one case—has been used as the basis for asserting jurisdiction over an absent defendant.

However, it is important to recognize that these traditional notions of personal jurisdiction in Europe have been modified within the EC by the 1968 Brussels Convention (Jurisdiction of Courts and the Enforcement of Judgments in Civil and Commercial Matters).[28] Under the Brussels Convention, a person's domicile is normally the controlling element in establishing personal jurisdiction—that is, a person may be sue where he is domiciled. In this instance, domicile in essence means where that person has his permanent place of residence. However, in something of a bow to the newer American long-arm statutes, the Convention also permits personal jurisdiction to be found in the place of performance of a contract or where a defendant has committed certain types of personal injury. The Convention also forbids French and German courts to invoke either Article 14 (French Code) or Article 23 (German Code) as a basis for jurisdiction when a lawsuit involves a citizen of another EU country.[29]

Issues of personal jurisdiction are not easily resolved, particularly when the lawsuit crosses national boundaries. Since there are rarely any conclusive answers and since personal jurisdiction is crucial to going forward with the lawsuit, many litigators simply take the path of least resistance and sue the defendant where the defendant can be found.

§12.6 SERVICE OF PROCESS

Service of process is sometimes confused with personal jurisdiction because courts occasionally use the term service of process when they are actually worried about personal jurisdiction—that is, a court's power over a nonresident person. In reality, service of process is a mechanical step by which the court notifies a person that she is being sued. In its simplest terms, service of process means getting papers relating to the lawsuit into the hands of the defendant. In certain circumstances, a plaintiff may also attempt to seize property belonging to the defendant when the suit is begun to guarantee satisfaction of any judgment that may be obtained. This is not to say that this

28. *See*, e.g., 18 Int'l Leg. Materials 8 (1979).
29. *Id.* The Brussels Convention is further discussed in §7.10. For a general discussion of the Convention *see*, Christian Kohler, *Practical Experience of the Brussels Jurisdiction and Judgments Convention in the Six Original Contracting States*, 34 Int'l & Comp. L.Q. 563 (1985).

step is unimportant. Virtually all courts have detailed service of process rules and a person is not subject to a court's jurisdiction until he is properly served.

In the United States, plaintiffs filing suits filed in federal court follow the requirements of Rule 4 of the Federal Rules of Civil Procedure. Basically, this rule requires that the plaintiff serve the defendant with a copy of the complaint and a summons which tells the defendant something of what the lawsuit is about and warns the defendant not to ignore his obligations to respond. In many instances, these papers may be served by registered mail or by a special process server. Usually, a defendant is properly served when the documents are placed in his hands either through the mails or by the process server.[30]

Service of process across national borders is always a little more difficult than domestic service of process; but most legal systems recognize that it is a necessary step in a lawsuit and provide special rules for transnational service. Between countries, even registered mail is sometimes faulty and using a process server can be enormously expensive and frequently not justified—particularly when, for example, the defendant's whereabouts are known and when he is not likely to flee to avoid process.

The United States Congress has greatly assisted international service of process by providing that federal courts may assist foreign courts and tribunals in making service of process on persons in the United States even when there is no prior judgment that the foreign entity is seeking to enforce.[31] Service of process by federal courts in the United States on persons in foreign countries is permitted under Rule 4 of the Federal Rules of Civil Procedure which allow service by mail, with some kind of return receipt, under any method allowed by the courts in that country including the device of a letter rogatory[32] and by special process server.

There is an important international convention governing service abroad—The 1965 Hague Convention on the Service Abroad of Judicial Documents in Civil or Commercial Matters (Service Convention).[33] The Hague Service Convention, now

---

30. For some of the hazards of service of process generally *see*, Frank Conley, *Service with a Smiley: The Effect of E-Mail and Other Electronic Communication on Service of Process*, 11 Temp. Int'l & Comp. L.J. 407 (1997); Linda Mullenix, *The New Federal Express: Mail Service of Process Under Amended Rule 4*, 4 Rev. Litig. 299 (1985). *See also*, Yvonne A. Tamayo, *Catch Me If You Can: Serving United States Process on an Elusive Defendant Abroad*, 17 Harv. J. of L. & Tech. 212 (2003).
31. 28 U.S.C. §1696. According to this section: "The order [of service of process] may be made pursuant to a letter rogatory issued, or request made, by a foreign or international tribunal or upon application of any interested person." Moreover, "[t]his section does not preclude service of such a document without an order of court." *Id.*
32. A letter rogatory used in this context means a written document "whereby one country, acting through its own courts and by methods of court procedure ... to assist the administration of justice in the former country" (Black's Law Dictionary (Rev. 4th ed., 1968)). *See also*, Kim M. Forcino, *Note, International Service of Process: The Trend Moves Away from Uniformity*, 8 Pace Int'l L. Rev. 485 (1996); Gary N. Horlick, *A Practical Guide to Service of United States Process Abroad*, 14 Int'l L. 637 (1980).
33. 20 U.S.T., 361 T.I.A.S 6638 (1965). American readers will find the Convention reprinted in 28 U.S.C., Rule 4, note. *See also*, Kevin W. Lewis, *E-Service: Ensuring the Integrity of International E-Mail Service of Process*, 13 Roger Williams U. L. Rev. 285 (2008); Emily Fishbein Johnson, *Privatizing the Duties of the Central Authority: Should International Service of Process be Up for Bid?*, 37 Geo. Wash. Int'l Rev. 769 (2005); Pamela R. Parmalee, *International Service of Process: A Guide to Serving Process Abroad under the Hague Convention*, 39 Okla. L. Rev. 287 (1986).

ratified by approximately fifty-nine countries including the United States and most of the Western European countries, requires each signatory country to designate a central authority to manage matters of service of process from abroad. Generally, this service will be accomplished in the same manner that its own courts serve process, although there are some grounds such as public policy on which the country may object to making the service. The Service Convention also sets out special rules for what might be done if a party who is served abroad fails to appear for the litigation. In this instance in the United States a default judgment is generally entered almost automatically. Under the Service Convention, however, the signatory countries commit themselves to examining closely the precise manner in which process was served and whether it was actually served before granting the default.

None of these procedures is inherently difficult. The practical problems in international service of process stem largely from: (1) the inability to locate the proper party; and (2) occasional mechanical breakdowns in transmitting the necessary papers. These are not problems of the law, but rather are problems inherent in all types of conflict resolution. There are relatively few legal barriers to proper service abroad, especially in the context of international commercial agreements between established companies. While it is faintly possible that our Singapore seller might flee the jurisdiction just to avoid a lawsuit brought in Singapore by the American buyer, it is highly unlikely. Corporate entities rarely resist service of process. They fight fiercely on all the other grounds.

§12.7 CHOICE OF FORUM, VENUE, AND FORUM NON CONVENIENS

As we have seen, many considerations dictate the place where the litigation takes place. Frequently, the parties simply have no choice as to the location of the lawsuit. A defendant who chooses to be uncooperative may require litigation in his home country to the exclusion of all other possibilities because his country's courts are the only legal system that has personal jurisdiction over him. In other instances, the location of the evidence may dictate litigation in that jurisdiction. In smaller cases, costs may severely limit the choices among locations.[34] However, when choice of forum is possible, the parties might well refer to the contract's choice of law clause for guidance. It makes a great deal of sense to try a case in the country whose substantive law is going to be applied to the dispute to avoid the complications inherent in attempting to prove another country's law in the forum court.[35] Having to "prove" foreign law normally requires bringing experts into the litigation to testify as to the foreign law and performing an elaborate review of applicable treatises. A court dealing with foreign law never feels perfectly comfortable and, on occasion, may make baffling mistakes of construction and interpretation simply because it is unfamiliar with the applicable law.

34. For a good general exposition of some of these issues *see*, Zelman Cowen & D. Mendes Da Costa, *The Contractual Forum: A Comparative Study*, 43 Can. B. Rev. 453 (1965).
35. von Mehren, *supra* n. 5, at 47.

All other things being equal, the parties might also consider the judicial procedure to be applied to the case by various courts. Litigating in a court with acceptable trial procedures is a benefit.

Chapter 4 explored the issue of whether it is possible for litigating parties to choose the forum for litigation when they draft the contract. Those choices are generally honored even when the forum is in a neutral country. In *The Bremen v. Zapata Off-Shore Oil Co.*,[36] the United States Supreme Court honored a forum selection clause in an international commercial agreement between an American and a German company that identified the High Court of Justice in London as the proper forum for any litigation, even though—in theory at least—the American courts could have exercised jurisdiction over the case. Clearly, the Supreme Court believes in forcing parties to live with the contract language that they drafted and is especially sensitive to the special considerations at issue in international commercial agreements. The Court noted that the choice of London was a rational one:

> Not surprisingly foreign businessmen prefer, as do we, to have disputes resolved in their own courts, but if that choice is not available, then in a neutral forum with expertise in the subject matter. Plainly the courts of England meet the standards of neutrality and long experience in admiralty litigation. The choice of that forum was made in an arm's-length negotiation by experienced and sophisticated businessmen and absent some compelling and countervailing reason it should be honored by the parties and enforced by the courts.[37]

At least in the United States, the touchstone for judging the validity of a contractual choice of forum is one of reasonableness. A prominent collection of what American law professors frequently refer to as black letter law, the newest Restatement on conflict of laws admonishes courts to give effect to such agreements unless the parties' choice is "unfair or unreasonable."[38] Courts in other countries may not be quite so amenable to such clauses, however. A number of decisions appear to worry about clauses that purport to oust local courts of jurisdiction or that bear no reasonable relation to the contract itself.[39]

But what of those instances in which the contract does not choose a forum, or where the choice strikes a court as improper? In these cases, a court will determine a forum after the plaintiff attempts to litigate it somewhere. Occasionally, a case may be tried in a number of different places, and it will be left to some court to determine the proper place for the litigation. This concept, usually referred to as venue, is closely related to the issue of forum non conveniens. While few scholars, practitioners, or

36. 407 U.S. 1 (1972).
37. *Id.*
38. Restatement (Second) Conflict of Laws, §80. This provision is nearly identical to a provision in the Restatement of the Foreign Relations Law of the United States (Revised) §421(2)(g).
39. *See*, the cases collected in Michael Gruson, *Forum Selection Clauses in International and Interstate Commercial Agreements*, U. Ill. L. Rev. 133 (1982). *See also*, Kevin M. Clermont, *Governing Law on Forum Selection Agreements*, 66 Hastings L.J. 643 (2015); Hannah Buxbaum, *Forum Selection in International Contract Litigation: The Role of Judicial Discretion*, Maurer Law Faculty Paper 326 (2004).

judges discuss or distinguish these two doctrines with clarity, for the purposes of this chapter, venue will be defined as a site for the litigation that is permissible under the law.

In many domestic cases, there is only one place where venue is proper. However, in international commercial agreements, there are almost always at least two places where a case might be litigated: the country of the buyer or the country of the seller. Forum non conveniens—the issue of the "best" or optimum place to bring a lawsuit—is a concept that comes into play when there are two or more locations in which it is legally permissible to bring the case.

Venue is normally dictated either by the rules of the court or by an underlying statute. For example, suits involving breach of contract in the U.S. federal courts may be brought, theoretically, in three places in the United States: the judicial district: (1) where any defendant resides; (2) where the defendants are subject to personal jurisdiction; or (3) where a substantial part of the events or omissions giving rise to the law suit have occurred.[40] These three sites are only theoretical possibilities. Issues of service of process and other factors may cancel out one or more of the sites for other reasons.

Most other countries have narrower venue rules. Foreign venue provisions, unlike American venue, tends to be more defendant-oriented. Note, for example, that Article 23 of the German civil procedure code limits certain suits to the district in which the defendant has property. Certain foreign jurisdictions are so small geographically that venue is not really a factor. In our shoe manufacturing hypothetical, if B wants to sue A where he lives, she will sue in the city of Singapore. By contrast, if her company has operations in, say, New York, Connecticut and California and she attempted suit in the U.S., she may be able to bring it in the courts of any of those states (again, so long as one of those states somehow can exert personal jurisdiction over the defendant; venue always takes a back seat to personal jurisdiction).

When there are options as to the site of the lawsuit, the question becomes slightly different. What is the most convenient place to try the case? In this instance, the choices are frequently left to the courts, rather than to the statutory law. The United States Supreme Court has identified a number of factors that it requires lower federal courts to apply and that constitute almost a codification of the American law of forum non conveniens. In the 1981 case of *Piper Aircraft Co v. Reyno*,[41] a wrongful death action was brought in a California state court and later removed to a federal court in California. The litigation stemmed from the fatal crash, in Scotland, of an aircraft manufactured by Piper. Only Scottish citizens were killed, but the American law of wills and trusts permitted the lawyer for the Scottish decedents to appoint his secretary, Ms. Reyno, as an administrator of their estates for the purposes of pursuing the wrongful death action where she lived in California.

Subsequently, the case was transferred to central Pennsylvania where the Piper Company at that time manufactured its aircraft. At that point, the defendants, Piper and Hartzell Propeller Company (the American company that manufactured the plane's

40. 28 U.S.C. §1391(a).
41. 454 U.S. 235(1981).

propellers) asked the court to dismiss the action entirely because a trial of this case in the United States would be inconvenient to the defendants and because an adequate forum existed, namely Scotland. Reyno resisted this request, arguing that Scottish law could not provide all the remedies that might be available under U.S. law.

On review in the United States Supreme Court, the Court held that the lawsuit should have been dismissed on forum non conveniens grounds. The Court stated expressly that "the possibility of an unfavorable change in law should not, by itself, bar dismissal."[42] The case is truly remarkable for a number of reasons. First, this is one of the first instances in which the Supreme Court has suggested that plaintiffs who are properly in a U.S. court can be kicked out of that court and forced to try the case outside the United States. Second, it was one of the few times that the Court fully articulated a number of grounds for assessing the issue of forum non conveniens.[43]

Briefly stated, there are what the Court calls private factors and others it refers to as public factors. Private factors which a court should consider include: access to sources of proof; availability of procedures for compelling the attendance of unwilling witnesses; possibility of view of the premises; "and all other practical problems that make trial of a case easy, expeditious and inexpensive." Public factors include: court congestion; the local interest in having local controversies decided at home; a forum that is at home with the law governing the action; and the avoidance of unnecessary problems in conflicts of law, or in the application of foreign law.[44]

What does this mean in practical terms? It is difficult to give the question a precise answer because the Supreme Court also made clear that trial courts in the United States have a great deal of discretion in deciding questions of forum non conveniens. In other words, if the trial court had considered the factors enumerated in *Piper v. Reyno* and concluded that the case should be heard in an American court, the Supreme Court would probably not disturb that decision. The Supreme Court was mainly troubled by the fact that the trial court's refusal to dismiss the American case and to send the case to a Scottish court was based on solely on the court's judgment that Scottish law was too pro-defendant, and that the U.S. plaintiff could not obtain all the remedies in Scotland that she had at her disposal in the United States. The mere fact that a plaintiff would be treated differently under the law of another country is not a proper basis for determining forum non conveniens.

How might *Piper* affect our shoe case, assuming other questions such as personal jurisdiction do not forestall the possibility of a U.S. forum? It is a tough question. On the one hand, the goods are now in the United States. They may be tested there and examined by American experts. Presumably, the specifications for the shoes are set out in the contractual documents; that is, it may not be necessary for a judge or jury to travel to Singapore merely to see what was said in the contract. By contrast, the Singapore defendant may have his own experts who might testify to the fact that the buyer's specifications were inaccurate or impossible to obtain—or, as often happens,

42. *Id.*
43. The factors were originally elucidated in slightly different form in *Gulf Oil Co. v. Gilbert*, 330 U.S. 501 (1947).
44. *Piper*, 454 at 265 n. 6.

merely that the plaintiff's experts are wrong and the defendant's experts are right. At bottom, a judge would simply have to balance all the interests and make a decision. In U.S. law, the plaintiff's choice of forum counts for a lot; but after *Piper* it is obviously not a controlling factor.

Professor Georges Delaume reports that English courts react much more mechanically to forum non conveniens problems than do American courts; and courts in civil law countries have failed entirely to develop a concept of forum non conveniens in part because civil system courts "do not enjoy the same discretion as those in common law countries and have little choice but to adjudicate a case on the basis of existing jurisdictional rules."[45]

§12.8 CHOICE OF LAW

The law applied to a commercial dispute is frequently dispositive of the case. As a consequence, it is no wonder that so many lawyers, judges and legal scholars spend a great deal of time on these issues. In the context of international commercial agreements, there are two ways in which law can be "chosen" for the dispute. First, the parties may insert a choice of law provision in the contract. Generally, if that choice is reasonable, a court will honor it. Reasonableness here is a matter of showing some kind of relationship between the body of law chosen and the contract. Chapter 4 contains a lengthy discussion of these issues.

But assuming that a contract does not specify the applicable law—or that a court refuses to honor the law chosen—what principles will a court apply to establish the applicable law? This issue is difficult to discuss in the abstract, so it may be helpful to reconsider our hypothetical dispute over the shoes manufactured in Singapore and sold to a U.S. buyer. The U.S. company intends to sell the shoes to industrial customers in the United States. The shoes traveled directly from Singapore to the United States and were not altered en route. To make the hypothetical a little easier to apply, assume that the shoe manufacturer came to the United States and signed the contract in New York.

Under these circumstances, it should be clear that if the contractual documents expressly choose, say, the UCC of some state in the United States or Singapore's law pertaining to sales of goods, choice of law should not pose further problems. A court or an arbitrator in all likelihood will simply honor that choice and apply the chosen law to the dispute. However, if the parties chose Soviet law (a concededly implausible situation inserted here purely for illustrative purposes), a court or arbitrator would probably feel free to disregard this choice. It bears no meaningful relation to the parties or their contract. At the same time, parties sometime choose the law of a country that is neither the country of origin or the country of destination. For example, in a major U.S. case between a Japanese car manufacturer and a car dealership in Puerto Rico, the contract chose Swiss law—a choice that all reviewing courts seemed to accept without question. It would seem that if two contracting parties choose the law of a major

45. Georges R. Delaume, *Transnational Contracts* (Booklet 11), 68–70.

trading nation, even if it is not the law of their respective countries, the choice will remain undisturbed by either arbitrator or courts.

When a contract is silent on choice of law, the court typically is forced to make the choice. When a court chooses law, it deals with an arcane but frequently crucial topic known as conflict of laws. Both courts and legislatures have worked out governing principles that are generally applied on a case-by-case basis. In the United States, codified principles of choice of law may be found in the UCC (indicating simply that the applicable law is the law of a state that "bears an appropriate relation to the transaction"[46] and the Restatements (both First and Second), Conflict of Laws. The Restatements must be discussed in tandem because some American states follow one document and some states abide by the other.

The First Restatement is concededly a mechanical approach to determining applicable law, but its mechanical nature also makes it a relatively simple system to apply. Under the First Restatement, the law applicable to a contract dispute is the place where the contract is to be made so long as the dispute concerns issues such as the capacity of the parties to make a contract, whether the contract contained all the proper formalities and the like. Put a little differently these are all the issues that tell us whether a contract was formed in the first instance.[47] That place is the place where "the principal event necessary to make a contract occurs;"[48] and for a formal contract, the principal event is the act of delivery.[49]

However, if the dispute involves issues of performance such as delivery of defective goods or a failure to abide by manufacturing specifications, another section of the Restatement provides that the applicable law will be the "law of the place of performance."[50] Thus, if we use Restatement First to solve the shoe manufacturing problem, the applicable law would almost surely have to be the law of some U.S. state since both delivery and performance (if one regards actually using the shoes or the act of reselling the shoes as the "performance" under the contract) occur in the United States.

Most mechanical rules in law eventually lead to trouble; and the First Restatement was no exception. The Second Restatement was deliberately made much fuzzier and more ambiguous to avoid some of the problems of the overly mechanical earlier version. Under Restatement Second, the choice of law depends on the type of contract and the issue in dispute, but at bottom, the law chosen is to be the jurisdiction that bears the "most significant relationship" with the contract,[51] a concept evaluated in terms of: (a) the place of contracting; (b) the place of negotiation; (c) the place of performance; (d) the location of the contract's subject matter; and (e) the domicile, residence, nationality, place of incorporation, and place of business of the parties.[52]

46. UCC §1-105.
47. Restatement (First) Conflict of Laws, §332.
48. *Id.*, §311.
49. *Id.*, §312.
50. *Id.*, §358.
51. Restatement (Second) Conflict of Laws, §188.
52. *Id.*

Applying this analysis to the shoe problem, the law chosen would again probably be the law of an appropriate U.S. state. While it is difficult to determine which state, it is unlikely that any court in the United States charged with choosing law for this dispute would consider itself bound to apply the law of Singapore.

Choice of law outside the United States appears to be moving away from purely mechanical principals to one of interest analysis and party autonomy. For example, the EU Convention on the Law Applicable to Contractual Assessments permits a court to infer a choice of law by the parties from such things as use of language that is unique to a particular legal system or by a choice of forum clause.[53] The Convention on the International Sale of Goods (CISG) adopts essentially the "substantial relation" approach of the UCC.[54]

Within the EU, the Rome Convention on the Choice of Law for Contracts provides a number of rules for choosing law that are applied by many of the European nations. While too complex for a lengthy discussion here, the Rome Convention sets out a number of detailed rules based on the subject matter of the litigation, for example, contract, personal injury, and the like.

§12.9 DISCOVERY AND GATHERING INFORMATION AND EVIDENCE ABROAD

Once the important threshold matters such as choice of forum and choice of law are made, the adversaries can get down to the business of actually litigating the dispute. Frequently, a contract dispute turns on questions involving facts that are not always readily apparent at the outset of the litigation. Many legal systems also require that information presented at trial be gathered and preserved in some specific form—that is, the originals of documents—or that oral evidence be taken under oath or in the presence of a magistrate. Finding, collating and evaluating the materials and information necessary to try a case is one of the most cumbersome and time-consuming aspects of litigation.

In the United States, pretrial gathering of evidence and information, referred to as discovery, is almost as important as the trial. U.S.-style discovery has become increasingly expensive and protracted. This has led to a great deal of criticism of the U.S. procedures abroad. In many other countries, the trial process tends to be more inquisitorial. Information gathering and analysis tends to be put into the hands of court officials and thus less under the immediate control of the parties or their attorneys. An in-depth analysis of the relative merits of the U.S. versus continental systems of litigation is not within the scope of this book. What is important, however, is to understand how both systems work.

---

53. §3(1). For an excellent, but more general discussion, *see*, Symposium, *The Influence of Modern American Conflicts Theories on European Law*, 30 Am. J. Comp. L. 1 (1982).
54. *See*, the discussion of the CISG, *supra* §2.9.4.

Discovery in the United States is based on three premises.[55] First, the U.S. system of litigation is adversarial in nature. That leads to the assumption that a determination of the truth of any matter is best and most efficiently reached when adversaries hammer at each other in court. Second, the adversarial process is best served by eliminating surprise, unfairness, or games playing at trial. That can be done by creating rules of procedure that tend, insofar as possible, to let the parties develop as much information as possible on the dispute before trial in order to eliminate surprise at trial. Third, as the adversaries come to know more and more about the case, they may choose to settle the matter rather than proceed to trial. Thus, comprehensive pretrial discovery may actually enhance the efficiency of the judicial system by promoting settlement and thereby eliminating the need for an actual trial.

While procedures differ in some states, the discovery rules used by the federal courts are a good example of a modern American system at work. The rules permit a party to inquire into virtually any kind of information pertaining to the litigation so long as the information is relevant to the case and is not privileged (this term is used in the sense of doctor/patient or attorney/client privilege—concepts drawn from the law of evidence).[56] The rules then establish several devices for the gathering or preserving of information and evidence:

(1) the deposition;
(2) written interrogatories;
(3) requests for the production of documents or physical inspections;
(4) requests for mental or physical examinations of persons; or
(5) requests to the other party that something simply be admitted so that proof on the point does not have to be adduced at trial.[57]

Some of these devices are used far more often than others. Perhaps the most frequently used discovery tools are depositions and interrogatories. In a deposition, a lawyer for one of the parties is permitted to question another person under oath in the presence of a court stenographer who takes down a verbatim transcript of the questions and answers. Interrogatories, as that term is used in the federal courts, are written questions proffered by one party to the other party to which that party responds in writing. Without going further into the nuances of federal discovery, the reader should be able to see how time-consuming and expensive this process can become. Its benefit, of course, is that both sides come to learn a great deal about the case long before they have to appear before a judge.

Legal systems outside the United States rarely give this much control and freedom of inquiry to the adversaries themselves. In most systems, a great deal of the

55. For elaborate commentary on discovery in federal courts, most lawyers refer to two multivolume treatises: Charles Alan Wright & Arthur R. Miller, *Federal Practice and Procedure and Moore's Federal Practice*. For two good commentaries on the system *see*, Arthur R. Miller, *The Adversary System: Dinosaur or Phoenix*, 69 Minn. L. Rev. 1 (1984); Marvin E. Frankel, *The Search for Truth: An Umpireal View*, 123 U. Pa. L. Rev. 1031 (1975).
56. Rule 26(a), Federal Rules of Civil Procedure.
57. *Id.* Rules 27–37.

elucidation of facts is done outside the context of the judicial proceeding (e.g., by private investigator) or under closely controlled orders issued by the court.[58] The court officials themselves are frequently the primary investigators. Of course, one reason why this is not ineffective is that the so-called trial in civil law countries extends over a number of sessions; it is usually not a single event; and, accordingly, the cases of each side may be developed as the proceeding moves along.[59] In these systems, the parties are far more passive. Discovery, as that term is used in the United States, is virtually unheard of.

Fact gathering for litigation within a particular country obviously requires the parties to use whatever procedures are allowed within that country by that country's judicial system. It is much more complicated to obtain information and take evidence outside the forum country.[60] Consider the problems faced by a lawyer in the United States who anticipates trying the case in the U.S., but who now wants to obtain information abroad. The rules applicable in the U.S. federal courts are a good starting place to illustrate U.S. practice. Federal Rule of Civil Procedure 28 now addresses these problems by providing for the taking of depositions in foreign countries either under procedures authorized by the law of the host country or by U.S. civil procedure rules. The request to that country for permission to take the deposition may be made either by commission or by letter rogatory; and the information discovered or the testimony taken abroad is not excludable in the U.S. court merely because it was not given under oath or because a verbatim transcript was not taken.

Some definition may be necessary here since even experienced American lawyers sometimes have a difficult time distinguishing between commissions and letters rogatory. First, readers should realize that the U.S. State Department cooperates in the taking of evidence abroad. When evidence is taken by commission, the commissioner is normally an employee of the State Department who is authorized to administer oaths. On occasion, he may also be a lawyer. Commissions come in two forms: open or closed. An open commission permits the commissioner to inquire of the witness on a particular matter without the structure of prepared questions. A closed commission requires the commissioner to submit written questions to the witness whose responses are recorded, normally in a verbatim transcript.

A letter rogatory, by contrast, is a formal request from one court to another to have the second court take evidence. The examining magistrate in the second country normally summarizes the testimony. At least one experienced international litigator has described letters rogatory as "useless" for obtaining evidence abroad because of the

58. For two principal articles on point *see*, Christopher Osakwe, *The Public Interest and the Role of the Prosecutor in Soviet Civil Litigation*, 18 Tex. Int'l L.J. 37 (1983); Benjamin Kaplan, Arthur T. von Mehren & Rudolf Schaefer, *Phases of German Civil Procedure*, 71 Harv. L. Rev. 1193 (1958).
59. John Merryman, *The Civil Law Tradition*, in *Comparative Law: Western European and Latin American Systems* (John H. Merryman & David S. Clark eds., 1978), 652–653.
60. *See* generally, the fine discussion on these issues in Charles Routh, *Representing the Foreign Client in Arbitration and Litigation*, in *International Trade for the Non-Specialist* (P. Vishny ed., 2d ed., 1997) and Born & Rutledge, *supra* n. 2, at 261–334. *See also*, Peter Metis, *International Judicial Assistance: Does 28 U.S.C. 1782 Contain an Implicit Discoverability Requirement?* 18 Fordham Int'l L.J. 332 (1994); Andreas F. Lowenfeld, *Some Reflections on Transnational Discovery*, 8 J. Comp. Bus. & Cap. Mkt. L. 419 (1986).

difficulties of working through another legal system and because of the time delays in the State Department's forwarding the letter rogatory to the appropriate foreign court.[61]

The United States is now a signatory to The Hague Convention on the Taking of Evidence Abroad in Civil and Commercial Matters (Evidence Convention).[62] The Evidence Convention permits a lawyer in one country to request permission through the host country's courts to take evidence on essentially the same terms as would be permitted in his home country without doing violence to the host country's legal system. As some commentary on the Evidence Convention indicates, the purpose of the Convention is to permit easier taking of discovery in ways that are "tolerable to the authorities of the State where [the discovery] is taken and at the same time utilizable in the forum where the action will be tried."[63]

One of the difficulties with the Convention is that Article 23 gives the country receiving the request a great deal of discretion in refusing to honor the request; and the Convention is still so underutilized that its precise boundaries remain unsettled.[64] It probably comes as no surprise to the reader that the U.S. was one of the moving forces behind the Evidence Convention. Few countries outside Western Europe have ratified it.

In 1987, the United States Supreme Court added to the legitimacy of The Hague Evidence Convention when it decided the case of *Societe Nationale Industrielle Aerospatiale v. United States District Court.*[65] In *Aerospatiale*, the Court addressed the question of whether parties must use the procedures set out in the Convention when seeking answers to interrogatories, the production of documents or admissions when the party from whom the information is sought is a French company over which a U.S. federal court has personal jurisdiction. The U.S. litigant argued that in this situation, it was free simply to use the discovery rules in the federal rules of civil procedure, rather than following the dictates of the Convention.

In a lengthy, troubled, and far from unanimous opinion, the Supreme Court refused to adopt a rule that would have required the litigants to first resort to the Convention. Rather, the Court enunciated a test requiring the lower court to consider and balance various interests such as particular facts of the case, interest of the sovereign governments, the likely effectiveness of the Evidence Convention devices and other matters in order to decide which mechanism (either the Convention or the U.S. federal discovery rules) are to be used. The dissenting justices spoke sharply to the

---

61. Harry J. O'Kane, *Obtaining Evidence Abroad,* 17 Vand. J. Transnat'l L. 69 (1984). Mr. O'Kane's article contains a parallel discussion of commissions and letters rogatory. *See also,* Hans W. Baade, *International Civil and Commercial Litigation: A Tentative Checklist,* Tex. Int'l L.J. 5 (1973). For a comment on some newer techniques of discovery *see,* Martin Davies, *Bypassing the Hague Evidence Convention: Private International Law Implications of the Use of Video and Audio Conferencing Technology in Transnational Litigation,* 55 Am. J. Comp. L. 205 (2007).
62. 23 U.S.T. 2555, T.I.A.S. 7444 (March 18, 1970).
63. Report of the United States Delegation to The Hague Conference, 8 Int'l Leg. Materials 785, 806 (1969).
64. von Mehren, *supra* n. 5, at 53–54.
65. 482 U.S. 522(1987). *See* William L. Wilks & Nancy E. Goldberg, *The Unresolved Problem in Taking Evidence Abroad: The Non-Rule of Aerospatiale,* 7 Penn State Int'l L. Rev. 65 (1988).

point that the Court's refusal to require a first resort to Convention discovery techniques effectively abrogated the United State's obligations under the treaty.

It is difficult to predict accurately where the *Aerospatiale* decision will lead. On the one hand, the Court acknowledged the fundamental legitimacy of the treaty. But on the other hand, the opinion seems almost to suggest that Convention discovery procedures are merely optional in many cases. Two highly regarded international lawyers in the United States have recently concluded:

> The majority opinion in Aerospatiale creates an undesirable and unworkable framework in which lower courts must make determinations about the appropriate use of the [Hague Evidence Convention]. Lower courts, inexperienced in transnational litigation and unfamiliar with [the Convention] have given little weight to concerns of international comity or to the legitimate interests of foreign states in their laws and sovereignty, and they have applied the [Supreme Court] majority's ad hoc test unevenly.[66]

It is hard to fault this conclusion. Fortunately for the international interests of the United States, some amendments to the federal rules of civil procedure intended to bring those rules closer to Convention practices are working their way through the system.[67]

§12.10 TRIAL PROCEDURE

Some of the sharpest differences between American practice and litigation elsewhere in the world are to be seen in the actual trial of a case. Indeed, the word inquiry, rather than trial, might be a better word to describe courtroom procedure in civil code countries. In those countries, as noted above, the process is a protracted series of hearings over time in which the presiding officer plays an important role in developing facts, questioning witnesses and generally shaping the outcome of the proceeding. The parties and their attorneys are in essence assistants to the magistrate for this purpose.

The trial process in the United States normally follows a prescribed format:

(a) Plaintiff's opening statement.
(b) Defendant's opening statement (which the defendant may delay until the close of plaintiff's case).
(c) Plaintiff's presentation of evidence (the so-called direct case).
(d) Defendant's presentation of evidence.
(e) Plaintiff's rebuttal evidence.
(f) Defendant's rebuttal evidence.
(g) Plaintiff's opening final argument.
(h) Defendant's final argument.
(i) Plaintiff's closing final argument.

66. Joseph P. Griffin & Mark N. Bravin, *Beyond Aerospatiale: A Commentary on Foreign Discovery Provisions*, 25 Int'l L. 331, 349 (1991).
67. The proposed amendments to Rules 26 and 28 would, in general, require parties to resort to the Convention's procedures if a party can take effective discovery under the treaty. *Id.*, at 343–345.

(j) Decision on the case by either judge or, if one has been empaneled, by the jury, who take the case after listening to instructions by the judge.
(k) Appeal, if any, to a higher court.

Because the trial process in civil code countries is organized much more around the activities of the presiding officer, the party's lawyers have far less maneuvering room. Nonetheless, the comparative legal scholar, Professor John Merryman, among others, warns that there may be too much emphasis put on the role of the judge in civil code litigation. As he describes it: "[In actual practice in civil code countries] the determination of what issues to raise, what evidence to introduce, and what arguments to make is left almost entirely to the parties. Judges in both traditions have some power to undertake inquiries on their own, but civil law judges seldom exercise this power."[68]

In Merryman's view, the sharpest distinguishing factor between the two legal systems is not the role of the judge. In fact it is the considerable emphasis on putting matters in writing in civil code countries as contrasted with the emphasis on oral presentations in common law countries. But even this comment may be a bit overbroad. In the United States the trial of complicated commercial matters relies heavily on documentary evidence, in contrast to oral testimony because so much modern business is conducted in writing, so even in U.S. trials the court must review a lot of paperwork. Nonetheless, writings in American trial practice are generally introduced and confirmed by live human witnesses. They do not normally stand on their own merits. This practice stands in sharp contrast to other legal systems in which the documents frequently speak for themselves.

This emphasis on what U.S. legal scholars frequently call orality comes into play in international commercial litigation even in areas involving the applicable law. As discussed in §12.4, a dispute involving an international commercial agreement may require the application of law different from the law of the jurisdiction in which the case is being tried. The problem of how to prove foreign law is common to all systems. In the United States, federal courts generally prove foreign law through the testimony of expert witnesses, rather than by relying on treatises or written documents. Treaties, by contrast, are frequently interpreted with the help of the U.S. State Department and, on occasion, by statements provided by other signatory countries.

U.S. trials are heavily dependent on rules of evidence, in large part because the system has devised certain principles for presenting matters to a jury composed of lay people. These rules are intended—at least in theory—to permit the jury to come to a rational, focused, unemotional decision. Rules of evidence are somewhat relaxed in American practice when the party's agree to a bench trial (trial before the judge sitting alone) and are virtually nonexistent in civil code countries.

Once a trial is completed, parties in the United States invariably have the opportunity to appeal to a higher court, although not all cases are appealed. Appeals, while even less common in other countries, are frequently permitted. This step has its own rules and procedures, protracts the dispute even further, and increases expenses.

68. Merryman, *supra* n. 59, at 655.

However, once both the trial and any appeals are concluded, the case is normally resolved once and for all. Rarely can a party reopen a judgment or bring another action challenging the first action.

§12.11 ENFORCEMENT OF JUDGMENTS AT HOME AND ABROAD

Once a final judgment has been rendered, the losing party must comply with the dictates of the court. Many parties comply voluntarily by paying damages or by obeying other orders of the court. When a losing party fails to comply, it is usually necessary to go back into either the same court or another court for an order compelling the losing party to abide by the judgment. This final step involves the issue of enforcement of the judgment. Enforcement is never easy even within a court's jurisdiction. It becomes even more difficult when a court judgment issued in one jurisdiction must be taken into another jurisdiction for enforcement. This issue—when and under what circumstances a court's judgment will be enforced elsewhere—is the last matter encountered in litigation.

In the United States, an important provision in the U.S. Constitution requires any state to fully abide by a final court judgment in any other state. Through the full faith and credit clause in the Constitution, each state is required to treat sister state judgments just as if they had been rendered in the state's own courts. The framers of the Constitution realized that such a provision was vitally necessary to break down the economic barriers which then existed among the former colonies. Now, in the United States, this point is taken for granted; and while lawyers can always argue about what constitutes a final judgment, the basic proposition—that states must enforce each other's judgments—is no longer subject to question.

The issue is not so clearly resolved on the international level. To put this discussion in perspective, consider once again the sale of those special shoes manufactured in Singapore and sold to the U.S. buyer. Let us assume that B, the buyer, has obtained a judgment in a Singapore court against A for USD 500,000 damages. Presumably, Singapore will enforce the judgments of its courts against a resident of Singapore, so in this case, enforcement should be no problem. But what might happen if, under a choice of forum clause, a U.S. court has rendered the same judgment—for USD 500,000 damages—but the Singapore manufacturer leaves the U.S. without paying the bill? In this case, B's lawyers will probably search for countries in which A has property and seek to enforce the U.S. judgment in those places. The question then becomes: do those countries' courts have to abide by the decision of the U.S. court?

To begin with, we are actually dealing here with two separate concepts: enforcement and recognition. A court enforces a foreign judgment when it orders the losing party to comply with the original judgments terms with no further proceedings. A court gives recognition to a foreign judgment when it gives only partial effect to the judgment, permitting the parties to relitigate certain issues in the case that had already been litigated abroad.

Tragically, there is no comprehensive international convention governing either recognition or enforcement of judicial decisions, although as will be seen in Chapters

8 and 9 there is such a convention for foreign arbitral awards. The existence of the arbitral award convention is one of the primary reasons why arbitration is the dispute resolution mechanism of choice in international commercial transactions. Since there is no worldwide treaty, courts sometimes enforce decrees and sometimes refuse enforcement based on much looser, more ambiguous doctrines.

To deal with these problems, most courts invoke the doctrine of comity when they are confronted with a foreign judgment. While comity is a somewhat elusive concept in actual practice, it is fairly easily stated: comity is the natural respect that one court should have for the judgments of another court irrespective of where those courts are located. A famous U.S. Supreme Court decision, *Hilton v. Guyot*,[69] expressed the doctrine in the following manner when the Court was asked to give effect to a French judgment:

> [The rule of comity—and thus recognition and enforcement—will be applied] where there has been an opportunity for a full and fair trial abroad before a court of competent jurisdiction, conducting the trial upon regular proceedings, after due citation or voluntary appearance of the defendant, and under a system of jurisprudence likely to secure an impartial administration of justice between the citizens of its own country and those of other countries, and there is nothing to show either prejudice...or fraud.

The Court examined all these criteria and determined that there was nothing wrong with the French judgment. However, it then moved to another level of analysis—whether the French courts would similarly enforce the judgments of a U.S. court—and concluded that there was no real reciprocity between the courts of the two countries. It therefore refused to give conclusive effect to the French decree.

The *Hilton* decision was not especially pleasing to many people in the United States. Many courts have chosen to disregard it as inappropriate. While the U.S. cases are sometimes difficult to harmonize, it appears that courts now consider four questions in deciding how to treat a foreign judgment: (1) did the foreign court have jurisdiction over both the subject matter and the parties; (2) was the defendant given proper notice; (3) was there any evidence of fraud or trickery in the earlier case; (4) will enforcement or recognition of the decision somehow violate U.S. public policy?[70]

Reciprocity, while discussed by some courts, appears not to be the sole determinant. In one case, a wealthy U.S. oil man, Nelson Bunker Hunt, became embroiled in a controversy with British Petroleum (BP) over oil assets that had been nationalized by Libya. BP brought suit in the English High Court of Justice claiming that the company had provided a number of oil field services for Hunt prior to expropriation from which he benefited and for which he should compensate the company. The court awarded BP

69. 159 U.S. 113 (1895).
70. On this topic *see*, e.g., Ronald A. Brand, *Federal Judicial Center International Litigation Guide: Recognition and Enforcement of Foreign Judgments*, 74 U. Pitt L. Rev. 491 (2013); Geoffrey C. Hazard & Michele Taruffo, *Transnational Rules of Civil Procedure*, 30 Cornell Int'l L.J. 493 (1997); Matthew Adler, *If We Build It, Will They Come?—The Need for a Multilateral Convention on the Recognition and Enforcement of Civil Monetary Judgments*, 26 L. & Pol'y Int'l Bus. 79 (1994); Arthur T. von Mehren, *Recognition and Enforcement of Foreign Judgments*, 167 Recueil des Cours 13 (1980).

roughly USD 20 million, but when BP came to the United States seeking the money, Hunt refused to pay and instead went to court in Texas arguing that U.S. courts should neither recognize nor enforce the British judgment.[71]

The U.S. court took a close look at the judgment itself, at the *Hilton* case and a number of other factors and concluded:

> There is little justification for judicial imposition of a reciprocity requirement [because, among other things, it penalizes individuals who have obtained foreign judgments in good faith].... [E]ven if reciprocity can be used to bring foreign pressure on foreign countries to recognize American judgments, such [actions] would probably be more effective and appropriate as part of executive or legislative action ...[72]

The U.S. court found Hunt's claim that the British courts did not afford him an adequate hearing by pointing out: "[T]he rendering forum's system of jurisprudence has been a model for other countries in the free world, and whose judges are of unquestioned integrity...."[73]

This seems to be a remarkably healthy decision in the highest traditions of comity. It also signals the strong movement among U.S. courts toward more generous recognition and enforcement of foreign court judgments. Within the United States, the various state legislatures have moved in the same direction. Over twelve states have enacted the Uniform Foreign Money-Judgments Recognition Act. This act provides generally that foreign money judgments are to be recognized and enforced on the same terms as a "sister state." Grounds for refusing recognition include a lack of personal or subject-matter jurisdiction, inadequate notice to the defendant, fraud, a judgment that is contrary to U.S. public policy, or the fact that the foreign court "was a seriously inconvenient forum for the trial of the action."[74] It appears from the legislative history of the uniform act that these exceptions are to be construed narrowly. In other words, it is expected that recognition and enforcement will be enhanced by the statute.

But is this same inclination toward greater enforcement and recognition typical of other countries? On a regional basis the most serious attempts to provide uniform treatment for another nation's court judgments has emerged from the work of the EC. The EC took serious steps to promote recognition and enforcement among its member nations when it devised the Convention on Jurisdiction and the Enforcement of Judgments in Civil and Commercial Matters (the Brussels Convention).[75] The Brussels Convention forbids each country from adopting special procedures for recognizing and enforcing judgments from other member countries and from making any substantive revisions (so-called revision Au fond) in those judgments. There are four exclusive grounds on which a court may refuse enforcement:

71. *Hunt v. BP Exploration Co. (Libya) Ltd.*, 492 F. Supp. 885 (N.D. Tex.1980).
72. *Id.*, at 893.
73. *Id.*, at 890.
74. 13 Uniform Laws Anno. 417.
75. *See*, e.g., Peter Herzog, *The Common Market Convention—An Interim Update,* 17 Va. J. Int'l L. 417 (1977).

(1) that the judgment violates the public policy of the enforcing country;
(2) that there was lack of adequate notice of the litigation to the defendant, preventing the defendant from mounting an adequate defense;
(3) that the enforcing country has adjudicated the matter prior to the judgment that it is being asked to enforce; or
(4) in limited instances, that the courts in the originating country failed to properly apply conflict of law principles.

Within Western Europe there was another major development in September 1988, when the Lugano Convention on Jurisdiction and the Enforcement of Judgments in Civil and Commercial Matters opened for signature. As of mid-1991 ten countries within the EC (Belgium, Denmark, France, Germany, Greece, Italy, Luxembourg, the Netherlands, Portugal, and the United Kingdom) and five other European countries (Finland, Iceland, Norway, Sweden, and Switzerland) had signed the convention, but at that time ratification had occurred in only two countries, France and the Netherlands.

Stated briefly, the Lugano Convention attempts to clarify and make simple the enforcement of judgments within signatory states in much the same fashion as the Brussels Convention accomplishes this within the EU. The Lugano Convention applies mainly to contractual matters and extends to all persons (both natural persons and corporations) domiciled in a signatory state who enters into a contract with a person domiciled in another signatory state. With regard to enforcement of judgments, the convention specifies that court judgments rendered in one signatory state are to be enforced in another signatory state without any special procedure or requirements.[76]

For non-EU judgments, most jurisdictions have mixed records on enforcement and recognition. For example, in France, a party seeking recognition and enforcement must apply for a writ of exequatur; and under the doctrine of revision, the French courts take the position that they may question virtually anything in the underlying judgment. Many countries place great weight on the reciprocity factor.[77] In other words, they refuse to enforce judgments if the country of origin does not give their judgments equal treatment. Reciprocity has become a barrier rather than an enhancement to enforcement.

What this means for our shoe purchaser, B, is not entirely clear. Singapore's legal system springs from the British common law; and courts within the Anglo-American system may well be predisposed to honor a judgment from another country within that same system. We might evaluate the prospects by simply applying the American criteria: the U.S. court had both subject-matter and personal jurisdiction. A, the seller, was properly served with process and thus had adequate notice of the lawsuit. There was no fraud, and it would be difficult to argue that it is contrary to Singapore's public policy to enforce a judgment for breach of contract emanating from a U.S. court. Of

76. Gautier & Stormann, *Lugano Convention on Jurisdiction and on the Enforcement of Judgments*, 19 Int'l Bus. Law. 410 (September 1991).
77. *See*, e.g., Henry J. Steiner & Detlev F. Vagts, *Transnational Legal Problems* (3d ed., 1986).

course, the result might be different if the U.S. court for some reason awarded punitive damages, contrary to Singapore law, or, if the underlying contract were for some transaction prohibited in Singapore.

Even if Singapore insists on some kind of reciprocity, the Hunt case stands for the proposition that U.S. courts would likely recognize and enforce a similar judgment emanating from the Singapore courts. Thus, B might well prevail in a recognition and enforcement action in Singapore. Whether she would prevail in other countries where A may have property is far more problematic.

§12.12 CONCLUSION

There are both similarities and differences among the world's litigation systems. On close examination, it is difficult to argue that one system is inherently better than another in ascertaining truth and providing satisfactory resolutions of disputes. Still, the legal process in some countries is flawed not so much by such things as rules of procedure and evidence (what some law professors refer to as law on the books) but rather by the ineptness and chauvinism of the court personnel, outright chicanery, or even by the imposition of inappropriate constraints through the country's political system (so-called law in action). Nationals from one country are frequently terrified of the courts of another country, partly because of the strangeness of the surroundings and partly because the courts may not be able to expunge bias against foreigners from the system.

Litigation is not a happy event in the best of circumstances. When one fears that a particular country's courts might produce an arbitrary outcome, litigation can be totally off-putting. One of the reasons for the establishment of our current system of international commercial arbitration is the preference, particularly among business executives, for a confidential dispute resolution mechanism that stands apart from the other party's legal system and domestic courts. For some countries, those fears are misplaced; for others they are quite well founded. Sometimes it is very difficult to determine which country fits into which category.

CHAPTER 13
Online Dispute Resolution

§13.1 INTRODUCTION

As we move toward the third decade of the twenty-first century there are some exciting new developments in the area of *alternative dispute resolution* (ADR). This phenomenon, usually referred to as *online dispute resolution* (ODR) appears to have obtained substantial traction over the past ten years. Indeed, it is showing all the signs of becoming one of the most important developments in the area of international commercial dispute resolution since the emergence of the major international arbitration institutions and the promulgation of the New York Convention on the Recognition and Enforcement of Foreign Arbitral Awards. ODR has been triggered in large part by all the technological and cultural developments fostered by improved computer technology and, perhaps most importantly, by the development of the Internet as a means of international communication. While we saw the earliest rudimentary attempts at ODR over ten years ago, the concept and its related processes are beginning to mature.[1]

1. The literature in the area is growing significantly. *See*, e.g., Ethan Katsh & Orna Rabinovich-Einy, *Digital Justice: Technology & the Internet of Disputes* (2017); The Hague Institute for the Internationalization of Law, ODR and the Courts: The Promise of 100% Access to Justice (2016); Mohamed S. Abdel Wahab, Ethan Katsh & Daniel Rainey, *Online Dispute Resolution: Theory and Practice: A Treatise on Technology and Dispute Resolution* (2012); Marta Poblet, *Mobile Technologies for Conflict Management: Online Dispute Resolution, Governance, Participation* (2011); Pablo Cortes, *Online Dispute Resolution for Consumers in the European Union* (2010); Faye Fangfel Wang, *Online Dispute Resolution: Technology, Management and Legal Practice from An International Perspective* (2008); Yun Zhao, *Dispute Resolution in Electronic Commerce* (2005); Gabrielle Kaufmann-Kohler, *Conflict Resolution in the Age of the Internet: Online Dispute Resolution* (2004); Colin Rule, *Online Dispute Resolution for Business* (2002); Ethan Katsh & Janet Rifkin, *Online Dispute Resolution: Resolving Conflicts in Cyberspace* (2001). For a comprehensive analysis of most of the pertinent legal issues, *see* Orna Rabinovich-Elny & Ethan Katsh, *Digital Justice: Reshaping Boundaries in an Online Dispute Resolution Environment*, 1 Int'l J. Online Disp. Res. 5 (2014). One of the early definitive articles by one of the pioneers of ODR is M. Ethan Katsh, *Dispute Resolution in Cyberspace*, 28 Conn. L. Rev. 953 (1996) (part of a symposium on ODR). A

There are a number of different varieties of ODR that will be of interest to the readers of this book. Because so much of this is new, it is generally helpful to set out some history and to establish some concepts and categories for further analysis. There are several different streams of activity that now fall within the broad definition of ODR. Among the first developments in ODR were initiatives prompted by the dramatic growth in electronic commerce that involved and affected consumers. Some of the unique elements of electronic commerce created a vital need for dispute resolution mechanisms that accommodated this new form of business arrangement. Just for illustration, examine the following case history and description of the dispute resolution system developed by the online auction company, eBay.

Consider the example of two consumers, one in Paris and the second in New York. The Parisian has sold a vase valued at USD 575 to the New Yorker via the eBay website. The buyer paid the full amount for the vase prior to receipt of the vase. On receipt of the vase by the buyer, the vase turns out to have a large crack that reduces its value to, say, USD 50. The crack was not disclosed by the seller. The buyer would not have paid the full price if she had known about it. In some circumstances, we might be able to criticize the buyer for sending payment prior to receipt of the good, but most sellers will not ship, in these circumstances, if payment is not in hand. At this point in time, it may not be clear who is responsible for the damage to the vase. The vase might have been shipped with the crack or the damage may have occurred during shipment. If the transportation company is the entity responsible for the crack, the dispute will, of course, be a relatively conventional problem of damage during carriage. But for our purposes, let us assume that the vase was shipped with a crack in it. The seller was simply not candid about the actual condition of the vase.

---

more recent article by Professor Katsh summing up more than 10 years' experience with ODR is Ethan Katsh, *Online Dispute Resolution: Some Implications for the Emergence of Law in Cyberspace,* 10 Lex Electronica No. 3 (Winter 2006), available at www.lex-electronica.org/articles. The University of Toledo School of Law has published a lengthy symposium on ODR: Symposium, *Enhancing Worldwide Understanding Through Online Dispute Resolution: Walking Along in the Mission,* 38 U. Tol. L. Rev. 1 (2006). Around 2001, the American Bar Association commissioned a task force on electronic commerce and dispute resolution. The final report of the task force is set out in: *Addressing Disputes in Electronic Commerce: Final Recommendations and Report,* 58 Bus. Law. 415 (2002). An article that is regarded by some as seminal but not exclusively devoted to ODR is David R. Johnson & David Post, *Law and Borders—The Rise of Law in Cyberspace,* 48 Stan. L. Rev. 1367 (1996). For another good overview of many e-commerce issues including dispute resolution *see,* Bruce L. Benson, *The Spontaneous Evolution of Cyber Law: Norms, Property Rights, Contracting, Dispute Resolution and Enforcement Without the State,* 1 J. L. Econ. & Pol'y 269 (2005). One innovative United States government agency doing fascinating work in ODR, including ODR for arbitrations, is the somewhat obscure National Mediation Board, an agency that helps to resolve labor-management disputes in the United States. The Board was formerly known as the Federal Mediation and Conciliation Service. The Board has worked closely with Professor Katsh and others in developing ODR techniques and concepts. The Board's website is www.nmb.gov. A very good website that serves essentially as a clearinghouse for ODR information is the National Center for Technology and Dispute Resolution, www.odr.info. The European Union and the Organization of Economic Cooperation and Development (OECD) have begun to deal with ODR: *see,* e.g., European Union, Statement of the European Union and the United States on Building Consumer Confidence in E-Commerce and the Role of Alternative Dispute Resolution, www.euruniion.org/partner/summit; the OECD has developed guidelines: OECD, Guidelines for Consumer Protection in the Context of Commerce, www.oecd.org.document.

In this posture, it is virtually inconceivable that the buyer would try to litigate this dispute in a national court or trigger traditional international arbitration. Concepts of personal jurisdiction would likely require the buyer to sue in a French court. The amount in controversy could not possibly support traditional arbitration.

Even so, it is clear that the buyer has been harmed and, if word gets out that there are lots of similar disputes connected with eBay transactions, eBay will lose a great deal of credibility which in turn will diminish its ability to conduct an online business. When eBay first started, it took the position that it was never a party to any transaction but merely served as a kind of conduit of information between potential buyers and sellers. But early on the company realized that this type of disclaimer would not work for long. Totally disclaiming any responsibility for transactions that went wrong would adversely affect the company's reputation, and, in truth, eBay's role in the auction transactions was considerably greater than that of a mere matching service. As a result, eBay worked with electronic payment systems such as PayPal that have developed their own mechanisms for resolving payment disputes.

But eBay needed to have some internal dispute resolution mechanisms as well. So, among other things, eBay set up the device now known as the "feedback profile" for parties that do business on eBay. This is information on individuals that might be called a "trustworthiness" index. The information is immediately available to participants.[2] The eBay also promotes a dialogue between seller and buyer if something is not right and will provide the buyer with some of the seller's contact information if the seller does not respond to the buyer's e-mails. But even that was not enough to satisfy eBay's customers. To keep the customers happy eBay set up a more formal dispute resolution mechanism, referred to as its *dispute process* and administered by the eBay security and resolution center. In this instance, the buyer must *open* a dispute by contacting eBay with an assertion that he/she either has not received the purchased item or that item is "significantly not as described." The filing of the dispute must take place between ten and sixty days after the purchase date. The eBay then contacts the seller and asks the seller to respond to the buyer's assertions within ten days. The seller and buyer then communicate with each other, hopefully resolving the dispute between themselves. However, if this does not work, the dispute moves into a more formal, more rigorous process that eBay calls its "Trust and Safety Team."

The trust and safety team further investigate the dispute and, if the seller is found to have behaved inappropriately may levy various sanctions against the seller that include: account suspension, cancellation of the seller's listings and forfeiture of any fees, specific limits on account privileges, or most drastically, a referral to an appropriate law enforcement entity. There are similar protections for sellers who are harmed by the activities of buyers.

There are several lessons to be learned here. First, a major e-commerce company such as eBay realized that it had to establish some process for resolving disputes and did so on its own by developing internal mechanisms rather than seeking legislation or regulation from some government entity. Second, as nearly as this author can

2. Most of this information is taken from the eBay website: www.ebay.com.

determine, these mechanisms are working in a satisfactory manner for the overwhelming number of eBay participants. Proof of that is simply that eBay continues as a robust, profitable e-commerce company. Third, the dispute resolution is low key and easily understood and accessible to all participants. In these instances, there seems to be no need for lengthy, turgid systems of "rules" that tie up the system in needless complexity. Fourth, the eBay system is quick. Disputes are supposed to be resolved within ninety days. Finally, virtually all of the process is accomplished online. But more recently eBay saw fit to take the process at least one step further and established a relationship with a separate ODR entity, Square Trade, for disputes that cannot be resolved internally. Square Trade is discussed more elaborately in §13.3.

The eBay experience is instructive but it is mainly suited for small amount transactions involving individuals.[3] What we will explore in this chapter is whether there are possibilities for ODR in larger-scale commercial disputes. The author's preliminary answer is "yes" as will be seen in the following discussion.

§13.2 ODR: CATEGORIES AND A SUGGESTED DEFINITION

We need to begin with some basic categories of analysis and at least an attempt at a definition for ODR. The best way to start is to recognize the two primary streams of activity in ODR: (1) resolution of disputes that occur solely in the context of online (e-commerce) transactions; and (2) resolution of disputes online when the underlying transaction has taken place in a traditional setting. ODR can be analyzed by looking at the identity of the parties as we frequently do in discussing e-commerce—for example, consumer-to-consumer (C2C), business-to-consumer (B2C), business-to-business (B2B), government-to-citizen (G2C).

ODR may also be sorted and categorized by reference to the subject matter of the dispute—for example, domestic relations disputes, student-faculty/administration disputes, employment and personnel disputes, etc. Another component of our analysis involves the type of dispute resolution mechanism utilized through ODR techniques, such as negotiation, mediation, or arbitration. But why should we limit ODR solely to ADR vehicles? There may be plenty of uses for ODR techniques in litigation even though everyone must concede that the municipal law of various countries could prohibit or severely limit ODR in certain litigation settings. For example, in the United States the Constitution requires that a criminal defendant be permitted to "confront" witnesses against the defendant. This has generally been interpreted as a true

3. For an excellent article that concentrates on the B2C component of ODR that also includes a solid discussion on the European Union's perspectives on ODR and B2C *see*, Lucille M. Ponte, *Boosting Consumer Confidence in E-Business: Recommendations for Establishing Fair and Effective Dispute Resolution Programs for B2C Online Transactions*, 12 Alb. L.J. Sci. & Tech. 441 (2002). For another good article on B2C initiatives that concentrates on international transactions *see*, Ivonnely Colon-Fung, *Protecting the New Face of Entrepreneurship: Online Appropriate Dispute Resolution and International Consumer-to-Consumer Online Transactions*, 12 Fordham J. Corp. & Fin. L. 233 (2007). For a very provocative article that examines many of the shortcomings and weaknesses of ODR, *see* Robert J. Condlin, *Online Dispute Resolution: Stinky, Repugnant, or Drab*, 18 Cardozo J. Conflict Res. 717 (2017).

face-to-face confrontation. At the far end of the ODR spectrum, there are some ODR experiments, used mainly in the real estate industry in disputes between buyers and sellers, that have effectively automated the dispute resolution: the parties put information on transaction into the computer and the computer makes a decision. This would provide a decision untouched by human hands.

But given the focus of this book, this chapter will largely confine itself to ODR in the context of relatively substantial international commercial transactions. At least in the short run, what we will likely see is the use of ODR techniques and systems to augment and enhance the traditional dispute resolution devices rather than completely replacing them.

Because ODR is a relatively new phenomenon, there is no single commonly accepted definition for ODR. It has been suggested that any mediation arbitration or other form of dispute resolution that takes place outside of court and at least partially online constitutes ODR.[4] But this seems far too broad. That could include a traditional arbitration with a standard face-to-face hearing under conventional rules of arbitration where the only thing the parties do is occasionally communicate via e-mail.

Another possible definition is any form of ADR that includes the use of the Internet or the use of web-based technological tools such as videoconferencing and webcasting. This is essentially a technology-driven definition. We could define ODR as pertaining solely to disputes that arise out of e-commerce transactions but doing so seems excessively narrow because it ignores all the contributions that ODR techniques could make to traditional dispute resolution. So as a working definition, this author suggests the following: ODR is the application of Internet techniques, equipment, and communications systems to the resolution of disputes when the use of the Internet comprises a substantial portion of the dispute resolution.

§13.3 THE POSSIBLE CONTRIBUTIONS OF ODR TO COMMERCIAL DISPUTE RESOLUTION

As we begin this discussion, it is important to recall the characteristics of a typical business dispute. A business dispute almost always develops as follows:

(1) Two or more parties enter into some kind of business agreement (sale of goods, agency or distribution, licensing, etc.).
(2) At some point, something occurs that causes one or more of the parties to stop performing as initially agreed. It might be a total cessation of a party's obligations; it might be a partial cessation; it might be a change in the manner of performance that was not expressed in the original agreement.
(3) The other party or parties discern and object to the failure to perform.
(4) At this point, the parties could simply walk away from the transaction. Abandonment of the underlying business transaction occurs more often than

4. Jason Krause, *Settling It on the Web,* ABA J. 21 (October 2007).

most people realize. There are plenty of times when the possible rewards growing out of dispute resolution simply do not exceed the costs associated with pursuing the dispute.

(5) If the injured party decides to pursue the dispute further, he/she has the options outlined earlier in this book, including renegotiation, mediation, arbitration, or litigation. Because, as noted above, litigation is very traditional and rules bound, and in some countries such as the United States, ties to the country's constitutional system, the remainder of this discussion will concentrate on renegotiation, mediation and arbitration.

§13.3.1 Renegotiation and ODR

Renegotiation mainly involves the disputing parties communicating with each other with regard to the elements of the dispute. If one or the other chooses not to participate in some form of communication, the affected party will likely have to resort to some other form of dispute resolution. Renegotiation is often handle with a few telephone calls. In which case, the concepts underlying ODR do not come into play. In this instance, ODR might be as simple as the exchange of e-mails with the possibility of other information in the form of documents attached to the e-mail. If the parties have the necessary equipment (none of which is terribly expensive these days) and decide that something more than e-mails are necessary, they might set up a web conferencing arrangement by which the participants can speak to each other, examine documents on their computer screen with the use of scanners and other document recognition devices and see each other by using cameras (so-called webcams) attached to their computer.

Readers who are new to international business and business dispute resolution should never discount the benefits of actually seeing and hearing the people on the other side. There is something about human behavior and human psychology that makes this type of communication much more effective than a mere e-mail. Frequently, in renegotiation, just being back in the presence of this person who was once a friend and who is not yet an adversary can go a long ways toward a resolution of the problem. A fuzzy picture on a computer screen is still warmer than an e-mail. There are times when more than just a webcam is needed. A number of companies, such as Webex, provide integrated webconferencing that includes not only picture transmission but also white boards, sharing of computer data, and document transmission at a relatively low cost with the added attraction that the communications are secure, unlike many e-mail systems.[5] There is a technology referred to as digital white board that permits online participants to share sketches and other hand written diagrams in the same way that people sitting around a conference table might jump up to make notes on a chalkboard or easel.

If the parties are widely separated—something quite common in international business—these same systems permit the storing of data and presentations so that the parties can view the documents and hear the other participants even when a "real

5. *See*, e.g., www.webex.com.

time" conference would not make sense because of the different time zones involved. In truth, there is very little these days that might have taken place during a face-to-face conference that cannot take place online.

There are a number of online services that engage in what is now called "assisted negotiation." These are services that provide the communication link between the parties, set up a framework for the negotiation and, if negotiation fails, provide a smooth segue into mediation or some other vehicle.[6] There is another online process referred to as "automated negotiation" that resolve a dispute by a type of blind-bidding on the part of the disputing parties. In this process, a party with a claim sends relevant information to the supervising online company which then contacts the other party to ask if the other party is willing to submit to the process. If the other side is willing, the parties make offers of settlement in particular amounts but these offers are never communicated to the other side. Based on an algorithm built into the software—usually when the competing offers are within 5%–30% of each other, the case is deemed resolved and the parties split the difference between the two offers. There has been some success with these processes in, for example, insurance claims. The ODR institution, Cybersettle, uses the technique in insurance disputes and reports a large success and satisfaction rate.[7] The online company, Square Trade, has partnered with eBay and other companies to establish a dispute resolution mechanism that begins with negotiation and then uses mediation if negotiation fails.[8]

§13.3.2 Mediation and ODR

One would think that mediation is particularly well suited for the ODR world.[9] Recall that mediation is essentially negotiation between the disputing parties with the assistance of a neutral, third-party mediator. Both Cybersettle and Square Trade utilize the services of independent mediators for any dispute that does not get resolved in the initial negotiation stage. Square Trade has its own stable of mediators who come into the process after a certain amount of training and investigation of credentials.[10]

§13.3.3 Arbitration and ODR

This is probably the area of most interest to the readers of this book since arbitration is so often the dispute resolution mechanism of choice for international commercial

6. *See*, e.g., www.ecodir.org for a lengthier description of the ECODIR process.
7. *See*, e.g., www.cybersettle.com for a more detailed explanation of the Cybersettle methodology.
8. *See*, the Square Trade website: www.squaretrade.com. The site is for B2C disputes and also sells product warranties.
9. *See*, e.g., David Allen Larson, *Artificial Intelligence: Robots, Avatars, and the Demise of the Human Mediator*, 25 Ohio St. J. on Disp. Res. 105 (2010); Joseph W. Goodman, *The Pros and Cons of Online Dispute Resolution: An Assessment of Cyber-Mediation Websites*, 2003 Duke L. & Tech. Rev. 4 (2003). Many of the ODR mediation websites did not survive the dot.com debacle.
10. *Id.*

agreements. It is also the mechanism with issues and protocols that interfere with an ODR approach. To begin with, arbitration is heavily rules-oriented which rules contemplate a traditional face-to-face adversarial hearing. In arbitration, unlike mediation, the arbitrator is required to decide the case and arbitrators who are schooled only in the traditional methodologies are clearly comfortable only with a face-to-face hearing. So there has been a fair amount of institutional resistance to ODR. In addition, there is some commentary to the effect that an ODR arbitration cannot be enforced under the New York Convention on the Recognition and Enforcement of Foreign Arbitral Awards. Article II(1) of the New York Convention requires the arbitration agreement to be "in writing," and some question has been raised as to whether an electronic agreement containing an arbitration clause is truly "in writing."[11] At this point in time, this would seem to be an issue not worth contemplating. First, it would appear that what the New York Convention was really getting at was a prohibition on purely oral arbitration agreements. That is not what we are worried about in e-commerce. Even an electronic contract is an agreement expressed in written words and is not a purely oral agreement. Second, the New York Convention, entering into force in 1958 long before the advent of e-commerce, must be informed by all the modern legal provisions such as the United Nations Commission on International Trade Law (UNCITRAL) Model Law on E-Commerce which provides expressly that a contract concluded in electronic form is just as valid as a contract put to paper.

There are a number of websites that claim to be online arbitration centers. Some of them have come and gone in just a few years and, different from negotiation or mediation websites, an online arbitration website must have substantial credibility to survive.[12] One such entity, the Virtual Magistrate, once heavily touted in the literature appears to be defunct.[13]

Perhaps the single, truly successful online arbitration program has been the Uniform Domain Name Dispute Resolution Policy (UDRP) established by the Internet Corporation for Assigned Names and Numbers (ICANN) to deal with disputes over Internet domain names.[14] At the outset, readers should understand that the UDRP may not be a true arbitration system because its decisions are not binding and enforceable in court. Also, there is some argument that the UDRP is not a true ODR system since the process now used by the World Intellectual Property Organization (WIPO) is not completely online. Whatever label we might place on this process, it seems to have had some success. WIPO reports having disposed of more than 25,000 domain name

11. *See*, e.g., Hong-Lin Yu & Motassem Nasir, *Can Online Arbitration Exist Within the Traditional Arbitration Framework?*, 20 J. Int'l Arb. 455 (2003). *See* generally, Giuditta Cordero Moss, *Form of Arbitration Agreements: Current Developments Within UNCITRAL and the Writing Requirement of the New York Convention*, 18 ICC Int'l Court of Arb. Bull. 51 (2007).
12. *See*, e.g., an article discussion online arbitration and an arbitration website: Robert B. Lubic, *Reducing Costs and Inconveniences in International Commercial Arbitration and Other Forms of Alternative Resolution Through Online Dispute Resolution*, 15 Am. Rev. Int'l Arb. 507 (2004).
13. *See*, e.g., Joseph Matthews & Karen Stewart, *Online Arbitration of Cross-Border, Business to Consumer Disputes*, 56 U. Miami L. Rev. 1111 (2002). Attempts to connect with the website, vmag.org. as of September 2008 proved fruitless.
14. All the details on the UDRP may be found on the ICANN website: www.icann.org/udrp.

disputes over the past several years. There may be additional use of Internet processes and techniques by WIPO in the near future.[15]

The traditional arbitration institutions appear to be gingerly dipping their toes into the ODR waters. The International Chamber of Commerce (ICC) has instituted its NetCase system. Based on the description provided by the ICC, the process has some built-in limitations. To begin with, the process may be used only if all the parties to the arbitration agree to its use and only so long as they all sign a "Statement of Acceptance of the Conditions of Access and Use of NetCase."[16] As described by the ICC and as viewed by most experienced arbitrators, NetCase, at this moment, is mainly an electronic document storage system. The ICC describes NetCase as "a service allowing arbitrations to be conducted in a secure online environment" but there appears to be no evidence that any arbitration has been handled exclusively through the NetCase system. Rather, NetCase permits the electronic exchange of documents between the parties and access to those documents through a secure website hosted by the ICC on a 24/7 basis. This information base also includes information on the arbitrators, the calendar for the proceeding and certain information relating to the financial aspects of the arbitration. The site can be used by the parties "to exchange views." But it does not appear that the arbitration hearing may take place online or that the arbitrators will work exclusively through online techniques. NetCase represents only a single small ICC toe in the water.

The American Arbitration Association (AAA) has a system similar to the ICC called the "AAA WebFile." WebFile is a document storage and retrieval system that permits parties electronically to: (1) file a new case; (2) managed a previously filed case; (3) access rules and procedures; (4) transfer documents; (5) select neutrals; and (6) use a special message board.[17] Both organizations appear to be taking only small steps toward full-blown ODR.

§13.4 THE FUTURE OF ODR

The concept of ODR holds out great promise for the future, not just in B2C or C2C disputes but also for large-scale international commercial agreements. While not necessarily perfect system of dispute resolution (there is no such thing), ODR offers cost savings, savings in time for all participants, savings in human energy, and many other things. Particularly for international agreements, it permits the participants to function while still at a long distance from each other. Some of the early qualms about ODR, such as concerns about transparency or due process, seem not to be a major problem at this point in time. In truth, one can do virtually everything by way of ODR techniques, including "live hearings" that are done in the more traditional, face-to-face

15. Virtually all the relevant information on the UDRP may also be found on the WIPO website: www.wipo.int. For an extensive discussion of domain names, intellectual property and ODR *see*, Haitham A. Haloush, *Internet Infrastructure and Online Alternative Dispute Resolution*, 25 J. Marshall J. Computer & Info. L. 217 (2008).
16. The information on NetCase may be found on the ICC's website: www.iccwbo.org.
17. The AAA's WebFile system is described on the AAA's website: https://apps.org/webfile.

settings. In the recent past, the traditional arbitration institutions appeared to be pricing themselves out of existence while applying outmoded and cumbersome rules of procedure. There is no question that the more traditionally minded dispute resolution specialists still have not fully accepted ODR, but this may be a situation that is driven by the consumers of ODR services, rather than the dispute resolution specialists.

CHAPTER 14
Future Trends in International Commercial Agreements and International Commercial Dispute Resolution

§14.1 INTRODUCTION

The reader should not be shocked to find that the one chapter in this book that attempts to predict matters is also one of the shortest. Most predictions seem useful only to show how wrong they were. A few readers may recall that at the turn of the twentieth century a U.S. Commissioner of Patents resigned from office because he believed that there was nothing more the human mind could possibly invent.

This chapter is a prediction of trends, not a statement of future certainties. Nonetheless, it seems to be a healthy exercise if only to try to suggest to readers of this book that a number of trends may have a significant impact on how they, and their clients, function as international lawyers and business people over the next several years.

§14.2 TRENDS IN INTERNATIONAL COMMERCIAL AGREEMENTS

As we move through the second decade of the twenty-first century the world continues to deal with serious financial problems. While some commentators continue to blame the financial sector meltdown in the United States in 2008–2010, it is clear that many problems persist wholly apart from the difficulty in the United States. The forces of free trade and the forces of protectionism remain locked in global battle.[1] While the United

1. The author of this book finds it necessary to get completely away from legal literature when he is searching for sound, well-though-out prognostications. In recent years, he has profitably consulted the following: Michael Pettis, the *Great Rebalancing: Trade, Conflict, and the Perilous Road Ahead for the World Economy*; J. Bradford Jensen, *Global Trade in Services: Fear, Facts, and*

States has frequently set the tone of this debate using its leverage as the world's largest trading nation, the U.S. no longer exercises the plenary economic power that it exercised after World War Two. Historically, the U.S. has never taken a consistent position on world trade; the country persistently vacillates between the promotion of global free trade and the narrowest sort of protectionism. The voices of protectionism have become particularly loud during this most recent economic crisis and following the 2016 presidential election in the United States and the decision of the United Kingdom to leave the European Union.

Following the election of Donald Trump as President of the United States, the U.S. has abandoned the Trans-Pacific Partnership (TPP), threatened massive new tariffs on Chinese goods entering the U.S., and undercut the authority of the World Trade Organization. These actions and others have led to a great deal of pessimism around the world. One journalist for the British Broadcasting System has asked "will Donald Trump mean the end of global trade?"[2] As he elaborates: "For decades there has been a consensus that globalization brought more jobs, higher wages and lower prices—not just for richer countries but also for developing and poorer nations. [But now] the future of free trade is looking very gloomy."[3]

On June 23, 2016 the United Kingdom voted in a referendum to leave the European Union.[4] No one is quite sure what this will mean either for the U.K. or for the EU. A great deal of the discussion in the U.K. echoed many of the pronouncements of President Trump in the United States: "too many rules on business," a decline in the U.K.'s "sovereignty," lack of control over the U.K.'s borders.

As the sixth edition of this book goes to press, no one can fully predict the end result of these initiatives.

But there is no question that the world remains economically interdependent and world trade must continue if we wish to survive.

While not without controversy, the fundamental world trade agreement, the World Trade Organization (WTO) treaty that incorporates the older General Agreement on Tariffs and Trade (GATT), remains highly important. It is unquestionably a major force for free trade. The day that the Peoples Republic of China became a member of the WTO was a major step in the progress of the Organization. It is not a perfect mechanism, of course. There are concerns with regard to how well the WTO serves developing nations.[5] Some nations continue to pursue narrower, more protectionist

---

Offshoring (2011); Elhanan Helpman, *Understanding Global Trade* (2011) and two significant works by a very prolific author, Thomas L. Friedman: *The Lexus and the Olive Tree: Understanding Globalization* (2012) and *The World Is Flat 3.0: A Brief History of the Twenty-First Century* (2007).

2. Mark Broad, BBC News January 25, 2017 (business segment).
3. *Id.*
4. *See*, e.g., *Britain after Brexit: A Nation Divided*, 28 J. of Democracy 17 (2017).
5. *See*, e.g., Tomer Broude, *The Rule(s) of Trade and the Rhetos of Development: Reflections on the Functional and Aspirational Legitimacy of the WTO*, 45 Colum. J. Transnat'l L. 221 (2007); Majorie Florestal, *Technical Assistance Post-Doha: Is There Any Hope of Integrating Developing Countries into the Global Trading System?* 24 Ariz. J. Int'l & Comp. L. 121 (2007). *See also*, John H. Barton, Judith L. Goldstein, Timothy E. Josling & Richard H. Steinberg, *The Evolution of the Trade Regime: Politics, Law, and Economics of the GATT and the WTO* (2008).

interests outside the WTO framework. The WTO dispute resolution has yet to prove truly effective.[6]

It remains to be seen whether the recent proliferation of bilateral investment treaties and the now significant regional trade authorities will impede or enhance the WTO.[7] In 2007, the WTO was sufficiently concerned with the impact of these other trade agreements to hold an important conference on the topic of *Multilateralizing Regionalism*. The WTO has taken steps to promote transparency and fairness in the processes developed by the regional trade organizations.[8]

The activities of the World Bank and the International Monetary Fund and the continuing and astonishing debt problems faced by a large number of developing countries suggest that the world is a long way from being able to solve those nearly intractable problems which are frequently characterized as the North-South controversy. Massive financial assistance to developing countries appears to have pushed them only deeper and perhaps inextricably into debt. Thus far they have not been able to extricate themselves either through austerity programs or increased trade.

As countries become more sophisticated in the ways of international business, it is clear that many of the old forms of commercial agreement, such as the much-criticized concession agreements are giving way to business arrangements over which the host country has more control.[9] Few countries will permit the export of either their natural resources or their economic capital without significant financial benefit to their citizens. This trend clearly favors such devices as joint ventures, with majority control vested within the host country, franchises (with close regulation of termination procedures) and various types of licensing and distributorship agreements.

But one of the most striking developments in international trade has come in the area of the sale of goods between merchants in different countries with the ratification, in January 1987, by the United States of the United Nations Convention on Contracts for the International Sale of Goods (CISG). It would appear that after centuries of unsuccessful attempts, the ratification or acceptance of the CISG by a large number of countries, including China, is a monumental achievement in international trade.[10] The

---

6. *See*, e.g., Petros C. Mavroidis, *No Outsourcing of Law? WTO Law as Practiced by WTO Courts*, 102 Am. J. Int'l L. 421 (2008); Shoaib A. Ghias, *A Theoretical and Political Analysis of the WTO Appellate Body*, 24 Berkeley J. Int'l L. 534 (2006); Petko D. Kantchevski, *The Differences Between the Panel Procedures of the GATT and the WTO: The Role of GATT and WTO Panels in Trade Dispute Settlement*, 3 BYU Int'l L. & Mgmt. Rev. 79 (2006).
7. *See*, e.g., Jason Webb Yackee, *Conceptual Difficulties in the Empirical Study of Bilateral Investment Treaties*, 33 Brook. J. Int'l L. 405 (2008); Jeswald W. Salacuse & Nicholas P. Sullivan, *Do BITs Really Work? An Evaluation of Bilateral Investment Treaties and Their Grand Bargain*, 46 Harv. Int'l L.J. 67 (2005). A book-length work with a distinct opinion on BITs is Amin George Forji, *Bilateral Investment Treaties as Instruments of Economic Hegemony: Qualifying the Implications for Developing Countries* (2011).
8. *See*, the report of the conference and related activities at the WTO website: www.wto.org.
9. *See*, generally, Pablo Zapatero, *International Trade and Commercial Law for the Twenty-First Century: Modern International Law and the Advent of Special Legal Systems*, 23 Ariz. J. Int'l & Comp. L. 55 (2005); Sandeep Gopalan, *New Trends in the Making of International Commercial Law*, 23 J. L. & Com. 117 (2004).
10. Any mention of the CISG would now be deficient without a citation to John Honnold's seminal book on the Convention, John Honnold, *The United Nations Convention for the International Sale of Goods* (1987). After Professor Honnold's death, co-authorship was assumed by Professor Harry Flechtner. The current volume is: John O. Honnold & Harry M. Flechtner,

CISG now appears to be recognized as such an achievement not only by academics but also by practicing lawyers, who are beginning, in greater and greater numbers, to accept the CISG as the choice of law for their sales of goods contracts.[11] It is entirely possible that the CISG, limited as it is to sales of goods, is simply one of the first steps toward the development of a truly comprehensive set of international contract rules.[12]

The CISG is striking and innovative but it is not the only point of interest in the development of international business law. As the earlier chapters in this book make clear, there is a great deal of "law" governing commercial agreements that is made by the parties themselves. These rules are sometimes described as *private ordering*. A recent term that seems to have captured the attention of many international legal academics is *soft law*.[13]

This is not a new concept. People in business have been making enforceable agreements for hundreds of years. Private ordering may have grown into something beyond mere words in a bilateral contract between two private companies. The supposedly private dealings of individual companies may be creating a new system of regulation of international business that stem from the negotiations that multilateral companies conduct with host countries.[14] This is sometimes referred to as the "Wal-Mart" factor:

> [T]he development of efficient systems of private law making by non-governmental organizations that sometimes supplement and sometimes displace traditional legal systems. [The Wal-Mart factor] arises in the shadow of, parallel with, and in response to the less successful attempts by national and international bodies to regulate economic behavior on a global scale. These systems are grounded in private law, contractual and business connections between the great multinational corporations and the many entities with which they have business relationships.[15]

Of course, international corporations are not totally free from governance either by host-country governments or by international bodies. There is a significant push,

---

Uniform Law for International Sales Under the 1980 United Nations Convention (4th rev. ed., 2009). *See also*, Ingeborg Schwenzer, Schlechtriem & Schwenzer: *Commentary on the UN Convention on the International Sale of Goods* (2010).

11. *See*, e.g., Alicia Jurney Whitlock & Boris S. Abbey, *Who's Afraid of the CISG? Why North Carolina Practitioners Should Learn a Thing or Two About the 1980 United Nations Convention on Contracts for the International Sale of Goods*, 30 Campbell L. Rev. 275 (2008).
12. *See*, e.g., Michael Joachim Bonell, *The CISG, European Contract Law and the Development of a World Contract Law*, 56 Am. J. Comp. L. 1 (2008).
13. *See*, e.g., Anna Di Robilant, *Genealogies of Soft Law*, 54 Am. J. Comp. L. 499 (2006); Ralf Michaels & Nils Jansen, *Private Law Beyond the State? Europeanization, Globalization, Privatization*, 54 Am. J. Comp. L. 843 (2006); J.H. Dalhuisen, *Legal Orders and Their Manifestation: The Operation of the International Commercial and Financial Legal Order and Its Lex Mercatoria*, 24 Berkeley J. Int'l L. 129 (2006).
14. *See*, e.g., Larry Cata Backer, *Economic Globalization and the Rise of Efficient Systems of Global Private Law Making: Wal-Mart as Global Legislator*, 39 Conn. L. Rev. 1739 (2007).
15. *Id.*, at 1740.

these days, to try to convince multinational corporations to act ethically.[16] There is a strong impetus to require businesses to pay attention to issues of human rights.[17]

No one working or writing in the area of international business transactions in the twenty-first century can ignore the significant impact of computer, the Internet, and what we now call "e-commerce." Two new chapters in this book discuss these issues in depth. One new development that bears watching is the recently promulgated, but not fully adopted, United Nations Commission on International Trade Law (UNCITRAL) agreement, the Convention on the Use of Electronic Communications in International Contracts. This Convention, if it eventually enters into force, will lend even more stability and legitimacy to electronic contracts than is now the case.[18]

§14.3 TRENDS IN INTERNATIONAL COMMERCIAL DISPUTE RESOLUTION

International commercial arbitration will remain the preeminent mechanism for resolving international commercial disputes for the foreseeable future. Litigation is usually too expensive and time-consuming; and court judgments—at least outside the EC—have little international impact. But cost-conscious business executives may begin looking more closely at what this book calls the less-drastic forms of commercial dispute resolution such as mediation/conciliation and minitrial. Granting that these devices lack finality and granting that the parties may still have to arbitrate or litigate if mediation or minitrial fail, these less-drastic devices still make sense in a large number of instances; and far too many lawyers disregard them. It may be that business executives rather than their lawyers will have to take the lead in insisting that the attempt be made. Too many lawyers are like many surgeons: they want to cut (read "litigate") without deeper analysis when there are plenty of ways to avoid cutting.[19] To be sure, arbitration is not without its critics. There are recent concerns that arbitration has become "judicialized"—i.e., "the proceedings are too lengthy, expensive and

16. *See*, e.g., Robert W. McGee, *Legal Ethics, Business Ethics and International Trade: Some Neglected Issues*, 10 Cardozo J. Int'l & Comp. L. 109 (2002).
17. *See*, e.g., Joseph E. Stiglitz, *Regulating Multinational Corporations: Towards Principles of Cross-Border Legal Frameworks in a Globalized World—Balancing Rights with Responsibilities*, 23 Am. U. Int'l L. Rev. 451 (2008); Ralph G. Steinhardt, *Soft Law, Hard Markets: Competitive Self-Interest and the Emergence of Human Rights Responsibilities for Multinational Corporations*, 33 Brook. J. Int'l L. 933 (2008). For a comparative view of these issues *see*, Anna Triponel, *Business and Human Rights Law: Diverging Trends in the United States and France*, 23 Am. U. Int'l L. Rev. 855 (2008). For a historical perspective on these issues *see*, Iris Halpern, *Tracing the Contours of Transnational Corporations' Human Rights Obligations in the Twenty-First Century*, 14 Buff. Hum. Rts. L. Rev. 129 (2008).
18. The full text of the electronic contract convention can be found on the UNCITRAL website: www.uncitral.org. *See*, e.g., Charles H. Martin, *The Electronic Contracts Convention, The CISG, and New Sources of E-Commerce Law*, 16 Tul. J. Int'l & Comp. L. 467 (2008).
19. *See*, e.g., Winston Stromberg, *Avoiding the Full Court Press: International Commercial Arbitration and Other Global Alternative Dispute Resolution Processes*, 40 Loy. L.A. L. Rev. 1337 (2007).

complex."[20] But these sentiments are strongly contradicted by other research and other pronouncements. A preeminent arbitrator has looked at some of the arguments (particularly strong in the United States) that arbitration is unfair to consumers and has concluded: "Whatever the benefits on the domestic scene of comparing the merits of arbitration with those of litigation, the comparison is neither interesting nor realistic on the international scene where arbitration is not only the *accepted* but realistically the *only* method of dispute resolution."[21]

For those disputes that must be arbitrated, there are in place a number of well-developed, efficient and effective systems of international commercial arbitration. In addition, individual countries are developing indigenous systems of effective, efficient arbitration by adopting the UNCITRAL Model Law on International Commercial Arbitration.[22]

The Model Law is intended to substitute modern, generally accepted arbitration principles for archaic domestic models; and it is finding acceptance nearly everywhere. Indeed, a number of countries who believe they have highly sophisticated forms of commercial arbitration would do well to look closely at the Model Law as an indication of some of the best recent thinking on the issue. Moreover, we may have reached a juncture in world history where uniformity in commercial arbitration is important. In that case, the Model Law could conceivably be adopted by all trading nations. If it were, many of the issues discussed in this book in Chapters 8–10 might be alleviated. Again, the Model Law may not be an issue in a new golden age of arbitration; but it is well-worth reading and understanding.

The Model Law began as an attempt in the 1960s by the Council of Europe to draft a Uniform Law for Commercial Arbitration—an attempt that was impeded by what Professor Pieter Sanders (the person many call the Father of the Model Law) describes as a tendency for each of the participants in such a venture (to try) to see that the Uniform Law will deviate as little as possible from his own national law.[23] Proposing and working on a model (as opposed to a uniform law) gave the drafters more freedom to introduce in the model the best solutions, which are not necessarily based on the national law of the drafters.[24]

The United Nations took some wise preliminary steps. Regarding the 1958 New York Convention on the Recognition and Enforcement of Foreign Arbitral Awards as a successful effort, the United Nations, by a 1966 resolution, created UNCITRAL and directed it to study additional steps to bring some uniformity to commercial arbitration

20. Leon Trakman & Hugh Montgomery, *The "Judicialization" of International Commercial Arbitration: Pitfall or Virtue?* 30 Leiden J. Int'l L. 405 (2017). *See also*, Remy Gerbay, *"Is the End Nigh Again? An Empirical Assessment of the 'Judicialization' of International Arbitration,"* 25 Am. Rev. Int'l Arb. 223 (2014).
21. W. Laurence Craig, *The Arbitrator's Mission and the Application of Law in International Commercial Arbitration*, 21 Am. Rev. Int'l Arb. 243, 251 (2010).
22. *See*, the UNCITRAL website for the full text of the Model Law at www.uncitral.org. *See also*, Assn. Int'l Arb., *The UNCITRAL Model Law on International Commercial Arbitration: 25 Years* (2010).
23. *International Council for Commercial Arbitration, UNCITRAL's Project for a Model Law on International Commercial Arbitration* 23 (Pieter Sanders ed., 1984).
24. *Id.*

as a step toward the progressive harmonization and unification of the law of international trade.[25] But rather than begin immediately to draft a Model Law, in 1976 UNCITRAL first developed and promulgated arbitration rules that could be used, at the option of private parties, in any number of international commercial arbitrations (*see* Chapter 8).

UNCITRAL then recognized that many business disputes could be resolved by some process less cumbersome than arbitration and promulgated the UNCITRAL Conciliation Rules (discussed at length in Chapter 6) in 1980 as a device which could be attempted before parties launch the comparatively more expensive and time-consuming process of arbitration. The conciliation rules were also sparked by the general aversion of many countries, including many nations in the Far East, to the antagonistic, gut-wrenching nature of the adversary process.[26]

But even with these developments, it became apparent to the members of UNCITRAL that creating a climate of uniformity in commercial arbitration required all countries to modify their internal arbitration laws since arbitration, as discussed in Chapter 8, always needs some kind of juridical "home"—that is, a country of origin in which the parties can invoke the supervisory and confirmatory powers of the domestic courts. As Sir Michael Kerr puts it:

> The necessary powers to give binding effect to the legal consequences of arbitration, which is the whole raison d'etre of the arbitral process, is invariably vested in the national courts by legislation....In the ultimate analysis the effectiveness of the private process must therefore rest upon the binding, and even coercive, powers which each State entrusts to its courts.[27]

There is some commentary to the contrary—that an international commercial arbitral award is not necessarily dependent for its validity and enforceability on having a home in some country's domestic court system, but that position is not well accepted.[28]

Thus, adopting the Model Law has had substantial consequences for each adopting state. For example, although the Model Law on its terms is restricted to international commercial agreements, it would make little sense for a country to have one process of commercial arbitration for purely domestic disputes and a wholly different process for international disputes. Accordingly, the Model Law appears to have had an impact on the arbitration of domestic disputes in the adopting countries, as well as controlling the arbitration of international commercial disputes. Representing some of the best recent thinking on commercial arbitration generally, adoption of

25. U.N. General Assembly Resolution No. 2205/21 (December 17, 1966), to be found in I Yearbook of UNCITRAL 1968–1970 (1971).
26. Carl August Fleischauer, *UNCITRAL and International Commercial Dispute Settlement*, 38 Arb. J. 9 (December 1983).
27. Michael Kerr, *Arbitration and the Courts: The UNCITRAL Model Law*, 34 Int'l & Comp. L.Q. 1 (1985).
28. *See*, e.g., the discussion by Professor Park in William W. Park, *The Lex Loci Arbitri and International Commercial Arbitration*, 32 Int'l & Comp. L.Q. 21 (1983).

the Model Law may well effect a great deal of arbitration, particularly in those countries whose current system of arbitration is rudimentary or whose courts have shown a great deal of hostility to arbitration.

Still, the difficulties, realized early on, of selling the Model Law to individual nations, did not discourage UNCITRAL. The UNCITRAL Working Group on the Model Law approved a final text in Vienna in June 1985 and that text was formally adopted by UNCITRAL itself on June 21, 1985. The Act is remarkable for both its brevity and its sophistication. To begin with, there are two crucial definitions which set the Act's boundaries. The term *commercial* is defined as broadly as possible to include such matters as:

> any trade transaction for the supply or exchange of goods or services; distribution agreement;...agency; factoring; leasing; construction of works; consulting; engineering; licensing; investment financing; banking; insurance; exploitation agreement or concession; joint venture...; carriage of goods or passengers by air, sea, rail or road.[29]

The term *international* is defined as a commercial agreement in which:

> the parties to an arbitration agreement have, at the time of the conclusion of that agreement, their places of business in different States; or [if] one of the following places is situated outside the State in which the parties have their places of business: (i) the place of arbitration...(ii) any place where a substantial part of the obligations of the commercial relationship is to be performed...or [where] the parties have expressly agreed that the subject-matter of the arbitration agreement relates to more than one country.[30]

To insure that courts let arbitration alone, the Act expressly states: "In matters governed by this Law, no court shall intervene except where so provided in this Law."[31] As discussed above, this provision alone should have the effect of curbing judicial interference with the arbitration process. Finally, the arbitration agreement must be in writing, although the concept of a writing is defined very broadly to include such things as telex messages and recorded telephone conversations.[32]

From that foundation, the Model Law moves to language and process that are very similar to the 1976 UNCITRAL Rules of Arbitration. The Act permits the parties to agree on the number of arbitrators, but in the absence of an expressly stated number requires that there be three arbitrators. The identity and credentials of the arbitrators may be agreed upon by the parties, but a court or other authority is permitted to appoint the arbitrators if the parties cannot agree.[33] The parties may specify rules of procedure and location or such matters may be prescribed by the tribunal if the parties cannot agree or if the agreement is silent on such issues.[34]

---

29. Model Law, Art. 1.
30. *Id.*
31. *Id.*, Art. 5.
32. *Id.*, Art. 7.
33. *Id.*, Arts. 10 and 11.
34. *Id.*, Arts. 19 and 20.

An arbitration is commenced by a claimant sending a request for arbitration to the respondent. Either in that notice or in a separate document, the claimant states his or her statements of claim to which the respondent files a defense or counterclaim. An oral hearing may be held, the tribunal may appoint and listen to experts and the tribunal may ask the country's courts for assistance in taking evidence.[35] The tribunal must make an award in writing that contains reasons for the award. While the tribunal may sit as an equitable body (*ex aequo et bono* or as *amiable compositeur*) only if the parties have expressly authorized it to do so, the tribunal may render a decision based on the terms of the contract and shall take into account the usages of the trade applicable to the transaction.[36]

Under the Model Law, courts are expected to recognize and confirm arbitral awards in the ordinary course without changing the terms of the award. A court is authorized to set aside an award only if: (i) a party was incapacitated or the underlying agreement was somehow invalid; (ii) a party was not given proper notice; (iii) the award "deals with a dispute not contemplated by or not falling within the terms of the submission to arbitration" or is somehow beyond the scope of the submission; (iv) the composition of the tribunal was not in accordance with the agreement; (v) the subject matter of the dispute is not properly subject to arbitration; or (vi) the award conflicts with the country's public policy.[37] The grounds on which a court may refuse to recognize and enforce a foreign arbitral award are set out in the Model Act in virtually the same terms.[38]

The Model Law has generally been given rave reviews. Even the delegation to the UNCITRAL Working Group from the United States—a country that appears to be constantly suspicious of anything the United Nations does or says—commented that the Model Law in conjunction with the 1958 New York Convention and the UNCITRAL Arbitration Rules:

> provide a comprehensive framework for the arbitral resolution of disputes arising from a broad range of international commercial transactions. Basic considerations of procedural due process are generally well protected and a proper balance is struck in the relationship between arbitration and the courts. The freedom of the parties to agree to arbitral procedures that best suit their specific needs is safeguarded throughout....The achievement of [adoption of the Model Law] will serve not only the cause of international commercial arbitration, but also as a stimulus to international trade and investment and thus the foreign policy objectives of the United States.[39]

At the same time, a few commentators and some semi-official bodies have reservations about the Model Law. In late 1989, the Mustill Committee (a British committee chaired by Lord Justice Mustill and charged with making a recommendation on British adoption of the Model Law) recommended that the Model Law not be

35. *Id.*, Arts. 21–27.
36. *Id.*, Arts. 28–33.
37. *Id.*, Art. 34.
38. *Id.*, Arts. 35 and 36.
39. Report of the United States Delegation set out in Am. Arb. Assn., *Arbitration and the Law 1985: AAA General Counsel's Report* 151 (1985).

adopted for England, Wales, and Northern Ireland.[40] By contrast, a similar committee investigating possible adoption in Scotland reported favorably on the Model Law and recommended adoption.[41] The Mustill committee took the position that while English arbitration law was not perfect, it nonetheless reflected the "unique richness of the English jurisprudence fully developed and tested in practice ..." concluding that the English system is "essentially satisfactory."[42] By contrast, the Scottish committee worried that Scottish arbitration law was based on common law rather than statute and the inherent lack of conformity with other nations' arbitration law might hinder the use of Scotland as a site for international commercial arbitration. This rationale appears to have been incorporated by most adopting jurisdictions. It is not so much that the Model Law is perfect; or, conversely, that a nation's existing arbitration law is defective. Rather, the absence of the Model Law or something close to it may inhibit contract drafters from choosing that jurisdiction as an arbitration site.

The Model Law has now come full circle and has become the statutory law of at least six states in the United States: California,[43] Connecticut,[44] Florida,[45] Georgia,[46] Hawaii,[47] and Texas.[48] However, the U.S. Congress has shown little or no interest in adopting the Model Law for the federal system. In each instance, the state legislatures enacted the Model Law in an attempt to encourage the siting of international arbitrations in that state.[49] This may mark the first time in U.S. history that a promulgation of the United Nations has been transmuted into a state statute.

There are other developments. The greatly expanded trade in intellectual property has prompted a number of initiatives in dispute resolution specifically for intellectual property issues.[50] The growth of Internet business has led to the creation of a number of interesting online dispute resolution processes.[51]

40. Ronald E.M. Goodman, *UNCITRAL Model Law on International and Commercial Arbitration: Divergent Approaches in England and Scotland*, 18 Int'l Bus. L. 250 (1990).
41. *Id.*
42. *Id.*, at 251.
43. Calif. Civil Procedure Code §§1297.11–1297.432.
44. 1989 Conn. Acts 89-179, approved June 1, 1989.
45. Fla. Stat. Ann. §§684.01–684.35.
46. Ga. Code Ann. §§9-9-30–9-9-43.
47. Haw. Rev. Stat. Ann. §§658D-1–658D-9.
48. Tex. Rev. Civil Procedure Code Ann., Arts. 249-1–249-43.
49. For a longer discussion of these state statutes and the Model Act *see*, Xavier E. Romeu-Matta, *New Developments in International Commercial Arbitration: A Comparative Survey of New State Statutes and the UNCITRAL Model Law*, 1 Am. Rev. Int'l Arb. 140 (1990). For a fascinating recent speculation on the future of international arbitration whose optimism can be discerned from its title, *see*, Bryan Garth & Yves Dezalay, *Dealing in Virtue: International Commercial Arbitration and the Construction of a Transnational Legal Order* (1996). A well-organized book, designed principally for law school classes, that takes a close and coherent look at a number of dispute resolution mechanisms is Klaus Peter Berger, *Private Dispute Resolution in International Business: Negotiation, Mediation, Arbitration* (2d rev. ed., 2009).
50. *See*, e.g., Peter K. Yu, *Toward a Nonzero-Sum Approach to Resolving Global Intellectual Property Disputes: What We Can Learn From Mediators, Business Strategists, and International Relations Theorists*, 70 U. Cin. L. Rev. 569 (2002).
51. *See*, Ch. 13.

§14.4 CONCLUSION

There are few matters in the world as important as international trade. It is through this process that wealth is built and shared, that information is transferred and that different cultures come to appreciate each other. The global problems of population, environment, and military conflict can be alleviated by a greater attention to trade and commercial relationships. We may have truly arrived at a time when no one on the face of the earth is immune from the consequences of international trade. If this book helps only a few transactions run a bit smoother, it will have accomplished its purpose.

Index

S

T

U

W